GLENCOE
INTRODUCTION TO
Networks and Networking

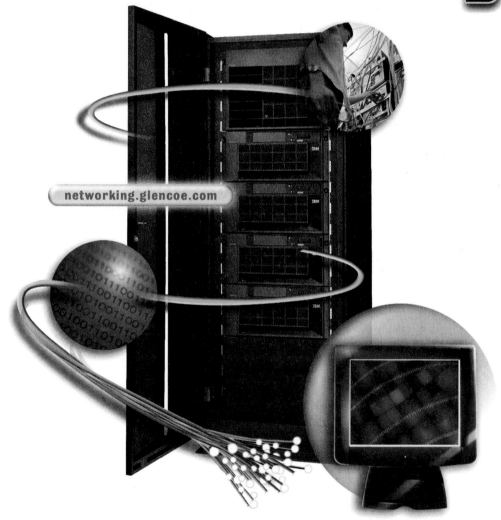

networking.glencoe.com

Dr. Paul J. Fortier
University of Massachusetts Dartmouth
North Dartmouth, Massachusetts

Hector J. Caban
Osceola County School District
Osceola, Florida

Glencoe

New York, New York   Columbus, Ohio   Chicago, Illinois   Peoria, Illinois   Woodland Hills, California

Glencoe

Copyright © 2005 by Glencoe/McGraw-Hill. All rights reserved. Printed in the United States of America. Except as permitted under the United States Copyright Act of 1976, no part of this publication may be reproduced or distributed in any form or by any means, or stored in a database or retrieval system, without the prior written permission of the publisher.

ISBN   0-07-861238-1 (Student Edition)
ISBN   0-07-861240-3 (Student Workbook)
ISBN   0-07-861239-X (Teacher Resource Manual)

2 3 4 5 6 7 8 9   079 09 08 07 06 05 04

Microsoft and all other Microsoft names and logos are registered trademarks of Microsoft Corporation and are used with permission.

All other brand names and product names are trademarks or registered trademarks of their respective companies.

Between the time that Web site information is gathered and published, it is not unusual for some sites to have changed URLs or closed. URLs will be updated in reprints or on the book's Web site when possible.

About the Authors

Dr. Paul J. Fortier is a Professor of Electrical and Computer Engineering at the University of Massachusetts Dartmouth. He holds a B.S. in electrical engineering from the University of Massachusetts Lowell, an M.S. in electrical engineering from Southeastern Massachusetts University, and a Doctorate of Science in computer science from the University of Massachusetts Lowell. He holds 7 patents, and is the author of 6 journal articles, 17 textbooks, and over 50 professional papers. He is an active member of the IEEE, IEEE Computer Society, and numerous technical committees of the IEEE, ACM, SIGMOD, SIGACT, ANSI, ASEE, and AMIA.

Hector J. Caban has been an instructor of networking and computer systems at Technical Education Center Osceola, Florida. He has also worked in the computer industry for over 10 years in the areas of technical support, network administration, system analysis, and computer programming. He holds a B.S. in information technology from the University of Central Florida, and holds the following certifications: A+, Net+, MCP, MCSA, MCSE, and CCNA.

Academic Review Board

E. Scott Huerkamp
Technical Instructor
Cisco Academy Network Instructor
Lincoln High School
Tallahassee, Florida

Steve Thompson
IT Instructor
Garden City High School
Garden City, Kansas
MOS, MCP

Louis Zulli Jr.
Network Administrator and Instructor
The Center for Advanced Technologies
St. Petersburg, Florida
CCA, CNE, MCSE

Academic Reviewers

Tammy Bradley
Academy of Information Technology
    Curriculum Coordinator
Chapel Hill High School
Chapel Hill, North Carolina
CCNA, CCAI, CAW

Charles B. Gallo
A+ Instructor, Computer Information
    Systems Instructor/Coordinator
John F. Kennedy High School
Bronx, New York

Eric A. Greve
Technology Instructor
Richard King High School
Del Mar Community College
Corpus Christi, Texas
CCNA, CCAI, MBA/A

Chuck Hostetter
Highland School of Technology
Gastonia, North Carolina
CCNA, CCAI, MCP, A+, Net+

Dr. Hong Liu
Professor of Computer Engineering
University of Massachusetts
    Dartmouth
North Dartmouth, Massachusetts

Sterling Mullett
SAIL High School
Tallahassee, Florida

Charles Robert Paige
Computer Science Instructor
Globe College
Oakdale, Minnesota

Kathleen Schrock
Administrator for Technology
Nauset Public Schools
Orleans, Massachusetts

Robert Tencza
Lakewood High School, The Center for
    Advanced Technologies
St. Petersburg, Florida

Gary M. Vale
Technology Department Chair
Santa Susana High School
Simi Valley, California

Christopher N. Wilson
A+, CCNA Instructor
Chapel Hill High School
Douglasville, Georgia
CCNA, CCAI

Technical Editor

Benjamin A. Rand
CAD/Engineering Software Manager
CADSolutions Instructor
Salt Lake City, Utah

Technical Reviewers

Emmett Dulaney
Technical Writer/Trainer
Anderson, Indiana
MCT, MCSE, MCP, Network+, Server+,
    A+, Linux+, LPI, CNE, CNA, CCNA

Michael Seibert
Director of Technology
Norwood, Ohio

E. Shane Turner
Technology Consultant
Orem, Utah

Table of Contents

Table of Contents

Table of Contents

Table of Contents

Table of Contents

You Try It Activity Contents

Features Contents

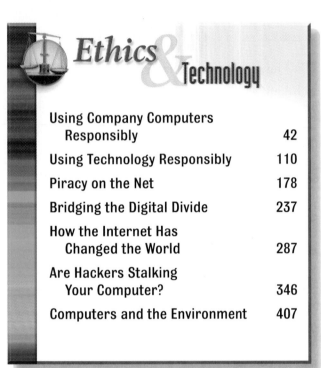

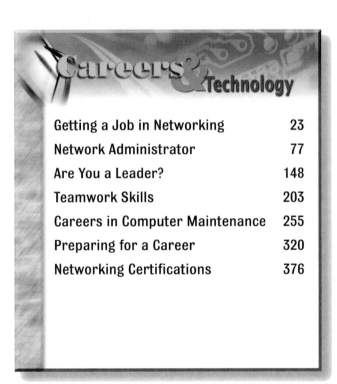

To The Student

Why Study Networking?

By understanding how networks function and how we use them to communicate with each other, you can learn how to build networks that work.

This book can help you develop skills needed to begin a career path in networking and information technology. Your textbook can also help you develop skills needed to succeed in any subject area and throughout your life. This book was written and designed to help you achieve each of the following goals:

Become a 21st Century Citizen

- ◆ Use technology wisely and safely
- ◆ Understand how networks, including the Internet, work
- ◆ Find and share information quickly, safely, and ethically
- ◆ Evaluate the accuracy and usefulness of information on the Web

Become a Networking Professional

- ◆ Demonstrate your understanding of fundamental networking principles
- ◆ Identify appropriate network topologies
- ◆ Plan and design functional, effective networks
- ◆ Evaluate network problems and troubleshoot solutions

Develop Learning and Study Skills for All Subjects

- ◆ Improve reading comprehension with both guided and independent reading strategies
- ◆ Develop critical thinking skills
- ◆ Build teamwork skills
- ◆ Integrate technology skills across the curriculum

BE AN ACTIVE READER!

When you read this textbook, you are gaining insights into technology and how it is used in the world around you. This textbook is a good example of non-fiction writing—it describes real-world ideas and facts. It is also an example of technical writing because it tells you how to use technology.

Here are some reading strategies that will help you become an active textbook reader. Choose the strategies that work best for you. If you have trouble as you read your textbook, look back at these strategies for help.

Before You Read

SET A PURPOSE
- Why are you reading the textbook?
- How might you be able to use what you learn in your own life?

PREVIEW
- Read the chapter title to find out what the topic will be.
- Read the subtitles to see what you will learn about the topic.
- Skim the photos, charts, graphs, or maps.
- Look for vocabulary words that are boldfaced. How are they defined?

DRAW FROM YOUR OWN BACKGROUND
- What do you already know about the topic?
- How is the new information different from what you already know?

As You Read

QUESTION

- What is the main idea?
- How well do the details support the main idea?
- How do the photos, charts, graphs, and maps support the main idea?

CONNECT

- Think about people, places, and events in your own life. Are there any similarities with those in your textbook?

PREDICT

- Predict events or outcomes by using clues and information that you already know.
- Change your predictions as you read and gather new information.

VISUALIZE

- Use your imagination to picture the settings, actions, and people that are described.
- Create graphic organizers to help you see relationships found in the information.

IF YOU DON'T KNOW WHAT A WORD MEANS...

- think about the setting, or context, in which the word is used.
- check if prefixes such as *un-*, *non-*, or *pre-* can help you break down the word.
- look up the word's definition in a dictionary or glossary.

READING DOs

Do...

- ✔ establish a purpose for reading.
- ✔ think about how your own experiences relate to the topic.
- ✔ try different reading strategies.

READING DON'Ts

Don't...

- ⊘ ignore how the textbook is organized.
- ⊘ allow yourself to be easily distracted.
- ⊘ hurry to finish the material.

After You Read

SUMMARIZE

- Describe the main idea and how the details support it.
- Use your own words to explain what you have read.

ASSESS

- What was the main idea?
- Did the text clearly support the main idea?
- Did you learn anything new from the material?
- Can you use this new information in other school subjects or at home?

Take the Networking Challenge!

Many features in this text—such as colored headings, illustrations with captions, and tables and charts—have been carefully constructed to help you read, understand, and remember key ideas and concepts. Taking advantage of these features can help you improve your reading and study skills.

Get Started

The scavenger hunt on these pages highlights features that will help you get the most out of your textbook. Collect points as you complete each step.*

1 What are the major topics you expect to learn about in Unit 1?
[6 points. *Hint: The Table of Contents gives you at-a-glance information about the major divisions and topics in the book.*]

2 How many times does the **Glencoe Online URL** networking.glencoe.com appear in the Chapter 1? [8 points]

3 What is the purpose of the **Think About It** activity on page 3? Why is it important? [4 points]

4 What is the best way to get an overview of what you will learn in Chapter 1? [5 points]

5 What are two study tips you learned from the **Read to Succeed** activity on page 5? [4 points]

6 What type of **Reading Strategy** graphic organizer is found in the Section 1.2 Guide to Reading? [5 points]

7 What three **key terms** are explained on the first page of Section 1.1?
[3 points. *Hint: Key terms stand out from the rest of the text because they are printed in bold, bright blue letters.*]

8 How many **Read Me!** margin features are found Chapter 1? What topics do they discuss? [8 points]

* When finished, see page xx for Networking Challenge answers and scoring rubric.

9 What is the main heading on page 6 and what are the two subheadings? [5 points]

10 What margin feature sends you to the Web to learn more about special topics? [4 points]

11 What skills are needed to successfully complete the **Building 21st Century Skills** project on page 98? [7 points]

12 How many steps will it take you to complete **You Try It Activity** 1B? [4 points. *Hint: You Try It Activities can be found easily by looking for the bright yellow arrow in the margin.*]

13 In Chapter 2, which **Show Me** video demonstrations will teach you more about bus networks? [5 points]

14 Why is it important to read the **Section Assessments** before you read the section? [5 points]

15 What are the four different types of full-page **feature articles**? [4 points. *Hint: Each chapter has two different full-page features.*]

16 On what page of each chapter will you find **Reviewing Key Terms, Understanding Main Ideas,** and **Critical Thinking**? [6 points]

17 What online study tools will help you check your comprehension of key ideas in the chapter? [4 points]

18 Which of the **Activities and Projects** on page 31 show you how standards relate to real-world situations? [3 points]

19 On which page in Chapter 1 will you find the **You Try It Activity** that helps you create a career development plan? [4 points]

20 Where can you find projects that will allow you to work on **Building Your Portfolio** of networking sample projects? [6 points]

To The Student

What's Your Score?

POINTS	CHALLENGE RATING
90 to 100	You really know how to let your textbook work for you!
70 to 89	Researching and organizing are skills you possess!
Less than 70	Consider working with your teacher or classmates to learn how to use your book more effectively—you will gain skills you can use your whole life.

1. Networking Basics, Network Architecture and Topology, and Modes of Transmission.
2. Eight times
3. Computer networks are everywhere. Each Think About It helps you connect what you will read to real-world situations. Reading experts have discovered it is easier to understand what you are reading if you first set a purpose for reading.
4. Look at pages 3–4, and note the chapter title, objectives, and activities listed. Or, read the main ideas from the Guide to Reading at the start of each section.
5. First, do a quick survey of the content by reading the colored headings. Second, jot down words you do not recognize so that you can look them up later.
6. The graphic organizer is a timeline.
7. Networking, file sharing, and resource
8. Four Read Me's. *Job Tip* describes the working hours of IT staff. The first *Caution* tells how to prevent security breaches. The second *Caution* notes security issues for doctors. *Jargon* defines the terms PC- and Mac-compatible.
9. The main heading is Reasons to Use a Network. The subheads are Sharing Information and Sharing Resources. (Did you notice that main topics use a large red font, but subheads use a smaller blue font?)
10. Go Online activities direct you to more activities on the Glencoe Web site.
11. Problem-solving skills
12. Nine steps
13. Show Me 2.1–2.8
14. By reading the questions first, you can focus on what to look for as you read.
15. Real World Technology, Careers and Technology, Emerging Technology, and Ethics and Technology
16. The Chapter Review and Assessment page
17. Study with PowerPoint and Online Self Check
18. Standards at Work
19. Page 22
20. At the end of each unit

Hardware and Software

Recommended Equipment

The majority of the hands-on activities in this textbook can be easily completed using Windows 2000 or XP. Other operating systems are also used throughout the book to expose students to a wide range of software. The table below lists the types of hardware and software that are covered in this textbook.

Minimum System Requirements

Windows 2000
- Pentium II or equivalent processor
- At least 256MB RAM
- At least 800MB available hard drive space (1GB recommended)
- 10 Mbps NIC

Windows XP
- Pentium II or equivalent processor
- At least 256MB physical RAM
- At least 2.5GB available hard drive space
- 10 Mbps NIC

DOS
(see Windows requirements above)

UNIX/Linux
Linux runs on most computers, laptops, and platforms.
- Pentium II or equivalent processor
- At least 256MB RAM
- At least 800MB available hard drive space
- Symmetrical Multiprocessing (multiple CPUs)
- 10 Mbps NIC

Mac OS X
- Macintosh with PowerPC G3, G4, or G5 processor
- At least 128MB RAM (256MB RAM recommended)
- At least 2.0GB available hard drive space (recommended), or 3.5GB if you have developer tools installed
- Built-in display or a display connected to an Apple-supplied video card
- Mac OS X does not support processor upgrade cards
- 10 Mbps NIC

Saving Your Work

You may need to save your documents and files while completing activities and labs.

- Your teacher will let you know where to save your work.
- Always double check to make sure you save to the correct location. Otherwise, you may not be able to find your work later.
- Do not ever overwrite or delete others' work. Think about how you would feel if someone did this to you.

Technology Standards

Most educators today believe that in order to live, learn, and work successfully in an increasingly complex society, students must be able to use technology effectively.

ISTE and NETS

The International Society for Technology in Education (ISTE) has developed National Educational Technology Standards to define educational technology standards for students NETS-S. The activities in this book are designed to meet ISTE standards. For more information about ISTE and the NETS, please visit **www.iste.com**.

Standards at Work

The ISTE standards identify skills that students can practice and master in school, but the skills are also used outside of school, at home, and at work. To reinforce how these standards are related to real-world situations, refer to the Standards at Work activities in each Chapter Review. Each activity emphasizes one of the six NETS student standards. Refer back to these pages for a full listing of all the standards and performance indicators for students.

Technology Standards

Technology Foundation Standards for Students

The NETS are divided into six broad categories that are listed below. Activities in the book are specifically designed to meet the standards within each category.

1. Basic operations and concepts
◆ Students demonstrate a sound understanding of the nature and operation of technology systems.
◆ Students are proficient in the use of technology.

2. Social, ethical, and human issues
◆ Students understand the ethical, cultural, and societal issues related to technology.
◆ Students practice responsible use of technology systems, information, and software.
◆ Students develop positive attitudes toward technology uses that support lifelong learning, collaboration, personal pursuits, and productivity.

3. Technology productivity tools
◆ Students use technology tools to enhance learning, increase productivity, and promote creativity.
◆ Students use productivity tools to collaborate in constructing technology-enhanced models, prepare publications, and produce other creative works.

4. Technology communications tools
◆ Students use telecommunications to collaborate, publish, and interact with peers, experts, and other audiences.
◆ Students use a variety of media and formats to communicate information and ideas effectively to multiple audiences.

5. Technology research tools
◆ Students use technology to locate, evaluate, and collect information from a variety of sources.
◆ Students use technology tools to process data and report results.
◆ Students evaluate and select new information resources and technological innovations based on the appropriateness of specific tasks.

6. Technology problem-solving and decision-making tools
◆ Students use technology resources for solving problems and making informed decisions.
◆ Students employ technology in the development of strategies for solving problems in the real world.

Educational Technology Performance Indicators for Students

In this text, all students should have opportunities to demonstrate the following performance indicators for technological literacy. Each performance indicator refers to the NETS Foundation Standards category or categories (listed on previous page) to which the performance is linked.

1. Identify capabilities and limitations of contemporary and emerging technology resources and assess the potential of these systems and services to address personal, lifelong learning, and workplace needs. (2)

2. Make informed choices among technology systems, resources, and services. (1, 2)

3. Analyze advantages and disadvantages of widespread use and reliance on technology in the workplace and in society as a whole. (2)

4. Demonstrate and advocate for legal and ethical behaviors among peers, family, and community regarding the use of technology and information. (2)

5. Use technology tools and resources for managing and communicating personal/professional information (e.g., finances, schedules, addresses, purchases, correspondence). (3, 4)

6. Evaluate technology-based options, including distance and distributed education, for lifelong learning. (5)

7. Routinely and efficiently use online information resources to meet needs for collaboration, research, publications, communications, and productivity. (4, 5, 6)

8. Select and apply technology tools for research, information analysis, problem-solving, and decision-making in content learning. (4, 5)

9. Investigate and apply expert systems, intelligent agents, and simulations in real-world situations. (3, 5, 6)

10. Collaborate with peers, experts, and others to contribute to content-related knowledge base by using technology to compile, synthesize, produce, and disseminate information, models, and other creative works. (4, 5, 6)

Technology *Handbook*

Contents

Ethical Computer Use

Computers are more common than ever before—almost every office desk in the country has a computer of some sort, and most schools have them in classrooms. The number of computers in the home is growing, too.

Computers can be used to do wonderful things, but they can also be misused. Knowing some simple ethical guidelines will ensure that you are always doing the right thing.

Using Computers at School

Whether in the classroom or at the library, you likely spend time working at a computer. Remember that the computer is there to help you get your work done. If you instead use the computer to play games, check your personal e-mail, or look at offensive material on the Internet, you are inappropriately using the resource that is being provided for you.

Many institutions are taking action to prevent such misuse. Hidden software applications watch everything users do while they are on a machine, including which Web sites they visit, what e-mails they send, even what keystrokes they type. If you are engaging in inappropriate activity on a school computer, you could be suspended from school, or perhaps even prosecuted.

> A good guideline to keep in mind: Do not do anything on a computer that you would not do if your teacher or parents were standing behind you, watching.

Using Computers at Work

While it might seem harmless to do a few small personal tasks while you are at work, the costs really do add up. According to research organizations, American businesses waste $85 billion every year due to personal use of company computers.

Plagiarism and Copying

Plagiarism is the act of taking somebody else's ideas and passing them off as your own, whether it be one or two sentences or an entire term paper. The "cut-and-paste" feature built into modern operating systems makes a lot of mundane tasks, like moving a paragraph of text, quick, and easy—but also makes plagiarism all too easy. Be on guard against falling into this trap.

It is acceptable to quote sources in your work, but you must make sure to identify those sources and give them proper credit. Also, some Web sites do not allow you to quote from them. Be sure to check each site or resource you are quoting to make sure you are allowed to use the material.

Tip — Using Internet Connections Responsibly

- Because your school may have a fast Internet connection, you may be tempted to use these connections to download large files. Check with your teacher first, as there may be policies forbidding this.
- E-mail systems leave a "digital paper trail." This means that what you type into an e-mail can be found by a system administrator. Be sure not to abuse company or school e-mail systems—it may come back to haunt you!
- If you download any files or applications, be sure to check with your system administrator before using them. Downloaded files are one of the chief sources of viruses, which cause millions of dollars in damages to computer networks every year.
- You would not steal office supplies from your office or school, so make sure you do not take home computer-related resources like CD-ROMs or floppy disks.

Copyright Laws

A copyright protects someone who creates an original work. When you create something—a book, a play, or a single sentence—you can copyright it, thereby claiming that you created it, and you are the owner. The goal is to prevent unauthorized copying of that work by another party.

Copyright protection is provided by the Copyright Act of 1976, a federal statute. At one time, if you wanted to copyright something you had to fill out a form, file your work with the Copyright Office in the Library of Congress, and pay a fee. Today, this is no longer the case. If you create an original work, it is automatically protected by copyright law—even if you forget to put the "© 2004" marker on the document. However, registering a copyright with the office does provide some additional protections, should you ever have to go to court over your creation.

Obtaining Permission

So what do you do if you want to use a portion of a copyrighted work in your own work? In order to do this, you need to obtain permission from the copyright holder.

Obtaining permission depends on the work in question. If you want to use an excerpt from a book, you will need to write a letter to the publisher, since they are the owner of the copyright.

(Sometimes the author, or an organization other than the publisher, owns the copyright. Check the copyright page in the front of the book to make sure.) Each instance is different, but many publishers are willing to grant permissions to individuals for educational purposes. If you want to reproduce information you found on the Web, contact the Webmaster or author of the article to request permission.

Duration and Public Domain

So once a copyright is in place, how long before it expires? The answer depends on when the work was created. For all works created since January 1, 1978, copyright lasts until 70 years after the creator's death. For works created before that date, the answer is considerably more complex. The copyright would last anywhere from 28 to 67 years from the date of creation, with possible options for renewal.

Once a work's copyright has expired, that work is considered to be in the public domain, meaning that nobody owns it and anybody can reprint it as they please. This is why you can find so many different printed versions of classic literature from writers like Dickens, Shakespeare, and the like—the publishers do not have to pay any fees for the right to print those books.

Some Common Misconceptions About Copyrights

- "If it does not say it is copyrighted, it is not copyrighted." Original work published after March of 1989 is copyrighted, whether it says so or not.
- "I found it on the Internet, therefore it is okay for me to copy it." Most of the text on the Internet is indeed copyrighted. Copying information from the Internet is a serious breach of copyright, and can result in prosecution.
- "It is okay to put copyrighted material on my Web site, because I do not charge people to look at it." It does not matter whether you are making a profit from the reuse of copyrighted material—you are distributing it, and that is illegal.
- "I have changed the material, so it is no longer copyrighted." Copyright law says that only the owner of the copyright can make "derivative works"— that is, new works based on the existing material.
- "I can reprint the material, because it is considered fair use." Be careful! "Fair use" refers to the right to reprint brief excerpts from copyrighted works. However, there are no clear definitions on how much of a work can be used. Some examples of fair use include quoting a book in a book report or parodying a work.

Word Processing Tips and Tools

One of the most common types of application software used in both business and school is the word processor. Word processing software allows you to create and edit documents such as reports, term papers, and essays. Many word processing programs will even allow you to create documents in HTML, which can be posted to the Web. To make the most of word processing, you will need to learn some of the features many of these programs offer.

Checking for Errors

Many people have come to depend on the spell-checker feature of word processing programs. Inside each word processor is a large file called the *dictionary*. Unlike the dictionaries that you will find on your bookshelf or online, this file does not contain any information about the meanings or pronunciations of words; instead, it knows how to spell them.

As you type into a word processor, the program constantly scans the dictionary. Every time you tap the space bar, the program knows you have just completed a word, so it looks up that word in the dictionary. If it cannot find it, the program will let you know, usually by placing a red line underneath the word.

Depending on the program, you may have a variety of options—for instance, looking at other words that the program thinks you meant to type, adding the word you typed into the dictionary so the program will recognize it, or telling the program to ignore it.

> **Remember that spell-checkers and grammar-checkers are not perfect.**

For instance, if you meant to type the word *stay* but accidentally typed *sty,* the program will not alert you to the error, because *sty* is a valid word. It is important to proofread each of your documents.

Many programs now also include grammar-checkers. Grammar-checkers compare sentence structures in documents to a file of common errors.

Tracking Changes

Sometimes, more than one person will need to work on a single document. Using the Versions feature (or Tracking feature) of a word processing program makes this easy. The program keeps copies of different versions of the document as changes are made, so you can refer back to earlier versions.

Another helpful feature is Comments. Comments allow you to make remarks about the document for other group members to see. They can make changes based on your comments, revise the comments, or leave more comments in return.

Tip → Online Calendars

Keeping track of all the work you need to do can be difficult—it is easy to get overwhelmed when you are faced with a mountain of books and papers and are not sure where to start. In cases like this, you might find that using an online calendar will help you get organized and handle your work efficiently.

Online calendars work much like paper day-planners that you buy at the office supply store, but instead of writing out tasks by hand, you type them into your Web browser. The calendar site keeps track of appointments, due dates, and to-do lists. Keeping all your tasks entered into an online calendar is one way of making certain you are accomplishing them in the smartest order.

You might also want to use the reminders feature; these are alarms that tell you when something must be done. The reminder might be a sound, a pop-up box, or an e-mail sent to you by the calendar site.

Also, since the information is stored online, you can check your calendar from anywhere—from home, school, or any place that has an Internet connection.

Etiquette for Digital Communication

New rules of etiquette have evolved for the new communication media provided by the Internet—e-mail, chat rooms, and newsgroups. Nicknamed "netiquette," these basic guidelines are important to keep in mind whenever you are communicating with someone online.

E-mail

Of all the conveniences provided by the Internet, e-mail is the most widely used. It has changed how people live, work, and socialize. Letters that used to take days to arrive in the mail now take mere seconds. Business communication has become much more efficient thanks to e-mail. Here are a few things to keep in mind when sending e-mail:

✔ Do not send large attachments, unless the recipient is expecting them.

✔ When forwarding e-mails, be sure to trim off unnecessary information like old headers and quotes—these can build up quickly!

✔ Keep your communication appropriate, and do not say anything about someone that you would not want them to hear. Even after you click Delete, e-mail records stay in the system for a long time, and can even be found years later.

✔ Never send or forward chain letters. Even if they seem like a good idea, they are often fraudulent—and will likely anger the people you are sending them to.

Chat Rooms

Chat rooms can be useful communication tools, but they can also be raucous free-for-alls. Some things to keep in mind:

✔ Choose the chat room wisely. Some chat rooms are populated with questionable people, so do some research first.

✔ For your safety, always remain anonymous.

✔ Take turns with the conversation. Just like in a real conversation, allow people to finish their thoughts, and do not interrupt.

✔ Be aware of "lurkers," people who are reading the conversation but not taking part. Try not to say anything that might hurt somebody's feelings.

Newsgroups

The Usenet system is made up of thousands of discussion groups, each on a particular topic. Having a rewarding newsgroup experience requires some basic netiquette, including the following guidelines:

✔ Stay on topic. Most Usenet groups are very specific, and readers do not appreciate posts that do not fit the topic.

✔ Avoid flaming. Newsgroups are particularly ripe for flaming— people tend to get passionate in these conversations. Never type something that you would not want to say out loud.

✔ Know your facts. There is no fact-checking process in Usenet—anybody can say anything he or she wants. Just because somebody says something in a newsgroup does not mean it is true—remember this when quoting or replying to someone.

Tip

General Netiquette Guidelines

● Behave as though you were communicating face-to-face.
● Remember that your words can be misinterpreted, and things like sarcasm, body language, and irony may not come across.
● Do not "flame." A flame is an aggressive or insulting letter.
● Do not "spam." Spam, or junk e-mail, is a billion-dollar problem, clogging mail systems and wasting time. Do not add to the problem.
● Do not SHOUT. Make sure your Caps Lock key is off.
● Do not distribute copyrighted information. Just because something is on the Internet does not mean it is free.
● Do not hide behind a screen name. Behave online as you would in the real world— honestly, ethically, and wisely.

Online Resources

One of the most useful elements of the Internet is the World Wide Web (also called "the Web"), which allows documents to be viewed by anyone anywhere in the world. This is particularly helpful when it comes to documents that are normally expensive or hard to find. For instance, many families do not own an encyclopedia, so a student who needs to do research would normally have to make a trip to the library. The Web makes it possible for documents like encyclopedias and dictionaries to be accessed by many people.

Dictionaries

There are hundreds of online dictionaries. Some specialize in certain types of information, such as law, medicine, or technology.

- **Dictionary.com** The name makes it easy to remember; this site also contains a fully searchable thesaurus. (www.dictionary.com)
- **OneLook Dictionaries** A "meta-dictionary," this site lets you type in a word once to search across more than 840 dictionaries. (www.onelook.com)
- **Merriam-Webster** A Web version of one of the best-known print dictionaries, this site includes a "word of the day" feature, a thesaurus, and links to other research sites. (www.m-w.com)

Encyclopedias

Encyclopedias need to be updated often, making them a perfect choice for online delivery. Online encyclopedias are searchable, and many contain photos and illustrations.

- **Brittanica Online** The online version of one of the most respected print encyclopedias offers both free and premium access, with more content and fewer ads in the premium version. (www.britannica.com)

- **World Book Online** The online version of World Book does not offer any free information; you have to pay a monthly fee to access the entries, which include all the contents of the print versions dating back to 1922. (www.worldbook.com)

- **Encarta** A popular encyclopedia by Microsoft, the Encarta Web site offers lots of free content, but to access all their information you will need to buy either a subscription or a copy of the CD-ROM. (www.encarta.msn.com)

Other Resources

While dictionaries and encyclopedias offer lots of useful information, other specialized resource sites can give you information about other subjects.

- **Roget's Thesaurus** The online version of the definitive thesaurus lets you search for words or browse them alphabetically or by category. The site also offers plug-ins that put dictionary and thesaurus buttons right in your browser window. (www.thesaurus.com)
- **RefDesk** A comprehensive site with links to every kind of information imaginable. If you do not know where to start looking for a particular fact or statistic, start here. (www.refdesk.com)
- **Bartleby** Bartleby is fully searchable and contains the complete text of Bartlett's Quotations, Simpson's Quotations, the Columbia World of Quotations, as well as dozens of biographies, articles, and books. (www.bartleby.com)

Safe Surfing

The Internet can be a wonderful place. There is much to learn, explore, and discover. You can find the answers to many of your questions on the Internet, often much more quickly than at the local library. And the Internet can put you in touch with people you might never have met—experts, writers, or just other students from around the world.

But the Internet can also be a dangerous place. There are Web sites that you would freely visit, and many others that you will want to avoid.

Privacy and Personal Information

Information is valuable. Companies that operate on the Internet are constantly seeking more information about customers, as well as potential customers. By building vast databases of names, addresses, and information about buying habits, those companies can market their products and services with increased efficiency, thereby increasing sales.

But in addition to legitimate sites that ask you for information like name, address, or age, there are many questionable sites that are looking for data as well. Before you type any information into an online form or in a chat room, be sure to evaluate to whom you are sending that information, and why you are sending it.

Here are some things to keep in mind:

✔ Know to whom you are giving the information. Check the URL in your browser—does it match the domain you visited? Or were you "redirected" to another site without your knowledge?

✔ Why are you giving the information? If, for example, you are ordering something online, you will need to give your address in order for the product to be shipped. There should always be a good reason for all information you provide. Never give out your social security number, your birth date, or your mother's maiden name without adult consent. These are often used to secure credit reports, and giving these to a dishonest source could ruin your credit.

✔ Never give personal information of any sort to someone you meet in a chat room. Always remain anonymous.

✔ If you are still unsure whether it is safe to give the information, check with a parent or other trusted adult.

Tip

Avoiding Physical Stress at the Computer

If you are going to be spending time in front of a computer, it is important that you minimize stress to your body. Here are some important things to keep in mind:

● Make sure you use a chair that provides strong back support. Be sure to keep your back straight while working, and keep your feet flat on the floor.

● Keep your wrists straight while you are typing. If your keyboard includes a "wrist rest," be sure not to use it while typing. Resting your hands while typing causes the wrists to bend, which causes muscle fatigue and can put you at risk for injuries.

● Position the monitor so that it is just a little below eye level and about two feet away. This will prevent strain on your neck muscles.

● Make sure there is enough light in the room so that you can easily see the monitor without straining your eyes.

● Keep your monitor's resolution set to a comfortable level. The highest possible resolution setting is not necessarily the best. Choose a resolution that displays images and text at a size that is comfortable to view.

Tips for Using the Internet for Research

The Internet is probably the single most important new tool for research since the public library. However, the advantage provided by the Internet can also be its greatest challenge: There is so much information out there that it is difficult to know where to begin.

Where to Start

A good place to begin work regardless of your research topic is Google. Arguably the most useful search engine, Google is an enormous "spider" (an automated piece of software that "crawls" the Web looking for information) that keeps an index of over three billion URLs.

Simply type your topic into Google's search bar. By default, Google looks for sites that contain every word you type. For instance, if you enter the words *sports medicine,* you will see a list of sites that contain both of those words, not just one or the other. To get better results, here are a few tips:

✔ Place quotes around your topic. Searching for **"sports medicine"** will find sites where that exact phrase appears.

✔ Use NEAR. Entering **sports NEAR medicine** will return sites that contain both words, and have the two words close to one another.

✔ Exclude unwanted results. Simply use a minus sign to indicate the words you do not want: **"sports medicine" - baseball**

When conducting a search online, be sure to spell all your search words correctly. Incorrect spellings can prevent you from getting good results.

✔ Stick to a single domain. If you only want to find information from a specific site, just add the domain after the search term along with the "site" tag, and Google will only look for documents on that site: **"sports medicine" site: www.espn.com**

Refining the Search

Your Google searches will likely give you page after page of hits, each with a brief summary of some of the text from that page. Some things to think about while browsing your Google results:

✔ Links on the right hand side of the page (and sometimes at the top, in a colored box) are sponsored links—this means that the company in question has paid to have their link show up. While this does not necessarily mean that the link is not worth exploring, it is usually an indicator that the site is selling a product or service, and might not be valuable for pure research.

✔ Google displays a few lines of text from each page and shows your search phrase in bold. Read the sentence surrounding the bold information to see if it is appropriate for your work.

✔ After you have entered your search phrase and have finished looking at the results, click on the "News" tab near the top of the page. This will show you recent news stories about your topic from a number of news services and wires.

Unique Online Research Tools

● **iTools** This "meta-research" tool lets you search not only the Web, but also discussion groups, dictionaries, and other sources. (**www.itools.com**)

● **RefDesk** This site contains links to hundreds of different Web resources, each designed for a very specific purpose. (**www.refdesk.com**)

● **eLibrary** This premium site searches the full text of hundreds of periodicals, newswires, books, maps, and more. (**www.elibrary.com**)

How to Evaluate Web Sites

While there is a lot of valuable information online, there is also a lot of information that can be deceptive and misleading. The books in your library have been evaluated by scholars and publishers; Web sites, however, are not verified. Learning to evaluate Web sites will make you a more savvy surfer and enable you to gather the information you need quickly and easily.

When you are trying to decide whether a Web site provides trustworthy information, there are a number of components to consider.

Authorship

When dealing with information from a Web site, the first and most important question to ask is "Who wrote this information?"

Once you have found the name of the author (usually located near the top or bottom of the page), do a quick Web search to see what else that author has written. Typing the author's name into Google will often return not only pages by that author, but also pages about that author, such as reviews of his or her work.

Check to see if the author has published in print. Search online for books that he or she has written. All this information will help you decide whether you should consider the person's information trustworthy.

Sponsorship/Publishing

Take a look at the domain that is offering the information. Why have they published this article? Are they trying to sell a product or service, or are they an impartial organization providing unbiased information?

Determining sponsorship or the publishing body will help you decide whether the information is biased. For instance, if an article that suggests a certain pesticide is very effective is posted on the Web site of a company that sells that pesticide, it is probably biased.

Accuracy

When you write a term paper, you are expected to provide sources for each of your facts. Look for Web sites that do the same thing by providing footnotes containing bibliographical information or references.

Also, look for clues that the information was written by someone knowledgeable. Spelling errors and grammatical mistakes are warning signs that the information provided may not be accurate.

Timeliness

Most articles will contain information about when it was written and when it was last updated. Recent update information normally appears at the very bottom of a Web site's main page, while date of authorship information usually appears near the title of the specific article.

The more recently something was written, the more likely it is to be accurate. An article from 1995 about "Internet trends," for instance, probably does not contain up-to-date information.

One Final Guideline

When using information from a Web site, remember to treat it just as you would print information. Never use information that you cannot verify with another source.

1 Fundamentals of Networking

Visit *Glencoe Online*

Go to this book's Web site at
networking.glencoe.com.

Click on **Unit Activities** and select
Unit 1 Scavenger Hunt. Complete the
online scavenger hunt to learn about
safe Internet use and the many
helpful features of this Web site.

Think About It

Networks Are Everywhere!
Even though you may not be able to see them, computer networks are part of our daily lives. From telephone networks to bank networks to the Internet, we are connected to the world at large.

Predicting the Future Activity
For many years, television networks affected more people than any other type of network. Do you think in the next ten years more people will access computer or television networks? Explain your answer.

YOU WILL LEARN TO...

WHY IT MATTERS.....................................

Everywhere you turn, networks are providing all sorts of services. When you use an ATM machine to withdraw cash from a bank account, a network is transmitting data back and forth. When you make a call, a network is connecting your telephone and sending the signal that carries your conversation. When you log on to a computer at school or work and print a document on a printer down the hall, you are using a network. Even when you are talking with your friends or family, you are using a social network.

Quick Write Activity

Whether you are aware of it or not, networks surround you. They are everywhere. Write a short paragraph that describes the networks that you use or that you are a part of.

WHAT YOU WILL DO..

READ TO SUCCEED

Survey Before You Read
Before starting the chapter, do a quick survey of the content by reading the colored headings. Think about what you already know about the topic. Look for the bolded terms and jot down words you do not recognize. Study the pictures and the charts. Do they help you predict what information will appear in the chapter? Finally, read the chapter summary and the review questions. This will help you pay attention to important concepts as you meet them in the reading.

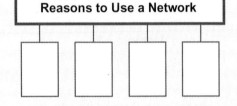

Guide to Reading

Main Ideas

Networks help us share data and resources. This increases efficiency and cost-effectiveness. Networks must be reliable, redundant, scalable, secure, and fast.

Key Terms

network
file sharing
resources
synchronous communication
asynchronous communication
reliable
redundant
scalable
throughput

Reading Strategy

Identify the four main reasons to use a network. Create a chart similar to the one below (also available online).

Reasons to Use a Network

TECH TRIVIA

Moore's Law Gordon Moore, cofounder of Intel Corporation, noted in the 1960s that engineering advances cause the processing power of computers to double every 18 months. Moore's Law has more or less held true over the last few decades.

Since computers were invented in the 1940s, they have grown more and more powerful at an astonishing rate. Early on, researchers could see that the full power of computers could be realized only if computers could share information and processing power with each other. Thus, networking was born. Today, networks affect nearly all aspects of our lives. Networks allow us to access more information than ever before.

REASONS TO USE A NETWORK

A computer **network** is two or more computer systems connected together so that they can share and exchange data. Networks connect systems together to make better use of limited resources. The definition of networking is very simple, but the details are much more involved.

Sharing Information

The most important reason to use a network is to share information. In business, sharing data is critical. For example, engineers designing an amusement park all need to reference the same documents to make sure they are all following the same plans. Putting documents such as blueprints on a network lets everyone use the same plans.

File sharing is the sharing of data between computers. Files store content such as text, graphics, music, videos, Web pages, and database records.

Sharing Resources

In addition to sharing files, networks also allow you to share resources. A **resource** is software or hardware that can be shared over the network, such as a hard drive, printer, or spreadsheet application. For example, anyone on the network can access the same network printer through his or her word processor, spreadsheet, database, or other software application, as shown in Figure 1.1 on the next page. It is much cheaper to buy one printer to share than it is to buy a printer for every computer.

 networking.glencoe.com

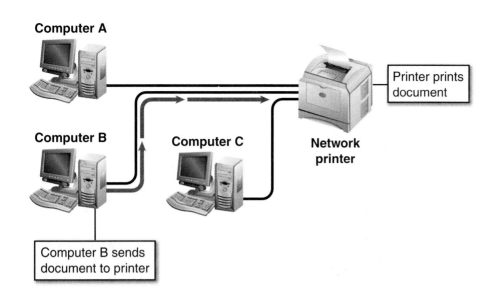

Computer A

Computer B

Computer C

Network printer

Printer prints document

Computer B sends document to printer

Centralizing Administration and Support

Another benefit of networking is the ability to centralize the administration and support of network users. Central control helps the network administrator handle many tasks, such as backing up data, creating new users, and maintaining the network—all from a single location.

One important administration job is to back up critical data and store it in a reliable place. If every user stored data on his or her computer, backing up this data would be very complicated. The administrator would have to look for new or changed files on tens, hundreds, or thousands of computers every day and then back all of them up. It is much easier to back up files if they are stored in a central location.

Better Communication

We use networks to improve communication. The phone system or plain old telephone system (POTS) is a complex web of cables, satellite systems, and transmission towers. Computer networks have made it easier for people around the world to communicate with each other using e-mail, instant messaging, and chat rooms.

Networking allows for two kinds of communications, called synchronous (real-time) and asynchronous, as shown in Table 1.1.

The Two Types of Communications

Type	Description	Examples
Synchronous	One person communicates and gets an answer immediately from one or more people.	◆ Phone calls ◆ Internet chat rooms ◆ Instant messaging
Asynchronous	One person communicates and has to wait for an answer.	◆ Letters and postcards ◆ E-mail

Table 1.1
Networks allow people to communicate and share resources through real-time or asynchronous communication. Which type of communication are you using if you leave a voice mail for a friend?

Networking in Real Time In **synchronous communication,** or real-time communication, people talk with each other at the same time. Examples include face-to-face conversations, phone calls, chat rooms, instant messaging, and videoconferencing. Business networks also use synchronous communication through videoconferencing. For example, employees in different offices around the world can work on a report using videoconferencing software and relying on the network to help them interact in real time (see Figure 1.2).

Networking Asynchronously Even though real-time conversations are an essential part of today's networked world, much more of our communication happens through **asynchronous communication.** Asynchronous communication does not happen instantly. There may be a delay of seconds, minutes, or even days. The two most common examples of this kind of communication are voice mail and e-mail. When you e-mail someone, you have to wait for a response. A shared printer on a network also uses asynchronous communication. If several people send files to the printer at once, the printer can only print one file at a time.

TRAITS OF A GOOD NETWORK

There are many traits that help define a good network. These traits include reliability, scalability, redundancy, security, and speed, as shown in Table 1.2. By using these traits, a network's strengths and weaknesses can be identified.

Five Traits of a Good Network

Trait	Description
Reliable	Is dependable, keeps data safe, and rarely fails
Scalable	Can expand with the needs of the organization
Redundant	Has multiple ways to ensure integrity and reliability of the network
Secure	Does not allow unauthorized access to important files
Speed	Transmits data quickly from computer to computer

READ ME!

Job Tip Downtime is costly to organizations. To avoid downtime, many network administrators and support staff must be available 24 hours a day, 7 days a week, just like doctors.

Reliable

A **reliable** network is dependable—users can trust that it will work. A good network is available to users all the time (except possibly during backups). It has few mechanical problems or failures. Electrical power to the network hardware remains continuous and stable.

The software on the network's central computer (also called a server) must also be reliable. The server software must handle any application "hiccups" or glitches, and it must recover quickly from more serious errors. Also, individual computers on the network must use operating systems and applications that can communicate and send information across the network. E-mail programs on users' computers, for instance, must be chosen so that they work with e-mail servers on the network to send, receive, download, and store mail messages correctly.

A network that does not work, or is "down" a lot, is in many ways worse than no network at all. Uptime is a term used to describe the amount of time a computer system has been running without needing a restart. Downtime, on the other hand, is the amount of time a system is out of service due to some problem. Figure 1.3 shows one way that a network administrator can tell if the network is reliable.

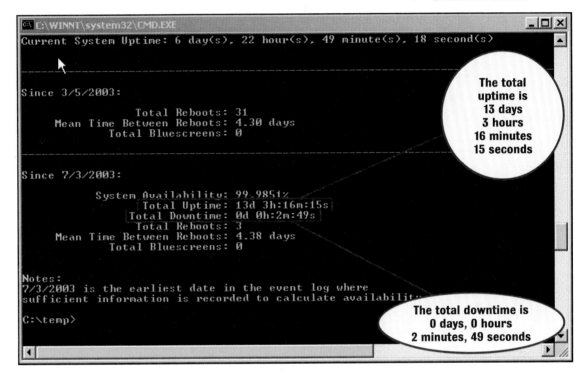

The total uptime is 13 days 3 hours 16 minutes 15 seconds

The total downtime is 0 days, 0 hours 2 minutes, 49 seconds

Redundant

A good network anticipates disaster. Hard drives fail, cooling fans die, and power supplies stop working. Fires, floods, earthquakes, and other natural disasters can all occur. To protect against these and other types of disasters, networks are redundant to keep the network running and to keep the data safe. **Redundant** networks duplicate data and resources to minimize downtime and data loss in the event of a disaster.

Scalable

A **scalable** network is one in which the hardware or software can grow (scale) up or down to meet an organization's needs. Organizations do not stay the same size or have the same needs forever. That is why scalability is a key issue that affects the entire network and its users.

There are different ways, however, in which a network and its software can scale. One way a network can scale upward is by simply adding more computers to support more users. A network can also grow by adding more power to a single server, or it can use a cluster of servers, joining them in a group that acts like a single system (see Figure 1.4 on the next page).

READ ME!

Caution The best way to prevent a security breach or disaster is to have a disaster prevention plan in place. The plan should include tactics for securing hardware, software, and data. Off-site software and data backups are strong elements of any disaster prevention plan.

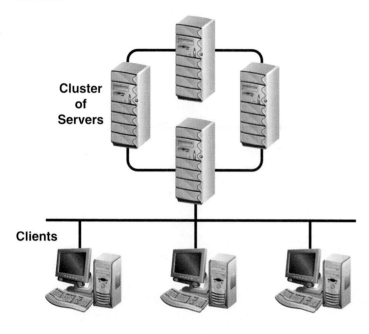

Cluster
of
Servers

Clients

Secure

Networks can be made secure through passwords, by servers that block unauthorized data, and by intercepting messages entering and leaving the network. Another safeguard is physical security. Server rooms are kept cool to prevent equipment from overheating. They are protected with specialized fireproofing techniques to prevent damage from fire sprinklers. Networking hardware is usually kept locked away to prevent unauthorized tampering.

Speed

The speed of the network is critical. Its speed is measured by several factors, such as the rate at which data travel, which is related to its throughput. **Throughput** refers to a network's capacity to handle traffic. On a relatively inactive network, a single message can speed along to its destination. However, on a congested network, messages must wait to be transmitted, and so the network slows down.

Other aspects of a network's speed include the number and power of its servers. For example, a Web server that processes credit card transactions must be extremely fast, or users will grow impatient and change service.

Section 1.1 Assessment

Concept Check

1. **Define** network, file sharing, resources, synchronous communication, asynchronous communication, reliable, redundant, scalable, and throughput.

2. **Explain** the reasons for using a network.

3. **Describe** the characteristics of a good network.

Critical Thinking

4. **Compare and Contrast** Describe the differences between synchronous and asynchronous communication. Provide examples of each.

5. **Analyze Information** Choose a network that you commonly use. Does the system qualify as a good network? Explain your answer.

Applying Skills

Describe the "Perfect" Network Based on your knowledge of a good network, describe what you think a "perfect" network would be. What kind of information and resources could users share on this network? What would the network administrator do? What kind of communication would be used?

Real World Technology

COMPUTER SAFETY IN THE CLASSROOM

Your computer probably does not seem like a dangerous piece of equipment. However, any classroom or workplace poses potential dangers, and you need to recognize and avoid them.

Always take proper precautions when working with electrical equipment such as computers.

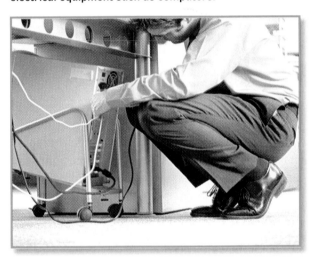

Safety-Conscious Attitudes

A good attitude can lead to a safer work environment:

◆ Know how to use equipment properly and safely.
◆ Stay alert for safety hazards, such as loose cords that can cause tripping or frayed wires that can cause shock.
◆ Stack or store equipment and materials properly.
◆ Avoid horseplay. It can cause accidents and damage equipment.

Fire Safety

Fire is always a concern in large buildings. Learn the location of fire alarms in your school or workplace. Be certain you know the procedures to follow in case a fire breaks out. Take fire drills seriously. They could save your life.

Using Computers Safely

As a result of sitting at a computer improperly, you could suffer from injuries. To avoid injuring yourself, make sure your workstation is adjusted for your physical comfort. Always readjust your seat if your workstation is used by many people. Make sure your feet are flat on the floor. Your wrists should be straight. The monitor should be about two feet away from you, at a height that allows you to look at it without twisting your neck.

Avoiding Common Injuries

Other kinds of injuries commonly happen at school and work. To avoid accidents:

◆ Always turn off and unplug equipment before repairing it.
◆ Never stick your hand or any object into an open piece of equipment. Shock results from touching electrical components or from handling damaged wiring.
◆ If you must move computer equipment, lift it by using your legs—not your back or arms. Get help or use a cart to move heavy objects.

Tech Focus

1. Review your school's safety procedures and emergency plan. Create a list of safety procedures for your classroom, and draw an evacuation map for your building.

2. Draft a report identifying safety issues related to computers. Describe safety standards regarding electrical equipment used with computers.

Guide to Reading

Main Ideas

Understanding how networks evolved in the past helps you understand today's technology. Future networks will enable us to connect almost anywhere, anytime, and faster than ever before.

Key Terms

multitask
timesharing
terminal
dumb terminal
ARPANET
hyperlink
distributed computing

Reading Strategy

Create a timeline of networking history milestones, similar to the one below (also available online).

Timeline of networking milestones

The history of networking plays an important part in its present state. Today's networks allow people and businesses around the world to communicate with each other quickly and reliably.

THE FIRST NETWORKS

In the 1960s, large, powerful computers called mainframes dominated the computing world. They were marvels of technology—lightning fast, complex, and very expensive. Mainframes were so large that it took entire rooms to house these giants, which consisted of multiple cabinets and assorted hardware.

Mainframes took their name from the fact that the processors and often the memory were housed in a single cabinet known as the "main frame." Unlike today's highly interactive PCs and Macs, mainframes did not allow direct interaction between human and machine. Instead of a keyboard, envelope-sized punch cards were used to enter data into mainframes.

Multitasking

In the early days of computers, mainframes could only perform one task at a time. Eventually, a new system of processing data emerged. The new system, called multiprogramming, opened the door to more efficient data processing. Computers learned to **multitask,** allowing them to turn their attention to another job if one was held up waiting for input or output. Within a few years, the concept of running multiple jobs at the same time led to yet another advance, called **timesharing.**

Figure 1.5
The terminal/host computing model made better use of the mainframe's resources. What advantages did this model of computing offer?

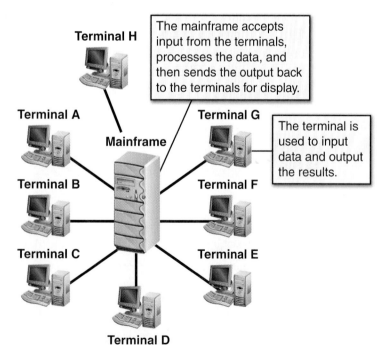

The mainframe accepts input from the terminals, processes the data, and then sends the output back to the terminals for display.

The terminal is used to input data and output the results.

Terminal H
Terminal A
Mainframe
Terminal B
Terminal C
Terminal G
Terminal F
Terminal E
Terminal D

networking.glencoe.com

Timesharing and Terminals Timesharing was based on the idea of switching the computer's processing from one task to another. Timesharing also allowed direct human/machine interaction in the form of **terminals** wired to the mainframe. A terminal is a device with a keyboard and a monitor that is directly connected to a mainframe. At this point, computing evolved from a localized, stand-alone model (mainframes only) to a more accessible, spread-out "networking" model in which many separate workstations could simultaneously access and use the processing power of the mainframe (see Figure 1.5).

Dumb Terminals The terminals used with timesharing computers were known as **dumb terminals**—that is, they had little or no processing power of their own. Nor did they have any local storage. Much like terminals, dumb terminals essentially consisted of keyboards for input and screens for output, and they were wired directly to the host computer.

ARPANET

In the 1970s, the United States Department of Defense developed a revolutionary new way of connecting computers. This network came to be known as **ARPANET,** named after the Advanced Research Projects Agency Network. ARPANET linked computers at universities and research labs around the country. It also provided a data highway for military communications. Through ARPANET, computers were finally able to communicate and to share files through an interconnected network, as shown in Figure 1.6. Through the use of mainframes, also called host computers, terminals were directly connected to ARPANET, which is the ancestor of the incredible worldwide Internet.

The development of personal computers (PCs) built processing power into desktop computers, which began to move computing away from the mainframe model. As these new PCs grew more and more capable, they eventually replaced terminals and freed users from central mainframe computers. New computer users also found PCs to be more user-friendly and interactive than the dumb terminals. While terminals can still be found in some work environments, they are not as popular as they once were. The world of hardware, software, and thus networks quickly evolved when PCs appeared.

● **Figure 1.6**
ARPANET allowed host computers around the country to communicate with each other. Why is ARPANET important?

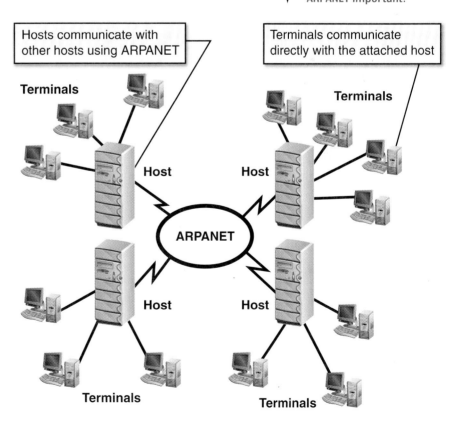

Hosts communicate with other hosts using ARPANET

Terminals communicate directly with the attached host

Terminals

Terminals

Host

Host

ARPANET

Host

Host

Terminals

Terminals

TODAY'S NETWORKS

Networks were once only used in governments, giant corporations, universities, or research groups. Now, networks have become a part of everyday life.

The Internet and the Web

The original Internet was primarily a text-based network mainly devoted to e-mail, file transfers, and newsgroups. In 1989, Tim Berners-Lee invented the World Wide Web (Web or WWW), a graphics-based interface used to access information on the Internet. Instead of using a keyboard and text to navigate the Internet, Berners-Lee used a mouse and hyperlinks. A **hyperlink** is text or an image that, when clicked on with a mouse, "links" you to another document. By building a collection of hyperlinked documents, users could share information more easily than ever before.

Although the Web is only one part of the Internet, most users think they are the same thing. The Internet is hardware connected together to create a massive worldwide network. The Internet's hardware consists of those computers, cables, telephone wires, and high-speed communication lines. The Internet is the world's largest, most widely used network.

Like all computer hardware, the Internet needs software that contains instructions that tell the hardware how to do work for the user. The Web includes software, such as Web browsers, that send information along the Internet's hardware. Web browsers allow you to view and interact with Web pages.

Networking in Society

Everywhere you turn in society today, networks are improving communications. We depend on networks to be reliable, redundant, secure, scalable, and fast in many aspects of our lives.

Business Companies are dependent on networks to efficiently store, back up, and secure data. Even businesses with just a credit card scanner are using networks to connect to a banking network. Today, many businesses rely on their network as part of their success.

Health Care In the past, families selected a family doctor. For all but the most serious problems, they returned to that same doctor year after year. In today's health climate, you might visit the same doctor's office, but rarely will you see the same doctor. Because of this, the health care and the insurance industry depend on reliable networks to transfer your medical records to the people who need the information most.

Education Teachers use networks to keep student records up-to-date and to communicate with parents. Students rely on networks to complete and store schoolwork and to use the Internet for research.

In education, scalability is an important factor. In many cities across the United States, new schools are being built to keep up with the growing numbers of students. As these schools (and their districts) grow, so too must the networks that support the staff's and the students' needs.

Leisure and Recreation At first, the Internet was used primarily as a research tool, allowing users at various educational and research institutes around the world to better collaborate on important projects. More recently, the Internet has become a big part of our leisure and recreational time. However, the more we turn to the Internet for entertainment purposes, the more we demand of it. For example, in order for a sporting event to be broadcast over the Internet, the connection to the Internet must be able to transmit continuous video and audio. The connection must be fast and reliable. Otherwise, a slow or intermittent connection could prevent the user from seeing fluid motion or hearing continuous audio (see Figure 1.7).

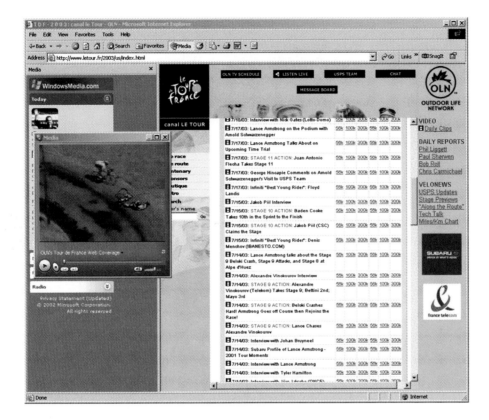

◀────────● Figure 1.7
The Internet provides content for our leisure and recreational activities. What do you think are the advantages of watching an event over the Internet versus on television?

TOMORROW'S NETWORKS

Internet access is becoming more readily available than ever before. Old, unused phone booths are being converted to wireless access points in some cities. New ways of using existing systems, such as the power lines in your house, are now being transformed into network cabling. There are even plans for networks in space!

In the past, massive computing power was solely the realm of expensive mainframe or so-called "super computers." Networks today and in the future will exploit the advantages of clustering less expensive computers to perform work more quickly and cheaply than the prohibitively expensive super computers of yesterday. **Distributed computing** uses the processing power of thousands of idle computers. It is the primary source of computing power for research into the human genome, protein folding, and the search for extraterrestrial life (see Figure 1.8 on the next page).

To do all this combined processing, the computers within the network must be able to communicate freely among themselves. The computers also need

Figure 1.8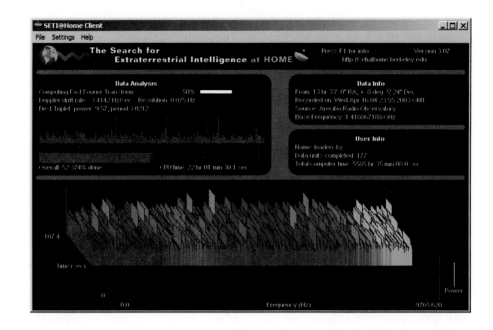

Distributed computing uses available processor time on many computers to process large data sets. One example is the Seti@Home project, run by Berkeley University in California. What promise does distributed computing hold for solving complex processing problems?

TECH TRIVIA

How Fast Is 983 Mbps?
A transmission speed of 983 Mbps would enable you to send a feature-length DVD quality movie every *36 seconds*.

Activity 1.1 Preventing Time Theft Spam, also known as junk e-mail, is hitting Web-enabled cell phones and PDAs. Discover what this type of spam is costing the subscribers. Go to **networking.glencoe.com** to locate information about these costly, and possibly illegal, messages.

to collaborate and share different tasks in order to contribute to the end result. Distributed computing represents a different way of using a network. Most current networking requires users to handle file management themselves. However, the computers in a distributed system take more of the file management burden on themselves and, in the process, reduce the burden on their users.

NGI and Internet2

In 1996, the U.S. government started the Next Generation Internet (NGI) initiative. This federally-funded program sought to develop next generation technologies, which are paving the way for a new, more capable Internet. In conjunction with NGI, a university-led Internet2 initiative is also working to bring new technologies to the world. Although Internet2 research is ongoing, the NGI initiative was recently completed. It had met nearly all of its original goals. New, advanced programs sponsored by the government are continuing under the Large Scale Networking (LSN) Coordinating Group.

Currently, over 200 universities are participating in Internet2 research, often with funding from NGI. The Internet2 is an ultrafast network. At the time this book was written, the current record for data transmission using Internet2 technology was 983 megabits per second (Mbps). This amazing transmission rate was sustained for over an hour across a distance of more than 4,000 miles.

Schools of the Future

With improved networking capabilities, classroom learning can evolve into more cooperative, team-oriented learning projects, possibly involving students from many countries. In some states, online cyber charter schools allow students to learn with the full benefits of Internet-enhanced content. Traditional classrooms may give way to webcasts, as students tune in to watch the day's lesson using their home or school computers. Webcasts are documents and videos that are sent through a network in real-time to multiple locations. Network infrastructure, such as that promised by Internet2 and NGI, could make such collaboration truly possible.

Networks in Health Care

In the future, when a physician needs accurate medical histories in emergency situations, she or he may rely on a wireless transmitter built into the patient's health-care card. The patient's file could be received on a handheld device (see Figure 1.9).

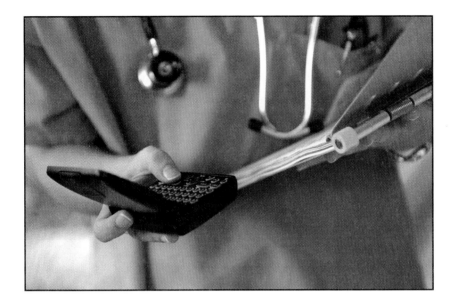

Figure 1.9
Wireless technology is becoming more and more common. What other uses for wireless services do you think will be developed in the future?

READ ME!

Caution A physician's code of ethics, specifically regarding confidentiality of patient information, requires that any information sent via a network be highly secured.

Coupled with the Internet2/NGI initiatives, a revolution in health care is developing. Medical researchers will be able to collaborate and exchange data in more ways than ever thought possible. Surgeons may be able to "scrub in" virtually and participate in complex surgical procedures with their colleagues on the other side of the world.

Section 1.2 Assessment

Concept Check

1. **Define** multitask, timesharing, terminal, dumb terminal, ARPANET, hyperlink, and distributed computing.

2. **Describe** various uses of networks in today's world.

3. **Explain** distributed computing.

Critical Thinking

4. **Synthesize Knowledge** Provide examples of how networks in business, education, and health care apply the traits of good networks.

5. **Predict Technologies** Make a list of devices that you, your friends, and your family use to access networks. Predict how these networks might change in the future.

Applying Skills

Research Technology in Education Research the technology that is available for student use in two colleges or universities. List each. For each school, describe the computer-related technology offered in that school's classrooms, dorms, and other buildings.

Section 1.3 Networking Careers

Guide to Reading

Main Ideas

There are many career paths in networking. Although educational backgrounds for many career paths in networking are similar, on-the-job experience and a continued interest in learning are keys to success in networking.

Key Terms

network administrator
network engineer
network architect
network support
    technician
outsourcing

Reading Strategy

Create a table similar to the one below (also available online) that lists the job titles, skills, and education needed for each networking career.

Job Title	Job Responsibilities	Technical Skills or Educational Requirements

Building and maintaining a network is a full-time job. There are so many different aspects of building and maintaining a network, that in many businesses it requires several people working full-time to handle the job.

CAREER PATHS

Networks should be carefully designed to meet the needs of their users. This job may fall to a network designer or systems analyst. Next in line are the network engineers, who are responsible for connecting everything together. The network administrators oversee the network once it is running. Finally, network support technicians help users deal with problems once the network is operating.

Network Administrator

Network administrators are responsible for setting up computers and installing operating systems. They also set up and administer servers and the software that runs on those servers. Network administrators apply upgrades and patches to configuration and security settings. Administrators in charge of Web servers, for example, must be on the lookout for viruses entering the system and for hackers attempting to gain unauthorized access to company data.

Job Skills Network administrators are typically people who enjoy the challenge of tinkering with computers and figuring out puzzles. People interested in this career continuously have to immerse themselves in the learning process. New technology is constantly updating old technology, and the job is always changing.

Education Many administrators study computer science or information science in college, whereas others choose technical schools focusing on building networking skills. On-the-job experience, coupled with a willingness to learn, is often the most valuable asset one can have.

Activity 1.2 Finding Job Openings Online Many jobs in networking can be found on the Internet. Go to **networking.glencoe.com** to locate sites that list job openings and common job qualifications for networking.

Network Engineer

Network engineers are responsible for connecting computers to the network and connecting networks to other networks. Little time is spent in front of a keyboard, as they are more responsible for planning and connecting networks (see Figure 1.10).

● **Figure 1.10**
Network engineers handle the physical components of a network. What skills are important for a career as a network engineer?

Job Skills Network engineers must be flexible. The work they do cannot stop business operations. A typical day might start at 10 or 11 A.M. and finish at 8 or 9 P.M. They are also typically on call 24 hours a day, in case anything goes wrong.

Education Network engineers commonly have strong educational backgrounds in math, computer science, or engineering. Employers generally look for intelligent individuals who are good at problem solving. A lot of the technology a network engineer works with is so new that few people have become experts at using it. Network engineers have to figure things out as they go.

Network Architect

A **network architect** is often called a systems analyst or network designer. This individual oversees the construction, maintenance, and expansion of a company's network. The architect works closely with the company to determine its needs, then decides whether it is best to use existing network infrastructure or to build new infrastructure.

Job Skills Network architects must have good people skills in order to communicate with many different people in their company. They have to learn how to differentiate between what people want and what they really need from their systems. They also need to enjoy making the most out of what they have. People in this profession often "inherit" an existing system that may be poorly designed or technically deficient. Architects who succeed relish the challenge this presents and make the most of the opportunity to make the system better (see Figure 1.11 on the next page).

Enrichment **LAB**

Lab 1.1 Troubleshooting Users' Problems Practice additional hands-on networking skills on page 428.

Education Most network architects study computer or information science, computer engineering, or computer systems analysis. With rapid changes in technology come the need to continuously upgrade skills by seeking out opportunities to learn new technology and networks.

Figure 1.11
Network architects plan how to build and expand a network to meet new demands. Why do network architects need to have good people skills?

TECH TRIVIA

Help Desk Technician Wanted Every day, newspapers all over the country advertise jobs for companies seeking help desk personnel. Beyond knowing about computer systems, these people must be solution-oriented and service-minded. Look at some job ads to see for yourself.

Network Support Technician

Network support technicians use specialized, technical knowledge to troubleshoot the many problems that arise in network usage. Some companies have their own in-house support personnel. Other companies employ outside contractors to provide technical support. Hiring an outside company to handle various information technology (IT) services, such as technical support, is called **outsourcing.**

Job Skills Above all else, support technicians must have patience and be able to work with people who may be upset about their technical difficulties. Technicians must be able to solve problems and communicate solutions to less tech-savvy individuals.

Educational backgrounds typically consist of computer science, information science, or computer systems analysis.

JOB SKILLS

The job skills required to succeed in a networking career are communication, problem solving, teamwork, and leadership. Because the technology is always changing, you can no longer count on going to college and learning all you will ever need to know for the rest of your career.

Communication

Communication skills are essential for a career in networking. You will have a very specialized and technical knowledge of what makes a network function. However, many of the people you work with may not have the same degree of understanding that you do. You must be able to communicate technology needs in clear terms that make sense.

Many times, you will encounter challenges that you do not know how to solve. Knowing how to ask questions and whom to ask are important skills. In some jobs, such as a network architect or support technician, being able to listen to the users' needs is crucial.

Problem Solving

You will encounter situations in which there is no easy solution, no manual to refer to, and no expert, other than yourself, to rely on. But there are steps that you can use to become a better problem solver (see Table 1.3).

Teamwork

Teamwork requires a good attitude, a willingness to participate, and the ability to help others and ask for help when necessary. You will often work with others to plan, implement, and configure network components. As part of a team, you can generally accomplish more than you would if every member of the team were working on his or her own. Teamwork often leads to increased productivity and better job satisfaction (see Figure 1.12).

Leadership

To advance in any career, including the field of networking, you must develop leadership skills. Good leaders exhibit all the skills previously described. They have the ability to communicate with team members and solve problems. In addition, they must be capable of making difficult decisions and accepting responsibility for their decisions. Mistakes are often part of the learning process, and good leaders are able to learn from past mistakes.

Table 1.3
Problem-solving skills are essential for a career in networking. What technology resources could you use to solve real-world networking problems?

Common Problem-Solving Steps

Step	Action
1. Identify the problem.	◆ Speak with others to determine the nature of the problem. ◆ Identify the most likely cause.
2. Find information that will help you solve the problem.	◆ Search the Internet. ◆ Talk with a colleague.
3. Create a solution.	◆ Generate possible solutions. ◆ Eliminate improbabilities.
4. Implement and evaluate the solution.	◆ Keep a journal of solutions and their outcomes. ◆ Identify other possible solutions and implement those if your original solution does not work.

Figure 1.12
Teamwork is an important skill in networking. Why are teams generally able to accomplish more than individuals?

> **YOU TRY IT**

ACTIVITY 1A Creating a Career Development Plan

It's not too early to start developing a career plan. Exploring networking careers can help you determine if you want to pursue this type of career path and, if so, which ones you find most interesting.

1 Make a list of networking careers that sound interesting to you. List the qualifications you already have and what you enjoy learning about.

2 Use your list to research career forecasts in your chosen areas. Consider how long you plan to be in school as you evaluate the career trends.

3 Find networking job postings and information about networking careers at career Web sites such as **www.monster.com** or **www.careerbuilder.com**.

4 Select two or three jobs that interest you. Research the qualifications and educational requirements that are necessary to get the job.

5 Select the career that sounds best to you.

6 Make a more detailed list of what you would need to accomplish or learn, what type of schools or courses you would need, and how long you think it will take to accomplish these objectives.

Whether or not you end up in this career is not important at this time. When it comes time to make a career decision, following these steps can help you plan for your future—for any type of job.

Section 1.3 Assessment

Concept Check

1. Define network administrator, network engineer, network architect, network support technician, and outsourcing.

2. Describe why it is important to have good communication skills in the field of networking.

3. Explain the role of a network architect.

Critical Thinking

4. Self-Assessment Assess yourself in communication, problem solving, teamwork, and leadership skills. Describe how you can improve your skills in each of these areas.

5. Compare and Contrast List the similarities and differences between the roles of a network administrator and a network engineer.

Applying Skills

Solve Problems Think of a problem you recently had, such as a conflict at school or work or a challenging assignment. Apply the problem-solving steps in Table 1.3 (page 21) to identify ways to solve this problem.

GETTING A JOB IN NETWORKING

Networking can be a lifelong career path, from entry-level jobs such as hardware technician all the way up to high-level positions such as Chief Information Officer.

Networking Jobs

Jobs in networking are as varied as the systems being used and the companies that use them. Many companies use PC-based networks, but others have complex networks including different platforms and operating systems. This environment rewards professionals with all types of skills and backgrounds.

Depending on your skills, you may find other networking jobs of interest. Many companies need administrators with security expertise, for example, whereas others look for systems analysts who can design corporate networks.

Preparing for a Networking Career

The training you need depends on the type of job that interests you. For example, if you are primarily interested in working with technology (such as setting up networks), then a networking certification such as the Network+ certification may be all you need. If you want to be an administrator, systems analyst, or IT manager, a degree in computer science can be helpful.

You should also map out a career path, marked by short- and long-term goals. That is, where would you like your career to begin and end, and what jobs do you hope to have during your career? These decisions can help you determine the kinds of credentials you will need and can help you target your job searches.

Looking for Jobs

You can find many resources for networking jobs, including newspapers, career-oriented Web sites, and corporate sites on which companies post their own job openings. The key to finding a job, however, is to focus your efforts. Decide what type of job interests you, and then look only for openings for that type of job.

Many networking professionals begin their careers as a hardware or installation technician. This type of job guarantees you plenty of exposure to hardware and software of all kinds.

Next, tailor your résumé to that job. List the exact education, experiences, and references that qualify you for that specific job. Your cover letter should also be tailored to the job and to the specific company to which you are applying.

Tech Focus

1. What should you list in your résumé and cover letter when applying for a networking job?

2. Participate in a career-related activity at your school or a local business. Describe the activity and the benefits you received from it in a class discussion or short report.

Guide to Reading

Main Ideas

A computer is made up of many components that interact with each other. Hardware is the physical components of the system. Software is a compiled set of instructions that tell the hardware what to do.

Key Terms

input
output
operating system (OS)
central processing unit (CPU)
reduced instruction set
    computers (RISC)
complex instruction set
    computers (CISC)
random-access memory (RAM)
read-only memory (ROM)

Reading Strategy

Categorize the four parts of a computer system. Create a chart similar to the one below (also available online).

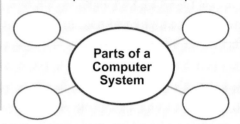

Parts of a Computer System

In this section, you will learn about the basic parts of a computer. These concepts and related terms are used by networking professionals every day. Because computers are part of every network, you will need to understand what is inside each individual computer to fully understand networks.

THE PARTS OF A COMPUTER SYSTEM

It is important in networking to understand how the different parts of a computer system work together. The four main parts of a computer system are hardware, software, data, and users.

Hardware

The first part of the computer system is hardware, which identifies all the physical components of a computer. The monitor, motherboard, RAM, and cables are examples of hardware. In later chapters, we focus on various hardware components related specifically to networking.

Input Devices Computers would not be very fun (or practical) to work with if you had no way to input or output data. **Input** allows you to provide instructions to your computer so that it knows what to do. Input devices include keyboards, mice, and microphones.

Most devices use ports to connect to the computer. A port is a socket in the back of a computer that connects input devices and output devices to the computer, as shown in Figure 1.13. Ports come in a variety of shapes, and different ports have different capabilities. Serial ports are used for devices that do not transmit a lot of information, such as a mouse, modem, or joystick. Parallel ports are used in conjunction with devices that need to transmit a larger volume of data, such as printers. Other types of ports, such as USB and FireWire, are capable of transmitting data at very high rates.

Enrichment
LAB

Lab 1.2 Comparing and Contrasting Input Devices
Practice additional hands-on networking skills on page 429.

Output Devices Data that displays on the screen, prints, and music that emanates from speakers are all forms of **output.** Output allows you to view or hear the results of what the computer is doing. Without output, you would have no way of knowing whether the computer was doing anything. Some examples of output devices include speakers, monitors, and printers.

Storage Devices Long-term storage of data is a broad topic. For now, it is important to understand the three basic storage categories: hard drives, optical drives, and flash memory. (See Table 1.4 for more details.)

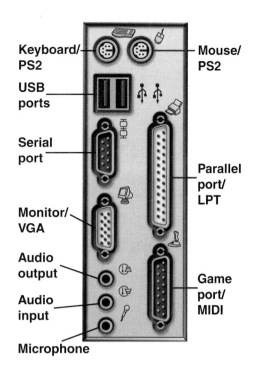

Keyboard/PS2 · Mouse/PS2 · USB ports · Serial port · Parallel port/LPT · Monitor/VGA · Audio output · Audio input · Game port/MIDI · Microphone

● Figure 1.13
Input devices provide simple ways for a user to interact with the computer. What input devices would you connect to each of the ports shown here?

Storage Devices		
Type	**Description**	**Example**
Magnetic	Information is quickly stored on magnetic platters, but is typically not very portable. Data can be lost with excessive jostling of the drive.	Hard drive or floppy drive
Optical	Optical devices are portable, but have slower write speeds compared to other technologies.	CD or DVD drive
Flash Memory	This technology is possibly *the* storage device of the future. It is small, and because it has no moving parts allows easy mobility. It is much more expensive per MB than the other types of storage devices.	Flash keychain drive

● Table 1.4
Different types of storage devices are intended for different purposes. List the different types of storage devices you have used and explain why each type was useful.

READ ME!

Jargon Software and hardware are generally classified as "PC-compatible" or "Mac-compatible." Typically, software applications are built for a specific operating system, such as Windows OS, Mac OS, and Linux.

Software

The second part of the computer system is software. Through the use of software, a user can tell the computer what to do. Software is basically a set of instructions for the computer's processor to follow. Software is often divided into two broad categories: systems software and applications software.

Systems Software Systems software includes the **operating system (OS)** and all utility programs that allow the computer to work. The OS software interacts closely with the hardware. This software makes it possible for users to interact with devices such as the processor, memory, hard drives, and other peripherals. Windows, Mac OS, and Linux are all examples of OS software.

Utility programs perform maintenance tasks that keep the computer operating at optimal settings. One common utility is a program that defragments a hard drive.

YOU TRY IT

ACTIVITY 1B Analyzing a Hard Drive

In this You Try It activity, you learn how to analyze your hard drive's fragmentation to determine if the hard drive should be defragmented. By defragmenting the hard drive, you will reorganize data to be stored more efficiently. The following steps apply to the Windows operating system (Mac OS X defragments in the background automatically).

Figure 1.14 ●
System utilities perform specialized jobs, such as defragmenting your hard drive.

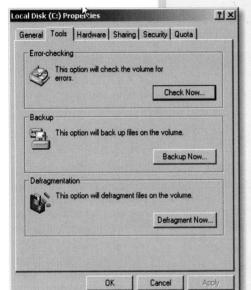

❶ Click the **Start** button.

❷ Point to **Programs** and select **Accessories.**

❸ Click **Windows Explorer.**

❹ Right-click the **C: drive.**

❺ Click **Properties.**

❻ Click the **Tools** tab (as shown in Figure 1.14).

❼ Click **Defragment Now.**

❽ Click **Analyze.**

❾ Click **View Report.**

A report appears informing you of the number of fragmented files and the overall percentage of the drive that is fragmented. If your drive is over 10% fragmented, it should probably be defragmented, with your teacher's permission. This operation can take up to several hours, depending on the capacity of the drive and the amount of fragmentation.

Another type of system software includes the device drivers that instruct an operating system how to interact with a device. For example, a graphics card driver allows the operating system to make use of the various capabilities of the graphics card in order to display an image on your monitor.

Application Software Application software is used to create or process data. This includes applications such as word processing, spreadsheet, presentation, and database applications. It also includes the many games available and the file-sharing applications that download and play music files.

Data

The third part of the computer system, data, are the information the computer works on. This includes the files you create, such as word processing documents, spreadsheets, images, and so forth. It also includes the system and program files that make up the operating system and software applications you use.

All data in a computer are stored in a digital form called binary, which uses ones and zeros. A computer "speaks" binary and only understands "on" (represented as "1") and "off" ("0"). For data to be read by humans, they must be translated from binary form to some form that you and I understand, such as text.

As you input data, such as text, into a word processor, the operating system translates data into this binary format so the computer can process and store the data.

Users

Finally, the fourth part of the computer system is a user. A user is another name for a person who uses a computer. Users include the people who program computers, as well as those who use the applications created by programmers.

INSIDE THE MACHINE

Underneath the cover of your computer case is a lot of very sophisticated and powerful hardware. For instance, the processor in your computer today is not much larger than a postage stamp. However, it is many thousands of times more powerful than the first room-sized computers created in the 1940s and 1950s. Most components in your computer have evolved to the point at which they are small, reliable, fairly inexpensive to manufacture. They are also easy to replace when newer and more sophisticated models come along.

Processor

The **central processing unit (CPU),** also known as the processor, is the brain of the computer. It is plugged into the motherboard. CPUs perform very basic functions, such as addition, subtraction, multiplication, and division. This is not so difficult—a calculator can do that. What makes a CPU so special is the fact that it can perform billions and trillions of calculations every second (see Figure 1.15).

The motherboard contains an intricate web of circuits. These circuits transmit data back and forth between the CPU and RAM, and between other slots that enable you to expand the computer's capabilities.

Today's CPUs fall roughly into two groups according to how they execute instructions. **Reduced instruction set computers (RISC)** rely on a relatively small set of simplified instructions, allowing them to operate very fast. Because the instruction set is simpler, the technology can also be implemented relatively cheaply. **Complex instruction set computers (CISC)** support more instructions. Due to the complexity of the instruction set, CISC chips are more difficult to design and build, leading to somewhat higher costs. Interestingly, most desktop (or personal) computers are built on CISC chip technologies, whereas many larger server and mainframe computers tend to be built on RISC technology.

● **Figure 1.15**
The CPU is the brain of the computer. What is the role of the CPU?

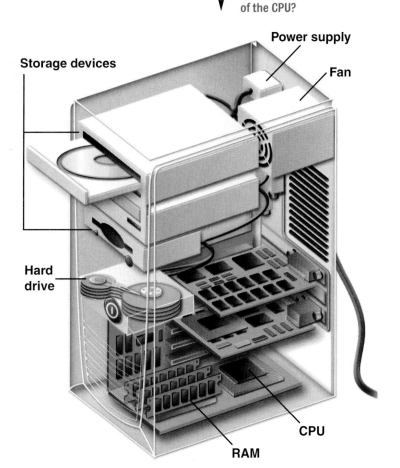

Power supply

Storage devices

Fan

Hard drive

CPU

RAM

Memory

Closely coupled with the CPU is a computer's memory, or **random-access memory (RAM).** RAM provides a storage area for data going into and out of the CPU. RAM is usually purchased in modules that can be plugged into special slots on the motherboard, making it easy for a user or system administrator to increase a computer's memory.

Despite its ability to retrieve and store large quantities of data very quickly, RAM is not a long-term storage solution. RAM requires power in order to hold onto its data. Thus, when your computer is turned off, the data cannot be stored in RAM. In fact, even while your computer is on, new data is constantly replacing old data as you work.

When the computer first boots or starts up, it accesses another kind of memory called **read-only memory (ROM).** ROM is a set of prerecorded instructions that tell the computer how to start, how to look for hardware devices, and how to check the operating system on the computer's disk drives. ROM is permanently written into a ROM chip and cannot be rewritten.

Communication Devices

Communication devices, such as modems and network interface cards (NICs), enable your computer to connect to other computers. For example, standard modems use a phone line to connect to another computer. NICs allow your computer to communicate with other computers on other networks. All of these types of devices are covered in much greater detail later in the book.

Section 1.4 Assessment

Concept Check

1. **Define** input, output, operating system (OS), central processing unit (CPU), reduced instruction set computers (RISC), complex instruction set computers (CISC), random-access memory (RAM), and read-only memory (ROM).

2. **Describe** the four parts of the computer system.

3. **Explain** the purpose of storage devices.

Critical Thinking

4. **Draw Conclusions** Why is RAM *not* considered a long-term storage device?

5. **Sequence Information** Suppose you are typing a report for science class. Explain how the information gets from your brain to the computer and then printed so that you can hand the report in.

Applying Skills

Categorize Hardware Make a list of the computer hardware devices used in your classroom, school, or at home on a regular basis. Categorize each device as an input or output device.

SECTION 1.1 Principles of Networking

Key Terms

network, 6
file sharing, 6
resource, 6
synchronous
  communication, 8
asynchronous
  communication, 8
reliable, 8
redundant, 9
scalable, 9
throughput, 10

Main Ideas

- Networks allow two or more computers to share data and resources.
- Networks allow data to be shared synchronously or asynchronously.
- Content is any type of data that can be saved and used later on.
- Networks must be reliable, scalable, redundant, secure, and fast.

SECTION 1.2 Networks Past, Present, and Future

Key Terms

multitask, 12
timesharing, 12
terminal, 13
dumb terminal, 13
ARPANET, 13
hyperlink, 14
distributed computing, 15

Main Ideas

- Past efforts in networking, such as ARPANET, have led to the technology and infrastructure of today's networks.
- Networks today appear in business, education, health care, and even in our homes.
- Tomorrow's Internet promises faster delivery of high bandwidth content that will further enable us to accomplish more.

SECTION 1.3 Networking Careers

Key Terms

network administrator, 18
network engineer, 19
network architect, 19
network support
  technician, 20
outsourcing, 20

Main Ideas

- There are many career choices in networking.
- Education and on-the-job experience are essential.
- Continued learning is a requirement for working in networking.

SECTION 1.4 The Computer System

Key Terms

input, 24
output, 25
operating system (OS), 25
central processing unit
  (CPU), 27
reduced instruction set
  computers (RISC), 27
complex instruction set
  computers (CISC), 27
random-access memory
  (RAM), 28
read-only memory
  (ROM), 28

Main Ideas

- Hardware comprises the physical components of a computer system.
- Input devices allow a user to input data into a computer.
- Output devices allow the user to see that the computer has performed instructions.
- Software is a set of instructions that tells the computer's hardware what to do.
- Systems software is the software that most closely communicates with the computer's hardware.
- Application software is the software you generally interact with to play games, create word processing or spreadsheet documents, or manipulate digital images and video.

READ TO SUCCEED PRACTICE

Survey Skills Develop a personal study tool by modifying the survey strategy introduced on page 5. Use the section and paragraph headings to create a topic outline, leaving enough room between topics to add key items. Then close your textbook and fill in as much information as you can remember about these topics. This is a good way to help you determine which topics you understand and which topics need the most additional review.

Reviewing Key Terms

1. Explain multitasking.
2. What does a network engineer do?
3. Explain what it means for a network to be scalable.
4. What is the difference between RAM and ROM?
5. What is the function of the computer's central processing unit?

Understanding Main Ideas

6. **Explain** how terminals and timesharing work.
7. **Explain** the advantages of flash memory versus optical disks.
8. **Identify** the job skills required for each of the following jobs:
   ◆ Network administrator
   ◆ Network engineer
   ◆ Network architect
   ◆ Network support technician
9. **List and describe** the five traits of a good network. Explain each trait in two or three sentences.
10. **Explain** how distributed computing works and how it can make more efficient use of computing resources.
11. **List** examples of three items that may be shared over a network.
12. **Explain** why it is important to keep only a single copy of a shared file.
13. **Describe** the four parts of a computer system and how they work together.

Critical Thinking

14. **Analyze Your Hardware** With your teacher's help, look at the back of a computer and then inside the case. Make sure it is *not* plugged in! Create a diagram and identify the following hardware components. Then, list the function of each component.
   ◆ USB port
   ◆ Serial port
   ◆ Monitor/VGA port
   ◆ Game/MIDI port
   ◆ CPU
   ◆ Storage devices
   ◆ RAM
   ◆ Hard drive
   ◆ Power supply
   ◆ Fan
15. **Compare and Contrast Networking Careers** Describe how the jobs of a network engineer and a network architect are similar and different.
16. **Evaluate Skills** Identify the four skills employers often look for when hiring someone for a networking job. Explain why these skills are important.
17. **Make Predictions** How do you think the use of audio and video on the Internet will change as new technologies make the Internet faster? Write a short paragraph and explain your predictions.

e-Review ....

networking.glencoe.com

Study with PowerPoint

Review the main points in this chapter. Choose **e-Review > PowerPoint Outlines > Chapter 1.**

Online Self Check

Test your knowledge of the topics covered in this chapter. Choose **e-Review > Self Check Assessments > Chapter 1.**

Making Connections

Social Studies – Compare Computer Networks to Social Networks Consider the similarities between a computer network and a group of people who interact within a cultural unit, such as a fishing village. Describe how both a group of computers and a group of people do each of the following:

a. Communicate
b. Share information
c. Share resources
d. Collaborate to solve problems
e. Change scale (that is, grow or shrink)

STANDARDS AT WORK

Networking History

Students are proficient in the use of technology. (NETS-S 1)

Create a Report

Use word processing software and an Internet browser to write a short report on the history of computer networking. In the report, describe how the technology evolved and identify significant, large-scale networks. Trace any networking development trends.

◆ With your teacher's permission, use the Internet to research your facts.
◆ As you find information, write three or four paragraphs in a word processing document.
◆ Compose a sources list of sites where you found facts you will include in your report. Follow the proper format.
◆ Edit your work using spelling and grammar checking.
◆ Prepare a cover sheet for the report that includes the title of the report, your name, the date, and class period.

TEAMWORK SKILLS

Discuss Real-World Networking

Form small groups, according to your teacher's instructions. In your group, take turns describing businesses or organizations with which you are familiar. If necessary, research types of organizations, such as schools, hospitals, restaurants, offices, etc. Each student should describe at least one business. Describe the day-to-day tasks of the organization.

When your discussion is finished, choose two businesses from those discussed that use a network or could benefit from having a network installed. As a group, prepare a short report on each that includes:

◆ **Scale of the business,** such as number of employees or offices, and service area
◆ **Type of information** dealt with on a daily basis, such as orders, invoices, schedules, payroll, and employee records
◆ **Commonly-used resources,** including databases, Internet access, printers, scanners, and other hardware
◆ **Day-to-day tasks** that involve employee interaction or the sharing of resources

CHALLENGE YOURSELF

Find Real-World Networks

Think about the networks that you have worked with or used before. Ask your teachers and classmates to describe networks with which they are familiar.

◆ Create a short presentation that highlights the purpose of two networks.
◆ Identify and explain the most important features, such as speed, scalability, and security.
◆ List three major responsibilities that come with the use of the two networks described. Be prepared to explain your reasoning.

YOU TRY IT
Networking Lab

1. Building Your Networking Résumé

Employers consider a large number of factors when hiring employees, so it is important to think carefully about the information you include in your résumé. This helps to ensure that your résumé is the best and most concise presentation of your goals, skills, and qualifications.

To prepare yourself for the important process of creating a résumé, write at least two paragraphs about yourself explaining each of the following:

A Your career goals, both long- and short-term

B Networking positions you would like to work in and how they relate to your career goals

C Educational experience, such as classes taken, test scores, and awards and honors received

D Work experience

E Familiarity with hardware and software, including commonly used programs, operating systems, and especially networking technologies

F Job skills, such as communication, writing, leadership, organization, and problem solving

2. Creating a Questionnaire

Create a questionnaire that you can use to interview people who have careers in networking. Write questions that cover the following topics:

◆ Education and technical experience necessary to find a networking job

◆ Benefits and drawbacks of a career in networking

◆ Skills most important for getting the job done

The questions that you write should be as simple as possible and should draw on the personal experience of the individual responding. For example, ask questions that start with, "In the organization that you work for . . ." as opposed to "When an organization hires for networking positions. . . ."

When preparing your questionnaire, be sure to word your questions clearly. Include adequate space or choices for responses.

Use your questionnaire to gather information from somebody with a career in networking. Write a short report summarizing your findings, and share your results with the rest of the class.

Networking Projects

1. Describe and Evaluate a Network

Evaluate the state of the network technology at your school.

A Begin by writing responses to the following questions:

- ◆ Do the networks used by students and teachers feature cutting-edge technology, or do they seem outdated and inefficient?
- ◆ Which specific features of the networks make them particularly well-suited for use at your school?
- ◆ Which features make them unreliable or hard to use?
- ◆ What could be done to improve your school's networks?
- ◆ Which factors limit your school's ability to implement newer technology?

B With your responses to these questions in mind, prepare a one-page proposal for improving the quality of networking at your school. Be specific about the changes you suggest and do your best to give a realistic estimate of the cost of implementing them.

2. Create a Networking Job Skills Presentation

Following your teacher's instructions, form small groups. In small groups, discuss and make a list of the job skills presented in Section 1.3. Consider the following job skills:

- ◆ Communication
- ◆ Problem solving
- ◆ Teamwork
- ◆ Leadership

Is this list complete? Add any other job skills to the list that you think are important in a networking position. For each skill in the preceding list, as well as each skill that you added to the list, write responses to the following questions:

A How is this skill learned?
B How do employers decide whether a prospective employee has this skill?
C How does this skill make an employee more efficient or valuable to the employer?
D Which on-the-job scenarios and tasks call for an employee to demonstrate this skill?

Use your final list and your answers to the preceding questions to create a presentation on the networking job skills that you identified. If possible, use presentation software. Select a spokesperson from the group to make the presentation.

Network Architecture and Topology

YOU WILL LEARN TO...

WHY IT MATTERS..

Networks are everywhere. An international corporation connects its employees to offices around the world. A travel agency links the computers in its office to each other and to airlines and hotels. At home, people network computers to printers or faxes. Each of these situations requires a different kind of network. Networking professionals must know which network works best for each situation.

Quick Write Activity

Write a short paragraph about all the different things that are connected by networks. These could be computers, data, people, and so on. Describe some advantages of being networked. What are some disadvantages that might result from being part of a network?

WHAT YOU WILL DO..

ACTIVITIES AND PROJECTS

Applying Skills

You Try It Activities

Chapter Assessment

You Try It Networking Lab

Networking Projects

Enrichment Labs

IN THE WORKBOOK

Optional Activities and Projects

Chapter Study Guide

Skills Practice

Networking Labs

ON THE WEB

Activities at networking.glencoe.com

Reading Strategy Organizers

Go Online Activities

Study with PowerPoint

Self-Check Assessments

READ TO SUCCEED

Key Terms

Knowing the dictionary definition of a word does not always help you understand the word's full meaning. To gain a more complete understanding and to help you recall the meaning, create a Key Term Journal. Divide a piece of paper into four columns. Label the first column *Key Term.* Then, label the other columns: *What is it? What else is it like?* and *What are some examples?* Write down each key term and answer the questions as you read the chapter.

Section 2.1 Networking Components

Guide to Reading

Main Ideas

Networks consist of client and server computers. Servers can be dedicated or nondedicated servers.

Key Terms

client
thin client
server
nondedicated server
dedicated server
peripheral
media
data
Redundant Array of Inexpensive Disks (RAID)

Reading Strategy

List at least two facts about each networking term. Create a chart like the one below to fill in the information (also available online).

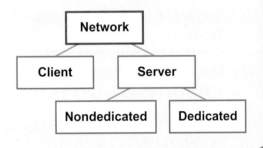

At first glance, networks appear to be a tangled web of hardware, software, and acronyms. Untangling the various technologies to see how they all fit together might seem difficult. But keep this in mind: all networks have the same basic parts. When you are familiar with these parts, it becomes easier to understand and explore the different kinds of networks.

THE PARTS OF A NETWORK

All networks are made up of the same basic components. These include servers, clients, media (such as cabling), data, peripherals, and shared resources. The most important of these are clients and servers.

Clients

When you go to a restaurant, you order dinner—the food is prepared by the chef, and the server brings (serves) the food to you, the client. In a network, a **client** is a computer that requests, or orders, information from a server. The server then responds to bring you what you ordered—a file, an application, or another service.

Typically, client computers are desktop computers with their own local storage and processing power. However, some networks use less powerful, less expensive equipment. A **thin client** is a network computer with no local storage. It processes information independently, but relies on servers for applications, data storage, and administration.

Servers

Servers are computers that work behind the scenes to provide (serve) the resources requested by the clients. Servers are categorized as either nondedicated servers or dedicated servers, depending on the type of work they do.

 networking.glencoe.com

A **nondedicated server** provides many different services to its client computers, such as file retrieval, printing, and e-mailing. On the other hand, a **dedicated server** provides only one type of resource to its clients, such as printing.

Nondedicated Servers Nondedicated servers are often found in home or small office networks. A nondedicated server in this type of setting might allow the different client computers (users) on the network to store and retrieve files and print to a shared printer. That computer might still be used for everyday tasks such as e-mail or word processing. Specialized services, such as high-level security and centralized administration and management, are not required on a nondedicated server.

A nondedicated server can be a traditional, stand-alone server or a desktop PC. You can set up a desktop PC for this task as long as it runs an operating system—such as Macintosh OS X or Windows NT—that enables it to share files and resources. A nondedicated server requires less processing power, memory, and disk storage than a dedicated server. Typically, a nondedicated server can be a desktop computer with one processor, as little as 256 megabytes (MB) of RAM and a single hard disk. For example, a Pentium III-class PC with 256 MB RAM and a 40-gigabyte (GB) hard drive could be a server. Many of the computers that you see in homes, offices, and schools *could* be used as nondedicated servers.

Dedicated Servers A dedicated server functions only as a server. It is not used as a client or workstation. It is dedicated to one purpose—being a server. Dedicated servers can simultaneously handle many requests from network clients. They also ensure the security of files and directories better than nondedicated servers because they can limit access. An example of a dedicated server is a Web server whose sole purpose is to store and provide access to Web pages. Another example is a print server whose single function is to allow multiple clients on a network to print on one printer, as shown in Figure 2.1. If the network is small enough, some dedicated servers could combine different roles into one machine. For example, a server could act as a print and file server.

Figure 2.1
Dedicated servers may function as both the print and file server. Why is this possible in a small network?

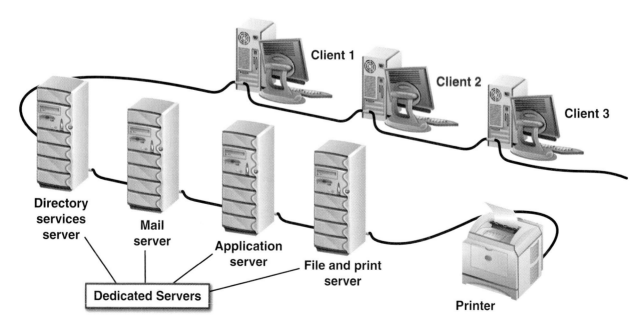

Directory services server

Mail server

Application server

File and print server

Printer

Client 1

Client 2

Client 3

Dedicated Servers

Dedicated servers are typically much more powerful than nondedicated servers. In high-demand situations, such as a server hosting a popular Web site, the server might contain eight or more processors. A dedicated server has large quantities of RAM—1 GB or more—and commonly has multiple hard disk drives. It is also protected by some type of backup power supply unit that carefully monitors performance and stability.

Other Network Components

Most networks are easier to understand when you know the different parts, or components, of a network and know what each part does. You have learned about the two main network components: clients and servers. Networks, however, are not complete with just clients and servers. Table 2.1 provides a list of components typically found in a network.

Table 2.1
In general, networks have certain components in common, as shown here. Name two other examples of shared peripherals.

Networking Components	
Component	**Role**
Servers	Computers that provide shared resources to clients.
Clients	Computers that access shared network resources provided by a server. Also known as network users, workstations, or desktop machines.
Shared peripherals	Shared hardware devices available on the network, such as printers, scanners, external storage drives, and so on.
Media	Cables that connect servers, clients, and peripherals to each other. Cables might be fiber optic or twisted-pair cabling. Wireless networks use wireless devices or beams of infrared light instead of cables.
Data	Files provided to clients by servers across the network.

Shared Peripherals A **peripheral** is a device that is connected to a computer and controlled by its microprocessor. Shared peripherals are devices that are available for use by more than one network client. Some examples include printers, scanners, and external storage devices.

Media Network **media** include the physical pieces used to transport data from one computer to another computer or peripheral on the network. Cabling, hubs, and switches that make up many networks are examples of media components. Media can also include the wireless or infrared devices that make up a wireless network.

Data Another component is **data,** also called packets. Data are distinct pieces of information, such as files or entries in a database. Data are almost constantly being transported around a network. Data might include files that a client requests from a file server or messages sent between computers.

How Do Network Components Work Together? Networks must allow clients and servers to communicate using a variety of media, such as cabling or wireless networking components. In many cases, the data transmitted across a network are intended for shared peripherals, such as printers. For example, a client might request an accounting file through a cable connection to the server. Another client might send a request to print a spreadsheet. The request is beamed to the printer using infrared light. A networked printer might inform the print server via a wireless connection that it is out of paper and needs to be refilled.

SPECIALIZED SERVERS

You are now familiar with the basic parts of a network—servers, clients, media, peripherals, and data. Because servers are at the heart of any network, it is important to know that there are different types of servers, particularly dedicated servers. Dedicated servers can be classified by the type of work they do. Specialized software services allow them to concentrate on providing access to files, printers, applications, mail, faxes, communications, and even backup services. Some of these servers and the jobs they perform are described below.

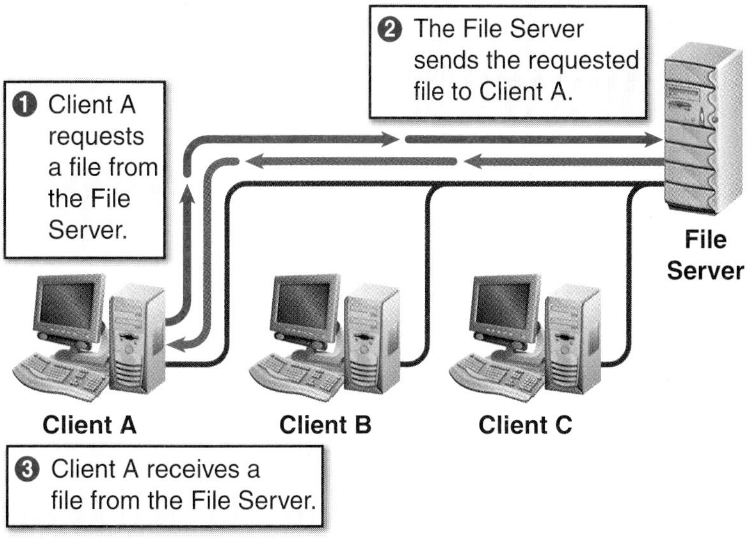

File Servers

File servers control access to file resources. For example, when you are running a word processing application, the application runs locally (on your computer). As shown in Figure 2.2, the actual document you are editing is stored on the file server. When you need to work on the document, it is loaded from the server into your computer's memory so that you can view or edit it from your computer. After you finish with the document, the changed data are then saved and transferred back to the server for storage.

● **Figure 2.2**
When a client requests a particular file from a file server, the server transfers the entire document to the client and does no processing of its own.
Where is the application that does the processing located?

❶ Client A requests a file from the File Server.

❷ The File Server sends the requested file to Client A.

File Server

Client A   **Client B**   **Client C**

❸ Client A receives a file from the File Server.

Print Servers

Print servers control access to printer resources. When you (the client) print the document, a print server receives the data and transfers it to the printer. The printer then prints the number of pages or the orientation that you requested. Neither the print server nor the printer change the document.

Application Servers

Application servers store large amounts of data and software that is only available on that server, such as Web services or databases. They process and deliver only the portion of data the client requests. By having the data stored centrally on the application server, multiple users can access and share the information.

For example, Katelyn in the college registration department needs to update one student's address. To do this, she must access the student's record, which is located in a database program. The application server quickly searches through the database. It locates only the requested record and transmits it to Katelyn's computer. This is much faster and more efficient than transmitting all of the data for all student records across the network.

As shown in Figure 2.3, an application server processes information before delivery to the desktop client, or front end. This is different from a file server. File servers perform behind-the-scenes, or back end, processes. They function as a storage area that transfers files through a local area network (LAN) or wide area network (WAN). Two excellent examples of application servers are the Microsoft SQL server and Linux MySQL. Both of these application servers provide database speed and ease of use.

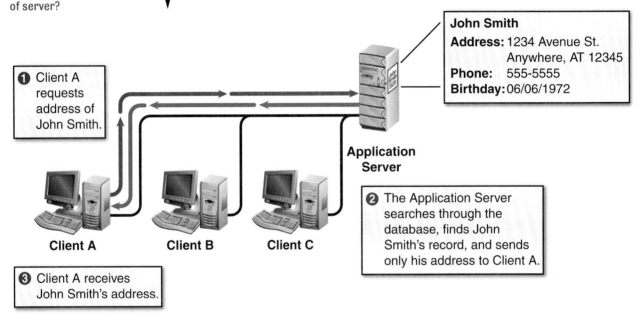

❶ Client A requests address of John Smith.

John Smith
Address: 1234 Avenue St.
Anywhere, AT 12345
Phone: 555-5555
Birthday: 06/06/1972

Application Server

Client A   **Client B**   **Client C**

❷ The Application Server searches through the database, finds John Smith's record, and sends only his address to Client A.

❸ Client A receives John Smith's address.

Mail Servers

Mail servers provide a centralized post office for e-mail message handling and storage. They deliver e-mail messages to network users either immediately or on a "when I ask for it" basis for remote users. Remote users are people who connect to a server using a dial-up or other off-site connection. At the very least, mail servers, such as Microsoft Exchange or Novell GroupWise, can also provide centralized scheduling and contact information to users on the network.

Communication Servers

Communication servers handle data flow between the servers' networks and other networks, mainframe computers, telecommunication, or remote users. This type of server essentially handles traffic inside the network and outside the network. This type of server differs from the e-mail server because it serves more network component types.

Directory Services Servers

Directory services servers, or directory servers, enable users to locate, store, and secure information on the network. For example, directory service server software, such as Suns' ONE directory software, provides a central location for storing and managing users' identity profiles and access privileges, among other tasks. Directory service servers combine computers into logical groups, called domains, which allow users to access resources on the network. These servers provide information about the network just like an address book provides contact information.

Backup Servers

Backup servers using software have the ability to perform regularly scheduled backups to archive the data and safeguard the networks' store of information. This information can be stored on storage media, such as disk or tape.

Many servers use a technique called "mirroring" to protect data. Mirroring employs an array of hard drives, called **Redundant Array of Inexpensive Disks (RAID).** When information is written to the primary hard drive, it is automatically duplicated on a second drive. Should the primary hard drive fail, the second drive can be substituted for the failed drive with little or no down time.

Planning for specialized servers becomes important when planning for future network growth. The network planner must take into account any anticipated network expansion so that network use is not disrupted if the role of a specific server needs to be changed. Network clients count on being able to access resources at all times.

Section 2.1 Assessment

Concept Check

1. **Define** client, thin client, server, nondedicated server, dedicated server, peripheral, media, data, and Redundant Array of Inexpensive Disks (RAID).

2. **List** five dedicated servers and describe what each one does.

3. **Describe** the main components of a network and how they work together.

Critical Thinking

4. **Compare and Contrast** Describe the differences between dedicated and nondedicated servers.

5. **Identify Roles** List each server in your classroom or lab, and identify whether it is dedicated or nondedicated. Then, describe the role each server plays in the overall network.

Applying Skills

Compare Memory and Storage Space With your teacher's approval, compare the amount of memory and storage space on client computers and server computers in your class or school. What conclusions can you make based on your information?

Ethics & Technology

USING COMPANY COMPUTERS RESPONSIBLY

With a computer on almost every desk, inappropriate use of Internet access is one of the most serious workplace issues for employers.

Inappropriate use of company computer resources costs billions of dollars every year.

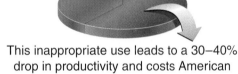

Approximately 40% of employee Internet use is business related.

Approximately 60% of employee Internet use is inappropriate.

This inappropriate use leads to a 30–40% drop in productivity and costs American business $85 billion every year.

Wasting Work Time

Over 60 percent of all employees admit to using the Internet at work for personal reasons at least once a day. A large portion of Web surfing by employees includes visits to unproductive and inappropriate sites. According to a recent study by Websense, businesses lose at least $85 billion dollars every year due to personal use of company computer resources.

Business Headaches

Besides losing productivity, companies face a number of threats from personal Internet use:

◆ In smaller businesses, streaming video or audio downloads takes up broadband space, which slows down the network.

◆ Peer-to-peer file sharing and instant messaging make the company's network less secure and open to viruses and hackers.

◆ Employers may be held liable if employees commit illegal acts using company equipment.

Who Will Know?

Although some companies may allow occasional personal e-mails, it should not happen often. Employers have the right to monitor Internet use, because employees use company-owned systems. In fact, employers have the right to read and permanently keep any data on your company computer because the data, as well as the computer, are company property.

As a network administrator, you might be responsible for tracking and monitoring workers' Internet and e-mail use. This is a privacy issue that many employers are facing. To avoid accusations of "spying," many companies prefer to block offensive Web sites instead of monitoring employees' Internet use.

It is wise to always follow your organization's computer-use policies. Serious abuses of a company's property by an employee could result not only in the loss of a job, but also in arrest and prosecution for a crime.

Tech Focus

1. Research one method employers can use to monitor employees' use of company computers. Explain why you think this method should be considered legal or illegal.

2. Find a company's acceptable use policy on the Web. What is considered objectionable use and what are the consequences? Write an acceptable use policy for your class.

Guide to Reading

Main Ideas

Networks can be classified according to how servers and clients are configured, or put together. They can also be categorized by the geographic area they cover.

Key Terms

peer-to-peer network
client/server network
local area network (LAN)
wide area network (WAN)
node
wireless local area network (WLAN)
bandwidth

Reading Strategy

List at least three characteristics of each type of network. Use an organizer like this one (also available online).

Types of Networks

Centralized	Peer-to-peer	Client/server

There are many different ways to classify, or group, networks. In this section, you will learn two main ways of classifying them. Networks can be grouped by their basic configuration, or they can be grouped by the geographic area that they tie together. We will discuss another way of distinguishing networks in Section 2.4.

CLASSIFYING NETWORKS BY CONFIGURATION

When you describe something's configuration, you describe how it is put together or how its parts are arranged. A network's configuration describes how the types of servers and clients are used in the network. Networks are generally divided into three broad categories based on their configuration: centralized networks, peer-to-peer networks, and client/server networks.

Centralized Networks

In a centralized network, an application runs on a large and powerful centralized computer, called a mainframe computer, as shown in Figure 2.4 on page 44. Users who want to use the application access the mainframe computer through a terminal. A terminal is a device with a monitor and keyboard that is connected to the mainframe through some sort of media. The terminal requests information from the mainframe computer.

Centralized networks are costly, but very powerful. Mainframe computers are also capable of handling hundreds or even thousands of simultaneous requests. Many large banks and financial institutions rely on mainframe computers for the huge amount of data processing that occurs on a daily basis. However, centralized networks are not easily scalable if the size of the network changes. Expanding a centralized network can mean replacing expensive hardware.

READ ME!

Jargon Networking professionals often use the terms configuration, design, and architecture to mean the same thing when they talk about a network's configuration.

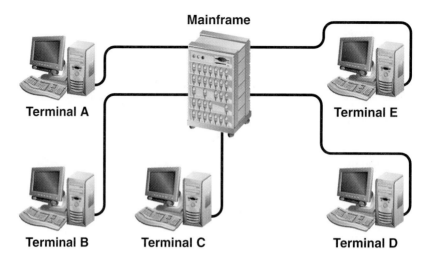

Figure 2.4 ●——▶
Centralized networks are built around mainframes and terminals. How is a terminal different from a PC?

Centralized Network

In the 1980s and 1990s, networks were planned with an emphasis on greater functionality, scalability, and cost-effectiveness. These newer networks were built around cheaper microcomputer technologies. Desktop processing capabilities and lower costs aided in reducing the demand placed on centralized servers. This change in technology helped usher in the era of peer-to-peer and client/server networks.

Peer-to-Peer Networks

In a **peer-to-peer network,** computers function as both clients and servers. There are no dedicated servers to handle specific tasks such as printing and file sharing. All the computers are "equal" and, therefore, are known as peers. Most peer-to-peer networks do not require an administrator, so each user determines which data and resources to share on the network, as shown in Figure 2.5. Peer-to-peer networks typically consist of a few computers sharing the same resources. For example, a building contractor works out of her home office. She networks together her few desktop computers in a peer-to-peer network so that the computers can share files, a scanner, and fax/printer.

Figure 2.5 ●——▶
In peer-to-peer networks, computers act as both clients and servers. How does a peer-to-peer network differ from a centralized network?

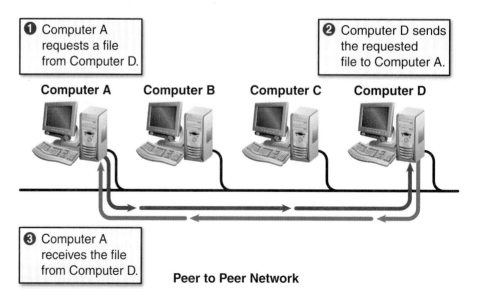

❶ Computer A requests a file from Computer D.

❷ Computer D sends the requested file to Computer A.

Computer A **Computer B** **Computer C** **Computer D**

❸ Computer A receives the file from Computer D.

Peer to Peer Network

Client/Server Networks

Like centralized networks, **client/server networks** (or server-based networks) are built around one or more dedicated servers. They are administered from a central location, as shown in Figure 2.6. Client/server networks are far more powerful than peer-to-peer networks. They can support hundreds or thousands of clients, and they can link multiple computer platforms. Client/server and peer-to-peer networks are the most common types of networks in use, and they are a mainstay of business, government, and education.

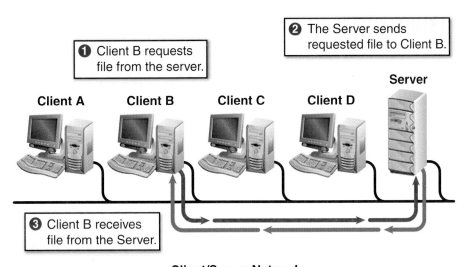

❶ Client B requests file from the server.

❷ The Server sends requested file to Client B.

Server

Client A   **Client B**   **Client C**   **Client D**

❸ Client B receives file from the Server.

Client/Server Network

← ● **Figure 2.6** Client/server networks are often found in corporations and other large businesses. Where else might client/server networks be used?

CLASSIFYING NETWORKS BY GEOGRAPHIC AREA

The second main way to classify networks is to group them by how much geographic area they cover. Networks that are relatively limited in size are called **local area networks (LANs).** Those that cover a larger area are called **wide area networks (WANs).** LANs and WANs are made up of centralized, peer-to-peer, and client/server networks.

Although many of the same underlying technologies are used in both LANs and WANs, they differ in the technologies required to help them do their jobs. A WAN, for instance, needs communications hardware and software, message-routing capabilities, and long-distance transmission technologies that a localized LAN does not.

Local Area Networks

Both peer-to-peer and client/server networks can be classified as LANs. LANs are computers connected in a small area, such as in the same office building. A true peer-to-peer network is a LAN because it can support only a limited number of clients and peripherals, also known as **nodes.** A client/server network is so flexible that it can be a LAN in a single building, or it can be one of many LANs spread across the country or around the world.

Wireless Networks

Some LANs make use of wireless technology to create **wireless local area networks (WLANs).** WLANs use media just like wired networks do, but you cannot see wireless media. Instead of cables, WLANs use either infrared (IR) light or radio frequencies (RF).

Wireless technology adds a new dimension to networking capabilities. For example, business conference attendees can use laptops equipped with a wireless PC Card, or wireless-capable handheld computing devices, such as PDAs or cell phones. With these devices, people can log on to their company's mail server to check e-mail, as shown in Figure 2.7. This is accomplished from anywhere within the conference center, without connecting a single wire!

Figure 2.7 ●———▶
Wireless networks eliminate cabling between clients and servers. Identify two other advantages of using a wireless network.

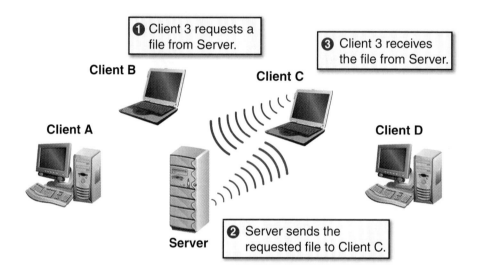

❶ Client 3 requests a file from Server.

❸ Client 3 receives the file from Server.

Client B

Client C

Client A

Client D

Server

❷ Server sends the requested file to Client C.

Wireless Network

Current WLAN technology is capable of transmitting data at speeds of up to 54 megabytes per second (Mbps). A wireless network means that you can roam an entire city with a wireless connection and remain plugged in to the Internet, or to your own workplace's network. Security on WLAN devices is a growing concern because transmissions can be intercepted. Unencrypted transmissions can be intercepted, allowing intruders unauthorized access to data on the network.

Wide Area Networks

WANs are computer networks that use long-range telecommunication links to connect networked computers across long distances. WANs, in simple terms, are made up of multiple LANs. Most WANs use media that can very quickly transfer large amounts of data. These media include wireless connections, satellite uplinks, or specialized types of cabling, such as T1/T3 telephone-type lines or fiber optic cables. Using these media allows the WANs to employ a large amount of **bandwidth.** Bandwidth is the amount of data that can be transmitted in a given amount of time.

ACTIVITY 2A Identifying the Type of Network

To understand types of networks, explore the ones in your school. This activity helps you understand how data flow to and from the school board office, departments, libraries, and individual student workstations.

1 Predict what type of network configuration your classroom or school uses: **centralized, peer-to-peer,** or **client/server.**

2 State the reasons why you think your school uses the predicted configuration.

3 Explain whether you think this type of configuration is a **LAN** or **WAN** and why.

4 With the help of your teacher or the network administrator at your school, find out what type of network is actually in use and why the school uses the particular network configuration.

5 Explain why your predictions were correct or incorrect.

6 Based on the type of network at your school, list reasons why another type of network may or may not be better suited to your school's needs.

7 Find out if your school plans to expand its network or networks. If so, are the plans anything like what you recommended in the previous step 6?

Although you may not yet be ready for a job as a networking consultant, you should now better understand the types of networks in general as well as the ones your school uses.

Other Kinds of WANs

Depending on the amount of ground they cover, WANs are often categorized in subgroups or smaller clusters. These WAN subgroups include campus area networks (CANs), metropolitan area networks (MANs), home area networks (HANs), global area networks (GANs), and storage area networks (SANs).

Campus Area Network (CAN) Networks found on a college campus or military base might be classified as campus area networks because they cover a limited geographic area.

Metropolitan Area Network (MAN) Towns and cities use metropolitan area networks. These networks link computers across a wider geographic area than CANs, such as neighborhoods and communities.

Home Area Network (HAN) To link computers and share common resources, such as printers and scanners, home area networks are used. HANs are becoming more commonplace as homes with multiple computers proliferate.

Global Area Network (GAN) Global area networks use satellites and other technologies to link networks spread across countries and continents.

Figure 2.8 ●——
SANs are used by businesses to backup or archive data. What is an advantage of using a SAN?

Storage Area Network (SAN) Specialized networks, called storage area networks, are used to store large quantities of data for backup or archival purposes, as shown in Figure 2.8. SANs are generally part of a larger network of computing resources, such as large file servers and/or mainframe computers.

Storage Area Network

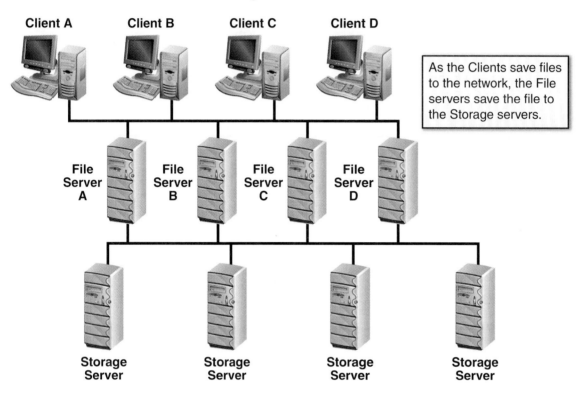

As the Clients save files to the network, the File servers save the file to the Storage servers.

Client A   Client B   Client C   Client D

File Server A   File Server B   File Server C   File Server D

Storage Server   Storage Server   Storage Server   Storage Server

---

Section 2.2 Assessment

Concept Check

1. **Define** peer-to-peer, client/server, local area network (LAN), wide area network (WAN), node, wireless local area network (WLAN), and bandwidth.

2. **List** the similarities and differences between centralized networks, peer-to-peer networks, and client/server networks.

Critical Thinking

3. **Compare and Contrast** LANs and WANs.

4. **Explain Business Needs** Name a type of business that might need a client/server network and one that might need a peer-to-peer network. Explain why each business needs that particular kind of network.

Applying Skills

Create Network Diagrams Create a diagram of a network used in your classroom or school. Identify the nodes as a server, client, or peripheral. Finally, label your diagram with the type of configuration.

Section 2.3 Network Architecture

Main Ideas

Choosing the right network architecture requires careful planning. The network's current and future needs must be balanced against the costs of implementing and maintaining the network. Each network architecture has advantages and disadvantages.

Key Terms

security
network interface card (NIC)
local user
remote user
network operating system (NOS)

Reading Strategy

Compare and contrast peer-to-peer and client/server networks. Use a Venn diagram like this one (also available online).

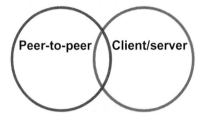

Different companies and organizations have different needs for their networks. It is important to understand the differences between peer-to-peer networks and client/server networks when deciding on a network architecture. Because of their overwhelming popularity, the focus of this book is on the more common of these two types of networks—the client/server network.

CHOOSING A NETWORK ARCHITECTURE

The distinction between peer-to-peer and client/server networks is important because each type has different capabilities. The type of network that is chosen depends on several factors, such as those in the following list. The information in Table 2.2 on page 50 will also help you understand when to use a peer-to-peer network or a client/server network.

- ◆ **Type of user**—Because each business has special needs, the type of business can determine how the network looks and operates. For example, computers in a travel agency need to be connected to other businesses with their own networks, such as airlines, hotels, and other travel-related companies.
- ◆ **Size of the organization**—Small companies can generally make do with a peer-to-peer network, whereas larger companies with more computers require a client/server network.
- ◆ **Administration**—The amount of network users dictates the level of administrative support necessary. A small office may not be able to afford a full-time network administrator.
- ◆ **Security**—The capability of the network operating system to secure data from unauthorized access is called **security.** The data at a financial institution need to be highly secure.

◆ **Network traffic**—Network traffic varies according to the number of clients accessing the network. Popular Web sites require powerful servers to handle the number of users accessing the site.
◆ **Cost**—Cost plays a role in how much money and time is allotted to create and maintain the network.
◆ **Scalability**—Scalability refers to the ability of the network to expand to accommodate more users. Companies often forecast their expected growth and network demands several years into the future to determine what type of network technology to implement.

Table 2.2
Several factors must be considered when choosing network architecture. What type of network architecture would be most appropriate for a large bank—peer-to-peer or client/server? Why?

When to Use a Peer-to-Peer Network or a Client/Server Network		
	Peer-to-Peer	**Client/Server**
Type of user	Homes and small businesses, such as a small construction or engineering company	Large corporations, schools, and hospitals
Size of the organization	Limited number of workstations	Large number of workstations
Administration	Users act as their own administrators	Central network administrator or team of network administrators
Security	Maintained by individual users	Maintained by the network administrators
Network traffic	Limited number of users sharing a small volume of files that are accessed infrequently	Large number of users frequently accessing databases or large files
Cost	Inexpensive to implement	Usually more expensive than peer-to-peer networks
Scalability	Limited network growth within the foreseeable future	High growth projected within the foreseeable future

PEER-TO-PEER CONSIDERATIONS

Peer-to-peer networks include capabilities beyond those listed above. For example, all of the computers on the network can act as clients and respond as servers.

Lab 2.1 Using System Tools to View System Information
Practice additional hands-on networking skills on page 430.

Hardware

Peer-to-peer networking software can run on minimal hardware. Since peer-to-peer networks are not intended to handle a high volume of traffic, they can use almost any computer. To communicate with one another, both client and server computers must be equipped with a **network interface card (NIC),** also known as a network adapter card.

Operating Systems

Peer-to-peer networking software does not require the same standard of performance and level of security as the networking software designed for dedicated servers. Many operating systems have built-in, peer-to-peer networking capabilities. For example, both Windows and Macintosh operating systems have built-in, peer-to-peer capabilities.

Performance

Workstations on a peer-to-peer network are not designed to handle many simultaneous requests for data. A user might notice a drop in the performance of his or her workstation while it is being accessed by another workstation. If this becomes a frequent problem, a client/server network model may need to be considered.

Administration

In a typical peer-to-peer network, no network manager oversees the administration for the entire network. Instead, individual users administer their own computers. Keep in mind whether users of peer-to-peer networks can perform these tasks. Typical administration tasks on a peer-to-peer network computer might include the following:

◆ Setting up shared folders
◆ Setting up a shared printer attached directly to the computer
◆ Connecting to shared folders or shared printers on other computers in the network
◆ Installing and upgrading applications and operating system software

Security

On a peer-to-peer network, security is low. Security means making computers and the data stored on them safe from harm or unauthorized access. Security measures might include encrypting data to make it unreadable to unauthorized users, and setting a password on a shared resource, such as a file or directory. In a peer-to-peer network, centralized control is very difficult to maintain because these network users set their own security. The shared resources can exist on any computer rather than on a centralized server. This lack of control has a big impact on network security because some users may not implement any security measures at all. If data on a network need a high level of security, a client/server network is probably a better choice.

Sharing Resources

All users can share any of their resources in any manner they choose. These resources include data in shared directories, files, printers, and so on. Each computer uses a large percentage of its resources to support the user at the computer, known as the **local user.** Additional resources are needed, such as hard disk drive space and memory, to support other users, known as **remote users,** accessing resources on the local workstation.

Cost

Peer-to-peer networks are relatively simple and less expensive than client/server networks. Each computer functions as a client and as a server. There is no need for a powerful central server or for the other components required for a large network. Peer-to-peer machines are typically desktop computers and are much cheaper than client/server networks.

TECH TRIVIA

Boot Disk An emergency boot disk or CD for Macintosh, Windows, and Linux operating systems is an important utility tool to have. The utility creates an image file of your system, requires you to identify yourself as an administrator, and copies the system's preferences, disk utilities, and, possibly, applications. An external drive that mirrors your system is another good way to make a boot disk.

READ ME!

Jargon Strong passwords are necessary tools of a network security administrator. These passwords utilize exact combinations of numbers and letters to guarantee that only valid users gain access to a company's computer network.

Enrichment **LAB**

Lab 2.2 Saving a Windows 2000 System Information File Practice additional hands-on networking skills on page 431.

Advantages and Disadvantages

A peer-to-peer network's advantages include ease of installation, no dedicated server or NOS, individual control of user resources, and low cost. Each computer in the network simply needs a NIC and an operating system to communicate.

The disadvantages of a peer-to-peer network are the limitations in geographic area, scalability, and difficulty in ensuring security. Peer-to-peer networks are useful only in offices with about ten or fewer workstations. Users might need a number of passwords and must safeguard their own files. Also, if one workstation goes down, resources can no longer be shared.

CLIENT/SERVER CONSIDERATIONS

One basic consideration for client-server networks is the size, which can be enormous and support thousands of client computers. The clients have their own local storage and processing power, but depend on the resources of a network.

Hardware

Client computer hardware can be limited to the needs of the user. Clients do not require the additional RAM and disk storage needed to provide server services. A typical client computer often does not need more then a Pentium III processor and 256 MB of RAM. Servers, on the other hand, need to be very powerful, fast, and capable of storing lots of information.

Operating Systems

The **network operating system (NOS)** used on a server in a client/server network must be much more robust than a peer-to-peer system. The NOS must quickly and effectively answer the demands of many users, and also provide administrative and security functions. NOS software includes Windows 2003 Server, Mac OS X Server, Unix, Linux, and Novell NetWare. Table 2.3 displays a list of other demands that a NOS must deliver.

READ ME!

Jargon The term robust indicates that a system does not break down easily, and that it provides a broad range of capabilities.

Table 2.3 ●
The NOS must satisfy a number of demands for the network to run properly and continuously. What operating system does your network use?

NOS Requirements	
Requirements	**Explanation**
Fault tolerance	The NOS has to be able to withstand severe problems that can bring a network to a standstill, cause hardware damage, or cause loss of data.
Different levels of access	The NOS allows the network administrator to give individual users different security clearances or network permissions based on their job or responsibilities.
Backup capability	A NOS is able to duplicate a copy of programs or data, which can be used in the event of data loss.
Centralized monitoring and administration	The NOS allows the network administrator to easily inspect the network by using NOS and various administration tools to make sure the network is running smoothly or to identify problems.
Control network traffic	A NOS can manage multiple applications as well as traffic generated by security needs, messages, and access limitations of numerous clients simultaneously using the network.

Performance

Servers are able to host specialized services, which allow workstations to focus on other tasks. This makes the network more efficient because data can be processed by the server and then sent to the client that requested the data. Servers are also specially designed to handle many simultaneous requests.

Administration

Network administration often includes adding and configuring workstations, setting up user accounts, and protecting the network against unwanted intrusions. Because these tasks can be administered from a centralized location, client/server networks are often preferred in larger companies.

Security

Security is often the primary reason for choosing a client/server approach to networking. In a client/server environment, a network administrator sets the security rules or policies and applies them to every user on the network, as shown in Figure 2.9.

Sharing Resources

A server is designed to provide access to many files and printers while maintaining performance and security for the user. Data sharing is centrally administered and controlled. This makes shared resources easier to find and support than resources on individual computers.

Cost

A client/server network can be significantly more expensive than a peer-to-peer network. Servers require more processing power, memory, and disk space. The hardware must be able to withstand more problems. In addition, operating systems for network servers usually cost much more than typical desktop operating system software. Often, the more nodes you need to access the server, the more you have to pay for the software.

Activity 2.1 Choosing Smooth Operators How do you know which network operating system to choose? Go to networking.glencoe.com to find out more about the different NOSs on the market.

● **Figure 2.9**
A centralized security system uses firewalls, passwords, and other security systems to protect the network. Why is it difficult to have centralized security on a peer-to-peer network?

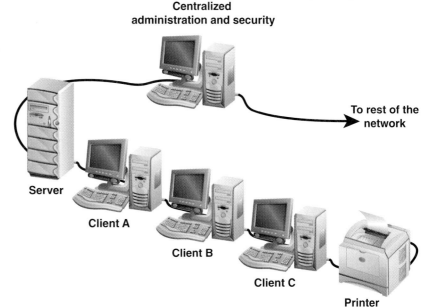

Centralized administration and security

To rest of the network

Server

Client A

Client B

Client C

Printer

Advantages and Disadvantages

Client/server networks are scalable and cost less than centralized networks. They support many users and are more powerful than peer-to-peer networks. You can centralize security and administration while controlling access to resources. Client/server networks communicate with other networks and support remote access, Internet sites, and multiple computing platforms.

Client/server networks are more expensive to implement and more complicated to administer than peer-to-peer networks. Another disadvantage is that server failures can bring down the entire network.

HYBRID NETWORKS

Hybrid networks utilize the capabilities of both peer-to-peer and client/server architectures. In a client/server network, the servers run a network operating system, and the desktop computers run a client operating system. For example, Windows Server can be used with clients that use Windows XP. Or, in a Mac environment, a Linux server might serve clients with the Mac OS X. Because client operating systems have built-in, peer-to-peer sharing capabilities, the desktop machines can make their own resources available to their peers without requiring support from their servers. Within a workgroup, for instance, the desktop PCs can share resources as peers, yet they can also take advantage of the server-based resources offered by a larger network.

Section 2.3 Assessment

Concept Check

1. **Define** security, network interface card (NIC), local user, remote user, and network operating system (NOS).

2. **Identify** three considerations you should make when choosing the best network architecture for a site.

3. **Describe** the demands that a NOS must meet to be used in a peer-to-peer or client/server network.

Critical Thinking

4. **Compare and Contrast** Why do large businesses want to use client/server networks instead of peer-to-peer networks?

5. **Draw Conclusions** Why is it harder to set up a client/server network than a peer-to-peer network?

6. **Understand Relationships** Why are client/server networks more secure than peer-to-peer networks?

Applying Skills

Choose an Architecture Megabyte, Inc. has 75 employees. Many work from home. Everyone sends large files back and forth. There is no network administrator. They want to limit costs, and they expect to stay the same size for the next two years. What kind of network do you recommend? Explain your answer.

SMART HOUSES

At the dawn of the computer age, futurists dreamed of "intelligent homes," with robotic lawn mowers and kitchens smart enough to prepare meals. In many ways, the "smart house" is becoming a reality.

Smart homes use technology, such as specialized televisions and phones, to monitor outside and inside the home.

Smart Appliances

Today's smart homes might have networks that monitor and automatically adjust lights, temperature, and TV volume in any room of the house. An emerging breed of Internet-enabled appliances will make homes smarter than ever. Next-generation refrigerators will warn you when the milk is about to expire, order more eggs for you, or schedule their own service when a repair is needed.

Independent Living

Imagine a home for an elderly or disabled resident with doors that open automatically or motion sensors that track movement. Such a house could call for help if no motion were detected, in case the resident had fallen or lost consciousness.

Such homes could also help the occupant lead a more independent life. Programmable appliances could be controlled automatically or by voice or breath.

Connecting the Smart House

Although most people think of a PC as the control center for a smart house, the future will more likely bring handheld, PDA-like devices that control all household functions wirelessly, even from remote locations. A smart house may be equipped with one or more of the following networking technologies or media:

◆ **Twisted-pair cable** is being installed in new homes during construction. By installing it in each room with a central hub, the home can be filled with network devices.
◆ **Wireless systems** are popular in older homes, because they free the owner from running cables through walls and floors.
◆ **Bluetooth** is still in its infancy, but it shows great promise for smart homes. It allows devices to communicate short distances via radio frequency.
◆ **x10** uses a building's electrical wiring to transmit data. Many smart home features can be added to existing houses by adding special electrical adapters to existing equipment, such as lamps.

Tech Focus

1. Do you think that smart houses will have a positive or negative impact on society? Explain why.

2. Research one type of current or emerging networking technology for smart homes. How does that technology compare to other current networking technologies?

Section 2.4 The Shape of a Network

Guide to Reading

Main Ideas

There are four basic network shapes, or topologies. When planning a network, the advantages and disadvantages of each type need to be evaluated to provide a solution that meets the needs of the network users.

Key Terms

topology
bus network
trunk
carrier sense multiple accesses with collision detection (CSMA/CD)
terminator
star network
hub
ring network
token
mesh network

Reading Strategy

Evaluate the advantages and disadvantages of each type of topology. Use a chart like this one (also available online).

	Advantages	Disadvantages
Bus		
Ring		
Star		
Mesh		

Once the network architecture is decided upon, you need to plan the network topology. In this section, you will explore the basic topologies. You will also learn the difference between the physical and logical topology of networks.

NETWORK TOPOLOGIES

The shape, or **topology,** of a network refers to the way the computers are cabled together. There are four basic designs that networks follow, known as bus, ring, star, and mesh. The network's physical topology, or actual shape, might not look like a bus, ring, or a star. The logical topology of a network, however, does describe the way data travel across a network. That is, network traffic travels in a line, a loop, or outward in a star-like pattern, based on the logical topology of the network.

To help you see how this works, Figure 2.10 shows a network based on a ring topology in which computers are connected to one another in a closed loop. If these computers are in different offices or even on different floors of a building, you can see that the network might not physically resemble a ring, but the logical connections do, indeed, form a closed circle.

In addition to the term topology, several other terms are used to define a network's design, such as physical layout, design, diagram, and map.

Figure 2.10
A network's physical topology is the wire itself. A network's logical topology is the way it carries signals on the wire. In what direction could a signal travel on this topology?

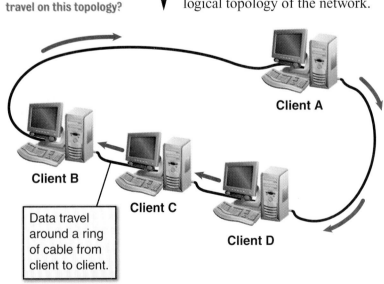

Client A

Client B

Client C

Client D

Data travel around a ring of cable from client to client.

A network's topology affects its capabilities. The choice of one topology over another has an impact on the following:

- Type of equipment needed
- Capabilities of the equipment
- Growth of the network
- Management of the network

Developing a sense of how to use the different topologies is a key to understanding the power of networks.

Bus Network

The simplest and easiest topology to implement is a **bus network** (or linear network). A bus network consists of a single cable, or **trunk,** to which the client computers and servers connect, as shown in Figure 2.11.

On a bus network, the nodes are passive participants. The nodes "listen" on the line and wait for messages addressed to them. They do not take an active part in moving messages from node to node through the network.

Any node on a bus network can transmit to any other node whenever it wants. Since each node has a unique network address, only the node to which a message is sent can actually intercept and read it. Transmissions are limited to one computer at a time, so at any given time, one computer is master of the network. Any other node wanting to transmit must wait until the line is free.

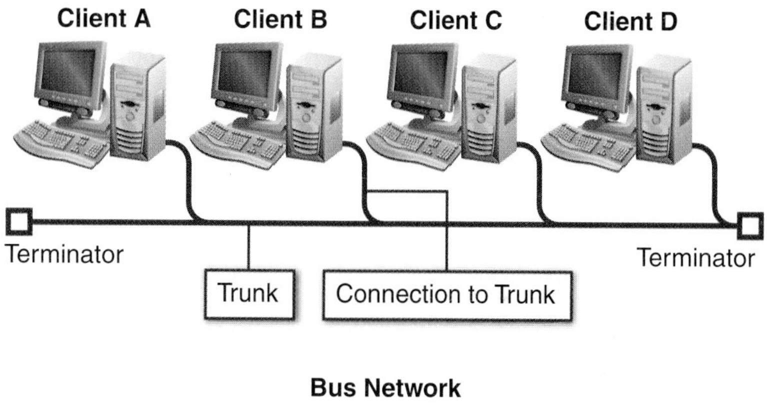

Collision and Signal Bounce Sometimes, two nodes on a bus network transmit data at the same time and the data run into each other. This is called a collision. The Ethernet, the most well-known type of bus network, manages this problem using a technique known as **carrier sense multiple accesses with collision detection (CSMA/CD).** When a collision is detected, both nodes must back off and wait for the line to be free before attempting to retransmit.

Messages on a bus network travel either left to right or right to left. When an electrical signal, or data, is sent to the entire network, it travels from one end of the cable to the other. Signal bounce is caused by a signal that continues uninterrupted to the end of the bus, and then keeps bouncing back and forth along the cable, preventing other computers from sending data.

To terminate a signal on a bus network, both ends of each cable segment must be plugged into something. For example, a cable end can be plugged into a computer or a connector. Any open cable ends must be equipped with a device called a **terminator** that absorbs the signals and keeps them from bouncing back along the trunk. Figure 2.12 on page 58 shows a properly terminated bus topology network.

● **Figure 2.11**
In a bus network, data are sent to all nodes, or computers, but only the destination computer accepts it. What possible problems occur in a bus topology?

Bus Network

SH⊕W ME!

Bus Network A bus topology is one of the simplest and least expensive networks to install. View the Show Me 2.1 to 2.8 at *networking.glencoe.com* to see how information is transferred in a bus network.

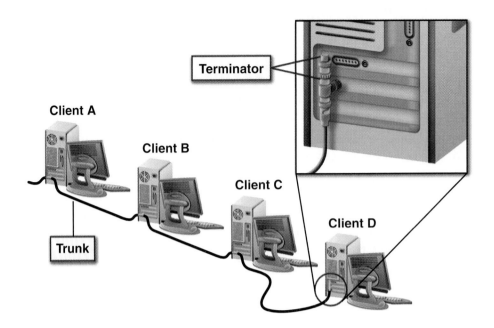

Figure 2.12 When a terminator absorbs a signal, it clears the cable so that other computers can send data. What happens to network activity when a signal bounces?

Terminator

Client A

Client B

Client C

Client D

Trunk

Figure 2.13 An unplugged cable is not terminated and takes down the network. Could you still edit a document on your computer if the network is down? Why or why not?

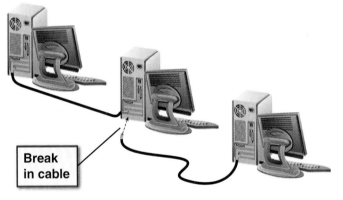

Break in cable

Disrupting Network Communication A break in the cable can occur if the cable is physically separated into two pieces or if at least one end of the cable becomes disconnected. In either case, one or both ends of the cable no longer have a terminator, causing the signal to bounce. All network activity stops when this occurs. Figure 2.13 shows a bus topology with a disconnected cable.

The computers on the network can still function as stand-alone computers. However, as long as the segment is broken, they cannot communicate with each other or otherwise access shared resources.

Network Expansion As the physical size of the site grows, the network needs to grow as well. Cable in the bus topology can be extended by one of the two following methods:

A component called a barrel connector can connect two pieces of cable to make a longer piece. However, connectors weaken the signal and should be used sparingly. One continuous cable is preferable to connecting several smaller ones with connectors.

A device called a repeater can be used to connect two cables. A repeater actually boosts the signal before it sends it on its way. A repeater is better than a connector or a longer piece of cable because it allows a signal to travel farther and still be correctly received.

Bus networks are easy to implement and require less cabling than other topologies. In addition, nodes are relatively easy to add and remove. On the negative side, problems can be difficult to pinpoint on such a network, and a break in the trunk means a breakdown in the entire network. Also, too many nodes slow the network, because the nodes must wait for longer periods before being able to transmit over an open line.

Star Network

A **star network,** like the arms of an octopus, stretches out in different directions from a central location. At the center of the star is a hardware device known as a hub, as shown in Figure 2.14. The **hub** connects the nodes in the arms. A hub can participate actively in the network by boosting signals as they pass through, or it can be a passive wiring panel that simply relays transmissions through the network. Regardless, the hub (or hubs in larger networks) forms the centerpiece of a star-wired network.

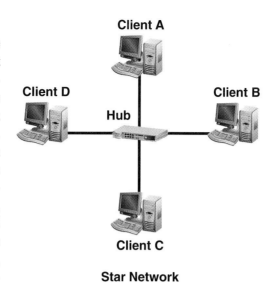

Star Network

● **Figure 2.14**
In order for data to be sent from one computer to the next, the data must pass through the hub. What is the difference between a hub that is active and one that is passive?

SHOW ME!

Star Topology A hub connects the nodes in a star network. View Show Me 2.9, 2.10, and 2.11 at **networking.glencoe.com** to see a demonstration of a star topology and network failure.

Star networks offer the advantages of centralized resources and management, as well as expandability. More nodes can be added easily when needed. In addition, because the cabling in a star network extends from hub to nodes, problems are easier to isolate, and a break in the cable brings down only the node directly affected by that cable.

However, because each computer is connected to a central point, this topology requires a great deal of cable in a large network installation. Also, if the central point fails, the entire network goes down.

Ring Network

In a **ring network,** the nodes form a circle. Network data travel from node to node, in one direction only, in a closed loop, as shown in Figure 2.15.

Notice that each node communicates directly with only two others: the node that transmits to it and the node to which it transmits. The nodes in a ring network participate actively by sending the signal around the ring. In some cases, the signal is boosted from node to node to strengthen the signal before passing it on.

Because the signal passes through each computer, the failure of one computer can bring the entire network down. A ring network can, however, add features that disconnect failed computers so that the network can continue to function despite the failure.

● **Figure 2.15**
Unlike a bus topology, a ring network has no terminated ends. Data travel around the ring from computer to computer. Why would signal bounce not be a problem in a ring topology?

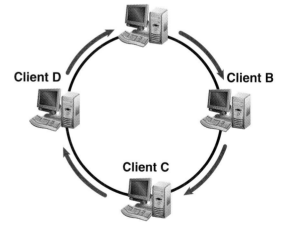

Ring Network

Token Passing To smooth the process of data transmission and to avoid collisions, ring networks typically rely on a well-known method of transmission called token passing. In token passing, computers pass a small collection of bits called a **token.** When a node has some information to transmit, it waits until it receives the token. A computer cannot transmit its data without the token.

The computer then modifies the token, in effect "stamping" it to inform the other nodes that the token is in use. The node passes the token and its

Figure 2.16 ●→
Token passing permits a computer to grab a token and then pass it around the ring. What would happen if a ring network did not use a transmitting method like token passing?

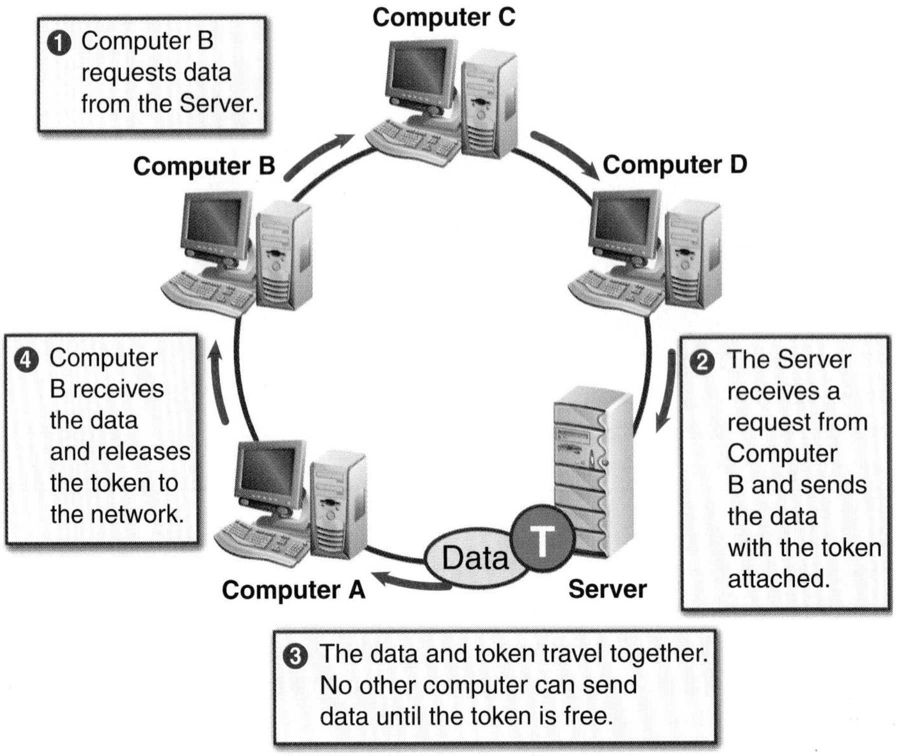

① Computer B requests data from the Server.

Computer C

Computer B

Computer D

④ Computer B receives the data and releases the token to the network.

② The Server receives a request from Computer B and sends the data with the token attached.

Computer A   Data **T**   **Server**

③ The data and token travel together. No other computer can send data until the token is free.

SHOW ME!

Signal Travel A signal in a ring network must travel through the hub before going to the next computer. View Show Me 2.12 to 2.16 at **networking.glencoe.com** to see how a signal flows through a network using a hub.

message along to the next node in line. When the token (and message) arrive at the recipient, the node acknowledges receipt of the message and creates a new, available-for-use token, which it then sends on its way around the ring.

It might seem that token passing, shown in Figure 2.16, would take a long time, but the token actually travels at roughly the speed of light (nearly 186,000 miles per second). A token can circle a ring 200 meters (656 feet) in diameter about 477,376 times per second.

Ring networks do not require massive amounts of cabling and fancy hardware to implement. One of their great advantages is giving each node an equal opportunity to transmit. As in bus networks, however, problems can be difficult to pinpoint and a break in the cabling brings down the entire network.

Mesh Network

In a **mesh network,** each computer is connected to every other computer by separate cabling, as shown in Figure 2.17. This topology provides redundant or backup paths throughout the network so that if one cable fails, another takes over the traffic. Although ease of troubleshooting and increased reliability are definite advantages, these networks are expensive to install because they use a lot of cabling.

Figure 2.17 ●
Every computer is directly connected to each other in a mesh network. Why would a receiving computer in this network have fewer problems receiving a transmission than a receiving computer in other networks?

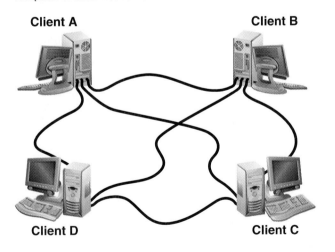

Client A   **Client B**

Client D   **Client C**

Mesh Network

Star-Bus Network

The star-bus network is a combination of the bus and star topologies. In a star-bus network, several star networks are linked together with linear bus trunks.

If one computer goes down, it does not affect the rest of the network. The other computers can continue to communicate. If a hub goes down, all computers on that hub are unable to communicate. If a hub is linked to other hubs, those connections are broken as well.

Star-Ring Network

The star-ring network (sometimes called a star-wired ring network) appears similar to the star-bus. Both the star-ring and the star-bus are connected at the center to a hub that contains the actual ring or bus. Linear-bus trunks connect the hubs in a star-bus, whereas the hubs in a star-ring are connected in a star pattern by the main hub.

SHOW ME!

Star-Bus Topology With a star-bus topology, if one computer goes down, the rest of the network is unaffected. View the Show Me 2.17, 2.18, 2.19, and 2.20 at networking.glencoe.com.

ACTIVITY 2B Planning a Network

How do you decide what kind of network or topology is best for a site? In this activity, you choose an example site for which you will plan a network. Just as a network professional would do, you answer a series of questions to help you determine a suitable network for the chosen environment.

1 With your teacher, choose a site that could be networked. For example, network your classroom or another on-campus site, such as an administrative office.

2 How many users will be served by the network?

- If it is more than ten, it should probably be a client/server network.

- If it is fewer than ten, it should be a peer-to-peer network.

- If two or more small networks need to be linked, consider a star-bus or star-ring topology.

3 Will users be allowed to share their own resources, set network policies for their own computers, and meet their own management needs?

- If security, central management, and shared resources are not issues, then a peer-to-peer network is suitable.

- If a central administrator (such as a teacher) will set network policies, then a client/server network should be used.

4 Will users' computers be used primarily as a client, server, or both?

- If a computer is being used primarily as a client computer or server computer, then it should be a client/server network.

- If a computer is going to be used as both a client and a server, you might think you need a peer-to-peer environment. However, in many client/server networks today, client computers can still share in a peer-to-peer fashion.

YOU TRY IT

Activity 2.2 Discovering Topologies The Internet is the "mother" of all networks. What kinds of topologies allow it to connect to all its users? Discover the kinds of topologies at networking.glencoe.com.

⑤ How many servers will there be and what tasks will be assigned to them?

◆ More than one server can be server-based or peer-to-peer, depending on the other factors discussed in this section.

◆ Servers can be designated for communication, backup, applications, databases, printing, storage, directories, and so on.

⑥ Is cost a consideration in choosing your network topology?

⑦ What are the physical elements you need to consider?

◆ Will servers be centrally located or spread out in different locations?

◆ Does the physical layout of the computers and office space, or existing wiring, naturally lend itself to a particular topology?

◆ Does the building have easy access to crawl spaces or wiring conduits?

◆ Is ease of reconfiguration important?

⑧ Based on your answers to the previous questions, what type of network topology do you recommend for your chosen site? Explain your reasons.

You can use the questions and information in this activity to learn the basic needs of a site and begin to plan a new network. The information can also be applied to an existing network environment to better understand its components and make suggestions for improvement.

Section 2.4 Assessment

Concept Check

1. **Define** topology, bus network, trunk, carrier sense multiple accesses with collision detection (CSMA/CD), terminator, star network, hub, ring network, token, and mesh network.

2. **Describe** why topologies are important for networking.

Critical Thinking

3. **Cause and Effect** Why is it hard to pinpoint a problem in bus or ring networks?

4. **Evaluate Information** Describe a business environment for each of the four topologies.

5. **Draw Conclusions** What are the advantages and disadvantages of each topology?

Applying Skills

Identify a Topology
Draw a diagram to illustrate how the computers in your classroom are connected to form a LAN. Label the diagram with the topology that the network uses. Is the network a peer-to-peer network or a client/server network?

SECTION 2.1 Networking Components

Key Terms

client, 36
thin client, 36
server, 36
nondedicated server, 37
dedicated server, 37

peripheral, 38
media, 38
data, 38
Redundant Array of Inexpensive Disks (RAID), 41

Main Ideas

- All networks are made up of the same basic components, such as servers, clients, media, data, peripherals, and shared resources.
- Dedicated servers are classified by the type of work they do.
- Servers can be dedicated or nondedicated servers.

SECTION 2.2 Types of Networks

Key Terms

peer-to-peer network, 44
client/server network, 45
local area network (LAN), 45
wide area network (WAN), 45

node, 45
wireless local area network (WLAN), 46
bandwidth, 46

Main Ideas

- Networks can be classified by configuration or the geographic area.
- There are three basic types of network configurations: centralized, peer-to-peer, and client/server networks.
- Networks can be classified as LANS and WANS, based on the geographic area covered.
- LANs are computers connected in a small area.
- WANs use long-range telecommunication links to connect networked computers over long distances.

SECTION 2.3 Network Architecture

Key Terms

security, 49
network interface card (NIC), 50
local user, 51

remote user, 51
network operating system (NOS), 52

Main Ideas

- Selecting a network architecture requires consideration of factors such as size, cost, security, traffic, scalability, and so on.
- The advantages and disadvantages of each architecture must be evaluated against the needs of the network.
- A NOS must be capable of meeting the demands of many users quickly and effectively.

SECTION 2.4 The Shape of a Network

Key Terms

topology, 56
bus network, 57
trunk, 57
carrier sense multiple accesses with collision detection (CSMA/CD), 57

terminator, 57
star network, 59
hub, 59
ring network, 59
token, 59
mesh network, 60

Main Ideas

- The topology, or shape, of a network describes how computers are connected.
- There are four basic network topologies: bus, ring, star, and mesh.
- The advantages and disadvantages of each topology need to be considered when planning a network.

READ TO SUCCEED PRACTICE

Key Term Journal Working in pairs or in small groups, compare entries in your Key Term Journal with those of the other students. How are the answers in the *What else is it like?* column similar or different? Note in your own journal any examples that are suggested by other students that you find helpful.

Reviewing Key Terms

1. Which type of network consists of a single trunk?
2. What function does a repeater provide?
3. What is a node?
4. What is a remote user?
5. What does the acronym NOS stand for?

Understanding the Main Ideas

6. **Define** the two most important parts of a network.
7. **Describe** two basic networking configurations.
8. **List** the differences between peer-to-peer and client/server networks.
9. **Identify** which topology is the most reliable, but also the most expensive to install.
10. **Explain** what makes a server a dedicated server.
11. **Identify** the type of WAN serving each of the following: a school district, a university, a city.
12. **Summarize** what information is needed in order to plan a network.
13. **Describe** the two different ways a network can be categorized.
14. **List** the advantages and disadvantages of implementing client/server architecture in a business that is growing.
15. **List** the differences between a desktop computer and a thin client computer.

Critical Thinking

16. **Analyzing** What kind of security problems might arise on a peer-to-peer network?
17. **Compare and Contrast** What type of hardware might a WAN have as compared with a LAN?
18. **Diagramming** Draw a diagram that indicates how information travels from one computer to another on a bus network with five computers and one printer.
19. **Evaluating Decisions** Allen's small business needs a server that will allow his employees to retrieve files and print to a centralized printer. He has only seven employees and may need to use the server as a workstation. Does Allen need a dedicated or nondedicated server? Defend your answer.
20. **Prioritizing** What factors would you consider to determine a network architecture for a small law office? Prioritize your list from most to least important.
21. **Troubleshooting** A network with a ring topology has gone down. How would troubleshooting this topology differ from troubleshooting a star topology?

e-Review · · · · · · · · · · · · · · ·

networking.glencoe.com

Study with PowerPoint

Review the main points in this chapter. Choose **e-Review > PowerPoint Outlines > Chapter 2**.

Online Self Check

Test your knowledge of the topics covered in this chapter. Choose **e-Review > Self Check Assessments > Chapter 2**.

Making Connections

Math – Calculate Network Cable Needs
For each of the following topologies, draw a diagram showing how five computers in the same office can be connected.

a. bus
b. star
c. ring
d. mesh

Use graph paper for the four diagrams, with each square equaling one foot. You may rearrange the workstations, but the dimensions of the office should not change.

Before you draw the diagrams, estimate approximately how much cable you will need to connect each topology. Which topology do you think will require the most cable and which will require the least cable?

After completing the diagrams, use the graph squares to calculate the amount of cable you might need for each topology. How accurate were your original estimates?

STANDARDS AT WORK

Students use technology tools to enhance learning, increase productivity, and promote creativity. (NETS-S 3)

Use Technology Productivity Tools
LANs and WANs used in business help users share resources and information from various sources. These networks make it possible for a company to safely share information, such as financial data, with stockholders and retail customers.

Describe a secure type of network server that could be used to share data and resources. Using a word processing or graphics application, or paper and pencil, create a diagram that shows how data can be placed on this server. Then show how the data flow through a LAN or WAN to a client.

TEAMWORK SKILLS

Cooperative Learning
Form small groups following your teacher's instructions. The owner of a floral shop would like you to design a network for the small company. You will need to choose a server, client computers, peripherals, media, and software for the shop's needs.

There are only five employees who are all local users, but they receive orders from customers through a Web site and e-mail. The owner has limited funds and does not think her networking needs will change for at least three years.

Prepare a network design proposal that could be given to the shop's owner.

a. Use the information learned in this chapter to develop the proposal.
b. Research the cost of the computers and resources, including servers, peripherals, media, and software.
c. As a group, draw the architecture for one of the three networks discussed in this chapter.
d. Provide diagrams in your proposal.

CHALLENGE YOURSELF

Research Network Architecture
Research the AppleTalk architecture, using either online or print resources.

◆ Write a short report or create a presentation describing the conditions in which it would be a suitable choice for a network.

◆ Specify any compatibility issues or other disadvantages to using AppleTalk. Describe how best to deal with the issue or barriers.

◆ Include at least one diagram or illustration in your report.

YOU TRY IT

Networking Lab

1. Identifying Advantages and Disadvantages of Networks

Recognizing networks is one of the first steps in finding your way around the information technology business. Also, recognizing inherent network strengths and weaknesses can help you understand how to troubleshoot and expand the network. Create a list of advantages and disadvantages for each of the topologies shown here:

Ⓐ Centralized network
Ⓑ Peer-to-peer network
Ⓒ Client/server network

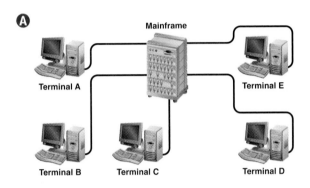

2. Creating a Topology Questionnaire

Create a list of questions that you would ask yourself or a client to help choose the best topology to use for a network. If possible, create the list using a word processing application. Your list should include information relating to the following:

◆ Purpose of the network
◆ Hardware
◆ Operating systems
◆ Performance
◆ Administration
◆ Security
◆ Sharing resources
◆ Cost of installation and maintenance

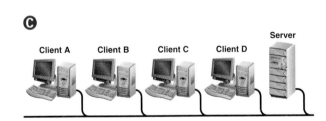

Networking Projects

1. Evaluate Network Configurations

Draw a diagram to show how the same components used in your current classroom network might work in a different configuration. Write an explanation of the following:

◆ Why you chose that topology
◆ What new components would need to be added
◆ How the new topology would change data flow
◆ How reliability of the network will be affected

2. Investigate Network Components

With your teacher's approval, examine the network interface cards used in your classroom computers.

◆ Determine how they connect to other major hardware components in the network.
◆ Draw the types of connectors and find out what they are called.
◆ Diagram the network's topology by either using a program like Microsoft Visio or drawing by hand. An example using Microsoft Visio is shown to the right.

Discuss your results with the class.

Server Client 1 Client 2

Client 3

Hub

Client 4

Printer Scanner Client 5

3. Research Network Configurations

Interview the technology coordinator in a local business or organization that has a client/server configuration. Report on the following:

◆ What kind of topology the organization uses and why that configuration was used
◆ Which network operating system is used
◆ What type of dedicated servers are being used
◆ What other services the network offers to the clients
◆ What type of media is used to connect the network
◆ How many employees administer the network

Write a report about your findings. Make sure to use standard rules of formatting, spelling, grammar, and punctuation.

Modes of Transmission

YOU WILL LEARN TO...

WHY IT MATTERS....................................

To facilitate international meetings, diplomats agree to follow rules of conduct known as protocols. Knowing your teacher's protocols, such as taking notes, may help you succeed in class. In network transactions, protocols are the rules for networking hardware and processes. They even control a task as simple as sending a friend e-mail. Protocols are means for networks to communicate and move data.

Quick Write Activity

Can you recall a discussion when many people tried to talk at the same time? This type of communication is ineffective. What are the rules for speaking or asking questions during class? Write down these rules. After you have read the chapter, compare your list of rules to the network protocols that help networks share data and communicate.

WHAT YOU WILL DO...

READ TO SUCCEED

Adjust Reading Speed

Effective readers not only think about what they are reading, they think about the process of reading. One action you can take to improve your comprehension is to adjust your speed of reading to match the difficulty of the text. As you read this chapter, slow down your reading speed when you have difficulty understanding a concept. If needed, re-read the text to give yourself enough time to absorb the material. It may take longer to read the assignment, but you will understand and remember more.

How Network Traffic Gets from Here to There

Guide to Reading

Main Idea(s)

Two important components needed to transfer data are data packets and network interface cards. Data can be transmitted using a digital or analog signal.

Key Terms

data packet
cyclical redundancy check (CRC)
bus
parallel transmission
serial transmission
analog
broadband transmission
digital
baseband transmission
multiplexing

Reading Strategy

List the three parts of a packet and describe their components. Create a chart similar to the one below (also available online).

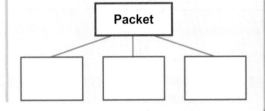

Now that you have a rough idea of what networks look like as a whole, the next step is to examine how the traffic, or data, moves to and from the various nodes on a network and, sometimes, between networks.

DATA PACKETS

Networks are very fast, but there is a limit to the amount of traffic networks can transport at one time. The challenge is to move large amounts of data as quickly as possible and still provide network access to all other users.

For example, Jamal is a graphic artist working on a magazine layout for this month's issue. He needs to send it over the network for approval to his supervisor. The file is quite large, over 100 MB. If his file was the only one that could be transmitted over the network, no one else would have access to the network while the file was being transmitted. Also, if there was an error during transmission, the entire file would have to be sent again.

The solution to this problem is to break this traffic into small pieces known as **data packets.** Breaking up Jamal's large file into many small packets allows other network traffic a chance to get transmitted at the same time as Jamal's data.

Anatomy of a Data Packet

A data packet, also called a packet, is a chunk of data that consists of three parts: a header, the data itself, and a trailer. A packet is a very small part of the entire piece of data that needs to be sent. By breaking large amounts of data into smaller portions, a network can let traffic from many sources flow in a more regular fashion. The size of a packet and how it is arranged is determined by a protocol. That protocol makes it possible for everyone on the network to send and receive information in the same format.

 networking.glencoe.com

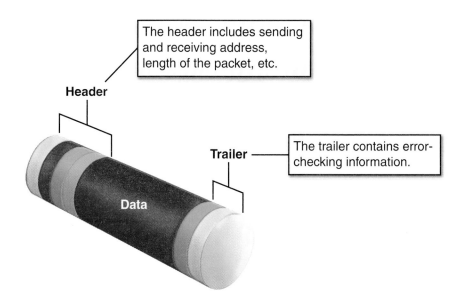

The header includes sending and receiving address, length of the packet, etc.

Header

Data

Trailer — The trailer contains error-checking information.

Figure 3.1
A data packet is made up of three parts. In what part of the packet are the sender and receiver nodes identified?

Header The packet's header is the part before the data (see Figure 3.1). The header includes the address of both the sending and the receiving computers. It also includes other information, such as the length of the packet and the time it was sent, to ensure the packet is transmitted appropriately.

Data The data section contains the actual chunk of information being transmitted. Depending on the network, this part of the packet is typically between 512 bytes and 4K in size. That means Jamal's file will be broken into thousands of small pieces. It will be reassembled when it gets to the receiving computer.

Trailer The packet's trailer is the "mop up" section of the packet. It contains the error-checking information that enables the receiving computer to verify that the data arrived intact.

Error Checking

It is important that a data packet arrives at the receiving computer intact and undamaged. In order to do this, networks commonly rely on the **cyclical redundancy check (CRC).** The sending node performs a mathematical calculation, and the result, the CRC, is attached to the packet's trailer. The receiving node then performs the same calculation on the packet it received. If the results match, the receiving node assumes that no errors occurred in the transmission and accepts the packet. If the results do not match, the receiving computer rejects the packet and signals the source computer to retransmit the data.

Data Packets and the NIC

With so much information whizzing through a network, you might wonder how it manages to get neatly chunked, addressed, and delivered with the receiver's address attached to each packet. Much of that job is handled by the network interface card (NIC) in each computer.

Role of the NIC The NIC is the network card in each computer that is the physical interface between the computer and the network cable. The NIC does all of the following:

◆ Provides the source, or hardware, address of the computer
◆ Prepares the data from the computer for the network cable
◆ Sends data to another computer
◆ Controls the flow of data between the computer and the cabling
◆ Receives incoming data from another computer
◆ Translates electrical impulses from the cable into binary code that the computer understands

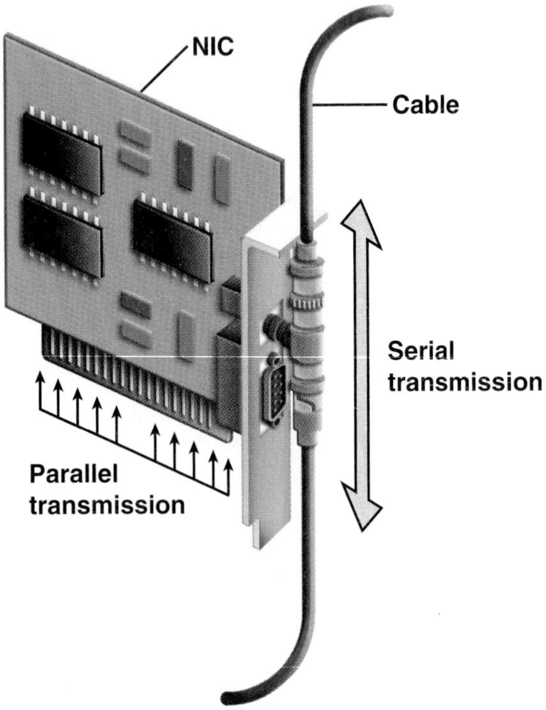

NIC in the Computer A NIC is either built onto the computer's motherboard, or can be installed as an add-in card not much bigger than a deck of cards, as illustrated in Figure 3.2.

Within the computer itself, information travels along pathways known as buses. A **bus** connects computer components, such as the NIC, video card, RAM, and CPU using parallel cabling or wire. Like freeways, a bus consists of multiple "lanes" (wires) set side by side. Figure 3.3 shows an example of a bus.

Data Packets in the Computer Data, like cars on the freeway, travel on these wires (lanes) side by side. Data travel in groups of 16, 32, or 64 related bits. Each group represents a text character or a memory address. This orderly procession of data is known as **parallel transmission.** Groups of bits are transferred simultaneously over two or more wires. The more bits the computer can move at once, the faster that information travels from place to place within the machine. Moving 32 bits of information at a time is faster than 16 bits, but moving 64 bits is even faster.

Figure 3.2 ●
The network interface card has a port for attaching a network cable. Why is it necessary to have a NIC to connect the computer to the network?

NIC

Cable

Serial transmission

Parallel transmission

Figure 3.3 ●
The computer's bus transfers data from the CPU to RAM and to other components. What is the difference between the computer's bus and a bus network topology?

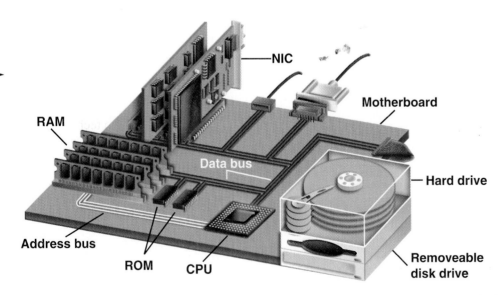

NIC

Motherboard

RAM

Data bus

Hard drive

Address bus

ROM   CPU

Removeable disk drive

Data Packets on a Cable Data must change when they move out of the computer bus onto a network cable. Although the bits transmitted still represent the same data, the groups of bits can no longer travel in parallel form or side by side. Unlike computers, network cables require information to travel bit by bit, or single file, as **serial transmissions.** Imagine multiple lanes on a freeway feeding their traffic onto a single-lane road. Similarly, data on a network move from the "multilane" computer cable to a "single-lane" network cable.

The Job of a NIC Bits cannot decide on their own to travel single file. They do not know how to go from the computer's bus to a packet ready to be sent on a cable. Converting the bits from the bus to the cable is done by the NIC. The sending and receiving NICs perform many important tasks to send and receive data. The tasks performed by each computer's NIC are listed in Table 3.1. Without the NIC, data would never get from one computer to another. It would never leave the sending computer.

NIC Tasks	
Sending NIC	**Receiving NIC**
Requests data from the computer	Watches network for packets addressed to NIC's address
Coordinates packet transmission size, speed, and timing	Coordinates packet transmission size, speed, and timing
Packages and addresses the data	Converts data from serial to parallel form
Adds CRC to packet's trailer for error checking on the receiving end	Performs CRC error checking and requests retransmit if errors are found
Converts parallel data stream to serial data stream	Removes addressing and other information from the packet
Moves packet onto network media	Passes the data from the computer to the application that will use the data

Table 3.1
Many tasks are performed by NICs at the transmitting and receiving end of a transmission. How do the jobs performed at each end of the transmission correspond to one another?

TRANSMITTING DATA PACKETS

After a data packet is prepared by the NIC, it is time for it to be transmitted over the network media. Baseband and broadband are two techniques used to transmit data packets over cable. We discuss how data are transmitted using both of these techniques below.

Bandwidth is the maximum speed at which a particular communications medium, such as cables, can transfer information. To understand how much traffic can travel on a given medium, you need to measure its bandwidth. Bandwidth measurement depends on the type of signal (analog or digital) and the media used to carry the information.

Type of Signal (analog or digital) + Type of Media = Bandwidth

Using Broadband to Transmit Analog Signals

In an **analog** signal, information travels as a continuously changing wave, as shown in Figure 3.4. This signal cycles up and down in a wavelike pattern. Radio and voice telephone are examples of analog signals.

Figure 3.4 ●———➤
Frequency is the number of cycles per second. If high frequency signals are close together like the ones shown here, how would low frequency waves look?

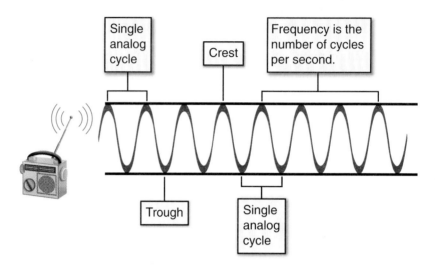

Activity 3.1 What's Your Frequency? The colors you see, the microwave you use to cook, and the radio you listen to all use a particular frequency. Visit **networking.glencoe.com** to learn more about frequencies in your life.

A single cycle is measured as the distance between wave top and wave top (crest to crest) or between dip and dip (trough to trough). The closer the cycles are to one another, the more often they occur so the frequency is higher. The further apart the cycles are, the less often they occur and the frequency is lower. Frequency is measured in Hertz (Hz), or cycles per second. This provides the basis for measuring analog bandwidth.

Broadband transmissions rely on an analog signal, a range of frequencies, and a communications medium. Broadband transmissions can be divided into multiple channels separated by small bands of unused frequencies to avoid one channel interfering with the signal being transmitted on its neighbors. Broadband is unidirectional—it moves in one direction only. To send and receive, the communications bandwidth is divided into two channels, one for each direction. Alternatively, two separate cables can be used for transmission and receiving. Figure 3.5 shows different types of cabling for broadband transmissions.

Figure 3.5 ●———➤
Broadband transmissions can run on fiber optic (shown on left) or coaxial (shown on right) cable. Are broadband transmissions analog or digital?

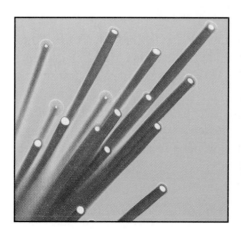
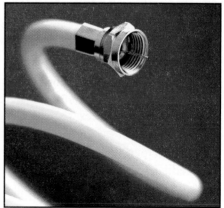

The bandwidth of a broadband transmission can also be reserved for separate channels carrying voice, data, and video. Cable television is based on broadband transmission and cable modems use broadband network technology.

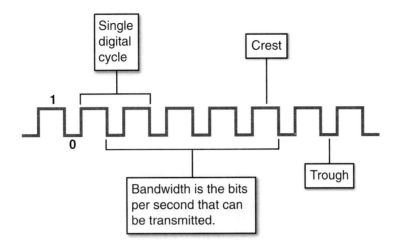

Figure 3.6
Digital signals are on/off pulses of information, rather than waves. What devices are used in a network to convert analog signals to digital signals?

Using Baseband to Transmit Digital Signals

Digital signals encode information numerically, using 0s and 1s. These simple signals convey information in separate on/off pulses over the communications medium, such as cables. A digital signal looks like Figure 3.6.

Digital signals are measured in bits per second (bps). Bps is a measure of the speed at which a device can transfer data. Digital signals do not have frequencies and are not continuously changing signals like analog. There is only the number of bits per second used to measure the bandwidth of a digital signal. All computers use digital signals to communicate.

You will find out more about digital bandwidth in later chapters that discuss advanced modem technologies, such as ISDN and xDSL. Other network architectures, such as ARCnet, Ethernet, ATM, and FDDI, are also discussed in later chapters. Because all of these technologies handle huge quantities of bits, most bandwidth measurements are shown as Kbps, Mbps, or Gbps, as shown in Table 3.2.

Baseband transmissions send digital signals over a single channel. One signal at a time travels over the network cable. The entire bandwidth is assigned to that signal. Although only one signal at a time is transmitted, a single message does not "hog" the network's entire bandwidth during transmission. Multiple transmissions can be sent through the channel simultaneously through a technique known as **multiplexing.**

READ ME!

Jargon Do not get confused between bits and bytes. Remember, there are 8 bits per byte.

Transmission Speeds and Abbreviations		
Abbreviation	**Full Name**	**Speed**
Kbps	Kilobits per second	1,000 bits per second
Mbps	Megabits per second	1,000,000 bits per second
Gbps	Gigabits per second	1,000,000,000 per second

Table 3.2
As the speed of the transmission increases on the network, the bandwidth must increase. What happens if the bandwidth is not increased to allow for greater speed?

Multiplexing By interweaving several transmissions into a single signal, multiplexing can separate each transmission by time or space. In Figure 3.7, a multiplexer is used to coordinate the transmissions of the signals. A multiplexer can be an application or a device that is used for connecting a number of communication lines in a computer. Because computers use digital signals to send and receive data, baseband transmissions are commonly used in networks such as LANs.

Figure 3.7 ●──────▶
With multiplexing, several signals from different sources can be fed into one cable for transmission. How do you think signals are kept apart using time?

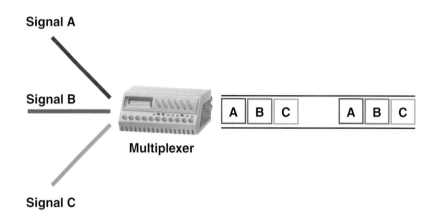

Signal A

Signal B

Multiplexer

Signal C

A B C   A B C

Baseband signals tend to deteriorate the faster they travel. Networks relying on baseband transmissions sometimes use repeaters. Repeaters act like hearing aids—they take a weak signal, amplify it, and pass it on. Well-known network architectures that rely on baseband transmission include Ethernet and Token Ring.

Section 3.1 Assessment

Concept Check

1. **Define** data packet, cyclical redundancy check (CRC), bus, parallel transmission, serial transmission, analog, broadband transmission, digital, baseband transmission, and multiplexing.

2. **Describe** the components of a data packet.

3. **Explain** how broadband transmission is different than baseband transmission.

Critical Thinking

4. **Understand Relationships** Why are data packets the basic building blocks of network data communication?

5. **Sequence** List the steps performed by the NIC as data are transmitted from one computer to another.

6. **Characterize Signals** What are the characteristics of digital and analog signals?

Applying Skills

Identify Data Transmission Types Data are being transmitted all around you. Identify at least four types of transmissions that you are familiar with (such as TV) and name the type of signal (broadband or baseband) used to transmit the signal.

Careers & Technology

NETWORK ADMINISTRATOR

Networks are now so important that most medium-sized companies have at least one network administrator on staff. Large companies may have multiple teams of administrators, whereas small businesses often turn to outside consultants to perform day-to-day network administration.

Responsibilities

Depending on factors such as the organization's size, number of locations and users, and geographic reach, a network administrator's job can include a wide variety of responsibilities, such as:

◆ Setting up and configuring network hardware and software
◆ Managing user accounts, such as passwords, storage space, and file-access privileges
◆ Creating and maintaining a system for backing up data and program files
◆ Ensuring the security of the network
◆ Managing the organization's e-mail system and access to the Internet
◆ Training users to utilize the network's resources

Preparing to Be a Network Administrator

A few years ago, only some basic networking experience was necessary. Increasingly, however, organizations demand specific qualifications, such as:

◆ An associate's or bachelor's degree in information technology
◆ Certification in one or more networking technologies, such as Windows Server technologies, NetWare, or Cisco products
◆ Demonstrable experience with computer networks
◆ Experience with key software, including NOS, desktop OS, LAN management tools, database systems, and productivity applications, such as word processing.

A Rewarding Career Path

For the beginning network administrator, the job can require long hours and irregular schedules. Many companies require an administrator to be on call 24 hours a day in case a problem arises.

Network administrators do not work only with technology. They also spend time with their system's users, learning about their needs and problems.

A career in network administration can be highly rewarding. A qualified administrator can easily make advances, which means more appealing and challenging responsibilities.

Tech Focus

1. Learn more about the role of network administrators. Write a paragraph about one aspect of the position, such as educational requirements or everyday tasks.

2. Assume you are planning a career in networking. If you started as a network support technician, what would you need to do to become a network administrator? Create a career plan for yourself that shows the path you want to take to reach this goal.

Section 3.2 Network Models

Guide to Reading

Main Idea(s)

Network models describe how different network devices communicate with each other. The OSI model consists of seven layers that describe the tasks a network component must handle.

Key Terms

protocol
Open Systems Interconnection (OSI) reference model
interface
session
data frame
Transmission Control Protocol/Internet Protocol (TCP/IP) reference model
Advanced Program to Program Communications (APPC)
Internetworking

Reading Strategy

Identify the purpose for each OSI layer. Create a flowchart similar to the one below (also available online).

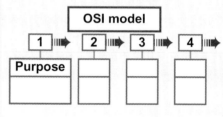

The simple act of sending an e-mail message to a friend is not really all that simple. You probably do not know whether your friend is using the same e-mail application, operating system, or type of NIC. But the beauty of it is that you do not have to know. The e-mail message is translated from your e-mail application into a data packet that is sent through your NIC over a LAN or the Internet. The data packet is then reassembled by the NIC on your friend's computer for use in the e-mail application. All of this translation is handled through a set of rules known as **protocols** that define how network devices communicate with each other.

MODELS VERSUS PROTOCOLS

To ensure that products from various manufacturers can communicate with each other, network models have been created. A network model is a conceptual description that divides the idea of a network into multiple layers. A protocol, which is part of software, is what makes a network work. The model describes what needs to be done and the protocol performs the work.

Protocols can be used for specific tasks, such as providing network access or addressing the data packet. The protocol can assume that other protocols are taking care of services needed to ensure that the sending and receiving of data packets happens correctly.

Protocols rely on models for standardization. By standardizing the services to be provided by each layer, the models effectively describe standardized protocols for each layer. The model standardizes the services and interfaces provided by protocols running at a particular layer in the model. This provides a standardized protocol "blueprint" that software can rely on.

These models define the tasks that must be performed so data can be sent successfully from one computer to another. By agreeing to use these models, manufacturers can be sure that their products will operate with other manufacturers' products.

THE OSI REFERENCE MODEL

One of the most prevalent models is the **Open Systems Interconnection (OSI) reference model,** also known as the OSI model, created by the International Standards Organization (ISO). The OSI model consists of seven layers that define how data are sent from a computer, through the network, and into a receiving computer. Understanding each layer and how each one interacts with other layers helps you understand how networks operate. To simplify tasks, each layer in the model is only concerned with the layer directly above or below it. A layer receives data from the layer above, performs the assigned tasks, then sends the data to the next layer.

The Seven Layers of the OSI Model

The OSI model provides a description of how network hardware and software work together in a layered fashion to make communications between computers possible. The model divides network communication into seven layers. Each layer includes different network activities, equipment, or protocols. Table 3.3 shows the seven layers of the OSI model.

Although there are other networking architecture models, the OSI model is the best known and most widely used guide for visualizing networking environments. Manufacturers adhere to the OSI model when they design network products to ensure compatibility. The model also helps network administrators to troubleshoot problems because it provides a common frame of reference for how components are supposed to function.

Activity 3.2 Where Do Standards Come From? Networking standards come from several organizations, such as the ISO. Go online to **networking.glencoe.com** to find out more about standards organizations.

The Seven Layers of the OSI Model

Layer	Name	Role or Purpose
7	Application	Provides applications with network access
6	Presentation	Adds a common format for data representation
5	Session	Establishes and monitors communication session between machines
4	Transport	Breaks up data into smaller pieces and ensures error-free delivery
3	Network	Addresses and routes messages
2	Data Link	Packages data in frames and establishes sessions
1	Physical	Defines hardware and transfers data as a serial bit stream

Table 3.3
The seven layers of the OSI model define the many tasks required to transmit data between computers. Why is it important for all manufacturers to follow the OSI model?

How OSI Layers Work Together

The OSI model defines how each layer communicates and works with the layers immediately above and below it. Each layer provides some service or action to prepare the data for delivery over the network. For example, the Transport Layer performs error checking to ensure that data are transmitted correctly. The Transport Layer communicates with the Session Layer above it and the Network Layer beneath it. Each layer builds upon the activities of the layer below it.

SHOW ME!

OSI Model View Show Me 3.1 to see an overview of the OSI reference model at networking.glencoe.com.

SHOW ME!

Sending Packets View Show Me 3.2 at networking.glencoe.com to look at a demonstration of data being transmitted through the OSI model.

SHOW ME!

Receiving Packets Watch the Show Me 3.3 and 3.4 videos at networking.glencoe.com to view layer transmission between computers using the OSI model.

Layers are separated from each other by boundaries called **interfaces.** An interface provides a means of communication between layers. It also shields neighboring layers from the details of how services are implemented. For example, the Session Layer expects to receive data from the Presentation Layer. The Session Layer does not care how the Presentation Layer does its job, as long as it passes the data in the expected format. All requests are passed from one layer, through the interface, to the next layer.

Data Packets and the OSI Model

Before data are sent from one layer to another, they are broken into packets. The packets are passed sequentially from one layer to the next. At each layer, more information is added to the packet, such as formatting or addressing information. This process is called encapsulation. This additional information is necessary for the packet to be successfully transmitted to the next layer. The sending computer passes its data packets in order, from the top layer to the bottom layer. Each complete packet is then transmitted from one computer to another on the network.

At the receiving end, each packet passes through the layers in reverse order, from bottom to top. All of the addressing and formatting information is stripped away, and the data are passed up to the next layer. This process is called decapsulation. By the time the packet reaches the Application Layer, all addressing information has been removed. The packet is back to its original form, ready to be reassembled with the other packets to create the complete data file.

OSI LAYERS

Beginning at the top of the OSI model (Layer 7), we work down to the bottom (Layer 1) as shown in Table 3.4. The lower layers in the OSI model support the tasks that are performed at the upper layers.

Layer 7 The Application Layer

Layer 7, the top layer of the OSI model, is the Application Layer. This layer relates to the services that directly support user applications, such as Web browsers, database applications, and e-mail applications. In other words, the Application Layer serves as a window through which application processes can access the network. A message to be sent across the network enters the

Table 3.4
The OSI model has seven layers. How is a data file sent through the layers?

OSI Model Stack	
Layer Number	**Layer Name**
7	Application Layer
6	Presentation Layer
5	Session Layer
4	Transport Layer
3	Network Layer
2	Data Link Layer
1	Physical Layer

OSI model at the Application Layer on the sending computer, travels through the other layers, and exits the Application Layer on the receiving computer, as shown in Figure 3.8.

Layer 6 The Presentation Layer

Layer 6, the Presentation Layer, defines the format used to exchange data among networked computers. Think of it as the network's translator. When computers from dissimilar systems—such as IBM, Apple, or Sun—need to communicate, a certain amount of translation and byte reordering must be done.

Within the sending computer, the Presentation Layer translates data from the format sent down from the Application Layer into a commonly recognized, intermediary format. At the receiving computer, the Presentation Layer translates the intermediary format into a format that can be useful to that computer's Application Layer.

Some of the tasks performed by the Presentation Layer include converting between protocols, translating the data, encrypting the data, and changing or converting the character set (such as EBCDIC to ASCII, which is discussed in Chapter 7). The Presentation Layer also manages data compression to reduce the number of bits that need to be transmitted.

Figure 3.8
Layer 7 of the OSI model enables applications to access the network. Why do you think this layer is the highest layer of the OSI model?

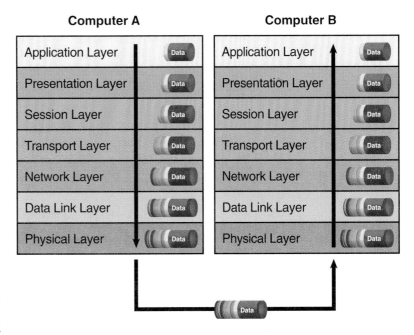

Layer 5 The Session Layer

Layer 5, the Session Layer, allows two applications on different computers to open, use, and close a connection called a **session.** A session is a highly structured dialogue between two workstations. The Session Layer is responsible for managing this dialogue.

To begin the process, the Session Layer on the sending computer establishes the connection. If required, the Session Layer also takes care of security measures, such as validating passwords. This part of the process is similar to dialing the phone at one end, and when someone answers it on the other end, asking whether the person speaking is the one to whom you want to talk.

After a connection is established, the Session Layer then ensures that the conversation, or dialogue, goes smoothly. It does this by monitoring and synchronizing the data flow, controlling who transmits, when, and for how long. This is comparable to having a third party "referee" a phone conversation, in which the two people on the phone take turns and do not speak at the same time.

When the data transfer is complete, the Session Layer ensures that the session ends smoothly—in this case, both parties "hang up."

Layer 4 The Transport Layer

Layer 4, the Transport Layer, ensures that packets are delivered error-free, in sequence, and without data losses or duplications.

On the sending computer, this layer divides long messages into several packets or collects many small packets into a larger package. This process ensures that packets are transmitted efficiently over the network. It also sequences the packets so the receiving computer knows how to reassemble the original message. In addition, the receiving computer sends an acknowledgment to the sending computer to confirm that the message was received. If a duplicate packet arrives, this layer recognizes the duplicate and discards it.

Layer 3 The Network Layer

Layer 3, the Network Layer, is responsible for addressing messages and finding the best path to move data across the network. It determines which path the data should take based on network conditions, the priority level of the transmission, and other factors. It also manages traffic problems on the network, such as the routing of packets and controlling the congestion of data. The Network Layer changes the size of a packet when it is routed from one network to another that accepts only certain packet sizes. At the receiving end, the Network Layer reassembles the data.

Layer 2 The Data Link Layer

Layer 2, the Data Link Layer, sends data frames from the Network Layer to the Physical Layer. A **data frame** is an organized, logical structure in which a data packet from the Network Layer can be placed (see Figure 3.9). A data frame is like a vehicle, in which the data are the people, or cargo, who ride inside the vehicle across the network.

On the sending computer, the Data Link Layer packages the packets into data frames, and then sends them to the Physical Layer. On the receiving computer, the raw bits of data received by the Physical Layer are repackaged into data frames, and passed on to the Network Layer to be broken down into packets.

The Data Link Layer is responsible for providing error-free transfer of these frames from one computer to another through the Physical Layer. This allows the Network Layer to anticipate virtually error-free transmission over the network connection.

Usually, when the Data Link Layer sends a frame, it waits for an acknowledgment from the recipient. The recipient Data Link Layer detects any problems with the frame that might have occurred during transmission. Frames that were damaged during transmission or were not acknowledged are then sent again.

Figure 3.9 ●
A data frame is used to transport data across the network. What tasks does the Data Link Layer perform?

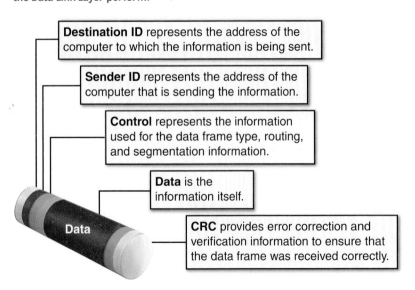

Destination ID represents the address of the computer to which the information is being sent.

Sender ID represents the address of the computer that is sending the information.

Control represents the information used for the data frame type, routing, and segmentation information.

Data is the information itself.

CRC provides error correction and verification information to ensure that the data frame was received correctly.

Layer 1 The Physical Layer

Layer 1, the bottom layer of the OSI model, is the Physical Layer. This layer carries the signals to transmit the data generated by the higher layers. The signal is transmitted as an unstructured, raw bit stream (1s and 0s) over a physical medium (such as the network cable). When a transmitting computer sends a 1 bit, the Physical Layer ensures that it is received as a 1 bit, not a 0 bit.

The Physical Layer is referred to as the "hardware layer." It is totally hardware-oriented and deals with all aspects of establishing and maintaining a physical link between communicating computers. It defines how the cable is attached to the NIC. For example, the Physical Layer defines how many pins the connector has and the function of each. It also defines how the data will be sent over the network cable.

Different types of media physically transmit bits (electrical impulses or light impulses in wireless networks) differently. The Physical Layer also defines the duration of each impulse and how each bit is translated into the appropriate electrical or optical impulse for the network medium, such as the cable.

ACTIVITY 3A Learning the OSI Reference Model

YOU TRY IT

The layers of the OSI model and their order is very important, especially when preparing to take a computer networking exam. To help you memorize the seven layers of the OSI model, you will create a mnemonic (pronounced nuh-**mon**-ick) device as shown in Figure 3.10.

1 Using a word processing or presentation application, create a chart listing the seven layers of the OSI model.

2 In the column next to each layer, list its role.

3 In the column next to the role, create two mnemonic devices of your own. One mnemonic device is for going up the OSI layers and one for going down the OSI layers.

It is critical for you to understand the OSI model and each of its layers. The purpose of each layer is to clearly define and separate the many tasks required to allow computers to communicate.

OSI Reference Model Layer Mnemonic

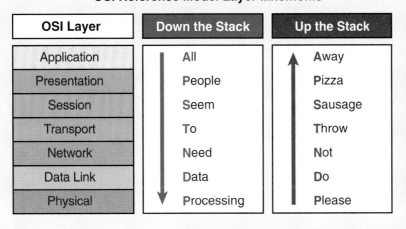

OSI Layer	Down the Stack	Up the Stack
Application	All	Away
Presentation	People	Pizza
Session	Seem	Sausage
Transport	To	Throw
Network	Need	Not
Data Link	Data	Do
Physical	Processing	Please

Figure 3.10
A mnemonic device is an easy-to-remember "hint" that can help you remember difficult information.

OTHER NETWORKING MODELS

The OSI reference model is the one most commonly referred to in descriptions of network layering and the various networking protocols. The OSI model is not the only networking model, however. Two other models, also layered, tend to pop up in descriptions of network architectures. One is IBM's network architecture for mainframe networks, known as Systems Network Architecture (SNA), and the other is an Internet-related model known as the **Transmission Control Protocol/Internet Protocol (TCP/IP) reference model.**

Systems Network Architecture

IBM designed its SNA in the 1970s as a means of enabling IBM products—mainframes, terminals, and printers—to communicate with one another and to exchange data. SNA was originally designed around the mainframe/terminal relationship but was later modified, in a specification known as **Advanced Program to Program Communications (APPC),** to include minicomputers and personal computers. The original SNA model consisted of five layers. It was later extended to complement the OSI model, as shown in Table 3.5.

Table 3.5
The SNA model was created by IBM. What kinds of products was this model used for?

SNA Seven Layers

Layer Name	Description
Transaction services	Responsible for application-to-application communication
Presentation services	Handles formatting, compression, and data translation
Data flow control	Describes rules for communication session
Transmission control	Starts, stops, and maintains sessions
Path control	Links nodes, manages links, and routes data
Data link control	Ensures reliable data transfer over physical network
Physical	Encompasses the physical network and electrical signaling

The TCP/IP Reference Model

The birth and evolution of the Internet gave rise to yet another model. This is the TCP/IP reference model, also referred to as the Internet reference model.

Unlike the OSI and SNA models, the TCP/IP model is not based on the idea of a communications session, but on a clearly defined link between communicating nodes. In other words, the TCP/IP model reflects the world of **internetworking.** Internetworking refers to the transfer and routing of information between a variety of network types. For example, a centralized network could transmit information to a client/server-based network.

Figure 3.11 shows the difference between the TCP/IP and OSI models, as well as rough—though not exact—equivalents between the layers in the two models. Note that the illustration draws no relationship between the TCP/IP internetworking layer and any layers in the OSI model. The TCP/IP model chooses not to include references to a physical layer, although any type of network relies on hardware and signaling standards.

The OSI, SNA, and the TCP/IP models are different in the layers they define. They are not, however, mutually exclusive. Modern networks can and do rely on protocols and services that fit more than one model. A LAN running the TCP/IP protocols, for example, can be based on a network operating system (NOS) designed with the OSI model in mind. That LAN can communicate with an IBM-based SNA mainframe network, given the appropriate "translation" software and gateways.

● **Figure 3.11**
The different layers in the TCP/IP and OSI models. How does the TCP/IP model differ from the OSI model?

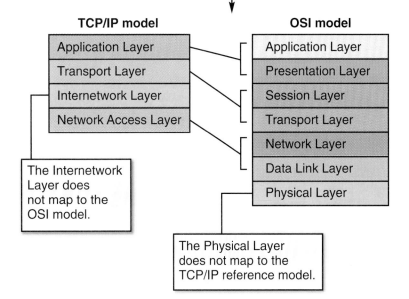

Section 3.2 Assessment

Concept Check

1. **Define** protocol, Open Systems Interconnection (OSI) reference model, interface, session, data frame, Transmission Control Protocol/Internet Protocol (TCP/IP) reference model, Advanced Program to Program Communications (APPC), and internetworking.

2. **Describe** the role an interface plays in a network model.

3. **Explain** the role of the OSI model. Include the functionality of each of the seven layers of the OSI model.

Critical Thinking

4. **Compare and Contrast** Describe the similarities and differences between the OSI, SNA, and TCP/IP networking models.

5. **Integrate Information** Use the OSI model to explain how an e-mail message is transmitted from your computer to a friend's computer.

6. **Evaluate Information** Explain how the TCP/IP model can coexist with components designed around the OSI model.

Applying Skills

Identify Network Applications Identify at least five applications that make use of network models. Draw a line down the center of a sheet of paper. On the left side of the column, list the applications. Opposite each application in the second column, write two or three sentences about that specific application.

STREAMING AUDIO AND VIDEO

Have you watched a movie trailer or listened to a radio station through your Web browser? If so, you have experienced streaming content.

Streaming Media

There are two ways to play audio or video from a Web site. One way is to download the entire media file from the Web server, and then use player software (such as RealPlayer, Windows Media Player, or QuickTime) to play it. But the user must wait for the file to download.

Streaming technology works by breaking a media file into pieces, then delivering them in order to the user's computer.

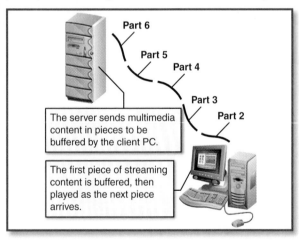

Part 6
Part 5
Part 4
Part 3
Part 2

The server sends multimedia content in pieces to be buffered by the client PC.

The first piece of streaming content is buffered, then played as the next piece arrives.

Streaming provides a more elegant solution. To stream media, the server breaks the audio or video transmission into pieces. The server sends the pieces, in order, to the user's computer. The result is a continuous stream of content, in which each downloaded piece plays as the rest of the file arrives.

Uses for Streaming Media

By using streaming technologies, Web sites provide access to information and cultures from around the world. Americans studying Spanish can listen to radio broadcasts from Latin America. Japanese teenagers can watch a live rock concert in London.

Technical Requirements

To stream content from a Web site, special hardware and software are needed:

◆ **Encoder**—The creator of the streaming content must specially encode the content to work with a specific type of player software, such as RealPlayer or Windows Media. Often, a dedicated computer is used for encoding.
◆ **Streaming media server**—This dedicated server delivers the media stream to the user.
◆ **Broadband connection**—Streaming works well only when the server is connected to the Internet (or a LAN) through a broadband link. Streaming audio and video requires a large amount of bandwidth, or the media's playback quality suffers.
◆ **Software**—Special software is required for streaming. You must use software that is compatible with the player format you want to use. The user must also have the correct player software to play your stream. Luckily, different players can coexist on most computers, so users could have RealPlayer, Windows Media, and QuickTime all installed on their systems, enabling them to play any type of streaming content.

Tech Focus

1. Compare and contrast how streaming video is accessed and plays back on a broadband Internet connection versus a dial-up connection.

2. If your school wanted to stream video content, what hardware and software would be required?

Section 3.3 Protocols

Guide to Reading

Main Idea(s)

Protocols are rules and procedures used to make network communications possible. Multiple protocols can be used by a NIC. Many protocols that operate in conjunction perform the various tasks needed to send and receive data.

Key Terms

protocol stack
binding process
binding order
Media Access Control (MAC)

Reading Strategy

Identify protocols and their descriptions that you read about in this section. Create a chart similar to the one below (also available online).

Protocol	Protocol Description

The layers within the various networking models merely provide a framework that describes where "work" is to be done in order for data to travel from the sending computer to the receiving computer. The actual work done on each layer is governed by protocols, or sets of rules.

THE FUNCTION OF PROTOCOLS

When data are transmitted over a network, they are sent in steps. A single step includes certain actions that cannot take place at any other step. Each step has its own rules and procedures, or protocols.

There are four points to keep in mind about protocols:

1. **There are many protocols.** Although each protocol facilitates basic communications, each has different purposes and accomplishes different tasks. Each protocol has its own advantages and restrictions.

2. **Some protocols work only at particular OSI layers.** The layer at which a protocol works describes the role of the protocol. For example, a protocol that works at the Physical Layer ensures that the data packet passes through the network interface card (NIC) and out onto the cable.

3. **Some protocols work at multiple layers.** Protocols can also work together in a protocol stack (also known as a protocol suite). Just as a network incorporates functions at every layer of the OSI model, different protocols also work together at different levels in a single protocol suite. The levels in the protocol suite "stack" on top of each other and correspond to one or more layers of the OSI model. Taken together, the protocols describe the entire stack's functions and capabilities.

4. **Protocols are consistent.** The protocol steps must be carried out in a consistent order that is the same on every computer on the network.

Each protocol concentrates on doing its own tasks as efficiently as possible. In a car assembly line, each worker (or machine) does one specific task. At one station, the doors are put on. At another, the body is painted. The paint station assumes that the door station did its job correctly and focuses on painting. Similarly, a network protocol addressing a data frame does not care how that data frame will be loaded onto the cable, or whether it will be retransmitted if necessary. Other protocols on other layers take care of those tasks.

PROTOCOLS IN A LAYERED ARCHITECTURE

The work of the various protocols must be coordinated so that no conflicts or incomplete operations take place. The results of this coordination effort are known as layering.

Protocol Stacks

A **protocol stack** is a combination of protocols as shown in Table 3.6. Layers within the stack, which generally correspond to the OSI model, specify various protocols for handling a function or subsystem of the communication process. Each layer in the stack has its own set of rules.

Table 3.6
A protocol stack is a combination of protocols. What protocols does the Transport layer in TCP/IP reference model use?

TCP/IP Protocol Stack		
TCP/IP Reference Model	**Function**	**Protocol(s)**
Application layer	Application protocols	FTP and SMTP
Transport layer	End-to-end reliability	TCP and UDP
Internetwork layer	Packet delivery	IP
Network Access layer	Frame creation, addressing, and routing	NDIS drivers in Windows NT

The lower layers in the OSI model specify how manufacturers make their equipment connect to equipment from other manufacturers. As long as the NICs use the same protocols, data can be sent and received from each computer regardless of the manufacturer.

Enrichment **LAB**

Lab 3.1 Displaying Local Area Connection Properties
Practice additional hands-on networking skills on page 432.

The Binding Process

The **binding process** is used to connect protocols, or protocol stacks, to the NIC. Protocols and NICs can be mixed and matched on an as-needed basis. Binding is the act of tying the protocols together to provide data with a route from the application level to the NIC. This is handled through a utility provided by the operating system or the NIC driver. For example, two protocol stacks can be bound to one NIC. If there is more than one NIC in the computer, one protocol stack can be bound to either or both NICs.

The **binding order** determines the sequence in which the operating system runs the protocol. When multiple protocols are bound to a single NIC, the binding order is the sequence in which the protocols will be utilized to attempt a successful connection. Typically, the binding process is initiated when either the operating system or the protocol is installed or initialized.

The binding process consists of more than just binding the protocol stack to the NIC. Protocol stacks need to be bound or associated with the components in the layers above and below them so that data can proceed smoothly through the stack during execution.

ACTIVITY 3B Discovering What Protocols You Use

YOU TRY IT

Most operating systems provide a utility that enables you to review and set the protocols bound to the NIC in your computer. On a Windows-based PC, you can use the following steps to identify the protocols on your computer.

❶ Click the **Start** button.

❷ Point to **Settings,** click **Control Panel.**

❸ Double-click **Network and Dial-up Connections.**

❹ Right-click the **Local Area Connection** icon, then click **Properties.**

❺ Write down any protocols you find listed there. A sample is shown in Figure 3.12. Note that your screen may not match the figure exactly.

❻ Also write down the information about your NIC, such as the manufacturer, model, and speed at which the NIC can operate.

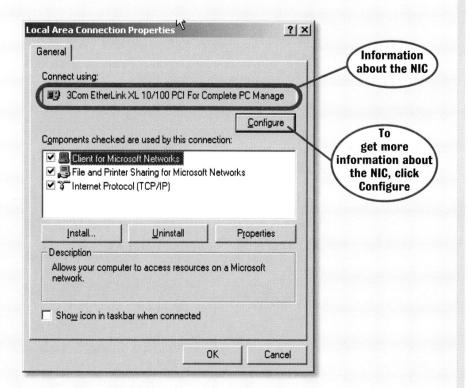

● **Figure 3.12**
The Local Area Connection Properties window provides a list of protocols used on your computer and information about the NIC.

The information you acquire about your NIC can be very useful if you need to troubleshoot a faulty NIC. For example, you may need the information to locate an updated driver in order to use the NIC with a new operating system.

Standard Stacks

The computer industry has designated several kinds of protocol stacks as standard models. Hardware and software manufacturers can develop their products to meet any one or a combination of these protocol stacks. The most important protocol stacks include:

◆ The OSI protocol suite
◆ Digital DECnet
◆ Novell NetWare
◆ Apple's AppleTalk
◆ TCP/IP
◆ The IBM Systems Network Architecture (SNA)

Protocols exist at each layer of these stacks, performing the tasks specified by that layer. However, the communication tasks that networks need to perform are grouped into one of three following types: application protocols, transport protocols, and network protocols. Each type is composed of one or more layers of the OSI model. As shown in Figure 3.13, these three protocol types map roughly to the layers of the OSI model.

Figure 3.13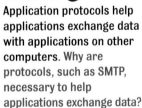
Communications are complete tasks within the OSI model. How are protocols connected to each other and to the NIC?

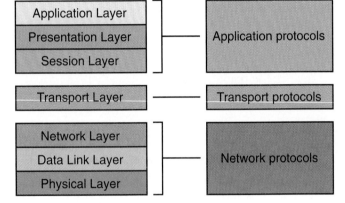

Application Protocols Application protocols work at the uppermost layer of the OSI model. They provide application-to-application interaction and data exchange. Popular application protocols are shown in Table 3.7.

Table 3.7
Application protocols help applications exchange data with applications on other computers. Why are protocols, such as SMTP, necessary to help applications exchange data?

Popular Application Protocols	
Protocol	**Description**
Simple Mail Transfer Protocol (SMTP)	An Internet protocol for transferring e-mail
File Transfer Protocol (FTP)	An Internet file transfer protocol
Simple Network Management Protocol (SNMP)	An Internet protocol for monitoring networks and network components
Telnet	An Internet protocol for logging on to remote hosts and processing data locally
Novell NetWare Core Protocol (NCP) and Novell client shells or redirectors	A set of service protocols
AppleTalk Filing Protocol (AFP)	Apple's protocol for remote file access
Data Access Protocol (DAP)	A DECnet file access protocol

Transport Protocols Transport protocols facilitate communication sessions between computers and ensure that data are able to move reliably between computers. Popular transport protocols are shown in Table 3.8.

Popular Transport Protocols	
Protocol	**Description**
Transmission Control Protocol (TCP)	The TCP/IP protocol for guaranteed delivery of sequenced data
Sequenced Package Exchange (SPX)	Part of Novell's IPX/SPX protocol suite for sequenced data
NetWare Link (NWLink)	The Microsoft implementation of the IPX/SPX protocol
NetBIOS Extended User Interface (NetBEUI)	The interface that establishes communication sessions between computers (NetBIOS) and provides the underlying data transport services (NetBEUI)
AppleTalk Transaction Protocol (ATP) and Name Binding Protocol (NBP)	Apple's communication-session and data-transport protocols

Table 3.8
Protocols at the Transport Layer ensure that data get from point A to point B intact. Why is it helpful to manufacturers of network components to have a reference model such as this?

Network Protocols Network protocols provide what are called "link services." These protocols handle addressing and routing information, error checking, and retransmission requests. Network protocols also define rules for communicating in a particular networking environment, such as Ethernet or Token Ring. Popular network protocols are shown in Table 3.9.

Enrichment
LAB

Lab 3.2 Exploring the AppleTalk and TCP/IP Protocols Practice additional hands-on networking skills on page 433.

Popular Network Protocols	
Protocol	**Description**
Internet Protocol (IP)	The TCP/IP protocol for packet-forwarding routing
Internetwork Packet Exchange (IPX)	NetWare's protocol for packet forwarding and routing
NetWare Link (NWLink)	The Microsoft implementation of the IPX/SPX protocol
NetBIOS Extended User Interface (NetBEUI)	A transport protocol that provides data-transport services for NetBIOS sessions and applications
Datagram Delivery Protocol (DDP)	An AppleTalk data-transport protocol

Table 3.9
Network protocols handle the link services. What job is handled by the NetWare Link protocol?

Protocol Standards The OSI model is used to define which protocols should be used at each layer. Products from different manufacturers that subscribe to this model can communicate with each other.

Figure 3.14
The OSI Reference model defines MAC driver activities. What role does the MAC sublayer play?

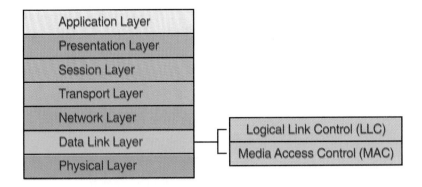

| Application Layer |
| Presentation Layer |
| Session Layer |
| Transport Layer |
| Network Layer |
| Data Link Layer | — | Logical Link Control (LLC) |
| | | Media Access Control (MAC) |
| Physical Layer |

The Data Link Layer is divided into two sublayers, known as the Logical Link Control (LLC) and the **Media Access Control (MAC)** sublayer as shown in Figure 3.14. A MAC driver is located at the MAC sublayer; this device driver is also known as the NIC driver. It provides low-level access to NICs by providing data transmission support and some basic adapter management functions.

A MAC protocol determines which computer can use the network cable when several computers try to use it simultaneously. The Ethernet protocol, otherwise known as the 802.3 protocol, allows computers to transmit data when no other computer is transmitting. If two hosts transmit simultaneously, a collision occurs, and all transmission is halted until the wire is clear. After a random wait period, each computer can begin to transmit again.

Section 3.3 Assessment

Concept Check

1. **Define** protocol stack, binding process, binding order, and Media Access Control (MAC).

2. **Describe** where the MAC sublayer is positioned in the OSI model.

3. **Explain** the relationship between network models, protocols, and protocol stacks.

Critical Thinking

4. **Analyze Information** In your own words, describe how the binding process works.

5. **Present Protocols** Using your knowledge of your school's network, list the protocols (and associated OSI layers) most likely involved in transmitting an e-mail message to a friend.

6. **Evaluate Information** Explain what happens when a computer fails to make a connection using a particular protocol.

Applying Skills

Explain PC and Mac Protocol Stacks In a large graphics firm, many of the artists use Macintosh computers, whereas other office staff use PCs running the Windows operating system. What standard protocol stacks are you likely to need for computers on this network to talk together? Explain your answer.

SECTION 3.1 How Network Traffic Gets from Here to There

Key Terms

data packet, 70
cyclical redundancy
   check (CRC), 71
bus, 72
parallel transmission, 72
serial transmission, 73

analog, 74
broadband transmission, 74
digital, 75
baseband transmission, 75
multiplexing, 75

Main Ideas

■ Data are broken into small chunks called packets prior to transmission.

■ All packets contain a header, the data, and a trailer.

■ Information is added to each packet to help the receiver put the data together again.

■ Bandwidth describes a network's capacity to send data.

SECTION 3.2 Network Models

Key Terms

protocol, 78
Open Systems
   Interconnection (OSI)
   reference model, 79
interface, 80
session, 81
data frame, 82

Transmission Control Protocol/
   Internet Protocol (TCP/IP)
   reference model, 84
Advanced Program to Program
   Communications
   (APPC), 84
internetworking, 84

Main Ideas

■ Network models provide a structured means of describing how network devices communicate.

■ The OSI, SNA, and Internet reference models are widely used models for describing network communication tasks.

SECTION 3.3 Protocols

Key Terms

protocol stack, 88
binding process, 88
binding order, 88

Media Access Control
   (MAC), 92

Main Ideas

■ Protocols establish the rules or tasks that must be accomplished at each level of network communication.

■ Various protocols work at different levels within a network reference model.

■ Protocol stacks, also called protocol suites, are groups of protocols that span multiple levels to accomplish many tasks.

Computer A	Computer B
Application Layer — Data	Application Layer — Data
Presentation Layer — Data	Presentation Layer — Data
Session Layer — Data	Session Layer — Data
Transport Layer — Data	Transport Layer — Data
Network Layer — Data	Network Layer — Data
Data Link Layer — Data	Data Link Layer — Data
Physical Layer — Data	Physical Layer — Data

Reviewing Key Terms

1. What is a protocol stack?
2. What information is stored in a packet's header?
3. What is multiplexing?
4. Explain what an interface does in terms of network layers.
5. What does the acronym OSI stand for?

Understanding Main Ideas

6. **Describe** what a bus connects.
7. **Explain** where dialog takes place in a session.
8. **Describe** how the binding process is used in an operating system.
9. **Show** in a diagram the three main parts of a data packet and label them.
10. **Describe** four important functions of a NIC.
11. **Interpret** what happens to a data packet during a parallel transmission.
12. **Recall** what repeaters act like when a baseband signal deteriorates.
13. **Explain** how CRC ensures data are transmitted correctly.
14. **Identify** the two sublayers of the Data Link Layer in the OSI model.
15. **Describe** how the binding order determines the behavior of a NIC.
16. **List** the function of each of the seven layers of the OSI model.
17. **Identify** the difference between networking and internetworking.
18. **Explain** why it is important to break data apart into packets before sending them across a network.

Critical Thinking

19. **Compare and Contrast** Describe the similarities and differences among the three basic protocol types: application, transport, and network.
20. **Draw Conclusions** Network transmissions take broadband and baseband forms. Write a paragraph that outlines broadband and baseband transmissions.
21. **Examine Relationships** Create a diagram showing how the OSI model and protocols in the TCP/IP reference models correlate to each other.
22. **Understand Layering** For a layering model to be effective, (1) each layer must have its own unique job, for which it alone is responsible, and (2) every stage of the communication process must be accounted for in the model. Explain why both of these conditions must hold for the model to be effective.
23. **Compare Networking Protocols** The Network Layer of the OSI model determines how data are moved from one computer to another on a network. Identify important features of the networking protocol for networks with the following topologies:
    a. Bus
    b. Token Ring
    c. Star

e-Review ·················

networking.glencoe.com

Study with PowerPoint

See a review of the main points in this chapter. Choose **e-Review** > **PowerPoint Outlines** > **Chapter 3**.

Online Self Check

Test your knowledge of the topics covered in this chapter. Choose **e-Review** > **Self-Check Assessments** > **Chapter 3**.

 networking.glencoe.com

Making Connections

Science – Take Advantage of Broadband Communication Electronic devices such as cable TV can distinguish between different signals and channels that are broadcast simultaneously and that have different frequencies.

Explain how this technique can be used to increase the bandwidth of a communication across a network. How do some businesses combine their telephone or video conferencing and network communications on the same media? How does a broadband signal make more efficient use of media than a baseband signal?

STANDARDS AT WORK

Students demonstrate an understanding of the nature and operation of technology systems. (NETS-S 1)

Identifying the Layered Network Model
Because of the layered model, protocols involved with a particular service operating on a particular layer do not have to concern themselves with protocols and services operating on other layers. Each network model's layer provides some service or action to prepare the data for delivery over the network. The model describes what needs to be done and the protocol performs the work.

◆ Research on the Internet or review this chapter to recall your understanding of protocols or discover different ideas about them. Gather diagrams and details of layered network models.
◆ Prepare a presentation in which you:
1. Outline at least three reasons why it is important to divide the communication process into separate layers, each governed by a protocol.
2. Create labeled models and provide one unique detail about each model.

TEAMWORK SKILLS

Developing a Protocol
At the direction of your teacher, form small groups, preferably four to six students. In your group, develop a protocol for communicating verbally. Have a group member take notes during the discussion. Your protocol should provide precise answers to the following questions:
◆ How is a discussion started and finished?
◆ Who may speak at any given time?
◆ What type of language and statements are acceptable?
◆ How do you handle situations when the protocol is not followed?

Create an electronic or flip chart presentation in which you answer the questions above on subsequent slides or charts. Make revisions to improve your protocol as necessary. Be certain to cover all of the questions completely. Finally, present your group's concept for developing protocols for communication.

CHALLENGE YOURSELF

Researching a Protocol
Use the resources available at your school's library and on the Internet to research one of the protocols for Windows, TCP/IP, Netware, or Mac OS.
◆ Prepare a report describing which layer or layers of the OSI model your protocol is involved with and the specifics of how it handles the responsibilities of the layer or layers identified.
◆ Include a history of the protocol's creation and development.
◆ Discuss the future of the protocol you chose. Will it be modified to work with new or changing technology, or will it be replaced by a different protocol after becoming obsolete? Be sure to give concrete reasons for your predictions.

YOU TRY IT
Networking Lab

1. Logging On and Off the Network

When you log on to a network, the protocol you follow is to provide your user name and password. This combination identifies you as a valid user, with rights to access certain resources (files or printers) on the network. Logging on in the Windows environment is simple.

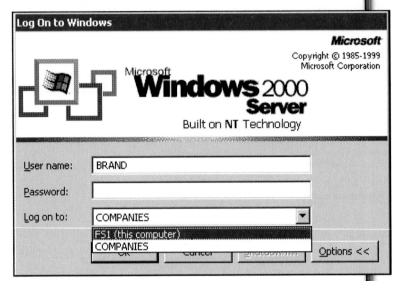

Ⓐ Start the computer and press **Ctrl+Alt+Delete** to open the Log On screen.

Ⓑ Enter your user name in the text box provided.

Ⓒ Press the **Tab** key to move to the Password text box and enter your password. Note: User names are usually not case sensitive, but passwords are. If your password is PassWord, typing in password does not work.

Ⓓ Click **OK.** After your password is validated, you can access the network resources you have rights to access.

Ⓔ To log off, press **Ctrl+Alt+Delete** to open the Task Manager and click **Log Off.**

2. Logging On to a Computer Locally

You do not always have to access the network. For example, a salesperson working on a laptop may not need to log on to the network. In this case, it can be logged onto "locally." This means that the computer ignores any network connection.

Ⓐ Press **Ctrl+Alt+Delete** to open the Log On screen.

Ⓑ Click the **Options** button to show the Log on to list box.

Ⓒ Click the **Log on to** list box and choose the computer you want to log on to (see figure). Your computer name will vary, but will say **(this computer)** after the **computer name.**

Ⓓ Enter your user name and password as usual.

Ⓔ Click **OK** to log on locally.

You can use similar protocols when logging on to other networks such as Unix or Mac OS.

Networking Projects

1. Describe Data Packet Life Cycles

Draw a diagram that shows the "life cycle" of data as it passes from one computer to another. Choose an application that might send data to another computer, and then trace the data from the Application Layer down the layers of the OSI model to the Physical Layer on the sending computer, then back up to the Application Layer on the receiving computer. For each layer of the model, do the following:

A Write a description of the changes made to the data in that layer.

B Draw an arrow to the next layer, labeling the arrow with a description of how the data make the transition between the two layers.

2. Research and Report Broadbands

Not all types of broadband technology are available in all places. Find out what types of high-speed Internet access are offered in your neighborhood. Report on the options that are available, being sure to include the following considerations in your report:

A Necessary hardware and installation fees

B Weekly, monthly, and yearly costs

C Peak (maximum) and average bandwidth

D Transmission medium (for example cable or DSL)

E Availability of troubleshooting and technical assistance and rates (if applicable)

F Future updates

G Included software packages and member services (e-mail and instant messaging, for example)

Using the information in your report, prepare a table comparing the different options available. Which type of Internet access would you suggest to someone in your area, taking all factors into consideration?

LOCAL BROADBAND OPTIONS		
Feature	**Local Cable Internet**	**Local DSL**
Hardware and installation fees	Cable modem, $75, with on-site installation included	DSL modem, $60, and on-site installation, $100
Monthly cost	$30	$28
Peak bandwidth	1 Mbps	750 Kbps
Average bandwidth	500 Kbps	600 Kbps
Technical assistance	Free with service	Free with service
Future updates	None	New transmission lines in 2004–2005 will increase bandwidth
Included software and services	5 free e-mail accounts	Free e-mail account

Building 21st Century Skills

Problem-Solving Skills: Choosing a Server

Servers make up an extremely important part of the networks to which they are connected. They must be very reliable or the network could shut down. For this reason, the hardware that comprises a server is generally more sophisticated than that found in its clients. Server manufacturers, such as Dell, Apple, and Sun Microsystems, offer servers with a broad range of hardware options and capabilities.

1. Research two server manufacturers online or use print catalogs. For each manufacturer, research the most popular servers offered and the hardware included with each server. For each server, include the following information:

   ◆ **Processor(s)** speed, type, and number

   ◆ **Storage** size and redundancy (i.e. RAID)

   ◆ **RAM** the amount of memory available on the server

   ◆ **Operating System**

   ◆ **Cost**

2. Use a spreadsheet application to create a chart that includes the information you collected. Create a column for each server and a row for each of the specifications listed in step 1. A sample table for one company has been provided to guide you.

SMALL BUSINESS SERVERS BY GATEWAY			
System Features	920 Series	960 Series	980 Series
Processor Speed (MHz)	2200	2400	2400
Processor Type			
Number of Processors			
Cache size (k)	256	256	512
RAM (Mb)	128	256	512
Hard drive storage (Gb)	60	36	36
Base price	$399	$1,099	$2,499

3. After filling in the appropriate information, use the application's chart wizard to create a graph that compares the following information for each server: the processor speed in megahertz (MHz), the RAM in megabytes (Mb), and the cost in dollars.

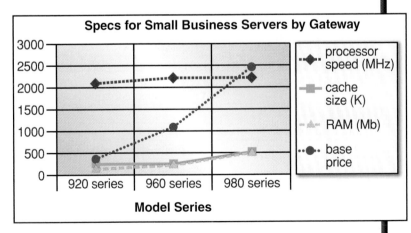

98   Unit 1

Building Your Portfolio

Researching Job Qualifications

Businesses, especially large ones, rely heavily on their networks as well as on the people who build and maintain them. If you are looking for a job in networking, it is a good idea to research the companies for whom you would like to work.

It is also a good idea to contact companies to see what jobs they have available and what qualifications are required for each position. This process can help you decide which jobs offer the best chance for your employment.

1. Following your teacher's instructions, research at least three businesses online. Try to research companies in different industries and of various sizes.

2. For each company, find out what types of networking jobs are available.

3. Determine which skills and qualifications are required for each position. Use the Job Research Checklist to guide your research.

4. Use a spreadsheet application to create a chart that summarizes your findings.

   ◆ Create a column for each job you researched.
   ◆ Include the name of the company that hires for that position.
   ◆ Create a row for each of the qualifications listed.
   ◆ Describe the requirements in each area for the jobs that you researched.

5. Inquire about the job application process for each of the businesses you researched. For example, many companies accept résumés only when a job is available. Others accept résumés continuously and keep them on file. Some companies prefer to interview job applicants at career fairs or other events where they can meet a lot of potential applicants at one time.

6. Write a brief review of the hiring process for each company.

Job Research Check List

Education
- ☑ Degree required
- ☑ Courses
- ☑ Grades
- ☑ Industry certifications

Software and Hardware Knowledge
- ☑ Network operating systems and workstation operating systems
- ☑ Network configuration
- ☑ Standards and protocols used by the company
- ☑ Kinds of software used on workstations

Work Experience
- ☑ Number of years
- ☑ Related job experience

Work Environment
- ☑ Hours to work
- ☑ In office or at home
- ☑ Travel required
- ☑ Overtime required

Job Responsibilities
- ☑ Types of daily duties
- ☑ On call support

Communication Skills
- ☑ Groups with whom you will work
- ☑ Company structure
- ☑ How you will interact with others

Company Profile
- ☑ Years in business
- ☑ Kinds of products or services provided
- ☑ Size of the company
- ☑ Type of industry

UNIT 2

Local Area Networks

→ Visit **Glencoe Online**

Go to this book's Web site at
networking.glencoe.com.
Click on **Unit Activities** and select
Unit 2 Internet Research Tips.
Practice skills and strategies that
will help you quickly find what you
are looking for on the Internet.

Think About It

Endless Computer Choices
There are hundreds of choices for computer hardware and software. To select the right pieces, you must first decide what tasks you (or the user) want the computer system to handle.

Design Your Ideal Computer System Activity
If you could create your ultimate computer system, what would you want it to do? List all the hardware and software you would buy. Remember to list any networking devices and media you would need to complete your system.

Network Hardware and Media

YOU WILL LEARN TO...

WHY IT MATTERS. ....

When you drive a car from place to place, you are guided by a vast infrastructure that allows you to get where you want to go. Highways permit you to travel quickly from one place to another. Intersections are controlled by traffic signals. Bridges help you cross geographic barriers. In a network, a similarly complex infrastructure exists to move data from one computer to another.

Quick Write Activity

Think about your ride to school or work every day. Describe each element you can think of that helps you get there safely, such as roads, bridges, traffic signals, and so on. Then describe how each of these things is similar to the elements of a computer network.

WHAT YOU WILL DO...

READ TO SUCCEED

Use Memory Tools
Successful readers use "mind tricks" to help them remember. An old—but proven—strategy is to make associations with new ideas you are learning. For example, the term WYSIWYG (WIZ-zee-wig) stands for "**W**hat **Y**ou **S**ee **I**s **W**hat **Y**ou **G**et" and illustrates the concept of a computer application that lets you see on the monitor exactly what appears when the document is printed. As you read this chapter, look for opportunities to make up your own memory tools.

Guide to Reading

Main Ideas

Nodes, hubs, switches, and routers are all connective devices that allow the transmission of communications traffic over networks. The traffic moves between nodes on the network. Modems are devices that allow remote nodes to access a network.

Key Terms

repeater
segment
bridge
switch
router
brouter
gateway
modulation
demodulation

Reading Strategy

Identify each of the network components listed in this section. Create a table similar to the one below (also available online).

Component	OSI Operating Layer

In most networks, data travel through many hardware devices. Each device performs specific jobs to help the data get to the intended destination. This section examines the role of each component that helps data get from one computer to another.

HUBS

The hub is a central hardware component for many LANs. Network devices are connected to the hub so they can share data, as shown in Figure 4.1. Hubs operate at the Physical Layer in the OSI model. Hubs contain multiple ports, and can connect to other hubs to expand the network. Status lights on the hubs help determine which nodes are not receiving data. Nodes are added to the network by being plugged into the hub.

As technology has improved, the cost of hubs has fallen. Expanding a network can be as easy as adding more hubs.

When a node on the network sends a data packet, it travels from the sending node, through the cable, and then to the hub. The hub repeats the data packet to all the other ports on the hub, and the data packet is sent to all of the nodes connected to that hub. Each node receives all of the data traffic and decides whether to keep it. Table 4.1 on page 105 outlines the capabilities of several different types of hubs.

Figure 4.1
A hub connects network devices so they can share data. How do you connect additional devices after all ports on a hub are full?

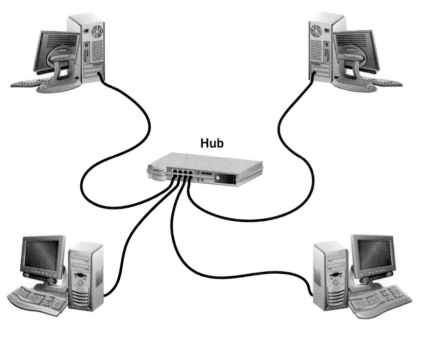

Hub

Types of Hubs and Their Capabilities	
Type	**Capabilities**
Passive	◆ Acts as connection point ◆ No signal amplification ◆ Does not require electrical power
Active	◆ Acts as connection point ◆ Regenerates and retransmits signal to extend length of network ◆ Requires electrical power
Switched	◆ Same capabilities as active hubs ◆ Examines packet address and sends it to a specific port on the hub to reduce network traffic ◆ More expensive than other types of hubs
Hybrid	◆ Same capabilities as active and switched hubs ◆ Uses several different types of cable

Table 4.1

Different types of hubs have different capabilities. What factors would you have to consider when choosing between types of hubs to use in a network?

SHOW ME!

Hubs View Show Me 4.1 to see a demonstration on how hubs work at **networking.glencoe.com**.

REPEATERS

Repeaters are simple devices used to extend the reach of a network. They are designed to receive a signal, clean it up, strengthen it, and pass it along. Repeaters operate at the Physical Layer of the OSI model. Essentially, repeaters allow smaller LANs to grow into larger LANs by moving transmissions from one network **segment** to another (see Figure 4.2). A segment is a section of the network that includes the cable and nodes that are connected to a device, such as a repeater, hub, or bridge.

To increase the size of the network and the distance between nodes on the network, repeaters are used. Repeaters are also used to move transmissions between different media types, such as coaxial and fiber optic cables. However, repeaters cannot be used to do the following:

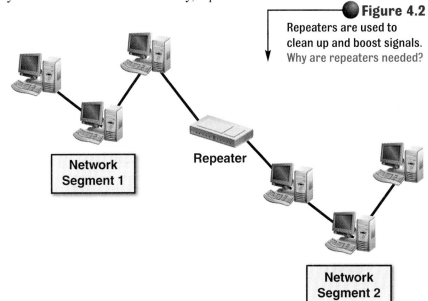

Figure 4.2

Repeaters are used to clean up and boost signals. Why are repeaters needed?

Network Segment 1

Repeater

Network Segment 2

◆ Enlarge a network beyond the capabilities of its underlying architecture.
◆ Connect network segments that use different ways of transferring data.
◆ Filter out bad or damaged transmissions.

BRIDGES AND SWITCHES

A **bridge** is used to connect two network segments together, just as a bridge over a river connects one side to the other. Bridges can be used to connect dissimilar network segments that use different methods of transferring data, such as Ethernet and Token Ring. Bridges are smart enough to transfer packets between the two segments, even though each segment uses different protocols. Bridges can also be used to isolate heavily trafficked segments or problematic nodes from the rest of the network.

A **switch** is basically a multiport bridge, allowing several segments of a network to communicate with one another. In today's networks, it is uncommon to find bridges because switches provide "multibridge" capability. However, to keep the explanation simple, we refer to the bridge. Just keep in mind that a switch allows multiple bridges to be formed.

Bridges operate at the Data Link Layer. They filter and pass packets between segments. To pass packets from one segment to another, the bridge must be able to determine whether the sender and receiver are on the same network segment.

- ◆ If the sender and the receiver are on the same segment, there is no need to transfer the packet to another network segment.
- ◆ If the sender and the receiver are on different segments, the bridge must find the receiver to forward the packet to the right party.

Routing Table

A bridge finds other nodes on the network by continuously monitoring all the traffic on the segments it connects. The bridge checks the source and destination address of the data flowing through it to determine to which segment the data will be sent. The bridge then creates and maintains a database, called a routing table. The routing table keeps track of the NIC's physical address of the node on the segments. The bridge starts with a blank routing table, but gradually builds an increasingly complete "picture" as packets pass back and forth through the bridge.

What happens when the bridge has built a routing table and it receives a packet sent from node 1 to node 2? It depends on which segments node 1 and node 2 happen to be. Figure 4.3 illustrates the following examples.

- ◆ If both node 1 and node 2 are on the same network segment, the bridge discards the packet and assumes that the network will deliver it.
- ◆ If node 1 and node 2 are on different segments *and* if the address of node 2 is in the routing table, the bridge forwards the packet to node 2.
- ◆ If node 1 and node 2 are on different segments *but* the address of node 2 is not yet in the routing table, the bridge forwards the packet to all segments except the one inhabited by node 1. The bridge broadcasts the packet to all segments except the one containing the sending node because the bridge never forwards packets between nodes on the same segment.

Figure 4.3 ●
Bridges connect segments of a LAN together. How are bridges different from hubs?

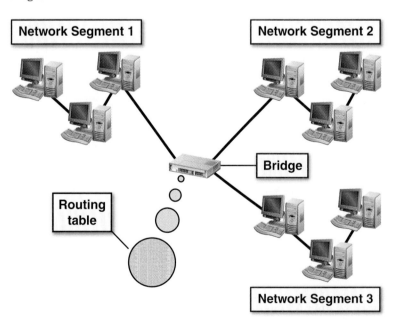

Network Segment 1

Network Segment 2

Bridge

Routing table

Network Segment 3

This method of building the routing table is referred to as backward learning. It is similar to learning your way around a new town. The more destinations you know, the more effectively you move around. Similarly, the more destinations the bridge knows, the more efficiently it can route packets and, in the process, relieve congestion by discarding intrasegment packets.

Collision Domains

An important function of bridges is to minimize collision of data packets by creating collision domains. A collision domain is a part of the network that includes a segment and its associated nodes, as shown in Figure 4.4. The collision domain receives all of the traffic and collisions generated by any node. Bridges and switches prevent the passing of collisions from one network segment to another. Therefore, bridges and switches contain collisions to one segment of the network. This can be helpful when used to isolate busy portions of the network from other segments.

● **Figure 4.4**
Collision domains are created to help reduce the number of collisions over a network. How do bridges prevent collisions?

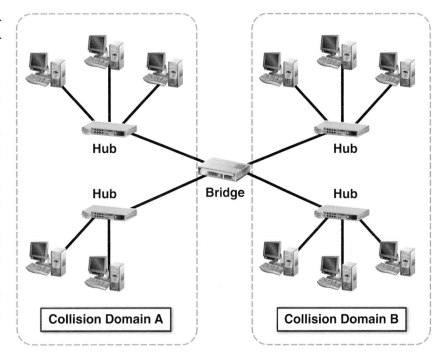

Collision Domain A

Collision Domain B

ROUTERS

Bridges are clever devices, but they are not as smart as routers. Whereas bridges forward data from one network segment to another, **routers** take the process one giant step further by doing the following:

◆ Forwarding packets from one network to another, even those separated by great distances and many networks in between
◆ Determining the best route to use to deliver the data

Like bridges, routers can transfer packets between networks built on different architectures, but routers operate at Layer 3, the Network Layer.

Routing Table

Routers communicate only with other routers. Routing tables are used to find other networks. Unlike bridges, which rely on physical addresses, routers rely on network addresses. Network addresses are numbers that identify the network and the subnetworks to which a node belongs.

A network address is similar to the zip code that identifies the town you live in. The subnetwork is similar to the name of the street you live on. A router sends data to another router located in the general area (the city you live in), but leaves the task of finding the exact node the data are intended for (the street and house address) to other devices within the intended network.

Data Routes

Another important job performed by routers is determining the route data will travel. This task includes finding possible routes, determining the distance between routers, and determining how many hops and how busy the route is at the time. A hop is one leg of the journey that the data packets travel between routers. Routers can even determine the cost of transmission. Figure 4.5 illustrates how a router identifies two possible paths a packet could take between Networks A and E.

Figure 4.5 ●———▶
This figure shows two possible paths for a packet traveling from Network A to Network E. One path takes 3 hops. The other takes 2 hops. At what layer of the OSI reference model do routers function?

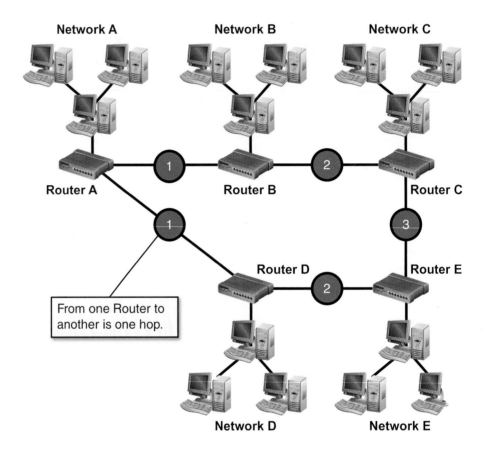

Network A   Network B   Network C

Router A   Router B   Router C

From one Router to another is one hop.

Router D   Router E

Network D   Network E

Collision Domains

Much like bridges, routers also create collision domains. Routers can also create broadcast domains. If two nodes can communicate with each other without the need to pass data through a router, the nodes are on the same broadcast domain. These broadcasts are not passed through the router to other networks. Broadcast domains are common in Ethernet networks in which the data are broadcast to all other nodes within the network.

Brouters

Brouters, as their name indicates, are hybrids that combine the capabilities of bridges and routers. Like bridges, they work at the Data Link Layer to transfer and filter network traffic. Like routers, they also work at the Network Layer to route packets from one network to another. They are sometimes referred to as bridging routers.

GATEWAYS

Repeaters, bridges, and routers enable data to transmit between similar networks. **Gateways** enable dissimilar networks to communicate. Gateways operate at higher levels in the OSI model such as the Application, Presentation, and Session layers. In some cases, they operate at all seven layers. For example, gateways could help a mainframe network based on IBM's SNA protocol to communicate with a network based on Microsoft Windows Server using the protocol TCP/IP.

Because of the complex jobs they perform, gateways are typically dedicated computers. Their job is to convert data packets from one network protocol to another. As each packet leaves the sending network, a gateway strips away the protocols, layer by layer. Prior to forwarding, the packets are repackaged in the protocol "wrappers" expected by the receiving network. This process enables different networks to communicate.

MODEMS

A modem is a computer-to-computer communication device that converts digital signals from the computer to analog signals for the telephone lines. Its name comes from the two operations it handles: modulation and demodulation. **Modulation** is the process of changing the digital signal to an analog signal on the sending computer. **Demodulation** is the process of converting the analog signal back to a digital signal on the receiving computer.

Modems and new modem technologies are discussed in greater detail in Chapter 7.

Section 4.1 Assessment

Concept Check

1. **Define** repeater, segment, bridge, switch, router, brouter, gateway, modulation, and demodulation.

2. **Explain** the differences between an active hub and a passive hub.

3. **Describe** the role modems play in network communications.

Critical Thinking

4. **Understand Relationships** Draw a diagram of a network that includes hubs, repeaters, switches, routers, gateways, and modems. Label each item with its purpose.

5. **Compare and Contrast** List the similarities and differences between the role of a hub versus the role of a switch.

Applying Skills

Identify Network Devices With your teacher's permission, identify the types of devices on your school's network that enable you to connect to the school's server(s). If possible, take a mini-field trip to view these devices. Write what you learn about the technology in place at your school.

Ethics & Technology

USING TECHNOLOGY RESPONSIBLY

The Internet has made it easy for anyone to find and duplicate all kinds of things. It is so easy that millions of people are sharing their favorite songs, posting copyrighted photos, and even copying software online.

The U.S. Copyright Office's Web site can give you basic information about copyright and trademark laws.

Copyright Laws

Unfortunately, in many cases it is illegal or at least unethical to duplicate material found on the Internet. Most people do not realize that they are violating copyright laws when they download or trade text, songs, photos, or software.

Text, pictures, media, software, and other products are the intellectual property of their creators. Copyright laws guarantee a work's creator certain rights pertaining to the work, such as the right to determine where and how it is published, who may copy it, and whether there is payment for use.

If you download a copyrighted work without paying for it or without getting permission from the copyright holder, you may be breaking the law. Selling a copyrighted work without the owner's knowledge is a crime. Even copying material to give to other people without profiting can be illegal.

Avoiding Problems

You can use the Internet legally by following some common-sense precautions:

◆ Consider anything you find online or on a disk to be protected by copyright.
◆ Avoid file-sharing services that provide access to songs, photos, movies, or software programs. These sites usually do not compensate the copyright holders and may encourage illegal file sharing.
◆ Never post a copyrighted item on the Internet, either via the Web, a newsgroup, or any other service.
◆ Follow the guidelines in your school's or employer's acceptable use policy (AUP).

You can use copyrighted materials in limited applications. It is usually legal to make a backup copy of a software program. It is also legal and ethical to copy small portions of a writer's work in a document you create, as long as you clearly quote the material and attribute it to its source.

Tech Focus

1. Report on how music companies are being affected by file sharing and the steps they are taking to protect themselves.

2. Write a paragraph about what you would be comfortable or uncomfortable doing to protect company resources.

Section 4.2   Network Media

Guide to Reading

Main Idea(s)

Cable is used to connect network devices. There are many types of networking cable in use today. Different types of cable have particular strengths and weaknesses, most notably in the speed at which they can transfer information.

Key Terms

shielding
noise
crosstalk
attenuation
BNC connector
twisted-pair cable
unshielded twisted-pair (UTP)
shielded twisted-pair (STP)
fiber optic cable

Reading Strategy

Identify each type of cabling you read about in this section. Create a chart similar to the one below (also available online).

Media Type	Description

One of the most basic components of a network is the cabling that connects devices together. Each type of cabling has its own capabilities, such as the speed at which it can transmit data and the distance at which it can reliably transmit the data.

CABLES

The vast majority of networks are connected by some sort of cabling. The cables are the network transmission media that carry signals between computers. Cable types can be confusing. Belden, a leading cable manufacturer, publishes a catalog that lists more than 2,200 types of cabling. Fortunately, only three major groups of cabling (coaxial, twisted-pair, and fiber optic) connect the majority of networks.

Coaxial

At one time, coaxial cable was the most widely used network cabling because it was relatively inexpensive, light, flexible, and easy to work with.

In its simplest form, coaxial cable consists of a core of copper wire surrounded by insulation, a braided metal shielding, and an outer cover. Figure 4.6 shows a coaxial cable and its layers. The core carries the electronic signals that make up the data. The insulating layer separates the core from the metal shielding. The core and the shielding layer must be kept separate to prevent shorts. A short in a coaxial cable will destroy the data being transmitted along the cable. An insulating outer shield—usually made of rubber, Teflon, or plastic—surrounds the entire cable.

The **shielding** layer grounds the cable and protects it from electrical noise and crosstalk so the data are not distorted. Stray electronic signals, called **noise,** interfere with data transmissions along a cable. **Crosstalk** is signal overflow from an adjacent wire.

Activity 4.1 Network Certification Preparation
When preparing for a networking certification examination, you need to have extensive knowledge of wiring requirements and uses. Visit **networking.glencoe.com** to find a helpful catalog of wiring types and uses.

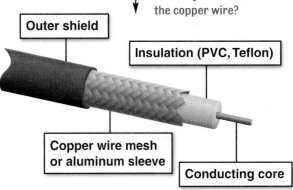

Figure 4.6

Coaxial cable consists of copper wire surrounded by three layers. What are the three layers that surround the copper wire?

Outer shield

Insulation (PVC, Teflon)

Copper wire mesh or aluminum sleeve

Conducting core

As data are transmitted along a cable, they begin to lose signal strength. The farther the signal travels, the more the signal fades. This is known as **attenuation.** Coaxial cable is more resistant to interference and attenuation than twisted-pair cabling.

Because of its resistance to attenuation, coaxial cabling is a good choice for longer distances and for reliably supporting higher data rates with less sophisticated equipment. Coaxial cable comes in a few different types, as summarized in Table 4.2.

Table 4.2
Coaxial cable comes in two main categories. When is coaxial cable a good choice?

Coaxial Cable Types

Type	Notes
10Base2 or thinnet	Thinnet cable (0.25" thick) is flexible and easy to work with. It is inexpensive and carries signals up to 185 meters before the signal suffers from attenuation.
10Base5 or thicknet	Thicknet cable (0.5" thick) is fairly rigid and difficult to work with. A thicker copper core enables thicknet cable to transmit data up to 500 meters. Thicknet is often used as a backbone for a network.

READ ME!

Jargon Cable that contains one layer of foil insulation and one layer of braided metal shielding is referred to as dual shielded. Quad shielding consists of two layers of foil insulation and two layers of braided metal shielding.

Connection Hardware 10Base2 and 10Base5 cabling use special connection components, known as **BNC connectors,** to connect the cable and the computers. There are several components in the BNC family, such as:

◆ **The BNC cable connector,** shown in Figure 4.7, is either soldered or crimped to the end of a cable.
◆ **The BNC T connector** joins the network interface card (NIC) in the computer to the network cable.

Figure 4.7
BNC cable connectors are used with 10Base2 and 10Base5 cables. How is the BNC connected to the end of the cable?

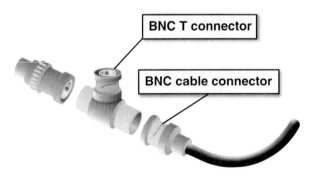

BNC T connector

BNC cable connector

◆ **The BNC barrel connector,** shown in Figure 4.8, is used to join two lengths of thinnet cable to make one longer length.
◆ **The BNC terminator** closes each end of the bus cable to absorb stray signals. Otherwise the signal bounces and all network activity stops.

Figure 4.8
A BNC barrel connector is used to make a longer length of cable. What type of cable is used with a BNC barrel connector?

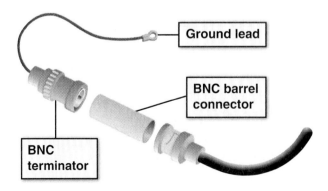

Ground lead

BNC barrel connector

BNC terminator

Coaxial cable is no longer king of the Ethernet cabling world. However, its prevalence in homes (thanks to cable television) coupled with cable Internet access promises to keep this type of cabling around for many years to come.

Twisted-Pair

In its simplest form, **twisted-pair cable** consists of two insulated strands of copper wire twisted around each other. The twisting of the wire cancels out crosstalk from adjacent pairs of cable. The higher the number of twists per foot of cable, the more effectively it cancels out crosstalk.

The total number of pairs in a cable varies depending on the purpose of the cable. Twisted-pair cable used for telephone systems often consists of two pairs, whereas most data-grade cable consists of four pairs.

UTP One type of twisted-pair cabling that does not have an extra shielding layer to help eliminate noise interference is **unshielded twisted-pair (UTP)**. Although this might seem to be a serious drawback, most business settings do not require the extra shielding, and they do not want to spend more for the shielding. The maximum length of a cable segment is limited to 100 meters (328 feet). UTP cabling is categorized according to its capabilities. The most important categories for you to know are as follows:

- **Category 5**—This type of cabling is often referred to as "Cat 5" and features four twisted pairs. It is suitable for transmission speeds up to 100 Mbps.
- **Category 5e**—This type of cabling also features four twisted pairs. It is suitable for transmission speeds up to 1 Gbps.
- **Categories 6 and 7**—These are emerging cable standards that can transmit data at speeds exceeding 1 Gbps. Expect to see more of these in the future.

STP Another type of twisted-pair cable is the **shielded twisted-pair (STP)** cable. It uses a woven copper-braid jacket to protect the transmitted data from outside interference. This allows STP cable to support higher transmission rates over longer distances than UTP. STP cable is more expensive.

Of the two types, UTP cable is most prevalent. Its popularity can be attributed to the fact that most buildings are prewired for telephone service. In many cases, new wiring does not have to be run through the building.

Connection Hardware Twisted-pair cabling uses RJ-45 connectors to connect to a computer, which are similar to RJ-11 telephone connectors. An RJ-45 connector is shown in Figure 4.9. Although RJ-11 and RJ-45 connectors look alike at first glance, they are different. RJ-45 connectors are slightly larger than RJ-11 connectors. The RJ-45 connector has eight cable connections, whereas the RJ-11 has only four.

Cabling a network requires custom sizes, lengths, and connector usages. With practice, you can install network cable quickly and accurately. However, you must first learn the basic skill of making a network cable.

● **Figure 4.9**

RJ-45 connectors look similar to telephone jacks. How can you tell the difference between an RJ-45 connector and an RJ-11 (telephone) connector?

ACTIVITY 4A Making Your Own Network Cable

Creating a UTP cable suitable for use in a network is a basic skill that you should learn. To complete this activity, you need your teacher's permission and the following supplies:

- A length of UTP cable, preferably Cat 5 or Cat 5e
- An RJ-45 connector
- A wire stripper
- A wire cutter
- A crimper tool

1 Cut a length of cable appropriate for the distance you need to cover from the computer to the connection device (that is, a hub or switch). Always add a few feet for mistakes or unanticipated rerouting of the cable.

Figure 4.10
Untwist the UTP cable following step 3.

UTP Cable

2 Strip approximately 1" of the cable's outer jacket. Go slowly to avoid cutting into the housing surrounding the wire inside the jacket.

3 Untwist the wires in the following order from left to right as shown in Figure 4.10: White/Orange, Orange, White/Green, Blue, Blue/White, Green, White/Brown, Brown.

- Note: You can use a different arrangement, but you must follow the same order on the other end of the cable.

4 Cut off ¹/2" of the wires, leaving ¹/2" exposed from the end of the outer jacket.

5 Push the wires into the RJ-45 connector. Ensure that the wires are pushed all the way to the end of the connector.

- Note: Always double-check your work at this point. If you have made a mistake and proceed to crimp the RJ-45 connector, you will have to cut it off and start over.

Figure 4.11
When you have finished crimping, your wire should look like this.

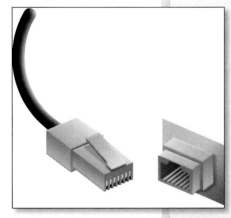

6 Plug the RJ-45 connector into the crimper and squeeze the handle. When properly crimped, the connector should not be easy to pull off the end of the cable.

7 Repeat steps 1–6 for the other end of the cable, double-checking that you arrange the wires on the other end in the same order you used in step 3. This is critical or your cable will not work!

8 When finished, your cable should look like Figure 4.11. Plug your cable into the computer's NIC and into a hub or switch device to test it.

- Note: To connect one computer directly to another, you must use a crossover cable. The steps are similar, but the wiring on one end of the cable must be reverse of the other end.

As you can see, creating UTP cabling is quite simple. Now, you are prepared to make your own custom network cabling whenever you need to.

Fiber Optic

In **fiber optic cable,** pulses of light travel down extremely thin tubes of glass or plastic to transmit data. Because fiber optic transmissions are not subject to electrical interference, they are extremely fast. The signal—a light pulse—can be transmitted over many miles.

Each glass tube passes signals in only one direction. A cable includes two strands in separate jackets. One strand transmits and the other receives. A reinforcing layer of plastic surrounds each glass strand, and Kevlar fibers provide strength, as shown in Figure 4.12. This reinforcing layer is used to protect the fibers from being broken or bent. As with twisted-pair and coaxial cables, fiber optic cables are encased in a plastic coating for protection. Fiber optic cables should be handled carefully. If the cable is bent too much, the fibers could break and prevent the flow of data.

Fiber optic cabling is more expensive than other types. It is also more difficult to work with, although recent advances have made it easier to use. It is a relatively secure way to send data because no electrical impulses are carried over fiber optic cable. This type of cable cannot be tapped, and its data cannot be stolen, unlike copper-based cables. Fiber optic cable is good for very high-speed, high-capacity data transmission because of the purity of the signal and lack of signal attenuation.

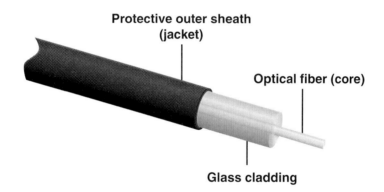

Protective outer sheath (jacket)

Optical fiber (core)

Glass cladding

● **Figure 4.12**
Fiber optic cable uses light pulses instead of electrical signals. What advantages does fiber optic cable offer over other types of cable discussed so far?

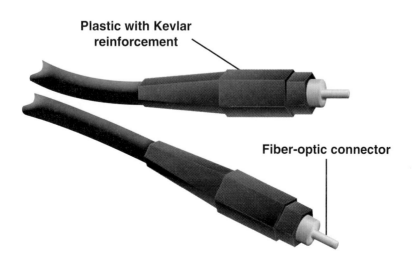

Plastic with Kevlar reinforcement

Fiber-optic connector

SELECTING CABLING

The cabling you select depends on the needs of a particular site. To determine which type of cable is best, consider the following guidelines.

Table 4.3
You should carefully consider which type of network cabling to use. What factors should you consider when evaluating different types of network cabling?

Cable Selection Guidelines

Consideration	Notes
Installation logistics	How easy is the cable to install and work with? Is security a main concern?
Shielding	Will the cabling run near "noisy" areas, such as power lines or motors? Is crosstalk a major concern?
Transmission rate	How fast does the network need to transmit data? Will the speed support growth in the future?
Signal attenuation	How far does the cable need to run?
Cost	What is the budget for cabling?

Enrichment **LAB**

Lab 4.1 Understanding Network Connectivity
Practice additional hands-on networking skills on page 434.

There are trade-offs with the type of cable you purchase. The least expensive cable might make the accountants happy, but the users will not be happy when speeds fall or security is compromised. Table 4.3 provides some guidelines you should consider when selecting cabling for a network project.

Section 4.2 Assessment

Concept Check

1. **Define** shielding, noise, crosstalk, attenuation, BNC connector, twisted-pair cable, unshielded twisted-pair (UTP), shielded twisted-pair (STP), and fiber optic cable.

2. **List** the types of cabling presented in this section. Include the maximum cable length, transmission speed, and cost (inexpensive or expensive).

Critical Thinking

3. **Analyze Information** What is the best type of cable to use if security is a major concern?

4. **Sequence Information** Arrange each of the following cable types by their usable cable length: fiber optic, 10Base2, UTP, 10Base5.

5. **Draw Conclusions** What factors must you consider when choosing network cabling?

Applying Skills

Choose Network Cabling Using your school's network as an example, explain what types of cabling would be most appropriate for each area, including within your classroom, from classroom to wiring closet or server room, and from building to building (if your school has separate buildings).

Guide to Reading

Main Idea(s)

The NIC is the direct link between the computer and the cable. Choose NICs carefully by identifying the computer's bus architecture and the connector type used on the network. Specialized NICs allow connections through different media.

Key Terms

programmable read-only memory (PROM)
boot-on-LAN

Reading Strategy

Identify what you currently know about installing and configuring NICs. Create a chart similar to the one below (also available online).

What I Know	What I Want to Find Out	What I Learned

Network interface cards (NICs) provide the interface between cables and computers. There are, of course, many types of cards, and there are also many types of connectors. The primary roles of network interface cards will be discussed in detail in the following section.

THE ROLE OF THE NIC

The NIC has four primary roles. First, the NIC prepares data from the computer for the network cable. Second, it sends the data to another computer. Third, it controls the flow of data between the computer and the cabling system. Finally, it receives incoming data from the cable and translates it into bytes that can be understood by the computer's central processing unit (CPU). Each of these roles makes an important contribution to a smoothly-run network.

To do its many jobs, the NIC uses its hardware and firmware. Firmware is the term for software routines that are permanently stored on the NIC. This storage is known as read-only memory (ROM) because it cannot be overwritten. Unlike your computer's RAM, read-only memory does not lose its contents when the power goes off. The programming stored in NIC firmware implements the Logical Link Control and Media Access Control functions in the Data Link Layer of the OSI model.

Preparing the Data

As you learned in Chapter 3, data inside a computer travel in digital form along parallel pathways called buses. Network cables, on the other hand, transmit data in serial (single file) data streams. To be transmitted, data must be converted from a parallel stream to a serial data stream. The NIC handles this conversion.

Signals must be translated into electrical or optical signals to travel on the network's cables. The component responsible for this task is the transceiver. A transceiver is a device that both transmits and receives signals. In the NIC, the transceiver is responsible for receiving and transmitting data.

READ ME!

Tech Tip 8-bit buses, used in the original IBM PC, moved 8 bits of data simultaneously. Over time, this bus size was increased to 32 bits. Some server architectures use 64-bit buses.

Sending and Controlling Data

Before data are sent over the network, a conversation between the sending and receiving NICs takes place. This conversation is necessary to establish the guidelines that will govern the transmission. The following items must be determined before any transmission can begin.

◆ The maximum size of the data groups to be sent
◆ The amount of data to be sent before confirmation of receipt is given
◆ The time intervals between sending data chunks
◆ The amount of time to wait before confirmation is sent
◆ How much data each NIC can hold before it overflows
◆ The data transmission speed

Each NIC communicates to the other indicating its own parameters and accepting or adjusting to the other card's parameters. After all the communication details have been determined, the two cards begin to send and receive data.

INSTALLATION OF A NIC

NICs act as the physical interface, or connection, between the computer and the network cable. For a long time, most NICs were installed in an empty expansion slot in your computer. These days, NIC functionality is built right into the motherboard, the main circuit board in the computer. A port on the motherboard allows you to connect the cable. Figure 4.13 shows a NIC with a coaxial-cable connection. NICs can also be found in other shared devices, such as printers and scanners.

Figure 4.13
NICs are now usually built into the motherboard of the computer. Does every computer on the network need a NIC?

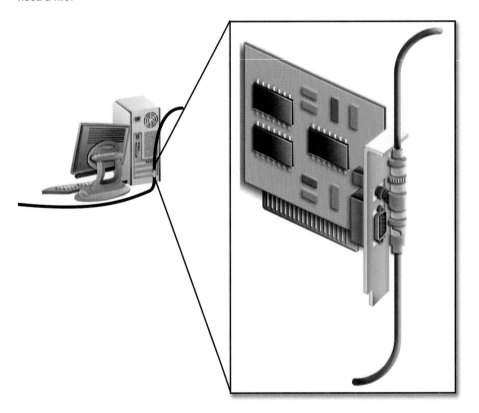

Although NICs are now typically built into the motherboard, many situations may require you to install a NIC manually. For example, you may need to add NIC functionality into an older computer. Or, you may want to upgrade existing NIC hardware to migrate to higher network speeds. First, watch the Show Me! 4.2 and 4.3 digital videos, which demonstrate how to install a NIC. Then, with your teacher's permission, complete You Try It Activity 4B, which guides you through the process of installing a NIC on your own. Make sure you understand both of these important procedures.

ACTIVITY 4B Installing a Network Interface Card

YOU TRY IT

Installing a NIC is one of the fundamental networking skills. If you are working with a computer that does not have a built-in NIC, or if you decide to upgrade to a faster network, you need to know how to install a NIC.

With your teacher's permission, perhaps using a test computer, perform the following steps:

1 Ground yourself by touching something metal that is in contact with the ground—a table or chair, for instance. Grounding discharges any static energy before you touch electronic equipment.

2 Turn the computer off, unplug the computer, and disconnect all peripheral devices plugged into the computer.

3 Remove the computer cover.

4 Locate an available PCI slot.

5 Insert the card into the slot. Be certain the card is seated completely in the slot.

6 Replace the cover.

7 Plug in all peripheral devices, including the network cable.

8 Plug the computer in, and turn it on.

9 Configure your network card:

- ◆ If your computer uses a plug and play compatible operating system (such as Windows 2000, Windows XP, or Mac OS X), follow the instructions to configure your NIC.

- ◆ If necessary, use the driver disk that comes with your NIC to configure it.

Installing a new NIC is simple. With a screwdriver and a few minutes, you can upgrade a PC from 10 Mbps to 100 Mbps, or even Gigabit Ethernet.

SHOW ME!

NIC Installation At networking.glencoe.com view Show Me 4.2 and 4.3 to watch demonstrations of a network interface card (NIC).

SELECTING THE RIGHT NIC

To ensure compatibility between the computer and the network, the NIC must:

- ◆ Fit with the computer's internal structure (data bus architecture).
- ◆ Contain the correct type of cable connector for the cabling.

For example, a card that works in an Apple computer communicating in a bus network does not work in an IBM computer in a ring environment. The IBM ring requires cards that are physically different from those used in a bus. In addition, Apple uses a different network communication method.

Data Bus Architecture

In the PC and Mac environments, you are most likely to encounter a bus architecture known as Peripheral Component Interconnect (PCI). A new version of PCI, called PCI-X is set to replace it. Older PC-based architectures

Table 4.4 ●

The data bus allows devices to communicate with the CPU. Which type of data bus are you most likely to encounter in today's PCs?

include Industry Standard Architecture (ISA), Extended Industry Standard Architecture (EISA), and Micro Channel. Because each type of bus is physically different from the others, the NIC must match the bus. For this reason, an ISA NIC cannot be used in a PCI slot. Table 4.4 summarizes the important facts to know about each bus architecture.

Types of Data Bus Architectures

Data Bus	Bus Speed	Throughput Rate	Description
Industry Standard Architecture (ISA)	16-bit	8 Mbps	Used in the IBM PC, XT, and AT computers and their clones.
Enhanced ISA (EISA)	32-bit	32 Mbps	Enhanced capabilities and speed. Backward compatible with the ISA bus.
Micro Channel Architecture (MCA)	16-bit or 32-bit	20 to 80 Mbps	Computers with MCA slots must use MCA. It is incompatible with the ISA and EISA.
Peripheral Component Interconnect (PCI)	32-bit or 64-bit	133 Mbps	Most common bus found in PCs and Macs.
PCI Extended (PCI-X)	64-bit	133 to 1 Gbps	Compatible with PCI. It is a key component of Gigabit Ethernet.
Universal Serial Bus (USB)	N/A	1.5 Mbps for USB 1.1 480 Mbps for USB 2.0	Hot swappable capabilities. USB 2.0 is also called Hi-Speed USB.
FireWire	N/A	400 to 800 Mbps	Used with digital video (DV) devices, such as DV cameras or external hard drives. Macs have built-in FireWire. PCs use add-on cards.

Network Cabling and Connectors

The NIC performs three important functions to coordinate activities between the computer and the cabling:

1. Makes the physical connection to the cable
2. Generates the electrical signals that travel over the cable
3. Controls access to the cable by following specific rules

To select the appropriate NIC for your network, you first need to determine the type of cabling and cabling connectors used. Coaxial, twisted-pair, and fiber optic are the most common cable types. Although most NICs accept a single type of cable, you may encounter NICs that can accept multiple types.

Connections NICs with more than one interface connector may be able to detect which interface to use automatically. Those without built-in interface detection must be set manually by setting jumpers on the card itself or by using a software-selectable option. Consult the NIC documentation for information on how to properly configure the card. Three examples of typical connectors found on NICs are shown in Figure 4.14 on page 121.

Caution Use care when choosing your NIC. The port on the NIC must accept the type of connectors used on your network. There is nothing quite like the feeling of showing up from a trip to the computer store with 100 NICs that accept RJ-45 connectors, only to find your network cabling is thinnet coaxial.

READ ME!

Tech Tip Be careful not to confuse a joystick port with a 15-pin transceiver port used by thicknet cabling. They look alike, but some joystick pins carry 5 volts DC, which can be harmful to network hardware as well as to the computer.

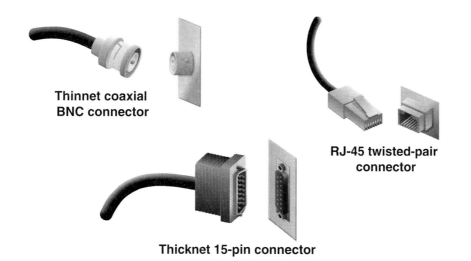

Thinnet coaxial
BNC connector

RJ-45 twisted-pair
connector

Thicknet 15-pin connector

Figure 4.14
NICs must be able to accept the type of connector associated with your network's cabling selection. How do you specify the interface connector to use when your NIC accepts more than one type of cabling?

Network Performance

The NIC has a significant effect on the performance of the entire network. A slow NIC cannot quickly pass data to and from the network. On a bus network, in which no one can use the network until the cable is clear, a slow card can increase wait times for all users.

After the physical requirements of the NIC are determined, there are several other factors to consider. Although all NICs conform to certain minimum standards and specifications, some cards feature enhancements that greatly improve server, client, and overall network performance.

You can speed up the movement of data through the NIC by adding the following enhancements:

1. **Direct memory access (DMA)**—The computer moves data directly from the NIC's buffer to the computer's memory, without using the computer's microprocessor.
2. **Shared adapter memory**—The NIC contains RAM that it shares with the computer. The computer identifies this RAM as if it is actually installed in the computer.
3. **Shared system memory**—The NIC's processor selects a section of the computer's memory and uses it to process data.
4. **Bus mastering**—The NIC takes temporary control of the computer's bus, bypasses the CPU, and moves data directly to the computer's system memory. This speeds up computer operations by freeing the processor to deal with other tasks. Bus mastering cards can be expensive, but they can improve network performance by 20 to 70 percent. EISA, Micro Channel, and PCI network interface cards offer bus mastering.
5. **RAM buffering**—Network traffic often travels too fast for most NICs to handle. RAM chips on the NIC serve as a buffer. When the card receives more data than it can process immediately, the RAM buffer holds some of the data until the NIC can process it. This speeds up the card's performance and helps keep the card from becoming a bottleneck.
6. **Onboard microprocessor**—With a microprocessor, the NIC does not need the computer to help process data. Most cards feature their own processors that speed network operations.

SPECIALIZED NICS

Most of the time, you use a standard NIC to connect each computer to the physical network. However, you may encounter some situations that require the use of specialized network cards. The remainder of this section introduces you to several varieties of these specialized cards.

Wireless NICs

In some environments, plugging a computer into a fixed cable is difficult or impossible. For example, a doctor making rounds in a hospital should not have to slow down to plug in her laptop at each stop. Wireless NICs allow computers to connect to the network without any physical cable attaching to the computer as shown in Figure 4.15.

Wireless NICs have many features, including the following:

◆ Indoor omnidirectional antenna and antenna cable
◆ Network software to make the NIC work with a particular network
◆ Diagnostic software for troubleshooting
◆ Installation software

These NICs can be used to create an all-wireless LAN or to add wireless stations to a cabled LAN. Wireless NICs usually communicate with a component called a wireless access point that acts as a transceiver to send and receive signals. Wireless access points can be thought of as wireless hubs. If multiple wireless access points exist in an office, users can roam around the office from one access point to another.

Fiber Optic NICs

"Fiber to the desktop" has become a catch phrase for the computing industry. As transmission speeds increase to accommodate the bandwidth-hungry applications and multimedia data streams that are common on today's intranets, fiber optic NICs (see Figure 4.16) allow direct connections to high-speed fiber optic networks. Fiber optic cable is generally more expensive than other types of cable, such as UTP or coaxial, and it is more difficult to work with. However, fiber optic network components have become cost-competitive with more traditional network components. At some point, it is expected that fiber optic networking will be commonplace.

Figure 4.15
Some wireless NICs use an antenna to communicate over the network. What does the wireless NIC antenna communicate with?

Activity 4.2 Exploring Wireless NICs To learn more about the current technology in wireless NICs go to **networking.glencoe.com**.

Figure 4.16
Using a fiber optic NIC, you can connect directly to a high-speed fiber optic network. Why is this option becoming more popular?

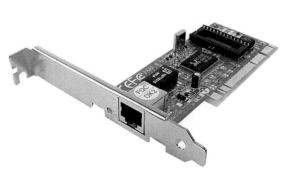

In some environments, security is so important that workstations do not have individual floppy-disk or hard drives. Without these, users are unable to copy information and, therefore, cannot take any data from the worksite.

Remote-Boot PROMs

However, the computer needs a source for the software that starts (boots) the computer. This is normally located on the local hard drive. In such an environment, the NIC can be equipped with a special chip called a remote-boot **programmable read-only memory (PROM).** This chip contains the hardwired code that starts the computer and connects the user to the network. With remote-boot PROMs, diskless workstations can join the network when they start.

Boot-on-LAN

A **boot-on-LAN** enables the PC to boot from a server rather than the local hard drive. Administrators can upgrade the entire network at once using this technology. In addition, boot files are protected from modification and corruption.

Erasable PROM (EPROM) is a special type of memory that can be reprogrammed using a unique device that exposes the memory to ultraviolet light. Electrically Erasable PROM (EEPROM) can be erased by exposing it to an electrical charge. The advantage of both types over PROM is that PROM cannot be reprogrammed if bug fixes or upgrades are required.

Enrichment
LAB

Lab 4.2 Troubleshooting New Network Components
Practice additional hands-on networking skills on page 435.

Section 4.3 Assessment

Concept Check

1. **Define** programmable read-only memory (PROM) and boot-on-LAN.

2. **Explain** two conditions that you should always consider when selecting a NIC that will ensure compatibility between the computer and the network.

3. **Identify** three reasons why wireless NICs are useful.

Critical Thinking

4. **Analyze Information** What are the primary roles of the NIC?

5. **Sequence Information** Arrange each bus architecture in order according to the bus capacity: Micro Channel, PCI-X, ISA, PCI, EISA.

6. **Interpret Information** Identify and describe each of the options you must consider when purchasing a network card for installation in a computer.

Applying Skills

Upgrade NICs
Suppose you are assigned the job of upgrading your company's network capabilities. Assume new NICs need to be placed in each computer. Create a plan that identifies how you would select a NIC that is compatible with your network. Then write a list of instructions for installing the NIC. The list should be easy to use by others who have been assigned to help you complete this task.

EMERGING TECHNOLOGY

WIRELESS TECHNOLOGIES

Wireless "zones"—public wireless LANs—allow people to access the Internet with wireless devices, such as notebook PCs, PDAs, and digital cell phones. Wireless zones are already available in hundreds of locations, such as cafes, hotels, and convention facilities.

Wired networks may one day be a thing of the past.

McDonald's, for example, is rolling out wireless Internet access at a number of its restaurants. Customers with wireless devices will be able to connect to the Internet at the restaurant for a small fee.

These zones can exist indoors and outdoors. They may be the best option for people in rural areas and other places with limited access to wired connections.

Wireless Dangers

Wireless networks pose unique security risks. The vast majority of home wireless networks, and a surprising number of corporate networks, are not secure against hacking. Someone with the right equipment can locate a wireless network's signal and tap into it, becoming a part of the network.

This security threat exists because wireless network transmissions can radiate in all directions. A home network's signal, for example, may extend several hundred feet beyond the home itself, allowing neighbors or passersby to pick up the signal.

A new breed of security measures, such as wireless firewalls and encryption schemes, are being introduced to handle these threats. Users of wireless networks will need to be more cautious than wired users for the foreseeable future.

Emerging Wireless Applications

A number of wireless standards have emerged, including:

- **Bluetooth** allows devices such as mobile phones, PDAs, and laptops to communicate with each other and the Internet via radio waves. Bluetooth's range is only about ten meters (30 feet).
- **Wi-Fi** is the most commonly used method for connecting to the Internet without wires. With a range of a few hundred feet, Wi-Fi is expected to become the backbone for home networks and wireless zones in hotels and restaurants.
- **IEEE 802.16** is a standard for wireless metropolitan area networks (MANs) technology. It has a range of 30 miles and data transfer rates of 70 Mbps.

Tech Focus

1. Design a simple wireless LAN for a small business with 12 people and two floors of a small office building.

2. Research a standard or protocol used in wireless LANs. Summarize your findings in a paragraph.

Section 4.4   Wireless Networking

Guide to Reading

Main Idea(s)

Infrared signals use light beams to transmit from computer to device. Narrowband radio signals use radio frequencies to transmit data. Spread-spectrum radio broadcasts data over a range of frequencies. Microwave technology includes ground to satellite transmission.

Key Terms

infrared
narrowband radio
spread-spectrum radio
hop
microwave
wired encryption privacy (WEP)

Reading Strategy

Identify each type of technology used in wireless transmissions. Create a diagram similar to the one below (also available online).

```
+--------------------------------------+
|      Wireless Transmission Types      |
+--------------------------------------+
   |        |          |          |
 [   ]    [   ]      [   ]      [   ]
```

Although much of the world uses cabling to interconnect computers and devices, a major shift to wireless communications is rapidly taking place. Wireless communication allows users to connect to various networks, as long as they are within the broadcast range of the network. Various technologies are used in wireless communications. Each of the primary wireless technologies will be discussed in the following section.

INFRARED LIGHT

Infrared wireless networks use an infrared light beam to transmit the data between devices. Strong signals are required because other light sources, such as windows, can interfere with weak transmission signals. Many of the high-end printers sold today are preconfigured to accept infrared signals. In the near future, it is quite possible that most printers will be preconfigured for wireless communication. An infrared network can normally broadcast at 10 Mbps, thanks to infrared light's high bandwidth.

There are four types of infrared networks:

- ◆ **Line-of-sight networks**—As the name implies, this version of infrared networking transmits only if the transmitter and receiver have a clear line of sight between them. All potential obstacles must be removed to ensure that a signal reaches its target.
- ◆ **Scatter infrared networks**—In this technology, broadcast transmissions are bounced off walls and ceilings and eventually hit the receiver. They are effective within an area limited to about 30.5 meters (100 feet).
- ◆ **Reflective networks**—Optical transceivers situated near the computers transmit to a common location that redirects the transmissions to the appropriate computer.
- ◆ **Broadband optical telepoint**—This infrared wireless LAN provides broadband services and is capable of handling high-quality multimedia requirements that can match those provided by a cabled network.

> **READ ME!**
>
> **Tech Tip** Wireless Markup Language (WML) is an emerging Web language designed to create documents for wireless communication hardware, such as PDAs or Web cell phones.

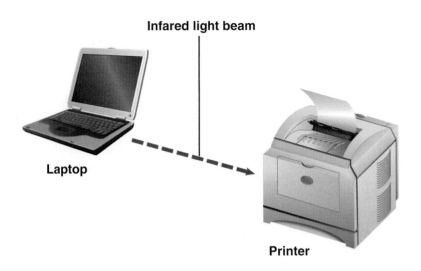

Infared light beam

Laptop

Printer

Figure 4.17 ●——→
Wireless portable comput-
ers can use an infrared
light beam to send data to
a printer. What are the
advantages of using
infrared communications?

Although infrared is fast and convenient (see Figure 4.17), it has difficulty transmitting data over distances greater than 30.5 meters (100 feet). Strong ambient light, such as that produced by fluorescent lights, also limits its effectiveness.

NARROWBAND RADIO

Narrowband radio is similar to broadcasting from a radio station. The user tunes both the transmitter and the receiver to a certain frequency. The broadcast range is 3,000 meters (9,842 feet), and does not require line-of-sight focusing. However, because the signal is high frequency, it is subject to attenuation from steel and load-bearing walls. Narrowband radio is a subscription service. The service provider handles all the Federal Communications Commission (FCC) licensing requirements. This method is relatively slow—transmission is in the 4.8 Mbps range.

SPREAD-SPECTRUM

Figure 4.18 ●——
Spread-spectrum radio
broadcast signals enhance
security. How does a hop
ensure security?

Spread-spectrum radio broadcasts signals over a range of frequencies. This helps it avoid narrowband communication problems. The available frequencies are divided into channels, known as hops. A **hop** is one portion of a journey between two points. For example, suppose you drive from New York City to Boston and you stop once along the way for snacks. This would be one hop along your route.

In spread-spectrum communications, the adapters tune into a specific hop for a predetermined length of time (as shown in Figure 4.18). After the time is up, they switch to a different hop, or channel. A hopping sequence determines the timing. The computers in the network are all synchronized to the hop timing.

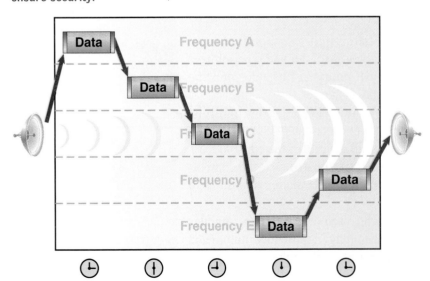

Frequency A

Frequency B

Frequency C

Frequency D

Frequency E

Data

Data

Data

Data

Data

This type of signaling provides some built-in security. For example, to tap into the data stream, the frequency-hopping algorithm of the network would have to be known. To further enhance security and to keep unauthorized users from listening in to the broadcast, the sender and the receiver can encrypt the transmission.

Using spread-spectrum network adapters, computers with networking capability built into the OS can establish a peer-to-peer network with no wiring at all. A spread-spectrum segment of the network can also participate in a traditional wired network. To do this, one of the computers must be connected to the wired network using an appropriate interface.

MICROWAVE TECHNOLOGY

Microwave systems are used in a wide range of applications. Microwaves are part of the electromagnetic spectrum and are, thus, a form of radiation. Microwave systems can be used for short- and long-distance communications. A good example of a microwave system is a TV van. The retractable dish on top of the van is used to transmit a microwave signal from the van back to its home office. Other systems are used to beam transmissions from building to building or even across a city (see Figure 4.19). Microwave systems can also be used for the following:

- ◆ Satellite-to-ground links
- ◆ Between two buildings
- ◆ Across large, flat, open areas, such as bodies of water or deserts

Figure 4.19
A microwave system can be used to transmit data from building to building. What are some other uses?

A microwave system consists of the following:

◆ Two radio transceivers: one to generate (transmitting station) and one to receive (receiving station) the broadcast.

◆ Two directional antennas pointed at each other to implement communication of the signals broadcast by the transceivers. These antennas are often installed on towers to give them more range and to raise them above anything that might block their signals.

SECURITY RISKS

Wireless technology is somewhat more prone to security risks. Due to the fact that the signal is broadcast in a certain radius, anyone within that radius can potentially intercept that signal.

An unauthorized user does not have to gain physical access to the building or to the computers. Nor does an unauthorized user need to hack through the company servers. He or she could simply sit in the parking lot, armed with a laptop and wireless NIC, and access the wireless network.

Unfortunately, many administrators fail to take the most basic precautions when setting up a wireless network. Most wireless NICs and access points have a built-in security feature, called **wired encryption privacy (WEP)**. When activated, WEP encrypts the data prior to transmission by the NIC. At the receiving end, the data are decrypted.

Many administrators fail to activate WEP, leaving their networks vulnerable to attacks by hackers or to unauthorized access by users who are not part of the company.

Section 4.4 Assessment

Concept Check

1. **Define** infrared, narrowband radio, spread-spectrum radio, hop, microwave, and wired encryption privacy (WEP).

2. **Describe** how spread-spectrum transmissions work.

3. **Explain** what WEP is and why it is important for wireless communications.

Critical Thinking

4. **Analyze Information** Military communications use spread-spectrum technology. What is it about spread-spectrum wireless that makes this a natural choice for the military?

5. **Compare and Contrast** Identify the differences between each type of infrared network.

Applying Skills

Identify Real-World Wireless Devices Identify several types of devices that use wireless technology. If possible, identify the type of wireless transmission technology each uses to send and receive data.

SECTION 4.1 Network Connectivity Devices

Key Terms

repeater, 105
segment, 105
bridge, 105
switch, 106
router, 107

brouter, 108
gateway, 109
modulation, 109
demodulation, 109

Main Ideas

- Hubs and switches are used for network communications within one segment of the network.
- Routers are used for communications between segments of a network or between other networks.
- Gateways are used for communications between incompatible networks.
- Modems are used for communications between computers over phone lines or other media.

SECTION 4.2 Network Media

Key Terms

shielding, 111
noise, 111
crosstalk, 111
attenuation, 112
BNC connector, 112
twisted-pair cable, 113

unshielded twisted-pair (UTP), 113
shielded twisted-pair (STP), 113
fiber optic cables, 115

Main Ideas

- Cable is used to connect devices on the network.
- Different types of cables have different capacities and capabilities.
- UTP is one of the most common types of cables used in networks.
- Fiber optic cable is expensive and difficult to work with, but it is used in high-speed, high-capacity data transmissions.

SECTION 4.3 Network Interface Cards

Key Terms

programmable read-only memory (PROM), 123
boot-on-LAN, 123

Main Ideas

- The network interface card connects a computer to the cable.
- The NIC must be the right type and configured correctly in order to work properly.
- NICs make physical connection to cable, generate electronic signal over cable, and control access to cable.
- The NIC has a strong impact on performance of the entire network.

SECTION 4.4 Wireless Networking

Key Terms

infrared, 125
narrowband radio, 126
spread-spectrum radio, 126

hop, 126
microwave, 127
wired encryption privacy (WEP), 128

Main Ideas

- Infrared technology uses infrared light to beam transmissions from a transceiver to devices.
- Narrowband radio uses a narrow range of radio frequencies and is regulated by the FCC.
- Spread-spectrum radio uses a wide range of radio frequencies.
- Microwave transmissions can be sent over long distances.
- Security is an important consideration when incorporating wireless technology.

READ TO SUCCEED

Exchange Memory Tools Work with three other students to create a poster or handout that illustrates or explains four of the most helpful memory aides developed by the group. These memory aids will help the group to remember important steps or concepts. Ask your teacher for permission to display the posters in the classroom.

Reviewing Key Terms

1. Explain what a hop is.
2. What categories of twisted-pair cable can be used for Gigabit Ethernet?
3. What is a collision domain, and how does creating a collision domain improve network communications?
4. Where is a PROM located?
5. How are microwaves used in networking?

Understanding Main Ideas

6. Explain why wireless networks are more prone to security risks. What can be done to secure a wireless transmission?
7. Describe how to select the appropriate type of cabling for setting up a new network.
8. List each device covered in Section 4.1 and identify the layer(s) of the OSI model at which the device functions.
9. List the enhancements that can be made to speed up the movement of data through the NIC.
10. Explain how spread-spectrum radio naturally offers a higher level of security than narrowband radio.
11. Describe the difference between passive and active hubs.
12. Explain the difference between an RJ-45 connector and an RJ-11 connection.
13. Describe the four different types of infrared networks.
14. List the different ways microwaves can be used in networking.

Critical Thinking

15. **Draw Conclusions** Think of the composition of fiber optic cable. Name three factors that should be considered when choosing materials with which to build a fiber optic cable. Name two of the limiting features. What conclusions can you draw about this type of wiring?
16. **Compare and Contrast** In your own words, write two paragraphs that compare and contrast the different types of wireless communications media, such as infrared, narrowband, spread-spectrum, and microwave.
17. **Investigate Hardware** Consider the functionality of passive, active, switched, and hybrid hubs. What are their functional similarities?
18. **Combine Network Media** When might a network combine different types of media, such as UTP and fiber optic cabling?
19. **Analyze Transmissions** List the distinctions between the functions of hubs, repeaters, bridges and switches, and routers and gateways. Explain your reasoning.
20. **Understand Relationships** Reread the section on infrared wireless transmissions types. Then sketch a diagram of one of them as you would expect it to look. Add captions and arrows to emphasis any notable features.
21. **Sequence Information** Explain the likely path of data (an e-mail message, for example) sent from your computer at school to a friend's LAN connected computer located in another city.

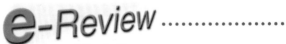

e-Review ··················

networking.glencoe.com

Study with PowerPoint

See a review of the main points in this chapter. Choose **e-Review > PowerPoint Outlines > Chapter 4.**

Online Self Check

Test your knowledge of the topics covered in this chapter. Choose **e-Review > Self-Check Assessments > Chapter 4.**

 networking.glencoe.com

Making Connections

Language Arts – Write a Cause and Effect Paper Research information from your text, library, or the Internet to write a cause and effect paper that is two well-thought-out paragraphs long. This paper is a vocabulary enhancing activity that focuses on the term *attenuation*. Practice good grammar, punctuation, and spelling skills. Take notes as you collect your ideas and develop your thoughts. As you write, ask yourself first what attenuation is as it applies to networks. Then build your paragraphs of the causes and effects of this condition.

STANDARDS AT WORK

Students demonstrate a sound understanding of the nature and operation of technology systems. (NETS-S 1)

Demonstrate an Understanding of Technology Operations

Use a spreadsheet application to create a table identifying the advantages and disadvantages of communications systems based on different types of network media. Open the spreadsheet application and label a row for each of the following types of media:

◆ 10Base2 (thinnet)
◆ 10Base5 (thicknet)
◆ UTP
◆ STP
◆ Fiber optic
◆ Wireless infrared

As shown below, label two columns "Advantages" and "Disadvantages." Identify the advantages and disadvantages of each type of media.

	ADVANTAGES	DISADVANTAGES
10Base2		
10Base5		
UTP		

TEAMWORK SKILLS

Develop a Network Proposal

Following your teacher's instructions, form small groups. With your group, develop a proposal for creating a network on a university campus. The campus is organized as follows:

◆ Dormitories were designed for network installation.
◆ Near the dormitories are two administration offices whose employees share files peer to peer.
◆ Three research facilities, rely heavily on peer-to-peer file sharing security and Internet connections.
◆ The research facilities' networks do not support the same protocols as the student and administration networks.

Your group should identify the following:

a. Important features of each part of the network
b. The type of cabling to be used in each building and to connect different buildings and groups of buildings
c. The hardware to be used, such as hubs, routers, and gateways
d. The architecture of the individual subnetworks and of the network as a whole
e. Which subnetworks are connected to one another and which subnetworks allow for peer-to-peer file sharing?

CHALLENGE YOURSELF

Identify Network Media

Using presentation software, create a slide show that identifies the different types of cabling used in your classroom. Include the transmission speed of each type of connection as well as the physical characteristics of the cabling you find. Finally, explain why you think each type of cabling was chosen for the purpose that it serves. Were good decisions made given the circumstances?

YOU TRY IT

Networking Lab

1. Building a Routing Diagram

Draw a network diagram using the following information:

- Four subnetworks are connected at a switching hub that uses backward learning to minimize network traffic.
- Computers 1–4 are on subnetwork A
- Computers 5–8 are on subnetwork B
- Computers 9–12 are on subnetwork C
- Computers 13–16 are on subnetwork D

The following data packets are received by the hub, in this order:

- Packet from computer 2 to computer 9
- Packet from computer 9 to computer 1
- Packet from computer 10 to computer 2
- Packet from computer 11 to computer 13
- Packet from computer 15 to computer 13

For each data packet, indicate on your drawing on which subnetworks the hub will broadcast the data packet.

2. Creating a Routing Table

A routing table tracks which computers are connected to which subnetworks. Using a word processing application, create a table using the information from You Try It Network Lab 1 above. List which subnetwork the packets travel through. Your table should include:

DATA PACKETS	ROUTE THROUGH SUBNETWORK
From computer 2 to computer 9	
From computer 9 to computer 1	
From computer 10 to computer 2	
From computer 11 to computer 13	
From computer 15 to computer 13	

Networking Projects

1. Research and Prepare a NIC Report

You are a network technician for a small company. The IT director has come to you because the company will be installing a new network. Prepare a report that identifies the factors you should consider when choosing cabling and NICs for a new network. Include how each factor influences the decisions made. Focus on the following factors:

Ⓐ Speed
Ⓑ Security
Ⓒ Scalability
Ⓓ Cost
Ⓔ Feasibility of installation
Ⓕ Existing infrastructure (such as phone and television cable systems)

Use the information presented in this chapter, as well as any other sources available in your classroom or on the Internet. If possible, talk with your school's network administrator or support technician or another computer networking professional. Be certain to cite the sources you use when preparing your report.

2. Examine and Diagram Network Media

You have applied for a networking technician's position in a large company's IT shop. As part of the interview exam you will demonstrate your knowledge and skills.

You will strip cabling and diagram different types of cabling. With your teacher's permission, take short lengths of at least two types of network cabling.

Ⓐ Using a wire stripper, remove 1.5 inches of the outer sheath from each type of cabling.

Ⓑ If there is an inner sheath (such as the shielding layer in coaxial cable), remove a smaller portion of the inner sheath—about 1 inch.

Ⓒ Draw an enlarged sketch of each type of cabling you have prepared. If the cable contains multiple wires (such as those in twisted-pair cable), note the color of each wire or use pencils or markers of the appropriate colors to draw them.

Ⓓ Label each part of your diagram, and mark whether it is structural or a signal carrier. For example, in twisted-pair cabling, the outer sheath is structural and the internal wires are signal carriers. Turn in your sketches along with the stripped cables you used.

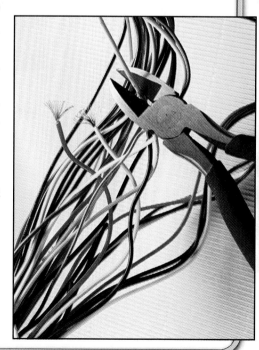

CHAPTER 5 Network Models and Protocols

YOU WILL LEARN TO...

Section 5.1

- Explain why standards are necessary for networking
- Explain how an Ethernet network functions
- List Ethernet classifications

Section 5.2

- Explain how a token-passing network functions
- List wireless network classifications
- Explain how wireless transmissions are sent

Section 5.3

- Map TCP/IP protocols to the OSI model
- Define TCP and IP
- Explain IP addressing

Section 5.4

- Describe the AppleTalk protocols
- Explain the protocols NetBIOS and NetBEUI
- Demonstrate knowledge of the NetWare protocols

WHY IT MATTERS.....................................

There are lots of different network models, just like there are lots of different kinds of roads. Sometimes, a small, two-lane street handles all the traffic, but at other times, a large freeway is needed. Building the right network is like building the right road. You need to know how much traffic will travel on a network. Network models help you plan a network that will handle the traffic on the network.

Quick Write Activity

Protocols control the way traffic moves through the network. For example, protocols determine which data are delivered first, next, and so on. In a short paragraph, explain what elements in the highway system help to control the flow of traffic. Why are these elements necessary?

WHAT YOU WILL DO ....

READ TO SUCCEED

Reading for a Purpose
Just as the author's purpose helped him or her determine what content to put in and what to leave out, your purpose for reading helps you decide what is most important to remember. Write down and complete this sentence for each section *before* you read: My purpose for reading this section is to _____. (Hint: You may want to use each section's Guide to Reading and the colored headings to help you finish the sentence.)

Section 5.1 Common LAN Models

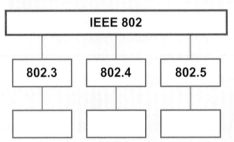
There are many manufacturers who supply products for linking computers in a network. Manufacturers need to make sure that their products can communicate with products manufactured by others. As networks and suppliers of networking products have spread across the world, the need for standardization has only increased. To address this need, several independent groups have created standard design specifications for computer-networking products. When manufacturers follow these standards, products produced by a variety of vendors can communicate.

IEEE 802.x

In the 1970s, as LANs emerged as potential business tools, the Institute of Electrical and Electronics Engineers (IEEE) saw a need to define certain LAN standards. The IEEE launched Project 802, named for the year and month it began (1980, February).

Project 802 defined network standards for the physical components of a network, such as network interface cards (NICs), wide area network (WAN) components, and components used to create twisted-pair and coaxial cable networks.

LLC and MAC

The Project 802 standards fit right into the OSI reference model, with only two differences.

First, 802 is limited to the Physical and Data Link Layers of the OSI model. These layers relate directly to hardware. Specifically, they relate to the NIC and the network media (cabling or wireless transmissions).

Second, 802 divides the Data Link Layer into two sublayers known as **Logical Link Control (LLC)** and Media Access Control (MAC). The LLC sublayer is responsible for establishing and terminating links to other computers and sequencing and acknowledging frames and controlling frame traffic. The MAC sublayer is responsible for sending data to and from the NIC.

The Standards Themselves

Today, the IEEE 802 committee is *the* standard-setting body. This committee is divided into different groups who are responsible for a distinct set of specifications.

In Table 5.1, the efforts of this group have resulted in the standards that define familiar LAN architectures. These include Ethernet, token bus, token ring, and others.

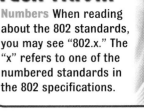

TECH TRIVIA

Numbers When reading about the 802 standards, you may see "802.x." The "x" refers to one of the numbered standards in the 802 specifications.

802.x Specification Categories

Specification	Description
802.1	Defines the standards related to network management.
802.2	Defines the general standard for the Data Link Layer.
802.3	Defines the MAC layer for bus networks that use carrier sense multiple access with collision detection (CSMA/CD). This is the Ethernet standard.
802.4	Defines the MAC layer for star and bus networks that use a token-passing mechanism (ARCnet is a variation of a token bus LAN).
802.5	Defines the MAC layer for token ring networks (token ring LAN).
802.6	Sets standards for metropolitan area networks (MANs).
802.9	Defines integrated voice/data networks.
802.10	Defines network security.
802.11	Defines wireless network standards.
802.12	Defines demand priority access LAN, 100BaseVG-AnyLAN.
802.14	Defines cable modem standards.
802.15	Defines wireless personal area networks (WPANs).
802.16	Defines broadband wireless standards.

Table 5.1
802.x specification categories refer to standards set by the IEEE 802 committee. Which specification is responsible for the Ethernet standard?

IEEE 802.3: ETHERNET STANDARD

Ethernet could be called the parent of LAN technology. Many, if not most, of the LANs in use today are based on this technology. Ethernet uses a bus topology and relies on CSMA/CD to regulate traffic on the main communication line. It was developed in the early 1970s at the famed Xerox Palo Alto Research Center (Xerox PARC). Xerox PARC was also the birthplace of the laser printer, the mouse, and the graphical user interface (GUI).

Ethernet was not the first type of network to use CSMA/CD. An earlier network, named ALOHA, first used CSMA/CD as its means of controlling network access and contention. **Contention** is the competition among stations on a network for the opportunity to use a communication line or network resource. Today, CSMA/CD is a primary feature of Ethernet networks.

READ ME!

Jargon Ethernet was named after the "ether" that was once thought to be the medium that conducted electro-magnetic energy.

CSMA/CD

Carrier sense multiple access with collision detection (CSMA/CD) functions on the MAC sublayer. Network nodes in Ethernet and other types of LANs rely on CSMA/CD to accomplish the following:

- ◆ Gain access to the network when they have packets to transmit.
- ◆ Ensure that two nodes do not try to transmit at the same time.

Carrier sense means that the nodes on the network *sense* a carrier signal on the line. A carrier signal indicates the network is busy. Multiple access means that more than one node might want to transmit at the same time. If two nodes actually do transmit simultaneously, the nodes rely on collision detection to resolve the situation.

Nodes on a CSMA/CD network are always listening for the carrier signal. If the signal is present, the line is busy. Sometimes, two nodes detect the line is free and try to transmit at the same time. On a CSMA/CD network, this results in a data collision—just like two people trying to telephone each other at the same time.

Collision Detection On the network, the nodes are able to detect a data collision (see Figure 5.1). When this happens, the nodes cancel their transmissions (the equivalent of saying, "oops" or "excuse me") and back off for a random period of time before trying to access the network again and transmit. The amount of time the nodes wait is called the deferral time. Assuming that each node backs off for a different amount of time, one or the other should be able to transmit successfully the second time around.

Figure 5.1
A collision occurs if two computers put data on the cable at the same time. How does a node know when it is safe to transmit data?

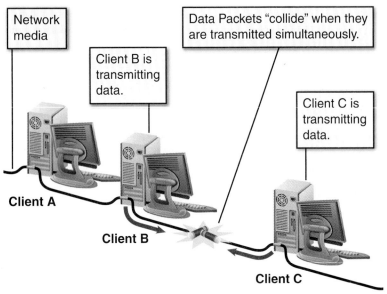

Network media

Client B is transmitting data.

Data Packets "collide" when they are transmitted simultaneously.

Client C is transmitting data.

Client A

Client B

Client C

Contention CSMA/CD is also known as a contentious means of gaining network access. The nodes are competing with each other for access to the network—the first one on the line wins. Later in this chapter, you learn about more "polite" means of networking.

Although CSMA/CD sounds like a brawling free-for-all, it works. However, it works so well that the majority of the world's networks are based on Ethernet.

The 5-4-3 Rule

One drawback of Ethernet networks, such as 10Base2 and 10Base5, is the limited number of nodes the network can support. Ethernet networks are divided into collision domains. If there are too many nodes or segments in one collision domain, there are higher amounts of data collisions. The network slows down or grinds to a halt, preventing further data transmissions.

The 5-4-3 rule was created to help maintain network efficiency. It specifies the maximum number of cable segments, repeaters, and populated segments that can exist in any collision domain, as shown in Figure 5.2 on page 139. A populated segment is the cable and all the nodes attached to it. The 5-4-3

SHOW ME!

Collision Detection
CSMA/CD is the access method used by Ethernet networks. View Show Me 5.1, 5.2, and 5.3 at **networking.glencoe.com** to see a demonstration of how CSMA/CD works.

rule states that there can be no more than 5 cable segments, 4 repeaters, and 3 populated segments in one collision domain.

The 5-4-3 rule does not apply to some newer Ethernet devices, such as switches. This is because a switch has the ability to temporarily store data before sending it to the correct node, thereby reducing the number of collisions.

● **Figure 5.2**
The 5-4-3 rule limits the number of users to reduce network congestion. Why is this rule not applicable with switched hardware?

Features Common to Ethernet Networks

Ethernet networks vary in topology, speed, and the types of cabling they use. However, all Ethernet networks have certain elements in common. Specifically, Ethernet networks:

◆ Use CSMA/CD as the means of gaining access to the network.

◆ Are all defined in the IEEE 802.3 specification.

◆ Rely on broadcast transmissions that deliver signals to all nodes at the same time. This broadcasting is necessary for CSMA/CD to work.

◆ Are primarily baseband networks.

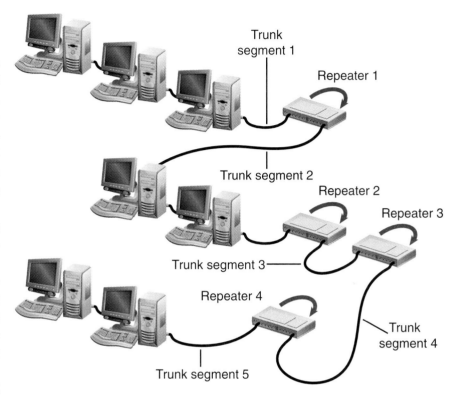

In addition, Ethernet networks all use the same unique Ethernet format, called a frame, for transmitting information (see Figure 5.3). The **frame** contains the preamble, source and destination addresses, data, type of protocol used to send the frame, and the CRC. Recall from Chapter 3 that a frame is the structure, like a vehicle, used to transport the data packet across the network.

The frame ranges from 64 bytes to 1,518 bytes in size. Regardless of length, however, all frames are built of the same pieces.

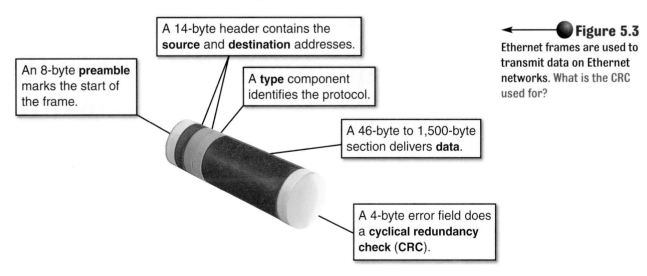

A 14-byte header contains the **source** and **destination** addresses.

An 8-byte **preamble** marks the start of the frame.

A **type** component identifies the protocol.

A 46-byte to 1,500-byte section delivers **data**.

A 4-byte error field does a **cyclical redundancy check (CRC)**.

◀━━━● **Figure 5.3**
Ethernet frames are used to transmit data on Ethernet networks. What is the CRC used for?

DRIVERS AND THE NIC

Network devices, like NICs, are frequently designed to work with any network model. But how can they do this? In Chapter 4, you learned that the NIC uses drivers to tie the NIC's hardware to a specific protocol. Rather than manufacturing the card to one set of specifications, manufacturers leave the functionality up to software device drivers that can be installed and updated whenever necessary. A **device driver** (or simply, driver) is software that helps a computer work with a particular device. A driver is a set of instructions that tells the OS how to interact with the device.

The drivers that control the NIC allow the computer and the NIC to communicate with each other. This, in turn, links the computer to the rest of the network. The NIC drivers operate in the MAC sublayer of the OSI reference model's Data Link Layer. The NIC drivers provide a virtual communications channel between the computer and the NIC. The virtual communication channel is temporary and not present until it is called into use.

YOU TRY IT

ACTIVITY 5A Locating NIC Drivers

In this activity, you learn how to locate and download (with your teacher's permission) the device drivers for the NIC in your computer. Because your computer likely has a different NIC and manufacturer than shown here, use these steps as a general guideline. You may have to perform your own search to find the manufacturer's Web site and download area. The following steps are for Windows-based computers.

Part One: Determine the manufacturer of your NIC

1 Click the **Start** button, point to **Settings,** and then click **Control Panel.**

2 Double-click **Network** and **Dial-up Connections.**

3 Right-click the **Local Area Connection,** and then click **Properties.**

4 Click the **Configure** button.

5 Click the **Driver** tab.

Information about your NIC, including the manufacturer, model, and driver version appear, as shown in Figure 5.4. Note that the information on your screen will probably differ from the figure.

Occasionally, you can simply click the Update Driver button to download an updated driver. More often, you must visit the manufacturer's Web site. In this case, the NIC manufacturer is 3Com.

Figure 5.4
Use the Driver tab to locate information about your NIC driver.

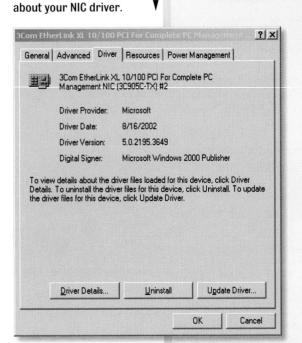

Part Two: Find the download area of the NIC's manufacturer

6 In your Internet browser, enter the address of your NIC's manufacturer. In this example, www.3com.com is the correct address.

7 Look for one of the following links, or some variation: Support, Downloads, Drivers. At 3Com's site, there is a "Downloads & Drivers" link.

8 Some manufacturers provide a list of available products. Companies with many products (such as 3Com) provide a search page to help you locate the device. Locate your NIC and its associated driver.

9 Click the link to the driver download.

At some point, you will be prompted to either open or save the downloaded file. You should always save the file and scan it for viruses *before* opening it. Even reliable vendors have been known to mistakenly post virus-infected files on their Web sites.

After the file is downloaded, the driver needs to be installed. Do NOT install the driver without your teacher's permission. Most installations feature a simple wizard interface to walk you through whatever steps are necessary to install and configure the driver. Because these steps can vary greatly, we do not continue the activity beyond this point.

READ ME!

Tech Tip Drivers for popular devices are often installed with the OS, but they are frequently out of date. Typically, drivers are also included on a disk with the equipment; however, these can also be out of date. The best choice is to download drivers from the manufacturer's Web site for the most up-to-date drivers.

It is important that you learn how to effectively gather information about hardware on a computer, locate the manufacturer's Web site, and quickly locate the desired information. This ability to gather information is another required, fundamental skill if you are considering a career in networking.

Section 5.1 Assessment

Concept Check

1. **Define** Logical Link Control (LLC), Ethernet, contention, frame, and device driver.

2. **List** the IEEE 802.x standards.

3. **Describe** the role of a device driver.

4. **List** the common features of Ethernet networks.

5. **Explain** why the 5-4-3 rule was created and what it specifies.

Critical Thinking

6. **Compare and Contrast** Differences and similarities appear in the 802.x standards from the OSI reference model. How do the two compare and contrast?

7. **Organize Data** List the steps that a computer takes to send data on the network. List what happens when two computers attempt to transmit at the same time.

8. **Synthesize Information** Explain how CSMA/CD works.

Applying Skills

Determine Latest Standards Even standards, such as IEEE 802.3, are divided into many classifications. Use the Internet to research the latest revision to the standards being considered in Ethernet networking. Also, research the different kinds of NIC cards currently available for Ethernet.

Section 5.2 Other LAN Models

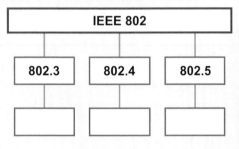
Although Ethernet is widely used in LANs, it is not the only LAN architecture. Two other important architectures called token ring and token bus are used. The networks differ in topology and other features, but in both forms, the network nodes use a small electronic "baton" known as a token to gain network access.

TOKENS AND TOKEN PASSING

Unlike the CSMA/CD method of gaining network access, token-passing networks rely on a more polite method. Rather than contending with one another for network access, each node simply waits for its turn. Each node takes an active role in managing access and avoiding collisions. At the heart of this access method is a small, special data frame only a few bytes in size, called the token.

This token is a unique frame—there is only one on the network at any given time. Like the baton in a relay race, it is passed from one node to another on the network. The token always moves in the same direction. It moves in a predetermined order that forms a logical, if not physical, ring. For example, if a network consists of nodes 1 through 25, node 1 passes the token to node 2, node 2 passes it to node 3, and so on. When the token reaches node 25, it is passed back to node 1, thus completing the "circle" and forming a logical ring. The token is critical to maintaining order on the network. Only the node that currently holds the token is allowed to transmit and it can only transmit a single packet.

When the network is very quiet and none of the nodes has any information to transmit, the token simply circulates around and around the ring. When a node has information to transmit, it waits until it receives the token. It then takes the token out of circulation by marking it "busy." It attaches its packet

READ ME!

Jargon Token-passing networks are called deterministic. This means you can calculate how long it will take before a node transmits again. Predictable network transmissions are required so that various parts and processes can be coordinated at precise times. Ethernet transmits at random times making it difficult to coordinate transmissions.

networking.glencoe.com

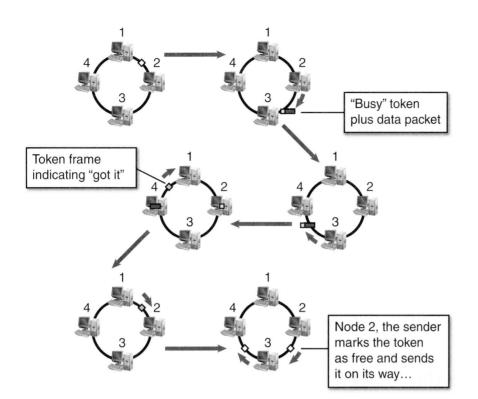

"Busy" token plus data packet

Token frame indicating "got it"

Node 2, the sender marks the token as free and sends it on its way...

of data, and then passes the token and data frame to the next node in line. And so it goes, until the package reaches the intended recipient.

The recipient strips the data from the frame, marks the frame as "read," and sends it on its way. When the sender receives the token, it checks to see whether the data were received, marks the token as "available for use," and sends it to the next node in line. Only one node at a time holds the token and no collisions occur. Figure 5.5 diagrams the token-passing process.

Now, on to the IEEE token-passing specifications. The token ring specification, and especially IBM's implementation, became very popular because it was the basis of IBM's own internal network. The IBM specification is found more commonly than the IEEE.

IEEE 802.4 AND ARCNet

Attached Resource Computer Network (ARCnet) is a PC-based LAN architecture that corresponds to the IEEE 802.4 specification. It was developed in the 1970s, before the IEEE formalized its specification. It became popular for smaller networks, in part because its components are inexpensive and because it is both flexible and relatively easy to set up.

An ARCnet is built using either a bus or a star topology and can support up to 255 nodes. ARCnets are built around three types of hubs—passive, active, or intelligent.

One advantage of ARCnets is that they can use twisted-pair, coaxial, and fiber optic cable on the same network. Because of this, it is a little harder to calculate the maximum length of a cable segment. The cable segment length is the length of an individual cable from one end to the other. The segment depends on the type of cabling, the type of hub, and the topology (bus or star) of the network.

SHOW ME!

Token Passing In token-passing networks, a token is passed around the network. To send data, a computer must have possession of the token. See how this works by watching Show Me 5.4 at networking.glencoe.com.

READ ME!

Tech History Fast Token Ring anyone? Like Ethernet, Token Ring specifications evolved to include a 100-Mbps specification. A 1-Gbps Token Ring architecture was developed. By the time it was developed, Fast Ethernet (100 Mbps) had gained so much ground and become so inexpensive that Fast Token Ring did not gain much attention and has largely died.

IEEE 802.5 AND TOKEN RING

There are two different forms of a token ring. One is the IEEE specification, which is spelled with a lowercase *t* and a lowercase *r*. The other, spelled with initial capital letters—**Token Ring**—is an IBM-designed architecture created to connect PCs with IBM's larger midrange and mainframe computers. What is the difference? The IEEE token ring specification was developed before IBM developed its Token Ring architecture. Although there are some differences between the two, the IBM Token Ring architecture is so successful and so widely used that descriptions of token ring architecture generally talk about IBM's implementation.

Token Ring is based on a ring topology, as its name indicates. In ring topologies, a break in the ring cabling can bring down the entire network. Token Ring networks rely on a safer, more reliable star-wired ring. Nodes are connected to one or more hubs called **Multistation Access Units (MAU).** The connections within (or between) the hubs form a logical ring, as shown in Figure 5.6. A Token Ring has a logical ring topology with a physical star topology.

Figure 5.6 ●——▶
This is a logical ring in a MAU-to-MAU-to-MAU connection. How does the Token Ring topology make a Token Ring network safer?

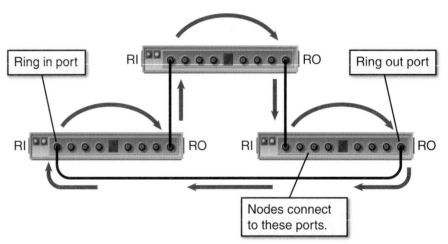

Ring in port

Ring out port

Nodes connect to these ports.

In addition to using token passing for both network access and contention control, a Token Ring network:

◆ Typically transfers information at 1 Mbps or 4 Mbps per second (in the IEEE specification) or at 4 Mbps or 16 Mbps (in the IBM version).
◆ Uses baseband transmission.
◆ Is based on twisted-pair or fiber optic cable.

OTHER IEEE LAN SPECIFICATIONS

In terms of popularity, Ethernet, token ring, and, to a lesser extent, ARCnet are the primary LAN architectures. The IEEE 802 specifications do, however, cover a few more, including isochronous networks and wireless networks.

IEEE 802.9 Isochronous LANs

When you attempt to open a text document over a network, it does not matter how it arrives as long as it all gets there in a reasonable amount of time.

 networking.glencoe.com

Certain types of data, such as audio and video, are a lot more time sensitive. If video frames do not arrive at a constant rate, the video will either be distorted, or cannot be viewed. Enter isochronous LANs.

Isochronous comes from the Greek *isochronos; iso* meaning equal, and *chronos* meaning time. It is often referred to as **Integrated Services LAN (ISLAN).** Isochronous LANs are used to transmit multimedia.

The IEEE started investigating Integrated Voice/Data (IVD) networks in the mid-1980s. An IVD network could transmit voice or data over the same line. At roughly the same time, another standards body, the Comité Consultatif International Télégraphique et Téléphonique (CCITT), set forth standards known as **Integrated Services Digital Network (ISDN).** ISDN is a technology that delivers voice, data, and video in digital form over standard telephone cabling.

IEEE 802.11 and Wireless Networks

The IEEE 802.11 specifications set standards for wireless LAN communications. These specifications are roughly comparable to Ethernet networks. Also known as wireless LANs (WLANs), these networks are especially useful in situations in which:

- Nodes must move around freely, as in a hospital, a supermarket (noting inventory, for example), or on a factory floor.
- Network connections are needed in a very busy area, such as an airport terminal.
- Connections are unreliable or dependent on external (unpredictable) factors, as in military operations.
- It is difficult or impossible to wire a building for a network. For example, a conference center with visitors moving throughout the facility would be unsuitable for wiring.

CSMA/CA One major difference in wireless networks is how a wireless device contends for network access. Wireless networks use a related technique, called **carrier sense multiple access with collision avoidance (CSMA/CA).**

In CSMA/CA, nodes "listen" to the transmission medium for a chance to transmit. However, the node does not simply grab the open "line" and begin transmitting, as it would in a CSMA/CD network. Instead, it holds up its digital hand and asks if it is OK to take a turn. This is known as a Request To Send (RTS). This request specifies the intended recipient and also warns all nodes in the vicinity to back off for a time. The recipient returns a Clear To Send (CTS) signal back to the node that started the transmission. Following the CTS signal, the node transmits its data.

After the data are received correctly, the recipient ends the transmission by sending an acknowledge (ACK) message to signify "A-OK." At this point, the medium is free for another node to use.

Wireless Standards The 802.11 specifications are one of the "hottest" areas of development in networking today. New variations are coming out as the standard evolves to become faster and more usable. Today, there are three major specifications that you should be familiar with.

The three standards 802.11a, 802.11b, and 802.11g are commonly referred to as **Wi Fi.** Be aware that devices built on one standard are not necessarily compatible with devices built around another standard.

READ ME!

Jargon The CCITT was later folded into the International Telecommunication Union (ITU), Telecommunication Standardization Sector. The ITU operates within the United Nations to develop international standards and regulations for telecommunications.

SHOW ME!

CSMA/CA CSMA/CA is used in wireless transmissions. See how devices use CSMA/CA to avoid collisions in Show Me 5.9 at networking.glencoe.com.

Table 5.2 ⬤ ━━━➤
Several variations of the 802.11 specification are in common use. Which of the variations does not specifically conform to an IEEE wireless standard? Why is it included in the list?

802.11 Specifications

Specification	Notes
802.11	Wireless devices operating at 2.4 GHz. Transmission speeds range between 1 and 2 Mbps.
802.11a	Wireless devices operating at 5 GHz. Transmission speeds up to 54 Mbps.
802.11b	Wireless devices operating at 2.4 GHz. Transmission speeds up to 11 Mbps. Incompatible with 802.11a devices.
802.11g	Wireless devices operating at 2.4 GHz. Transmission speeds up to 54 Mbps. Compatible with 802.11b devices.
Bluetooth	Technically not an IEEE standard. Wireless devices operating at 2.45 GHz. Transmission speeds up to 2 Mbps. Does not support IP, so not useful for LAN transmissions. Good for transferring data between smaller devices.

TECH TRIVIA

Line-of-Sight Transmission Diffused infrared signaling is different from "line-of-sight" transmission. Line-of-sight devices, such as a TV remote control or a wireless computer keyboard, are called transmitters. They require a straight line to transmit a beam to a "bull's eye" or receiver, like the TV or computer.

As noted in Table 5.2, 802.11a and 802.11b devices are not compatible, but 802.11b and 802.11g devices are compatible.

Because wireless technology is more expensive, and typically slower than physically cabled devices, most "wireless" environments are not completely wire free. A user with a wireless network card might connect to a wireless hub, called a wireless access point (WAP). This access point can detect wireless signals within a certain radius. Although the access point could beam the transmission to another access point and eventually to a wireless network card installed on the server, this is uncommon. The access point is generally wired using a faster, more reliable cable connection to the server (see Figure 5.7).

Diffused Infrared Light Signals At the Physical Layer, wireless LANs rely on two different methods of transmission, diffused infrared light signal and radio signals. Diffused infrared light signal is infrared light spread out and

Figure 5.7 ⬤ ━━━➤
Wireless networking enables devices to connect to network resources without cables. What are the advantages of the 802.11g standard?

not beamed in a straight line. This signal is broadcast to all nodes within the area. Diffused infrared signals bounce around off walls, floors, and ceilings until they reach the recipient. An advantage of diffused infrared light is that it provides a fair amount of freedom for its users. A disadvantage is that all the bouncing slows and weakens the signal. The range is limited to about 33 meters (100 feet).

Radio Signals There are two categories of radio signals: Frequency Hopping Spread Spectrum (FHSS) and Direct Sequence Spread Spectrum (DSSS). Radio signals are broadcast over the 2.4 GigaHertz (GHz) radio band. FHSS requires the transmitter and receiver to hop in unison from one frequency to another. If your favorite radio station used this technique, you would have to constantly change the channel to keep up with the transmission. The time spent at each frequency is called dwell time. This timing, plus the choice of channels, are all predetermined, so the devices on the network know what to do. DSSS is a little more complicated. In this system, data are broken up into a pattern of particles, called chips. These chips can then be loaded onto the radio signal over a broad range of frequencies. One advantage of this technique is that the "chipping" process automatically encrypts the data. Only a receiver with the correct chipping code can decrypt the data stream.

Wireless offers greater freedom of movement, and there is no hassle trying to route new cabling through buildings, offices, and cubicles. As the 802.11 standards continue to evolve, and new technology is developed, better speed and reduced costs will bring wireless technology right to the front of networking.

Section 5.2 Assessment

Concept Check

1. **Define** Attached Resource Computer Network (ARCnet), Token Ring, Multistation Access Unit (MAU), Integrated Services LAN (ISLAN), Integrated Services Digital Network (ISDN), carrier sense multiple access with collision avoidance (CSMA/CA), and Wi Fi.

2. **List** wireless network classifications set by the 802.11 standards.

3. **Explain** what a MAU does and what type of network it is used in.

Critical Thinking

4. **Draw Conclusions** Explain why Bluetooth technology is incompatible with LAN technology.

5. **Sequence Information** Describe how a computer sends information in a token-passing network.

6. **Compare and Contrast** List similarities and differences between CSMA/CD and CSMA/CA.

Applying Skills

Compare Network Costs Suppose you want to set up a wireless network at your house. Go online to find current prices for wireless NICs and a wireless access point. For comparison, find prices for 802.11a, 802.11b, and 802.11g compatible devices.

Careers & Technology

ARE YOU A LEADER?

If your career plan leads to a management position, then leadership skills will be essential to your success. Good management skills make you more employable and can help you work better with others.

In many businesses, leadership skills are just as in demand as technical skills.

What Makes a Leader?

Effective leaders often share certain characteristics:

- **Trustworthiness**—Managing people means motivating and directing them. For this to happen, people must believe they can trust you. Good leaders deliver on promises, keep confidences, and are honest.
- **Communication skills**—Good managers are diplomatic but straightforward when giving directions and offering assistance. They communicate in a positive and evenhanded manner and know that people are not motivated by negative or emotional outbursts.
- **Decision-making skills**—Managers understand what tasks need to be done and determine the best method to accomplish them. Being decisive can be scary. Decision making is easier when you learn as much as possible about the organization, its mission, and its resources.

- **Accountability**—A manager may be called upon to justify decisions, to accept credit, or to explain failures. Accountable leaders take responsibility for their group's achievements and shortcomings. They accept responsibility without blaming others and give credit to those who deserve it.
- **Professional skills**—Good leaders are tuned into their professional surroundings and learn as much as they can about the responsibilities of others. This helps them to understand people's needs and to give appropriate instructions and feedback.

Developing Leadership Skills

There are many things you can do to build leadership qualities. For starters, get involved in classroom or community activities and make an active contribution. Find opportunities to practice the skills described in this article.

In school, make a point of taking business, communications, and management courses whenever possible. These studies will provide you insights into business leadership.

Consider joining the Business Professionals of America and Future Business Leaders of America. Both might have chapters in your school or community.

Tech Focus

1. Make a list to identify and assess your own decision-making and leadership skills. Why are these skills valuable?

2. Form a team. Each team member will take a turn as the leader and must direct and motivate other members to do specific tasks, as directed by your teacher. Assess each person's leadership skills.

Section 5.3 TCP/IP

The Internet is a vast universe of networks. ARPANET, the original Internet, had some important goals. First, it allowed networks using different technologies to communicate with each other. Second, it found alternative routes of communication if something went wrong. These goals were accomplished using a protocol stack known as TCP/IP.

INTRODUCTION TO TCP/IP

TCP/IP rode to fame along with the rise of the Internet in the 1990s. As more and more businesses found it essential to "internetwork" with other networks, TCP/IP emerged. Although TCP/IP is grouped together, TCP and IP perform distinct roles in transmitting information.

Transmission Control Protocol

A connection between the sending and receiving computers is created by the **Transmission Control Protocol (TCP).** Because TCP operates at the Transport Layer, it makes sure that all the data arrive safely. TCP is a connection-oriented protocol. Although it takes longer to establish this type of connection, it usually provides a more reliable communication.

Internet Protocol

Internet Protocol (IP) is responsible for routing packets, sometimes through many different networks. It operates at the OSI Model's Network Layer or in TCP/IP's Internet Layer. IP is like the truck driver who decides which route to take in order to get the product, or data, to the destination as quickly as possible. IP is a connectionless protocol and does not need to establish a complete channel of communications. When Computer A wants to transmit to Computer B, it simply addresses and broadcasts its message, and hopes that the message finds its way to Computer B.

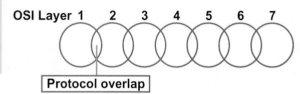

GO Online

Activity 5.1 Discover TCP/IP Standards **How are standards set for TCP/IP and its protocols? Find out how at networking.glencoe.com.**

Addresses

IP is able to route data from one network to another through a system of addressing. In this system, every computer, or host in TCP/IP terms, is given an address. This address is a globally unique, 32-bit number. These numbers look similar to 216.239.53.99.

Every time you use the Internet, you are working with these numeric IP addresses. A Web site address is a domain name, such as **www.google.com**, that makes it possible to access a particular computer somewhere in the world. The domain name is really just a mask for the IP address. Fortunately, we do not have to keep track of all those 32-bit numbers. Instead, your Web browser uses a **Domain Name System (DNS)** to locate the IP address of the domain name you entered in the address bar of your browser. After it finds the IP address, the IP figures out a route to connect to that host, and communications follow.

Services

Building on the TCP/IP stack are various protocols. Some of these protocols operate at the Application Layer and provide a variety of services, including the following:

- ◆ File Transfer Protocol (FTP) moves files between networked computers.
- ◆ Telnet enables a user to log on to another computer on the network and remotely operate another computer.
- ◆ Simple Mail Transfer Protocol (SMTP) transfers e-mail messages.
- ◆ Simple Network Management Protocol (SNMP) provides network management services.
- ◆ Hypertext Transfer Protocol (HTTP) is the protocol used by the WWW. Its job is to format and transmit Web pages.

TCP/IP AND OSI

Although there are many similarities, TCP/IP does not match up exactly with the OSI reference model. Instead of seven layers, it uses only four. TCP/IP is broken into the following four layers.

Each of these layers corresponds to one or more layers of the OSI reference model, as shown in Figure 5.8 on page 151.

Network Interface Layer

The Network Interface Layer in the TCP/IP suite corresponds to the Physical and Data Link Layers of the OSI reference model. TCP/IP communicates directly with the network. This layer provides the interface between the network architecture (such as token ring or Ethernet) and the Internet layer.

Internet Layer

The Internet Layer corresponds to the Network Layer of the OSI reference model. Several protocols, such as IP and IPX, run at this layer to route and deliver packets. Routers work at this layer to move packets from one network to another. One useful protocol is Time to Live (TTL). It is called this because a packet must reach its destination in a predetermined period of time or it dies.

READ ME!

Caution The Internet Layer uses a protocol that leaves a computer open to a type of computer attack, known as Denial of Service (DoS). One type of DoS attack is known as the "ping of death." An IP packet larger than 65,536 bytes is sent to another computer. This packet size is illegal and can cause the recipient to freeze, crash, or reboot.

Activity 5.2 Explore Internet Protocol (IP) To learn about the Internet Layer protocols and how packets of data are transmitted, go online at **networking.glencoe.com**.

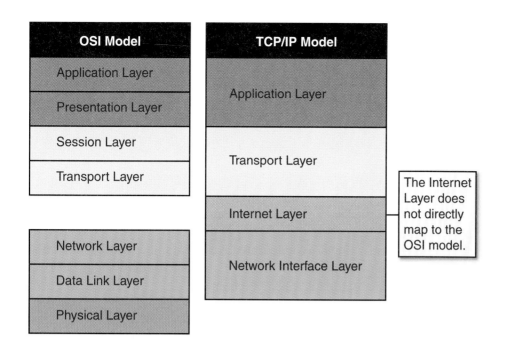

The Internet Layer does not directly map to the OSI model.

Transport Layer

The Transport Layer in the TCP/IP suite corresponds to the Transport Layer of the OSI model. It establishes and maintains end-to-end communication between two computers. Like a mother duck putting her ducklings in a line, the Transport Layer sequences packets, handles flow control, and provides acknowledgment of receipt. If any of the packets fail to make it, TCP retransmits them. The Transport Layer can use either TCP or **User Datagram Protocol (UDP)** depending on the requirements of the transmission. UDP is a connectionless transport protocol. It does not establish a path between the sender and receiver computers before transmitting and does not verify that packets arrive correctly.

Three-Way Handshake Because TCP is a connection-based protocol, it needs to establish a link between two computers. The link is called a connection or session. TCP uses a sequence of steps, called a three-way handshake, to create a reliable connection.

First, the sending computer sends a packet of information to the receiving computer that includes an initial sequence number (ISN). The ISN is used to verify that data arrived safely. Second, the receiving computer sends an acknowledgment back to the sending computer. Third, the sender acknowledges the acknowledgment. After this process is complete, the data can begin to flow.

Ports IP addresses are used to identify the address of a host on the network. Similarly, protocol port numbers are used to reference the location of a particular application or process running on a machine. The Application Layer and the Transport Layer communicate through this port.

Application Layer

The Application Layer of the TCP/IP stack corresponds to the Session, Presentation, and Application Layers of the OSI model. It is responsible for connecting applications to the network. Many of the services explained earlier in this section, including FTP, DNS, HTTP, and SMTP, run at this layer.

PHYSICAL ADDRESS

Every computer in the world is assigned a unique IP address. In many ways, this is similar to a person's phone number or home address. The IP address in decimal form is arranged in four sets of numbers: 216.239.53.99. Each set of numbers ranges between 0 and 255. In reality, an IP address is a 32-bit binary number, separated into four octets. 216.239.53.99 translates to the binary number:

$$1011000.11101111.110101.1100011$$

The address consists of two parts, a network address and an address that identifies the node, or host. Every host within a given network shares the same network prefix, but is assigned a unique host number within that prefix.

Depending on your network configuration, your IP address may be fixed, or assigned to your computer when you boot up.

YOU TRY IT

ACTIVITY 5B Finding Your IP Address and MAC Address Using Windows

❶ Click the **Start** button, and then click **Run.**

❷ Type cmd on Windows 2000 or XP, or if you are using Windows 9x command.

❸ Click **OK** or **Run.**

❹ At the DOS console, type ipconfig /all and press **Enter.**

❺ A list of information about your computer's configuration is displayed, as shown in Figure 5.9.

❻ Find your IP address and MAC address and write them down.

Figure 5.9
Using the ipconfig command at a DOS console displays your IP address and a lot of other interesting facts about your network.

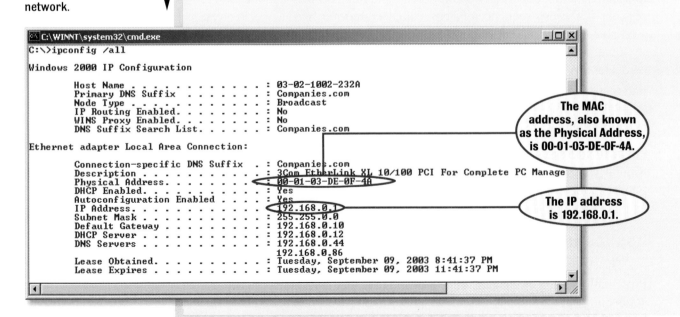

ACTIVITY 5C Finding Your IP Address and MAC Address Using Unix

1 At the command prompt, type ifconfig.

2 A list of information about your computer is displayed, as shown in Figure 5.10.

3 Find your IP address and MAC address and write them down.

Knowing where to find important network information is an important skill. This can be useful when trying to troubleshoot problems, such as when a computer cannot connect to the Internet (often, the Gateway IP address is missing or incorrect).

● **Figure 5.10**
The IP address for this computer can be found next to "inet," whereas the MAC address can be found next to "HWaddr."

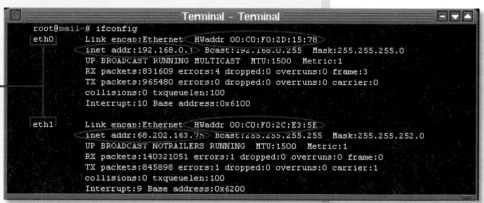

This computer has two NICS—one called "eth0" and the other called "eth1." Each NIC has a unique MAC address and IP address.

In this section, you have learned about one of the most important protocols, TCP/IP, which is the foundation of all communications on the Internet. It has become the standard for almost all LANs in use today.

Section 5.3 Assessment

Concept Check

1. Define Transmission Control Protocol (TCP), Internet Protocol (IP), Domain Name System (DNS), and User Datagram Protocol (UDP).

2. Describe the roles of TCP and IP.

3. Explain how IP addresses are used.

Critical Thinking

4. Deduce Explain how IP can be a connectionless protocol, whereas TCP, which uses IP to transport data, can be a connection-oriented protocol.

5. Analyze Consider how TCP establishes a connection with another host. What is the process involved?

Applying Skills

Find IP Addresses
Use an online service such as **www.internic.net** or **www.whois.net** to find the IP address of a Web site you visit often, such as Google or Yahoo!

ELECTRICITY BASICS

There are two types of electricity, direct current (DC) and alternating current (AC). Batteries use DC current. With DC, electrons move from one place to another—from one connection on a battery, through the device the battery powers, and back into the other connection. The movement of these electrons generates energy.

With AC, the electrons move rapidly back and forth, creating a field of energy, but individual electrons never make the complete trip. Most American electrical outlets currently use 120 volts of AC, meaning that the electricity moves back and forth 120 times every second.

Electricity moves in a circuit and is always trying to evenly distribute itself. Be aware of the devices you use which conduct electricity—even a small amount can be deadly.

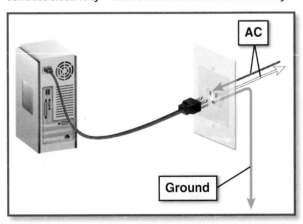

Grounding and Discharging

Electricity always moves from a position of greater energy to one of less energy. It is always trying to even itself out. This means that if a highly charged object is placed in a circuit with something that has a lesser charge, electricity moves through the circuit until it is evenly distributed.

This is bad news for humans because our bodies are excellent conductors of electricity, but our electrical levels are relatively low. If a person gets hooked into a circuit with a device that is plugged into a 120V outlet, enormous amounts of electricity flood through the body, trying to reach that state of balance. This is often fatal.

Grounding is the process that pulls away electricity before it has a chance to do damage. A grounded electric current goes into Earth itself, which can suck up any excess charge safely. If you look at a wall outlet, you will see three holes. The third one, either above or below the other two, is the "ground."

Using Electricity Safely

Follow these safety guidelines:

◆ Our bodies build up static electricity, particularly when moving across carpet. Discharge this energy before dealing with any electronic equipment. Do this by touching something metal that is in contact with the ground—a table or chair, for instance. Antistatic pads work well underneath chairs to help keep static electricity to a minimum.

◆ Never remove the third prong from an electrical cord or use "cheater adaptors" that allow you to plug such cords into a nongrounded outlet.

◆ Unplug any electronic equipment from the wall before servicing. Even if it is off, current might still be stored somewhere inside. This is particularly true with computer monitors, which should only be serviced by trained professionals.

Tech Focus

1. Describe the differences between AC and DC currents. How is voltage related to current?

2. Describe safety standards you should observe when handling electrical equipment.

Section 5.4 Other Models and Protocols

Guide to Reading

Main Ideas

Many protocol stacks provide services and communication on different types of networks. AppleTalk is used for Macintosh networks. Microsoft Windows-based computers use the NetBIOS interface. NetWare is hardware-independent network software that allows networks running on different architectures to be joined together.

Key Terms

AppleTalk
Network Basic Input/ Output System (NetBIOS)
NetBIOS Extended User Interface (NetBEUI)
NetWare
Internetwork Packet Exchange/Sequenced Packet Exchange (IPX/SPX)

Reading Strategy

Identify and describe the protocol stacks that map to the OSI model. Use an organizer similar to the one below (also available online).

OSI Reference Model

TCP/IP is not the only protocol stack on the block. Many other protocols have been created by various manufacturers to work with their line of products. Although no protocol compares to TCP/IP in its popularity and almost universal acceptance, many of these protocol stacks are significant in their own right.

These protocols are proprietary. This means that the technology belongs to the company that created it, and does not necessarily conform to any standard. Proprietary protocols often limit the pool of manufacturers. Because these proprietary protocols are controlled by the manufacturers, this can lead to higher prices for consumers.

APPLETALK

Apple Computer's LAN hardware and software for Macintosh computers use a protocol stack called **AppleTalk.** The AppleTalk protocol stack corresponds to five of the seven layers in the OSI reference model, as shown in Figure 5.11.

In an AppleTalk network, data are delivered using a connectionless service called Datagram Delivery Protocol (DDP). DDP, like UDP, delivers packets of data, but provides no means of guaranteeing delivery. Protocols at higher levels establish sessions between computers and ensure reliable delivery. As you would expect, protocols in each layer provide services to the protocols above and below them. Table 5.3 on page 156 briefly describes the protocols in each layer, starting from the top layer.

● **Figure 5.11**
The OSI reference model layers correspond to the AppleTalk protocols. Identify the differences between the AppleTalk network model and the OSI reference model.

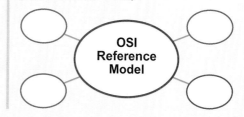

OSI Model	AppleTalk Protocol Stack		
Application Layer	No Protocols		
Presentation Layer	No Protocols		
Session Layer	ADSP	PAP	ZIP
Transport Layer	ATP		NBP
Network Layer	DDP		
Data Link Layer	Link access protocols, e.g., EitherTalk and TokenTalk		
Physical Layer	Ethernet, LocalTalk, FDDi		

Table 5.3

The AppleTalk network model features many protocols to accomplish networking tasks. How does the AppleTalk protocol stack correspond to the TCP/IP protocol stack?

Layers and Protocols of AppleTalk

OSI Layer	Protocols	Description
Session Layer	AppleTalk Data Stream Protocol (ADSP)	Establishes full, two-way communications sessions
	Printer Access Protocol (PAP)	Provides bidirectional communications between PostScript printers and the client computer
	Zone Information Protocol (ZIP)	Locates nodes on the network
Transport Layer	AppleTalk Transaction Protocol (ATP)	Transports packets
	Name-Binding Protocol (NBP)	Makes connections between devices and their network names
Network Layer	Datagram Delivery Protocol (DDP)	Prepares datagrams for routing and delivers them—a datagram is a packet of data with addressing information, sent through a packet-switching network
Data Link Layer	EtherTalk	Allows communication over Ethernet networks
	TokenTalk	Allows communication over token-passing networks
Physical Layer	LocalTalk	Uses cabling and configuration specially designed for AppleTalk networks
	FDDITalk	Allows communication on high-speed, token-passing ring networks over fiber optic cables

NetBIOS

Most of the services and applications that run within the Windows OS use the **Network Basic Input/Output System (NetBIOS)** interface or interprocess communication (IPC). This interface has evolved into a standard method for applications to access protocols in the Transport Layer. NetBIOS interfaces exist for NetBEUI, NWLink (a Microsoft protocol used to connect to Novell networks), and TCP/IP. NetBIOS requires an IP address and a NetBIOS name to uniquely identify a computer. NetBIOS performs four primary functions.

Name Resolution NetBIOS maintains a table of the names and any aliases (made up names) for the workstations on a network. The first name in the table is the unique name of the NIC. Optional user names can be added to provide a user-friendly identification system. NetBIOS then cross-references the names as required.

Datagram Service This function allows a message to be sent to any name, group of names, or to all users on the network. However, because this service is connectionless, there is no guarantee that the message will arrive at its destination.

Session service This service opens a point-to-point connection between two workstations on the network. One workstation initiates a call to another and opens the connection. Because both workstations are peers, each can send and receive data concurrently.

NIC/session status This function makes information about the local NIC, other NICs, and any currently active sessions available to any application software using NetBIOS.

Enrichment **LAB**

Lab 5.2 Designing a Token Ring Network Practice additional hands-on networking skills on page 437.

NETBEUI

NetBEUI, which is pronounced "net-boo-ie" by some and "net-byou-ie" by others, is short for **NetBIOS Extended User Interface.** This protocol was developed by IBM in the mid-1980s. It was designed for LANs of up to 200 computers. NetBEUI operates at the Transport Layer.

On the Microsoft Windows OS, NetBEUI acts as a go-between. To communicate with lower levels, NetBEUI uses NDIS. NDIS allows a NIC to support multiple protocols. Higher up, NetBEUI communicates with higher levels (the Session, Presentation, and Application Layers). It uses a programming interface called the Transport Driver Interface (TDI). Figure 5.12 shows simply how NetBEUI fits between the TDI and NDIS interfaces in relation to the OSI model.

Figure 5.12
NetBEUI helps applications communicate with the NIC. What layers does NetBEUI tie together?

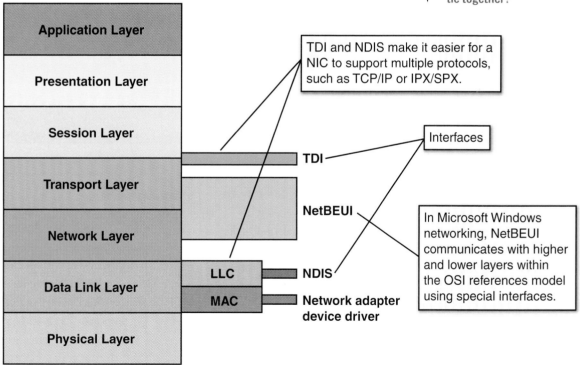

Although NetBEUI is small and fast, it does not support routing. This limitation restricts its usefulness to only a single segment of a LAN. With the growth of WANs, internetworking, and the Internet, NetBEUI has been replaced by TCP/IP.

NETWARE PROTOCOLS AND IPX/SPX

Figure 5.13 ●———
IPX/SPX provides services similar to TCP/IP. What advantage does IPX have over NetBEUI?

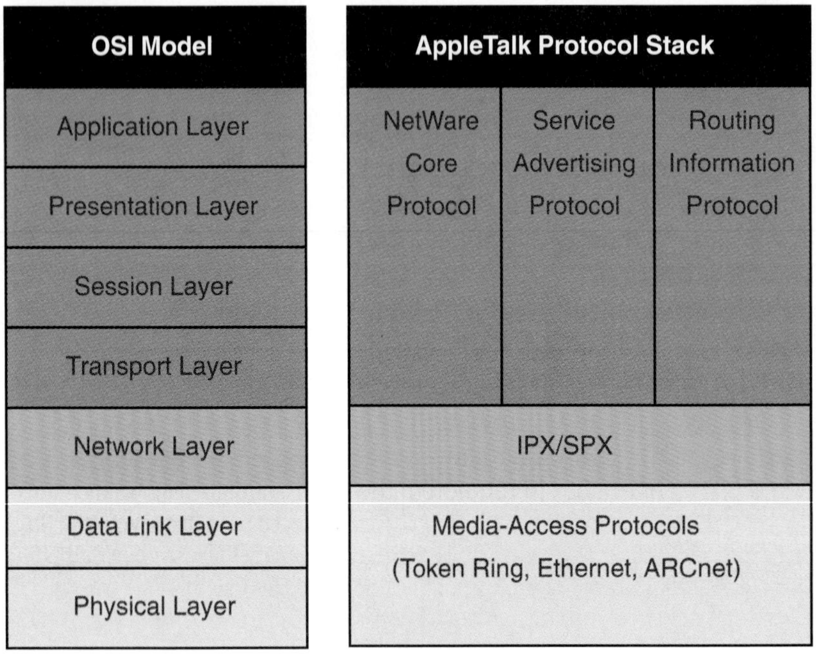

One of the earliest and largest forces in networking technology was Novell Corporation. Novell **NetWare** is a software networking product that runs on top of existing hardware, such as that used in Ethernet and Token Ring networks. Figure 5.13 shows how various NetWare protocols map to the OSI model. Notice that some of the NetWare protocols operate at several OSI levels simultaneously.

IPX/SPX (Internetwork Packet Exchange/Sequenced Packet Exchange) refers to two protocols designed by Novell for its NetWare networks and is a routable protocol. It can be used for larger internetworks. Like IP, IPX operates at the Network Layer of the OSI reference model and transports data through connectionless communications.

SPX, which corresponds to the TCP protocol, runs on the Transport Layer. SPX creates connection services similar to TCP, and controls data flow and acknowledges delivery.

OSI Model
Application Layer
Presentation Layer
Session Layer
Transport Layer
Network Layer
Data Link Layer
Physical Layer

AppleTalk Protocol Stack		
NetWare Core Protocol	Service Advertising Protocol	Routing Information Protocol
IPX/SPX		
Media-Access Protocols (Token Ring, Ethernet, ARCnet)		

Section 5.4 Assessment

Concept Check

1. **Define** AppleTalk, Network Basic Input/Output System (NetBIOS), NetBIOS Extended User Interface (NetBEUI), NetWare, and Internetwork Packet Exchange/Sequenced Packet Exchange (IPX/SPX).

2. **List** several AppleTalk protocols.

3. **Explain** what a NetWare protocol is.

Critical Thinking

4. **Recognize Limitations** Explain the critical limitation of NetBEUI.

5. **Categorize** Create a chart that shows how NetBIOS and NetBEUI work together.

6. **Design a Network** Identify which protocol would be used to integrate computers running the Microsoft Windows OS on a Novell NetWare network.

Applying Skills

Integrate AppleTalk
Show how an AppleTalk network can be integrated with an Ethernet network. Using a drawing application or paper and pen, create a diagram illustrating the different types of hardware needed to integrate the two types of networks.

SECTION 5.1 Common LAN Models

Key Terms

Logical Link Control
(LLC), 136
Ethernet, 137
contention, 137

frame, 139
device driver, 140

Main Ideas

- Standards enable devices made by different manufacturers to communicate with each other.
- Drivers provide the OS with instructions on how to work with a hardware device.
- IEEE 802.x standards define communications at the lowest layers of the OSI model.
- 802.3 is the standard that defined Ethernet networks.
- Ethernet networks use CSMA/CD for gaining access to the network.

SECTION 5.2 Other LAN Models

Key Terms

Attached Resource
Computer Network
(ARCnet), 143
Token Ring, 144
Multistation Access Unit
(MAU), 144
Integrated Services LAN
(ISLAN), 145

Integrated Services Digital
Network (ISDN), 145
carrier sense multiple
access with collision
avoidance (CSMA/CA), 145
Wi Fi, 145

Main Ideas

- Token-passing networks pass a token around the network and each node takes its turn to avoid collisions.
- 802.4 defines the ARCnet token bus standards.
- 802.5 defines the token ring standards.
- 802.9 defines the isochronous LAN standards.
- 802.11 defines the wireless standards.
- Wireless networks use a variety of transmission methods resulting in a variety of transmission speeds, security levels, and incompatible devices.

SECTION 5.3 TCP/IP

Key Terms

Transmission Control
Protocol (TCP), 149
Internet Protocol (IP), 149
Domain Name System
(DNS), 150

User Datagram Protocol
(UDP), 151

Main Ideas

- TCP/IP is one of the most important protocols used in networking.
- TCP/IP permits communication across a wide range of components.
- TCP/IP is routable, allowing it to move through a variety of networks and reroute around problem areas on the network.
- The TCP/IP stack consists of many protocols operating at various levels of the OSI reference model.

SECTION 5.4 Other Models and Protocols

Key Terms

AppleTalk, 155
Network Basic Input/
Output System
(NetBIOS), 156
NetBIOS Extended User
Interface (NetBEUI), 157

NetWare, 158
Internetwork Packet
Exchange/Sequenced
Packet Exchange
(IPX/SPX), 158

Main Ideas

- Other protocol stacks operate on different types of networks.
- AppleTalk is a set of protocols used in Macintosh networks.
- NetBEUI and NetBIOS are used in Microsoft networks.
- NetWare is networking software that runs independent of the network architecture.

READ TO SUCCEED PRACTICE

Reviewing the Purpose Go back to the Reading for a Purpose sentences you completed before each section. Did you succeed in your stated purpose? Use your Key Term Journal, class notes, and your memory to write down a brief explanation for each purpose statement. This exercise helps you determine what topics you need to review.

Reviewing Key Terms

1. Explain what an IP address is and what information it gives about a host.
2. What is the LLC sublayer responsible for?
3. Identify the specification that enables network cards to communicate with multiple protocols at the same time in Microsoft networks.
4. What is the purpose of the 802.x standards?
5. What was the first network to use CSMA/CD? Why was this significant?

Understanding Main Ideas

6. Summarize the 5-4-3 rule of Ethernet networks.
7. Describe how token-passing networks differ from Ethernet networks in their access methods.
8. Identify the primary difference between AppleTalk and NetBIOS.
9. List the OSI layers at which the Network, Internet, and Transport Layers of the TCP/IP protocol operate.
10. Explain the purpose of a Domain Name System (DNS).
11. Describe the two components of TCP/IP.
12. Explain how a single NIC can be made to work with different types of networks.
13. Describe the process of collision avoidance in wireless networks.
14. List the interfaces used in NetBEUI.
15. Explain the common features of an Ethernet network.

Critical Thinking

16. **Draw Conclusions** Explain why a token-passing network is better for networks involved in manufacturing. Why is token passing not desirable in all network situations?
17. **Compare and Contrast** What are the similarities and differences of CSMA/CD and CSMA/CA?
18. **Understand Relationships** Draw a diagram of an Ethernet frame. Label each portion of the frame and give a brief description of the information that it contains.
19. **Analyze Network Topology** What is the physical topology of an IBM Token Ring network? Why is its physical topology different from its logical topology?
20. **Compare and Contrast** Briefly describe these three technologies: diffused infrared light signals, Frequency Hopping Spread Spectrum radio, and Direct Sequence Spread Spectrum radio for wireless LANs. How are they similar and different?
21. **Analyze Wireless Networks** When would a wireless network be appropriate? When would it not be appropriate?

e-Review

networking.glencoe.com

Study with PowerPoint
To review the main points in this chapter, select **e-Review** > **PowerPoint Outlines** > **Chapter 5**.

Online Self Check
Test your knowledge of the material in this chapter by selecting **e-Review** > **Self Checks** > **Chapter 5**.

Making Connections

Math – Use Binary Numbers As you learned in this chapter, IP addresses are stored and transmitted between computers as binary.

In a binary number, only one of each digit, or bit, may be set to zero or one. Thus, a one-bit binary number can store only one of two values (zero or one). By adding another bit to a binary number, you double the number of values it can store. Thus, a two-bit binary number can store four values, a three-bit binary number can store eight values, and so on.

How many values may be stored in the following binary numbers?

a. 4-bit binary number
b. 8-bit binary number
c. 16-bit binary number
d. 32-bit binary number

STANDARDS AT WORK

Students use productivity tools to collaborate in constructing technology-enhanced models, prepare publications, produce creative works. (NETS-S 3)

Create a Slide Show Presentation

Work with a partner to create a slide show that demonstrates the life cycle of a token in a Token Ring network.

Using at least six slides, show what happens to the token, as well as any data being sent with it, before, during, and after the transmission of a frame from one computer on the network to another. Indicate on each slide whether the token is "busy," "ready," or "available for use." Design your presentation so that the final slide shows a complete model of a Token Ring network.

Edit and finalize your slide show with your partner. Save your slide show on either a floppy disk, CD, or other media, and exchange the show with another group. Ask for constructive feedback about your show. Implement the changes that will enhance your presentation.

TEAMWORK SKILLS

Collaborative Discussion

Following your teacher's instructions, form small teams to discuss company proprietary standards and draw conclusions.

As mentioned in the chapter, some standards are owned by private corporations. These standards, called proprietary standards, may not be used in new hardware or software without the owner's permission.

Discuss and take notes on the following:
1. What are the advantages and disadvantages of proprietary standards for their owners?
2. Under what circumstances might a company choose to make its standards available to the public?

Write a report summarizing your group's discussion, being sure to include at least two advantages and one disadvantage of working with proprietary standards.

CHALLENGE YOURSELF

Identify IEEE Standards

The IEEE standards govern the behavior of most types of hardware and software involved in networking.

There are standards that define which types of media can be used with networks, how data is exchanged between the computers connected to a network, how data is prepared for transmission, how data is interpreted after being transmitted, and so on.

◆ Identify which of the IEEE 802 standards apply to the hardware and software that makes up your school's network(s).
◆ Prepare a spreadsheet and list at least three standards along with their 802.x number and the part of the network where it functions.

YOU TRY IT

Networking Lab

1. Upgrading Your NIC

Research the other types of NICs provided by your NIC's manufacturer and identify two other computer's NICs. Find upgrade information.

Ⓐ Using a Web browser, go to the Web site for the manufacturer of your computer's NIC.

Ⓑ After you have located the manufacturer's Web site, look for a link labeled "product catalog," "network hardware," or something similar. Follow the link and locate a list or catalog of the NICs offered by this manufacturer.

Ⓒ Find your NIC and select two other NICs that you want to learn more about. If possible, choose NICs that are newer or more powerful.

Ⓓ Prepare a report on the three NICs that includes the following information:

- The standard with which the NIC complies, such as 10BaseT or 100BaseTX
- The type of connectors needed
- The operating system needed
- The system requirements of the NIC
- Any special features of the NIC, such as multiple connectors or support for multiple standards or protocols
- The price of the NIC

2. Comparing IP Addresses

Find and compare the IP addresses of several computers. The way that you locate each computer's IP address depends on its operating system.

Ⓐ Find the IP address of another computer by using its Web address:

- At the DOS console, type ping Web address and press **Enter.** In this case, to find the IP address of the Library of Congress, type ping loc.gov. Information on the specified server, including its IP address and response time is displayed.
- Write down the IP address.

Ⓑ Using the ping command, find the IP addresses of the following computers. Be forewarned that some computers or Web sites may not respond to your ping.

- At least three computers on your classroom's network
- Two computers on another network at your school, if possible
- Three other servers, using the Web addresses of sites with which you are familiar

Ⓒ Using a word processing or spreadsheet application, create a table that compares computers and servers with their IP addresses.

Ⓓ Within the same document, write the answers to the following questions:

- What similarities of the IP addresses do you find?
- What seems to determine the level of similarity between two IP addresses?

Networking Projects

1. Redesign Networks

A small public relations firm leases space in two buildings in an office park. The business staff, including the human resources and accounting departments, has 12 people and is located in one office in Building A. The creative staff, including the copy writing, graphics, and production departments, with a total of 22 employees, are in Building B. Buildings A and B are about 600 meters (about 1970 feet) apart.

The business staff is networked with a four-year-old coaxial bus that ties their PC-compatible computers together in a peer-to-peer workgroup. The creative staff in Building B has a group of computers including Macs and PCs. They are not networked.

The owners of the company want to network all the computers for the creative staff and connect the creative staff network to the business staff network. They also want to standardize the type of network used in both buildings to keep troubleshooting issues to a minimum.

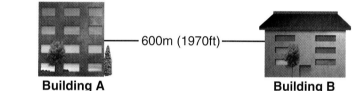

Building A
Business Staff with 12 people

600m (1970ft)

Building B
Creative Staff with 22 people

Based on the information above, answer the following questions.

A What kind of network should be installed for the creative staff in Building B? Explain your answer.

- client/server
- peer-to-peer

B What type of network should the company implement in each building? Explain your answer.

- fiber optic Ethernet
- fiber optic Token Ring
- fiber optic ArcNet
- Ethernet 10BaseT

- Ethernet 10Base2
- Token Ring
- LocalTalk
- ArcNet

C What type of network should the company install between the two buildings? Explain your answer.

- fiber optic Ethernet
- fiber optic Token Ring
- fiber optic ArcNet
- Ethernet 10BaseT

- Ethernet 10Base2
- Token Ring
- LocalTalk
- ArcNet

Network Operating Systems and Software

YOU WILL LEARN TO...

WHY IT MATTERS......................................

Learning about complex systems, such as how an engine works, can be difficult. Looking under the hood of the car to see the system in operation is very helpful. Computers rely on an operating system much the same way that a car relies on its engine. Without an operating system, the computer cannot function.

Quick Write Activity

Learning how the operating system and applications work can help you to understand networks. Think about a computer task that takes many steps to accomplish, such as sending an e-mail or copying a file to a floppy disk. How would you teach that task to someone who has never used a computer before? Write a set of steps that explains how to perform this task from beginning to end.

WHAT YOU WILL DO ....

READ TO SUCCEED

Stay Engaged

You are an active reader when you stay engaged in the material. One way to stay engaged is to turn each of the colored section heads into questions, then read the section to find the answers. When you can think of a good question and find complete answers, you will be engaged in learning.

Section 6.1 Common Operating Systems

Operating systems essentially perform two important tasks. First, they manage the hardware and software on your computer. Second, OSs provide a consistent interface for applications. UNIX, Mac OS, Windows, Novell NetWare, and Linux are just some of the popular OSs available for personal computers and servers.

UNIX

In the 1960s, researchers from Bell Labs, General Electric, and MIT created an OS that allowed timesharing. Timesharing was an automated system of allocating processor time to various jobs submitted by multiple users. The OS was called Multiplexed Information and Computing Service (Multics). However, it turned out to be too expensive and too difficult to maintain. A determined group of researchers still sought an OS that could be used on different kinds of hardware. In the end, they came up with UNIX. **UNIX** is a uniquely powerful and flexible OS that stands for **Uniplexed Information and Computing System.** The name was a play on the earlier Multics.

UNIX was developed in a programming language that was independent of the hardware on which it needed to operate. The key to UNIX's success was that very little code was written using assembly programming languages. Most of the code was written in the programming language C. C provides a close correspondence between high-level language and machine-level instructions.

Another key characteristic of UNIX was that it took a modular approach to its development. Rather than trying to do everything for everyone, developers were free to basically "plug in" new tools, utilities, and capabilities as the need arose. This includes tools for networking and administration. If you wanted to communicate with a colleague at another university, you could write an e-mail program and add it to the OS. Developers could add to the OS because it is an open system. This means that anyone is free to add to and improve the code.

Many different vendors have created their own versions of UNIX. Some popular versions include FreeBSD and Solaris. Most variations of UNIX are command–oriented as shown in the diagnostics utility in Figure 6.1 on page 167,

Lab 6.1 Working with UNIX Commands Practice additional hands-on networking skills on page 438.

which makes the system less user-friendly. They do not have a **graphical user interface (GUI),** which makes computing simpler by using easy-to-understand graphics to represent various objects or commands within the OS. However, a lot of work has been done in recent years to provide UNIX with a GUI interface to make it easier to use. Perhaps no system has been more successful than Mac OS X, which is built on top of UNIX.

● Figure 6.1
UNIX is a command heavy OS. What is the command code shown in this UNIX diagnostic utility?

```
$> prtdiag

System Configuration: Sun Microsystems sun4u Sun Ultra
450 (4 X UltraSPARC-II 248MHz)
System Clock frequency: 83 MHz
Memory size: 256 Megabytes

$> prtdiag
```

DOS

In the 1980s, IBM and Microsoft developed **Disk Operating System (DOS).** DOS was not a very pretty OS. There was no GUI. DOS was capable of many important tasks, such as file and directory management, disk formatting, and simple text editing. Although the days of DOS are pretty much over, power DOS and UNIX users are still very comfortable working at a text console, otherwise known as the "command prompt."

ACTIVITY 6A Using DOS Commands

In this activity, you learn how to use an important DOS command, and then generate a results file to capture the output from the command.

❶ Using a computer running Windows OS, click the **Start** button, and then click **Run.**

❷ Type cmd if you are using Windows 2000 or XP, or type command if you are using Windows 95 or 98.

❸ At the command prompt, type help and then press **Enter.** Read through the list of available commands. You can view help about a specific command by entering help and the command name at the command prompt. In this case, we want to learn about the dir command, which displays the contents of the current directory.

❹ Type help dir at the command prompt and press **Enter.**

❺ Type dir at the command prompt and press **Enter.** If there are a lot of files in the directory, you probably saw a long list of files fly by. You could not read the name of each file.

❻ Many DOS commands support options, called switches, which change the function of the command. In the case of the dir command, switches control how the list is sorted and how you want the output directed. Type dir /p and press **Enter.** The switch /p pauses the list after each screen full of information as shown in Figure 6.2 on page 168.

❼ To sort the list, type dir /odn /p and press **Enter.** Now, the list is ordered by date first, then by name.

❽ Output this information to a text file suitable for printing or later review. Type dir /odn /p > filelist.txt and press **Enter.** Surprise! Nothing was output to the screen. That is because the information was output to a new file, rather than to your screen.

YOU TRY IT

GO *Online*

Activity 6.1 Research DOS
The real power of the command prompt lies in its ability to be controlled from a batch command or script. In either case, a set of predetermined commands is saved into a file that can be called and executed whenever needed. Go to **networking.glencoe.com** to learn more about DOS batch commands and scripts.

Command Prompt

Figure 6.2
Switches can be used to
change the behavior of
the command.

9 To view the contents of the file you created, you can use one other simple DOS command, edit. Type edit filelist.txt and press **Enter.**

10 Press **Alt+F** then **X** to exit the Edit window when you are finished reviewing the file.

11 Type exit to close the command prompt window when you are finished looking at the DOS commands.

DOS continued to play an important role in PC history. The first versions of Windows were simply a graphical interface, placed on top of DOS. In recent years, DOS has been completely phased out, although you can still get to a DOS command prompt in any Windows OS.

MACINTOSH OPERATING SYSTEM

As PC users struggled at the DOS command prompt, other manufacturers sought to make computers easier to use. In 1984, Apple Computers introduced the Macintosh computer with a graphical user interface. Instead of typing strange DOS commands, the **Macintosh** OS GUI allowed users to click a mouse and graphical icons to manage files (see Figure 6.3 on page 169). In an OS, an icon is a picture, or graphic, that represents files, folders, drives, or applications.

Apple's operating system OS X uses UNIX as its underlying architecture. This makes the Mac OS more stable and easier to customize than it had been in past OS versions. From early on, the Mac OS has included built-in networking tools such as AppleShare.

Even though Macintoshes make up only a small percentage of the computer market, networking professionals must still be familiar with the Mac hardware and the Mac OS. Many networks include PCs running Windows as well as Macintosh computers. Newer Macintosh features, such as AirPort® and Rendezvous™, greatly simplify attaching a Mac to almost any type of network.

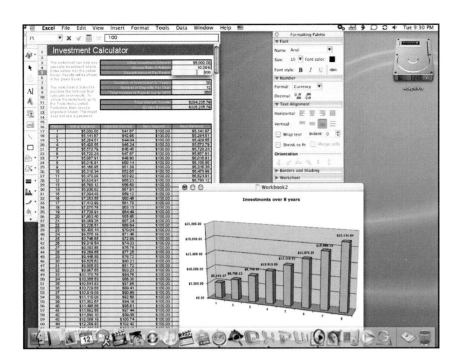

Figure 6.3
The Macintosh OS paved the way for GUIs. What aspects of the Mac OS made it successful?

MICROSOFT WINDOWS

The Microsoft answer to the Macintosh OS came in the form of an OS named **Windows.** Built on top of DOS, the first versions of Windows were not very successful. However, version 3.1 changed all that. Released in 1992, more than a million copies were sold within the first two months of its release.

In DOS, each application took the entire screen to display and the user could only work on one task at a time. In Windows, like Mac OS, multiple applications could run at the same time, each in its own "window." This is an example of multitasking, which enables users to accomplish many tasks at the same time. Each window could be moved, resized, and reordered to an individual's liking.

Windows 95 was the first OS to claim rock-star status. Customers lined up at midnight the day it was released in 1995 to be the first to own it. The first million copies were sold in four days. Windows 95 improved the graphical interface and stabilized the OS. One of the most notable additions was the now familiar "Start" menu. The Start menu organized access to applications and utilities installed on the computer.

The Windows 9x family (including Windows 95, 98, and Millennium Edition) continued its relationship with DOS. Windows NT, however, was not based on DOS. Windows NT provided a stable, reliable OS for business. Because of this, Windows NT gained popularity in client/server LAN environments. Windows NT eventually evolved to Windows 2000. Both Windows NT and 2000 were sold in workstation and server versions. Windows NT and 2000 workstation versions can operate in peer-to-peer or client/server networks.

Microsoft eventually merged the Windows 9x family of OSs and the Windows NT OSs into today's Windows XP (see Figure 6.4 on page 170). This merger provided the same stability and performance of the Windows NT line for business, while retaining the plug-and-play capabilities and ease of use of the Window 9x family for home users. Today, Windows is the OS of choice on nearly 90 percent of computers.

READ ME!

Jargon The NT stands for "New Technology." Windows NT was written from the ground up without DOS as its underlying OS.

Figure 6.4
The Windows OS uses a system of virtual windows to organize running applications. How does this feature make a user more productive?

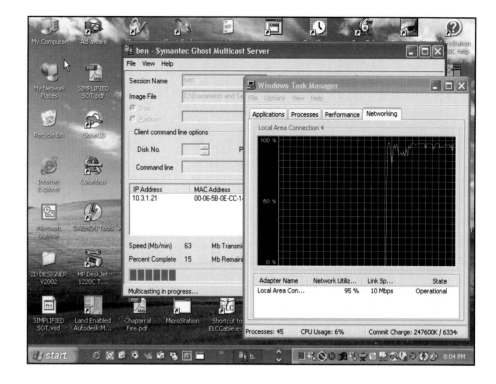

READ ME!

Tech Tip Novell is committed to a growing market of Linux users. GroupWise® offers cross-platform client and server services, and runs completely on Linux. GroupWise handles communication, document management, and workflow services across NOSs, including Novell's own NetWare.

NOVELL NETWARE

Novell's NetWare OS is distinct from the other OSs in this chapter. NetWare is technically a network operating system (NOS), and is, therefore, devoted entirely to the client and server software required to create a LAN environment. NetWare is built to run on top of an existing OS and hardware to provide networking services.

In the early days of networking, vendors often tied their network OS to a particular brand of software products, usually their own. Customers did not like this approach because it meant replacing expensive hardware to support different network software.

Novell recognized this problem and chose to concentrate on the software. Similar to the UNIX approach, Novell wrote its software to run on any hardware. This approach allowed NetWare to run on Macintosh and UNIX-based computers, as well as on PCs using Microsoft Windows. NetWare introduced many important protocols that are still in use on many networks today. For example, the IPX/SPX stack of protocols you learned about in Chapter 5 is still in use.

LINUX

Linux, a derivative of UNIX, has gained popularity in recent years as an alternative to Windows. Linux was written by a computer science student, Linus Torvalds, in 1991. Torvalds chose to make Linux **open source,** which meant that anyone was free to add and improve on the code. To this day programmers freely contribute to the Linux source code. Today, Linux (see Figure 6.5 on page 171) runs on everything from handheld devices to massive parallel super computing clusters.

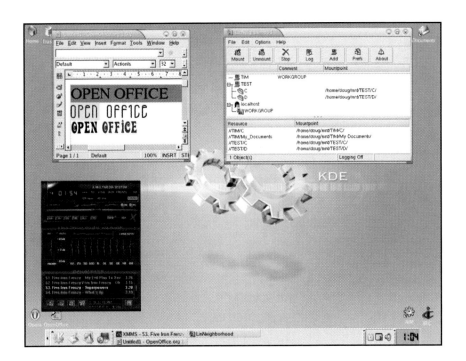

Figure 6.5
Linux, a popular derivative of UNIX, has many alternative GUIs to choose from. Why do you think the originator of Linux made it open source?

Linux source code is completely free to anyone who wants to download the files, compile, and install the operating system. However, this is a complicated, technical task. Most people prefer to buy a pre-compiled version and follow the setup wizard. The companies that sell the products do not make money off Linux itself. They charge for packaging of the utilities, and the installation software they have created to make it easier for users to install and configure.

Section 6.1 Assessment

Concept Check

1. **Define** Uniplexed Information and Computing System (UNIX), graphical user interface (GUI), Disk Operating System (DOS), Macintosh, Windows, Linux, and open source.

2. **List** the common OSs and state whether they are available for workstations or servers.

Critical Thinking

3. **Analyze Information** What factors made UNIX such an important operating system?

4. **Sequence Information** Describe the development of Windows OSs starting with DOS and ending with Windows XP.

5. **Understand Relationships** In what ways does NetWare differ from other operating systems?

Applying Skills

Conduct an OS Survey Conduct a survey to find out which operating systems are in use at your school, among your friends, and in local businesses. Create a table using a word processor or spreadsheet application to tally the results. Which OS is the most popular? The least popular? Why do you think people use these particular OSs?

EMERGING TECHNOLOGY

NEW BREEDS OF SECURITY THREATS

For years, firewalls and antivirus software made networks as secure as possible. But new threats are emerging quickly, putting network administrators on alert.

Antivirus software developers continually update information about the newest threats, including some types of malware and blended threats.

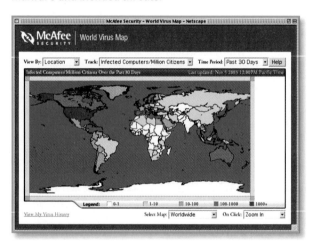

Malware

Malware (malicious software) is any program that can cause damage or instability in a computer. Viruses can be malware. Other examples of malware include the following:

◆ **Spyware**—Sometimes, free programs that can be downloaded from the Internet contain spyware. These programs can gather information from a user's PC without the user knowing it. Spyware uses the PC's Internet connection to transmit information about the PC and its user back to the program's creator. This information is then used for personalized advertising or sold to third parties. Often, spyware is poorly programmed and may cause computers to crash or freeze.

◆ **Peer-to-peer (P2P) file sharing programs**—Like spyware, some P2P programs create a

"tunnel" that allows their creators access to a computer through an Internet connection. A hacker may use this opening to bypass firewalls and gain unauthorized entry to the computer and its P2P network. The computer's data and systems can then be hijacked for unethical purposes, such as a denial-of-service attack.

Many commercial programs include spyware and most are harmless. For example, programs such as Apple's QuickTime and Microsoft Windows automatically check back to their developers' Web sites for updates.

Current antivirus programs do not look for malware. Future "anti-malware" programs may be able to distinguish innocent programs from destructive ones.

Blended Attacks

A blended attack is a virus that uses hacking techniques to defeat network security measures. In a blended attack, the virus scans computers for security weaknesses. After a virus infects a Web server, it can copy itself onto the computers that access that server. It may also reconfigure the network to allow unauthorized access. For example, the virus may allow drives and folders to be shared, or create a "guest" account with privileges that allow the virus to perform any action on the system.

Tech Focus

1. How do viruses, malware, and blended attacks damage networks?

2. Research new trends in computer and network security. Predict how threats such as viruses and hackers will be handled in five years.

Guide to Reading

Main Ideas

The graphical user interface includes icons, and menus which organize related commands, and make computers easier to use. Help systems aid users learning about the software. File system directories organize files to provide easy, organized access to data.

Key Terms

menu system
file system directory
tree structure
file allocation table (FAT)
NT file system (NTFS)
Hierarchical File System (HFS)
Extended File System Version 2 (EXT2)

Reading Strategy

Identify the components of a graphical user interface. Create a chart similar to the one below (also available online).

Components of a graphical user interface

The GUI introduced by Apple in 1984 made computers truly easy for anyone to use. People with no prior computing experience found it easy to move, copy, and delete files. This type of interface has continued to become simpler and more intuitive for people to use. At the same time, it has grown to enable users to do more, faster than ever before possible.

PARTS OF THE GUI WINDOW

The GUI is an essential part of most operating systems today. In the Windows OS, each application runs in its own "window." Each window can be opened, closed, or resized. The windows can be arranged in just about any order that makes sense to the user.

In Figure 6.6, many of the important elements of the Windows GUI are shown. In the lower-left corner is the Start menu button. Clicking this button displays a menu of icons and folders. Pointing to a menu selection often leads to a submenu, as shown in the figure.

The windows concept allows users to run many applications at the same time. The user can switch quickly back and forth between applications. For example, suppose you are writing an e-mail message. You need to check a calculation. Therefore, you open the Calculator application or switch to a spreadsheet application. After you have collected the necessary data, you switch back to your message.

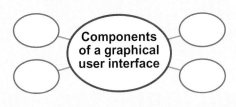

● **Figure 6.6**
The Windows interface relies heavily on graphics to simplify user interaction with the OS. What are the visual characteristics of this GUI interface?

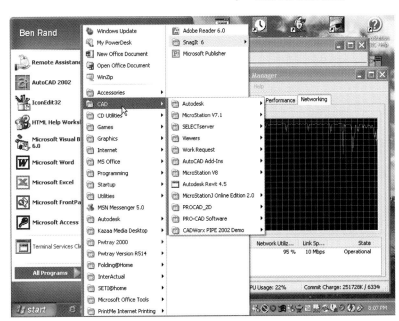

Activity 6.2 Common Keyboard Shortcuts

Keyboard shortcuts abound in most any OS you are likely to use. Go online at networking.glencoe.com for a list of common Windows and Mac OS keyboard shortcuts.

Icons

Icons are an important part of most GUIs. An icon can represent many different things, such as files, folders, drives, or applications. An icon displays a picture, or graphic, that makes it easy to identify what the icon represents.

In most OSs, clicking an icon opens the object the icon represents. An application icon launches the application. A file icon opens the file in its related application. For example, clicking a Word document icon opens the document within Microsoft Word.

Sometimes, icons represent the actual file. Deleting or moving the icon deletes or moves the file. Other times, icons are merely links, or shortcuts, to the object they represent. For example, Mary needs to work on files that are stored in a folder on the file server. Because she needs to access these files frequently, she can make a shortcut—an icon that points to the real folder on the file server. This is better than copying the files to her computer, because the files need to be accessed by other people. Also, the files on the file server are backed up nightly by the company's backup server.

Figure 6.7

Menus combine similar commands into logical groups. How do menus organize commands and information?

Menu Systems

Menu systems represent another method to organize commands and information within an application. Most applications with a GUI interface use

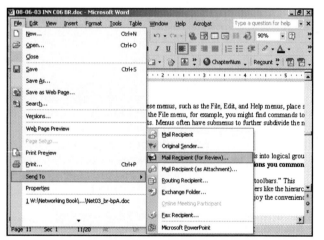

menus across the top of the application window, as shown in Figure 6.7. These menus, such as the File, Edit, and Help menus, place similar commands together. On the File menu, for example, you might find commands to open, save, and print documents. Menus often have submenus to further subdivide the menu into logical categories.

In many applications, menu commands are also duplicated on "toolbars." This duplication provides the best of both worlds for users. Some users like the hierarchical approach to locating a command that menus provide. Others enjoy the convenience and graphical nature of a toolbar.

HELP SYSTEMS

At one time, software vendors included printed documentation with every product they sold. Today, most vendors still provide documentation. However, it is usually in electronic form, rather than printed documentation. Electronic format help systems provide many advantages over printed documentation.

Printing documentation is expensive. It is also usually out of date by the time it has been published. Electronic documentation, on the other hand, can be updated until the product ships. It can then be kept up-to-date via a download from the vendor's Web site. These are all advantages for the software vendor.

For the user, electronic documentation is nice primarily because it is searchable. As fast as you can type in a keyword and press Enter, you can find every place in the documentation that mentions your keyword.

In addition, you do not have to worry about where to place those dozens of software manuals.

Help systems are available with almost every software application, from games, to business software, to operating systems. Sometimes, the help documentation is in simple text files. More often, though, graphical help systems are highly organized, with pictures, hyperlinks, and even embedded animations to show you how to perform a particular task.

ACTIVITY 6B Using Online Help

In the preceding chapter, you learned about TCP/IP. Online help available within your system can help you configure your TCP/IP settings. In this activity, you use the help system to find out how to configure TCP/IP settings. The following instructions are for computers running Microsoft Windows 2000/XP.

❶ Click the **Start** button, then click **Help** (Windows 2000) or **Help and Support** (Windows XP), or press **F1.**

❷ Click the **Search** tab (Windows 2000). For Windows XP, there is a **Search** box in the upper-left corner, as shown in Figure 6.8.

❸ Type TCP/IP in the Search box, and then press **Enter.**

❹ Browse through the list and double-click **Configure TCP/IP settings.**

Online help is easy to access. Using the help system, you can quickly accomplish many important tasks.

┌─**READ ME!**─
Tech Tip On the Windows platform, press **F1** to access help. On the Macintosh platform, press **⌘+?**.

YOU TRY IT

● **Figure 6.8**
Using a Help system allows you to find answers to questions on your own.

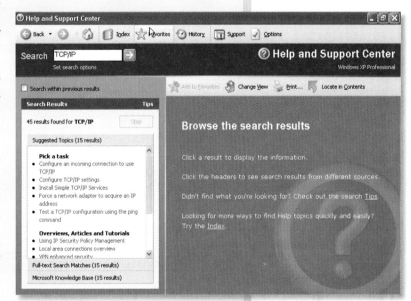

FILE SYSTEM DIRECTORIES

An essential part of any OS, including GUIs, is the **file system directory.** This important tool represents the organizational structure of the files stored on the hard drives, network drives, and other removable storage devices, such as Zip disks or CD-R disks. Like the Dewey Decimal system used to categorize books, the OS file system is used to catalog and find files stored on a storage device.

Most OSs use a tree structure to represent the files stored on disk. In a **tree structure,** a drive often represents a "root," or base, that has folders or directories for its branches, as shown in Figure 6.9. Each directory can store files, or other directories, often called subdirectories or subfolders.

● **Figure 6.9**
Tree structures display drives, files, and folders in a hierarchy. What is the "root" directory?

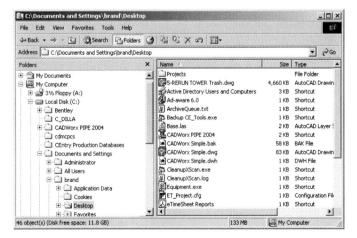

Figure 6.10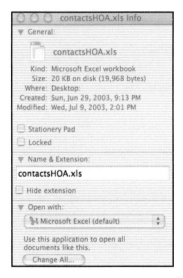
Mac files are stored in two parts: the data and the resource fork. What is stored in the data fork?

Different OSs have different ways of storing files. Even different OSs from the same vendor may utilize different file structures, which are not always compatible with each other. These file systems have different capabilities in regard to securing access, file compression, and physical storage of the data on the disk. Some attributes you should know about common file systems are identified in the following list.

◆ **FAT/FAT32**—**FAT** stands for **file allocation table.** This file system is used by the Windows 9*x* line of operating systems (and optionally by operating systems based on Windows NT). FAT32 is an extension to FAT, which uses 32 bits to store a file's address location. Hard drives can store up to 2 terabytes of data.

◆ **NTFS**—Short for **NT File System, NTFS** is used by Microsoft Windows NT-based operating systems (Windows NT, Windows 2000, and Windows XP). NTFS is more reliable than FAT/FAT32. It allows an administrator to set access permissions for directories and/or individual files.

◆ **HFS**—The Mac OS uses the **Hierarchical File System (HFS)** to store files. Mac files are normally stored as two "forks" or parts. The data fork stores the actual data contained within the file. The resource fork is used to identify the type of file and the application that created the file (see Figure 6.10).

◆ **EXT2**—The most common file system on Linux systems is called **Extended File System Version 2 (EXT2),** or EXT2FS. Linux uses something called a virtual file system (VFS), which it uses to mount, or load, file systems. This enables Linux to read other file systems, such as FAT or NTFS. After being mounted, files can be accessed as though they are "native" to Linux.

YOU TRY IT ACTIVITY 6C Sharing Folders with Peers

Using Windows OS, users can share folders and their contents with other users on the network as in a peer-to-peer network. No server would be needed to store the data, since the data would remain on the user's computer. The user would only need to change the permissions to allow others access to the folder's contents.

Figure 6.11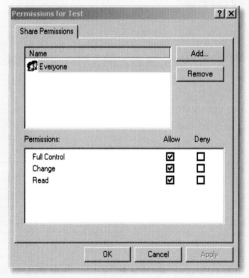
You can control who has access to the directory by using the **Add** and **Remove** buttons.

❶ Create a folder called **Test.** To do this, open **Windows Explorer.**

❷ Select **File,** choose **New,** and click on **Folder.**

❸ Type Test as the folder name.

❹ To share the folder, right-click on the folder and choose **Sharing** from the pop-up menu.

❺ On the Sharing tab, click **Share this Folder.**

📄 Test

◄─── ● **Figure 6.12**
You can tell a folder is shared by looking at the icon.

My Documents

Select an item to view its description.

See also:

My Documents

My Network Places

My Computer

❻ Click **Permissions** to set who will be able to get to your data. In Figure 6.11 on page 176, all users are able to access the folder called Test. However, by clicking on **Add** or **Remove,** you can customize who does and does not have access to the folder and the contents.

❼ When finished, click **OK** to exit the Permissions dialog.

❽ Click **OK** to exit the Sharing dialog box.

❾ Go to the **Windows Explorer** window. The Test directory has a new icon associated to it as shown in Figure 6.12.

Sharing folders is the basis for creating a peer-to-peer network. By allowing files and directories to be shared, users on the network can cooperatively work together without the added expense of a server.

┌READ ME!─┐

Tech Tip The Mac file system has some unique advantages over the Windows file extension system. In Windows, each extension, such as .doc, is associated with one type of application. However, a file in some other format could be renamed to use the .doc extension. Although Windows attempts to open the file in Word, the file may be incompatible. The Mac resource file prevents this from happening by storing the application association separate from the file name.

Section (6.2) Assessment

Concept Check

1. **Define** menu system, file system directory, tree structure, file allocation table (FAT), NT file system (NTFS), Hierarchical File System (HFS), and Extended File System Version 2 (EXT2).

2. **Explain** how an icon works in a GUI system.

3. **Describe** what the file allocation table does for DOS/Windows OSs.

Critical Thinking

4. **Compare and Contrast** What are the similarities and differences between FAT/FAT32 and NTFS?

5. **Sequence Details** Think of a difficult-to-learn skill in an application you use frequently. Find this topic in the application's help system. Then write down the steps for another user to access the same information.

Applying Skills

Illustrate Directory Structures Although the "tree structure" is the most common method of illustrating a directory structure, it is not the only method that can be used. Work in groups to brainstorm two other graphical ways files could be displayed to make information easier to find.

Ethics & Technology

PIRACY ON THE INTERNET

The term piracy once meant copying or installing a software program or operating system without purchasing it. Today, piracy is no longer limited to software.

Many Web sites tell you whether they grant permission for others to copy or use their content, and how to request permission.

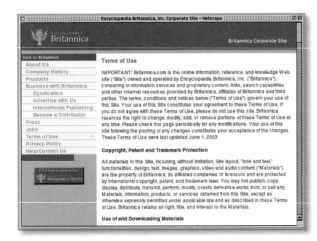

Using or Stealing?

Online pirates often do not understand that software, songs, photographs, movies, and written works are usually someone's property. A photograph is the property of the photographer. A copyrighted song is the property of its writer or publisher.

When copyrighted material is downloaded illegally from the Internet, that material is being stolen. The material's creator receives no payment for it.

Peer-to-Peer File Sharing

Online piracy became a major issue in the late 1990s when Web-based, peer-to-peer (P2P) file-sharing services appeared, such as Napster, KaZaa, and Gnutella. These systems turned the Web into a giant P2P network, allowing users to search each other's disks for files. P2P services are most commonly used for sharing music files, but are also used for sharing software, movies, and other types of data. File sharers swap millions of files weekly without paying for them.

Getting Permission

Some people believe that copyrighted works become "public domain" (meaning they are no longer protected by copyright) after they are posted on the Internet. This is not true.

You cannot assume that a Web site's developer owns the copyright to items on the site. The material may have been published with the actual owner's permission, but that permission does not extend to you.

Most Web sites post information about whether you can use material from a site and how to get permission. Look for a link to a "terms of use" page, or contact the Webmaster to determine whether you can use the material.

Taking copyrighted items without paying for them or without getting the owner's permission is unethical and illegal. Always make sure you have permission to use any item before copying or downloading.

Tech Focus

1. How has piracy affected the software, music, movie, and publishing industries? Research the estimated losses from piracy and write a short report on this issue.

2. Do you use such a service to share music files? Do you think it is legal or ethical to do so? Support your views.

Section 6.3 Network Operating System Software

Guide to Reading

Main Ideas

All network operating systems provide administrative tools and security utilities. Network services are used for e-mail, groupware, and other important business functions.

Key Terms

administrative tools
domain
group
Microsoft Active Directory
Novell Directory Services (NDS)
Post Office Protocol (POP)
Simple Mail Transfer Protocol (SMTP)
groupware

Reading Strategy

Scan the headings in this section. Create a chart similar to the one below (also available online).

What I Know	What I Want to Find Out	What I Learned	How I Can Learn More

The software that makes up a network operating system (NOS) is important. Administrative tools make it easier for a network administrator to do the job. Directory services simplify administrative tasks by providing many tools in one easy-to-use interface. Other software enables services that are run on the server. These services handle e-mail and specialized duties such as groupware.

ADMINISTRATIVE TOOLS

One of the key differences between an ordinary OS and a NOS lies in the **administrative tools** that are part of the NOS. These tools can often be run remotely, allowing a network administrator to manage servers, users, and resources from virtually anywhere on the network. Each of the major NOSs has its own organization scheme and corresponding set of administrative tools.

Directory Services

NOSs use directory services to organize and manage objects that belong to the network. These objects can be many different things, from servers and computers, to printers, to files and directories, to users and groups. Directory services organize these objects, often in a tree hierarchy, similar to the method in which file systems are organized.

Directory services allow administrators to manage everything from domains to individual computer and user accounts. A **domain** is a grouping of computers and devices that are administered as one unit. Security policies, such as minimum password length, can be established for the entire domain.

Groups are used to automatically assign permissions to many users at once. For example, accounting files are often restricted to only those users who work in the Accounting Department. By creating an Accounting group, an administrator can easily add or remove users to the group to set access permissions. Anyone belonging to the group gets access, whereas everyone else is out of luck.

Enrichment LAB

Lab 6.2 Choosing a Password System Practice additional hands-on networking skills on page 439.

Windows Active Directory Although most people are familiar with the standard Windows OS, networking professionals are more familiar with the NOS versions such as Windows 2000 Server or Windows Server 2003. This powerful NOS is used to administer networks both large and small. In Windows 2000 Server and Windows Server 2003, **Microsoft Active Directory** is the central database system for administering the network.

Figure 6.13 shows Active Directory. Within a domain, organizational units can be set up. In the figure, you can see a folder named "Users" and another named "Workstations." Within the Users folder, an administrator can set up new user accounts, disable accounts, and reset passwords.

Novell Directory Services Novell Directory Services (NDS) is the central administration for NetWare-based networks, as shown in Figure 6.14. Similar to Active Directory, NDS provides a single tool for administering the network. Network resources are represented as objects within a hierarchical tree structure.

NDS provides security administration for resources at three levels:

◆ **Accounts**—Creating and editing users' names, passwords, workstation time
◆ **Rights**—Creating, reading, erasing, or writing files
◆ **Directory/file elements**—Directory/file sharing, deleting, copying, editing

Like Active Directory, NDS simplifies administrative chores for a NetWare administrator. All network resources and users can be managed from one application, which can be run remotely by the administrator, wherever he or she happens to be at the time.

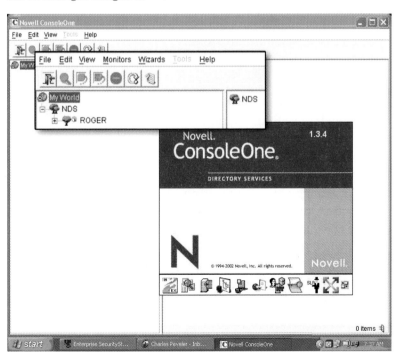

Network Security Utilities

Network security is an important aspect of any network, and many different methods exist to secure a network. Network administrators, like security guards, must always be on alert, watching for potential security problems.

Policies and Permissions One of the primary means of securing network access is through the use of passwords. Administrators can set policies that dictate how passwords are created. Another technique used to protect access to network resources is through the use of permissions. Permissions grant access to certain users or groups of users. These access rights may allow users to view, edit, or add and delete documents.

Event Notification Tools Event notification tools monitor the network and alert the network administrator when certain events have taken place. For example, a server handling network logons can create a log when someone attempts to log on and uses an incorrect password. Several unsuccessful log on attempts could signify an unauthorized attempt to gain access to the network.

External Threats External threats involve people outside the organization gaining unauthorized access to the network. After they have access, they can do anything from disrupting network activity to stealing important information. Hackers are computer users who attempt to break into, or hack, a network. They can do this by finding a password or by exploiting bugs in application code that allow them to launch programs. Viruses are malicious programs, which are created by programmers, that infect other files. If the file is opened, the virus can delete files, copy themselves to other files, and perform other malicious acts. A Trojan horse is a type of application that embeds itself in another file. When its host file is launched, the Trojan horse program can steal information and send it back to the programmer who created it.

Network administrators guard against external threats using many utilities. Antivirus software can be set up to monitor all files and e-mail on the network (see Figure 6.15). If a virus is detected in an e-mail attachment, the attachment is removed and deleted. Firewalls and proxy computers (explained in more detail later in this book) protect the network from hackers.

● **Figure 6.15**
Applications like Norton AntiVirus help administrators detect infected files.
What other tools are used to protect the network?

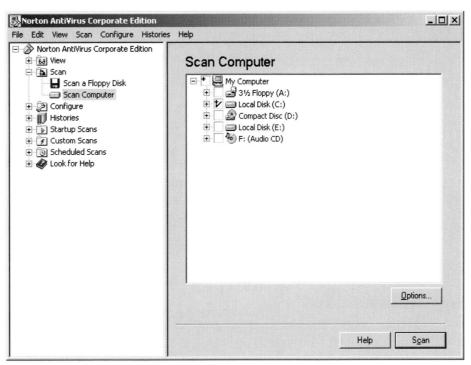

Network Backup and Recovery Utilities

A company's data are its most important resource. For this reason, utilities to back up and restore data are an essential part of most network software. Most networks back up critical data daily, although there are a number of different strategies. For example, one strategy backs up all new or changed data daily. The entire system is backed up weekly. Once a month, the entire system is backed up, and the backup tapes are stored at an off-site location.

If a file is deleted, an administrator can easily restore the file from the previous day's backup. In a worst case scenario, such as a flood, fire, or other natural disaster, off-site tapes can be used to restore the system. Data can be backed up to a variety of removable media, including floppy disks, writable CD or DVD, or tape. Although slow, tape is the most commonly used backup media because of its low cost and high capacity.

OTHER SERVER SOFTWARE

In addition to administration tools, servers run a number of other specialized software applications. Servers in smaller organizations can often run many of these services simultaneously. However, in larger companies, it is more common to find each service running on a server dedicated to just that function.

E-mail and SMTP

An e-mail server acts as the central post office for an organization. This electronic post office is actually split into two distinct functions: sending and receiving messages.

Incoming messages are received by a server called a POP3 server. **POP** stands for **Post Office Protocol** and the 3 stands for the current version in use. The POP3 server scans incoming messages and organizes them by the addressee. When you send a message to jim@somewhere.com, a POP3 server at somewhere.com places the message you sent in the mailbox or file belonging to "jim."

Outgoing messages are sent through an SMTP server. SMTP stands for **Simple Mail Transfer Protocol.** The SMTP server must perform several jobs in order to send a message. Suppose Jeff, an accountant, needs to send a message to Holli, a client of his who works at Busy Business. Jeff's message, addressed to Holli@busybusiness.com is sent by Jeff's e-mail client to his SMTP server. The SMTP server locates the domain name, busybusiness.com. To send the message, the domain name must be resolved into an IP address. The SMTP server contacts a DNS server to locate the IP address of busybusiness.com. The DNS server sends back this address. Then, the SMTP server at Jeff's company contacts the SMTP server at busybusiness.com. If Holli@busybusiness.com is indeed a valid address, Jeff's SMTP server sends the message to the POP3 server at busybusiness.com. Most e-mail servers can be configured to block certain types of attachments, or can automatically scan messages for viruses, helping to keep the network safe.

YOU TRY IT

ACTIVITY 6D Configuring E-mail Accounts

A common task performed by a network administrator is configuring user e-mail accounts. In this activity, you will configure an e-mail account using Microsoft Outlook on Windows 2000.

Note: Your school may or may not use POP3 mail servers. If not, you can follow most of these instructions to understand how to do this. However, you may not be able to complete the entire exercise.

❶ Open the **Control Panel.**

❷ Double-click the **Mail** icon.

❸ Click the **E-mail Accounts** button.

❹ Click the **View or change existing e-mail accounts** option, and then click **Next.**

❺ Click **Add.**

❻ Click **POP3,** and then click **Next.**

7 Enter the information requested (see Figure 6.16). Ask your teacher for the server name and other information you need to enter. Most POP3 and SMTP server names are something like **pop3.mycompany.com** and **smtp.mycompany.com**.

8 After you have completed the required information, click the **Test Account Settings** button to test the connection to your mail servers. If everything is entered correctly, you should see a confirmation page acknowledging your ability to send and receive e-mail. If not, recheck your settings and try again.

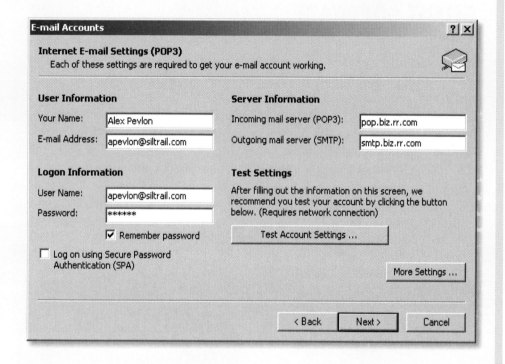

← ● **Figure 6.16**
POP servers organize incoming e-mail.

9 Unless instructed by your teacher, do not save your settings. Click **Cancel** to close the dialog box.

This activity covers the basics of how to configure an e-mail account. However, it is good to recognize that the specific nature of exact e-mail server addresses are different for every organization.

Groupware

Groupware represents a special class of software. This class is often referred to as workgroup productivity software. Groupware can generally be divided into two types, though many groupware applications provide the functionality of both types. One type of groupware can provide centralized scheduling, e-mail, and even telephone utility services to users on a LAN. Microsoft Exchange, Lotus Notes, or Novell GroupWise are examples of this type of groupware software.

Team groupware, another type of groupware, permits users located at remote sites to collaborate on projects. For example, using groupware, team members can:

◆ Participate in online meetings.
◆ Present online presentations.
◆ Share documents for team review.
◆ Share applications.
◆ Assign tasks to team members.
◆ Track progress of assigned tasks.
◆ Use an electronic "whiteboard" to draw diagrams to communicate ideas.

CLIENT SOFTWARE

Client software runs on the client machine, rather than on the server. One example of client software is an e-mail application, such as Eudora or Microsoft Outlook. Client software requires server software to do all the things it is supposed to do. When a user sends the message, an e-mail server contacts the recipient's e-mail server to verify that the address really exists, and sends the message. The same server software handles receiving and distributing incoming e-mail messages.

In some networks, such as Novell NetWare, client software is used for all network access functions. This client software is loaded and configured on each machine. Then, the software loads automatically each time the computer boots. Microsoft OSs, such as Windows 2000 and Windows XP Professional, have built-in networking client software.

Section 6.3 Assessment

Concept Check

1. Define administrative tools, domain, group, Microsoft Active Directory, Novell Directory Services (NDS), Post Office Protocol (POP), Simple Mail Transfer Protocol (SMTP), and groupware.

2. List the directory services of each of the major NOSs.

3. Identify two distinct functions of an e-mail server.

4. Explain some of the functions common in groupware products. Give examples of each.

Critical Thinking

5. Analyze Information Explain what client software is. Provide examples and explain how it differs from server software.

6. Sequence Information List the steps taken when an e-mail message is sent. Include the steps taken by the SMTP server to locate the destination and deliver the message.

7. Hypothesize Explain why it is important to store backup data off site periodically.

Applying Skills

Explore Security Threats Security threats impact everyone who connects to the Internet. One of the most important jobs of a network administrator is to stay current on emerging threats. Use the Internet to find information about a recent virus. Write a summary report that describes the security threat and how it can be stopped.

SECTION 6.1 Common Operating Systems

Key Terms

Uniplexed Information and Computing System (UNIX), 166
graphical user interface (GUI), 167
Disk Operating System (DOS), 167
Macintosh, 168
Windows, 169
Linux, 170
open source, 170

Main Ideas

- UNIX is one of the oldest and most powerful OSs.
- DOS was first used on the IBM PC.
- Macintosh OS popularized the GUI interface.
- Windows became the most popular OS in the world.
- Linux is a derivative of UNIX and can run on almost any type of computer.
- Novell NetWare is a NOS and is hardware independent.

SECTION 6.2 Graphical User Interface

Key Terms

menu system, 174
file system directory, 175
tree structure, 175
file allocation table (FAT), 176
NT file system (NTFS), 176
Hierarchical File System (HFS), 176
Extended File System Version 2 (EXT2), 176

Main Ideas

- GUI interfaces make computers easier to use.
- Icons use pictures to represent objects on the computer.
- Menus organize common commands.
- Help systems can teach users how to use software.
- File directory systems are used to organize files and directories.

SECTION 6.3 Network Operating System Software

Key Terms

administrative tools, 179
domain, 179
group, 179
Microsoft Active Directory, 180
Novell Directory Services (NDS), 180
Post Office Protocol (POP), 182
Simple Mail Transfer Protocol (SMTP), 182
groupware, 183

Main Ideas

- NOSs provide administrative tools, called directory services, to manage the network.
- Network services provide e-mail and groupware services.
- Password policies are used to help prevent unauthorized access to the network.
- Antivirus software monitors files for virus and Trojan horse programs and helps protect the network.
- Client software runs on the local machine and interacts with server software to provide full services.

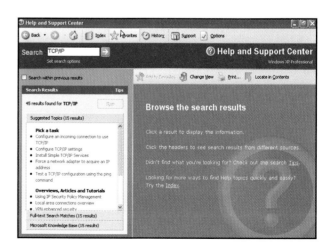

Reviewing Key Terms

1. Explain what a graphical user interface is. How is it more user-friendly than a text-based interface?
2. Describe domain.
3. What is a file system directory?
4. What does open source mean?
5. Describe a tree structure. Give an example of when using a tree structure would be helpful in networking.

Understanding Main Ideas

6. Explain how groups are used to manage access to files on a network.
7. Describe how programming in the C language contributed to the success of the Unix operating system.
8. Explain how software companies can sell Linux, an open source operating system, for profit.
9. List the administrative tools offered by a network operating system.
10. Analyze why people prefer to purchase a pre-compiled version of Linux.
11. Describe the similarities and differences between an operating system and a network operating system.
12. Evaluate when password policies are used.
13. Describe the NDS security administration.
14. List the different types of groupware.
15. Explain when POP3 is used.
16. Describe the purpose of an HFS.

Critical Thinking

17. Analyze Why do GUI operating systems use windows instead of a command-line interface to accept input and display program output? What role do windows play in multitasking?
18. Diagram Create a diagram showing how a computer's hardware, OS, and applications communicate with the network to which they are connected.
19. Draw Conclusions Explain why, in large networks, certain important processes usually run by themselves on dedicated computers. Why not just have multiple computers, each working on several tasks simultaneously?
20. Compare and Contrast Discuss the similarities and differences among the file allocation table (FAT/FAT32) file system used by Microsoft Windows, the Hierarchical File System (HFS) used by the Mac OS, and the Extended File System Version 2 (EXT2) used by most Linux operating systems.
21. Explain Describe how SMTP uses domain names to send and receive e-mail messages.
22. Make Recommendations List at least four features of an operating system that you frequently use. Predict how these features might be improved for future versions of the operating system.

e-Review ···················

networking.glencoe.com

Study with PowerPoint

To review the main points in this chapter, select **e-Review** > **PowerPoint Outlines** > **Chapter 6**.

Online Self Check

Test your knowledge of the material in this chapter by selecting **e-Review** > **Self Checks** > **Chapter 6**.

Making Connections

Language Arts—Using Technical Documentation There are a number of technical manuals available to help you work with your operating systems. Some are easy to read and understand, while others are more difficult. These manuals can be found on the Internet, in your classroom, and in the OS itself.

a. Locate the technical documentation for the operating systems used on the computers in your lab or classroom.

b. Find and read the instructions on how to create, view, and delete directories or folders.

c. With your teacher's permission, actually create, view, and delete directories or folders based on the instructions you found.

d. Evaluate which documentation was the easiest to read and understand. Explain your reasoning.

STANDARDS AT WORK

Technology problem-solving and decision-making tools. Students use technology resources for solving problems and making informed decisions. (NETS-S 6)

Communicating Information

Each operating system has its own set of utilities for backing up and recovering data.

Explore your operating system's tools for handling these tasks and answer the following questions:

1. What kinds of data does the utility back up and recover?

2. What are the steps to back up the data? Write out the steps so another user can easily follow the directions.

3. What are the steps to restore data? Write out the steps so another user can easily follow the directions.

4. How often do you think data on your computer should be backed up? Explain your answer.

TEAMWORK SKILLS

Cooperative Learning

Following your teacher's instructions, form small groups. Identify a complicated task that computer users complete using the operating system or an application.

1. Write a help file, describing in detail how to accomplish that task using the chosen operating system or application. Do not look at any help files that already exist.

2. Work as a group to determine the exact steps required to complete the task.

3. When you are finished, trade help files with another group. Follow their instructions and provide any feedback to clarify instructions.

4. When your group receives its help file, make any necessary changes based on the feedback provided.

CHALLENGE YOURSELF

Use a Command-Based OS

On a computer using the Windows OS, go to the command prompt. Use the following commands to browse through and save the contents of your computer's "Program Files" directory to a file:

1. At the command prompt, type cd [name]. This changes the current directory to [name]. The [name] directory may be a full path, such as c:\Windows\System, or simply the name of another directory in the current directory.

2. At the command prompt, type cd .. . This moves to the directory one level above the current directory, that is, the directory in which the current directory resides.

3. Type dir /p to show the contents of the current directory, pausing after each page for large directories.

4. Type dir > [filename].txt to saves the contents of the current directory to a text file with the given name.

5. Using DOS help files, find the appropriate print command to print the text file. Print the text file.

YOU TRY IT
Networking Lab

1. Creating a Batch File

People who use command-based operating systems often execute the same sequence of commands many times to accomplish a repetitive task. Most OSs that accept text commands offer a way to create a collection of commands, saved as a file, that can be executed without retyping each command again. DOS saves such collections as "batch" files with the extension .bat.

In this activity, you create a batch file using the standard DOS text-editing command, edit. You must be careful when creating batch files, especially if you use the del or deltree command to delete files or folders because running such commands from the wrong directory may destroy important data.

Use the following steps to write a simple batch file on a computer running Windows 9x or above:

Ⓐ At the command prompt, type cd plus the letter of your computer's main hard drive and press **Enter** (for example cd C:\).

Ⓑ Type edit testbat.bat and press **Enter.** This creates a new batch file and opens it in the editor.

Ⓒ Type the following commands, in order, on separate lines as shown in the following example. Be certain to type them carefully and exactly as they are written to avoid unexpected behavior:

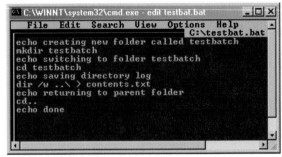

```
echo creating new folder called testbatch
mkdir testbatch
echo switching to folder testbatch
cd testbatch
echo saving directory log
dir /w ..\ > contents.txt
echo returning to parent folder
cd ..
echo done
```

Ⓓ To save the file, press the **Alt** key and open the **File** menu. Select **Save** from the menu.

Ⓔ To exit the editor, press the **Alt** key and open the **File** menu. Select **Exit** from the menu.

Ⓕ To execute the batch file, type testbat.bat at the prompt and press **Enter.**

Ⓖ Type exit to exit the command window.

Ⓗ Look for the folder named **testbatch** on your computer's main hard drive.

Ⓘ Open the file in the folder. What does it contain?

Networking Projects

1. Create a Directory Structure Diagram

In this activity, you create a tree representing the directory structure of your computer. Because most computers have hundreds, or even thousands, of directories, you only include a few of the subdirectories in each directory. Complete the following steps to create your directory tree:

Ⓐ Obtain a large sheet of paper, turned so that it is longer in the horizontal direction.

Ⓑ At the top of the sheet, at the center of the long side, draw a picture to represent the hard drive on your computer.

Ⓒ Below the picture, write the names of at least one file *and* three folders stored at the top level of your computer's file system, that is, files and folders on the hard drive and not in any other folder.

Ⓓ Write the names from left to right, connected with horizontal lines, with a single line extending upward to the hard drive. Be certain to include any folders important to the OS, such as the "Windows" and "Documents and Settings" folders in Windows, or the "System" folder in Mac OS X.

Ⓔ Below each folder, write the names of one file and a few folders that each contains, as in step C, with a line connecting them to the parent folder.

Ⓕ Continue this process, moving down through the hierarchy until you have mapped out your computer's directory structure.

2. Create Network Support

Ⓐ Find three computers running at least three different OSs.

Ⓑ For each OS, write instructions for accessing network information and directories. Your instructions should be detailed enough that a user can obtain network information and access network controls without any additional assistance.

Ⓒ In addition, provide the following information:

◆ How is the computer connected to a network?

◆ Is it necessary to change any settings to make a connection, or is it a plug and play system?

◆ What protocols does the OS use to connect to a network, send and receive mail, and so on? Note that an OS may support more than one protocol, or that the protocol may be chosen by the software responsible for a specific service.

Building 21st Century Skills

Communication Skills: Teach Operating System Basics

Networking professionals must often teach new users how to perform basic computing and networking tasks. Imagine that you are asked to teach basic computer skills to a group of novice computer users. Use a word processing application, such as Microsoft Word, to prepare a brief lesson plan or outline of several tasks.

1. List five essential tasks involving networking, such as connecting to a printer or sending an e-mail message.

2. Include specific step-by-step instructions to accomplish each task.

3. If possible, include screen shots or diagrams with the instructions.

4. Present your lesson to another student. Note any improvements your partner suggests. Then switch places. Listen carefully and follow the steps. Make suggestions to help the other student improve the presentation.

5. Update your lesson plan according to your partner's suggestions.

6. If possible, give your presentation to new networking students or to another class learning these skills.

Decision-making Skills: Calculate Media and Component Costs

Your business has just added a new building to its small group of offices. The new server room will be connected to the old server room in an existing building, which is located 500 feet away. Create a table using a spreadsheet application, such as Microsoft Excel, to list the information described below.

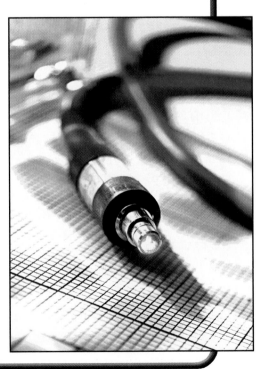

1. Make a list of cable types that could be used to wire the new room to the existing room. Don't forget to convert feet to meters to check the cable length!

2. Use the Internet or other resources to find the per-foot cost of each type of cable.

3. If necessary, list the type and cost of equipment needed to extend cables to the required length.

4. Determine costs for NICs that will work with each type of cable.

5. List the pros and cons of each type of cable.

6. Once the table is created, answer the following questions:
   - What are two types of cable that could be used? Explain your answer.
   - How much cabling will be needed?
   - How much will each cost?
   - Which solution is the most cost effective? Explain your answer.

Building Your Portfolio

Diagram Your School's Network

In any networking job you need to be able to identify the hardware components in use, operating systems used on both clients and servers throughout the network, and the protocols your network uses to communicate.

Create a diagram of the network(s) you and your teachers and administrators use at school. Your diagram will be a complete representation of the topology, hardware, operating systems, and protocols in use, as well as the different types of connections that exist between the computers and shared resources on the network.

Use the Network Diagram Checklist to help you decide what information should be included in your diagram.

To create your diagram, follow these steps:

1. On a large piece of paper, or with an application such as Microsoft Visio, draw each computer and list its operating system next to it. Identify any computers that are not connected to the network

2. Determine the type (centralized, client/server, or peer to peer) and topology (bus, ring, star, etc.) of your classroom's network(s). Add any hardware that is used in your classroom, such as hubs, switches, or wireless access points. You may need help from your teacher if these devices are not visible.

3. Repeat steps 1 and 2 for the other networks on your school's campus, including labs, classrooms, and, if possible, administrative buildings. Draw your diagrams on the same piece of paper (or document) that you started in step 1.

4. Draw the connections between the separate networks you diagrammed. If you discover that the computers in more than one classroom actually belong to the same workgroup, modify your diagram to show this configuration.

5. Add your completed diagram to your portfolio. Your diagram should now show all of the networks in use at your school. These individual networks may function together as a single overarching network, depending on how they are connected.

Network Diagram Checklist

Computers
- ☑ Operating system
- ☑ Processor type/speed
- ☑ Amount of RAM
- ☑ Size of hard drive
- ☑ Connected to network?

Network Components
- ☑ Hubs
- ☑ Switches
- ☑ Wireless Access Points

Media
- ☑ Type of media
- ☑ Show connections to network components in classroom

Servers
- ☑ Dedicated or non-dedicated
- ☑ Operating system
- ☑ Processor type/speed
- ☑ Amount of RAM
- ☑ Size of hard drive

Shared Resources
- ☑ Type of resource
- ☑ Show connection

UNIT
3

Wide Area Networks

Visit *Glencoe Online*

Go to this book's Web site at **networking.glencoe.com**.

Click on **Unit Activities** and select **Unit 3 Evaluating Web Sites.** Learn how to evaluate Web sites to make sure the information is current and reliable.

Think About It

Networks of Highways
The streets and highways you travel on every day are a kind of network. Each system of roads connects other road systems to form large networks of highways. Each road serves a specific purpose—to help keep traffic moving and connected to other networks.

Compare Networks Activity
What can happen to the flow of traffic on the road when there is construction or an accident? Describe how this is similar to what can happen to network traffic in computer networks.

Local Area Networks to Wide Area Networks

YOU WILL LEARN TO...

Section 7.1

- Explain how modems function
- Describe how satellites transmit data
- Identify the role of a multiplexer
- Explain how synchronous and asynchronous communications work

Section 7.2

- Explain different computer numbering systems
- Demonstrate how to convert numerical values between decimal, binary, and hexadecimal systems

Section 7.3

- Describe different transmission technologies that can run on POTS
- Explain how various digital transmission technologies work

WHY IT MATTERS.....................................

Using a variety of technologies, including satellites and the Internet, climbers can use cell phones or other wireless devices on a mountaintop. Remote expeditions can even broadcast live transmissions using wide area networks (WANs). This illustrates the idea of the "shrinking globe," where we can now communicate with anyone virtually anywhere on the planet at any time.

Quick Write Activity

Write about a time in your life when some form of technology helped you communicate with someone far away. How did the technology you communicated through help you learn more about this person?

WHAT YOU WILL DO...

READ TO SUCCEED

Get Creative

An excellent way to stay engaged in your reading is to make associations while you read. For example, drawing an image of a piece of computer hardware and labeling it reinforces your memory. Thinking of an easy-to-remember rhyme or setting a series of short steps to music is another way to help your brain make associations for easier recall. Your memory trick doesn't have to be beautiful or impressive—it only has to mean something to you.

Section 7.1 Communications

Guide to Reading

Main Ideas
Modems are one of the most common ways for computers to connect to each other. Satellite systems are used to connect WANs across the globe. Multiplexers are a key component of WAN technology. Transmissions can be asynchronous or synchronous.

Key Terms
V series
AT command set
PC Card standards
cable modem
geostationary earth orbit (GEO)
medium-earth orbit (MEO)
low-earth orbit (LEO)
asynchronous
synchronous
frame

Reading Strategy
Identify each main topic you read about in this section. List two details about each topic. Create a chart similar to the one below (also available online).

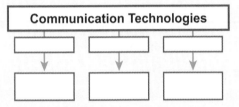

Communication Technologies

Before satellites began digitally transmitting data over WANs, modems were the primary means of connecting two computers over long distances. Modems are still the method most people use to access the Internet at home. However, they are quickly being replaced by newer, faster technologies, such as ISDN, DSL, and cable modems.

MODEMS

Figure 7.1
Modems modulate and demodulate computer-to-computer transmissions by converting digital signals to analog form. **How do modems act like translators?**

The term modem comes from the two primary tasks it performs: **mo**dulation and **dem**odulation. Modulation is the process of changing the digital signal to an analog signal on the sending computer. Demodulation is the process of converting the analog signal back to a digital signal on the receiving computer. In many ways, a modem is like a language translator (see Figure 7.1).

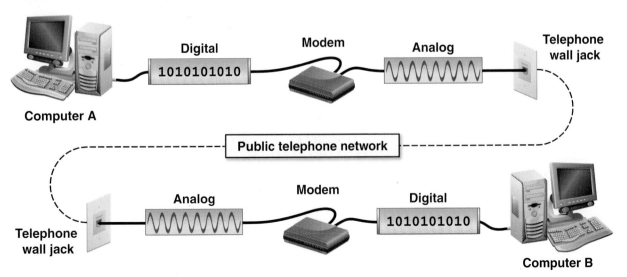

Modem Standards

Almost since they were invented, modems have been identified with two different sets of standards, the V series and Hayes-compatible standards.

V Series Standards The first important set of standards was developed by AT&T in the 1970s and early 1980s. These were known as the Bell standards. These standards applied to modems operating at speeds of 300 and 1200 bps. The **V series** of standards covers today's modems, with speeds up to 56 Kbps. These standards were developed by the Comité Consultatif International Téléphonique et Télégraphique (CCITT). Several of the V series standards are noted in Table 7.1.

SHOW ME!

How Modems Work View Show Me 7.1 through Show Me 7.5 at networking.glencoe.com to see how modems transmit data.

Modem Standards	
Standard	**Definition**
V.42bis	Older compression standard for 56 Kbps transmission
V.44	Compression standard optimized for Web access
V.90	Combines the two technologies used in 56 Kbps transmission: x2 from 3Com/U.S. Robotics and K56flex from Rockwell
V.92	Improved standard for 56 Kbps modems that works hand in hand with V.44 to improve Web access and upload speeds

Table 7.1
V series modem standards are used for today's modems. Who is responsible for the V series modem standards?

Hayes-Compatible Standards A special set of commands for controlling modems, called the **AT command set,** was developed by Hayes Microcomputer Products. For example, the **ATL0** command turned the modem speaker down, whereas the **ATM0** command turned the speaker completely off. These commands were so popular that other manufacturers adopted them and advertised their modems as "Hayes-compatible." Almost all modems manufactured today are Hayes-compatible.

PC Card Standards Once known as Personal Computer Memory Card International Association (PCMCIA) cards, **PC Card standards** target a broad range of devices, including modems, intended for laptop users. These cards are known for their versatility, small size, and their ability to be hot swappable (see Figure 7.2). Hot swappable means that you can plug in a modem PC Card when a dial-up connection is needed. Then it can be swapped for a micro hard drive to store a large file without shutting down the notebook.

READ ME!

Jargon The *bis* or *ter* portion of the standard name indicates that the number refers to a revision (bis) or a revision of a revision (ter) of the original recommendation. The words are derived from the Latin for second (*bis*) and third (*ter*).

Figure 7.2
PC cards add new capabilities to laptops. Why is the ability to "hot swap" PC cards an important feature?

Performance

In theory, the fastest data transmission rate for analog phone lines is 33.6 Kbps. However, developments in the past few decades enabled modem speeds to transmit at 56 Kbps (56K, for short). They can achieve this speed because many telephone companies have steadily been moving to digital technologies.

Today, most of the telephone network is digital. Most of the transmission can travel along super fast digital channels, and it only needs to be converted and transmitted as an analog signal when it hits the wire system connecting to a house. Because the signal is only converted once, less data are lost.

However, the 56K transmissions can occur in only one direction: downstream. A downstream transmission is an incoming transmission to the modem. The upstream, or outgoing transmission from the modem, is limited to 45 Kbps. This is because the upstream flow involves more than a single digital-to-analog conversion. Every time the signal is converted, more *noise* is introduced. Noise, in this case, is garbage that is added to the signal. This reduces the quality of the signal and slows the speed of transmission. 56K technologies are effective as long as:

◆ 56K technologies are in effect from end to end (if a user on the other end has a 33.6K modem, you are both stuck at the lower speed).

◆ The transmission involves only one analog-to-digital conversion.

◆ The connection to the server is digital.

◆ The phone line is not noisy.

YOU TRY IT

ACTIVITY 7A Installing an Internal Modem

Installing a modem is another fundamental networking skill. Although many computers are now shipped with modems already installed, you may need to upgrade or troubleshoot modems in your network.

With your teacher's permission, perhaps using a test computer, perform the following:

1 Be certain you are grounded. Discharge any static energy before dealing with any electronic equipment. Do this by touching something metal that is in contact with the ground—a table or chair, for instance.

2 Turn the computer off, unplug the computer, and disconnect all peripheral devices plugged into the computer.

3 Remove the computer cover.

4 Locate an available PCI slot.

5 Insert the modem card into the slot. Be certain the card is seated completely in the slot.

6 Replace the cover.

7 Plug in all peripheral devices, including the network cable and phone cable.

8 Plug the computer in, and turn it on.

 networking.glencoe.com

9 Configure your modem:

◆ If your computer uses a plug and play compatible operating system (such as Windows 2000, Windows XP, or Mac OS X), follow the instructions to configure your modem.

◆ If necessary, use the driver disk that comes with your modem to configure the modem.

10 To test whether your modem is properly installed and configured, open the **Control Panel** and double-click **Phone and Modem Options.**

11 Select the **Modem** tab and click **Properties.**

12 Select the **Diagnostics** tab and click **Query Modem.** The computer will then try to find and communicate with your modem. If the communication is successful, you will receive a notification. If it is not, you will receive an error message like the one shown in Figure 7.3. You may need to see if the modem is properly seated in the slot. Also make sure that the phone cable is properly plugged into the back of the computer and the wall jack.

It is also good to understand this process when working over the phone with customers. You will be able to step the customer through the installation process.

● **Figure 7.3**
If the modem is not responding, you can use Help to assist you in diagnosing the problem.

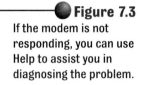

Types of Modems

New technologies are poised to replace traditional modem technology. Some of these new "modems" technically do not perform the same job as a standard modem. However, since they allow your computer to interface with the Internet, they are still called modems.

Cable Modems To get faster transmission rates, a **cable modem** uses a cable television connection. A cable modem downloads information at rates from 10 Mbps to about 36 Mbps. Like traditional modems, cable modems are faster downstream than upstream. Although an upstream rate of 10 Mbps is possible, a maximum of 2 Mbps is more likely. Altogether, a working cable modem connection involves a system of devices, as shown in Figure 7.4.

ISDN Modems Integrated Services Digital Network (ISDN) transmissions are digital, and provide bandwidths of up to about 2 Mbps. ISDN modems are not

● **Figure 7.4**
Cable modems use bandwidth available for cable TV. What is the potential download speed for a cable modem connection?

Typical Home Cable Modem Installation

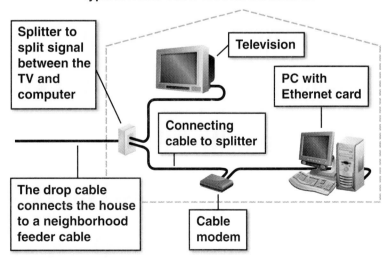

really modems. An ISDN adapter adapts the signals—which are transmitted in several separate channels—to the communications standards understood by the computer. ISDN is covered in more detail later in this chapter.

DSL Modems Another type of digital communications technology is called Digital Subscriber Line (DSL). DSL is a fast transmission technology, with transfer rates of up to 7 Mbps. DSL requires two specialized modems: one connected to the computer accessing the Internet or other network, and another installed at the phone company. DSL comes in a wide range of types and transmission speeds. We cover DSL modems later in the chapter.

SATELLITE SYSTEMS

Large WANs separated by oceans or other geographic boundaries often use satellite systems as the best means to connect and transfer data. Satellites can carry all sorts of data, including television, telecommunications (telephone calls), and computer data.

Satellites orbit Earth in one of three tiers. Fewer satellites are required for global coverage at higher altitudes. Satellites in a **geostationary earth orbit (GEO)** fly at 22,000 miles above Earth. From this position, only about eight satellites are needed to cover the entire planet. Imagine placing Earth inside a huge box, with a satellite at each corner of the box. Because of the distances involved, it is more expensive to launch satellites into a GEO because more fuel is required. Also, the satellite must be capable of generating a more powerful signal to transmit its data back to Earth. GEOs are fixed in a stationary position, which means they always "look" at the same point on Earth (see Figure 7.5).

Satellites orbiting between 6,250 and 12,500 miles above Earth are in a **medium-earth orbit (MEO).** Because of their closer proximity to Earth, about 20 satellites are required to create a constellation of satellites. A constellation of satellites is a group of satellites working together to provide global communications coverage. MEOs have less round-trip latency than GEOs. Latency is the time it takes for a transmission to go from one point to another.

Low-earth orbit (LEO) satellites orbit between 310 and 1,240 miles above Earth. From their low position, LEOs have much higher rates of transmission. However, it takes nearly 48 satellites to form a constellation of satellites, all of which must be in position before data can be transmitted.

Figure 7.5
Satellites are used to transmit all types of communications data. Why is it more expensive to use a geostationary earth orbit?

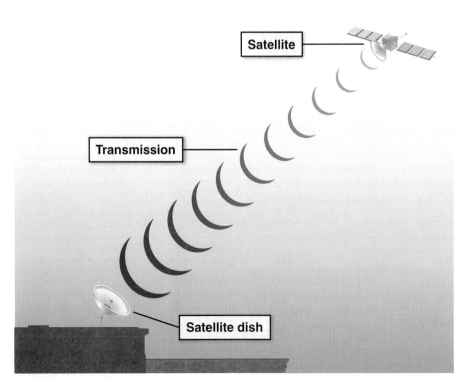

Satellite

Transmission

Satellite dish

MULTIPLEXERS

Multiplexers are commonly used in WANs. Several data signals are combined from many sources into a single signal, which is fed into one cable transmission. Transmitting data in this manner reduces cost.

On the sending end, a multiplexer, also known as a "mux," is used to combine the signal. At the receiving end, a demultiplexer, or "demux," is used to break the high data rate stream back into its original lower rate stream. Normally, the multiplexer and demultiplexer are built into a single piece of equipment. Multiplexing can be achieved using several different methods.

- **Frequency Division Multiplexing (FDM)** assigns each signal to a different frequency.
- **Time Division Multiplexing (TDM)** assigns each signal a fixed time frame that rotates in a fixed order between each signal.
- **Statistical Time Division Multiplexing (STDM)** dynamically assigns time slots to signals. This allows the bandwidth to be utilized more fully. It is also the most common method used for cell phone transmissions.
- **Wavelength Division Multiplexing (WDM)** assigns each signal to a particular wavelength. This type of multiplexing is used in conjunction with fiber optics.

TRANSMISSION TYPES

For two computers to communicate, they must exchange data in a form that both can recognize and handle. The rules of the game are dictated by standards and protocols. On the broadest levels, transmissions are divided into two basic types: asynchronous and synchronous.

Asynchronous Transmissions

Modems typically rely on serial, asynchronous transmission. Communications that are not governed by timing are called **asynchronous.** In other words, the sending and receiving computers do not have to synchronize timing before a transmission can take place. The sending computer can transmit when it is ready, stop, and transmit again after an indeterminate time period. The receiving computer is able to determine where any particular byte—representing one character—begins and ends within the flow of transmitted bits.

Until now, we have primarily discussed bits, those long strings of 1s and 0s that computers are so fond of. Bytes, a group of eight bits, form a fundamental unit of measure for computer data. Take a look at what this string of bits—representing the letters **h** and **i**—looks like, as shown in Figure 7.6.

When data are transmitted asynchronously, the receiving computer cannot rely on timing to determine where each byte starts and stops. The computer uses start bits and stop bits. These bits act as signals that frame the bits making up

● **Figure 7.6**

Each 8-bit sequence forms a byte, representing one character. What is the difference between a bit and a byte?

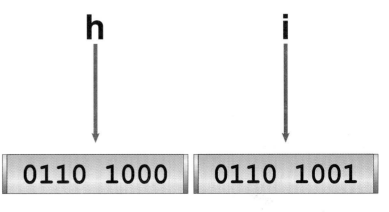

h

i

0110 1000   0110 1001

Figure 7.7

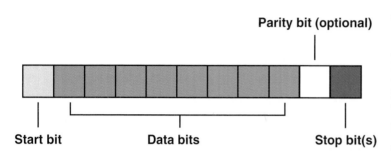

Figure 7.7
Asynchronous transmissions rely on start and stop bits to mark the beginning and end of a character. What is the parity bit used for?

one character. The start bit indicates the start of the character. The stop bit marks the end of the character. Between the start and stop bits are the bits representing the character itself. An optional additional bit, known as the parity bit, is used for error checking. A byte transmitted asynchronously could be diagrammed as shown in Figure 7.7.

Parity bit (optional)

Start bit   Data bits   Stop bit(s)

Synchronous Transmissions

Asynchronous transmission is the norm for modem-to-modem communications. However, digital systems and networks rely more on **synchronous** communications. This method results in faster transmissions, but it is also more complex and more expensive. In asynchronous transmissions, the "building blocks" are bytes delineated by start and stop bits. In synchronous transmissions, the "building blocks" are based on **frames:** blocks of bits separated by equal time intervals.

To communicate synchronously, the sending and receiving computers must coordinate closely. Internal clocks in each computer help coordinate this communication. Before and during transmission, both computers use special synchronizing characters to initiate communication and to carry out periodic checks on the accuracy of the timing. Synchronous communications are required in high-precision, fast-moving environments, such as an automobile factory. Data must be passed precisely at known intervals to machines for the manufacturing process to continue without interruption.

Section 7.1 Assessment

Concept Check

1. **Define** V series, AT command set, PC Card standards, cable modem, geostationary earth orbit (GEO), medium-earth orbit (MEO), low-earth orbit (LEO), asynchronous, synchronous, and frame.

2. **Explain** the job performed by a modem.

3. **Describe** a satellite data transmission.

4. **Identify** what "muxing" is.

Critical Thinking

5. **Draw Conclusions** Explain how advances to telephone systems enabled modems to transmit at speeds higher than the supposed 33.6K limit.

6. **Evaluate Information** Create a list of the three orbits commonly used by communications satellites, the distances each orbit covers, and the number of satellites required in each orbit to create a constellation.

Applying Skills

Research High-Speed Internet Options Not all high-speed Internet technologies are available in certain areas. Find out which technologies are available in your area and create a table that summarizes the costs and transmission speeds of each technology.

TEAMWORK SKILLS

As a network professional, you will be part of a group or team. You will be working with administrators, coworkers, customers, and possibly your own networking team. For this reason, you must have people skills as well as technology skills.

Teamwork requires good communication skills.

Meeting Needs
Whether you are a hardware technician or a network administrator, your success depends on how well you meet the different needs of the people who use your network. Your employers may have a budget you must follow. A customer might have specific security requirements. A coworker might need to access e-mail away from the office.

You have the knowledge to solve problems. But first, you have to be certain you understand what the problem is.

Communicating
Networking is a technical field and many of the people you work with will not understand networking technology. This makes it essential to sharpen your communication skills.

Here are some communication tips:

- Listen carefully without interrupting.
- Ask questions to ensure you understand what an individual wants.
- Use language that people understand. Most people will not understand networking jargon.
- Be polite and sympathetic. Stay positive even if you do not agree with someone.

Collaborating
Collaborating means cooperating. Team members need collaboration skills to solve problems and to complete tasks effectively. To collaborate productively, consider the following guidelines:

- Team members with different skills should be assigned roles that suit their interests and abilities.
- Decisions can be made by voting or negotiating. Teams should work out procedures for solving conflicts and working toward agreements.
- Teams should develop communication strategies. Members can use meetings, e-mail, phone calls, or other methods to exchange work and ideas on a regular basis.

Tech Focus

1. Can you explain networking concepts clearly? Teach a friend or family member about a basic networking concept, such as simple LAN topology or data transmission.

2. In a group, work out the ideal modes of communication for team members to stay in touch at all times. Use those methods to collaborate on a report. Describe the communication methods and skills your team used to collaborate.

Guide to Reading

Main Ideas

Computers use numerical values to transmit data. Computers understand only binary numbers. Hexadecimal is a numbering system that simplifies complex binary numbers. Decimal is a numbering system people use.

Key Terms

decimal
base 10
binary
base 2
bit
hexadecimal
base 16
American Standard Code for
 Information Interchange (ASCII)
Extended Binary Coded Decimal
 Interchange Code (EBCDIC)
Unicode

Reading Strategy

Compare the values of base 2, base 10, and base 16 to each other through the power of 7. Create a chart similar to the one below (also available online).

Power	Base 2	Base 10	Base 16
0			
1			
2			
3			
4			
5			

No matter what technology is used to send data around a network or the Internet, all data must be converted into numerical values. The only values that computers understand are 1s and 0s. Humans speak a variety of languages, use many types of complex characters to represent linguistic concepts, and use different numbering systems. Through various conversion and encoding processes, computers are quite capable of handling all of this complexity.

NUMBERING SYSTEMS

To fully understand computers and how data are transmitted between computers, you need to understand a few things about numbering systems. There are many different methods for representing numerical data. For example, the following shows different ways to represent the concept of "27."

```
27
XXVII
```

Decimal System

The **decimal** system is based on the use of ten digits (0, 1, 2, 3, 4, 5, 6, 7, 8, and 9). The number of digits forms the base of the system. Ten symbols give us **base 10.** Each column of digits from left to right in a decimal number represents another power of ten. The value 3,245 is broken down in the box.

$$3 \times 1000 = 3000 = 3 \times 10^3$$
$$2 \times 100 = 200 = 2 \times 10^2$$
$$4 \times 10 = 40 = 4 \times 10^1$$
$$5 \times 1 = 5 = 5 \times 10^0$$

This is the system that you have been using since you first learned to count. To distinguish base 10 values from other numbering systems, these values are often noted with a subscript$_{10}$. So, $1,245_{10}$ indicates that the value is noted in base 10.

networking.glencoe.com

Binary System

The most important system for computers is the **binary** system. The binary system uses only two digits: 1 and 0. Because of this, it is called **base 2.** This numbering system is critical for computers, which only understand two concepts: on (1) and off (0). A binary digit is commonly called a **bit,** which is a combination of **b**inary dig**it.**

Each digit has a position in the binary system. The position represents a different power of two. Table 7.2 shows the first eight positions of the binary system.

Position Values of an 8-bit Binary Number								
Position	8th	7th	6th	5th	4th	3rd	2nd	1st
Power of Two	2^7	2^6	2^5	2^4	2^3	2^2	2^1	2^0
Value$_{10}$	128	64	32	16	8	4	2	1

Table 7.2
Each position of a binary number signifies a higher power of two. Why do computers "think" in binary?

Each position of a binary number represents a different power of 2. The binary number 11 (pronounced "one one") has two positions. This number's conversion would look like the following:

$$2^0 = 1 = 1 \times 1$$
$$2^1 = 2 = 2 \times 1$$

Adding these together gives us $2 + 1 = 3$. Table 7.3 compares decimal and binary values zero through fifteen.

Decimal and Binary Representations			
Decimal	**Binary**	**Decimal**	**Binary**
0	0	11	1011
1	1	12	1100
2	10	13	1101
3	11	14	1110
4	100	15	1111
5	101	16	0001 0000
6	110	17	0001 0001
7	111	18	0001 0010
8	1000	19	0001 0011
9	1001	20	0001 0100
10	1010	21	0001 0101

Table 7.3
This table lists decimal and binary values. How would you translate a number from decimal to binary?

ACTIVITY 7B Converting Decimal Numbers to Binary Numbers

Converting decimal numbers to binary numbers and back is an important skill. For example, when setting up a network, such conversions help to configure IP addresses and subnet masks (covered in Chapter 9). This activity uses the value 187. Then, you will try a few conversions on your own.

1 On your own paper, create a table like the one below (Table 7.4).

2 Start at the left column. Does 187 have the value 128 in it? $(187 - 128 = 59)$ Yes, so write **1** in the left column.

3 Use the remainder 59. Does 59 have the value 64 in it? $(59 - 64 = -5)$ No, so write **0** in the second column.

4 Does 59 have the value 32 in it? $(59 - 32 = 27)$ Yes, write **1** in the third column.

5 Repeat steps 3 and 4 until you get to the last column. You should end up with the binary 1011 1011. (Binary numbers are written in groups of four, with a space between each grouping.)

6 Fill in the rest of your table, converting the decimal numbers 200 and 84 to binary numbers.

Table 7.4
The decimal system is based on base 10.

Decimal Conversion Worksheet

Decimal Number	Binary Values								Binary Number
	128	64	32	16	8	4	2	1	
187	1	0	1	1	1	0	1	1	1011 1011
200									
84									

7 Now convert binary to decimal numbers. Create a table like the one below (Table 7.5). For every column in row two with a "1," write the corresponding value from row one in row three. Otherwise, write "0." Based on the binary value 1011 1011, you should write 128, 0, 32, 16, 8, 0, 2, 1 in row three.

8 Add the values in row three $(128 + 0 + 32 + 16 + 8 + 0 + 2 + 1 = 187)$.

9 Fill in the rest of your table, converting the binary numbers to decimal numbers.

Table 7.5
Base 2 is the numbering system for binary.

Binary Conversion Worksheet

Binary Number	Binary Values								Decimal Number
	128	64	32	16	8	4	2	1	
1011 1011	128	0	32	16	8	0	2	1	187
1011 1101									
1111 1111									

Practice converting values from binary to decimal and back again on your own.

READ ME!

Tech Tip Binary numbers are often indicated with a subscript$_2$. The value 10_2 indicates that this is a binary value.

Hexadecimal System

Binary digits are difficult to read, particularly when you are faced with large values. One way to simplify these values is to use a different system, called hexadecimal. In **hexadecimal,** 16 characters are used for each place, including the numerals 0 to 9 and the letters A to F. Hexadecimal is called **base 16.** Base 16 values are often noted with a subscript$_{16}$. Hexadecimal is commonly used in HTML documents to represent color values, which are often broken down into three 8-bit values representing various amounts of red, green, and blue.

Counting in hexadecimal from 0 to 16 is shown in Table 7.6.

● **Table 7.6**
HTML documents use hexadecimal to show color values. How are these values broken down?

Base 16																
Number	0	1	2	3	4	5	6	7	8	9	10	11	12	13	14	15	16
Hexadecimal	0	1	2	3	4	5	6	7	8	9	A	B	C	D	E	F	10

Why does $10_{16} = 16_{10}$? First, look at Table 7.7 to see the value of each column in a hexadecimal number.

The far right position represents the values 0 to 15. The second position represents the values 0 to 15 *times* 16^1. From left to right, the value 10_{16} is calculated as follows:

$$1 \times 16^1 = 16$$
$$0 \times 16^0 = 0$$
$$16 + 0 = 16$$

● **Table 7.7**
Each position of a hexadecimal number represents a power of 16. Why is the hexadecimal system used?

Hexadecimal Column Values				
Position	4	3	2	1
Power of Sixteen	16^3	16^2	16^1	16^0
Value$_{10}$	4096	256	16	1

ACTIVITY 7C Converting Binary to Hexadecimal

YOU TRY IT

Converting from binary to hexadecimal is often easier when you break the binary value into 4-bit chunks, or quartets, and convert each "chunk" into decimal. The value $1011\ 1011_2$ from the previous activity will be used here.

❶ Break the first quartet of bits, and convert it to hexadecimal: $1011_2 = 11_{10} = B_{16}$.

❷ Convert the second quartet to hexadecimal. This provides the value BB_{16} as shown in Table 7.8.

● **Table 7.8**
Make short work of converting binary to hexadecimal to decimal by working with separate quartets of binary values.

Converting Binary to Hexadecimal to Decimal		
Value	**Operation**	**Calculation**
1011 1011	Separate into quartets and convert to decimal	Binary 1011 to decimal (digit values from right to left): 1 + 2 + 0 + 8 = 11
11 (decimal)	Convert to hexadecimal	11 in decimal equals B in hexadecimal, both quartets together = BB
BB (hexadecimal)	Convert each digit to decimal	B in the first (right) digit equals 11×16^0 equals 11 B in the second (left) digit equals 11×16^1 equals 176
	Add together the value of each hexadecimal digit	176 + 11 = 187

❸ Now convert the hexadecimal back to decimal. Multiply the value of each column by the power of 16. In hex, B = 11_{10}.

    a. $11 \times 16^1 = 176$

    b. $11 \times 16^0 = 11$

    c. $176 + 11 = 187$

❹ On your own, convert the following values:

    a. 248_{10} (convert to hex)

    b. $C4_{16}$ (convert to decimal)

    c. $1001\ 0111\ 1011\ 1010_2$ (convert to hex)

TEXT REPRESENTATION

Normal communication among people is not numerical in nature. Most of the time, you use words to communicate with other people via e-mail or word processing documents. How does the computer transmit something like "Hello"? The answer is that letters are replaced by numerical values. In addition to numerical systems, there are text-representation systems.

ASCII

American Standard Code for Information Interchange (ASCII) is one of the oldest and most commonly used binary codes. In the ASCII system, each letter, character, or nonprinting character is given a specific numerical code. For example, character 'A' is 65 in decimal numbering or 41 in hexadecimal. 'Z' is 90_{10} or $5A_{16}$. Nonprinting characters such as Space and Tab are represented by 32_{10} and 9_{10}, respectively.

As people began to use more complex characters, an extended set of additional characters was developed. Although there are some variations, the ASCII set of codes is limited to 255 characters.

EBCDIC

Extended Binary Coded Decimal Interchange Code (EBCDIC) was developed for IBM computers. EBCDIC values were assigned for easy use with punch cards. Punch cards were commonly used to feed data into early mainframes. Because of this, EBCDIC values are often not contiguous. For instance, values A through I are represented by decimal values 193 through 201, but values J through R are represented by decimal values 209 through 217.

ASCII and EBCDIC values do not correspond to each other, nor do they contain the same characters. For example, EBCDIC has the cent sign (¢), whereas ASCII does not. On the other hand, EBCDIC does not include symbols such as [ ] or { }. It is unlikely that you will encounter EBCDIC outside of IBM mainframe environments.

Unicode

The **Unicode** standard was developed to combat limitations of systems like the ASCII system. Human languages are very complex. For example, the 255 characters of ASCII are simply not enough to represent the broad range

Lab 7.1 Converting Binary to Decimal Numbers
Practice additional hands-on networking skills on page 440.

Activity 7.2 Find ASCII and Unicode Charts You can find a complete listing of ASCII characters and their Unicode equivalents online at **networking.glencoe.com**.

networking.glencoe.com

of characters needed for the Arabic, Japanese, and Chinese languages. Unicode originally used 16-bit encoding to provide room for over 65,000 characters. 32-bit Unicode extensions provide even more flexibility and room for the character set to grow.

In Unicode, characters such as 'A' are represented by a unique hexadecimal value. The value **U+0041** is the Unicode value for 'A' (see Table 7.9).

Character Representations in ASCII

ASCII Character	Decimal (ASCII)	Hexadecimal Equivalent	Unicode
A	65	41	U+0041
B	66	42	U+0042
C	67	43	U+0043
D	68	44	U+0044
E	69	45	U+0045
F	70	46	U+0046
G	71	47	U+0047
X	88	58	U+0058
Y	89	59	U+0059
Z	90	5A	U+005A

Table 7.9
Unicode expands the 255 character set of ASCII to over 65,000 possible characters. Why do we need 65,000 characters?

Notice that the ASCII hexadecimal code corresponds to the Unicode value. Because of its universal approach, Unicode is widely used for exchanging data between computers worldwide.

Section 7.2 Assessment

Concept Check

1. **Define** decimal, base 10, binary, base 2, bit, hexadecimal, base 16, American Standard Code for Information Interchange (ASCII), Extended Binary Coded Decimal Interchange Code (EBCDIC), and Unicode.

2. **Explain** how the hexadecimal system complements the binary system.

Critical Thinking

3. **Compare and Contrast** Identify the similarities and differences between the ASCII system and the EBCDIC.

4. **Analyze Information** Which is the best system for encoding characters? Explain your answer.

Applying Skills

Convert an IP Address to Binary Using the IPCONFIG utility you learned in Chapter 5, find the IP address of a computer on which you work. Convert your IP address to its 32-bit binary value (just convert each of the four 8-bit "chunks").

FREE VERSUS FEE OPERATING SYSTEMS

Many organizations and individuals are switching from proprietary operating systems (OSs), such as Microsoft Windows, to open software such as Linux.

You can learn more about open source software, and download many examples, on the Internet.

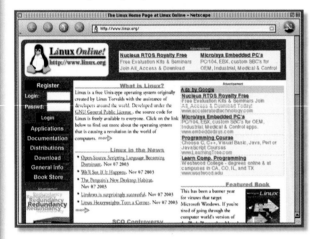

Proprietary and Open Operating Systems

Proprietary software belongs to the developer. You may have a copy of Microsoft Windows, for example, on your PC. Although you paid for the OS, you do not own it. You purchased a license that allows you to use the OS. The software and its source code (original programming instructions) remain the property of Microsoft Corporation. This is true of nearly every commercial software program you purchase.

The developer of open software (or open source software) does not claim the same type of ownership. Open software is available to anyone and is often free. The program's source code is also available, and anyone can modify the program. Open source software is created by a community of developers who share ideas and code.

Linux

The best-known example of open source software is the Linux OS. In the early 1990s, a programmer named Linus Torvalds created the core elements of Linux. He published the code on the Internet so other developers could freely use, test, and change it.

Like many open source applications, Linux is available for free, although you can also purchase packaged versions with enhancements, such as a graphical user interface, utilities, and improved network support. But freeware Linux is so powerful and flexible that it has become the OS for nearly one-quarter of all network servers.

Hardware vendors such as IBM and Hewlett-Packard have begun supporting their own versions of Linux. This means Linux is now accepted throughout the computer industry, despite its humble beginnings as "freeware."

Disadvantages of Open Software

But openness is not everything. As developers of proprietary software will testify, using open source software can be risky, especially in critical applications, such as corporate servers or databases.

For example, open source software may not have a toll-free number for technical support. Security is an even bigger concern. Although Linux is known as a secure OS, its source code is freely available to everyone, including hackers.

Tech Focus

1. Research the basic features of the Windows, Linux, and Macintosh OSs. Create a chart that summarizes, compares, and contrasts these OSs.

2. Write an essay about the history of Linux and why it has become so popular today. Discuss why you think open source software is a good or bad idea.

Section 7.3 Communications Carriers

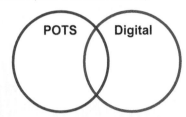
Where WAN communications are concerned, practically everything eventually boils down to telecommunications carriers. A telecommunications carrier or provider, such as AT&T, provides the lines, equipment, and connection services that enable communications to happen. For example, a modem might connect via telephone or microwave satellite transmission. Either way, a telecommunications provider is involved. A business connection made over an ISDN line or a T1 line involves a telecommunications provider. About the only exception is broadband cable using cable modems, which were discussed earlier. The following sections discuss various telecommunications systems providing both analog (telephone-based) and digital communications.

POTS

Analog communication via a modem generally uses **Plain Old Telephone Service (POTS).** This service is provided by the phone company. Originally, POTS was intended only for voice communications. In the past decade, both telecommuters needing remote access to corporate networks and home users seeking e-mail and Internet access have grown to rely on POTS.

POTS is a service provided by the **Public Switched Telephone Network (PSTN).** For networking, it can be used in two forms: dial-up or leased lines.

Dial-Up Connections

When Ray needs to call in to the office network or access the Internet via modem, he is using dial-up networking. The call temporarily connects him to the remote computer. When he hangs up, the connection is terminated. Dial-up networking works well for individuals needing remote access to a company network. It can also be suitable for intermittently connecting two LANs.

The following types of connections are dial-up connection protocols that are commonly used.

SHOW ME!

Dial-Up Lines Dial-up lines use public telephone lines. To see a demonstration of how dial-up lines provide a connection between a remote user and the network, view Show Me 7.6 at networking.glencoe.com.

SLIP Developed during the 1980s, Serial Line Internet Protocol (SLIP) was used for connecting to the Internet when modem speeds were limited to 2400 bps. Computers used SLIP to connect to an Internet Service Provider's (ISP) computer, which provided access to the Internet.

CSLIP A version of SLIP that compresses (hence the 'C') the TCP header of each packet of data transmitted, Compressed SLIP (CSLIP) reduces the overhead of a TCP transmission, which is important when transmitting small packets of data at low speeds.

PPP Far more common today than SLIP, Point to Point Protocol (PPP) provides more features than SLIP, including more stable connections and error-checking features. PPP works at the Data Link Layer.

PPTP To create a Virtual Private Network (VPN), Point-to-Point Tunneling Protocol (PPTP) is used. VPNs use the public Internet to create a private "tunnel" to connect two computers. In this manner, a remote user can securely access his or her network using an Internet connection.

Figure 7.8
Modems connect computers to the Internet via phone lines. Why is this considered a slow connection?

PPPoE Whereas PPP is a serial-based transmission protocol, Point-to-Point Protocol over Ethernet (PPPoE) creates point-to-point communications over Ethernet connections. A typical scenario might be several users on an Ethernet network using a DSL line to connect to the Internet.

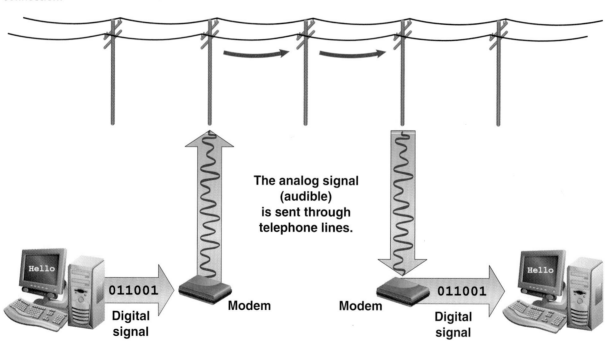

With a maximum attainable speed of 56K, dial-up connections, shown in Figure 7.8, are considered slow. Under some conditions (such as noisy lines), they can also be unreliable. However, they are easy to install and terminate, and they are inexpensive compared to other faster and more reliable options, such as ISDN, DSL, or cable modems.

Leased Lines

Leased lines are a step up from dial-up networking. When a customer leases a line from the phone company, that line is dedicated full-time to the customer's own use. The quality of a leased line and the speed at which data can be transferred are higher than that of dial-up lines.

Data transfer rates can range from 56 Kbps to many megabits per second. The many megabits cost more. Leased lines are often described as direct connections that are not routed through the phone company's switching system. Although this can be true, long-distance connections are usually routed through switched circuits. A switched circuit is a connection that is created temporarily for the duration of the transmission. It is not a permanent connection between the two points. However, the resulting connection appears to be a dedicated connection.

Leased lines are generally thought of as permanent versions of dial-up lines, but digital communications lines, such as ISDN and T1, are also leased lines in the sense of being reserved for use by a single customer. We cover both types of digital lines later in this section.

SHOW ME!

Leased Lines Leased lines provide a full-time connection between a user and the network. View Show Me 7.7 at networking.glencoe.com to see a demonstration of how leased lines provide a permanent connection for a remote user and the network.

DIGITAL

As multimedia becomes more popular on the Internet, speed is of the essence. We want speedy connections to download music files, view streaming sports broadcasts, and one day even watch DVD-quality movies over the Internet. Connecting at a paltry 56 Kbps does not fill this need.

Digital communications come into play in all these areas, and you have several options from which to choose.

DDS

Digital data service (DDS) lines are dedicated, point-to-point connections. These lines transmit digital data rather than voice calls. DDS lines rely on a two-part device called a Channel Service Unit (CSU) and a Data Service Unit (DSU) to connect two networks (see Figure 7.9). The device, usually referred to as the CSU/DSU, takes the place of a modem and performs the following tasks:

- The CSU processes the signals being sent over the digital line and isolates the line from network equipment problems.
- The DSU converts the data from their network-oriented, computer-based format to the form needed for synchronous transmission. The DSU also controls the flow of data to the CSU.

● **Figure 7.9**
A DDS connection relies on a CSU/DSU unit at each end to mediate between the network and the digital line. What job does the CSU perform?

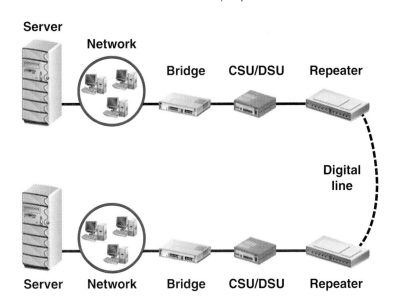

ISDN

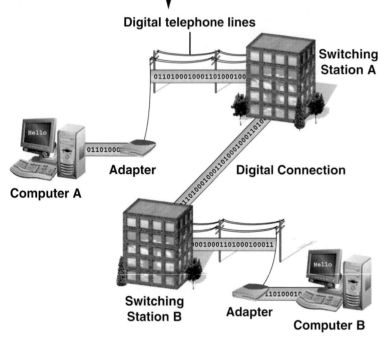

Figure 7.10 ●

ISDN can transfer data up to 1.544 Mbps. How is this achieved?

Digital telephone lines

0110100010001101000100

Switching Station A

01101000

Adapter

Digital Connection

Computer A

0010001101000100011

Switching Station B

Adapter

110100010

Computer B

Developed in 1984 as a means of providing end-to-end digital service over the telephone network, ISDN is currently used by businesses and by individual (home) subscribers, where it is available (see Figure 7.10). ISDN is designed to deliver voice, data, and images including video at a speed of 64 Kbps.

ISDN is available in two different forms known as **Basic Rate Interface (BRI)** and **Primary Rate Interface (PRI).** In the BRI form of ISDN, there are two B (bearer) channels that carry data at the rate of 64 Kbps. A single D (data or delta) channel carries signaling and other control information at the rate of 16 Kbps. BRI is the type of ISDN typical in home use.

In the PRI form of ISDN, the line is divided into many more channels. In North America and Japan, PRI includes 23 B channels and 1 D channel. In other parts of the world, including Europe, PRI consists of 30 B channels and 1 D channel. The PRI form of ISDN is generally used to connect a company's telephone network—called a Private Branch Exchange (PBX)—to the local or long-distance phone company.

You should remember the following about ISDN:

◆ It is digital.
◆ It is divided into either 2 B channels and 1 D channel (BRI) or into 23 or 30 B channels and 1 D channel (PRI).
◆ It carries voice, data, and video.
◆ It is used by both individual subscribers and businesses.
◆ It is less expensive than T1 service.

T1/T3

T1, sometimes referred to as T1 carrier, was developed by Bell Laboratories. It was introduced in the 1960s as a means of enabling telephone wires to carry more than one conversation at a time. Today, T1 is one of the most widely used—and one of the most expensive—technologies in digital communications. Much faster than ISDN, T1 lines carry information at the rate of 1.544 Mbps. T1 connections are widely used in schools and universities as well as in businesses (see Table 7.10 on page 215). A fractional leased line means that only a portion of the line's bandwidth is available.

T1 transmits in full-duplex, which means that devices on both ends of the transmission can send and receive simultaneously. Originally, it was designed for use over four twisted-pair copper wires. Two pairs were used for sending and two were used for receiving. Today, however, T1 lines can also be fiber optic cable, coaxial cable, and microwave.

Percentage of Public Schools with Internet Access Using Various Types of Connections: 2001

Type of Connection	Percentage	Type of Connection	Percentage
T3/DS3	5	DSL	1
Fractional T3	1	ISDN	5
T1/DS1	55	56KB	6
Fractional T1	14	Dial-up connection	5
Cable Modem	8	Wireless connection	4

(Source: U.S. Department of Education, National Center for Education Statistics, Fast Response Survey System, "Internet Access in U.S. Public Schools, Fall 2001." FRSS 82.)

Table 7.10
Public schools use T1 "drops." What is the percentage of schools with a T1 connection?

To attain such a high transmission speed, T1 multiplexes 24 separate 64 Kbps channels into a single digital data stream. When you encounter T1 details, you often see 64 Kbps—the speed of a single T1 channel—referred to as DS-0, for Digital Services (or Digital Signal) level 0. The higher 1.544 Mbps speed is known as DS-1. The DS-1 rate, in turn, can be multiplexed further to provide even higher transmission rates, including the following:

◆ DS-2, which is the basis for T2 lines, incorporates four T1 channels and transmits at 6.312 Mbps.

◆ DS-3, which is the basis for T3 lines, incorporates 28 T1 channels and transmits at 44.736 Mbps.

◆ DS-4, which is the basis for T4 lines, incorporates 168 T1 channels and transmits at a blistering 274.176 Mbps.

Of these, T1 and T2 can be used on copper wire. T3 and T4 require fiber optic cable or microwave.

To save on the potentially considerable expense of leasing a T1 line, businesses can opt for an alternative known as **fractional T1,** in which they lease part rather than all of the T1 bandwidth. At the other end of the scale, they can choose to use T3 lines in place of multiple T1 lines. Public schools, on the other hand, generally receive funding assistance from various governmental agencies and commercial concerns to lease expanded bandwidth.

Enrichment **LAB**

Lab 7.2 Updating Network Communications Practice additional hands-on networking skills on page 441.

xDSL

Digital Subscriber Line (xDSL) represents a family of digital communications technologies. The *x* in xDSL stands for any of several letters that represent different versions of basic DSL communications. These services provide high-speed network access over the standard copper wires run into homes and offices by the telephone company. To achieve high data rates—ranging from 8 Mbps to as much as 52 Mbps—DSL relies on modulation and on the fact that digital signals do not have to be converted to analog form.

In truth, the data only run over copper wiring for a short distance, from the telephone switching station to the house or business office. This so-called "last mile" connection is limited to around 20,000 feet. This limitation is perhaps the biggest drawback of xDSL service. If the house or office is not located close enough to a central office, you cannot get DSL service. Table 7.11 lists several variations of xDSL, along with the range limits from the central office.

Table 7.11 ●——→
DSL comes in many different "flavors." What is the main limitation of DSL?

Version of xDSL	
Version of DSL	**Range Limits**
Asymmetric DSL (ADSL)	8 Mbps Download, 640 Kbps upload
DSL Lite	1.544 Mbps download (maximum), less complex and less expensive
High bit-rate DSL	1.544 Mbps in both directions (same as T1), 15,000 foot maximum range
Single-line DSL (SDSL)	Similar to HDSL but 10,000 foot maximum range
Rate Adaptive DSL (RADSL)	Software adjusts transmission rate according to the quality of the line and the distance of the transmission, 2.2 Mbps download, 1.088 Mbps upload
Very high rate DSL (VDSL)	52 Mbps download, 2.3 Mbps upload, 4,500 foot maximum range

As you can see, there are many exciting and speedy alternatives for WAN connections. Each technology has its own positive and negative aspects, including transmission speeds, availability, and cost.

Section 7.3 Assessment

Concept Check

1. **Define** Plain Old Telephone Service (POTS), Public Switched Telephone Network (PSTN), digital data service (DDS), Basic Rate Interface (BRI), Primary Rate Interface (PRI), fractional T1, and Digital Subscriber Line (xDSL).

2. **List** the different types of protocols that can be used in dial-up networking.

3. **Explain** how a T1 line achieves high-speed data transmission.

Critical Thinking

4. **Analyze** Interpret in a short paragraph how DSL differs from ISDN in achieving high data transmission speeds.

5. **Draw Conclusions** Explain what PPTP is used for and why it is important for dial-up networking.

6. **Understand Relationships** List the various types of DSL by speed of transmission.

Applying Skills

Learn About WAN Technology More than likely, your school's LAN (or CAN) is connected to the school district's WAN. Find out what technology is used to link together the schools in your district. Using a drawing application or pencil and paper, draw your school's LAN. Label the technology used to connect the networks.

SECTION 7.1 Communications

Key Terms

V series, 197
AT command set, 197
PC Card standards, 197
cable modem, 199
geostationary earth orbit (GEO), 200

medium-earth orbit (MEO), 200
low-earth orbit (LEO), 200
asynchronous, 201
synchronous, 202
frame, 202

Main Ideas

■ Modems have been an important means for computers to communicate with each other.

■ Satellite systems connect systems over large geographic distances.

■ Multiplexers combine signals from multiple sources onto one data line.

■ Asynchronous transmissions rely on start and stop bits to mark the beginning and end of each data packet.

■ Synchronous transmissions rely on precise timing to regulate the flow of data.

SECTION 7.2 Data-Encoding Basics

Key Terms

decimal, 204
base 10, 204
binary, 205
base 2, 205
bit, 205
hexadecimal, 207
base 16, 207

American Standard Code for Information Interchange (ASCII), 208
Extended Binary Coded Decimal Interchange Code (EBCDIC), 208
Unicode, 208

Main Ideas

■ The base 10 or decimal system uses 10 digits to designate values.

■ Base 2 or binary uses two digits to designate values.

■ Base 16 or hexadecimal uses 16 digits (0–9 and A–F) to designate values.

SECTION 7.3 Communications Carriers

Key Terms

Plain Old Telephone Service (POTS), 211
Public Switched Telephone Network (PSTN), 211
digital data service (DDS), 213
Basic Rate Interface (BRI), 214
Primary Rate Interface (PRI), 214
fractional T1, 215
Digital Subscriber Line (xDSL), 215

Main Ideas

■ Almost all WANs rely on telecommunications.

■ POTS provides many options beyond simple modem connections and speeds.

■ Digital communications use a variety of technologies to achieve very high-speed transmissions.

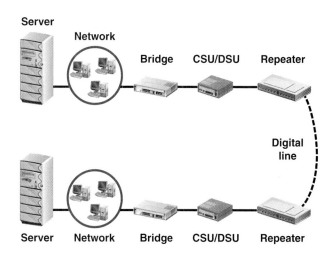

READ TO SUCCEED PRACTICE

Using Creative Study Tools Choose a topic from the chapter and create some artwork or compose a brief song based on the content. Give this to a classmate and take one from him or her. Evaluate how this study tool helps you remember the topic. Does the friend's study tool mean as much to you as the one you developed yourself?

Reviewing Key Terms

1. Describe each of the following types of modems. Then, describe how they are alike.
   ◆ Cable
   ◆ ISDN
   ◆ DSL
2. Identify the four types of multiplexing. Give a description of each.
3. What is the basic numbering system that computers understand?
4. How fast is a single T1 channel? How does this compare to the speed of a fractional T1 line?
5. Can a T1 handle both data and voice? Why or why not?

Understanding Main Ideas

6. List the different types of WAN connections.
7. Explain why a standard modem is not as stable as a cable or DSL modem.
8. Describe why a company would use a satellite if there is a mid-Atlantic cable between the United States and Europe.
9. Explain how a company could save money by separating channels of a T1.
10. Describe the dial-up connections you could use for VPNs. Explain your answer.
11. Explain why a company would use a leased line.
12. List each type of modem and provide an example of the best environment to use it in.
13. Describe the three types of numbering systems.
14. Summarize the uses for each type of text representation.
15. List the transfer rates for T1, ISDN, and DSL in order from slowest to fastest.

Critical Thinking

16. **Draw Conclusions** If a company had to choose between the following, which one should they choose? Why? What are the factors they need to consider?
    ◆ T1
    ◆ DSL
    ◆ Cable connection
17. **Compare and Contrast** Identify the similarities and differences between synchronous transmissions and asynchronous transmissions.
18. **Investigate Hardware** What are the similarities and differences between the different types of satellites?
19. **Combine Connections** Why would a company combine a dial-up network connection and a leased line?
20. **Understand Connections** Why are dial-up connections considered slow? What other types of connections can be used instead of dial-up?
21. **Evaluate Hardware** List the hardware needed for an ISDN connection, dial-up connection, and cable modem connection.
22. **Make a Recommendation** Your company is deciding to upgrade its dial-up connection, but wants to minimize the cost. What is one cost-effective solution? Explain your answer and include examples.

e-Review ....

networking.glencoe.com

Study with PowerPoint

To review the main points in this chapter, select **e-Review > PowerPoint Outlines > Chapter 7.**

Online Self Check

Test your knowledge of the material in this chapter by selecting **e-Review > Self Checks > Chapter 7.**

Making Connections

Math – Understanding Conversions

By understanding how to convert between various number systems, such as binary and hexadecimal, you will build a better understanding of how computers around the world communicate and translate data.

Following the instructions below, convert numbers from decimal to binary and hexadecimal.

◆ Pick four decimal numbers (at least three digits long).
◆ Convert the numbers to binary and hexadecimal.
◆ Use the tables and steps provided in the You Try It Activities 7B and 7C.
◆ Be certain to show your work and be able to explain how you converted the numbers.

STANDARDS AT WORK

Students demonstrate a sound understanding of the nature and operation of technology systems (NETS-S 1)

Understand Carriers and Modems

Using the Internet, classroom resources, and what you have read in the chapter, do the following:

◆ List the advantages and disadvantages for each of the following technologies.
◆ List the types of hardware needed, from modems to cables.
◆ Put the technologies in order from least expensive to most expensive.
◆ In a short paragraph, defend your rationale.
◆ List under which circumstances each technology is most effective. Explain your answer.
  a. PSTN
  b. ISDN
  c. xDSL
  d. Cable modem
  e. Dial-up modem

TEAMWORK SKILLS

Help Desk Role Play

Following your teacher's instructions, form groups of two students. Use the scenarios below. One of you will be the network support technician and the other will be the user.

◆ The user will explain the problem while the technician helps to solve the problem with the user.
◆ Role-plays can be an in-person visit or a telephone conversation.
◆ You can use help documentation, Internet resources, or other resources you have available to solve the problem.
◆ After you have solved one of the scenarios, switch roles and work on the next one.

Scenario 1: The modem will not dial out.
Scenario 2: The operating system is not detecting the modem.

On a separate piece of paper, answer the following questions:

1. What kinds of questions helped you gather the most useful information? Explain your answer.
2. What documentation was the most effective in solving the user's problem?

CHALLENGE YOURSELF

Know Your Hardware

This challenge will give you a good understanding of how drivers and software are made for modems.

◆ Using the Internet or other sources, research the AT commands used with Hayes-compatible modems.
◆ With your teacher's permission, use a Hayes-compatible modem and Microsoft Hyper-Terminal to dial out a number with only AT commands. Were you able to connect to another computer? List the commands you used and explain your results.

YOU TRY IT

Testing a Modem

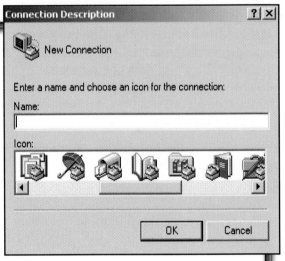

Using Microsoft's HyperTerminal, test that the modem installed is functioning properly.

Windows 2000

Ⓐ Select **Start,** select **Programs,** select **Accessories,** choose **Communications,** and click on **HyperTerminal.**

Ⓑ When the application opens, click **Cancel** on the Connection Description window as shown.

Ⓒ In the HyperTerminal window, type at and press **Enter.** Depending on your modem, you may not see the characters "at" as you type them. If the modem is working properly, "OK" or "0" will appear in the window.

Ⓓ If "OK" or "0" do not appear, use the Modem Troubleshooter. Select **Start,** select **Help,** and click the **Contents** tab.

Ⓔ From the list, select **Troubleshooting and Maintenance** and click on **Windows 2000 Troubleshooters.**

Ⓕ From the table, select **Modem.** This troubleshooter will help you diagnose basic problems with a modem.

Windows XP

Ⓐ Select **Start,** select **Programs,** select **Accessories,** choose **Communications,** and click on **HyperTerminal.**

Ⓑ Click **File** and select **Properties.**

Ⓒ Select the **Connect to** tab and click on your modem in the Connect using box. Click **OK.**

Ⓓ Click **File** and select **New Connection.**

Ⓔ Click **Cancel** in the Connection Description window.

Ⓕ In the HyperTerminal window, type ate1 and press **Enter.** Depending on your modem, you may not see the characters "ate1" as you type them. If the modem is working properly, "OK" or "0" will appear in the window.

Ⓖ If the modem is not functioning properly, "OK" or "0" will not appear in the window. Select **Start,** select **Help and Support,** and click the **Fixing a Problem.**

Ⓗ From the list, select **Hardware and system device problems** and click **Modem Troubleshooter.** This troubleshooter will help you diagnose basic problems with a modem.

Networking Projects

1. Create a WAN Structure

A magazine publisher has three offices, one in Seattle, Washington; one in Fort Lauderdale, Florida; and one in New York City, New York. The offices primarily use the telephone and send packages to pass information to each office. The company would like to cut phone and mail expenses by connecting the offices together with a WAN.

The internal networks have had frequent cable problems, and each time they have a problem, the entire office network goes down until the problem is resolved. Each network has a coaxial linear-bus topology supporting Ethernet 10 Mbps traffic.

The management team would like a network design that offers easier troubleshooting, less down time, and provides WAN communication between sites. They would like the WAN connection to be able to support about 256 Kbps of data and several analog telephone conversations between sites.

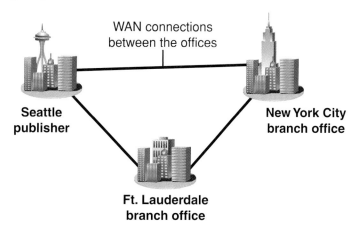

On a separate sheet of paper, answer the following questions based on the above scenario:

Ⓐ List the problems with the current networks.

Ⓑ Identify at least two network items that need upgrading in each office network site.

Ⓒ The separate branch offices need to maintain voice and data communications with each other. Which type of WAN connection (link) might you use to connect the three sites to each other?

Ⓓ Which type of device could be used to collect the multiple signals from voice and data and put them on the same WAN link?

Ⓔ Which type of connectivity device should be used to connect the LAN to the multiple paths in the WAN illustrated in the diagram above?

WAN Technologies

YOU WILL LEARN TO...

WHY IT MATTERS......................................

The Mississippi River is over 2,300 miles long. More than 286 million tons of goods are shipped on its surface every year. Like a great river, WAN technologies merge various flows of data to transmit them over great distances as quickly as possible.

Quick Write Activity

Suppose you were the president of a large automobile manufacturer. You need to get your product (cars) to your many distributors throughout the country. Brainstorm the various ways a large quantity of goods could be transported. What advantages and disadvantages are there to each option?

WHAT YOU WILL DO...

READ TO SUCCEED

Prior Knowledge
Imagine some friends are talking about a new movie you have not seen. You soon lose interest. However, when they talk about your favorite movie, you become interested. Reading works much the same way. The more you know about a subject, the more you understand. That makes it easier to be an active, interested participant. Look over the "You Will Learn To" at the beginning of the chapter. Write down what you already know about each objective and what you want to find out by reading the chapter. As you read, find examples for both categories.

Section 8.1 How a WAN Works

Main Ideas

Circuit-switched networks use a direct, physical connection to transmit data back and forth. Message-switched networks send entire transmissions between intermediaries. Packet-switched networks route packets through virtual circuits.

Key Terms

carrier services
remote access
dial-up networking (DUN)
Virtual Private Network (VPN)
circuit-switched network
message switching
packet switching
Packet Switching Exchange (PSE)

Reading Strategy

Identify at least three facts about each main topic. Create a diagram like the one below (also available online).

How a WAN Works	

WANs exchange information across wide geographic areas. They depend on communication services, called carriers, for covering vast distances. The most common public carrier is the telephone network. Because of the distances involved, WANs typically have longer delays, and a higher number of errors than usually occur on a LAN. However, WANs are the most effective of the currently available means of transferring computer-based information. In this section, we explore many different ways to move data across a WAN.

CARRIERS

It is difficult and expensive to move data over long distances. After a network grows beyond the confines of the LAN, you need some sort of carrier service. **Carrier services** are provided by telecommunications companies, such as AT&T, Sprint, or Verizon. There are many types of carrier services, such as dial-up and leased lines, which were discussed in Chapter 7. If you want more speed and you have to cover longer distances, you will likely have to pay more.

Carriers provide a wide range of services, depending on the needs of the organization. Many individuals are more familiar with services a little closer to home. For example, many people telecommute, or work from home. With a modem and dial-up networking software, users can connect to a server at the workplace and access network resources. This connection is often established using the phone line. Alternatively, they might use a DSL or cable modem connection to access their ISP (a telephone or cable company). Then they can connect to the network via a VPN, which we explain momentarily.

Lab 8.1 Choosing a Remote Access System Practice additional hands-on networking skills on page 442.

Remote Access

To establish a direct connection to the network using regular dial-up lines, **remote access** is used. Two conditions must be met to establish a remote access connection. First, users need to connect to the network using a client service called **dial-up networking (DUN).** Second, the receiving server (or the remote access server) must have a service ready to accept incoming DUN

networking.glencoe.com

calls. The remote access server authenticates users and permits access to the network. After the connection is made, users can work on the network as if they were at their desk in the office (see Figure 8.1). Many people, such as traveling sales representatives, use a remote access service (RAS) to check e-mail and update sales databases while they travel.

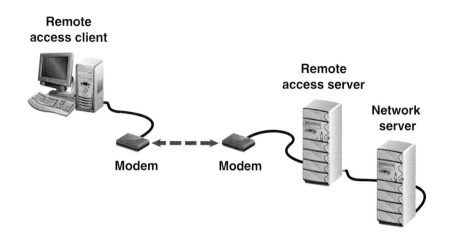

Remote access client

Remote access server

Network server

Modem **Modem**

Figure 8.1

The RAS allows remote users to access the network. What are the advantages and disadvantages of dial-up networking?

ACTIVITY 8A Setting Up a DUN Connection

YOU TRY IT

To allow users to connect to a remote network using a modem, you need to set up a dial-up network connection. In the Windows OS, this service is called Remote Access Service (RAS). Practice setting up this type of connection using the Windows XP operating system.

❶ Click **Start,** and then click **Control Panel.**

❷ Click **Network and Internet Connections** in Category view, or **Network Connections** in a Classic view.

❸ Click the **Create a connection to the network at your workplace** task.

❹ Click **Dial-up connection,** and then click **Next.**

❺ Enter the name of the company, organization, or school to which you are connecting.

❻ Enter the phone number of the RAS server. This is available through your network administrator (see Figure 8.2).

❼ Select the connection availability option that applies to your computer, and then click **Next.**

❽ Check the box to add a shortcut to the desktop, and then click **Finish.**

Figure 8.2

Enter the phone number of the line connected to the RAS server.

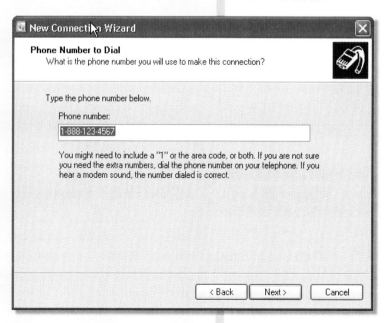

New Connection Wizard

Phone Number to Dial
What is the phone number you will use to make this connection?

Type the phone number below.

Phone number:
1-888-123-4567

You might need to include a "1" or the area code, or both. If you are not sure you need the extra numbers, dial the phone number on your telephone. If you hear a modem sound, the number dialed is correct.

< Back   Next >   Cancel

Figure 8.3
Each time you want to connect to the network, you must make a connection using DUN.

⑨ After the DUN is set up, you can connect to the network (assuming you have an installed modem that is connected to a phone line). To make the connection, double-click the DUN icon on your desktop.

⑩ Enter your network user name and password in the text boxes provided, and then click **Dial** (see Figure 8.3).

Remote access services differ, depending on the server or the client. For example, Windows 2000 Server permits up to 256 simultaneous incoming RAS connections. The client, however, can connect to only one server at a time.

Virtual Private Networks

An alternative to using DUN is the creation of a **Virtual Private Network (VPN).** A VPN uses a network connection (often via the Internet) to connect to a particular network (such as a corporate intranet). The advantages of a VPN are that users benefit from faster network connections and the network connection is private and secure. After the VPN connection is established, it is as if the user were in the office. For example, a telecommuter with a broadband cable connection to the Internet could use a VPN to connect to the network at work.

A VPN provides a secure, private "tunnel" to the network to which you are connecting. VPNs use the Point-to-Point Tunneling Protocol (PPTP) you learned about in Chapter 7. PPTP supports many protocols, such as TCP/IP, IPX, and AppleTalk, so it can be used to connect by employing any of the common network protocols. In addition, PPTP secures transmissions by encrypting its connections. Encrypting data is essentially converting data into a secret code. Even if the encrypted data are intercepted, the data cannot be read. Creating a VPN connection is another important task you will need to perform if you choose a career in networking.

YOU TRY IT

ACTIVITY 8B Setting Up a VPN Connection

VPN connections allow you to create a secure, private network connection by tunneling through an existing public network, such as the Internet. In this activity, you use Windows XP to create a VPN connection.

❶ Click **Start,** and then click **Control Panel.**

❷ Click **Network and Internet Connections.** Note: Some systems give different choices.

❸ Click **Create a new connection.** Click **Next** in the New Connection Wizard.

❹ Click **Virtual Private Network connection,** and then click **Next.**

❺ Enter the name of the company, organization, or school to which you are connecting and click **Next.**

❻ Select the option regarding whether to dial into an initial connection. For now, choose **Do not dial an initial connection.** This option assumes you have access, perhaps through a cable modem or other type of LAN connection. Then click **Next.**

❼ Enter the host name (for example, www.yahoo.com) or the IP address of the network server (see Figure 8.4).

❽ Select the connection availability option that applies to your computer, and then click **Next.**

❾ Check the box to add a shortcut to the desktop, and then click **Finish.**

❿ Some VPN settings are not established through the wizard. For example, many of the security options can only be found in the VPN properties window. To access these settings, double-click the **VPN** icon on your desktop.

⓫ Click **Properties.**

⓬ Click the **Security** tab (see Figure 8.5).

⓭ After you have configured the VPN settings, click **OK** to return to the log on window.

By understanding how to configure a DUN and VPN, you, as a network support technician, can help troubleshoot connections and set up new users. Knowing the process can also help you guide new users through problems over the phone.

● **Figure 8.4**
Enter the host name or IP address of the server to which you want to connect.

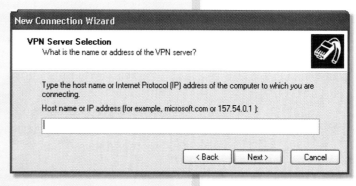

● **Figure 8.5**
Depending on your network configuration, you may need to adjust VPN security settings.

How do those data get transferred from here to there? In the sections that follow, you learn about many different ways data can be transmitted across the WAN.

SWITCHING TECHNOLOGIES

After data enter the WAN, they can be transported using a variety of different technologies. As telecommunications companies improve and update their capabilities, different technologies are introduced and older technologies are phased out. Here, you learn about some of the more common types of technologies used to transmit data from one point to another over a WAN connection.

Circuit Switching

A **circuit-switched network** creates a direct physical connection between the sender and receiver. This connection lasts as long as the two parties need to communicate. One example of a circuit-switched network is the Plain Old Telephone System (POTS). When you dial the telephone to speak to a friend, a direct connection is made from your phone, through the phone network, to your friend's phone. After the connection is made, you and your friend can count on "owning" the circuit for as long as you remain connected.

Circuit switching allows for a fixed, rapid rate of transmission. The primary drawback to circuit switching is the fact that any unused bandwidth remains exactly that—unused. Because the connection is reserved only for the two communicating parties, unused bandwidth cannot be "borrowed" for any other transmission.

Message Switching

Unlike circuit switching, **message switching** does not involve a direct physical connection between the sender and receiver. Message switching is an older technology used to route an entire message from one system to another. That message is routed through intermediate (go-between) stations or, possibly, to a central network computer. E-mail is one early system that used message switching to transport a message from one computer to another.

Each station along the way accepts the entire message and studies the address. Then, it forwards the message to the next party, which might be another intermediary or the destination node. A defining feature of message-switching networks is that the intermediaries do not have to forward messages immediately. Instead, they can hold messages before sending them on to their next destination. This is one of the advantages of message switching. Because the intermediate stations can wait for an opportunity to transmit, the network can avoid or reduce heavy traffic periods. It also has some control over the efficient use of communication lines (see Figure 8.6).

Figure 8.6 Message switching sends the entire message to intermediary stations that decide which route to use and when to forward the message. What are the advantages of a message-switched network?

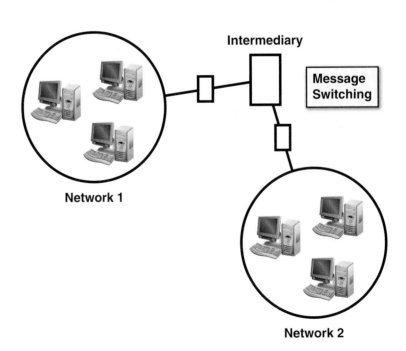

Network 1

Intermediary

Message Switching

Network 2

Sending data along a message-switching network is similar to shipping goods on a train. Although there are many alternative routes for the train to take, all the train cars must stay together as they travel from station to station. At each station, a decision is made determining the best route and whether to wait until traffic is lighter along the route.

ACTIVITY 8C Tracing Packets

YOU TRY IT

Using the utility "tracert" for the Windows OS and "traceroute" for the Unix OS, you can discover the route and number of hops the data packet took to arrive at its destination. You can trace the route on which data packets travel to various servers, such as a Web server.

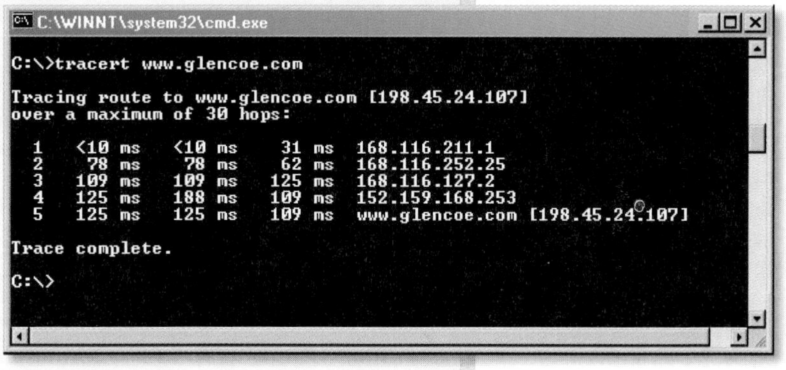

1 On a computer with Windows OS, click the **Start** button, and then click **Run.**

● **Figure 8.7**
Use tracert or traceroute to track data packets.

2 Type cmd if you are using Windows 2000 or XP, or type command if you are using Windows 95 or 98.

```
C:\WINNT\system32\cmd.exe                              _|□|×|

C:\>tracert www.glencoe.com

Tracing route to www.glencoe.com [198.45.24.107]
over a maximum of 30 hops:

  1   <10 ms   <10 ms    31 ms  168.116.211.1
  2    78 ms    78 ms    62 ms  168.116.252.25
  3   109 ms   109 ms   125 ms  168.116.127.2
  4   125 ms   188 ms   109 ms  152.159.168.253
  5   125 ms   125 ms   109 ms  www.glencoe.com [198.45.24.107]

Trace complete.

C:\>
```

3 At the C: prompt, type tracert www.glencoe.com. You can use the URL of any Web site to follow the path of the data packet (see Figure 8.7). This utility allows the tracking of up to 30 hops.

4 Click the **Close** button to exit the cmd windows.

5 On a computer with the Unix or Linux OS, type traceroute www.glencoe.com at the command prompt.

Unlike circuit switching, packet switching typically does not tie up a line indefinitely for the benefit of sender and receiver. Transmissions require only the bandwidth needed for forwarding any given packet, and because packet switching is also based on multiplexing messages, many transmissions can be interleaved on the same networking medium at the same time.

Packet Switching

In **packet switching,** all transmissions are broken into units called packets. Packet switching acts as a dispatching system and, to some extent, the cargo containers that carry the data from place to place. Packet switching is commonly found in LANs. It is also the backbone of WAN routing.

Each packet contains the sending node and receiving node addressing information. These packets are routed through various go-betweens, called **Packet Switching Exchanges (PSEs),** until they reach their destination. At each stop along the way, the PSE inspects the packet's destination address, consults a routing table, and forwards the packet at the highest possible speed to the next link in the chain leading to the recipient.

As they travel from point to point, packets are often carried on virtual circuits. A virtual circuit is a temporary allocation of bandwidth between the sending and receiving computers. Each computer must agree to certain "ground rules," including packet size, flow control, and error control (see Figure 8.8).

Figure 8.8 ●——————▶
Packet-switching networks send individual packets along the best route available. **What job is performed by a PSE?**

Activity 8.1 Explore Connection Services Explore in detail how networks make the connection between the sender and the recipient at **networking.glencoe.com**.

Packet-Switched Network

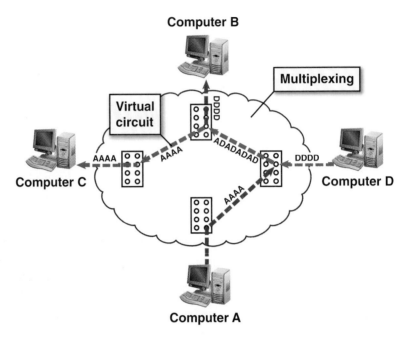

Section 8.1 Assessment

Concept Check

1. **Define** carrier services, remote access, dial-up networking (DUN), Virtual Private Network (VPN), circuit-switched network, message switching, packet switching, and Packet Switching Exchange (PSE).

2. **Explain** the role carriers play in WAN transmissions.

3. **Describe** how data are transmitted in a packet-switched network.

Critical Thinking

4. **Compare and Contrast** How are DUN and VPN connections alike and how do they differ?

5. **Analyze Information** Based on what you know about circuit switching, message switching, and packet switching, which is the most promising technology? Explain your answer.

6. **Contrast Information** How does message switching differ from packet switching? Why is this important?

Applying Skills

Modify a DUN Setup
Your company just moved to a new town. Your salespeople all have DUN connection shortcuts on their desktop that dial to the wrong RAS phone number. Write a list of instructions that informs the users how to change their DUN connection to dial the correct number.

networking.glencoe.com

EMERGING TECHNOLOGY

PERSONAL AREA NETWORKS

Imagine carrying a network wherever you go. This is already possible with new personal area network (PAN) technologies.

PANs manage all your personal computing devices.

What Is a PAN?

A PAN is a wireless network with a coverage area the size of a single person. A PAN serves two main purposes:

◆ It can connect all computing devices a person carries, such as a laptop, PDA, cell phone, and portable printer. A PAN could let your cell phone look up a phone number stored in your PDA's contact list. Someday, PANs may connect devices such as MP3 players, wristwatches, and headsets.

◆ It can connect personal devices to a LAN or the Internet. Imagine carrying a PAN-enabled PDA. When you go to work, the PAN identifies you to the building's security system so you can enter the building. When you reach your office, the PDA connects to the company's e-mail server and downloads your newest messages.

You Are the Network

PANs must work wirelessly—you would not want to connect all your portable devices with wires. An early idea (proposed by researchers at the Massachusetts Institute of Technology and supported by IBM Corporation) suggested that a PAN might use its wearer's body as its communications link.

PAN devices could transmit signals through the user's body tissues. This transmission method would prevent signals from straying too far from the user, making the system secure. PAN-to-PAN communication could be enabled when two PAN users touch each other.

Bluetooth PANs

Another approach bases PAN communication on the Bluetooth standard, which uses short-range radio waves to carry data. Hardware and software vendors like this idea because Bluetooth is an existing standard that is already being used in many kinds of devices. For example, you can already use a Bluetooth connection to wirelessly connect your cell phone and PDA, or to connect peripherals such as a keyboard to a PC. All devices are not currently Bluetooth-compatible, but this is changing as Bluetooth becomes more broadly available.

Tech Focus

1. Think of some possible personal and business uses for PANs in the near and distant future. Discuss your ideas with the class.

2. Research two networking technologies that will be used to create PANs. Write a brief report summarizing your findings.

Guide to Reading

Main Ideas

X.25 is a packet-switching protocol originally designed for analog telephone lines. Frame relay uses permanent, virtual circuits and reliable, digital lines to transmit data. ATM transmits data, voice, and video over many types of lines.

Key Terms

X.25
Data Terminal Equipment (DTE)
packet assembler/disassembler (PAD)
Data Circuit-terminating Equipment (DCE)
frame relay
Asynchronous Transfer Mode (ATM)
cell relay
broadband ISDN (B-ISDN)

Reading Strategy

Identify unique facts and common traits about two types of networks in this section. Create a chart similar to the one below (also available online).

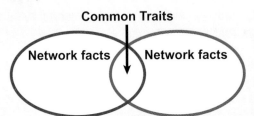

Common Traits

Network facts   Network facts

Packet-based data transfer defines a packet-switching network. However, there are different kinds of packet-switching networks, just like there are different breeds of dogs. In this section, you learn about some of the different "breeds" of packet-switching networks: X.25, frame relay, ATM, and SMDS.

X.25 PACKET-SWITCHING PROTOCOL

In the 1970s, **X.25** was created as a connection-oriented, packet-switching protocol. It was originally designed for use on ordinary analog telephone lines. Computers on an X.25 network can receive and transmit data at the same time. This is also called full-duplex communication.

The X.25 protocol is not concerned with how a packet is routed from switch to switch between networks. It concentrates on the interface through which the transmissions flow. This interface is composed of a series of devices that are explained in the following list:

- ◆ **DTE**—In X.25 terminology, there are no computers, hosts, or nodes. Instead, sending and receiving computers are referred to simply as **Data Terminal Equipment (DTE).**
- ◆ **PAD**—A **packet assembler/disassembler (PAD)** is used to prepare packets for transmission and disassemble the packets that come in. The PAD also buffers (stores temporarily) data before processing takes place.
- ◆ **DCE**—From the DTE or PAD, packets are sent to the **Data Circuit-terminating Equipment (DCE).** A DCE might be a modem or packet switch, usually located at the carrier's facilities. A DCE is located at each end of the connection.
- ◆ **PSE**—Within the carrier's network, Packet Switching Exchanges (PSEs) take care of moving packets along the best route available.

Diagrams of X.25 networks often show the WAN as a big cloud. This may sound odd, but keep in mind that X.25 does not have control over the path the packets take. After a packet enters the carrier's network, the PSEs determine the best route available (see Figure 8.9).

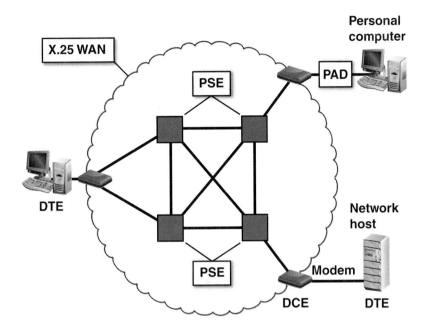

Figure 8.9
Packets in an X.25 network travel the best route available, not necessarily the same route for every packet in a transmission. Which device is responsible for determining the route of a packet across an X.25 network?

X.25 relates to the three lowest layers of the OSI model: the Physical, Data Link, and Network Layers (see Table 8.1). On an X.25 network, transmissions are typically broken into 128-byte packets. However, they can be as small as 64 bytes or as large as 4,096 bytes.

Table 8.1
The X.25 focuses on the lower three layers of the OSI model. How does X.25 control the path that packets take?

X.25 and the OSI Model

OSI Layer	Description
Physical	Specifies the physical means by which communications take place. This includes electrical, mechanical, or other means.
Data Link	Covers the link protocol, known as the Link Access Protocol Balanced (LAPB). LAPB defines how packets are framed. It also ensures an error-free connection.
Network	Handles packet formats. Also routes and handles the multiplexing of transmissions between devices.

FRAME RELAY

Frame relay is a newer form of packet switching that relies on digital technologies, such as fiber optic and ISDN. Because digital media is more reliable, frame relay does not need to include as much error correction and flow control information with each frame. This streamlining makes it faster than the X.25 protocol (see Figure 8.10 on page 234).

Figure 8.10 ●——➤

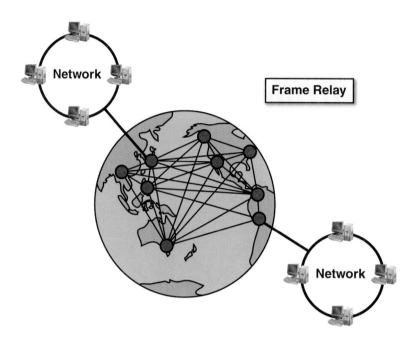

In essence, frame relay provides end-to-end service over a known, fast, digital communications route. Frame relay operates over permanent virtual circuits (PVCs). A PVC appears to be a permanent, fixed connection between two points, such as two offices located in different cities. Because the route is fixed, transmitting devices do not have to waste time finding the best route available.

Although frame relay does not include any facilities for error correction, it does check for corrupted transmissions using a cyclic redundancy check (CRC). The CRC is used to detect whether any bits in the transmission have changed between the source and destination. To control the flow of transmission, special bits in the frame header are used. If too much data are delivered to the receiver, it can signal the sender to slow down. If the receiver is still overwhelmed, it begins discarding lower priority deliveries. Think of it as if you were throwing cargo off a plane running out of fuel to lighten the load so that you make it to the airport.

Frame relay networks connecting LANs to a WAN rely on routers and switching equipment. The equipment is capable of packaging data into frames for transmission across the WAN.

ATM

Another type of switching technology is **Asynchronous Transfer Mode (ATM).** ATM is capable of delivering not only data, but also voice and video simultaneously—and over the same communications lines. ATM is a connection-oriented networking technology. Like frame relay, ATM is designed to take advantage of digital media. In fact, ATM transmission speeds *start* at 155 Mbps, and go up from there.

Transporting Data

ATM is useful for high-speed LAN and WAN networking over a range of media types. These types range from traditional coaxial cable, twisted-pair, and fiber optic to communications services of the future, including Fiber

Channel, FDDI, and SONET (described later in this chapter). ATM relies on **cell relay,** a high-speed transmission method based on fixed-size units (tiny ones only 53 bytes long) that are known as cells. These cells are multiplexed onto the carrier. An example of a cell is shown in Figure 8.11.

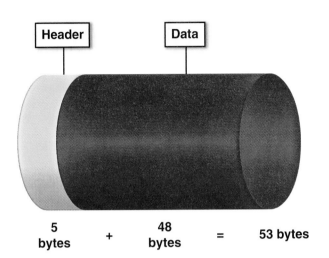

Header   **Data**

5 bytes   +   48 bytes   =   53 bytes

● **Figure 8.11**
ATM transmits data in 53-byte cells. What are the main features of ATM networks?

How ATM Works

Imagine a "universal" packaging machine. This machine takes in any type of data, whether they are delivered in spurts or in a constant stream, and turns those data into look-alike packages. On the transmission end, this is basically what ATM does. It takes incoming data, voice, and video, and it packages the contents in uniform, 53-byte cells. At the receiving end, ATM sends its cells out onto a WAN in a steady stream for delivery, as shown in Figure 8.12. The ATM-capable node handles the conversions using a three-layer ATM model. This model is summarized in Table 8.2.

● **Figure 8.12**
ATM converts all incoming data to same-size cells. How does this help make ATM networks so fast?

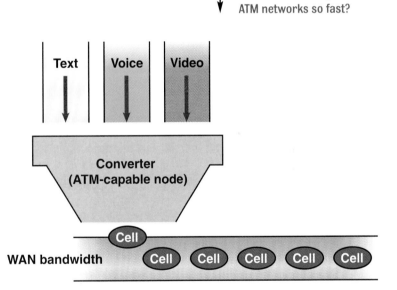

Text   Voice   Video

Converter (ATM-capable node)

WAN bandwidth   Cell   Cell   Cell   Cell   Cell   Cell

ATM Model	
ATM Layer	**Notes**
ATM Adaptation Layer (AAL)	Repackages incoming data (voice, data, video, and so on) into a 48-byte payload.
ATM Layer	Attaches header to payload to form an ATM cell. This header includes addressing as well as path and circuit information to get the data to the intended destination.
Physical Layer	Moves the ATM cell along the physical medium, whether modem, T1, or fiber optic cable.

● **Table 8.2**
The ATM model specifies how data are prepared and sent over an ATM network. How does the ATM Layer form an ATM cell?

After the cells arrive at their destinations, they go through the reverse of the sending process. The ATM Layer forwards the cells to the appropriate services (voice, data, video, and so on) in the ATM Adaptation Layer (AAL), where the cell contents are converted back to their original form. Everything is checked to be sure it arrived correctly, and the "reconstituted" information is delivered to the receiving device.

Enrichment LAB

Lab 8.2 Understanding the Digital Divide Practice additional hands-on networking skills on page 443.

B-ISDN

ATM was created for **broadband ISDN (B-ISDN).** B-ISDN is the next-generation ISDN, capable of delivering high quantities of data. Whereas normal ISDN (also called narrowband ISDN) works over traditional copper telephone wires, B-ISDN is intended to work over fiber optic cabling. B-ISDN services are divided into two basic categories, interactive services and distributed (or distribution) services.

◆ Interactive services include you-*and*-me types of transactions, such as videoconferencing, instant messaging, and information retrieval.

◆ Distributed services include you-*to*-me types of information that are either delivered or broadcast to the recipient. These services are further divided into those that the recipient controls (for example, e-mail or videoconferencing) and those that the recipient cannot control other than by refusing to "tune in" (for example, audio and television broadcasts).

In a sense, B-ISDN is comparable to a catalog shopping service that delivers everything from food to clothing. ATM is like the boxes in which those products are packaged and delivered.

Section 8.2 Assessment

Concept Check

1. **Define** X.25, Data Terminal Equipment (DTE), packet assembler/disassembler (PAD), Data Circuit-terminating Equipment (DCE), frame relay, Asynchronous Transfer Mode (ATM), cell relay, and broadband ISDN (B-ISDN).

2. **Explain** the advantages of frame relay.

3. **Describe** how ATM is used to transmit any type of data.

Critical Thinking

4. **Compare and Contrast** Describe the similarities and differences between how X.25 and frame relay networks transmit data.

5. **Synthesize Information** How does an ATM cell differ from a frame?

6. **Categorize B-ISDN** Categorize the attributes of broadband-ISDN and compare and contrast them.

Applying Skills

Choose a WAN Technology You have been asked to investigate WAN technologies for a large university hospital. In particular, they need the ability to videoconference with other hospitals. The ultimate goal is to allow physicians around the world to participate in live surgeries. Which technology is best suited to this application? Explain your answer.

Ethics & Technology

BRIDGING THE DIGITAL DIVIDE

Although it seems like computers are everywhere, many people around the world do not have computers or have access to the Internet.

The Digital Divide Network's Web site provides more information on the digital divide.

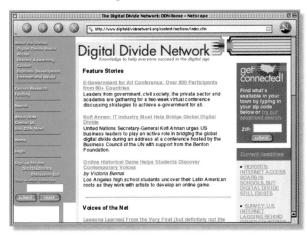

The Digital Divide

The gap between people who have access to technology and those who do not is often referred to as the digital divide. Although many Americans still do not use computers, computer literacy is rapidly increasing in the United States. However, according to The Digital Divide Network, only about 6 percent of the world's population has Internet access.

Why Is This a Problem?

The digital divide is about more than having computers or Internet access. It is really about the benefits and opportunities those technologies provide, including job skills, educational opportunities, and information.

Without technology, people could fall increasingly behind. In poor American neighborhoods and cities, children with limited access to computers lack computer skills. As adults, they may have a hard time competing for jobs that require basic proficiency.

Technology is sometimes out of reach for people in developing nations. These countries are often more concerned with finding adequate nutrition, medical care, and jobs for their citizens.

What Is Being Done?

A huge effort is under way to close the digital divide. Large companies, such as IBM and Microsoft, have donated millions of dollars of hardware and software to communities in need. Schools, libraries, and organizations such as Boys and Girls Clubs and the YMCA often provide computers and free technology classes. In Africa and Asia, small computer centers are set up in isolated villages to give people access to communication and education.

You can help shrink the gap. Donate used computer hardware or software. There are organizations that will recycle the computers and give them to groups that need them. You can also donate your skills. Volunteer with a local organization to help others become better computer users.

Tech Focus

1. Estimate the percentage of jobs from a listing that require computer skills. Discuss the impact of computer access on job opportunities.

2. Contact a local charitable organization that recycles computers or needs volunteers to teach computer skills. Choose one that the class can support as an ongoing project.

Guide to Reading

Main Ideas

FDDI transmits data over fiber optic cabling using a ring topology. SONET multiplexes incoming signals for transmission over very-high-speed optical cabling. SMDS transmits data in any format between networks.

Key Terms

Synchronous Optical NETwork (SONET)
Synchronous Digital Hierarchy (SDH)
optical carrier (OC)
Synchronous Transport Signal (STS)
Switched Multimegabit Data Services (SMDS)

Reading Strategy

Contrast two of the technologies you read about in this section. Create a chart similar to the one below (also available online).

Technology ⎯⎯⎯ Contrasting Features ⎯⎯⎯ Technology

Nothing in technology ever stands still for very long. For all its strengths, ATM is but one of many competing technologies. Another technology, Fiber Distributed Data Interface (FDDI), is well known for its use in both LANs and WANs. Two others are Synchronous Optical NETwork (SONET) and Switched Multimegabit Data Services (SMDS). All three—FDDI, SONET, and SMDS—tie in with ATM. In this section, you learn more about each of these technologies.

FDDI

FDDI was developed based on ring topology and token passing. It uses fiber optic as its medium of transmission. FDDI was developed for two primary reasons. First, it was designed to support and extend the capabilities of older LANs, such as Ethernet and Token Ring. Second, it provides a reliable infrastructure for businesses moving mission-critical applications to networks. Mission-critical applications or devices are essential to business operations. Failure of a mission-critical application or device could have serious consequences. For example, Wall Street trading companies are absolutely dependent on the applications and devices that handle billions of dollars of trading transactions.

FDDI transmits data at very high speeds (100 Mbps). However, its physical rings are limited to a maximum length of 100 kilometers (62 miles). This limitation puts FDDI into a "more than a LAN, but not quite a WAN" status. It is a good choice as the backbone covering a number of smaller LANs. It can also provide the core of a network as large as a metropolitan area network (MAN). FDDI is often used to connect high-end servers or mainframes or other high-performance devices, such as video/graphics workstations, within a LAN. These types of devices benefit from FDDI because a considerable amount of bandwidth is needed to transfer large amounts of data at satisfactorily high speeds.

Although FDDI was developed specifically for use with fiber optic cable, it can operate on a variety of cable types. A variation of FDDI, Copper-Distributed Data Interface (CDDI) operates on copper cabling. It is cheaper

Activity 8.2 Mission Critical
Discover the vast array of mission-critical requirements related to business networking practices at **networking.glencoe.com**.

to implement, but CDDI is limited to cable lengths of 200 meters. CDDI could be used to connect servers to nearby switches or hubs within a LAN. In all, FDDI supports four different types of cable:

- **Multimode fiber optic cable**—This type of cable can be used over a maximum of 2,000 meters and uses light emitting diodes (LEDs) as a light source.
- **Single-mode fiber optic cable**—This type of cable can be used over a maximum of 10,000 meters and uses lasers as a light source. Single-mode cable is thinner at the core than multimode cable, but it provides greater bandwidth because of the way the light impulse travels through the cable.
- **Category 5 Unshielded Twisted Pair (Cat5 UTP) copper wiring**—This cable contains eight wires and, like the next category, can be used over distances of up to 30 meters.
- **IBM Type 1 Shielded Twisted Pair (STP) copper wiring**—This is a shielded cable that contains two pairs of twisted wires, with each pair also shielded.

FDDI Topology and Fault Tolerance

As mentioned previously, FDDI topology is similar to Token Ring, except that it operates using optical transmissions. Another important distinction is that FDDI is characterized by two counter-rotating rings (known as a dual-ring topology). An FDDI topology by itself usually does not make use of hubs, as shown in Figure 8.13.

● **Figure 8.13**
FDDI uses two counter-rotating rings to provide fault tolerance. What is the second ring used for?

The second ring is there mostly for insurance. Normally in an FDDI network, the primary ring carries the tokens and data. The secondary ring remains idle and is used as a backup for fault tolerance. Should a node break the primary ring, traffic "wraps" around the problem node and data are carried in the opposite direction on the secondary ring.

Sometimes both rings are used for data. In this case, the data travel in one direction (clockwise) on one ring and in the other direction (counter-clockwise) on the other ring. Using both rings to carry data means that twice as many frames can circulate at the same time and, therefore, the speed of the network can double—from 100 Mbps to 200 Mbps.

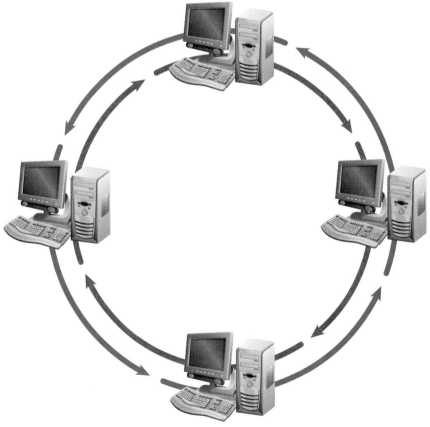

FDDI Token Passing

FDDI puts a slight twist on the Token Ring concept. Similar to Token Ring, nodes can only pass data when they have the token. However, to increase the fault tolerance, FDDI allows nodes to detect problems. When a problem is detected, the node can generate a special beacon frame, which it sends to the network. This beacon signifies that there is a problem. Neighboring nodes detect the beacon and transmit their own beacons. Eventually, a beacon reaches the node that started the transmission. This node can then generate a new token and begin transmitting again.

Structure of an FDDI Network

FDDI networks are limited to rings no longer than 100 kilometers apiece. They are also limited to no more than 500 nodes per ring. Although the overall network topology must conform to a logical ring, the network does not have to look like a circle. It can include stars connected to hubs or switches, and it can even include trees—collections of hubs/switches connected in a hierarchy. As long as the stars and trees connect in a logical ring, the FDDI network is happy.

Nodes on FDDI Networks The nodes that connect to the network come in two varieties. The type depends on how they are attached to the FDDI ring. One variety, called a single attachment station, or SAS, connects to a hub-like concentrator and, through the concentrator, to the primary ring. Because an SAS connects to a concentrator, the latter device can isolate the node from the rest of the ring if it happens to fail. The second type of node, called a dual attachment station, or DAS, has two connections to the network. These can link it either to another node and a concentrator or—if their operation is critical to the network—to two concentrators, one of which serves as a backup in case the other fails. This type of two-concentrator connection for a single resource, such as a mission-critical server, is known as *dual homing*. It is used to provide the most fail-safe backup mechanism possible.

Network Speed FDDI is a high-speed, high-bandwidth network based on optical transmissions. It is relatively expensive to implement, although the cost can be lowered by mixing fiber optic with copper cabling. Because FDDI has been around for quite some time, it has been fine-tuned to a high level of stability. It is most often used as a network backbone for connecting high-end computers (mainframes and peripherals) and for LANs connecting high-performance engineering, graphics, and other workstations that demand rapid transfer of large amounts of data.

SONET

Synchronous Optical NETwork (SONET) is an American National Standards Institute (ANSI) standard for the transmission of different types of information—data, voice, and video. In the United States and Japan, SONET is transmitted over the fiber optic cables that are widely used by long-distance carriers, such as AT&T, MCI, and Sprint. In Europe, this standard has been adopted by the ITU and was renamed **Synchronous Digital Hierarchy(SDH)**. Together, SONET and SDH represent a global standard for using optical media to transmit digital data around the world.

> **READ ME!**
>
> **Jargon** A concentrator is a communications device that combines signals from multiple sources before sending them along to their network destination.

Multiplexing Signals

SONET works at the Physical Layer. It is concerned with the details related to framing, multiplexing, managing, and transmitting information synchronously over optical media. In essence, SONET specifies a standard means for multiplexing a number of slower signals onto a larger, faster signal for transmission. Two signal definitions lie at the heart of the SONET standard regarding multiplexing capability:

◆ **Optical carrier (OC)** levels, which are used by fiber optic media and translate roughly to speed and carrying capacity

◆ **Synchronous Transport Signals (STSs),** which are the electrical equivalents of OC levels and are used by nonfiber media

● **Figure 8.14**
SONET multiplexes many incoming signals for high-speed transport. What is the difference between SONET and SDH?

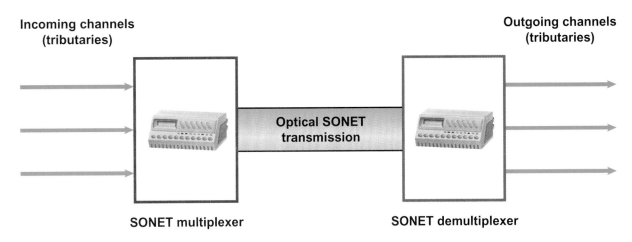

Incoming channels (tributaries)

Outgoing channels (tributaries)

Optical SONET transmission

SONET multiplexer

SONET demultiplexer

Charging the Transmission

Why is STS required if SONET is an optical transport technology? Remember that it is a long-distance transport. Although transmissions flow through the SONET system in optical form, they do not begin and end that way. Transmissions are multiplexed onto the SONET optical medium from—and to—other electrically-based types of digital transport such as T1. You might think of SONET as something like the Mississippi River, with channels it connects to as tributaries that flow into and out of it. (In SONET terminology, those channels are called tributaries, so the analogy is reasonably accurate.) Figure 8.14 shows the basics of what happens during a SONET transmission.

Because SONET is a synchronous transport, the signals it works with are tied to timing. The transmission speeds it handles are based on multiples of a single base signal rate known as STS-1 (Synchronous Transport Signal Level-1) and the equivalent optical measure, OC-1. Table 8.3 summarizes the various speed levels of SONET.

Before you run out and lease an OC-192 line, keep this in mind. OC-48 costs several thousands of dollars to set up and several hundreds of thousands of dollars *per month* to maintain. Large communication companies are the typical users of SONET.

● **Table 8.3**
SONET speeds are measured as multiples of a single base rate. What is the difference between STS and OC?

SONET Transmission Speeds	
Rate	**Speed**
STS-1/OC-1 (base)	51.84 Mbps
STS-3/OC-3	155.52 Mbps
STS-12/OC-12	622.08 Mbps
STS-48/OC-48	2.488 Gbps
STS-192/OC-192	10 Gbps

How SONET Works

SONET converts electrical (STS) signals to optical (OC) levels for transport. It also "unconverts" them (OC to STS) at the point in which the transmissions leave the SONET media.

Transmissions travel along fiber optic cables. It is impossible to stretch a single fiber optic cable over too great a distance. As it travels from source to destination, a transmission can pass through more than one intermediate multiplexer. It can also pass through switches, routers, and repeaters that boost the signal. Each part of this route is given a different SONET name:

◆ A section is a single length of fiber optic cable.
◆ A line is any segment of the path that runs between two multiplexers.
◆ A path is the complete route between the source multiplexer (where signals from tributaries are combined) and the destination multiplexer (where the signals are demultiplexed so they can be sent on their way).

SONET transmissions are made up of 810-byte frames. These are sent out at a rate of 8,000 per second. Each frame contains a number of bytes that are used to monitor and manage the data. In addition, there are two remarkable aspects about SONET frames.

1. First, the frames pour out in a steady stream, whether or not they contain any information. In other words, they are like freight cars on an endless train.

   ◆ If some data happen to arrive at the time SONET is putting a frame together, those data get popped into the frame—and the freight car is loaded.
   ◆ If no data arrive, the frame leaves the "station" empty, as shown in Figure 8.15.

2. Second, because SONET is a synchronous transport, each frame contains a device called a pointer that indicates where the actual data in the frame begin.

   ◆ This pointer is necessary because it is impossible for incoming data streams to be synchronized to the same clock.
   ◆ Instead, SONET allows for a certain amount of variation in timing. The pointer ensures that the beginning of the data payload is clearly marked for retrieval at its destination.

Figure 8.15
SONET frames are sent continuously, like freight cars—whether they contain data or not. What do "pointers" signal in SONET frames?

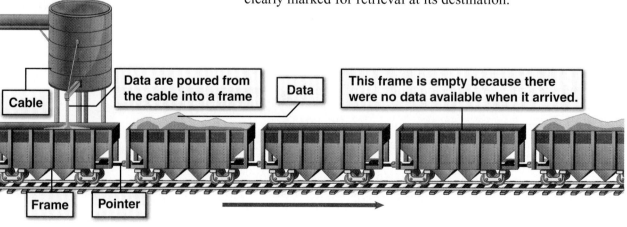

Cable

Data are poured from the cable into a frame

Data

This frame is empty because there were no data available when it arrived.

Frame   Pointer

Protocol Layers in the SONET Standard

In doing all of the work of organizing, multiplexing, transmitting, and routing frames, SONET relies on four protocol layers, each of which handles one aspect of the entire transmission, as shown in Table 8.4.

SONET Protocol Layers

Layer	Duties
Photonic Layer	Converts signals between electrical and optical forms
Section Layer	Creates frames and monitors for errors in transmission
Line Layer	Multiplexes, synchronizes, and demultiplexes
Path Layer	Gets the frame from source to destination

Table 8.4
SONET protocol layers sound nothing like OSI layers. How would you map the SONET layers to the OSI model?

These are the basics of SONET, and they should help you understand at least roughly how SONET works. Perhaps the most important lesson to carry away from this is the realization that SONET represents a fast, reliable transport for developing our future WAN technologies, including B-ISDN and, by extension, ATM.

SMDS

Switched Multimegabit Data Services (SMDS) technology is a broadband public networking service offered by communications carriers. It is a means for businesses to connect LANs in separate locations. It is a less expensive alternative to dedicated leased lines. SMDS is a connectionless, packet-switched technology well-suited to the type of "bursty" traffic characteristic of LAN (or LAN-to-LAN) communications.

One way to think of bursting is this: Suppose you are shipping goods via trucks on the freeway. Most of the time, the trucks have to share the road with lots of other people (transmissions). Occasionally, the road clears and you get the benefit of the whole freeway for transmission. This is called a burst, which happens regularly in LAN communications.

Instead of being "on" all the time, SMDS is connectionless, which means that it is available as needed. It is also a fast technology, transmitting at speeds between 1 Mbps and up to 45 Mbps.

The basis of an SMDS connection is a network address designed as a telephone number that includes country code and area code, as well as the local number. This address is assigned by the carrier and is used to connect LAN with LAN. A group address can also be used to broadcast information to a number of different LANs at the same time (see Figure 8.16 on the next page). SMDS takes it from there and makes a "best effort" to deliver the packets to their destinations. It does not check for errors in transmission, nor does it make an attempt at flow control. Those tasks are left to the communicating LANs.

SMDS packets vary in length, up to 9,188 bytes of data. They include the source and destination addresses. These packets are routed individually and can contain data in any form with which the sending LAN works—Ethernet packet, Token Ring packet, and so on. In other words, SMDS acts somewhat like a courier service—it picks up and delivers but does not concern itself with the contents of its packages.

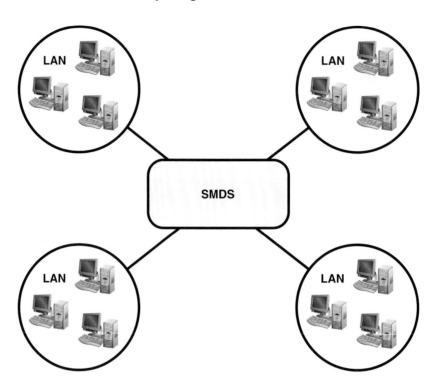

Figure 8.16
SMDS is a connectionless service that provides WAN transmissions on an as-needed basis. **Are "bursty" transmissions a good thing?**

Section 8.3 Assessment

Concept Check

1. Define Synchronous Optical NETwork (SONET), Synchronous Digital Hierarchy (SDH), optical carrier (OC), Synchronous Transport Signal (STS), and Switched Multimegabit Data Services (SMDS).

2. Identify which areas of the world use SONET.

3. Explain some of the benefits of SMDS for smaller businesses.

Critical Thinking

4. Analyze Information Explain how FDDI maintains a high level of fault tolerance.

5. Sequence Information List the steps multiple data streams would go through as they are transmitted across a SONET network.

6. Compare and Contrast Describe the similarities and differences between OC and STS signal definitions used in SONET.

Applying Skills

Apply the Right Technology You are consulting for a midsize company with offices in four cities located in several states. Each office needs to transmit data periodically during the day to other offices, but the amount of traffic is not high. The company does not have the ability to spend a lot of money for its WAN carrier service. Which technology would you recommend and why?

SECTION 8.1 How a WAN Works

Key Terms

carrier services, 224
remote access, 224
dial-up networking (DUN), 224
Virtual Private Network (VPN), 226
circuit-switched network, 228
message switching, 228
packet switching, 229
Packet Switching Exchange (PSE), 229

Main Ideas

- Carriers provide the means to transmit data across long distances.
- DUN and VPN can be used to connect to a network over long distances.
- Circuit-switched networks use dedicated physical connections to transmit data.
- Message-switched networks transmit entire messages from one intermediary to another.
- Intermediaries on a message-switched network can hold messages until an optimal time for transmission.
- Packet-switched networks create virtual circuits that disappear once the packets are transmitted.
- Packets can travel along many paths to reach their destination.

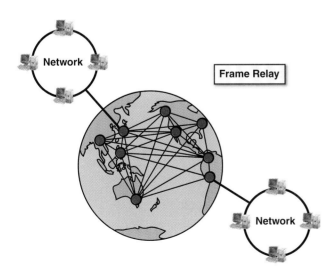

SECTION 8.2 Sending Data across a WAN

Key Terms

X.25, 232
Data Terminal Equipment (DTE), 232
packet assembler/disassembler (PAD), 232
Data Circuit-terminating Equipment (DCE), 232
frame relay, 233
Asynchronous Transfer Mode (ATM), 234
cell relay, 235
broadband ISDN (B-ISDN), 236

Main Ideas

- X.25 was designed to transmit packets across analog phone lines.
- Frame relay uses permanent, virtual circuits and less error control to speed transmissions.
- ATM transmits all types of data in fixed-size cells.
- B-ISDN and ATM were designed for each other.

SECTION 8.3 Developing Technologies

Key Terms

Synchronous Optical NETwork (SONET), 240
Synchronous Digital Hierarchy (SDH), 240
optical carrier (OC), 241
Synchronous Transport Signal (STS), 241
Switched Multimegabit Data Services (SMDS), 243

Main Ideas

- FDDI uses a unique double-ring topology to provide high fault tolerance.
- SONET is used to transmit data at very high speeds across long distances.
- SMDS uses fixed network addresses to transmit data in any format between networks.

READ TO SUCCEED PRACTICE

Add to Your Knowledge Look over the Main Ideas listed in the Reading Review on page 245. Which main ideas did you know before you read the chapter? Which did you learn more about as you read? What did you learn that is not listed? Write down any topics that you want to know more about but were not covered in the chapter. Use these as follow-up questions for your teacher or a class discussion.

Reviewing Key Terms

1. Explain what DUN does in remote areas.
2. What network function does VPN support?
3. What is the function of ATM in network communications?
4. What are the two digital technologies on which frame relay relies?
5. Where is packet switching commonly found?

Understanding Main Ideas

6. **Explain** why B-ISDN is considered the next generation ISDN.
7. **Describe** what the acronym SONET represents.
8. **Explain** the difference between circuit switching and packet switching.
9. **Describe** how SONET and SDH are related.
10. **Describe** what a carrier service and a remote access do together to transfer information among users in a WAN.
11. **Explain** why a VPN might be used instead of a DUN.
12. **Identify** the three major switching techniques to move data across a WAN and name one real world example for each.
13. **Describe** the difference between DTE and DCE.
14. **Identify** how OC and STS are related.
15. **List** the five techniques or "breeds" of packet switching and/or services that send data across a WAN.
16. **Explain** how FDDI offers high fault tolerance for a network backbone as large as MAN (Metropolitan Area Network). Refer to Figure 8.13 in your text.

Critical Thinking

17. **Analyze Information** Think about all of the network components used when someone telecommutes. Identify which components would be used.
18. **Compare and Contrast** Circuit-switched networks and packet-switched networks are the two dominant kinds of WANs in use today. What are the advantages and disadvantages of circuit switching and packet switching, and why?
19. **Evaluate** After reading the text, which technology for WANs is the most promising, and why?
20. **Sequence Information** Create a list of equipment required to transmit data across an X.25 network and briefly describe the function of the equipment in communications.
21. **Contrast Information** Why do single mode fiber optics allow for greater distances when compared to multimode fiber?
22. **Synthesize Information** The data transmitted in different "breeds" of packet-switched networks have different names. How do these data transmissions differ in their general format and operational function?
23. **Evaluation** Based on SONET transmission speeds, what is the fastest connection speed you would recommend that a large communication company make available? Explain your reasoning.

e-Review
networking.glencoe.com

Study with PowerPoint

To review the main points in this chapter, select **e-Review > PowerPoint Outlines > Chapter 8.**

Online Self Check

Test your knowledge of the material in this chapter by selecting **e-Review > Self Checks > Chapter 8.**

Making Connections

Social Studies—Develop a Timeline About every ten years WAN technologies adjust for market demand, implementation limitations, timing, and politics.

Use the Internet or available resources to research the approximate year in which each following WAN technology was launched:

- X.25
- frame relay
- ATM with B-ISDN
- SMDS

Create a timeline that shows the growth and decline of these technologies. For the last item on the timeline, show your view of the Internet for the decade to come.

STANDARDS AT WORK

Students use technology resources for solving problems and making informed decisions. (NETS-S 6)

Categorize Decision-Making Information

As you read in this chapter, broadband ISDN (B-ISDN) is capable of delivering high quantities of data. This is the next-generation technology that is intended to work over fiber optic cabling. B-ISDN provides two basic categories of services: interactive and distributed services.

Create a table that shows the B-ISDN interactive and distributed services that would help customers choose a service suitable for their particular communication needs. Include the following:

- A list of the ways of communicating
- The number of participants
- Who is in control of the transaction
- The service that allows broad interaction marked with a highlighter

TEAMWORK SKILLS

Debate a Position

Distance learning is a means of moving the classroom to allow people to study online anytime. Distance learning takes various forms.

1. With your teacher's permission, form groups of three to five students.
2. Analyze the following methods for delivering distance learning services and their features:
   - Pre-recorded lecture—students study at their own pace by postal mail, e-mail, and/or fax.
   - Live delivery—students observe what's going on in the instructional area without physically commuting to the area.
   - Interactive method—students at remote sites participate in both lecture and discussion. B-ISDN is a popular example of this type of distance learning.
3. Within your group, choose the above method that best describes your group's position, or create a hybrid form of the methods outlined, and list your reasoning for the choice.
4. Prepare to debate your position, according to your teacher's instructions and Robert's Rules of Orders.

CHALLENGE YOURSELF

Packet-Switching Performance

The two fundamental switching technologies for WANs are circuit switching and packet switching.

1. Calculate the maximum number of customers a 128 Kbps link can take with circuit switching and with packet switching if all the customers' traffic patterns are 16 Kbps with 50% on and 50% off.
2. Discuss which switching technology is better for performance and which is better for utilization based on your computation results.

YOU TRY IT

Networking Lab

1. Configuring Remote Connections

With the permission of your teacher, set up a computer using Windows XP to allow for remote connections. Note: The machines in this lab activity will need to be connected to a network.

A Use the Help and Support center found in Windows XP for specific instructions on how to set up your machine to accept remote connections. Click the **Start** button and then the **Help and Support** feature.

B On another computer with Windows XP, click **Start,** select **Programs,** select **Accessories,** choose **Communications,** and click on **Remote Desktop.**

C Enter the computer's name or IP address that you wish to control remotely.

D Log on to the machine and see how it interacts.

E Answer the following questions on a separate piece of paper:

- ◆ How might this type of connection tool allow for improved technical support?
- ◆ How might this process allow for improved productivity in the workplace?
- ◆ Describe issues on your network that may slow down or hinder the performance of this remote control session.
- ◆ What kind of security issues does this type of technology create?

2. Comparing DUN and VPN

DUN and VPN are the two popular ways to access networks remotely. Perform the following test to see which is faster, DUN or VPN.

A Connect to the Internet via DUN and send your partner an e-mail message with a large file attached.

B Disconnect from the Internet.

C Reconnect to the Internet via VPN and send your partner the same message.

D Ask your partner to tell you the sent and received times of both the messages.

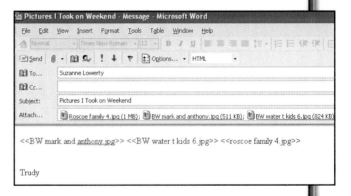

E Repeat steps 2 to 5 several times and calculate the average for each message's duration times, i.e., the difference between the received and sent times.

Compare your results with others in the class. Does VPN consistently take longer time than DUN? Explain your findings.

Networking Projects

1. Recommend ISP for Home Users

Imagine you own a small company that helps homeowners subscribe to ISPs for their Internet connections. Currently, the common methods for remote accessing an ISP have three forms:

◆ Dial-up modem connection via telephone line, such as American Online
◆ DSL modem connection via telephone line, such as AT&T Broadband Internet
◆ Cable modem connection via TV cable company, such as Comcast Online

Making a choice could be quite frustrating for the home user. There is no hard and fast rule. Conduct a survey about ISPs in your area. Consider the following attributes:

◆ transmission speed, that is, whether the claimed transmission speed is dedicated to the subscribed customer or shared with the users on the same transceiver (typically in your neighborhood)
◆ operational costs
◆ all the necessary devices, such as modem types and wiring categories for each form of the remote access
Write a recommendation explaining your results to the client.

2. Investigate Regional WAN Carrier Services

Each region's WAN carriers often provide different services to suit diverse demands for long-distance communications.

◆ Investigate what kinds of carrier services are available in your region and by whom they are offered.
◆ Study those offers and organize them into a spreadsheet by attributes such as transmission speed, geographic spacing, cost function, and so on.
◆ Next, with your teacher's permission, contact your school's network administrator to find out what carrier service your school system uses.
◆ Finally, investigate the traffic statistics running on your school's network.
◆ Include your findings in a spreadsheet similar to the one you just created for your regional data.

Compare the two spreadsheets. Justify why your school chooses to use this particular WAN technology.

CHAPTER 9

The Internet and the Web

WHY IT MATTERS......................................

The Internet is a giant network built of millions of pieces of hardware that are all interconnected. The individual pieces of hardware form small networks that are then joined together into larger networks and finally into the largest network—the Internet. The Internet is a lot like a large building, which is created with millions of pieces of building materials. Individual rooms are built that then make up larger offices that are all part of the main building.

Quick Write Activity

When you build a network, that network may become part of other larger networks. Write a brief paragraph that explains how your small network could be connected to other networks. Explain why it is important for you to plan a network that works with other existing networks.

WHAT YOU WILL DO..

READ TO SUCCEED

Prepare With a Partner

You might find it easier to work with a partner as you read through a chapter. Before you read, you and your partner can ask each other questions about the topics that will be discussed in the chapter. (Use the section headings or the "You Will Learn to . . ." objectives to identify the topics.) What do you both think is important to know after reading the section? Write down the questions you both have about each section. Keep these questions in mind as you read.

Section 9.1 Structure of the Internet

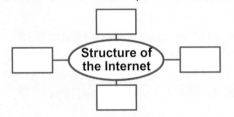
You have traveled the road from small peer-to-peer networks to clients and servers, LANs, extended LANs, and WAN technologies. You have now come to the biggest and most far-reaching network of them all—the Internet.

Many people see the Internet as entertainment and a shopping medium. It has fueled the explosion of interest in "Net" technologies ranging from:

◆ Web browsing
◆ Cross-platform software development
◆ E-commerce
◆ Intranets and extranets
◆ Electronic mail

Figure 9.1
The backbone is the foundation of the Internet.
What is the purpose of the backbone?

THE BACKBONE

The Internet is an internetwork. In other words, it is a global collection of smaller networks that communicate and transfer data among themselves. Although it has existed for far longer, the popular explosion of the Internet came in the early to mid-1990s. In just a few years, the Internet went from a purely academic forum, to a pop-culture icon, to a major influence on the world economy. Today, it is the ultimate collection of networks.

If you were able to see the structure of the Internet, you would see it as a global mesh of different networks and network levels, as shown in Figure 9.1.

The foundation of the Internet is a **backbone** of high-speed communications lines that interconnect many regional networks. Attached to these regional networks is an intricate web (no pun intended) of

networking.glencoe.com

other networks, servers, gateways, routers, and the numerous communications lines connecting them (see Figure 9.2).

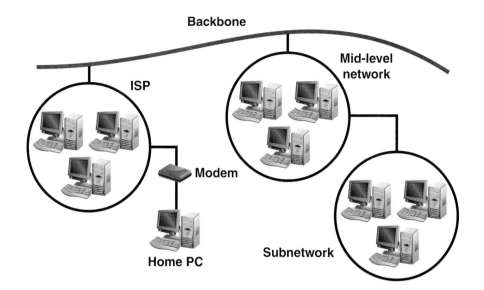

Figure 9.2
The Internet is the largest network of networks. What new technologies do you know of that are part of the ever-growing Internet?

REGIONAL AND OTHER NETWORKS

Geography played a significant role in determining the structure of the Internet. In the United States, for example, the Internet is made up of a number of **regional networks.** These networks serve the Northeast, Midwest, West, East, Southeast, Northwest, and central California. To join the larger Internet, these regional networks connect to a national backbone through one of many major locations known as **Network Access Points (NAPs).** Most NAPs are created and maintained by major telecommunications companies, such as Qwest, MCI, and AT&T, among others. NAPs are located near many major cities, such as San Francisco, Washington, D.C., Chicago, and New York.

On the cutting edge of the Internet is the Abilene network. This network serves the Internet2 project and connects approximately 220 universities across the United States. This high-speed, research-oriented network uses OC-192 optical cable technology to transmit data at 10 Gbps. New technologies developed on this network will become tomorrow's standard for high-speed data exchange.

INTERNET SERVICE PROVIDERS

To connect to the Internet, an **Internet Service Provider (ISP)** or an online service provider is needed. Microsoft Network (MSN) and America Online (AOL) are just two examples of the many ISPs available. Both ISPs and online service providers are the agents, so to speak, that provide a pipeline to the Internet. There is usually a connection to a regional network and, through that connection, to the Internet backbone.

As a group, these providers are businesses with the equipment and technology needed to provide high-speed access to the Internet over communications lines such as a T1. Some of these providers are national or international companies, such as MCI and AOL. Others are small organizations that provide

Activity 9.1 Investigating Internet Statistics The Abilene Project provides statistical information on the amount of data being transmitted across the Abilene network. Go to **networking.glencoe.com** to learn more.

Figure 9.3
Small ISPs provide a valuable Internet service.
Where on this page would you find this ISP's charges?

access to individual cities or relatively small geographic regions. As shown in Figure 9.3, ISPs charge a fee for accessing their services. The cost ranges from a few dollars a month for simple dial-up connections, to several thousand dollars a month for high-speed leased line services, such as T1 and T3.

Section 9.1 Assessment

Concept Check

1. **Define** backbone, regional network, Network Access Point (NAP), and Internet Service Provider (ISP).

2. **List** several cities where major Network Access Points can be found.

3. **Explain** the role of an ISP.

4. **Identify** two types of high-speed leased line Internet services.

Critical Thinking

5. **Draw Conclusions** Who is responsible for providing Network Access Points?

6. **Sequence Information** List the sequence of networks a user would likely pass through using a dial-up connection to connect to a university network through the Internet.

7. **Predict** What is the name of the network used for Internet2 research? What is your prediction for its future?

Applying Skills

Find Network Access Points Using the Internet and other resources available, find information about regional networks and Network Access Points. Is your city a major NAP for the Internet backbone? If so, make a list of the major companies that maintain NAPs in your city. If your city is not an NAP, what is the closest city with NAP?

Careers & Technology

CAREERS IN COMPUTER MAINTENANCE

Businesses use technology that includes desktop PCs, laptops, network servers, cabling, printers, and other peripherals. Because computer hardware often needs servicing, the demand for qualified PC hardware maintenance technicians is strong.

Hardware technicians often work in workshop-style offices.

The Hardware Technician's Job

Generally, a PC technician (also known as the hardware technician, PC technology specialist, or break/fix technician) is responsible for these tasks:

◆ Installing and configuring new computer hardware and peripherals
◆ Upgrading computers (installing new cards, memory, drives, and so on)
◆ Dealing with network-related hardware issues (installing network interface cards, working with cabling, installing hubs or routers, and so on)
◆ Troubleshooting and repairing hardware of all types

Many companies rely on their hardware maintenance technicians for input when planning for new system development, expansion, or acquisitions. This is because technicians are in daily contact with end users and develop a good understanding of their needs.

Skills and Job Requirements

The exact skills and educational requirements for a hardware maintenance technician's job depend on the organization. In a small company, the technician needs only basic PC troubleshooting skills and certification in electronics or computer maintenance.

In a demanding corporate environment, job requirements may include several years of work experience and a degree in electronics or computer science.

A technician may also need certification in the following:

◆ One or more operating systems (such as the Microsoft Certified Systems Administrator or Microsoft Certified Systems Engineer certifications)
◆ Network operating systems (such as Novell's Certified Novell Engineer certification)
◆ Networking hardware (such as one of the many certifications available through Cisco Systems, Inc.)

Tech Focus

1. Use the Internet to learn more about the role of hardware maintenance technicians. Describe various aspects of the position, such as educational requirements, everyday tasks, or one's role in an organization's IT department.

2. Assume your career goal is to become a hardware technician. Create a career plan that maps the path for reaching your goal. Show the career paths you might take after reaching this goal.

Guide to Reading

Main Ideas

Internet sites are categorized into domains according to organization type or geographic location. Domain names are resolved to IP addresses by DNS servers. ICANN is the organization responsible for assigning IP addresses.

Key Terms

DNS name server
root server
cache
Internet Corporation for Assigned Names and Numbers (ICANN)

Reading Strategy

Illustrate the process needed to resolve a Web site address you are trying to view on the Web. Create a chart similar to the one below (also available online).

Resolving a Web Site

READ ME!

Tech Tip In most Internet browsers, you no longer have to input the **www.** portion of a Web address. If you input **apple.com**, the browser assumes you mean **www.apple.com**.

It is a common misconception that the Internet and the World Wide Web (WWW or Web) are the same thing. The Web is a subset of the Internet. The "real" Internet is entirely text-based. Early on, the Web was not much more than a collection of easily viewed text documents with hyperlinks linking to other documents. Because the Web is part of the global Internet, there are a few common similarities, for instance, how the Internet and Web sites are organized and named.

DOMAINS

In addition to its physical structure and organization, the Internet is built upon the concept of domains. A domain, and the conventions used in creating and managing them, was devised as a means for:

◆ Maintaining order in the "virtual" world
◆ Allowing for orderly, continued growth of the Internet

DNS

Internet domains contribute to a classification system, similar to that used in the plant and animal kingdoms. The Internet classification is called the Domain Name System (DNS). DNS is used to uniquely identify sites based on a treelike hierarchy. This hierarchy includes a top-level domain, a second-level domain, and, often, one or more subdomains. A DNS site name looks like **www.microsoft.com**. Figure 9.4 breaks down the URL.

Figure 9.4 Each part of the URL is used to identify a specific Web site or page on the Internet. Why are so many sites part of the .com domain?

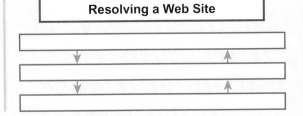

www . microsoft . com

This Web site is part of the WWW.

This portion represents the second-level domain—in this case, the name of a rather familiar business.

The period (pronounced "dot") separates the top-level and second-level domain names.

This portion represents the top-level domain.

Because DNS is based on a treelike hierarchy, domains at one level can be "parents" to multiple domains on the next (lower) level, as shown in Figure 9.5. For example, a domain name like **www.microsoft.com** can be extended further to include multiple subdomains within the site and, possibly, the names of host computers within the subdomains. For example, in the address **support.microsoft.com**, the **.com** represents the top-level domain. The **microsoft** portion of the address is the second-level domain. And **support** is a sublevel domain of **microsoft.com**.

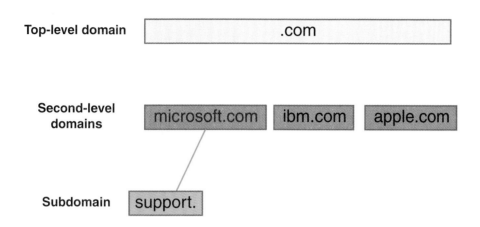

Figure 9.5
DNS creates an orderly hierarchy of sites. What level domain does **apple.com** represent in this figure?

Notice that even though your eye probably reads domain names from left to right, the name is *resolved* from right to left, with the highest-level domain at the far right (see Figure 9.6).

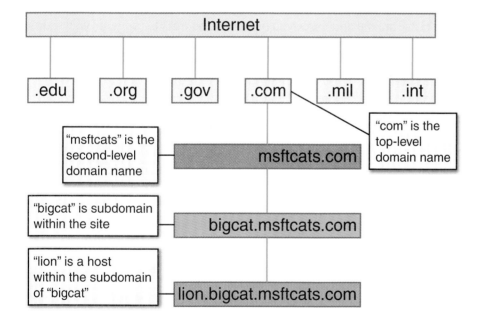

Figure 9.6
Domain names are resolved from right to left. What is the top-level domain in the address bigcat.msftcats.com?

Top-Level Internet Domains

The word *domain* can be thought of like a *kingdom.* Internet domains are, in some aspects, like virtual "kingdoms." The virtual kingdoms are united by the fact that all members of the kingdom have something in common. For the top-level domains, that "something" is either geography or type of organization.

Table 9.1 lists several geographic and organization domains. Within all these domains is the vast array of Internet sites that are created, owned, and maintained by various individuals and organizations.

Table 9.1 ●——→

Top-level domains organize sites by geography or organization type. What do sites with .gov have in common?

Top-Level Internet Domains			
Geographic Domain	Country	Organizational Domain	Type of Organization
.fr	France	.com	Commercial
.de	Germany	.org	Noncommercial organizations
.ca	Canada	.gov	U.S. Government
.jp	Japan	.net	Network-related groups
.za	South Africa	.edu	Educational institutions
.us	United States	.mil	U.S. Military
.ru	Russia	.int	International organizations

DNS DATABASES AND IP ADDRESSES

The preceding pages have described DNS in terms of naming Internet sites. These are the addresses you type in the address bar of your Web browser to visit a Web site. DNS also refers to databases distributed among a number of **DNS name servers.** For example, how do computers contact each other on the Internet? When you type **www.apple.com** to visit the Apple Web site, does your computer send out that particular stream of characters and hope that another computer named **www.apple.com** answers?

In reality, *apple.com* is just an easy name you and I can remember. Computers prefer working with numbers. On the Internet, sites are identified by an Internet Protocol (IP) address. You will recall that an IP address is a 32-bit number. It is divided into four 8-bit groups that look like this: 192.168.1.100. You learn more about what an IP address signifies in the next section of this chapter. For now, understand that an IP address uniquely identifies one computer from the millions of other computers out there in the world.

YOU TRY IT ▶

ACTIVITY 9A Finding Domain Registration Information

If you start your own business, you may want to register your own domain name, or even check an expiration date for a domain name. First, check to see if the domain name you want to use is already registered.

❶ Open your Web browser.

❷ Type http://www.networksolutions.com/ in the address bar of your Web browser. This site can look up registered domain names and provide you with the registration information.

❸ Click the link **WHOIS.**

❹ In the **Search All WHOIS Records** field, type www.apple.com, and then click **Search.**

❺ Type the computer-generated security code, and then click **Verify Code.**

❻ A Web page appears with information about the registrant. Record the expiration date for apple.com.

You may also need to locate important information, such as who owns the domain name. Using the WHOIS service on the Web makes this an easy task.

DNS and its databases are used to match domain names to IP addresses. This is called address resolution. When you type **www.apple.com** into your address bar, a DNS server looks through its database to find a matching entry, then resolves the IP address of 17.254.0.50. In Figure 9.7, a simplified version of the process is shown.

● **Figure 9.7**
DNS servers match domain names to IP addresses. *Why are DNS servers so important?*

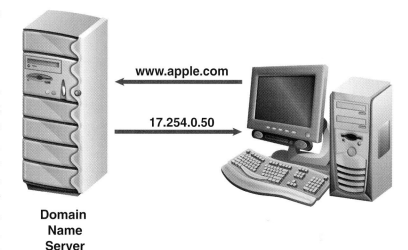

www.apple.com

17.254.0.50

Domain Name Server

Root Servers

The job performed by the DNS name servers is critical. You might imagine that these servers must be huge machines that survey the entire Internet, but this is not true. The Internet hierarchy, remember, is composed of different domain levels. DNS servers do their matchmaking at different levels, too. The DNS name server at any given level is considered the name/address authority for that level.

At the very highest level, DNS servers referred to as **root servers** are responsible for tracking top-level domain names (.com, .org, .net, and so on). The root server (or servers) responsible for sites within the .com domain contains the information needed to locate the server for **apple.com**. That is all it does. The root server does not concern itself with any lower levels—subdomains—within **apple.com**. At each subdomain level, another DNS server locates subdomains within its realm of responsibility.

Making Connections

When you type in a Web address, such as **info.apple.com** (Apple's support site), how is the address resolved?

A name resolution process known as an iterative query is used. This means that the request is sent repeatedly (iteratively) through name servers in the domain hierarchy until the complete address—or a "no such site exists" response—is produced.

Although the process sounds tedious and time-consuming (shown in Figure 9.8 on page 260), the DNS system speeds things along in two ways. First, the top-level database is replicated (reproduced) on many root servers located throughout the world. The task of resolving addresses at the highest level does not need to be handled by one or two overworked machines.

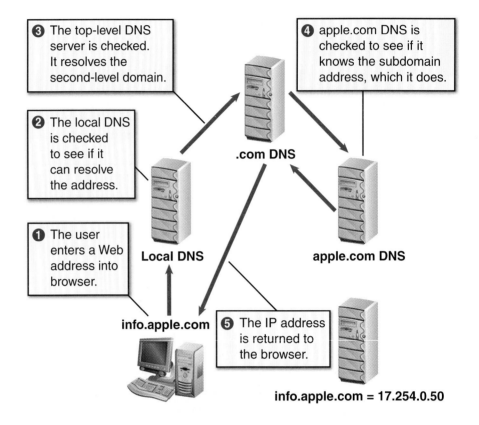

Figure 9.8 Requests are passed up the chain of DNS servers until an address is resolved or is not found. Why don't all DNS servers store the entire database of domain names and IP addresses?

❸ The top-level DNS server is checked. It resolves the second-level domain.

❹ apple.com DNS is checked to see if it knows the subdomain address, which it does.

❷ The local DNS is checked to see if it can resolve the address.

.com DNS

❶ The user enters a Web address into browser.

Local DNS

apple.com DNS

info.apple.com

❺ The IP address is returned to the browser.

info.apple.com = 17.254.0.50

Second, servers at all levels cache the addresses they have already resolved. A **cache** is a storage area in memory. When a request for a particular location arrives, these servers consult their cache first. If they find the requested address, they can send an immediate response to the requesting computer. If the address cannot be found in the addresses stored in the cache, then the servers have to go through the string of iterative queries to resolve the name.

YOU TRY IT

ACTIVITY 9B Displaying the DNS Cache

Whenever you visit a Web site, the domain name must be resolved to an IP address by DNS servers scattered throughout the Internet. A small amount of cache memory is used on your computer to remember these IP addresses for future use. You can view the contents of the local DNS cache by performing the following on Windows-based computers (including Windows XP and Windows 2000):

Figure 9.9 A small DNS cache is stored on the local computer temporarily.

❶ Click the **Start** button, and then click **Run**.

❷ Type cmd, and then click **OK**.

❸ At the command prompt, type ipconfig /displaydns. Be certain to enter a space between ipconfig and /displaydns. If you have been on the Web in the last few minutes, you should see a list (sometimes fairly long) of domain names and the associated IP addresses (see Figure 9.9).

4 You can also clear the DNS cache. At the command prompt, type ipconfig /flushdns. This clears the contents of the DNS cache. You might need to do this when a Web site is being updated frequently, yet you are still seeing the old pages.

5 Leave the command prompt window open, then open your Internet browser, and go to your home page.

6 Reactivate the command prompt window and type ipconfig /displaydns again.

The DNS cache on your local computer makes it faster when you need to return to a site repeatedly in a short amount of time. These two options of the ipconfig command can provide interesting and valuable information.

ICANN

DNS involves some heavy-duty tracking and record keeping to ensure that site names are not duplicated, site names and IP addresses are correctly maintained, and new sites and their corresponding IP addresses are added to the appropriate databases.

Within an organization, it is the responsibility of the organization itself to keep track of its subdomains, hosts, and various subgroups (called zones). The responsibility for registering domain names, such as **apple.com**, is handled by a corporation known as **Internet Corporation for Assigned Names and Numbers (ICANN).** ICANN is a nonprofit organization that was founded in 1998 to assign IP addresses, preserve the operational stability of the Internet, and oversee the Internet's root server system.

Activity 9.2 Defining the Internet's Future In addition to ICANN, other organizations and standards groups play important roles in defining, managing, and shaping the future of the Internet. Read more about some of these organizations at **networking.glencoe.com**.

Section 9.2 Assessment

Concept Check

1. Define DNS name servers, root server, cache, and Internet Corporation for Assigned Names and Numbers (ICANN).

2. Describe what an IP address is used for and how it is formed.

3. Explain the role of the ICANN organization.

Critical Thinking

4. Sequence Information Suppose you want to view the site at **support.microsoft.com**. Take apart this domain name and show to which hierarchy level each portion of the name belongs.

5. Draw Conclusions How are kingdoms and top-level domains similar?

Applying Skills

Make Connections Suppose you are using your school's LAN to access the Internet and do research for an upcoming project. You need to visit the **google.com** Web site. In as much detail as possible, describe how your computer resolves the name **google.com** to an IP address to make the connection.

The Internet relies on TCP/IP to transmit data between computers. To tell one computer from another, IP addresses are assigned to every computer. In this section, you learn all about IP addresses.

IP ADDRESSING

Just imagine reading an advertisement that told you to visit the Web address:

11001111.00101110.10001010.00010100

Only slightly better would be the decimal version:

207.46.138.20

As you know, domain names are resolved to IP addresses through DNS. As you recall, an IP address, such as 207.46.138.20, is really a 32-bit number. It is separated into four octets (8-bit groups). Each group of numbers in an IP address is limited to values between 0 and 255.

Every computer needs an IP address. In an isolated network, it does not matter what IP address is assigned, as long as all the addresses fall within the same network designation. However, after you connect to the Internet, every computer must be assigned a unique number. When a domain is registered, an IP address, or block of IP addresses is assigned to that domain. This address identifies two things: the network and a host (computer) on that network. A system of IP address classes is used to keep one network separate from other networks.

Classes of IP Addressing

A range of assignable IP addresses technically runs from 0.0.0.0 to 255.255.255.255. This is called the **address space.** However, not all these addresses are available for assignment, as some are reserved for special use. For example, the address 0.0.0.0 always represents the local network. The address 255.255.255.255 is used to broadcast messages to the entire local network. The address 127.0.0.1 is another special reserved address, called a loopback address. A **loopback address** is used to test whether a computer's network capabilities are functioning.

The assignable address space is divided into five classes and is identified by the binary form of the IP address, as shown in Table 9.2.

IP's 32-bit address space allows for over 4 billion unique addresses, but there are some problems. For example, a small business with ten computers applies for a public IP address. Falling under Class C, the IP network address (the first 24 bits) is assigned, and a chunk of 254 host addresses is given to the small business. The business only needed ten, but all 254 addresses are now gone. The problem grows for those businesses with a Class A address. Because only the first eight bits identify the network, a huge chunk of 16.7 million addresses goes with it. Subnetting helps alleviate some of this problem, but the future lies in IPv6, which you learn about shortly.

IP Address Classes

Class	First Octet Values	Maximum Number of Networks	Maximum Number of Hosts within Network
A	1–126	126	16,777,214
B	128–191	16,384	65,534
C	192–223	268,435,456	254
D	224–239	N/A	Multicast addresses
E	240–254	N/A	Experimental addresses

Table 9.2

IP addresses are divided into separate network classes. What is the reserved address 127.0.0.1 used for?

Subnetting and Subnet Masks

For an IP address to be valid, it must use a combination of an IP address, along with a subnet mask. A **subnet mask** is used to determine the portion of the IP address that identifies the network and the portion that identifies the host. In a Class C address, the first three octets identify the network, and the remaining octet identifies the host. In Table 9.3, an example is provided showing the IP address and a typical (default) subnet mask.

Enrichment LAB

Lab 9.1 Locate IP Addresses with NSLookup Practice additional hands-on networking skills on page 444.

Default Subnet Mask

IP (decimal)	207.46.138.20
IP (binary)	11001111.00101110.10001010.00010100
Subnet mask (decimal)	255.255.255.0
Subnet mask (binary)	11111111.11111111.11111111.00000000
What the subnet mask represents	nnnnnnnn.nnnnnnnn.nnnnnnnn.hhhhhhhh

n = network, h = host

Table 9.3

Subnet masks identify which portion of an IP address represents the network and which portion represents the host. What would the default subnet mask be for a Class B IP address?

Table 9.3 on page 263 shows the IP address and a default subnet mask. The subnet mask identifies the first 24 bits as the network address, with the remaining eight bits identifying the host. This is the most common scenario for a Class C address.

In some situations, it is necessary to further divide the host addresses into subnetworks. This may be done for security purposes or to divide the network into smaller pieces to keep a busy portion of the network separate from the rest. In this case, the subnet mask can be used to identify a subnet or subnetwork. This subnet mask rigidly defines which IP addresses are available. In Table 9.4, another scenario is presented in which the network is divided into two subnets.

Creating a Subnet

Subnet mask (decimal)	255.255.255.192
Subnet mask (binary)	11111111.11111111.11111111.11000000
What the subnet mask means	nnnnnnnn.nnnnnnnn.nnnnnnnn.sshhhhhh

n = network, s = subnet, h = host

In this case, the first two bits of the host portion are reserved to identify the subnet. The remaining six bits are used to identify the host. In this scenario, hosts on subnet #1 can have an address between 223.46.15.65 and 223.46.15.126. Hosts on subnet #2 can have an address between 223.46.15.129 and 223.46.15.190.

You can use an easy formula to calculate the number of subnets a given number of subnet bits will create: 2^n = number of subnetworks. The n represents the number of bits used as the subnet ID. If three bits are used as the subnet ID, then calculating 2^3 results in eight possible subnetworks.

Another simple formula, $2^x - 2$, reveals the number of available hosts. The x represents the number of bits available to the host ID. In the previous example, three bits were used for the subnet ID, leaving five bits for the host ID. Thus, $2^5 - 2 = 30$, the number of available hosts per subnet. Keep in mind that for every subnet, the host ID of all 0s is reserved as the network ID, and the host ID of all 1s is reserved for broadcast messages. Also keep in mind that subnetting always reduces the number of available host addresses. From there, it is a relatively easy matter to calculate the IP address ranges for each subnet, as shown in Table 9.5.

Calculating IP Address Ranges

Subnet Value (Binary)	Subnet Value (Decimal)	Host addresses (decimal) = subnet bits + host bits Host bits of all 0s are reserved for subnet Host bits of all 1s are reserved for broadcasting
000	0	1–30
001	32	33–62
010	64	65–94
011	96	97–126
100	128	129–158
101	160	161–190
110	192	193–222
111	224	225–254

IPv6

One of the main problems with the 32-bit IP address space (called IPv4 because it is the fourth version of IP) and the IP class system is that we are running out of IP addresses. Consider this: for every Class B address that is assigned, 65,534 host addresses go with it, regardless of whether all of those are ever used. There are bound to be a lot of wasted addresses.

Internet Protocol version 6 (IPv6) is the latest generation of the IP protocol. It is also called Next Generation IP, or IPng. IPv6 uses 128-bit addresses, which works out to 4 billion times 4 billion times 4 billion times the current number (4 billion) of IP addresses. Yes, it is a pretty huge number.

Besides dramatically increasing the address space, IPv6 includes several other very important capabilities. First, IPv6 hosts can configure themselves, eliminating the need for manual IP addressing or even DHCP, which assigns IP addresses automatically (you learn about this momentarily). Second, IPv6 includes built-in security capabilities that far exceed what the current implementation of IP has available. In addition, IPv6 uses a compressed header format that eliminates a lot of the wasted space.

IPv6 is here now. It operates with the current IP standard (IPv4), and can be installed as a software upgrade on existing devices. Mac OS X 10.2 and Linux 2.2 (and higher) have built-in IPv6 functionality. Windows XP comes with it, but it must be installed and is currently included only for development and testing. Future versions of Windows will likely have full IPv6 support built into the OS.

WORKING WITH TCP/IP ADDRESSES

Many important services are involved for IP packets to get transmitted between Internet-networked computers. These services handle important tasks, such as assigning IP addresses, resolving hardware addresses from IP addresses, and resolving domain names to IP addresses (as you learned with DNS).

ARP

Before an IP packet can be forwarded to another host, the hardware address of the receiving machine must be known. **Address Resolution Protocol (ARP)** is used to determine the hardware address (MAC address) that corresponds to an IP address. If ARP does not know the address, it asks for help. All hosts on the network process the request. If any of the hosts contain the map to that address, they pass it back to the requestor. The packet is then sent on its way, and the new information address is stored in the router's cache.

RARP

Reverse Address Resolution Protocol (RARP) works the reverse of ARP. When the hardware, or MAC address, is known, but not the IP address, RARP is used to look it up. RARP is a service that normally runs on a server. It maintains a database of machine numbers, which is used to match the physical address to its associated IP address.

DHCP

The **Dynamic Host Configuration Protocol (DHCP)** is used to automatically assign IP addresses within a network. As you know, all IP addresses in a network must be unique. An administrator could assign all these IP addresses by hand by going from computer to computer. However, assigning and keeping track of hundreds or thousands of IP addresses in a large network would quickly become unmanageable.

A DHCP server automatically maintains a database of IP addresses. As a computer logs onto the network, the DHCP server locates an available IP address and assigns it to the computer. This IP address is "leased" to the computer for a certain amount of time.

WINS

Computers running the Windows OS are assigned a computer name that is unique within the network. Although DHCP is used to dynamically assign IP addresses, it does not keep track of which Windows computer name is matched to which IP address. The **Windows Internet Naming Service (WINS)** is used to match computer names to IP addresses in a Windows network. As computers log on to the network and are assigned IP addresses by DHCP, WINS updates its own database automatically.

Gateways

As you learned earlier in this book, a gateway connects two networks together. Often, a gateway connects a LAN to the Internet and provides security features. However, the term gateway is often used for nodes that serve to connect two subnetworks together. In this context, routers and even switches fall under this description. The main thing to remember is that each computer must be assigned to a gateway if it wants to communicate with other computers outside of its network or subnetwork. Assigning a gateway is simply a matter of inputting the correct IP address of the node functioning as the gateway.

YOU TRY IT

ACTIVITY 9C Configuring DHCP, WINS, and Gateway

Configuring a Windows computer's IP settings is relatively easy to do, as long as you know the necessary IP addresses for each device. In this activity, you learn how to check your computer's configuration. The following steps are for the Windows XP OS.

1 Click **Start,** and then click **Control Panel.**

2 Click **Network and Internet Connections** in Category view.

3 Click **Network Connections.**

4 Right-click the **Local Area Connection** icon, and then choose **Properties.**

5 Select **Internet Protocol (TCP/IP),** and then click **Properties.**

6 Click **Advanced.** As shown in Figure 9.10 on page 267, the Advanced TCP/IP Settings window has tabs where you can configure DHCP, DNS, WINS, and Gateway settings.

7 Select the **Settings** tab, and then click **Add** in the **Default Gateways** group.

8 Enter the Gateway IP address, and then click **Add** (only if told to do so by your teacher—otherwise, click **Cancel**).

Adding a DHCP, DNS, or WINS server(s) is a repeat of the same process. Assigning these servers is an important step in configuring a Windows OS computer to participate on the network.

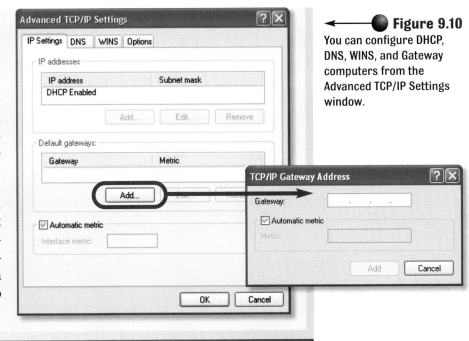

Figure 9.10
You can configure DHCP, DNS, WINS, and Gateway computers from the Advanced TCP/IP Settings window.

There is much to know to properly configure a TCP/IP network. It helps that services such as DHCP and WINS automatically assign IP addresses and resolve Windows computer names.

Section 9.3 Assessment

Concept Check

1. **Define** address space, loopback address, subnet mask, Internet Protocol version 6 (IPv6), Address Resolution Protocol (ARP), Reverse Address Resolution Protocol (RARP), Dynamic Host Configuration Protocol (DHCP), and Windows Internet Naming Service (WINS).

2. **Identify** how a loopback address is used for and the IP address reserved for that function.

3. **List** some of the devices that can act as a gateway.

Critical Thinking

4. **Categorize** Describe the five classes of IP addresses and list the address ranges of each class.

5. **Contrast Information** Explain the difference between the roles of a DHCP and a WINS server.

6. **Analyze Information** What are the advantages of IPv6 over the current IPv4?

7. **Compare Information** Compare the IP classes and explain why public addresses are not useful for all businesses.

Applying Skills

Calculate Subnet IP Addresses You work for a small company with about 150 employees. The company needs two subnetworks. What class of IP address should the company apply for? What subnet mask should be used? Identify the ranges of IP addresses that can be used in each subnet.

THE WEB IN BUSINESS TRANSACTIONS

Companies that use the Internet for business use many different strategies to make their Web sites faster, more reliable, and more secure.

Bigger Is Sometimes Better

Many large companies with busy Web sites need to use powerful computers, such as mainframe systems. This is especially true for e-commerce businesses such as retailers, airlines, banks, insurance companies, and credit card services. These online businesses maintain huge and constantly changing databases of information.

Mainframe systems are still used to support e-commerce Web sites.

The computers for business networks must provide information to internal workers and managers. They must also feed data to the company's Web servers at a rapid rate. That is why some companies also use mainframe systems such as Web servers. They are fast and reliable enough to handle thousands of transactions every day.

Many companies use "server farms" to meet internal and e-commerce needs. Server farms may connect dozens of servers to storage systems.

Security Is Everything

Companies must protect their internal data from viruses, hacking, and other threats. E-commerce sites must also protect customer data, to prevent identity theft, fraud, and other crimes.

Businesses use three primary means to keep online transactions secure:

- ◆ **Firewalls**—A firewall is hardware or software that prevents unauthorized requests from entering a network.
- ◆ **Encryption**—This technology allows server and client computers to "garble" data, which makes it unusable to anyone else. Secure Internet protocols such as Secure Sockets Layer (SSL) and Transport Layer Security (TLS) are used by many businesses to encrypt data.

  Encryption is commonly used to protect transactions, such as electronic fund transfers or electronic purchases. It protects customers' personal information, such as account numbers and addresses.
- ◆ **Virtual Private Networks (VPNs)**—Many companies conduct business-to-business (B2B) transactions online. Instead of using the public Internet, however, they may use a Virtual Private Network (VPN).

Tech Focus

1. Research one of the security threats facing businesses on the Web. Discuss the social and economic impact of these practices.

2. What components would you need for a basic e-commerce Web site? Bear in mind that it must tie into a company's internal systems.

Section 9.4 Internet and Web Services

Guide to Reading

Main Ideas

Web browsers display pages written in HTML format. Search engines index and categorize sites on the Web to make information easy to find. Services like FTP, NNTP, and Telnet add capabilities such as file transfer and remote control of computers. The Web provides a variety of entertainment options.

Key Terms

Hypertext Markup Language (HTML)
search engine
Network News Transfer Protocol (NNTP)
newsgroups
Usenet
Telnet
online gaming
multiuser dungeon (MUD)
instant messaging (IM)

Reading Strategy

Show various services available on the Internet. Create a chart similar to the one below (also available online).

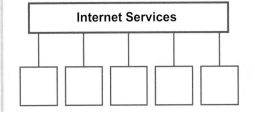

In this section, you quickly survey some of the services and protocols that make the Internet and the Web what they are today.

WEB BROWSER

A Web browser is a software application that is used to view Internet documents written in **Hypertext Markup Language (HTML).** This type of document uses a series of formatting codes that the Web browser understands. The Web browser then formats the contents of the page and displays it for you to read. You learn more about HTML in Chapter 10.

Popular browser software includes Microsoft Internet Explorer and Apple's Safari. Other popular browsers can be downloaded for free, including Netscape Navigator, Opera, and Mozilla. Using any of these Web browsers, you can shop securely, download software, play games, watch streaming video, or research your latest project.

SEARCH ENGINES AND SERVICES

Finding information on the Internet is easy. Just start clicking one hyperlink after another and you find all sorts of information. But finding the information you want to find requires a little more knowledge. In the "old days," you could go to the library and use the card catalog to search for a book by title, author, or subject. Search engines and information services are like the card catalog—only many times faster and more capable.

Searching by Category

Many sites attempt to categorize Web sites. One of the best known examples of this type of site is Yahoo!. This site helps you locate information by organizing sites in a hierarchy. With this type of navigation system, it is fairly easy to navigate from broad categories to narrow topics to find information.

In the next You Try It activity, you can practice navigating through Yahoo!'s Web site to find specific information about solar eclipses.

YOU TRY IT

ACTIVITY 9D Searching By Category

Search sites that categorize information hierarchically make it easy to navigate from broad topic to specific detail. Yahoo! is one of the best examples of this type of site. These instructions should work on any OS with a Web browser and an Internet connection.

1 Open your Web browser.

2 Enter the address www.yahoo.com in the address field, and then click **Go.**

3 Click the link to **Science.**

4 Click the link to **Astronomy.**

5 Click the link to **Solar System.**

6 Click the link to **Sun.**

7 Click the link to **Solar Eclipses.** See Figure 9.11.

Figure 9.11
Many search sites allow you to search using a hierarchy of categories.

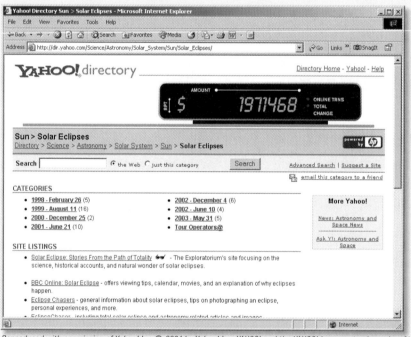

Reproduced with permission of Yahoo! Inc. © 2004 by Yahoo! Inc. YAHOO! and the YAHOO! logo are trademarks of Yahoo! Inc.

8 Browse through some of the pages and, with your teacher's permission, print out a page that shows when the next solar eclipse is due.

As you can see, hierarchical sites make it easy to find specific information (solar eclipses) by starting from broad categories (science).

Unlike many other sites that use software to automatically categorize sites, Yahoo! is cataloged by actual people. Although human beings are nearly obsolete, we still seem to have an edge when it comes to properly evaluating and placing sites in the right categories. The human touch is what makes Yahoo! particularly good. The links that turn up under the subcategory "solar eclipses" are likely to be highly relevant. Of course, most indexed sites (including Yahoo!) allow you to input a search term such as "solar eclipses" and automatically locate links related to the search term.

Using a Search Engine

A **search engine** is a Web site that uses automated software to index the Web. This type of software, called a spider or robot, "crawls" the Web on a regular basis. As it does this, it creates an index of every page it can find. Based on a complex set of criteria, pages can be ranked. When you input a search term of "solar eclipses," the pages are displayed in order of importance, according to the site's ranking criteria. Excellent examples of search engine sites include Google and AltaVista. In the next You Try It activity, you use Google to find specific information about the next scheduled solar eclipse.

ACTIVITY 9E Narrowing a Web Search

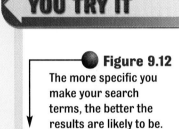

Narrowing your search is extremely important when searching the Web. Google claims to index over 1 billion pages. Even with a good search engine, you must learn to make your searches as relevant as possible.

1 Open your Web browser.

2 Type the address www.google.com in the address field, and then click **Go.**

3 Type the search term solar eclipses in the search box, and then click **Google Search.** Your results may vary, but Google finds something in the neighborhood of 157,000 results. To narrow this search, you can use a technique called natural language query. A natural language query allows you to input a question as though you were speaking to a person.

4 Type the phrase solar eclipses in 2010 in the search box, and then click **Google Search.** The more specific the question or search terms, the more relevant the returns are likely to be (see Figure 9.12).

● **Figure 9.12**
The more specific you make your search terms, the better the results are likely to be.

Most search engines also provide the user with the means of performing either a simple search based on one or more keywords or a more elaborate search that allows the use of logical (Boolean) operators, such as AND, OR, and NOT.

In this way, you might search for pages including both the terms "solar" AND "eclipse," or the pages including either the word "solar" OR "eclipse," or possibly only pages including "solar" but NOT "eclipse." It is important to understand the consequences of using those three statements. OR searches tend to return the most results because pages with either term (not necessarily both) will be returned. AND searches narrow the results because both terms must appear on the page. NOT searches are a good way to exclude certain topics you do not care about.

FTP

Although search engines and the Web make finding information a snap, there are also other ways to find and retrieve information. One of the most widely used is the File Transfer Protocol (FTP), which makes downloading both text and binary files extremely fast and easy (see Figure 9.13).

Figure 9.13
FTP capabilities are built into most of today's browsers. What is FTP used for?

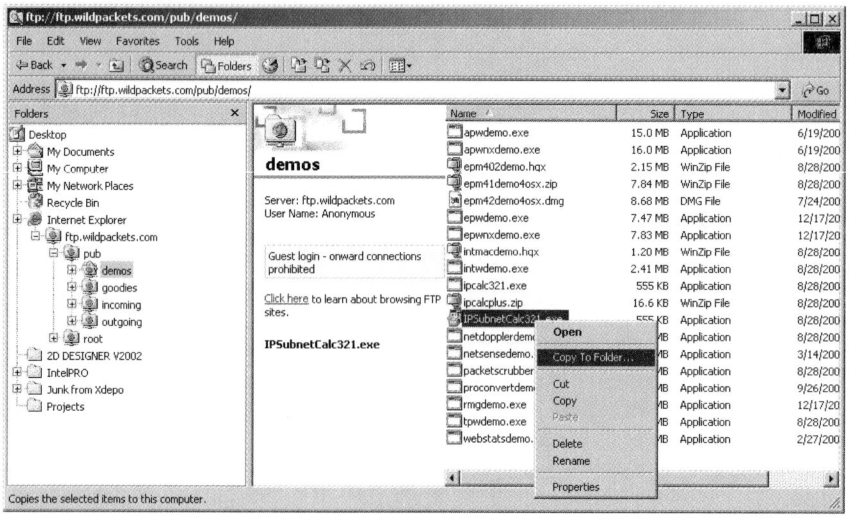

FTP functionality is built into today's Web browsers, making other software largely unnecessary. All you have to do is point your browser to an FTP site, log on, and start copying files. FTP sites are often used by businesses to post large files that cannot be e-mailed. An FTP site address usually starts with "ftp." instead of "www." for Web pages. Remember, the Internet and Web are not one and the same. The WWW and FTP are merely two aspects of what the Internet provides.

E-MAIL

Figure 9.14
E-mail addresses indicate where a message is supposed to go. What is required to receive and send e-mail?

One of the most popular uses of the Internet is e-mail. This global message service enables families, friends, business associates, and even complete strangers to communicate with one another. All that is needed is an e-mail account, Internet access, and a Web browser or e-mail software, such as Microsoft Outlook. E-mail addresses are used to identify the "mailbox" of the person you are sending a message to, as shown in Figure 9.14.

Internet mail transport and delivery standards are supported by the Simple Mail Transfer Protocol, or SMTP, which runs at the Application Layer. As you recall, SMTP is part of the TCP/IP protocol suite and provides a simple e-mail service.

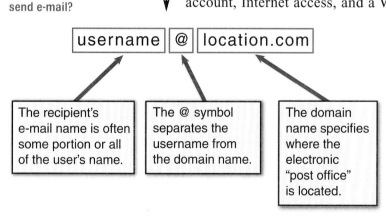

| username | @ | location.com |

The recipient's e-mail name is often some portion or all of the user's name.

The @ symbol separates the username from the domain name.

The domain name specifies where the electronic "post office" is located.

NEWS

News on the Internet has two different meanings. First, there is news broadcast by television anchors, newspapers, and various magazines and journals. Some of it is subscription-based. Then, there is the news that people like to personally exchange through online posts to discussion groups and real-time chats. This type of news is handled on the Internet by services based on the **Network News Transfer Protocol (NNTP).** NNTP is a protocol that is used to distribute collections of articles called newsfeeds to a bewildering array of interest-based **newsgroups.**

NNTP provides for downloads just like FTP. However, it also offers more in terms of interactivity and selectivity. NNTP supports communication between two news servers and also between clients and servers. Because of this interactivity, NNTP enables clients to download newsfeeds and newsgroups selectively, omitting those that are of no interest. In addition, NNTP supports the ability to query servers and to post news articles.

To access a newsgroup, you need a program called a newsreader. Then, subscribe to the newsgroup(s) in which you are interested. Subscribing to a newsgroup does not cost anything; it just tells your newsreader to watch for new posts in that group.

Usenet is one of the most well-known news services that implements NNTP. **Usenet** is basically a huge bulletin board where users can post and respond to posted messages 24 hours a day, 365 days a year. When more than one user responds to a message, the original topic is called a thread (see Figure 9.15).

Lab 9.2 Command Prompt FTP Practice additional hands-on networking skills on page 445.

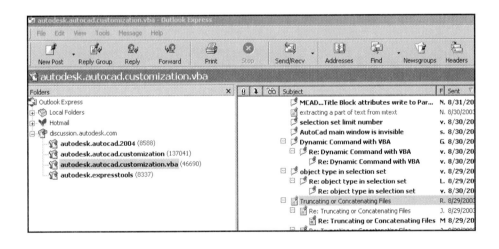

Figure 9.15
Newsreaders allow you to view and post messages to newsgroups. What must you do to read and post messages to a newsgroup?

TELNET

Telnet is like remote control for computers. It is a TCP/IP protocol that runs on the Application Layer and allows a computer to log on to a remote computer and pretend it is attached directly to the host. As long as the connecting computer has terminal emulation capabilities (available, for example, in Windows NT and Windows 95/98), it can use the resources and programs installed on the remote machine. For example, a network administrator could telnet into a server located in a building in another city. Once logged on, she could run applications and configure the server as if she were sitting in front of the actual server.

ONLINE GAMING, MUDS, CHATS, AND INSTANT MESSAGING

And, finally, what about some of the really fun things people get involved in on the Internet? Of course, it depends on your definition of fun.

Online gaming pits players from around the world against one another in real time, such as the extremely popular National Football League (NFL). Players choose teams and control simulated action. Many online gaming communities charge a monthly fee that allows you to connect and play several games against other subscribers.

Multiuser dungeons (MUDs) are an outgrowth of the popular dungeons and dragons type of interactive, multiplayer role playing games (RPGs). On the Internet, a MUD provides participants with a virtual game environment. Here, each can play the part of a different character and all can interact in real time.

Chat rooms are a sort of natural extension to newsgroups. Chats enable multiple people to "get together" in one environment and carry on real-time conversations. A chat room is similar to a conference call with many participants.

In recent years, chat rooms have spawned a whole new service called **instant messaging (IM).** Instant messaging enables two (or more) people to establish a private, real-time communications channel, similar to calling someone on the phone. It reduces the need (to some extent) for e-mail and long-distance phone calls.

READ ME!

Caution Unfortunately, the Internet is not a safe place. You should NEVER give out personal information, such as your name, address, or credit card number in a chat room.

Section 9.4 Assessment

Concept Check

1. **Define** Hypertext Markup Language (HTML), search engine, Network News Transfer Protocol (NNTP), newsgroups, Usenet, Telnet, online gaming, multiuser dungeon (MUD), and instant messaging (IM).

2. **List** the different parts of an e-mail address.

3. **Identify** the protocol used for distributing newsgroups.

4. **Explain** how FTP sites differ from WWW sites.

Critical Thinking

5. **Analyze Information** Explain how search engines index sites on the Web.

6. **Formulate** How will results from the following search queries differ?
   1) lunar OR solar + eclipse
   2) lunar AND solar + eclipse
   3) lunar NOT solar + eclipse.

Applying Skills

Search for Information In the preceding section, you learned about IP addresses and subnet masks. Use your favorite search engine to locate an online IP address calculator. Use the application to calculate your school's IP address and subnet addresses.

SECTION 9.1 Structure of the Internet

Key Terms

backbone, 252
regional network, 253
Network Access Point (NAP), 253
Internet Service Provider (ISP), 253

Main Ideas

■ The Internet is a global connection of smaller networks.

■ The Internet ties regional networks to a common communications backbone.

■ Major telecommunications companies, such as AT&T, MCI, and Qwest, provide the communications backbone of the Internet.

■ ISPs provide access to the regional networks.

■ People and organizations pay fees to ISPs to access the Internet.

SECTION 9.2 Internet and Web Communities

Key Terms

DNS name server, 258
root server, 259
cache, 260
Internet Corporation for Assigned Names and Numbers (ICANN), 261

Main Ideas

■ The Internet is divided into domains representing various organization types or geographic locations.

■ DNS is used to uniquely identify sites based on a tree-like hierarchy.

■ Domain names are resolved to IP addresses using Domain Name System.

■ ICANN is the organization responsible for assigning IP addresses.

SECTION 9.3 Internet Connections and Addressing

Key Terms

address space, 263
loopback address, 263
subnet mask, 263
Internet Protocol version 6 (IPv6), 265
Address Resolution Protocol (ARP), 265
Reverse Address Resolution Protocol (RARP), 265
Dynamic Host Configuration Protocol (DHCP), 266
Windows Internet Naming Service (WINS), 266

Main Ideas

■ The IP address space is divided into classes for various sizes of networks.

■ Subnet masks are used to identify which part of the IP address identifies the network ID and which part identifies the host ID.

■ Subnet masks can be used to divide a network into smaller subnets.

■ Many devices and functions assist in resolving IP addresses, domain names, and Windows computer names.

SECTION 9.4 Internet and Web Services

Key Terms

Hypertext Markup Language (HTML), 269
search engine, 271
Network News Transfer Protocol (NNTP), 273
newsgroups, 273
Usenet, 273
Telnet, 273
online gaming, 274
multiuser dungeon (MUD), 274
instant messaging (IM), 274

Main Ideas

■ Web browsers are used to display HTML documents.

■ Search engines index the Internet and make it easy to find information by keywords or hierarchical categories.

■ Services such as FTP, NNTP, and Telnet increase the capabilities of the Internet.

■ The Web provides many entertainment opportunities.

Reviewing Key Terms

1. Where do NAPs connect to the national Internet backbone?
2. What is ICANN?
3. What is the address space of assignable IP addresses?
4. When does an IP packet use ARP on a network?
5. When is RARP, which usually runs on a server, used on a network?

Understanding Main Ideas

6. Explain what a search engine is. Give an example of a search engine and its URL.
7. Explain how FTP works.
8. Describe the purpose of Usenet.
9. Describe briefly the structure of the Internet.
10. List the seven original generic top-level domain names and, for each, give its meanings and a working URL.
11. Explain the Internet addressing system.
12. List five services available on the Internet.
13. Describe how a host's domain name, its IP address, and its MAC address are all related.
14. Summarize what a loopback address is used for.
15. Explain how IPv6 will help with the problem of dwindling IP addresses.
16. Summarize why IP addresses must be unique. What would happen if duplicate IP addresses existed?
17. Describe the role of a gateway.
18. Compare DHCP and WINS. How are they alike and how are they different?
19. List eight client/server applications from the chapter.

Critical Thinking

20. Sequence Information List the steps involved in the process to resolve a Web site address that is in a different domain from your computer where you view the site. What happens when you first visit this site? What happens when you visit it again?
21. Identify Internet Services Create a table that identifies at least four services available on the Internet. For each service, give its name, functionality, and the supporting protocol (acronym and full name) if available.
22. Analyze Information Imagine that you have been asked to install a new Web server in your classroom that connects to the Internet. Assume that this new computer has a NIC card with a RJ-45 slot. You want to get a unique name for this computer before you acquire an IP address for it. Who do you contact to negotiate a favorable name? Do you have to contact ICANN and why?
23. Explore Subnets Subnet masks are used in conjunction with IP addresses to identify the network ID and the host ID of an IP address class. For a small business with a class B network and about a dozen departments, what is its subnet mask supposed to be if each department is given a separate net? And about how many hosts can be connected in each subnet?

e-Review

networking.glencoe.com

Study with PowerPoint

To review the main points in this chapter, select **e-Review > PowerPoint Outlines > Chapter 9.**

Online Self Check

Test your knowledge of the material in this chapter by selecting **e-Review > Self Checks > Chapter 9.**

Making Connections

Social Studies – Geography of the Internet

The Internet has over 250 top-level domains (TLDs): generic (Organizational) and countries. Some newly approved generic TLDs by ICANN are .biz for business, .info for information, and .pro for professions. With your teacher's permission, visit ICANN online to find how the Internet domain name system is administered. Then go to IANA's ccTLD Database to find seven more country TLDs, one for each continent.

Write a paragraph outlining how a TLD is assigned. Next draw the continents and place a top-level domain on each.

STANDARDS AT WORK

Students use technology research tools to evaluate and select new information resources and technological innovations based on the appropriateness of specific tasks. (NETS-S 5)

Search for Internet Architecture Standards

Most standards for the Internet and operations have been processed and issued by the Internet Engineering Task Force (IETF).

The IETF Web site has a RFC Index Search Engine. With your teacher's permission, go the RFC Editor Web site and access the search engine. Click the HELP feature to learn how to use the search engine. Then record the RFC Number and Status for each of the following TCP/IP protocols:

◆ DNS (Concepts)
◆ IPv4 (Internet Protocol)
◆ IPv6 (Specification)
◆ ARP (Ethernet)
◆ RARP
◆ DHCP
◆ HTTP
◆ FTP
◆ SMTP
◆ NNTP
◆ Telnet (Specification)
◆ Instant Messaging (Session Initiation)

TEAMWORK SKILLS

Sharpen Web Searching Skills

Following your teacher's instructions, form small teams. Identify a topic from your science or math class.

1. Have each team member use a different Web search site to find information on the topic. Use both category sites, such as Yahoo!, and search engine sites, such as Google.
2. Develop a list of the criteria for the evaluating Web searches, including ease of locating information, matches to topic search, coverage for linked sites, flexibility for entering the search criteria, limited time for responses, and access to special features.
3. Begin searching each assigned Web site and record the search process and results.
4. Get together as a group to compare and contrast the searching process and results against the criteria.
5. Deliver a multimedia presentation that summarizes your group's discoveries.

CHALLENGE YOURSELF

Understand Relationships Among Protocols

A networking technician must know the relationships between protocols in order to connect a computer to the Internet and get it working. What protocols are used to install and to configure the computer for the Internet? Which role does each protocol play in the setup? How are the protocols related? Are the versions compatible?

Create a technician's "quick-start" guide for installing a Web server. Include:

◆ Hardware Preparation—minimum requirements for hardware components
◆ Software Preparation—minimum requirements for software components
◆ Provider Essentials—possible ISPs and their requirements for devices and wiring
◆ Setting Up Your Server—setup procedures
◆ Configuring Your Server—procedures for configuring the protocols on the computer
◆ Testing Your Server—procedures to test the server's performance

YOU TRY IT

Networking Lab

1. Evaluating a .name-domain

Many ICANN approved registrars are available on the Web in addition to Network Solutions. Be aware that some registrars claim to be free for a period of time but then charge your credit card. Therefore, never provide your credit card number unless you really want to register for a domain name. Before you decide which registrar to obtain your own name domain from, evaluate many registrars' costs and features.

A Launch your Web browser.

B Complete an online search to find Web sites that offer a .name-domain registration. Or, go to the InterNIC Web site to find a list of ICANN approved registrars.

C Create a spreadsheet that lists each Web site's name, registration costs for a .name domain, the monthly charges, and annual fees for at least five registrars.

D Chart the data in order to see at a glance which site offers the best pricing.

E Include a column in your spreadsheet to type any special features of the site. (For example, free registration.)

Note: Make sure you are *not* registering for a name. You want to avoid billing.

2. Showing and Clearing Web Browsing History

In addition to the DNS cache that maps the URLs that you visited and their IP addresses, your Web browser also records the history of your most recently visited Web pages in a cache. You can re-configure the history to keep pages for a specified time.

A Launch your Web browser.

B Use the pull-down arrow on the right end of the address field to view a list of the URLs that you visited at other times.

C Open your Web Preferences, or Internet Options (as shown here), dialog box.

D Choose the number of days you want to keep pages in history (for re-configuration) or click to clear history from the cache.

E Now, go back to the pull-down button on the right end of the address field.

With your teacher's permission, e-mail the results of this activity to two or more classmates.

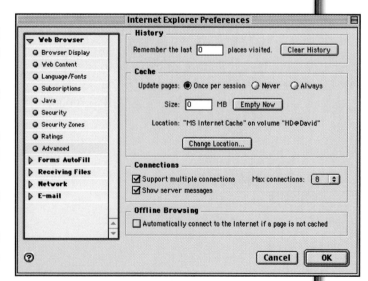

Networking Projects

1. Set Up a VPN

In your newly formed online pet supply company, you want to provide all of your national stores secure Internet access to the home office.

There is a gateway at the boundary of the VPN that guides incoming traffic by translating the publicized IP address, such as Glencoe's Web server's address 198.45.24.107, into the internal address such as 1.1.1.1. Hiding the server's true identity effectively reduces the risk of outside hackers attacking your company stores' computers. You found out that an important security feature is a VPN. The following will help illustrate how such a network could be developed.

A Draw and label a diagram of a network topology similar to the one shown here. One computer is a gateway, one a Web server, and the other is an FTP server.

- There are three computers.
- Each computer has two NIC cards installed so every computer is connected to the other.
- The gateway has an additional NIC card for the Internet access.

B List as many steps as you can that would enable you to set up the hardware and software for a VPN.

C Draw any other diagrams that would help demonstrate this type of network's concept.

2. Demonstrate How to Use Web Searches

Knowing how to find relevant information from the Web is an important life and business skill. You have been asked to create a presentation that outlines the use of two major methods for finding information online.

- Category—To locate information with category sites such as Yahoo!, follow the hierarchy of categorized information.

- Search engine—To use search engine sites such as Google, key logically combined keywords.

Show the two choices by stating each one's advantages and disadvantages.

The World Wide Web

YOU WILL LEARN TO...

WHY IT MATTERS......................................

Even before 9/11, security was a major concern—from personal travel to Web sites. You simply cannot walk into an airport anymore and *not* notice the security. There are metal detectors, security personnel, dogs, and machines to detect explosive residues. We all want to be safe. However, many of us take our own security for granted when "travelling" on the Internet. Take time to learn how to protect your computer and your privacy whenever you are on the Internet.

Quick Write Activity

What sorts of online activities do you participate in? What possible risks are involved in these activities? Write down several ideas of what you can do to prevent privacy and security abuses. Divide the list into two categories: computer safety and personal information safety.

WHAT YOU WILL DO..

READ TO SUCCEED

Use Notes

When you are reading, you may not want to stop to look up a word or review a difficult concept. To avoid interruptions, keep a note pad handy. Whenever you come upon a section or term you want to go back to, write the word or question on the note paper and mark the place. After you have finished the chapter, go back to the places you marked. Look up the terms or try to answer your questions based on what you have read.

Section 10.1 The Internet and the World Wide Web

Guide to Reading

Main Ideas

Web sites present an organized collection of Web pages in HTML format. Individual pages are located using URLs. Web servers and browsers communicate using HTTP.

Key Terms

Uniform Resource Locator (URL)
Active Server Page (ASP)
Hypertext Transfer Protocol (HTTP)
Secure HTTP (HTTPS)

Reading Strategy

Identify how Web sites, pages, hosting services, and HTTP are interrelated elements. Create a chart similar to the one below (also available online).

Web Elements

☐ ➡ ☐ ➡ ☐ ➡ ☐

The World Wide Web (WWW or Web) certainly has come a long way from Tim Berners-Lee's original vision. It has grown into a critically important electronic marketplace for business and an indispensable tool for communication and information.

With all sorts of products and services advertised, sold, and traded online, the Web has become an everyday source of information, entertainment, and shopping. Web technologies and protocols in business transactions now account for billions of dollars in sales every year.

WEB SITES

Web sites present information using combinations of text, graphics, sound, animation, video, and, of course, hyperlinks. Using nothing more than a mouse, a visitor can navigate from page to page and from site to site.

At the time this book was written, 3.3 *billion* Web pages were indexed by Google.com, one of the leading search engines. These pages are organized hierarchically within individual Web sites. This means that from one page, you can jump to many subpages. Some sites are one-stop, single-page affairs, whereas others contain a handful of pages. Some sites, such as **www.microsoft.com**, contain thousands of pages. No matter the size of the site, any or all of these pages can contain links to other pages. Some links are within the same site, whereas others link to pages on related sites.

Home Pages

Generally, a visitor can work through the site's hierarchy by starting at the main page, or home page. The home page usually includes links to pages within the site. In the sample Web site displayed in Figure 10.1 on page 283, the home page guides visitors to products, resources, and information pages.

READ ME!

Tech Tip The Web is a vast resource of information, but you have to learn to discern between opinion and fact. Always find multiple sources to verify facts, and choose reliable, unbiased Web sites when using the Web for research.

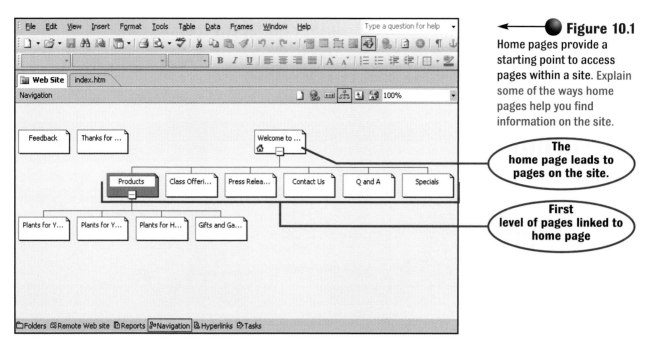

Figure 10.1
Home pages provide a starting point to access pages within a site. Explain some of the ways home pages help you find information on the site.

The **home page leads to pages on the site.**

First level of pages linked to home page

Web Site Hosting

For other people to view a Web site on the Web, it must be available to the public. Many businesses purchase their own Web servers that are connected 24/7, usually through an ISP, to the Internet. For smaller companies and home users, Web site hosting is a cheaper, easier alternative.

Many companies, including ISPs, offer Web site hosting for very reasonable rates (sometimes free). Usually, the amount is determined by the amount of space needed for the Web site's pages and associated files, as well as the amount of traffic the site generates.

Hosting involves a company that rents space for Web sites. These companies are called Web hosts. All the files that constitute the Web site are transferred to the Web hosting computer. These files are usually transmitted via the File Transfer Protocol (FTP). The Web server connected to the Internet then allows other computers to connect to the site(s) stored on the server (see Figure 10.2).

Web hosts can generally support many sites at a time. Hosting makes it very easy for small businesses and individuals to gain a Web presence. They do not have to buy and house the equipment, nor possess the technical know-how to set up or maintain the Web server.

Activity 10.1 Find Free Web Page Hosting There are many ways to establish your own Web site. Many services offer free space and easy-to-use tools to help you set up your page. Visit **networking.glencoe.com** to find out how you can get your own Web page online.

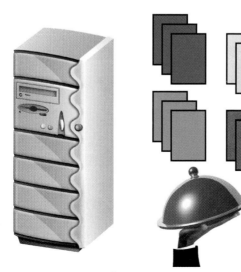

Figure 10.2
Web site hosts provide a server and space for many companies' Web sites. What are the advantages of using a Web hosting service?

ACTIVITY 10A Uploading and Downloading Documents Using FTP

Sometimes you might need to upload or download files from FTP servers, such as Web documents, applications, patches, and so on. There are a variety of applications available that are free or cost a fee. Microsoft Internet Explorer allows you to not only access FTP sites, but to upload and download files. Note: For this activity, you will need to access an FTP site that allows you to upload files. Ask your teacher for an appropriate FTP site.

Figure 10.3 ●
Some FTP sites can be logged into anonymously, while others use passwords.

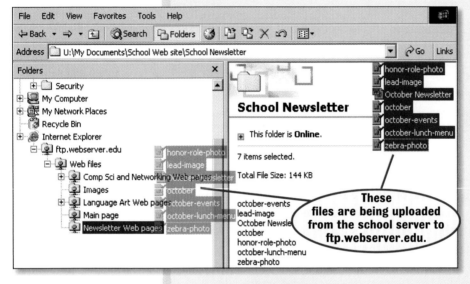

❶ Open **Internet Explorer** and go to the FTP site.

❷ On the toolbar, click **Folders.** On the left, the list of folders will appear.

❸ Navigate to the folder where the files that need to be uploaded are located. In this example the October Newsletter files are uploaded for the school Web site.

❹ Select all of the files or folders to be uploaded as instructed by your teacher.

❺ Click and drag the files and folders down to the appropriate folder on the FTP site as shown in Figure 10.3. The files are now being uploaded to the selected folder.

Figure 10.4 ●→
Downloading files can be done easily by right-clicking on the file and selecting **Copy to Folder** from the pop-up menu.

❻ To download files from the FTP site, right-click on the file(s) and select **Copy to Folder…**

❼ A new window titled "Browser for Folder" will appear as shown in Figure 10.4.

❽ Select the folder where the file is to be stored or create a new folder.

❾ When finished, click **OK.**

WEB ADDRESSES AND URLS

In the previous chapter, you learned that domain names, such as microsoft.com, are resolved to IP addresses by DNS servers. This is how the Web browser locates a particular site. But how does the computer know what page to go to? It uses the page's Web address. This Web address is called the **Uniform Resource Locator (URL).** URLs are used to specify the exact location and name of a resource on the Web. Although URLs differ as do street addresses, they all use a format similar to that shown in Figure 10.5.

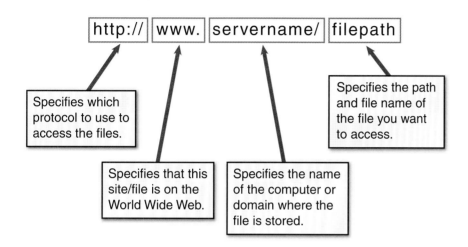

● Figure 10.5
Each part of the URL plays an important role in locating a specific document somewhere on the Web. What does http:// tell the browser?

For example, the following URL:

http://www.microsoft.com/windows/ie/default.asp

tells the browser to use the HTTP protocol to connect to the World Wide Web (www). Somewhere out on the Web is a server named *microsoft.com.* On that server in a directory called *windows* is a subdirectory named *ie.* Within that folder is a file called *default.asp.* This URL is the path the browser software follows whenever a link is clicked on a Web page. It can also be entered by the user in the address field of the browser application.

The ".asp" is a file name extension that identifies the document as an **Active Server Page (ASP).** ASP is capable of generating customized Hypertext Markup Language (HTML) pages on the fly. Sites such as **Amazon.com** can customize the pages you see based on recent purchases you have made. You learn more about ASP and HTML pages later in this chapter.

WEB TRANSPORT SERVICE

HTML is the language used to display pages and text within a browser window. It does not, however, transport a page to the browser. That job belongs to the Web protocol **Hypertext Transfer Protocol (HTTP).** HTTP appears at the beginning of every URL clicked or typed with the purpose of visiting a Web site or to request a specific document within the site.

HTTP operates between Web browsers and Web servers. It carries requests from browsers to servers, and it transports requested pages (if available) from servers back to browsers. HTTP uses several commands that enable it to interact with Web pages.

You will rarely use these commands directly, but when you enter an address and click the Go button, the browser uses the HTTP command "get" to go get the file you requested. A typical HTTP interaction between a browser and a Web server is a simple, two-step process such as the following:

◆ The browser sends an HTTP command, such as GET, to request a particular Web page from a server.
◆ The server finds the page, if it is available, and sends it back to the browser (see Figure 10.6).

Figure 10.6
HTTP enables Web browsers and Web servers to exchange information. How are communications secured using HTTP?

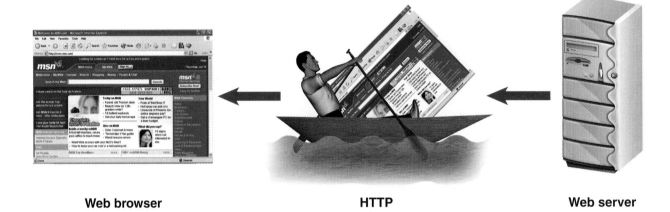

Web browser　　　　　　　　**HTTP**　　　　　　　　**Web server**

HTTP is widely used and has deliberately been designed for improvement and evolution. However, it was not designed with high security in mind. An extension to HTTP, called **Secure HTTP (HTTPS),** adds encryption and security features to HTTP. This helps secure private information, such as your credit card number, when you purchase something online.

Section 10.1 Assessment

Concept Check

1. **Define** Uniform Resource Locator (URL), Active Server Page (ASP), Hypertext Transfer Protocol (HTTP), and Secure HTTP (HTTPS).

2. **Explain** the organization of most Web sites.

3. **Describe** when you might use the HTTPS protocol.

Critical Thinking

4. **Analyze Information** Discuss why a company would or would not want to use a Web hosting service. What are some of the factors that would lead to this decision?

5. **Compare and Contrast** Explain the similarities and differences between a URL and a domain name.

Applying Skills

Find Web Hosting Services Web hosting services are usually easy to find and inexpensive. Some are even free. Find a few Web hosting services and make a table comparing their prices, their amount of disk space, and their limitations.

Ethics & Technology

HOW THE INTERNET HAS CHANGED THE WORLD

Has the Internet made the world a better place? Consider some of its benefits and drawbacks.

Although many people believe that the Internet is beneficial, there are risks. Be careful about giving out personal information.

Benefits of the Internet
The Internet has become a positive force in many respects:

◆ **Education**—Distance learning brings the classroom into the home, allowing people to study online from anywhere.
◆ **Society**—People use the Internet to voice their opinions about societal issues, from the merits of a movie to the morality of a war.
◆ **Politics**—Voters are better informed than ever, thanks to the Internet. Someday, you may be able to vote via the Internet in state or national elections.
◆ **Business**—Both large and small businesses can serve customers and partners anywhere in the world.

Drawbacks of the Internet
The Net also has critics, for many reasons:

◆ **Reliability**—Information about almost anything can be found online, but not everything is accurate or true. It is easy to find out-of-date, misleading, and even dangerous, information about health and other issues online. Be sure to verify information that you find online with another trustworthy source before acting on it.
◆ **Privacy**—Each day, we give away more of our privacy as businesses and government agencies collect personal data online. Hackers can go online to steal personal information or disrupt our computers with viruses.
◆ **Depersonalization**—You cannot see the people who communicate on the Internet, and they do not have to tell you their real names, ages, or genders. Because of this, some people may do things on the Internet they would not do in person.
◆ **Predators**—Some people intentionally post false information to deceive others. They may convince people to buy nonexistent products. Worse, they can pretend to be a friend or a chat room "pal" and lure children or other innocent people into dangerous situations.

Tech Focus

1. Describe one positive and one negative aspect of the Internet on society. Explain why you have chosen these examples. Support your conclusions with research.

2. How would you function without access to the Internet? Describe how the Internet has affected your life.

Guide to Reading

Main Ideas

Web technologies play important roles in networking and everyday computing. E-commerce is a primary way of doing business today. There are many ways to secure documents and communications on the Web.

Key Terms

intranet
extranet
portal
Authenticode
digital signature
data encryption standard (DES)
Multipurpose Internet Mail Extensions (MIME)
Secure Sockets Layer (SSL)
firewall
proxy server

Reading Strategy

Identify how a firewall helps protect a network. Create a chart similar to the one below (also available online).

Firewall

Web technologies already play important roles in business networking. The Web's all-important hyperlinks, for instance, are now routinely embedded as active links within documents and e-mail. Users have the ability to jump from information source to information source randomly and easily.

Some Web technologies are blurring the line between a public network and a local network. Features that were introduced in browser software, such as hyperlinks, are now commonly found in all types of documents, including word processing and spreadsheet documents. These features help erase the difference between local and remote files. Users can now concentrate on what they want to see, rather than where they must look to find it.

INTRANETS AND EXTRANETS

Two of the most significant applications of Web-related technologies in corporate networks are **intranets** and **extranets.** An intranet is a network that can only be accessed by employees of the corporation. An extranet is a network that makes it possible for employees of a corporation and trusted outside parties to access the network. Intranets and extranets are like miniature Webs. Browser software is used to access, view, and use documents and applications important to the business. These might include employee handbooks, phone directories, or 401(K) account management.

Both intranets and extranets rely on Internet protocols and technologies, including HTTP and TCP/IP for transport and HTML for displaying documents. Large enterprises may also cover multiple LANs or spread across an entire WAN. Basically, intranets and extranets overlie a corporate network to give it the look and feel of the World Wide Web.

Intranets and extranets can also provide access to the Internet. Making the internal network secure from strangers on the Internet is a priority. Typically, corporations protect these networks by using firewalls and proxy servers,

Enrichment LAB

Lab 10.1 Creating an Intranet Home Page
Practice additional hands-on networking skills on page 446.

which are discussed later in this section. Basically, these devices shield the rest of the network from outside intruders.

ELECTRONIC COMMERCE AND PORTALS

Electronic commerce, or e-commerce, is the term used to describe business transactions performed on the Web. For example, you can buy anything from clothing to books to movie tickets online. Service-oriented businesses, such as travel sites, allow you to buy airline tickets and place hotel and car reservations for an upcoming trip. You can even manage bank and investment accounts and pay bills online.

Many businesses, from Eddie Bauer clothing to Dell Computer and Amazon.com, maintain their own Web sites. But many businesses are also extending their visibility by entering into partnership with the owners of a few large and heavily used sites known as portals.

Portals act as an entryway, or a gateway, to the Web. The site provides visitors with all the comforts of a familiar home page. Many sites can be customized to show content in which the user is interested. For example, you might want to see localized weather, local and national news, stock reports of your favorite high-tech companies, and the latest scores of your favorite team (see Figure 10.7). Some well-known portals are maintained by Web technology companies, including Microsoft (MSN) and America Online (AOL), and search providers, such as Excite, Yahoo!, and Infoseek.

Portals can also provide access to electronic stores or malls. Some of the sites and services offered are owned by the organization that maintains the portal, but many are supplied by partners that rent space on the portal screen much as merchants rent shops in a mall.

● **Figure 10.7**
The MSN portal allows users to customize the content to show items of personal and local interest. What services are offered by portals?

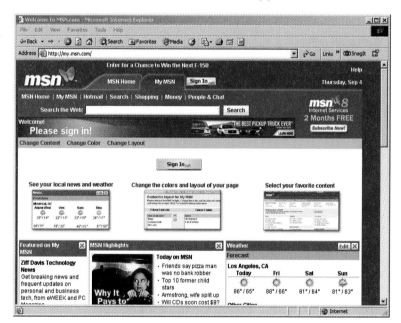

SECURITY

Network security covers a range of different issues. There are the physical aspects of ensuring uninterrupted power to servers, mirroring, and backing up data. From a personnel standpoint, user names, passwords, and user groups are used to control access to documents, databases, and company files. In terms of the Web, there are issues that a network faces, including:

◆ Protecting the internal network from access by unauthorized individuals.
◆ Protecting information as it is transported over the Internet.
◆ Protecting the privacy and security of people's personal and financial information.

It is no wonder that people are concerned about privacy and security on the Internet because they may have posted credit card and bank account numbers around the Internet. Another legitimate concern is whether they can trust that a given document, e-mail, or application is from the person it is supposed to be from. Although security concerns will likely always be an issue with the Internet, technologies in the discussions that follow are in place to help people feel more at ease.

YOU TRY IT

ACTIVITY 10B Accessing and Reviewing Local Security Settings

You will access and review local security on a computer running Windows 2000. A network administrator and support technician should be familiar with these settings so they can change or set the policies to maintain the network.

① Log on to your computer.

② Click **Start,** point to **Programs,** select **Administrative Tools,** and choose **Local Security Policy.** The Security Settings console will appear as shown in Figure 10.8.

Figure 10.8
The Security Settings console allows you to review various security policies set up by the network administrator.

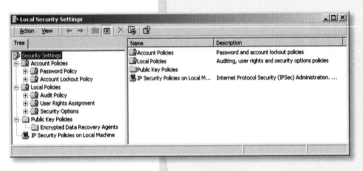

③ Click on **Account Policies** and review the **Password Policy** and **Account Lockout Policy.**

④ Click on **Local Policies** and review the **Audit Policy, User Rights Assignment,** and **Security Options.**

⑤ Click on **Public Key Policies** and review **Encrypted Data Recovery Agents** to find out whom you ask to retrieve files.

Authenticode

You may have seen a certificate-like window appear when you downloaded a piece of software from the Web. This window is the viewable portion of a Microsoft code-verification feature known as **Authenticode.** Authenticode is a means of assuring end users that the code they are downloading:

◆ Has been created by the group or individual listed on the certificate.
◆ Has not been changed since it was created.

It is true that Authenticode verifies that the code has not been tampered with after it was completed and signed by the creator. However, it cannot verify that the program to be downloaded is either bug free or completely safe to use.

Digital Signature

At the heart of Authenticode is an important security feature known as a **digital signature.** A digital signature verifies the creator of a program or other electronic document. Digital signatures rely on a set of two keys, known as a public key and a private key. The public key can be given out to other people.

The private key, like the password, is one that should be known by only one person, its owner. These keys must be acquired from a valid organization known as a certification authority (the equivalent of your town's locksmith).

Suppose Dave wants to send the latest revision of a contract to his lawyer. His lawyer needs to be sure that Dave really sent it, when he sent it, and that it was not changed between the time Dave sent it and the time the lawyer received it (see Figure 10.9).

Dave provides his lawyer with a copy of his public key. Anyone can have Dave's public key. It can be used only to verify whether Dave's private key was used to sign a message supposedly coming from Dave. The digital signature created using Dave's private key is like an electronic fingerprint—no two can be alike. If even a single character of the document is changed, there is a mismatch and the recipient can tell that the file has been changed or tampered with.

Figure 10.9
Digital signatures consist of a public key and a private key. Where can someone acquire a digital signature?

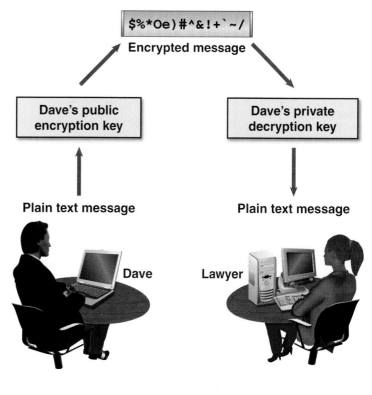

Encryption

Although digital signatures are valuable in authenticating and validating programs and messages, an even higher level of security is provided in the encryption of important files before transmission—essentially, turning the files into unreadable gibberish to all but the sender and receiver. Encryption can be used either in addition to or instead of a digital signature.

The process of encryption turns a readable message (known to cryptographers as plaintext) into a garbled version (known as ciphertext) for transmission (see Figure 10.10). The coding itself relies on one of several encryption algorithms—roughly, sets of steps or instructions—that are based on the use of either a public key (asymmetric algorithm) or a private key (symmetric algorithm).

Figure 10.10
Encryption encodes information to protect privacy. What is required to decode an encrypted message?

◆ Asymmetric encryption uses a public key and a private key. Messages encrypted with the public key can be decrypted only with the corresponding private key.

◆ Symmetric encryption uses the same (presumably secret) key or uses a decryption key that can be derived from the one used to encrypt the transmission.

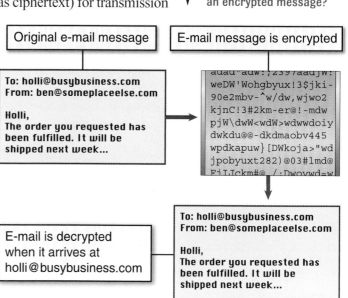

The strength of encryption itself is dependent on the number of bits used for the key. The general rule of thumb is the longer the encryption key, the more secure the encryption. However, as computers become more powerful and distributed computing makes brute force attacks more feasible, the security of a given key length is reduced considerably. The following standard key lengths have been commonly used:

- 40-bit keys, once a standard, would take about 1 trillion attempts to crack by brute force (that is, by trying every possible bit combination in sequence). These keys are no longer considered secure.
- 56-bit keys, known as the **data encryption standard (DES),** were the maximum length keys allowed for U.S. export just a few years ago.
- 128-bit keys are currently used to secure transactions in Microsoft Internet Explorer and in the PPTP protocol used to secure VPN connections. A popular product, Pretty Good Privacy (PGP), also uses 128-bit keys. This and higher key lengths are considered reasonably secure (at least for now).

MIME

MIME (Multipurpose Internet Mail Extensions) is a well-known and widely used protocol for Internet e-mail. It was designed to allow mail messages to include not only text, but also sound, graphics, audio, and video. To do this, the message header is used to define the content of the message. In other words, if the message includes a sound file, the header says so. At the receiving end, software can use the information in the header to call on appropriate programs to display, play, or otherwise handle the different media types. MIME does not provide much in the way of security. To handle this task, Secure MIME (S/MIME), MIME with support for digital signatures and encryption, is used.

Figure 10.11
SSL encrypts communications between clients and servers. How can you tell if you are on a secure page?

SSL

Secure Sockets Layer (SSL) was developed by Netscape Communications. SSL uses authentication and encryption to protect communications between client and server. Most URLs requiring an SSL connection start with *https,* as shown in Figure 10.11, instead of the usual *http.* In addition, you can look for the lock image in the lower-right corner of your browser.

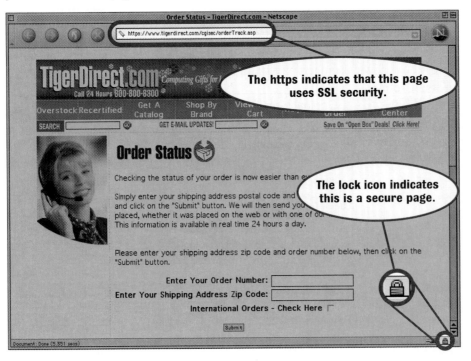

The https indicates that this page uses SSL security.

The lock icon indicates this is a secure page.

The SSL protocol is used in all major browsers and can encrypt data using either 40-bit or 128-bit keys. Nearly all sites that allow you to pay online using a credit card use SSL to encrypt the data you transmit back and forth between the servers.

Proxies and Firewalls

Secure protocols, encryption, and digital signatures are essential for guarding the data that travel over the Internet. However, they cannot protect an internal network from outside intruders. That job is handled nicely by **firewalls** and, to a lesser extent, by software/hardware known as proxies, or proxy servers.

In buildings, a firewall is used to prevent fire from spreading from one area to another. A network firewall, like the firewall in a building, is a barrier designed to keep intruders out. Firewalls can also be used to block outbound traffic. For example, some companies block users from using music-sharing applications. A firewall can be a router, bridge, or gateway that sits between the network and the outside world (see Figure 10.12).

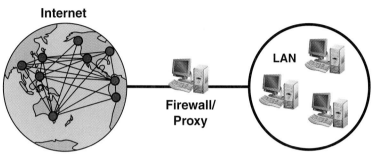

● **Figure 10.12**
Firewalls and proxies act as barriers to protect the LAN from outside intruders. How does a firewall protect incoming information?

Firewalls protect the network by examining packets. Using a table of acceptable and unacceptable addresses, the firewall determines if a packet is allowed to pass through. If the address or port on a packet is on the unacceptable list, the packet is blocked. In this way, ports associated with a particular service, such as Telnet or FTP, can be shut down. Firewalls can operate at the Application Layer to filter e-mail based on content, size, or some other important feature.

A **proxy server,** or proxy, forms a barrier between the internal network and the outside world, like a firewall. The proxy's job is a little different. The proxy presents a single IP address to the world, and hides identities (addresses) of the computers within the network. A hidden address helps defend against intruders.

ACTIVITY 10C Enabling Windows XP Firewall

YOU TRY IT

Windows XP features a built-in firewall, called Internet Connection Firewall (ICF). Home users with permanent Internet connections, such as DSL and cable, should definitely consider activating ICF, or use another third-party firewall application. To enable ICF:

❶ Click **Start,** and then click **Control Panel.**

❷ Click **Network and Internet Connections.**

❸ Click **Network Connections.**

❹ Right-click your main connection—this may be a dial-up, LAN, or other type of connection—and then click **Properties.**

❺ Click the **Advanced** tab.

Figure 10.13
The Windows XP ICF dialog box makes it easy to shut down commonly used (and exploited) ports.

⑥ Check the box in the ICF (Internet Connection Firewall) group to "Protect my computer. . . ."

⑦ Click **Settings** and look at the options given in Figure 10.13.

⑧ Click **Cancel** twice to discard your changes to the current firewall settings.

Firewalls are an important security feature that anyone connected to the Internet should consider using.

Like firewalls, proxies can also be used to limit Internet access. For example, proxies can be used to prevent employees from visiting undesirable Web sites, or they can block sites that are not related to work.

Proxies serve another useful purpose—they cache Web sites as they are requested by users. From that point on, the proxy quickly displays those Web sites from the cache rather than retrieve them from the external network. This ready access saves download time and bandwidth.

Section 10.2 Assessment

Concept Check

1. **Define** intranet, extranet, portal, Authenticode, digital signature, data encryption standard (DES), Multipurpose Internet Mail Extensions (MIME), Secure Sockets Layer (SSL), firewall, and proxy server.

2. **Explain** how you can tell if you are viewing a secure Web page.

3. **Describe** how a firewall can shut down access to a certain type of application, such as music sharing.

Critical Thinking

4. **Compare and Contrast** List the similarities and differences between SSL and MIME.

5. **Formulate Information** You work for a software company and want to assure your clients that downloads on your site have not been tampered with. Explain how a digital signature would help your software company accomplish this.

Applying Skills

Acquire a Digital Signature Use the Internet to find out where you can acquire a digital signature. With your teacher's permission, use a search engine such as Google, AltaVista, or Dogpile. Write down the name of the company, the cost of the signature (if any), and how long the key is valid.

EMERGING TECHNOLOGY

ENTERPRISE STORAGE

Large organizations, such as enterprises, are using specialized technologies to manage storage needs.

SANs are used by businesses to backup or archive data.

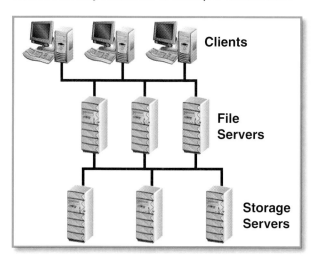

Huge Demands, New Strategies

In the enterprise, storage systems must be:

◆ **Massive**—Many corporate storage systems can hold several terabytes of data.

◆ **Reliable**—Many companies insist on 99.99 percent uptime for their storage systems.

◆ **Fault tolerant**—Enterprises nearly always store data in several places, so they are not lost if a disk fails.

A growing number of large companies are separating their storage systems from their network by using one of the following three methods.

SAN

A storage area network (SAN) is appropriate for enterprises with data storage requirements over one terabyte. SANs are networks that store and retrieve data. They are part of the larger enterprise network.

A SAN can include hard disks, tape drives, and optical drives. These storage components are connected together and to the enterprise network. Companies can make any of these storage devices accessible to any network user. Users may see the SAN as one storage device or a collection of drives.

NAS

Network-Attached Storage (NAS) devices are a good choice for companies with data storage requirements up to one terabyte. NAS devices are separate from the network servers, but "plug into" the network directly. This gives users direct access to the drives contained in the devices.

SSP

Instead of adapting its own network to accommodate a SAN or multiple NAS devices, a company can turn to a Storage Service Provider (SSP) to meet its storage needs. SSPs generally provide off-site storage, which is accessed via a secure Internet or VPN connection. SSP-based storage is scalable, secure, and can be cost effective for many companies that do not want to build their own massive storage systems.

Tech Focus

1. Find an example of a company currently using enterprise storage solutions. What storage method are they using?

2. Imagine you are the network administrator for a retailer that has an illustrated online catalog, a large customer database, and a huge amount of sales transactions both online and in stores. Which enterprise storage would you choose? Why?

Section 10.3 Languages of the Web

Guide to Reading

Main Ideas

The Web uses a number of different languages to format, structure, and present data. Some of these languages are capable of automatically generating Web pages.

Key Terms

tags
attributes
Dynamic HTML
cascading style sheets (CSS)
Extensible Markup Language (XML)
document type definition (DTD)
Extensible Style Sheet
script
JavaScript
Common Gateway Interface (CGI)

Reading Strategy

Identify three facts about each language covered in this section. Create a chart similar to the one below (also available online).

Language	Fact #1	Fact #2	Fact #3

The Web is evolving rapidly. The first Web pages were hand coded and, with few exceptions, all looked the same. Still pictures and colored fonts could only go so far. New languages and capabilities have emerged so today's Web is nothing like the Web of five years ago. Web pages can now react to user activity. Users can even customize pages to their own liking. These advancements are made possible by the many languages of the Web.

HTML

Hypertext Markup Language (HTML) is the language used to define the structure and layout of a Web page. HTML acts as a set of instructions that tells browser software how and where to place the page's content. By using a standard set of instructions, any browser running on any operating system can display an HTML page the same way.

HTML uses a system of **tags** and **attributes** to identify formatting and layouts. A tag tells how to display an element, such as text or an image, within a browser. Most tags require a closing tag to identify the beginning and end of a specific formatting function. For example, the following displays the text "**This text is bold**" in a bold font style.

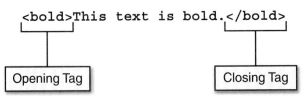

An attribute modifies a certain instruction. For example, the tag <hr> is used to insert a horizontal rule (a line) into a document. But the <hr> tag has certain attributes that allow you to change the line's size and even its color. In the next You Try It activity, you create your own HTML page, using a variety of tags and attributes.

 networking.glencoe.com

ACTIVITY 10D Creating an HTML Page

YOU TRY IT

Creating a simple HTML page is just that, simple. All you need is a text editor, such as Microsoft Notepad, and a browser to test your finished product.

1 Start **Notepad** (or another text editor).

2 Type the HTML code shown in Figure 10.14.

3 Click **File** and then click **Save.**

4 Change the Save As Type from **Text Documents** to **All Files.**

5 Select a folder where you are allowed to save files, and then type the file name firstpage.html.

6 Click **Save.**

firstpage.html
```
<html>
<title>Welcome to my web page</title>
<center>
<h1>This is a heading</h1>
</center>
<hr size="10" color="000000">
<body>This is the body text.</body>
</html>
```

Figure 10.14
HTML uses tags and attributes to describe how the page should look.

7 Using your file manager, locate the file you just saved and double-click it to open the file in your browser.

- Alternatively, you can open the file from within the browser. Click **File** and then click **Open.**

- Click **Browse,** use the Open dialog box to locate and select your file, and then click **Open.**

8 Your file should look similar to Figure 10.15.

Figure 10.15
Attributes are used to modify tags in HTML documents.

Experiment with this simple page. For example, you could modify the <hr> tag to adjust the size and color of the line. By the way, colors in HTML are specified in hexadecimal format. Each pair of digits specifies red, green, and blue values from 00 to FF (0 to 255).

Most Web designers today use applications, such as Microsoft FrontPage or Macromedia Dreamweaver, to generate the HTML code automatically. However, it is still very helpful to understand the basics of how Web pages work and are built.

Welcome to my web page

file:///Users/Shared/firstpage.html

Apple   .Mac   Amazon   eBay   Yahoo!   News▼   fedex.com

This is a Heading

This is the body text.

DHTML

HTML is nice for defining the layout of Web pages that never change, but users wanted more. They wanted Web pages that were more interactive, or dynamic. In other words, they wanted Web pages that changed in response to their actions. **Dynamic HTML (DHTML)** provides that capability.

DHTML embeds a special type of program, called a script, within a regular HTML page. These scripts can perform a variety of functions. For example, a Web page can be coded to show patriotic graphics on the 4th of July, or Halloween graphics during the month of October. DHTML is also used to provide dynamic menus. When a user points to a menu item, the menu pops open, and submenus can cascade, just like a regular application. HTML has no ability to perform this type of action.

Enrichment **LAB**

Lab 10.2 Adding Attributes to an Intranet Home Page Practice additional hands-on networking skills on page 447.

CASCADING STYLE SHEETS

Web designers ran into major problems in the early days of the World Wide Web. Because HTML was designed to present a static, unchanging document, it was very difficult to change a site's *look* without disturbing the content. **Cascading style sheets (CSS)** were developed to make it easier to apply formatting rules to one or more HTML documents.

CSS documents define rules for how certain elements are to appear. For example, it might define that the <H1> tag uses the Arial font, 16 point size, and the color red. The CSS document is then referenced by the HTML page, or pages. When the browser loads the HTML page, it sees the reference to the CSS file. The CSS file is checked for formatting instructions. Anytime an <H1> tag is encountered, the formatting instructions contained in the CSS file are used instead of the default formatting. Making a single change in the CSS file can change the look of an entire site at once.

XML

Activity 10.2 XML and Web Services An emerging technology called Web services goes hand in hand with XML. Web services enable applications to communicate with each other, using XML to exchange data, with no human intervention. Visit **networking.glencoe.com** to read more about this important new technology.

Although HTML is fine for defining how a Web page looks, it cannot tell you what the data represent. For example, suppose someone has the idea to sell books online. This site is going to have to display dozens of books from many different publishers. The problem is the publishers all store their information in different database systems. It is going to be difficult to pick out the important information, such as the title, author, and book summary from all the data they are going to send you.

The **Extensible Markup Language (XML)** was designed for just this situation. XML is used to define the structure of the content. XML does not care how the online bookseller wants to format book titles or italicize author names. It is "extensible" because you are free to define the structure any way you want to. There is no fixed, predefined set of tags that you have to use to describe your data. You can make them up any way you want, as long as you follow the rules of XML.

In our publishing example, XML can be used to describe each portion of a book's information sent to us by the publisher. For example:

```
<title>Introduction to Networks and Networking</title>
<publisher>Glencoe</publisher>
<summary>Introduction to Networks and Networking
provides an in-depth overview...</summary>
```

In this format, it is very easy to see what each portion of the data represents. The primary goal of XML is to provide a structure to transmit data between applications. It does not tell those applications what to do with those data. For XML to actually do something, it needs some companions.

◆ A **document type definition (DTD)**—Defines which tags are legal in an XML document. For the XML file to be valid, it must follow the rules set by the DTD.

◆ An **Extensible Style Sheet (XSL)**—Displays XML data (in a browser, for example). An XSL document sets up formatting for display of XML data as an XHTML document. XHTML, as you might have guessed, is an extension of regular HTML that is used to display XML data.

◆ A parsing program—Is used to read through the XML document. Parsing is a way of analyzing language, or a computer file. For example, words in a sentence could be counted by parsing for spaces within the sentence. An XML document's structure could be analyzed using a parsing program. Then, data from the supplier could be read into Amazon's own Web site however they saw fit.

SCRIPTING

Scripting has changed the face of the Web. Web pages can change their appearance and even their content using scripted programs embedded within an HTML document. These scripts are based on several different programming languages and bring a lot of new capabilities to the Web.

Scripts are usually fairly short programs that limit interaction within the confines of the Web page and browser. Also, the scripts do not have to be written with any particular operating system or computer hardware in mind. Instead, the script rides along as part of the HTML code. It is up to the browser to recognize the script commands and do what the script tells it to do.

ASP

Active Server Pages (ASP) are Web pages that are created dynamically. These pages have an .asp extension instead of the familiar .htm or .html extensions. You see examples of ASP almost anytime you visit an online shopping site. For example, if you search for the musician Tori Amos, a database retrieves all of her available albums. Then, a new Web page is generated with current pricing information and is returned to your browser.

● **Figure 10.16**
Web pages using scripts can react to what the user is doing. How do interactive Web sites enhance the usability of the Web?

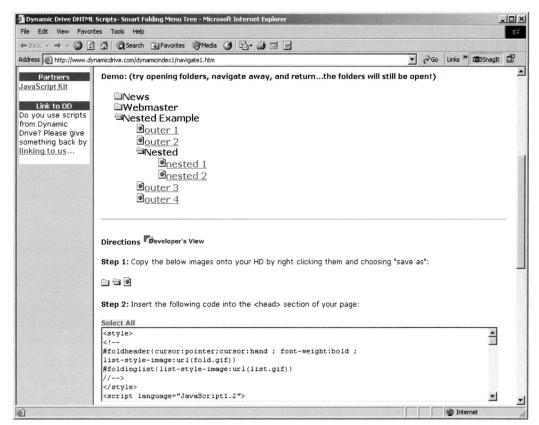

JavaScript

JavaScript utilizes the Java programming language. JavaScript can be used to add all sorts of interesting features and dynamic effects to an HTML page. For example, rollover buttons respond to the mouse cursor by changing their appearance. This feature creates more interaction between the user and the HTML page. Such interaction can lead to a much more satisfying user experience. Figure 10.16 on page 299 shows an example of a JavaScript program that uses an expanding folder concept to provide enhanced navigation.

CGI

The **Common Gateway Interface (CGI)** allows Web servers to interact dynamically with users. CGI programs are commonly used to process online forms. For example, you might visit a page that requires you to register your user name and password. You input your information in an HTML form. When you click the Submit button, a CGI program verifies that the information you input is valid. The program then stores the information in a database. The CGI program can later return information to you. CGI programs typically run on the server, so all processing occurs there and the results are sent to your Web browser. These results are just one more example of how the old, static pages of the past are being replaced by dynamic sites in which users can interact with content. Perhaps users will come to rely on or even expect such interactions on nearly all the pages they visit.

Section 10.3 Assessment

Concept Check

1. Define tags, attributes, Dynamic HTML, cascading style sheets (CSS), Extensible Markup Language (XML), document type definition (DTD), Extensible Style Sheet, script, JavaScript, and Common Gateway Interface (CGI).

2. Explain how a script differs from an application.

Critical Thinking

3. Sequence Explain how data could first be extracted from a database in XML format and then how they are displayed in a Web page.

4. Formulate Information How do scripting languages make the Web more interesting and more useful? Write a paragraph that highlights the uses of language.

Applying Skills

Create a Web Page
Use your online research skills to learn more about basic HTML tags. Find out how to include an image and a hyperlink. Revise your firstpage.html to include both an image and a hyperlink to one of your favorite sites. If possible, post your page to your school (or class) intranet.

SECTION 10.1 The Internet and the World Wide Web

Key Terms

Uniform Resource Locator (URL), 285
Active Server Page (ASP), 285
Hypertext Transfer Protocol (HTTP), 285
Secure HTTP (HTTPS), 286

Main Ideas

- Web sites present pages in an organized manner.
- You must learn to identify reliable and unreliable sources of information on the Web.
- Small businesses and home users can use Web hosting services to get a site on the Web.
- URLs are used to locate pages within a particular domain.
- A Web browser communicates with Web servers using HTTP.

SECTION 10.2 Business and the Web

Key Terms

intranet, 288
extranet, 288
portal, 289
Authenticode, 290
digital signature, 290
data encryption standard (DES), 292
Multipurpose Internet Mail Extensions (MIME), 292
Secure Sockets Layer (SSL), 292
firewall, 293
proxy server, 293

Main Ideas

- Intranets and extranets provide businesses with a Web-like interface for document and application access.
- Electronic commerce describes any type of business transaction on the Web.
- Securing networks, transactions, and personal information on the Web is critical.
- Digital signatures and encryption are used to protect documents and transmissions.
- Firewalls and proxy servers prevent unauthorized traffic from flowing into and out of networks.

SECTION 10.3 Languages of the Web

Key Terms

tags, 296
attributes, 296
Dynamic HTML, 297
cascading style sheets (CSS), 298
Extensible Markup Language (XML), 298
document type definition (DTD), 298
eXtensible Style Sheet, 298
script, 299
JavaScript, 300
Common Gateway Interface (CGI), 300

Main Ideas

- HTML describes the appearance of a Web page.
- Scripts embedded in Web pages can be used to provide interactive Web pages.
- XML describes the structure of data and is used to allow applications to exchange data.
- ASP and CGI are used to allow a Web page to interface with databases, and can create HTML code on the fly.

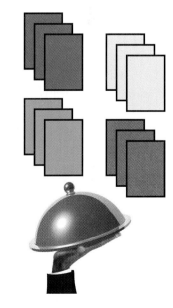

Reviewing Key Terms

1. Explain the role of a URL.
2. What is the purpose of HTTP?
3. Where on a browser can you see that a Hypertext Transfer Protocol is secure?
4. What is S/MIME?
5. What does CGI stand for?

Understanding Main Ideas

6. **Explain** why HTML is an important part of Web technology.
7. **Illustrate** the structure of a typical Web site. Show the relationship between the Web browser, Web server, Web page, URL, HTTP, and HTML.
8. **Explain** how JavaScript enhances an HTML page.
9. **List** at least six methods to secure online documents and transactions, and describe each one's function(s) and disadvantage(s).
10. **Describe** what a portal is and give an example.
11. **Identify** the underlying use of scripting languages for developing a Web site.
12. **Explain** the reason why intranets have become an important Web technology used by businesses.
13. **Discuss** a situation in which a scripting language is suitable for use in developing a Web site.
14. **Identify** the means SSL uses to protect communications between client and server.

Critical Thinking

15. **Compare and Contrast** Examine the similarities and differences of HTML and XML.
16. **Evaluate Information** For a company to run electronic commerce, there are choices of maintaining a Web server by itself, using a Web hosting service by outsource, or joining a well-known portal offered by a third party. List the factors that would influence the decision making.
17. **Draw Conclusions** List the four general categories of goals (services) of network security and explain why the methods/protocols in these categories should be used.
18. **Compare and Contrast** Firewall and proxy servers have similar roles in network security, but they are different in many ways. Compare and contrast their roles, then answer why a firewall is more popular in home networking.
19. **Formulate Information** Your company is moving to electronic commerce. You are assigned the job of enhancing the company's old Web site. The old Web site contained text, images, and hyperlinks for product and sales representative information. What are the functions needed for online selling? Explain how using them will grow your present Web site into an e-commerce site.

e-Review ·················

networking.glencoe.com

Study with PowerPoint

To review the main points in this chapter, select **e-Review > PowerPoint Outlines > Chapter 10.**

Online Self Check

Test your knowledge of the material in this chapter by selecting **e-Review > Self Checks > Chapter 10.**

Making Connections

Social Studies—Comparing Highways In the past, automobiles were designed with large combustible engines that violate today's highway safety standards. Research automobile safety campaigns from the 1960s until now. For example, manufacturers installed airbags in new vehicles.

Nowadays, the Internet, the information highway, brings many hazards to home, business, and government computer networks. Create a chart that compares both types of highway safety systems. The chart can also show cause and effect examples. A tip to remember as you are plotting your chart is to ask yourself why it is important to provide secure transportation on both highways.

STANDARDS AT WORK

Students evaluate and select new information resources and technological innovations based on the appropriateness of specific tasks. (NETS-S 5)

Selecting New Information

It is an ongoing task trying to keep up with current Internet network HTTP specifications and any new developments. Up to the time that this book was published, the Internet Engineering Task Fork (IETF) had two HTTP standards versions, Hypertext Transfer Protocol—HTTP/1.0 (RFC1945) and Hypertext Transfer Protocol—HTTP/1.1 (RFC2616).

◆ Using a Web browser, go to IETF's RFC pages to find these two RFC documents.
◆ Type 1945 in the space labeled "RFC number".
◆ Use the browser's **Find** function and search for Web page HTTP request commands that are generally called "methods."
◆ Go back to the search page and type 2616.
◆ Again, look for "methods" in the document.
◆ On a separate piece of paper, list the 11 methods and write one or two sentences stating its purpose.
◆ Choose one method and draw a diagram of what happens to the Web page because of that method.

TEAMWORK SKILLS

Web Design Thumbnails

With your teacher's permission, form groups of at least three people. Using a Web browser, go to a Web portal like **yahoo.com** or **msn.com**. Based on what your group sees, draw thumbnail sketches that show portal designs that include the following:

◆ Subjects
◆ Weekly topics and assignments
◆ Term papers or portfolio projects
◆ Online study resources
◆ Teachers, students, and parents
◆ News and events

Evaluate your own group's Web portal sketches. Use the following criteria to help create and evaluate a final sketch:

◆ Is it well organized and consistent in appearance?
◆ Does it grab your attention?
◆ Are there too many images that will slow its transfer over networks?

Finalize one design and submit the group's portal to your teacher.

CHALLENGE YOURSELF

Study HTTP Performance

The major improvement of HTTP/1.1 over HTTP/1.0 is the type of connection used to data transfer. HTTP/1.0 uses a nonpersistent connection, with which only a single Web page is transferred over a transportation connection. HTTP/1.1 uses a persistent connection as its default mode, in which multiple Web pages can be transferred during the lifetime of a single connection.

Assume that the time for connection setup is **s seconds,** the size of the base HTML file is **b bytes,** the size of the image GIF file is **j bytes,** and the speed of data transfer from the Web server to the Web browser is **r bits** per second.

Write an equation of the total time it takes from the moment when a user clicks a URL of a base file containing ten images to when the user sees the complete page displayed on his screen for each version of HTTP.

YOU TRY IT

Networking Lab

1. Viewing the Firewall Security Log

After you enable the Windows XP Firewall in "You Try It Activity 10A Enabling Windows XP Firewall", you can enable the Security Log and monitor suspected attacks. Note: The log file grows which could eat up your disk space, so you should disable the log after this lab activity. You will need two different computers.

A Click **Start,** click **Control Panel,** and choose **Network and Internet Connections.**

B Click **Network Connections.**

C Right-click your main connection—this may be a dial-up, LAN, or other type of connection—and then click **Properties.**

D Click the **Advanced** tab. The box "Protect my computer..." should be checked.

E Click **Settings,** and then click the **Security Logging** tab.

F Verify that **Log dropped packets** and **Log successful connections** are both checked. Make a note of the log file location (**c:\windows\pfirewall.log**).

G Click the **ICMP** tab and check the box to **Allow incoming echo request.**

H Click the **Services** tab and check the box to allow **Web Server (HTTP).**

I Click **OK** twice to save your changes to the firewall setting.

J Find out your computer's IP address:
   ◆ Open a command window.
   ◆ Type in ipconfig which will show you the IP address and other information about your computer.

K Find another computer on the same network as your computer or with the Internet connection, and issue some traffic connections to your computer:
   ◆ In the command window, type in ping 198.188.8.8 and observe what message you get.
   ◆ Open your Web browser and type in http://198.188.8.8/<*type the path to where you saved the "firstpage.html" file you created in "You Try It Activity 10B>* /firstpage.html and observe what message you get. You may or may not see a page.

L Go back to your original computer and view the security log file named "pfirewall.log" under the default folder "Windows". Pay attention to the values under the titles "Log dropped packets" Date, time, action and "Log successful connections".

M Does your finding match your connection attempts?

```
pfirewall.log - Notepad

File  Edit  Format  View  Help

#version: 1.0
#Software: Microsoft Internet Connection Firewall
#Time Format: Local
#Fields: date time action protocol src-ip dst-ip src-port dst-port size tcpflags tc

2003-12-11 19:45:13 OPEN UDP 10.3.1.30 10.3.0.37 1027 53 - - - - - - -
2003-12-11 19:45:13 OPEN TCP 10.3.1.30 10.3.0.40 3449 445 - - - - - - - -
2003-12-11 19:46:17 CLOSE UDP 10.3.1.30 10.3.0.37 1027 53 - - - - - - - -
2003-12-11 19:46:17 CLOSE TCP 10.3.1.30 10.3.0.40 3449 445 - - - - - - -
2003-12-11 19:46:27 OPEN TCP 10.3.1.30 213.222.11.9 3451 80 - - - - - - - -
2003-12-11 19:47:17 CLOSE TCP 10.3.1.30 213.222.11.9 3451 80 - - - - - - -
2003-12-11 19:47:22 OPEN-INBOUND TCP 10.3.1.62 10.3.1.30 1838 80 - - - - - - - -
2003-12-11 19:47:23 OPEN-INBOUND TCP 10.3.1.62 10.3.1.30 1839 80 - - - - - - - -
2003-12-11 19:47:30 OPEN UDP 10.3.1.30 10.3.0.40 123 123 - - - - - - - -
2003-12-11 19:47:30 OPEN-INBOUND TCP 10.3.1.62 10.3.1.30 1840 80 - - - - - - - -
2003-12-11 19:47:31 OPEN-INBOUND TCP 10.3.1.62 10.3.1.30 1841 80 - - - - - - - -
2003-12-11 19:47:39 OPEN-INBOUND TCP 10.3.1.62 10.3.1.30 1842 80 - - - - - - - -
2003-12-11 19:47:44 OPEN-INBOUND TCP 10.3.1.62 10.3.1.30 1843 80 - - - - - - - -
2003-12-11 19:48:01 OPEN-INBOUND TCP 10.3.1.62 10.3.1.30 1844 80 - - - - - - - -
2003-12-11 19:48:06 OPEN-INBOUND TCP 10.3.1.62 10.3.1.30 1845 80 - - - - - - - -
```

Networking Projects

1. Plan a Web Site

You are a newly hired Webmaster for your school. Your first assignment is to create a Web site for your school.

Ⓐ Create a slide show or flip chart presentation that follows the Web development cycle shown in the diagram.

Ⓑ Include what you would do at each stage of the development and how you would do it. You should consider what might be in the Web site in order to prove your concepts.

Use the information presented in this chapter and other sources available in your classroom, such as texts, or Web sources. Cite the sources you use when you prepare your presentation and acknowledge any persons you interviewed.

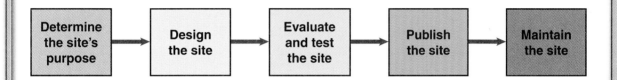

| Determine the site's purpose | → | Design the site | → | Evaluate and test the site | → | Publish the site | → | Maintain the site |

2. Create an HTML Page

Re-create the simple HTML page you made in You Try It Activity 10D on page 297. Use Microsoft Word and save the file as an HTML document.

Ⓐ Launch Word and type This is a Heading, and click the **Center** icon.

Ⓑ Click **Format, Borders and Shading,** and **Borders.** Pick the style and location and insert a horizontal line, and click **OK.**

Ⓒ Type This is the body text. and click the **Align left** icon.

Ⓓ Insert a "GIF" file by clicking **Insert, Pictures, From File....** Choose the folder where the image file is located, highlight the flag GIF file, and click **Insert.**

Ⓔ Save the file as a Web page in the folder where you are allowed to save files. Type the file name wordpage.html and save the file.

Ⓖ Locate the file you just saved and double-click it. Note: you may have noticed that there is now a new file in that folder with "gif" as the extension name.

Ⓗ Within your Web browser, click **View,** and then **Source** to see the HTML code of the Web page you just created. **Tip:** This is a quick way for you to learn to write HTML code—by "reading" another's fine work. This is similar to the way you learn writing—by reading literature.

Problem-Solving Skills: Converting Binary and Hexadecimal Numbers

Many different numbering systems are used with computers and networking. The decimal numbering system is used by people. Computers use the binary system of 1s and 0s. The hexadecimal system can be used as a go-between system to help humans convert back and forth between the binary and hexadecimal systems.

One of the most common conversion tasks is converting an IP address to its binary equivalent. Refine your abilities to convert between systems by solving the following problems.

1. Use the IPCONFIG utility in DOS to obtain your computer's IP address, or use the address 192.168.0.1.

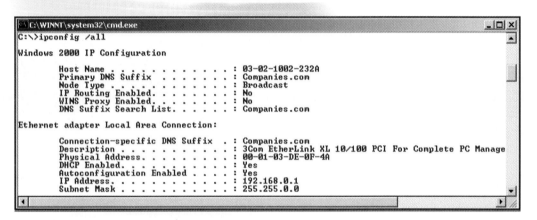

```
C:\WINNT\system32\cmd.exe

C:\>ipconfig /all

Windows 2000 IP Configuration

        Host Name . . . . . . . . . . . . : 03-02-1002-232A
        Primary DNS Suffix  . . . . . . . : Companies.com
        Node Type . . . . . . . . . . . . : Broadcast
        IP Routing Enabled. . . . . . . . : No
        WINS Proxy Enabled. . . . . . . . : No
        DNS Suffix Search List. . . . . . : Companies.com

Ethernet adapter Local Area Connection:

        Connection-specific DNS Suffix  . : Companies.com
        Description . . . . . . . . . . . : 3Com EtherLink XL 10/100 PCI For Complete PC Manage
        Physical Address. . . . . . . . . : 00-01-03-DE-0F-4A
        DHCP Enabled. . . . . . . . . . . : Yes
        Autoconfiguration Enabled . . . . : Yes
        IP Address. . . . . . . . . . . . : 192.168.0.1
        Subnet Mask . . . . . . . . . . . : 255.255.0.0
```

2. Convert your IP address to its binary equivalent (convert each four-bit portion individually).
3. Convert the four binary values you calculated in step 2 to their hexadecimal equivalents.

Information Skills: Discovering ASCII and EBCDIC

To further understand how computers and humans interact, research ASCII and EBCDIC. ASCII is a common code used to represent characters in a text file. EBCDIC is an IBM code used for the same purpose. However, the two code sets do not match one another. Suppose you need to write a program that will convert capital letters from one system to the other.

1. With your teacher's permission, search online for tables listing ASCII and EBCDIC code values.
2. Make a chart that lists the decimal equivalent of letters A–Z in ASCII and EBCDIC codes. You do not need to include lowercase letters, numbers, or other characters unless your teacher instructs you to do so.
3. Translate the phrase "NETWORKING COMPUTERS IS FUN" to ASCII values.

Building Your Portfolio

Surveying WAN Services

Your publishing company is expanding from a single office to new offices located in Los Angeles, New York, and Miami. Obviously, your current LAN technology cannot serve the needs of the new remote users who will be accessing the servers.

Prepare a report that analyzes the various WAN technology options. Use online resources to help you determine what services are available and to show costs associated with various technologies.

1. Use a word processing application to prepare your report.
2. Analyze the value of modems as a means of establishing a WAN connection.
3. Discuss WAN technologies such as ISDN, SONET, and SMDS.
4. Include in your report a chart or table that compares each of the WAN technologies in terms of cost, speed, and availability in your area.
5. Identify the important terms and features of X.25 and Frame Relay and ATM.
6. Explain the difference between packet-switched and circuit-switched transmissions.

WAN Report Check List

Modems
- ☑ Speed
- ☑ Cost
- ☑ DUN vs. VPN

WAN Technologies (ISDN, SONET, SMDS)
- ☑ How are data transmitted?
- ☑ Equipment needed
- ☑ Costs (installation, equipments, monthly fees)

Data Transmission (X.25, Frame Relay, ATM)
- ☑ Key terms
- ☑ Devices used
- ☑ Primary uses
- ☑ Speed of transmission

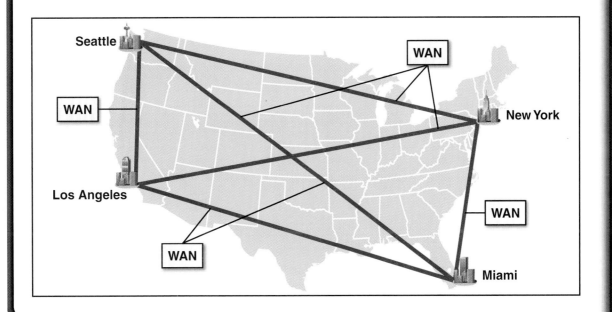

Network Design and Implementation

Visit *Glencoe Online*

Go to this book's Web site at **networking.glencoe.com**.

Click on **Unit Activities** and select **Unit 4 Copyright and Fair Use**. Recognize the importance of understanding copyright policies, and learn what information you can and cannot use legally.

Think About It

Your Networking Toolbox
To support a network, you need various tools, such as screwdrivers, wire strippers, volt-ohmmeters, and so on. Just as important to your effectiveness is the ability to use "soft skills" that improve communication and problem-solving.

Discover Networking Skills Activity
What soft skills (also called "people skills") do you think you need to have to support a network? Name as many as you can think of and explain why the skill is important.

CHAPTER 11 Network Planning and Design

YOU WILL LEARN TO...

Section 11.1

- Identify customer requirements
- Recommend appropriate network topologies
- Gather data about existing equipment and software

Section 11.2

- Demonstrate knowledge of RAID levels and how to choose between them
- Identify planning strategies for network growth
- Describe hardware compatibility issues

Section 11.3

- Identify methods to measure server performance
- Demonstrate OS performance
- Identify methods to measure network performance

WHY IT MATTERS......................................

You have probably heard the phrase, "Fail to plan, plan to fail." Most successful people learn early that planning is an important part of success. These individuals set goals for themselves, and plan exactly what steps they will take to accomplish their goals. After the plan is formulated, they act. Planning is absolutely critical when designing a network. Fail to plan, and you can count on your network failing.

Quick Write Activity

Think about a recent goal you were trying to accomplish. Write a short paragraph about why you set that goal and the steps you took to prepare for and accomplish that goal. In retrospect, state if there was anything you could have done early during the planning stage to make achieving the goal easier.

WHAT YOU WILL DO...

ACTIVITIES AND PROJECTS

Applying Skills

You Try It Activities

Chapter Assessment

You Try It Networking Lab

Networking Projects

Enrichment Labs

IN THE WORKBOOK

Optional Activities and Projects

Guided Reading

Study Guide

Networking Labs

ON THE WEB

Activities at networking.glencoe.com

Reading Strategy Organizers

Go Online Activities

Study with PowerPoint

Self-Check Assessments

READ TO SUCCEED

Organize Information

If you were told to remember the names of everyone in your class on the first day, it would probably be difficult. But what if you grouped people in ways that made it easier? You could remember the names of one row at a time. Grouping information also helps when you have to remember material that you have read. When you take notes, think about how topics relate to each other. Organizing them as a group makes them easier to remember.

Guide to Reading

Main Ideas

Designing a network requires careful planning. Decisions about an existing network should always be made with future growth in mind.

Key Terms

budget
legacy application
patch cable

Reading Strategy

Identify each issue you should consider when designing a network. Create a chart similar to the one below (also available online).

Design Issues

It is important to lay a good foundation as you build a functional network. Throughout this section, we examine a fictional company that hired you to install a computer network. Keep in mind that the choices we make are based on the requirements of this hypothetical company and do not address every company's networking situation and needs.

CUSTOMER REQUIREMENTS

The "Ski Shack" company manufactures custom-made skis (see Figure 11.1). They have hired you to install a computer network. The network will bring the company up-to-date in communication technology. Your design needs to be flexible enough to allow for future expansion.

The company's network goals are to:

- Network the existing computers so that they can share information and printers.
- Add two additional computers to the network—one for the Product Design Group and one for the Manufacturing Department.
- Allow for the possible addition of three computers at a later date.
- Provide an Internet connection for the Product Design Group.

Figure 11.1
Ski Shack is looking to expand their network. According to their goals, how are they planning for future growth?

networking.glencoe.com

Table 11.1

Ski Shack Company Technology Data	
Location	Boulder, Colorado
Number of employees	23
Product	Ski Equipment and Supplies
Facility	Single-story building: 245 square meters (2,625 square feet)
Current distribution of computers	Managing Director: Pentium IV 2.2 GHz
	Accounting Department: Pentium III 800 MHz
	Sales Department: PowerPC G5
	Shipping Department: AMD Athlon 1.8 GHz
	Product Design Group: Pentium IV 2.2 GHz
Operating systems	Managing Director and Product Design Group: Windows 2000
	Accounting Department: Windows 98
	Shipping Department: Windows XP
	Sales Department: OS X
Peripheral equipment	Managing Director: modem, Internet connection, and a color ink-jet printer
	Design Department: laser printer
	Accounting and Sales Departments share a second laser printer on a switch box
	Shipping Department: dot matrix printer

Table 11.1
Planning a network requires a careful evaluation of existing equipment. **What can you determine from the following background information?**

Table 11.1 provides background information about the company. Refer to this table as you work toward achieving the company's networking goals.

Figure 11.2 illustrates the layout of the ski company. As you can see, the layout includes public areas, department offices, and manufacturing facilities.

In addition to the customer's technical requirements for the network, you also have to work within a budget. A **budget** is a summary stating how much money and time will be used toward a specific purpose, such as the maintenance of a network. Working within the budget often means making difficult decisions regarding all aspects of the network. It can mean choosing a different type of media, another brand of switch or hub, or using a less powerful computer for the server. However, you should always try to make the best long-term decision. You do not want to make a decision that saves a few dollars today, only to find the network fails to meet tomorrow's requirements.

Figure 11.2
A facility map of the ski company displays the business space. **Why do you think information like this facility map is important when planning a network?**

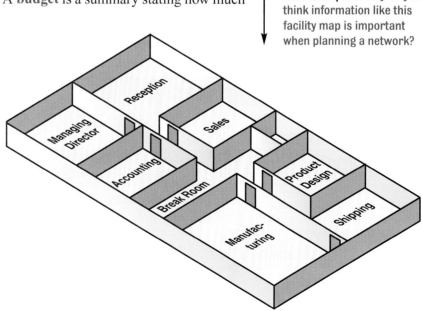

PEER-TO-PEER OR CLIENT/SERVER?

The first decision we need to make for this new network is whether it should be a peer-to-peer or a client/server network. The factors we need to examine include the following:

- Size of the network
- Level of security
- Type of business
- Level of administrative support available
- Amount of network traffic
- Needs of the network users
- Network budget

Because of the small number of users (less than ten) and lack of budget for a full-time administrator, a client/server network is not feasible. However, to provide flexibility for future expansion, a hybrid peer-to-peer network is selected. One new computer will be installed and configured as a file server to centralize company information.

TAKING INVENTORY

Our next step is to inventory the existing hardware and software, and determine what needs to be replaced or purchased. Taking inventory is an important step because it sets the stage for future network expansion. Ski Shack currently has a mixture of computers, ranging from a PowerPC to an older Pentium III, to some new Pentium IV and AMD Athlon computers.

For example, if all the computers run Microsoft Windows 95 or Windows 98, the type of network is limited to using a peer-to-peer network. Upgrading to a client/server network would require either purchasing a new server or upgrading an existing computer to run a NOS, such as NetWare, one of the Windows Server editions, or Linux.

A proper inventory involves at least four categories, including hardware, software, telecommunications equipment, and network requirements.

Hardware Survey

To begin a hardware survey, you will need to record the specifications of each computer. The details you gather at this stage can save time in the long run. To function effectively, networks often require that hardware and software meet certain minimum standards. If you know the specification details of the available equipment in advance, you can prevent many problems later.

YOU TRY IT

ACTIVITY 11A Surveying Network Hardware

For this activity, survey the computer equipment available in your own classroom or lab. Use a spreadsheet application to record the following information for each computer:

1 Record the make and model of the computer.

2 List the make, model, and size of the monitor.

3 Document the following information in as much detail as possible. In the Windows OS, you can find most of this information by going to the **Control Panel** and opening **System** (see Figure 11.3). **Note:** Some of this information is found by going to the **Hardware** tab, and then clicking **Device Manager.**

- Processor manufacturer
- Amount of installed RAM
- Make, model, and size of hard drive(s)
- Make, model, and amount of memory of the video card
- Make, model, and driver versions of any installed devices, such as NIC, CD or DVD burners, and so on

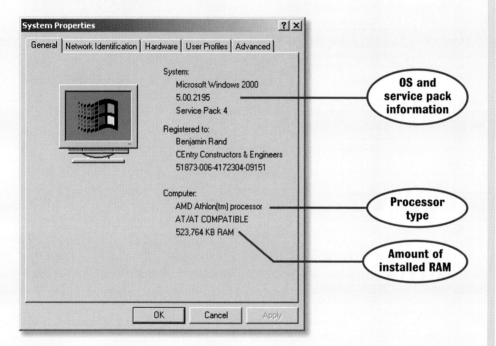

Figure 11.3
The System utility can provide information about hardware installed on Windows OS computers.

4 Following your teacher's instructions, open the computer case to view the type of bus slots available. This is important in case you need to install network interface cards.

Performing a detailed survey helps you be prepared for incompatibility problems that you may encounter later. This survey can also be used to keep inventory of the hardware. Eventually, you could expand it to include information about who installed the hardware and the problems encountered. It could track when the hardware was bought and the cost. All of this information could be used to plan for future upgrades and track problematic hardware.

This is also a good time to survey the network's storage capacity. For a client/server network, this means finding out if a file server has the capacity to store the amount of files it will be required to store. In a peer-to-peer network, each computer needs the capacity to store the OS, installed applications, and whatever files the computer is going to share with other users.

Software Survey

Be aware of all the software currently in use throughout the organization. You need to be especially cautious about older legacy applications. A **legacy application** is software that may use older technology, which may be considered outdated compared with today's applications. However, many companies have invested a large amount of time and money in these legacy applications, so they continue to be used. Legacy applications include database management systems that run on mainframes. Some of these programs may not run on newer operating systems and a solution will need to be found to continue accessing the legacy application. Contact the software developer for information about running the application on the network. Not all of these will run in a network environment. The software licensing arrangement might not allow network operations.

> **YOU TRY IT**
>
> ## ACTIVITY 11B Inventorying Software
>
> A software survey can help track software currently used. Create a spreadsheet to list the following data you collect using your classroom or lab computers.
>
> **❶** Application name.
>
> **❷** Version number. In most applications, you can click the **Help** menu and then select **About** to determine the application version.
>
> **❸** Availability of the original installation media.
>
> **❹** Availability of upgrades or patches.
>
> **❺** Any licensing information (critical).
>
> Collect as much detailed information about each application as you can. It is extremely important that you locate installation media and license information. You will need this if you need to reinstall applications following an OS upgrade.

Activity 11.1 Cost of Illegal Software Illegal software costs software companies billions of dollars per year. It also carries with it the possibility of large fines and potential jail time for those caught using illegal software. To find out more, go to networking.glencoe.com.

As you carry out a software survey, be sure to note any potential software incompatibilities within and among company departments. For example, the Accounting Department might be using WordPerfect, whereas the Sales Department is using Microsoft Office. If you are planning to upgrade some day, now is the time to make any changes needed to ensure that the same system is used company wide.

It is also critical to examine the licensing of all software in use throughout the network, including the OS. Many software licenses permit installation on only one computer. Copying the software to other computers is illegal and could result in large fines.

Telecommunications Equipment Survey

Surveying the existing telecommunications equipment is an important element of your survey, especially if you intend to use Internet connections or some form of remote access server. Overlooking something as simple as the number of phone lines wired into each office can have a major impact later if you need modem and telephone connections at the same time.

For example, suppose a company has an automated telephone system. Although telephone outlets might be located in every office, they might not be capable of a modem connection. In this case, a separate telephone outlet might be required for voice and data communication. Also, if the company is using a high-speed digital telephone service, you might not be able to connect with standard modems. Do not assume a standard RJ-11 telephone jack is going to be sufficient for you to connect a modem and start surfing the Web.

Requirements of the Network

After you have examined the existing facility and equipment, you need to define the requirements of your network. You then match these requirements to the existing hardware, software, and telecommunications features available and determine what steps need to be taken to develop the network.

ACTIVITY 11C Determining Network Requirements

YOU TRY IT

Using your own classroom or lab environment as an example, create a document using a word processing or spreadsheet application that shows the following:

1 Physical size of the facility (located on a single floor versus multiple floors)

2 Number of users

3 Whether the LAN will be extended to other buildings

4 Physical environment (office, manufacturing, outside, and so on)

5 Current network media (type of cable, wireless)

6 Technical competence of users

7 Amount of network traffic (initially and anticipated in the future)

8 Level of security required to protect network data

This information can help you make important decisions regarding the type of network media and the type of infrastructure components required, such as NICs, hubs versus switches, or server capabilities.

BUILDING A MAP

Now, it is time to lay out the network. Before you recommend a network plan, it is a good idea to make a map of all the elements involved. During this step, you should consider two aspects of the network: the physical layout, including the location of each piece of hardware and how it relates to the others, and the physical and logical topology of the proposed network.

ACTIVITY 11D Mapping the Facility

YOU TRY IT

Using your own classroom or lab environment, create a physical map of the facility.

1 As accurately as possible, create a scaled map of the facility using graph paper or a drawing application such as Microsoft Visio.

② Show the locations of each computer, printer, server, or other device attached to the network. Include hubs, switches, or other connecting devices.

③ Identify each device by providing its name. Alternatively, number each device on the map.

④ Show cable type(s) and routing from each device to a connection point or where it exits the room.

A detailed map can help you determine quantities for the network cabling, NICs, and other network devices you will need to purchase. It also helps when you need to locate a specific device for maintenance or troubleshooting later.

You need to consider several factors when choosing the network topology. For example, bus networks are economical because they tend to use less cable. However, a break in the cable can affect many users. Ring topologies are favorable in certain situations, such as manufacturing, when transmission timing is important. Star topologies are the most common, especially in Ethernet networks. Problems can be harder to isolate, but failure of one node does not affect the rest of the network.

INSTALLING NETWORK MEDIA

Installing network media requires special skills and is best left to a professional cable installer if the topology is complex. With a simple topology, such as the one at Ski Shack, the necessary skills are well within our reach.

The simplest layout for a network in our small-office environment is to use a physical star. The focal point of the star is a 16-port Ethernet switch. A hub could be used, but switches generally give better performance and do not cost a great deal more. Also, the choice of a 16-port switch rather than an 8-port switch leaves room for more devices to be added in the future.

Cable is run from the network equipment closet (or a room dedicated to network equipment) to each of the rooms. The cable is connected to an RJ-45 outlet, which is installed in the walls, like a power or telephone outlet.

After the media is installed, connecting the computers is straightforward. A short length of cable with connectors at each end, called a **patch cable,** is used. One end of the patch cable is plugged into the NIC at each computer (or printer, if it has a built-in NIC) and the other end is secured to the RJ-45 outlet. Figure 11.4 shows one complete connection from a workstation to the switch.

A lot of effort is required when planning a larger network. However, the time spent planning pays off down the road if you choose the right technologies from the beginning.

Figure 11.4 ⬤
Connecting the media is a simple step. What two important factors affect the choice of network media?

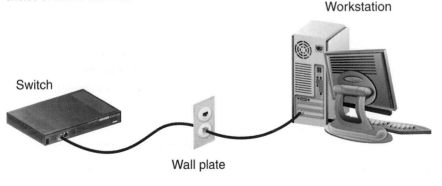

Workstation

Switch

Wall plate

DESIGNING WITHIN AN EXISTING INFRASTRUCTURE

Most network installations or upgrades have to happen within an existing infrastructure. This presents many challenges. Cost is usually the first and biggest concern. For example, a company that wants to move to fiber optic cable must consider both the higher price of the cable itself and also the cost of having a certified technician install the cable. Twisted-pair cable is not only less expensive, but also easy to install with little or no training. However, this may not be a feasible choice over longer distances or if the site suffers from too much electronic interference.

Physical factors, such as distance between buildings or sites, also play a role. Two offices situated a few blocks apart may not have the option of physically running cable between sites. However, a rooftop mounted microwave system could be used to transmit data, as long as the systems are in a direct line-of-sight (or can access repeaters).

Supporting the new infrastructure may also require some thought. For example, moving from peer-to-peer to a client/server network may require more technical expertise than is available within the company. If there are a large enough number of users, a full-time network administrator may be required.

As with any important undertaking, it is important to plan every aspect. This section has identified some of the things you can do to prepare to install a new network. In the sections that follow, we take a look at other factors that play a role.

Section 11.1 Assessment

Concept Check

1. **Define** budget, legacy application, and patch cable.

2. **Explain** what type of cable is used to connect a computer to a wall jack.

3. **List** several points to consider when examining the requirements of the network.

Critical Thinking

4. **Design Strategies** Identify five factors you should consider when designing a network.

5. **Theorize** Complete an inventory of materials needed to install the network media for the company's computers.

6. **Draw Conclusions** Which topology, star or bus, is best for the ski shop? Explain your answer.

Applying Skills

Design a Home Network Consider a scenario in which a family has three computers, a printer, and a cable modem connected to one of the computers. They want to share the scanner and the printer. Design the home network. Identify the equipment needed and consider the network media type.

PREPARING FOR A CAREER

Although your education is a big step in preparing for a networking career, it is just one step toward reaching your career goal.

An internship can be an excellent way to break into an industry and start your career.

Building Your Résumé

Get experience and build your résumé by taking part in volunteer activities, professional organizations such as the Future Business Leaders of America, or school-to-work activities, such as a career-oriented workshop or a nonpaying internship.

These activities can improve your ability to manage time and communicate effectively. They also can lead to important contacts with professionals.

Practicing Interviewing

Work with a career counselor or an experienced manager to polish your interviewing skills:

◆ Create a list of potential interview questions and prepare answers for each one.
◆ List questions you want to ask interviewers.
◆ Think about your posture, eye contact, and body language. These things say a lot about you.

Looking for a Job

A job search can be daunting, but these skills can help you succeed:

◆ **Writing résumés**—There are many resources on résumé writing, including books, Web sites, and career counselors. Target your résumé to the specific job for which you want to apply.
◆ **Checking ads**—Read print or online advertisements carefully. Trustworthy employers supply complete job descriptions. This includes qualifications, salary, and contact information. Avoid ads that do not reveal the employer's name or contact information. Such ads may be connected to scams.
◆ **Making a good first impression**—Employers expect workers not only to act professionally, but to look that way, too. Always wear business attire to an interview. Make sure you are well groomed. Be aware of your language and mannerisms.
◆ **Applying for a job**—Completing a job application can be tedious, but it is very important. Be certain the facts and timeline on the application match your résumé. Fill out applications completely, neatly, and accurately.

Tech Focus

1. Find a job in the classified ads for which you would want to apply. Prepare a résumé targeted to that job.

2. Pair up with another student in your class. Based on the jobs you chose in Exercise 1, conduct practice interviews with one another.

Main Ideas

Servers make use of RAID hard drive technology to provide faster disk access and better data security. It is important to plan for change when designing a network. Select hardware carefully to ensure it is compatible with existing hardware.

Key Terms

array
striping
mirroring
parity
pilot deployments

Reading Strategy

Identify three important points about each RAID level. Create a table similar to the one below (also available online).

RAID 0	RAID 1	RAID 3	RAID 5
1.	1.	1.	1.
2.	2.	2.	2.
3.	3.	3.	3.

Choosing network hardware requires a great deal of research. There are different technologies involved at every level, from the server's hard drives, to the NICs, to the network media itself. When choosing hardware, find out which technologies are applicable to your project, and then begin the search for reliable manufacturers.

RAID LEVELS

The hardware chosen for a network is of high importance due to expense and the welfare of the business. But hardware costs rarely, if ever, exceed the value of an organization's data. A dynamic, inexpensive manner in which to provide storage becomes an important issue.

One of the key decisions regarding the storage of data on the file server(s) is the implementation of Redundant Array of Inexpensive Disks (RAID). RAID combines hard drives to minimize the loss of data if one of the hard drives in the array fails. An **array** is an ordered collection, such as hard drives.

There are several levels of RAID, each with its own specific capabilities. RAID levels are sometimes combined to provide the capabilities of multiple levels at the same time. For example, RAID 1+0 combines the capabilities of RAID 1 with those of RAID 0 to provide the benefits of both. The most common RAID levels are described in the following sections.

RAID 0

A technique called striping is used at the RAID 0 level. **Striping** spreads segments of data across each drive in the array (see Figure 11.5 on page 322). Because each disk in the array can read a small portion of the data quicker than a single disk can read all the data, the array's read and write speeds are increased. The storage capacity of two or more drives in RAID 0 is combined. So, two 80 GB drives appear as a single 160 GB drive. RAID 0 is used when

---

READ ME!

Jargon RAID is also known as Redundant Array of *Independent* Disks. This name is probably more accurate because the high-performance hard drives traditionally used in RAID configurations are usually anything but inexpensive.

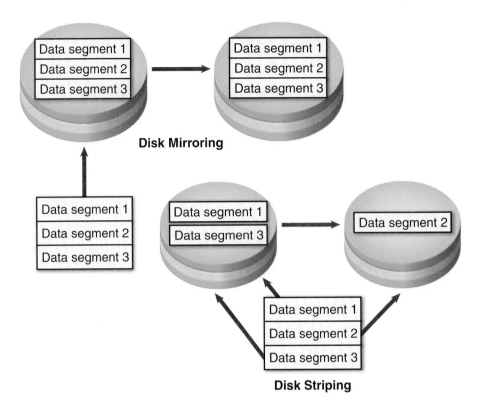

Figure 11.5
RAID 0 uses a method called striping, while RAID 1 uses mirroring. What is a benefit of mirroring?

Disk Mirroring

Disk Striping

READ ME!

Jargon In servers, failed drives can often be "hot swapped." Hot swapping a device means that it can be removed and replaced without shutting down the computer. A network technician could replace a failed hard drive without taking the server down.

Activity 11.2 More RAID What about levels 2, 4, 6, and 7? Go to **networking.glencoe.com** to find out more about these other RAID levels.

read and write speeds are critical, as in video or audio editing. However, it is not a good choice for fault tolerance. If any drive in the array fails, all data in the array are lost.

RAID 1

A technique called mirroring is used at the RAID 1 level. **Mirroring,** as shown in Figure 11.5, duplicates segments of data on the primary drive to the other drive(s) in the array. Although speed is not as good as RAID 0, fault tolerance is much better. If the primary drive fails, one of the other drives can kick in from the point at which the first drive failed.

RAID 3

A method for detecting errors in information, called **parity,** increases fault tolerance at the RAID 3 level. Similar to RAID 0, RAID 3 requires three or more drives. The first two store the data, whereas the third drive is dedicated to storing parity information. The parity information can be used to rebuild the array and restore data in the event that one of the drives fails.

RAID 5

Instead of using a dedicated parity drive, the parity information at the RAID 5 level is distributed among the drives in the array. This improves performance. Because parity information for any given block of information is stored on a different drive, fault tolerance is also high. This is one of the most popular choices in RAID because of its reasonable performance and good fault tolerance.

At one time, RAID was found exclusively in servers and high-end computers. Today, RAID can be added to many computers through the use of an add-on controller card, or is built on to many consumer motherboards. Another major change is that RAID is no longer limited to the more expensive SCSI drives.

SCALABILITY AND PLANNING FOR CHANGE

Enrichment LAB

Lab 11.1 Writing Standard Operating Procedures
Practice additional hands-on networking skills on page 448.

When a business expands, its networking needs change. Scalability describes a network's ability to grow in response to increased demands. Three approaches to consider for scalability are described in the following list:

◆ A server may require additional RAM or CPUs to keep up with additional users.
◆ More disk space may be needed to provide more storage space.
◆ Servers may need to be clustered to meet increased demand. Clusters operate in tandem and appear as a single server to the rest of the network.

When changes will affect the entire network, a period of testing usually happens before the solution is deployed throughout the network. For example, before a new service pack is applied to a NOS, it is usually installed on a test server. This test server would be connected to a test network, separate from the regular network. Only after the service pack is thoroughly tested, is it installed on the company servers.

Pilot deployments, also known as test installations, can also make changes easier. For example, new software may be installed on a few user systems. After a period of testing, the software is installed throughout the network.

HARDWARE COMPATIBILITY

Hardware incompatibilities are a fact of life. In today's computer industry, hundreds of manufacturers develop hardware and software. Each developer wants to accomplish the same task, and each provides a unique solution. Copyright and patent issues further complicate the matter.

Evaluating and selecting hardware is a major part of planning for network implementation. If you have the luxury of designing a network from the ground up, you can choose vendors and place the burden of compatibility on them. Often, you can provide vendors with a list of the hardware you plan to use and ask them to certify that those items are compatible with their products (see Figure 11.6).

Most of the time, you must create a network out of an existing collection of hardware. Any time you work with existing (often outdated) hardware, the likelihood of encountering compatibility problems is very high. It is sometimes more cost-effective to discard the old hardware and start over.

● **Figure 11.6**
Some manufacturers work very hard to help you identify potential conflicts with your existing hardware and software and new versions in which you are interested. What is the major source of incompatibility problems?

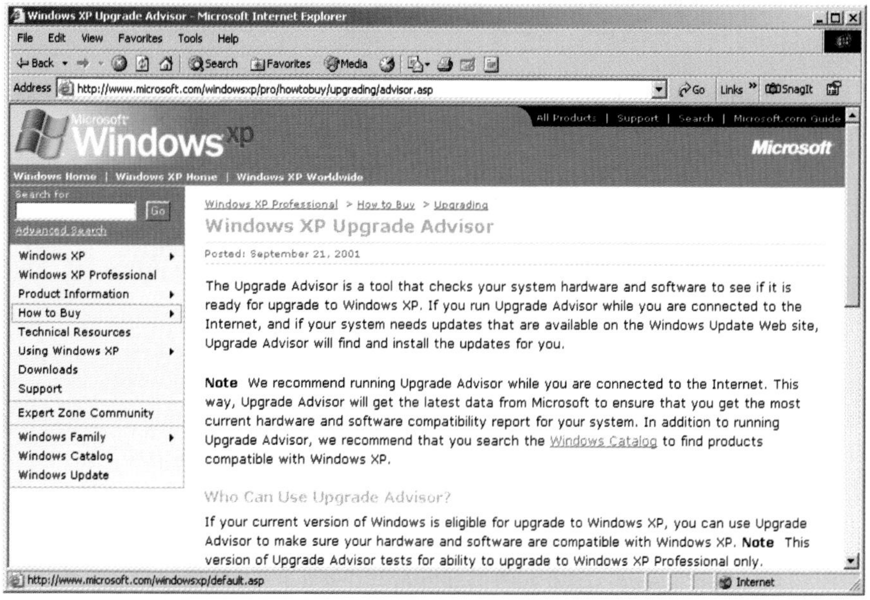

The most common incompatibilities occur between hardware and software. Changing or upgrading a computer or network operating system can lead to major problems. Be certain to address compatibility issues between new software and existing hardware before you start any upgrades.

You should consider the following list when implementing new hardware:

◆ **Read the documentation**—Chances are the manufacturer has already documented incompatibilities with other products. Check the manufacturer's Web site for additional or updated information.

◆ **Verify that devices are detected during installation**—Most hardware today is plug and play, which means that the OS should recognize not only the type, but also the specific model of device being installed.

◆ **Check minimum requirements**—Most manufacturers publish a list of minimum requirements your computer needs to have in order to use the hardware or software.

Network hardware does not suffer from compatibility issues as often as software. Network hardware operates at the lower, Physical and Data Link Layers of the OSI reference model. It works mainly with data packets. As a result, compatibility conflicts with hardware are less likely. Hardware maintains strict adherence to the IEEE 802.x standards. Therefore, any device that meets an IEEE standard can communicate with another device that meets the same standard. The only situation in which you can expect compatibility issues to arise is when two devices meet different standards.

Section 11.2 Assessment

Concept Check

1. **Define** array, striping, mirroring, parity, and pilot deployments.

2. **Explain** why RAID 0 level does not really provide data redundancy.

3. **List** several ways a network's server might be upgraded or modified to increase its capabilities.

Critical Thinking

4. **Evaluate** What factors would help you determine which RAID technology to employ when selecting server hardware?

5. **Predict** A small business with eight computer users is hiring eight more employees. There is currently a peer-to-peer network. What network changes will be required to add these new employees? List any new equipment or software you predict the company will need.

Applying Skills

Select RAID Technology
A video editor needs the fastest drive speed possible for editing video footage. After being edited, the final video will be stored on some other medium, so long-term storage on the computer's hard drive is not much of a concern. Which RAID technology is most appropriate for this user? Explain your answer.

Real World Technology

LONG-DISTANCE LEARNING

People have been studying at home for decades by using mail, educational television, and tapes. But the Internet has made distance learning an increasingly important form of education.

Online courses often allow interaction between students and teachers with Internet tools, such as e-mail or chat rooms.

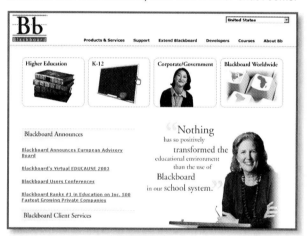

Uses for Distance Learning

Distance learning is a form of education that uses computer technology so that students can take courses in their home or office or at a computer center. Students can take a single course or earn degrees or technical certifications.

Many companies use computer-based training (CBT) to teach workers about products, policies, and customers. This allows workers to study at their own pace, from their own office, whenever they have free time.

Most important, distance learning brings the classroom to people who cannot easily attend classes. This is especially helpful for people who live in rural areas, work during regular class times, or are homebound.

How Distance Learning Works

Distance learning courses require a multimedia computer and an Internet connection. The computer should include a sound card, microphone, and speakers. For videoconferencing, the system needs a Webcam with an appropriate video adapter and software.

Distance-Learning Technologies

A variety of methods and technologies are used in distance learning:

◆ **The Internet**—You can register for a class, view prerecorded or live lectures, complete assignments, interact with teachers and students, and take tests.
◆ **Videoconferences**—Provide a "virtual classroom" where students can gather online for live discussions and lectures.
◆ **E-mail**—Lets students participate in discussions, receive homework assignments, and deliver completed assignments to the instructor.
◆ **Chat rooms**—Let students share messages in real time. Many schools set up private, Web-based chat rooms, where students and teachers can exchange audio or video messages.
◆ **Optical discs**—Are the basis for computer-based training (CBT), a popular tool in distance learning. CBT programs use text, audio, and video recorded on compact discs (CDs) or digital video discs (DVDs).

Tech Focus

1. Describe how people around the world benefit from distance-learning technologies.

2. Use the Internet to find and compare three educational organizations that offer online courses and exams for networking-related certifications.

Section 11.3 Server and Network Performance

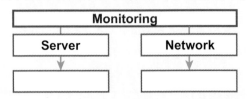
Users do not really think much about the network or its servers as long as everything is running smoothly. But as soon as something goes wrong, the network technicians are expected to find the problem and fix it, fast. To pinpoint problems, it is important to know how to monitor the server's performance and the network's performance. System tools are available to help you do this.

SERVER PERFORMANCE

When the network is first set up, it is very important to create a baseline. A **baseline** measures the server's performance in a number of key areas. This baseline can be used to compare performance over time. For example, when the server baseline was established, its average processor usage hovered around 20 percent. Several months later, users complain that the server seems slow. After monitoring the server, you notice that the processor usage is at 75 percent. Without the baseline, you would not know if 75 percent was normal or not. After this is determined, you can begin to track down the source of the increase.

The Windows 2000 and XP OSs feature a tool called Performance Monitor. This tool is capable of monitoring many vital statistics, some of which are explained in the following sections. There are dozens of processes, or counters, that can be monitored. Among these are processor activity, TCP, IP, and UDP traffic, and NIC statistics. These processes are categorized into "objects." For example, the Processor object contains a number of activities related directly to the CPU that can be monitored and measured. An explanation of some of the Processor-related counters follows.

Processor Time

The processor time is a measure of how much time the processor spends actively doing work. Believe it or not, most of the time, your computer's processor has little to do. For example, if you are working in a word processing document, your processor is probably using less than five percent of

networking.glencoe.com

its potential. If your processor is performing at 100 percent all the time, your system will most likely not be very responsive (see Figure 11.7).

Interrupt Time

Interrupt time is the amount of time the processor spends receiving and processing interrupts. Interrupts are requests from various devices, including the keyboard, mouse, NIC, and other peripheral devices. When a device sends an interrupt request to the processor, the processor stops working on whatever it was doing, and processes the request. A high level of interrupt time could indicate a problem with one of the devices attached to the computer.

Privileged Time

When the processor is working, it divides its time between processing applications and processing OS components and hardware drivers. Privileged time is time spent processing the OS and hardware drivers. A high percentage of privileged time could be due to a failing hardware device generating a large number of interrupts.

User Time

User time is time the processor spends processing applications. For example, a spreadsheet application calculates formula results during user time. Most of the time, applications should not require full use of the processor, or the system will be very unresponsive. However, some calculation-intensive applications require a great deal of processor power for a long period of time. For example, rendering is a process used in computer-generated animation. Each frame of a movie, such as *Finding Nemo,* requires a great deal of processing time. In this case, using 100 percent of the processor's time is not only normal, it is desirable. The more processing time is dedicated to the process, the faster the rendering process gets finished.

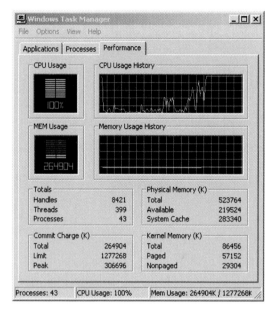

● **Figure 11.7**
Processor usage is an important indicator of system performance. Why is it important to establish a baseline of server performance?

ACTIVITY 11E Configuring Performance Monitor

YOU TRY IT

Performance Monitor is a utility you can use on Windows 2000 and XP systems. This tool can monitor a variety of system processes and even create log files of the results. The log file can be saved to establish a baseline of system performance.

❶ Open **Control Panel.**

❷ If you are using Windows XP, click **Performance and Maintenance.** Otherwise, go to step 3.

❸ Double-click **Administrative Tools.**

❹ Double-click **Performance.**

❺ Select **System Monitor** in the left pane.

READ ME!

Tech Tip The processor is not the only thing Performance Monitor can track. Click the Performance Object list for a complete list of objects you can monitor.

6 Right-click in the right pane and choose **Add Counters.** At the top of the window, you can specify whether you want to monitor the local computer or monitor another computer on the network (see Figure 11.8). You specify another computer by its Windows name.

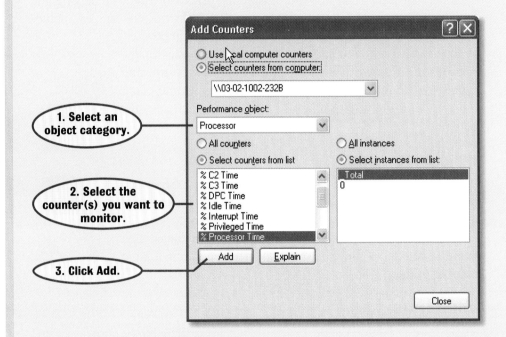

1. Select an object category.

2. Select the counter(s) you want to monitor.

3. Click Add.

7 You can choose different performance objects to monitor using the list provided. Here, we concentrate on the Processor object's counters, but there are many others you can choose, depending on which aspect of the server's performance you want to monitor. Hold the Ctrl key and click each of the following items in the left-hand list:

◆ **% Interrupt Time**

◆ **% Privileged Time**

◆ **% Processor Time**

◆ **% User Time**

8 You can click the **Explain** button to view an explanation of each counter. Click **Add,** and then click **Close.** Figure 11.9 shows the added counters to the System Monitor.

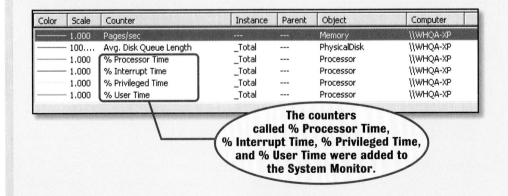

The counters called % Processor Time, % Interrupt Time, % Privileged Time, and % User Time were added to the System Monitor.

9 You can click any of the counters below the graph to view the associated data. You can also use the Highlight feature to highlight the selected counter. Click the **Highlight** button, and then click the **% Processor Time** in the Counter list (see Figure 11.10).

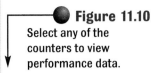

● **Figure 11.10**
Select any of the counters to view performance data.

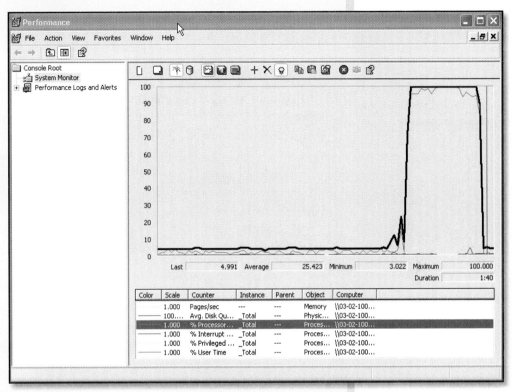

10 After a few minutes, you can save the monitor results as an interactive HTML page. You can view this page in your Web browser. Click any of the counters to view the results. After a few minutes of monitoring, right-click the graph area and choose **Save As.**

11 Select a folder and choose a name for the file.

12 Exit the application.

Using Performance Monitor is a good way to start troubleshooting problems with a server. However, it is very important that you establish a baseline so that you have a basis for comparison in the future. You should periodically monitor important systems, such as servers, so that you can be aware of any increasing trends in server usage.

NETWORK PERFORMANCE

Network monitors are software tools. They are similar to performance monitors because they can track all network traffic. They can also be used to track a selected part of network traffic. Network monitors examine data packets and gather information about packet types, errors, and packet traffic that is directed both to and from each computer.

Network monitors are very useful for establishing part of the network baseline. After the baseline has been established, you can troubleshoot traffic problems and monitor network usage to determine when it is time to upgrade. As an example, after installing a new network, you determine that network traffic is utilized at 40 percent of its intended capacity. When you check traffic one year later, you notice that it is now being utilized at 80 percent capacity. If you had been monitoring it all along, you would have been able to predict the rate of increased traffic and predict when to upgrade before failure occurs.

Protocol Analyzers

Lab 11.2 Upgrading a Network Practice additional hands-on networking skills on page 449.

Protocol analyzers perform real-time network traffic analysis using packet capture, decoding, and transmission data. Network administrators who work with large networks rely heavily on protocol analyzers. These are the tools used most often to monitor network interactivity.

Protocol analyzers look inside the packet to identify a problem. They can also generate statistics based on network traffic to help create a picture of the network, including:

- Cabling
- Software
- File servers
- Workstations
- Network interface cards

The protocol analyzer can provide insights and detect network problems, including the following:

- Faulty network components
- Configuration or connection errors
- LAN bottlenecks
- Traffic fluctuations
- Protocol problems
- Applications that might conflict
- Unusual server traffic

Protocol analyzers can identify a wide range of network behavior. They can be used to:

- Identify the most active computers.
- Identify computers that are sending error-filled packets. If one computer's heavy traffic is slowing down the network, the computer should be moved to another network segment. If a computer is generating bad packets, it should be removed and repaired.
- View and filter certain types of packets. This is helpful for routing traffic.
- Determine what type of traffic is passing across a given network segment.
- Track network performance to identify trends. Recognizing trends in performance can help an administrator better plan and configure the network.
- Check components, connections, and cabling by generating test packets and tracking the results.
- Identify problem conditions by setting parameters to generate alerts.

Microsoft Network Monitor

Windows 2000 Server includes a utility called Network Monitor that allows a network administrator to analyze network traffic. This utility can be used to analyze a number of different network statistics.

Using Network Monitor, the network administrator can analyze individual frames. This powerful tool can actually isolate each portion of a TCP/IP data frame, including the IP header, data portion, and so forth. In the next You Try It activity, you learn how to use this powerful tool.

ACTIVITY 11F Analyzing the Network Using Network Monitor

YOU TRY IT

To complete this activity, you must have access to Windows 2000 Server. If you do not have access, you can still learn how to use the monitor utility by reading the following information.

1 Log on to a Windows 2000 Server machine.

2 Open **Control Panel.**

3 Double-click **Administrative Tools.**

4 Double-click **Network Monitor.**

5 Press **F10** to start capturing network statistics (see Figure 11.11).

● **Figure 11.11**
Tools such as Network Monitor can provide lots of information about network traffic.

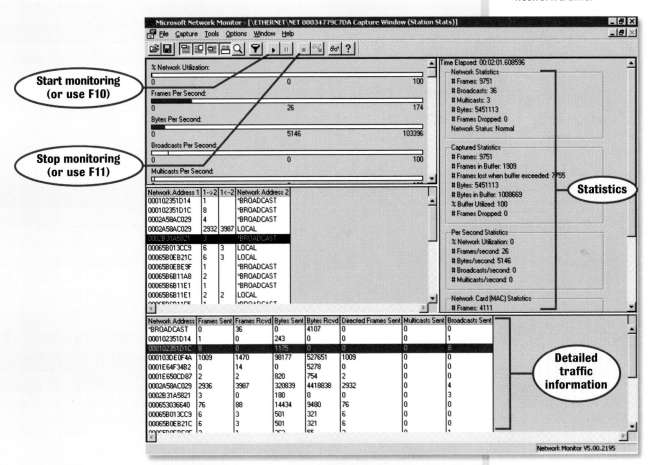

Figure 11.12
The detailed report shows information about all the data being transmitted around the network.

6 After monitoring for a few minutes, press **F11** to stop capturing.

7 Press **F12** to view a detailed report of the traffic captured while you were monitoring the network (see Figure 11.12).

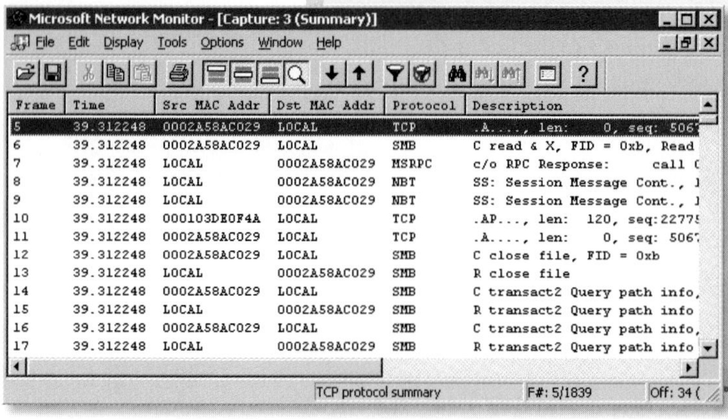

8 Close Network Monitor and do not save the captured data.

9 Log off the server if you are finished using it.

The information generated by Network Monitor can help you analyze and resolve a large number of network problems. Other NOSs feature similar tools to help you with this important task.

This information is often critical when trying to isolate potential intrusions. For example, certain types of hacker attacks use one of the TCP/IP protocols, called **Internet Control Message Protocol (ICMP)**. Ordinarily, ICMP is used to help hosts control network traffic and respond to various error conditions. However, it can also be responsible for flooding a network with ICMP messages, creating a **Denial of Service (DoS)** attack. This type of attack "paralyzes" a system because it has so many messages to which it is trying to respond. Information generated by Network Monitor can help an administrator find the exploited machine and close the security hole.

Section 11.3 Assessment

Concept Check

1. **Define** baseline, network monitors, protocol analyzer, Internet Control Message Protocol (ICMP), and Denial of Service (DoS).

2. **Name** the protocol that is often used in Denial of Service attacks.

3. **Explain** what a high level of interrupt time might indicate.

Critical Thinking

4. **Cause and Effect** A new database application is installed on a server. Server response is now very slow. How can you identify whether this application is the source of the problem?

5. **Propose** After using a protocol analyzer, you notice that several computers generate 80 percent of the network's traffic. What can you propose to reduce the network congestion?

Applying Skills

Monitor TCP/IP Traffic Using the Performance Monitor introduced in the You Try It Activity 11B, monitor the TCP/IP traffic sent and received by your computer. (*Hint:* Select the TCP and IP objects to select appropriate counters.) Leave the monitor active while you copy a large file to the network, and search the Internet for information about RAID technology.

SECTION 11.1 Network Design

Key Terms

budget, 313
legacy application, 316
patch cable, 318

Main Ideas

- Evaluating customer requirements is an important part of designing a network.
- Choose the appropriate network architecture with future growth in mind.
- Perform a detailed survey of all hardware (including telecommunications hardware) and software.
- Use a map to help you locate equipment and plan the installation of network hardware and media.
- Select network media that meets client requirements, working environment conditions, and future needs of the network.

SECTION 11.2 Selecting Hardware

Key Terms

array, 321
striping, 321
mirroring, 322
parity, 322
pilot deployments, 323

Main Ideas

- Servers use different levels of RAID technology to provide various levels of fault tolerance.
- Always plan a network so that it can be changed easily as the demands increase.
- Avoid hardware incompatibility issues by checking manufacturer recommendations and performing a careful survey.

SECTION 11.3 Server and Network Performance

Key Terms

baseline, 326
network monitors, 329
protocol analyzer, 330
Internet Control Message Protocol (ICMP), 332
Denial of Service (DoS), 332

Main Ideas

- After a server is installed, you should use performance monitoring tools.
- It is important to establish a performance baseline.
- Network and protocol analyzers can be used to pinpoint and solve network problems.

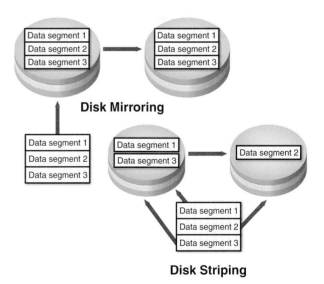

Disk Mirroring

Disk Striping

Reviewing Key Terms

1. What is the problem with legacy applications?
2. Sketch a diagram to show how patch cable is used in connecting computers and peripherals.
3. What does RAID stand for?
4. Which RAID levels use striping and which level uses mirroring?
5. What does ICMP stand for and what is its purpose?

Understanding Main Ideas

6. Identify the steps involved in network planning and design. Discuss the issues of each step.
7. Support the statement "It is important to plan when you design a network."
8. List the most common levels of RAID technology discussed in your textbook, the techniques that each deploys, and the degrees of fault tolerance that each provides.
9. Describe why is it important to establish a performance baseline when a server or a network is set up.
10. Explain how pilot deployment lessens the difficulty in upgrading or changing a network.
11. Identify the major pitfall to watch for when you upgrade a networking system.
12. List factors for choosing network media.
13. Explain the function of a network monitor.
14. Describe how parity information can be used.
15. Identify the best use of a protocol analyzer.
16. Explain the functionality of parity for RAID 3 level.

Critical Thinking

17. **Classify Strategies** Network planning and design involves two major activities: information collection and decision-making. Classify the five steps of network planning and design into these two categories above. If a step fits into both the categories, place it on both lists.
18. **Analyze Media** Network media selections are made based on certain conditions. How do these conditions guide a selection?
19. **Understand Relationships** What factors affect the choice of network topology and how do these factors guide a selection?
20. **Evaluate Information** Each of the four RAID technologies discussed in your textbook has a specific goal and deploys a specific technique. Evaluate how each technique fulfills the specified goal for that particular RAID technology.
21. **Synthesize Information** What additional items do you need to upgrade a peer-to-peer network to a client/server network? Categorize your items in terms of hardware, software, telecommunication, networking, and personnel.
22. **Apply Knowledge** You are the network administrator of a company. Your company has just finished upgrading its peer-to-peer network to a client/server network. What kind of tools would you need to prepare annual reports about the current network performance and its usage growth trend?

networking.glencoe.com

Study with PowerPoint
To review the main points in this chapter, select e-Review > PowerPoint Outlines > Chapter 11.

Online Self Check
Test your knowledge of the material in this chapter by selecting e-Review > Self Checks > Chapter 11.

 networking.glencoe.com

Making Connections

Math – Find the Bottleneck Your company's business has been successful in recent years since your company initiated an online order service. Recently, you have received complaints from your customers that your Web site is very slow in responding to their requests.

Your baseline for the server is 20%. This was the recorded average processor usage. The baseline of your network is 30% average link utilization. Now your recent monitoring statistics report 75% for both processor usage and link utilization.

If the budget only allows you to upgrade either the Web server or the network, but not both, which one would you choose in order to decrease the performance deterioration? Where is the bottleneck: in the server or in the network?

STANDARDS AT WORK

Students use technology resources for solving problems, and making informed decisions. (NETS-S 6)

Test Network Bandwidth
Use a bandwidth speed test to determine the speed of different networks and connections.

◆ Use a Web browser to locate a bandwidth speed test, such as bandwidth.com.
◆ Test the speed of your school's connection before school, during class, and after school.
◆ If possible, do the same thing from home and from a friend's or neighbor's computer.
◆ Answer the following questions:
  ■ Based on your results, what conclusions can be made?
  ■ What are the limitations of this experiment?
◆ Write a two-page essay explaining your results. Make sure to include possible reasons for any variations in your results.

TEAMWORK SKILLS

Debate a Position
Which of the following two printing solutions would you choose if you were given only a limited initial investment budget for a small company with a dozen computers?

1. Buy several cheaper printers so that each small cluster of computers has one printer
2. Buy one expensive printer for all the computers to share

The first choice implies a peer-to-peer network while the second one implies a client/server network.

Following your teacher's instructions, form small teams.

◆ Choose a position. Be sure to consider as many issues as possible, such as printing speed, space occupancy, convenience, cost of cartridges, and cost of maintenance.
◆ Use a word-processing application to draft a brief justification of your position.
◆ Share your team's position with the rest of the class.
◆ Which position was the most popular? Why?

CHALLENGE YOURSELF

Economics and Technology Connections
Conduct a survey of railroad history in the United States and compare it to network planning and design.

◆ Describe how economics, such as the stock market and the employment rate, and railroad development affected each other.
◆ Identify how some newer transportation technologies, such as commercial airlines and automobiles, caused a decline in railroad use.
◆ Write an essay that draws lessons from railroad history to understand the issues of network planning and design.

How could you utilize the new technology and stay in the economic mainstream?

YOU TRY IT

Networking Lab

1. Installing RAID 1 Level

RAID 1 level is the most common technique for providing fault tolerance by mirroring. Usually, one additional drive is installed on a computer to duplicate data on the primary drive. If the primary drive fails, this extra drive kicks in to keep the computer running and to back up the valuable data.

Ⓐ Shut down the computer, ground yourself, and unplug the computer and any connected devices.

Ⓑ Open the computer case and insert the new disk drive on an available bus slot.

Ⓒ Close the computer case, attach devices, and plug in the computer.

Ⓓ Open the **Control Panel** and select **Add/Remove Hardware.**

Ⓔ On the Welcome to the Add/Remove Hardware wizard page, click **Next.**

Ⓕ On the Choose a Hardware Task page, click **Add/Troubleshoot a device,** and then click **Next.** You may have to wait briefly while the wizard searches for the new hardware.

Ⓖ In Devices, click **Add a New device,** and then click **Next.**

Ⓗ On the Find New Hardware page, click **No, I want to select the hardware from a list,** and then click **Next.**

Ⓘ In Hardware types, click **Hard disk devices,** and then click **Next.**

Ⓙ In Manufacturers, click the manufacturer.

Ⓚ Click **Next,** and then follow any additional instructions to install the drive.

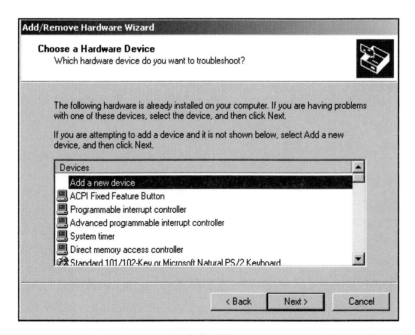

Networking Projects

1. Network a Home

Wireless home networking is growing. It avoids the problem of wiring in the house and offers convenience. Consider a scenario in which a home has three desktop computers in separate rooms sharing a printer and a scanner. They use a cable modem for the Internet access. It also has a laptop that can be on and off the network. IEEE 802.11 is the standard for wireless LAN.

A Find out what devices and connection media are needed to set up a wireless LAN for this scenario.

B Conduct a survey of wireless LAN products. In addition to compatible devices and connection media, address other issues, such as spanning distance limitation and unauthorized access.

2. Document the Network

As a network engineer, it is your responsibility to maintain operational documentation for aspects of the network. There are many tools for network management available on the Web. These tools run on a variety of platforms. A standardized way to categorize network management tools is shown here. It is accessible in text form at the IETF Web site. This location presents a Network Management Tool Catalog. The diagram shown here is an example of the documentation you want other IT professionals in your corporation to keep.

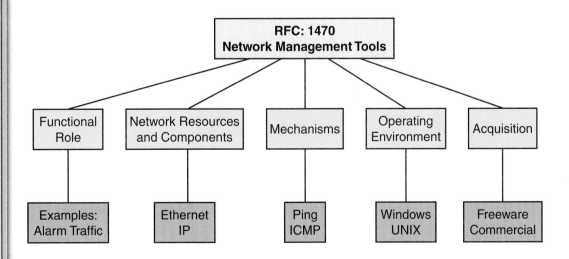

Choose two of the categories of management tools in the diagram and write a paragraph that summarizes each tool's performance.

CHAPTER 12

Installing and Upgrading Networks

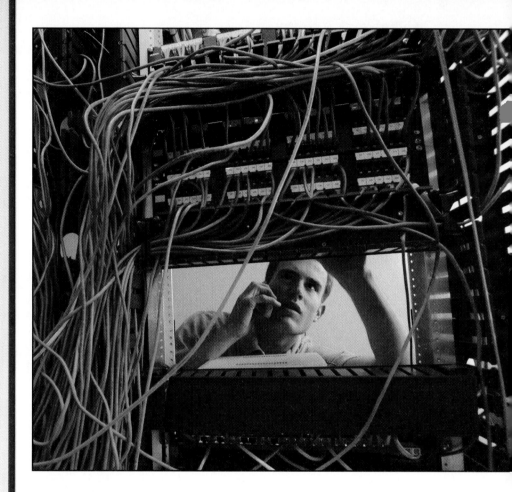

WHY IT MATTERS......................................

When the economy is good and businesses are profitable, companies are more willing to spend money upgrading computers and software. But when the economy takes a downturn, companies may hold off on new technology purchases or make only essential upgrades. Learning to make the most out of your technology dollar is important both for corporate budgets of millions of dollars and for small personal budgets.

Quick Write Activity

Do you have a job or an allowance? Do you manage your money? Write about a time when you wanted something you could not afford. What did you do to (a) earn or save money to buy it, or (b) live without it?

WHAT YOU WILL DO . . . .

READ TO SUCCEED

Take Good Notes

By now, you should understand that the chapters in this book are organized so that main headings describe the main ideas and subheadings introduce supporting details. You can organize your notes by this method. Think of main ideas as Level 1 ideas. Supporting details can be Level 2, 3, or 4. Every time you read a main idea, write down a brief Level 1 note. Under that, write down the Level 2 support details. Level 2 may also have its own supporting information. Those are Level 3 details. Note those details beneath Level 2. Continue this method as you read through the chapter.

Section 12.1 Installing Operating Systems

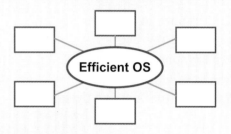
Many of today's major operating systems (OSs), including Microsoft Windows, Mac OS X, and Linux, feature easy-to-follow installation routines. Despite this, setting up a computer is still a fairly major task. It is a very good idea to familiarize yourself with the things you can do to prepare for the installation of an operating system.

CONFIGURATION OF AN OS

Many computers purchased today come with an OS preinstalled. This is nice for many consumers, who simply want to plug their new computer in, turn it on, and start using it. There are many cases, however, when you need or want to install and configure an OS from scratch. For example, you might want to:

- Upgrade an older OS to a new version.
- Reinstall an OS when problems arise.
- Run several different OSs, such as Windows XP and Linux, on the same computer.
- Build a computer from the ground up.
- Use a custom standardized configuration to make technology support easier.

In large organizations, a standardized disk image may be used for all computers. A **disk image** is a complete copy of a configured OS, with all applications and options already set up. Using a disk image makes troubleshooting and support easier for the Information Technology (IT) staff because they know exactly what hardware and software they are dealing with. Products such as Symantec Ghost make the process of creating a disk image very simple (see Figure 12.1 on page 341). A completed image can be loaded onto multiple computers simultaneously. Within minutes, dozens of computers can be prepared with a custom OS configuration.

READ ME!

Tech Tip Although some OSs can be upgraded to a newer version, most IT personnel prefer reformatting the hard drive and installing the OS "clean." This gets rid of unneeded (and often incompatible) drivers from the previous OS and applications that are no longer needed. Of course, you must back up all data before formatting the hard drive. Any applications must be reinstalled.

---

networking.glencoe.com

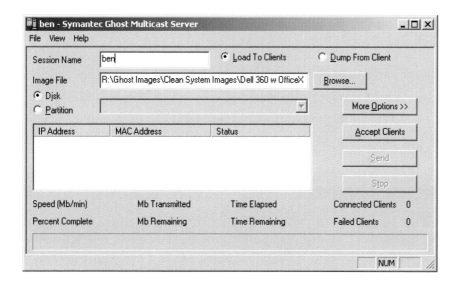

Figure 12.1
Disk images are used by IT personnel to install and configure an OS on many machines at the same time. What advantages are there to using the same configuration throughout an organization?

Most OS installations are now highly automated. In most cases, you put the CD in a CD-ROM drive, boot the computer, and follow a series of prompts to install the OS. Typical installations take 20 minutes to about an hour.

There are several points you should be aware of when installing an OS:

- ◆ Verify that the hardware meets the minimum requirements of the OS. Some hardware may have to be upgraded for use with the new OS.
- ◆ Have all software installation disks and license numbers available. Double-check to find out if your software will operate on the new OS.
- ◆ To participate in a network, you need to know the domain name, IP address (unless DHCP is used), and a unique computer name (Windows networks).
- ◆ If the computer connects to the Internet using dial-up modem, DSL, ISDN, or cable, write down all required configuration information. This can save time on the phone with the ISP tech support team.
- ◆ If you are installing a new OS on an old computer, *back up your data.*

INSTALLATION OF A SERVER OS

The actual installation of a server OS is largely the same as installing a normal OS on a personal computer or workstation. In fact, many of the differences between a server OS and a normal OS are not that noticeable. However, because of the important role the server plays, you often have to do a lot of planning before you put a new server into service on a network. Some of the planning steps you should take include the following:

- ◆ Organize the team members if the deployment is a large-scale project. Be certain each member of the team knows exactly what is required.
- ◆ Create an accurate inventory of your network's hardware and software.
- ◆ Clearly define the goals and reasons for the deployment. Ask questions such as, "Why are we choosing this particular server OS? What do we hope to gain by using this OS?"
- ◆ Create diagrams or flowcharts showing how your existing network directory structure will fit within the context of the new network directory structure. In general, this means categorizing users into groups and

TECH TRIVIA

OS Minimum Requirements Minimum requirements are often just that—minimum. For example, Windows XP lists 64 MB of RAM as a minimum. Although 128 MB (or more) is recommended, many users find that Windows XP does not perform well until the system has 256 MB of RAM.

identifying how folders and files will be organized on the file server to restrict access.

◆ Set up a pilot installation. This often means setting up a functional network in a lab, disconnected from the main network. After the testing and troubleshooting period, the server(s) are placed into the main network.

Server OSs do not appear to be drastically different from a workstation OS. It is the services, such as file and print sharing services that run quietly in the background, that make the biggest difference (see Figure 12.2).

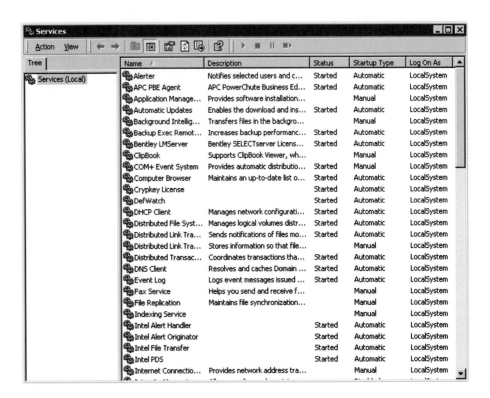

Figure 12.2
Specialized services are provided by servers. What information should you know before setting up a server OS?

Before installing a server OS, you should know the following:

◆ How (or if) you will **partition** the server hard drive(s). Partitioning divides the usable space on a hard drive into two or more virtual disks. They are called **virtual disks** because the computer recognizes them as individual disks, even though all the storage space is contained on one physical drive. Drives may be partitioned so that one portion contains the OS and installed applications, while other partitions hold the data.

◆ The file system that will be used. For Windows 2000 Server and Windows Server 2003, the best choice is NTFS, which offers superior security to FAT32.

◆ The domain name your server will be connected to and whether the server will act as a domain controller. A **domain controller** stores the logon and security information for a network.

◆ The server's computer name and administrator account's password.

During installation of the server OS, you may need to select and configure networking components. In Windows 2000 Server and Windows Server 2003, the TCP/IP protocol is automatically installed as part of the "Typical" install. However, if your network requires another protocol, such as AppleTalk or IPX/SPX, you need to select those options and configure them.

After the server OS is installed, you need to install and configure the services running on the server. For example, many organizations use networked application licenses. This allows licenses to be checked out by a user on an as-needed basis. For many companies this is more cost-effective than purchasing individual licenses for users who may only use the software occasionally. Configuration of services in the Windows OSs is handled from an application called the Services console. You will learn to use this application in the following You Try It activity.

ACTIVITY 12A Accessing and Configuring Services

Client services run on desktop machines, whereas server services run on servers. In either case, you can access the Services console to configure available services. **Caution:** You should not start, stop, or change service configurations unless you know exactly what you are doing. By shutting off a key service, you could disable an important component of the OS. The following steps apply to Windows 2000 or Windows XP.

● **Figure 12.3**
The Services console in the Windows OS is used to manage services.

❶ Open **Control Panel.**

❷ Double-click **Administrative Tools.**

❸ Double-click **Services** (see Figure 12.3).

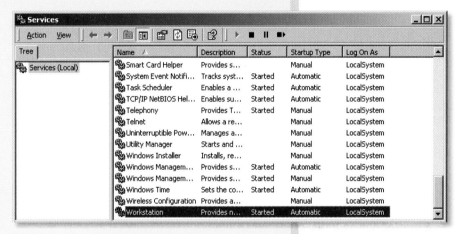

❹ Scroll through the list and double-click the **Workstation** service. On the General tab, you will find information about the service. For example, you can find a description of the service, as well as the path to the executable file. You can also start, stop or pause a service, and change the startup option.

● **Figure 12.4**
Some services depend on other services.

❺ Click the **Dependencies** tab. Some services depend on, or are depended upon by, other services. Figure 12.4 shows that several services depend on the "Workstation" service in order to function. If this service were stopped or disabled, the computer would not be able to logon to the network, or maintain a list of other computers on the network.

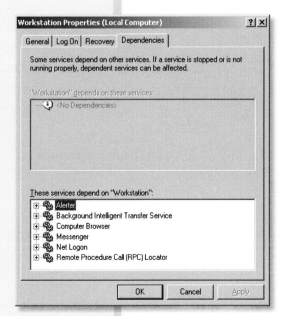

❻ Click **Cancel** in the Workstation Properties window, and then close the Services console.

It is very important that you know precisely what you are doing whenever you start or stop services on your computer. Stopping a critical service could prevent important network functions, such as printing, from working.

You may need to access services if a problem arises on the server. For example, Print Services may need to be stopped and restarted if the printers maintained by a certain print server suddenly stop printing. Another example of an important service in the Windows server environment is **Internet Information Services (IIS).** IIS provides Web server services, such as file transfer (FTP), e-mail (SMTP), and Active Server Pages (ASPs) for interactive Web applications.

CONFIGURATION AND INTERNETWORKING BETWEEN OSs

In some network environments, many different OSs are in use. For example, a graphics design company may use Macs for their graphics application, whereas the administration and accounting departments use PCs running on Windows. Meanwhile, the company's Web server might run on Linux. How can computers running on these various OSs communicate with each other?

Protocols can be installed on each computer to allow computers to speak the same language. You might, for instance, install the AppleTalk protocol to allow Windows computers to communicate with the Mac computers.

In a Novell NetWare environment using the IPX/SPX protocol, two services may be used. **Client Services for NetWare (CSNW)** allows Microsoft clients to connect to file and print resources on NetWare services. **Gateway Services for NetWare (GSNW)** provides a gateway for Microsoft clients and services to access resources on NetWare services (see Figure 12.5).

The primary reason to use GSNW is to avoid having to install CSNW on all the client computers. In such a scenario, the client computers connect to the NetWare resources through the gateway server. Of course, if the gateway server goes down, none of the client computers can access the necessary resources. If each of the client computers have the client services installed, then they can make their own connections.

Figure 12.5
Connecting OSs requires appropriate client or gateway software. What disadvantage could there be to using GSNW instead of installing the client on all client computers that need to access NetWare resources?

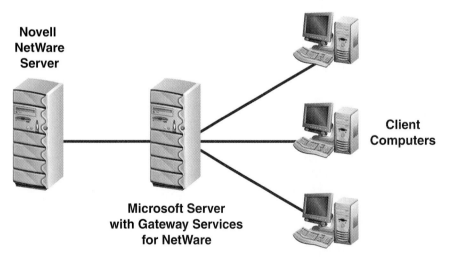

Novell
NetWare
Server

Microsoft Server
with Gateway Services
for NetWare

Client
Computers

EFFICIENT USE OF AN OS

There are many ways to use your OS efficiently. Naturally, you should learn its capabilities. Most OSs have dozens, if not hundreds, of utilities built into them. If you learn to use an OS skill one way, you should not be afraid to try something else when a new application comes along. Using a skill in only one way is a pretty limiting strategy, especially when computers are concerned. Applications created 10 years ago are not as user-friendly, nor as capable, as many of today's applications. New, more efficient techniques are constantly being added. Challenge yourself to find out all you can about the operating system and applications you use on a regular basis.

Here are tips to make sure you make the most efficient use of your OS:

- Back up your data frequently. If your data are backed up, you can fix the computer, restore your data, and get back to work.
- Keep your data saved separately from your application and OS files. You can store your data in a special folder, or on a separate hard drive. This will help keep data organized.
- Install antivirus software and keep it up-to-date.
- Keep your operating system and drivers up-to-date.
- If you install shareware programs that you do not use, uninstall them. **Shareware** are programs you try before you buy them.
- Delete temporary and other unnecessary files.
- Defragment the hard drive regularly. A fragmented hard drive occurs when the computer tries to store files wherever there is space on the hard drive. **Defragmenting** the hard drive optimizes the disk by bringing together scattered files in like clusters.
- Empty your Web browser cache from time to time.
- Create keyboard shortcuts that can make repetitive tasks easier.

Activity 12.1 Find Shareware
Shareware is an important marketing tool for many software companies. Visit **networking.glencoe.com** to find sources for shareware.

Section 12.1 Assessment

Concept Check

1. **Define** disk image, partition, virtual disk, domain controller, Internet Information Services (IIS), Client Services for NetWare (CSNW), Gateway Services for NetWare (GSNW), shareware, and defragment.

2. **Explain** why partitioning a disk can be useful.

3. **Describe** the role of a domain controller in networking.

Critical Thinking

4. **Analyze** Emphasize in a slide presentation at least three issues you may need to address before installing an operating system.

5. **Cause and Effect** A user reports that, after changing some service settings, he can no longer log on. What is the likely cause of this problem?

6. **Contrast** Prepare a brief report that outlines the difference(s) between installing a client operating system versus a server operating system.

Applying Skills

Prepare to Use Your OS Efficiently Using the list provided in this chapter, prepare a schedule for performing maintenance on your computer. Identify which tasks you think should be performed daily, weekly, or monthly.

Ethics & Technology

ARE HACKERS STALKING YOUR COMPUTER?

If your computer is connected to the Internet, either directly or through a LAN, you need to take precautions against hacker attacks.

Hackers do not think of the harm they do to individuals when they invade corporate networks.

What Is a Hacker?

A hacker is usually defined as a knowledgeable computer user, often with a programming background, who intentionally tries to find the weaknesses in computers or networks. Some hackers are true criminals, relentlessly trying to access data they can sell or use to enrich themselves, like credit card information and account numbers.

Other hackers are bent on destruction or disruption. Some hackers break through network security measures to corrupt or delete files.

Most hackers, however, get a thrill from being on the outside, taking risks, and constantly testing the boundaries of technology. They find hacking fun, despite the fact that it is almost always unethical and illegal.

Protecting Yourself

Hackers have learned how to take control of multiple computers (often home PCs with permanent Internet connections). They use the hijacked computers to launch Denial of Service attacks against network and Web servers. In these attacks, a server is flooded with requests for data or services. The huge volume of requests can slow the server or cause it to stop responding altogether.

With the popularity of always-on Internet connections (via cable modems, DSL service, and LANs), individual users are just as vulnerable to hacking as business systems. Hackers can easily locate vulnerable home PCs by using software that searches for Internet-connected computers with open ports and other weaknesses.

To thwart hackers, you should always:

- Password-protect your computer using your operating system's protection features.
- Turn off file and printer sharing unless you absolutely need to use them.
- Install either a software or hardware firewall, and be certain it is always operating.
- Get updates or patches for your operating system or applications.

Tech Focus

1. Create a presentation about an actual corporate network or e-commerce site that was victimized by a hacker. Assess the security that was used and the results of the attack.

2. Conduct research to learn more about the precautions organizations or individuals can take to protect their networks from hackers. Share your findings with the class.

Guide to Reading

Main Ideas

Many techniques exist to connect hardware to a computer. The operating system communicates with hardware using device drivers. Most organizations have policies regarding installation of software. Use the ping utility to help test network connectivity.

Key Terms

expansion slot
Advanced Technology
  Attachment (ATA)
Serial ATA (S-ATA)
license server
ping (Packet Internet
  Groper)

Reading Strategy

Identify three details or examples of each heading within this section. Create a chart similar to the one below (also available online).

Setting up hardware and drivers	Configuring workstations and software	Testing network connectivity
1.	1.	1.
2.	2.	2.
3.	3.	3.

Hardware added to a system enhances its capabilities. For example, sound cards allow a computer to output sound effects from your favorite game and play your favorite music on CD. However, without proper drivers your hardware would be useless because the operating system would not know what to do with it.

HARDWARE SETUP AND DEVICE DRIVER INSTALLATIONS

From time to time, you may find it necessary to install new hardware. As you have already learned, there are different categories of hardware. For convenience, we have grouped these categories as add-in cards, external devices, and storage devices. Keep in mind that these categories cross functionality boundaries, but it is important for you to know the physical aspects of how each device attaches to the computer system.

Add-In Cards

You should remember the following when installing add-in cards, such as NICs, sound cards, or hard drive controller cards.

◆ Always turn off the computer and unplug it before you start.
◆ Ground yourself properly to avoid damaging sensitive components with static electricity buildup. You can use a grounding strap (available at many electronics or computer stores) or touch the edge of the metal case *before* touching any of the electronic components.
◆ Always handle add-in cards by the edges. Avoid touching the surface or other parts, including the plug-in edge, of the card. Touching the surface of delicate electronics can leave behind an oily residue that may contribute to heat buildup and possible malfunction of the device.

◆ Verify which type of bus interface your computer uses. Most computers use the PCI or PCI-X bus for expansion slots and an Accelerated Graphics Port (AGP) for the video card (see Figure 12.6).
◆ Verify that there are empty **expansion slots** if you are installing a new device. Expansion slots are thin, rectangular slots on the motherboard that accept add-in cards to increase the computer's capabilities.
◆ Check to ensure the new device is the correct type for the expansion slot. A NIC built to run on the EISA bus does not fit into a PCI slot.

Figure 12.6 ●———▶
Always verify that the computer has the proper type of slot available before purchasing an add-in card. What will happen if you try to put the wrong type of card into an expansion slot?

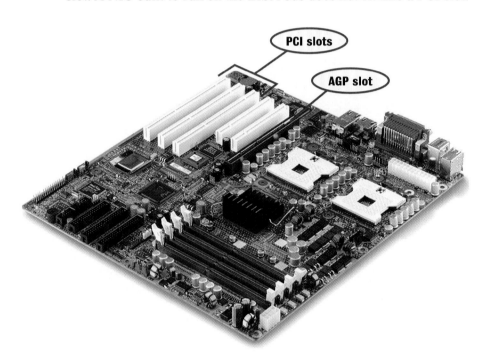

PCI slots

AGP slot

Figure 12.7 ●———
USB devices are automatically detected by the OS. What advantages do USB devices have over add-in cards?

External Devices

External devices, such as printers, scanners, some modems, and flash memory storage devices, are connected to the computer in a variety of ways. As you learned earlier, some older devices use parallel or serial ports. Most devices you are likely to encounter today use either USB or FireWire. Connecting these types of devices is much simpler as they plug into a port located on the front or back of the computer. The computer does not have to be turned off or restarted when USB and FireWire devices are connected or removed from the computer (see Figure 12.7).

USB hubs, like their network counterparts, allow many different USB devices, including other USB hubs, to connect to a single USB port. The OS automatically detects these devices and prompts to install drivers, if necessary.

Storage Devices

Hard drive and other types of storage devices, including CD and DVD burners, require some additional planning. You might need to install a new hard drive to increase the computer's capacity or to replace a failed drive. Or, you might purchase a DVD burner to use for data backups. For these types of devices, you need to be aware of the following interface technologies:

◆ Many hard drives, CD and DVD burners, and other storage devices use the **Advanced Technology Attachment (ATA)** interface to connect to the motherboard. This interface is also known as EIDE. Ultra ATA devices are faster than standard ATA devices but must use a special 80-pin ribbon cable, rather than the standard 40-pin cable (see Figure 12.8).

◆ A new technology known as **Serial ATA (S-ATA)** is replacing the aging ATA interface. S-ATA can transfer data much more quickly than either ATA or Ultra ATA devices, and uses a thinner cable. Serial ATA requires a special connection interface that is either built onto the motherboard or can be added via an add-in controller card.

◆ In servers, the Small Computer System Interface (SCSI) is the general standard. These drives, although expensive, have traditionally led the performance race by a wide margin. These drives are usually configured in a RAID array, increasing read/write performance, data redundancy, or both. In some systems, SCSI drives can be hot-swapped, meaning that the computer does not have to be turned off in order to safely remove and install a new hard drive.

◆ Verify that your computer's power supply can handle any additional drives. Most important, the power supply must be able to supply enough power to keep all the devices running smoothly. The power supply provides a limited number of connectors that you can use to power devices such as hard drives and CD-ROM devices. If you do not have a free connector end, you can purchase inexpensive "Y" splitters to provide additional connectors.

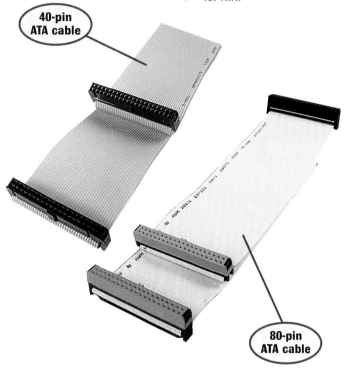

● **Figure 12.8**
A comparison of a standard 40-pin ATA cable and an 80-pin Ultra ATA cable. What is another common name for ATA?

40-pin ATA cable

80-pin ATA cable

Device Driver Setup

Most devices require a driver for the OS to communicate with the device. These drivers are usually supplied with the device on a floppy disk or CD-ROM. In most cases, you can also download drivers from the manufacturer's Web site. Keep in mind that many older devices are not supported by the manufacturer indefinitely, and may not function with the latest OS. Many devices, such as USB flash storage, are plug and play compatible, which means the OS detects the device. If the OS does not have a driver for the device, you are prompted to install the driver supplied by the manufacturer. Although each driver installation program differs, it is usually a simple matter of following instructions to install the driver and configure the device.

WORKSTATION CONFIGURATION AND SOFTWARE LOADING

In networking terminology, a workstation is a computer on the network on which applications are installed. Both desktop and laptop computers can be considered workstations. A user within the organization uses this computer to get work done. A server, by contrast, is generally not used directly by anyone, other than network administrative personnel. The workstations access the server(s) for whatever services they require. Servers often use specialized hardware, such as RAM and hard disk arrays, to increase their reliability.

In many organizations, workstation configurations are standardized to reduce the burden on IT support. A standardized workstation configuration usually consists of:

◆ **Similar hardware components**—This reduces the number of potential conflicts, and makes it much easier to swap components that have failed.

◆ **OS configured similarly from workstation to workstation**—All settings, network protocols, and drivers have the same setup.

◆ **Identical software applications throughout the company**—It is easier for IT support personnel to troubleshoot and respond to requests when the same office productivity suite or utility applications are used throughout the organization.

Software is generally loaded on computers using a CD-ROM. Automated installation routines guide the installer and prompt for any required information. In most cases, the user can select the destination folder where the application files will be stored. Options for the type of installation, such as "Typical," "Custom," or "Minimal," allow the user to specify which portions of the program are installed.

Licensing information is generally input during the installation (see Figure 12.9). Applications that use network licensing may need to be configured to find the appropriate license server. A **license server** acts like a librarian who issues licenses to clients. After the application is closed, the client computer "checks in" the license and it is made available to someone else on the network.

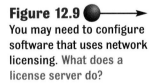
Figure 12.9
You may need to configure software that uses network licensing. What does a license server do?

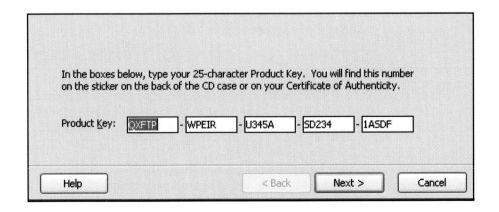

In the boxes below, type your 25-character Product Key. You will find this number on the sticker on the back of the CD case or on your Certificate of Authenticity.

Product Key: QXFTP - WPEIR - U345A - SD234 - 1ASDF

Help   < Back   Next >   Cancel

Most organizations have policies regarding users configuring and loading software onto their systems. In many cases, users are strictly forbidden from doing either. There are many reasons for this:

◆ **Licensing**—Users within an organization who install unlicensed software put the organization at risk.

◆ **Support**—Nonstandard software may not be supported by IT personnel. Contrary to popular belief, IT personnel do *not* know everything about every application ever written.

◆ **Security**—Software brought in from outside sources (downloaded, for example) may contain viruses, or bugs, that can potentially damage the network.

You should *always* check the organization's policy before installing any software on a computer that is not your own.

NETWORK CONNECTIVITY TESTING

After the OS is properly set up and configured, it needs to be tested to ensure it can connect to the appropriate network resources. These resources may include a DHCP server if IP addresses are assigned automatically, an e-mail server, file and print servers, and so on. Of course, the NIC and its drivers must already be installed, and the appropriate media connection must be attached.

A simple test can be performed just by looking at the back of the computer. Most NICs include at least one or two status light-emitting diode (LED) lights. One of the LEDs usually indicates a link status if it senses other network traffic. On many 10/100 Ethernet NICs, a LED may indicate whether the card is connected at 10 Mbps or 100 Mbps.

The next step is to determine whether the computer can detect other computers on the network. There are means to do this, depending on your operating system. One tool that works on many operating systems is the **Packet INternet Groper (ping).** This command-line utility "pings" other computers, similar to the way a submarine uses sonar pulses to detect the presence of other ships. However, ping is used to test a computer's connectivity to another computer.

ACTIVITY 12B Using Ping to Test Network Connectivity   **YOU TRY IT**

There are tools available to test network connectivity. One of the best tools is called ping, which works on many OSs.

❶ Open the command prompt window in Windows OS. (In Mac OS, open the Applications folder, then open the Utilities folder, launch the Network Utility application, and select the PING tab.)

❷ You should determine whether your computer has an IP address assigned to it. Type ipconfig /all at the command prompt. Write down the IP address and Default Gateway address.

❸ At the command prompt, type ping /?. This displays help for the ping command. The basic format for the ping command is **ping *ip address*,** where *ip address* is replaced by the actual IP address you are trying to detect. For example, you might want to test the IP address of your gateway server or the IP address of an Internet site. You can also use the domain name, such as **microsoft.com**, instead of the IP address.

4 Type ping 127.0.0.1. This is your local computer's loopback address. This is a special reserved IP address used for testing. A successful result means that your NIC is capable of sending and receiving packets.

5 Type ping *gateway*, but instead of *gateway* type the IP address of your default gateway (see Figure 12.10).

Figure 12.10
ping is a helpful tool to test network connectivity.

```
C:\WINNT\system32\cmd.exe                                    _ □ ×
C:\>ping 10.3.0.1

Pinging 10.3.0.1 with 32 bytes of data:

Reply from 10.3.0.1: bytes=32 time<10ms TTL=255
Reply from 10.3.0.1: bytes=32 time<10ms TTL=255
Reply from 10.3.0.1: bytes=32 time=10ms TTL=255
Reply from 10.3.0.1: bytes=32 time<10ms TTL=255

Ping statistics for 10.3.0.1:
    Packets: Sent = 4, Received = 4, Lost = 0 (0% loss),
Approximate round trip times in milli-seconds:
    Minimum = 0ms, Maximum =  10ms, Average =  2ms
```

If the address cannot be reached, you see a "Request timed out" message. This can indicate a problem with your computer, or possibly that the computer you are trying to connect to is having a problem.

One of the most common problems you will encounter using TCP/IP is using an incorrect IP address and/or subnet mask or supplying an incorrect Gateway IP address. The ping command makes it easier to determine if this is the problem. More troubleshooting tools are covered in Chapter 14.

Section **12.2** Assessment

Concept Check

1. **Define** expansion slot, Advanced Technology Attachment (ATA), Serial ATA (S-ATA), license server, and ping (Packet Internet Groper).

2. **Describe** the difference(s) between a workstation and a server.

3. **Explain** what a loopback address is used for. What is the default loopback IP address?

Critical Thinking

4. **Evaluate** Suppose you need to buy a new hard drive to replace one that failed in a workstation. List the items you should check before you purchase a replacement.

5. **Draw Conclusions** The company you work for has recently fired several people for installing unauthorized software. Why would the company be taking such drastic measures?

Applying Skills

Compare OS Prices
You are shopping for a new operating system. Use available resources to compare the prices of Windows XP Professional, Mac OS X, and a commercial version of Linux.

TELECOMMUNICATIONS AND THE CORPORATE NETWORK

At one time, the term telecommunication was used to describe voice communications over the telephone network—now known as the Public Switched Telephone Network (PSTN) or Plain Old Telephone System (POTS).

Voice and data networks should continue to merge in the coming years until they become seamlessly integrated.

Conversely, the term data communications described the transmission of digital data over a computer network. This included any kind of data, from text to video, transmitted over a LAN, WAN, or the Internet.

Today, the two terms are used interchangeably and the concepts are merging together. As organizations demand more from their data networks and the public demands more from the PSTN, data networks and the telephone system are becoming more alike in some ways.

Meeting Corporate Needs

A decade ago, most companies were happy if their networks could handle e-mail and basic file sharing. Today, many of those businesses want their networks to handle teleconferencing. Some organizations even want to shift their telephone calls from the PSTN to their LANs and the Internet to allow for cheap or even free phone service.

If companies merge their voice and data networks into a single system, they will be able to:

◆ Save on management and maintenance.
◆ Offer new services to employees and customers, such as more sophisticated call forwarding, interactive voice mail, and voice-enabled e-mail.
◆ Take advantage of customized computer-telephone integration (CTI) programs. These programs might allow a customer service representative to access information about callers in real time, via the company's data network.

What Lies Ahead

In the future, new protocols and standards will make it easier to transmit real-time phone calls on data networks. In fact, the next version of the PSTN will be called the *new public network,* and will be a packet-switching data network from end to end, transmitting all types of data in digital form.

Tech Focus

1. What are the advantages and disadvantages of using a LAN or WAN for telephone communications?

2. Research the PSTN to learn about its history, its development, and its future. What impact has it had on business and society?

Section 12.3 System and Network Upgrades

Guide to Reading

Main Ideas

Network components and software should be closely monitored to prepare for necessary upgrades. A network administrator must calculate cost and investment to justify spending money for hardware and software.

Key Terms

Total Cost of Ownership (TCO)
Return On Investment (ROI)

Reading Strategy

Identify four factors to consider when upgrading a network. Create a chart similar to the one below (also available online).

Network Upgrade

Computer hardware and software licenses are not cheap. In fact, network hardware is often very expensive. Upgrading any portion of a network must be planned and budgeted. In many cases, network administrators must justify why an upgrade is necessary and show how the cost will help the company's bottom line. You may need to examine many of the issues that must be considered before hardware and software purchases are made. You also learn about calculating the costs associated with upgrading.

NETWORK EXPANSION

Various factors offer clues that an upgrade might be needed. If your network was configured several years ago, it is possible that the CPU and network are no longer responsive enough. This may be due to increased user demand and the requirements of new software. Documenting performance and listening to end users helps to determine when the time has come to upgrade.

Hardware

Network hardware can include servers, hubs, switches, routers, and other types of devices that connect all the devices on the network together. Trained technicians complete the tasks connecting hardware (see Figure 12.11). How do you know when it is time to upgrade or expand the network?

Servers should have enough RAM, disk space, and processing power to allow end users to use their software applications efficiently without having to wait for the server to retrieve, process, or store their

Figure 12.11
Expanding the network involves installing and configuring new hardware devices. What tools can be used to help determine when network devices need to be upgraded?

networking.glencoe.com

information. Time spent waiting for a server to respond quickly adds up. Monitoring the server periodically against a known baseline is important. If the CPU is busy over 80 percent of the time, the CPU or the amount of memory might need to be upgraded.

Sometimes server components operate well, but end users complain of slow system response. In this case, the network might need to be upgraded to a speedier technology. For example, exchanging hubs for switches can greatly improve the speed at which data can be transmitted across the network.

READ ME!

Tech Tip Always check with the server manufacturer to find out how much and what type of RAM can be added to the server. Servers are much more particular about the type of RAM they can use.

Software

One of the most common upgrades is software. In the past, major software upgrades happened once every few years. Periodic maintenance releases, or patches, were released a few times a year. Today's software release schedule is much more hectic. Major releases of software happen yearly, if not more often. Patches are sometimes released weekly or daily (see Figure 12.12).

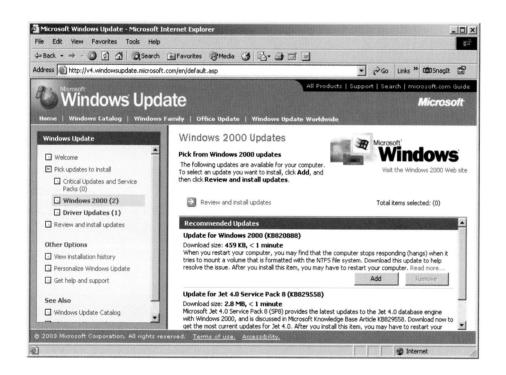

Figure 12.12
Software patches are released as often as necessary by the manufacturer. Why is it important to keep software as up-to-date as possible?

In addition to the cost of the software upgrade, there are other costs the end users often do not realize. For example, there is a cost associated with installing and configuring the software throughout the organization. There are also costs involved with training users to use the new software and supporting problems that inevitably arise with new software.

The current trend among major software companies is to use a maintenance or subscription program, such as those found with virus protection software. A yearly maintenance fee is paid for each license. Any upgrades to the software are automatically sent to the organization. For many organizations, this is a good way to stay current on the latest software. It also makes budgeting easier because the maintenance fee is a fixed cost every year.

CALCULATING THE COST

Upgrades for network hardware and software are often expensive and are frequently necessary. However, IT departments are not just handed a blank check to purchase equipment and software. The costs of most purchases extend beyond the initial purchase price and must be carefully budgeted. Also, IT departments often must justify purchases by proving that the company will realize some significant savings or generate earnings. In other words, they have to show how upgrades will be beneficial to the company.

TCO

The cost of upgrading or installing hardware or software in a network is not simply the total purchase price of the equipment. In fact, there is much more to it. The **Total Cost of Ownership (TCO)** is the calculation of the initial purchase price of the hardware and software involved in the upgrade and the costs associated with installation, management, training, and insurance.

For example, suppose you are considering servers from two different manufacturers with a price difference of several hundred dollars. If the less expensive model is more difficult to install and configure, and tests prove that it is less reliable than the more expensive model, then its TCO is going to cost more in the long run. The TCO includes not only the purchase price, but also the expense of installing and configuring the device. There are also costs associated with repairing it if it fails, not to mention losses incurred due to downtime.

ROI

Many IT departments must justify purchases by calculating the **Return On Investment (ROI).** ROI attempts to calculate how the cost of new equipment or software will result in increased savings or earnings. This is often calculated using a formula such as:

$$\text{(Earnings + Savings)} - \text{(Cost + Finance Charges + Operational Charges)} = \text{ROI}$$

Although calculating the potential earnings or savings may not be much more than an educated guess, there are methods to quantify it. Consider a company evaluating a software upgrade. In a trial, a user learns that a three-minute process now takes only two minutes, thanks to an improved workflow in the new software. Using this command five times a day, 240 times a year means the user saves approximately 20 hours per year. At a $40,000 per year salary, that is a productivity gain of over $400 a year. This and other potential productivity gains can be compared against the cost of upgrading to the new software to find out if it makes good business sense to do so.

Activity 12.2 Investigate Current Computer Costs
Computer prices are always changing as new hardware is developed and put on the market. Find current prices for a personal computer, workstation, and server. Go to networking.glencoe.com and make a list of what hardware is in each system. If possible, check these prices again in several weeks or in a few months.

YOU TRY IT

ACTIVITY 12C Calculating the ROI for an IT Purchase

IT departments must justify expenses, often to managers who do not understand why Technology X is superior to Technology Y. Learning how to figure ROI is an important skill for IT managers, network administrators, and network architects. In this simple scenario, you have been asked to justify adding more RAM to a user's computer in your ski company.

1 Calculate the TCO of the purchase. Purchase price of the RAM is $200, installation will be handled by IT staff whose salary + benefits for the 15 minutes to install the RAM amounts to about $10. There will be little or no maintenance for this item over its three-year lifespan.

2 Calculate the estimated potential time-savings this purchase will create. When working on large files, the user frequently must wait up to 30 seconds for the file to open. It is estimated that the additional memory will help the file to open 20 percent faster. Figure that the user opens 20 such files per day throughout an average work year (approximately 220 days).

3 Calculate how much the user's time costs the company (salary or wage plus benefits divided by the number of workdays divided by the number of work hours per day). Figure the total salary and benefits package for this user at $45,000 per year.

4 Multiply the user's cost per hour times the calculated potential time-savings times the life expectancy for the part.

5 Subtract the TCO from the potential earnings/savings calculated in step 4. A positive value indicates a worthwhile investment, whereas a negative number indicates that this may not be a good investment.

It is often difficult to estimate the potential savings or earnings a new hardware or software can generate. You should test tasks or network performance by quantifiable means to make your argument convincing.

READ ME!

Tech Tip Some organizations adopt an "every-other-release" policy to control the cost and frequency of upgrades. Rather than purchase every major upgrade, they sit out every other one. Of course, there could be compatibility issues when an application changes its document format to support new features.

Network administrators spend a lot of time researching and analyzing network hardware and software before finalizing any purchase decisions. In a cost-conscious business environment, it is important to make the right choice the first time.

Section 12.3 Assessment

Concept Check

1. **Define** Total Cost of Ownership (TCO) and Return On Investment (ROI).

2. **List** some of the reasons a server might need to be upgraded.

3. **Explain** why it is important to monitor the network periodically.

Critical Thinking

4. **Strategize** Write a paragraph that highlights the main strategies companies use to minimize software upgrade costs.

5. **Draw Conclusions** A company upgrades its computers every year to the best hardware available. Is this a wise idea? Explain your answer.

Applying Skills

Justify IT Costs You are the network administrator and must review next year's budget. You have money to replace some aging computers and to upgrade software to a new version. Prepare a statement explaining why these purchases will benefit the company.

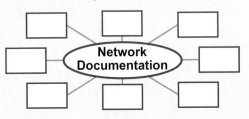

Main Ideas

Documenting a network is an important task for IT personnel. Proper documentation can help restore important system settings in an emergency. Testing network components must be carefully planned and executed to provide meaningful results.

Key Terms

service agreements
logbook
drive assignment
test life cycle

Reading Strategy

Identify eight important elements of documenting a network. Create a diagram similar to the one below (also available online).

Documenting a network and planning tests are probably not on any Top 10 Most Fun Tasks of IT Personnel lists, but they are a necessary function. Organized documentation makes it easy to recover from disasters and easy to pass the network "torch" on to someone else. Testing can be done for many reasons, but always must be carefully planned and executed. With so many factors playing a part, proper test planning helps provide meaningful results.

DOCUMENTING A NETWORK

Preparing and maintaining network records are essential tasks that pay off when you need to make changes to a network. Up-to-date documentation provides information about how the network should look, perform, and where to seek help if there are problems. Documentation developed for maintenance, upgrading, and troubleshooting should contain the following:

◆ A map of the entire network that includes the locations of all hardware and details of the cabling

◆ Server information, including the data on each server and the schedule and locations of backups

◆ Software information, such as licensing and support details

◆ Essential names and telephone numbers for vendors, suppliers, contractors, and other helpful contacts

◆ Copies of all **service agreements.** A service agreement is a contract with an outside business that maintains and repairs certain types of equipment, such as printers and copiers.

◆ A record of all problems and their symptoms and solutions, including dates, contacts, procedures, and results

Documentation should be thorough, well-organized, and stored in an easily accessible location. Remember that it is easy for documentation to be lost and that these records must be available should the person who created them leave the organization without training a successor.

If there is more than one network administrator, it is important that all records are kept in a shared logbook. The **logbook** contains a written record of all changes that affect the network. This log can become an invaluable guide to future administrators. It might be necessary to trace a performance problem or resolve network issues related to system growth as well as equipment, maintenance, and system configuration changes.

In addition to the items listed previously, the documentation should also include:

◆ Purchase and installation dates and descriptions of all key equipment.
◆ Vendor, model, and warranty information, including serial numbers.
◆ The installation process and the results. You should record any configuration settings you made and note whether the installation process was successful.
◆ The initial and subsequent network configurations.
◆ Network usage policies and procedures.
◆ Network resources and drive assignments. A **drive assignment** maps a network folder or drive to a logical drive on a user's computer. A logical drive appears to be a physical hard drive attached to the user's computer. In reality, the "drive" could be a folder stored on a remote network server.
◆ Copies of crucial network configuration files, such as Config.sys and .bat files. Files like Config.sys and Autoexec.bat are used by certain operating systems at startup to configure various devices to operate correctly.
◆ Any unusual application program configurations.
◆ Any particular computer, motherboard, or peripheral settings.
◆ Hardware or software changes.
◆ Any activities that affect the topology or architecture.

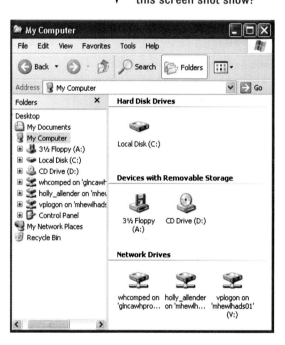

● **Figure 12.13**
Screen shots are a good way to document network information. What does this screen shot show?

It is important that all network historical documentation be easy to access and easy to read. Graphics, such as screen shots showing configuration settings, or even hand-drawn sketches can be very helpful. (See Figure 12.13.)

The logbook can be kept online or in a notebook. However, if the computer that stores the logbook should crash, it may not be possible to access the logbook. By the way, this is exactly the type of incident that the logbook should show.

ACTIVITY 12D Mapping a Network Drive and Folder

Sometimes, computers lose their connection to the network. As a network administrator or support technician, you may need to walk a user through reconnecting to the network. The following steps are for Windows 2000.

❶ Click the **Start** menu, point to **Programs,** point to **Accessories,** and click **Windows Explorer.**

❷ Click the **Tools** menu and select **Map Network Drive.**

3 In the new window that appears, click the **Drive** drop-down menu (see Figure 12.14) and select the network drive.

Figure 12.14 ●——▶
To reconnect a computer to a network drive, Windows OS uses a utility called Map Network Drive.

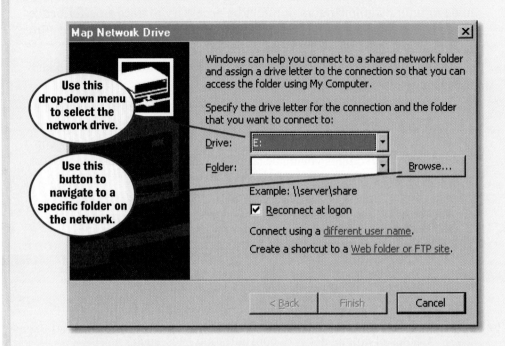

4 You can also connect directly to a specific folder. For example, users might have their own working folder on the network. Click the **Browse** button and navigate to the specific folder.

5 When done, click **Finish.**

6 To find the network drive or folder, go the Windows Explorer window. Click **My Computer** and a list of all the network drives and folders are listed.

A quick way to see if the computer is no longer connected to the network is to view the network drives and folders in Windows Explorer. If there is a red "X" on the network icon, the computer has lost its connection to the network.

Some companies have scripts that automatically reconnect the computer to the network when a user first logs on. However, you may still need to manually reconnect a computer to a network drive or folder.

Lab 12.1 Executing the Test Life Cycle Practice additional hands-on networking skills on page 450.

TESTING THE NETWORK

You test components of the network for many reasons. For example, you might need to evaluate a new server to find out if it helps alleviate a current problem on your network. Or, you might test a new software package to see if it is compatible with existing software on the network. Or, you might try to identify the source of a problem that is causing your network to fail.

Proper testing follows several distinct stages. These stages are often referred to as the **test life cycle** (see Table 12.1).

Table 12.1

Testing the components of a network is completed in stages. What must occur if a test is inconclusive?

Test Life Cycle

Stage	Description
Stage 1 Test is planned.	It is critical to identify exactly what questions you are trying to answer and how you are going to answer them. Above all else, test one thing at a time. (Many people try to test several things simultaneously, which makes it impossible to determine if the test was successful.)
Stage 2 Test strategy is defined.	In some cases, a test lab may need to be created to support the testing.
Stage 3 Test plan and test cases are designed.	A test case describes the conditions and parameters of the test. This describes the specifics of how the testing will proceed, exactly what will be tested, and possibly identifies the individuals who will be involved in the testing.
Stage 4 Actual execution of the test takes place.	Careful planning in the earlier stages pays off here as you have a clearly defined test and recognizable results at the end of the test. Some tests may need to be run in off-hours to avoid downtime during critical business hours.
Stage 5 Results of the test are evaluated and analyzed.	If the results are inconclusive, testing parameters may need to be adjusted and the testing life cycle may need to start over.

The test life cycle is illustrated in Figure 12.15. Successful deployment of any new network component depends heavily on following each stage of the test life cycle.

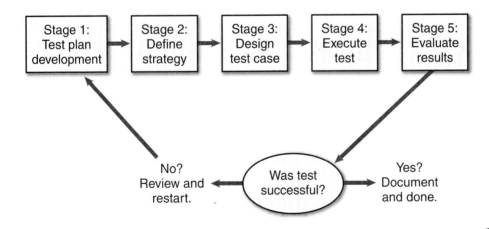

Figure 12.15

The test life cycle may require several loops through the cycle before testing is conclusive. Why is it important to follow this methodology?

ACTIVITY 12E Implementing the Test Life Cycle

YOU TRY IT

A designer in an engineering firm reports a problem with her Computer Aided Drafting (CAD) software. Whenever she tries to shade a 3-D model of the plant she is designing, the software crashes. You suspect that the video card driver is to blame. Implement the test life cycle to test this theory.

❶ Identify the problem and what you are trying to answer. In this case, the problem is that the CAD software is crashing whenever a specific set of steps is followed. You have verified that the same set of steps reproduces the same error.

2 Define the test strategy. Depending on the test, you may decide to try this on a test machine before attempting to fix the problem on a network wide basis. In this case, the problem affects one user, so you test the user's machine.

3 Create the test plan and test case. In this case, you plan to download the latest driver for the video card, install it, restart the user's computer, and then try the same sequence of steps that caused the crash.

4 Execute the test. Here, you follow the steps you outlined in step 3. Do not allow yourself to get distracted and make other changes at this stage! Otherwise, you cannot determine for certain whether the change was successful.

5 Analyze the results. After rebooting the user's computer, you execute the same steps that produced the error. This time, the steps work flawlessly and the designer can get back to work.

6 Create a document that summarizes the problem and its solution for future reference.

If the solution had not worked, you would need to begin the entire process all over again. It is critical that you remember to test only one thing at a time.

Lab 12.2 Re-Implementing the Test Life Cycle Practice additional hands-on networking skills on page 451.

It is very tempting to try a variety of things in rapid succession. Even if you are successful in fixing the problem, you may never know exactly what it was that solved the problem.

Whether the component is software, hardware, or combinations of the two, an organization must be certain that its network will continue to function after the new component is added to it.

Section 12.4 Assessment

Concept Check

1. Define service agreements, logbook, drive assignment, and test life cycle.

2. List at least 10 items that should be included in network documentation.

3. Identify the most important thing to remember when preparing to test network components.

Critical Thinking

4. Diagram Make a detailed map of your classroom, lab, or school's network. List as much information as you can about the location, type, and quantity of equipment.

5. Hypothesize Identify several scenarios in which proper documentation could help resolve a network problem.

Applying Skills

Apply the Test Life Cycle A user complains that his video card does not perform as well as another user's video card. Use the test life cycle to prepare a test that clearly demonstrates whether one video card is better than another. Document the five stages.

SECTION 12.1 Installing Operating Systems

Key Terms

disk image, 340
partition, 342
virtual disk, 342
domain controller, 342
Internet Information
    Services (IIS), 344

Client Services for NetWare
    (CSNW), 344
Gateway Services for
    NetWare (GSNW), 344
shareware, 345
defragment, 345

Main Ideas

■ There are many reasons to install an operating system (for example, upgrade, get rid of problems, multiple OSs, standard configuration).

■ Prepare for an OS installation by checking the minimum requirements and writing down important information.

■ Server OSs require more information about the network, the server's role, and the services the server will provide.

■ Operating systems and servers use client and gateway software to communicate with other operating systems.

SECTION 12.2 Implementation

Key Terms

expansion slot, 348
Advanced Technology
    Attachment (ATA), 349
Serial ATA (S-ATA), 349

license server, 350
ping (Packet Internet
    Groper), 351

Main Ideas

■ Hardware can be added to a computer using a variety of connection interfaces.

■ Always check to ensure that your computer has room for and will accept a particular type of hardware.

■ Find out about, and adhere to, your organization's policy regarding system configuration and installation of software.

■ Test network connectivity using the ping utility.

SECTION 12.3 System and Network Upgrades

Key Terms

Total Cost of Ownership (TCO), 356
Return On Investment (ROI), 356

Main Ideas

■ Monitor network hardware to prepare for necessary upgrades.

■ The need for software upgrades should be closely evaluated.

■ Total Cost of Ownership includes the purchase price of equipment or software, plus all costs associated with the product throughout its useful life.

■ Return On Investment is an important calculation that identifies the potential earnings or savings a purchase can bring to the organization.

SECTION 12.4 System Testing and Documentation

Key Terms

service agreements, 358
logbook, 359
drive assignment, 359
test life cycle, 361

Main Ideas

■ An important task for IT personnel is recording network documentation.

■ Up-to-date documentation is critical during system emergencies.

■ Components are tested for reasons such as evaluating new equipment, checking software compatability, or identifying the source of a problem.

■ Network component tests must be completed in stages.

■ A test life cycle includes seven important stages.

Reviewing Key Terms

1. Why is disk image necessary for IT staff?
2. What does IIS stand for and how is it used?
3. What is the other name for ATA?
4. What is your computer's loopback address and its functionality?
5. Why do you use drive assignment in a networked environment?

Understanding Main Ideas

6. **Describe** why it is important to document a service agreement.
7. **Explain** what a license server is and why it is important to install only licensed software.
8. **Identify** why a software company would want to distribute shareware.
9. **Explain** why defragmenting a disk increases computing efficiency.
10. **Describe** how drive partitions, virtual disks, and domain controllers are related to installing a server operating system.
11. **Identify** two details you should remember when installing add-in cards.
12. **List** three connection (bus) interfaces that can be used for adding hardware to a computer. Tell when it is appropriate to use the interface.
13. **Contrast** TCO and ROI in the role of system and network upgrades.
14. **Describe** the differences among (standard) ATA, Ultra ATA, and S-ATA as interfaces that connect storage devices to the motherboard.
15. **Explain** why is it necessary to keep a shared logbook.
16. **List** the five important stages in a test life cycle of a system and network.

Critical Thinking

17. **Evaluate Information** Installing an operating system involves important decision making. Understanding your company's role and services is crucial for you to choose the right method to make you a productive IT staff member. Identify the methods discussed in your textbook for installing an OS and discuss the situation in which it is appropriate to use the method.
18. **Analyze Information** List the ideas discussed in your textbook about how to use your operating system efficiently. Explain why each of the methods is recommended.
19. **Compare and Contrast** In a network, different operating systems are often installed on computers that need to communicate with each other. So that they understand each other, protocols can be installed on each to have them speak the same language. In a Novell NetWare environment with the IPX/SPX protocol, CSNW or GSNW can be used. Compare and contrast CSNW and GSNW for remote accessing resources.
20. **Analyze Practices** Software instructions come with licensing agreements for its use. IT personnel must follow the conditions and capabilities of the network. Analyze licensing and software use practices.

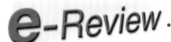

networking.glencoe.com

Study with PowerPoint

To review the main points in this chapter, select **e-Review > PowerPoint Outlines > Chapter 12.**

Online Self Check

Test your knowledge of the material in this chapter by selecting **e-Review > Self Checks > Chapter 12.**

Making Connections

Math – Calculating Total Cost of Ownership
Many IT managers are asked to make hardware and software recommendations for an entire company, and they typically justify their recommendations based on the Total Cost of Ownership (TCO) of various products. Using basic mathematical functions, develop an algebraic equation that will allow you to calculate the TCO of a particular software application over a period of five years. Include in your equation the initial purchase price, plus the annual cost of support and upgrades, training and certification, and the salaries of application support personnel.

STANDARDS AT WORK

Students use technology resources for solving problems and making informed decisions. (NETS-S 6)

Understanding TCP/IP Configurations
In order for workstations to communicate with each other on a network, it is essential that the workstation operating system (OS) be configured properly via the active network protocol. Using the following procedure, locate the configuration information for a Windows XP-based workstation running on a TCP/IP network.

a. Open the **Windows Control Panel.**
b. Locate the control panel icon labeled **Network Connections** and open it.
c. Right-click on the **Local Area Connection** icon and select the **Properties** option.
d. Locate and double-click the entry labeled **Internet Protocol (TCP/IP).**
   Use the dialog box (labeled Internet Protocol Properties) to answer the following:
1. Does your workstation use an automatic (dynamic) or static IP address?
2. If it is static, what values are used for the IP address, subnet mask, and default gateway?
3. Does your workstation use an automatic or static Domain Name System (DNS) address?
4. If they are static, what values are used for the primary and alternate server?

TEAMWORK SKILLS

Prepare an Oral Report
Under the supervision of your teacher, divide your class into four small groups. Using the Internet or other available resources, each group should research one of the following operating systems:
a. Microsoft Windows XP
b. Novell NetWare 6
c. Red Hat Linux 8
d. MacOS X
   Prepare a spreadsheet that allows for potential advantages and disadvantages of your assigned OS. Include information about the following:
◆ Minimum system requirements
◆ Initial purchase price and upgrade pricing
◆ Training and/or certification programs
◆ Technical support and any associated costs
◆ Features, limitations, versatility, interoperability, scalability, etc.
   Each group presents its work to the class.

CHALLENGE YOURSELF

Share a Folder
Within the classroom network and with your teacher's permission, create a share. The process in Windows XP is as follows:
a. Launch **Windows Explorer** and navigate to the folder you wish to share.
b. Right-click on the folder name and select **Sharing and Security....**
c. Select the radio button **Share this folder.**
d. Type a name for the share in the **Share name** field. Windows will enter a default name for you, but you may change it if you wish.
e. Type a comment in the **Comment** field.
f. To limit the number of network users who may access the share at the same time, click the radio button **Allow this number of users,** and set the desired value in the corresponding number field.
g. Click **OK** to make the share active.
   Create a drive map to the shared folder for quick access.

YOU TRY IT

Networking Lab

1. Defragmenting a Hard Drive

Many network administrators are given the responsibility to periodically defragment server hard drives. This helps the operating system perform file operations (reads and writes) more efficiently. Defragmenting a hard drive is especially valuable when this particular drive is to be used as the source of a disk image. If the disk is defragmented before the image is created, then every hard drive that is setup up with that image will be defragmented also.

Several versions of the Windows operating system include a utility called Disk Defragmenter. You may access and use this program from within a standard installation of Windows XP by following the steps below. Keep in mind that the task may have been completed only a short time ago. Only complete this activity with the permission of your teacher.

Ⓐ Click **Start, Programs, Accessories, System Tools,** and **Disk Defragmenter** to open the Disk Defragmenter tool from the main Windows menu. The main screen will look similar to the one shown here.

Ⓑ Click **Analyze** to initiate an analysis of your hard drive's data files. The tool will report the amount of file fragmentation it finds, and it will give a recommendation as to whether disk defragmentation is warranted or not.

Ⓒ Click **Defragment** to begin the defragmentation process. Depending on the speed of your computer and the severity of fragmentation, this operation may take several minutes to complete.

Ⓓ When the defragmenting process is finished, click **View Report** to see some interesting information that the Disk Defragmenter has prepared.

Ⓔ Keep the **Disk Defragmenter** tool open while you answer the following questions.
1. What percentage of your disk was fragmented?
2. Was defragmenting recommended?
3. How long did it take to defragment your hard drive?
4. What information was included in the defragmentation report?
5. What other useful or interesting observations can you make?

Ⓕ **Close** the Disk Defragmenter tool.

Networking Projects

1. Research and Prepare a Device Driver Report

Disk images can be a very useful tool when setting up user computer systems with a standardized software configuration. The disk image will only function correctly if the proper device drivers are installed. Windows OSs include hundreds of device drivers in order to support many different types of devices, so it is critical for the disk image to contain the correct drivers.

Fortunately, Windows XP includes a useful tool called Device Manager that can tell you exactly what drivers are currently in use on any given workstation. Prepare a written log of the active device drivers on your workstation for several common devices, including the display adapter, keyboard, mouse, network adapter, etc. Start by including the computer's general properties information.

Ⓐ Right-click **My Computer** and select **Properties.**

Ⓑ Click the **Hardware** tab in System Properties, and then click the **Device Manager** to open the Device Manager utility. The resulting window should look like the one shown here.

Ⓒ Navigate through the device tree, and right-click the device you wish to research. Select **Properties** from the pop-up menu.

Ⓓ Click the **Driver** tab on the Properties dialog. Click the **Driver Details** button. Include the driver file information in your device driver report.

2. Examine System Logs with Event Viewer

One responsibility of IT personnel is to maintain a logbook of server problems as well as solutions. Changes made to the network should also be noted in the logbook. Network administrators can use Event Viewer in a Windows environment to detect server problems or changes made to the network. As a member of the IT staff, you should be able to document this information if called upon by the network administrator. Prepare an entry for the logbook. Event Viewer is accessed in Windows XP as follows:

Ⓐ Launch the Windows control panel and double-click **Administrative Tools.**

Ⓑ Locate and double-click **Event Viewer** to open the Event Viewer Utility. The resulting window should look similar to the one shown here.

Ⓒ Click on the **Application, Security,** and **System** folders in the left-side navigation tree to view a list of log messages on the right side of the Event Viewer window.

Ⓓ Note that there are three types of log messages: information, warning, or error. Double-click any log message to view the details of the message.

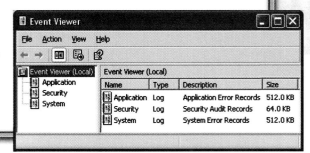

Ⓔ Record one of the messages and describe your interpretation of the message.

Network Security and Maintenance

YOU WILL LEARN TO...

WHY IT MATTERS.....................................

In this day and age, network security is (or should be) on every network administrator's mind. Some dream of a powerful "fire and forget" method of security that, once established, would silently tick away in the background repelling any and all attempts to break into the network. Unfortunately, the reality is that network systems must be constantly monitored and managed against a variety of threats.

Quick Write Activity

Computer virus attacks are occurring with alarming frequency. You can often find reports of the latest damaging attack reported on nationwide network news programs. Write a paragraph about the latest computer security problem you have seen or read about in the news.

WHAT YOU WILL DO..

ACTIVITIES AND PROJECTS

Applying Skills

You Try It Activities

Chapter Assessment

You Try It Networking Lab

Networking Projects

Enrichment Labs

IN THE WORKBOOK

Optional Activities and Projects

Guided Reading

Study Guide

Networking Labs

ON THE WEB

Activities at **networking.glencoe.com**

Reading Strategy Organizers

Go Online Activities

Study with PowerPoint

Self-Check Assessments

READ TO SUCCEED

Two-Column Notes

Two-column notes are a useful way to organize and study what you read. Divide a piece of paper into two columns. In the left column, write down main ideas. They can be written as a word, phrase, or question. In the right column, write down supporting details. Use short phrases rather than sentences. For example, for the main idea *"monitors (2 examples),"* the details could be: *1) CRT (cathode ray tubes) are less expensive. Take lots of power and space. 2) Flat screens use LCD (liquid crystal display.) Images may not be as clear as CRT.*

Guide to Reading

Main Ideas

SNMP-compliant devices can store and communicate information about themselves. Individual users can be added to groups, and groups can be assigned to resource permissions to make access management easier.

Key Terms

Simple Network Management Protocol (SNMP)
Management Information Base (MIB)
username
account policies
permissions

Reading Strategy

Identify each of the acceptable password policies. Create a chart similar to the one below (also available online).

Password Policies	
1.	4.
2.	5.
3.	6.

Network management involves managing equipment and users. These jobs would be very time-consuming if every piece of equipment and every user had to be dealt with individually. A variety of tools and methods simplify network management.

MANAGING EQUIPMENT AND SNMP

After a network grows beyond a handful of computers, management of those computers becomes an important issue. Suppose the IT staff of a credit card company was asked to inventory all the network hardware. This could be very time-consuming and expensive.

Instead, what if each device on the network could store information about itself, then return that information when asked? The **Simple Network Management Protocol (SNMP)** was designed to do exactly that. SNMP-compliant devices are able to store information about themselves. An SNMP device, called an agent, stores this information in a database called a **Management Information Base (MIB).** This information can then be retrieved by special applications known as SNMP management applications (see Figure 13.1).

Most devices found on networks today, including routers, switches, or computers, are SNMP-compliant. Operating systems can include SNMP client software as an optional installation component, or you can purchase SNMP software from third-party sources.

Figure 13.1
SNMP agents store information about themselves and can respond when asked questions about themselves. What information can be returned from an SNMP agent?

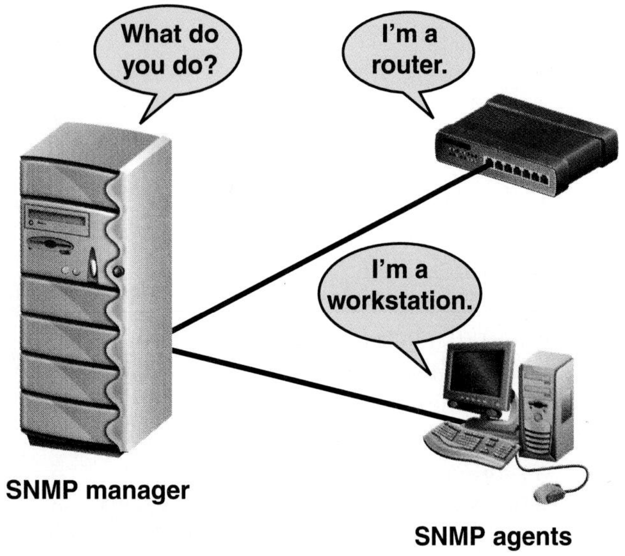

What do you do?

I'm a router.

I'm a workstation.

SNMP manager

SNMP agents

The many uses of SNMP include:

◆ Configuring remote devices. For example, you could change a network copier's default settings using SNMP (see Figure 13.2).
◆ Monitoring network performance.
◆ Detecting network faults.
◆ Detecting inappropriate access to network resources.
◆ Auditing network usage.

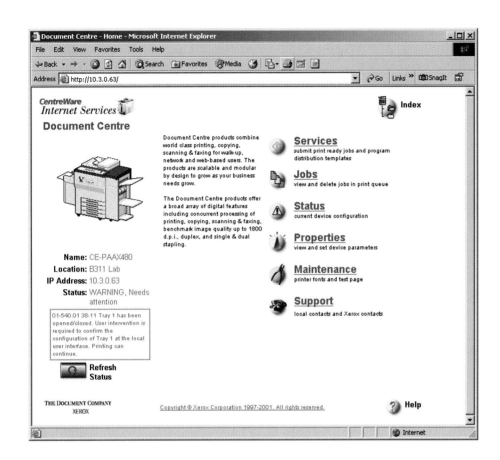

◀━━●Figure 13.2
Information and configuration of this networked copier is available using SNMP. What are some other uses of SNMP?

Because all of these functions can be performed remotely, the IT staff of our fictional credit card company can smile and say, "Sure, no problem," when asked to inventory the entire network.

MANAGING PEOPLE

People, otherwise known as "users," are network resources that must be managed. User accounts must be created. Permissions must be set. Resources must be mapped so the user can access them.

At the network level, user access to resources is carefully defined. For example, only certain individuals might be allowed to create files within a certain folder on the network. Anyone else attempting to create a file there gets an access denied message (see Figure 13.3).

●Figure 13.3
Permissions are used to control what users are allowed to do on a network. Why would an administrator want to deny users from creating files in a certain folder?

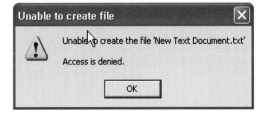

Figure 13.4 ●────────
A user account must be
added before a user can
log on to the network. What
information can be stored
in the user account?

User Accounts

An account must be created for a user before that user can log on to the network. Directory services applications, such as Microsoft Active Directory and Novell Directory Services, are used to set up user accounts and manage network resources. User accounts can be created, disabled, or deleted. An account can store such user data as job title, phone numbers, e-mail address, and so on.

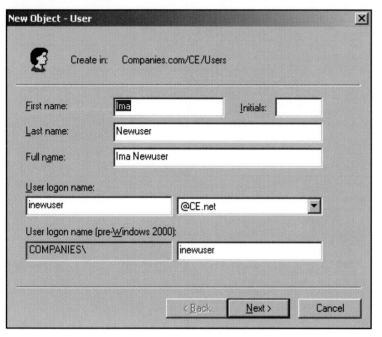

The user account also establishes the username and password. A **username,** or logon name, identifies a specific user on the network. Usernames are often created by combining letters from the user's first and last name. In Figure 13.4, the username was created using the first initial of the first name and the full last name.

When a user account is first set up, a temporary password may be assigned. The first time the user logs on, the password must be changed. Passwords are often the key that opens the door to the network. Because of this, passwords must always be kept secret and should not be easy to guess. Passwords are covered in more detail later in this section.

Account Policies and Permissions

After the user account is established, permissions can be assigned. For example, a traveling salesperson may need to use Remote Access Service (RAS) networking to log on to the network and access her e-mail or files on the server while on the road (Figure 13.5).

Figure 13.5 ●────▶
RAS allows people to
remotely connect to net-
works. What kinds of net-
works can the application
connect to?

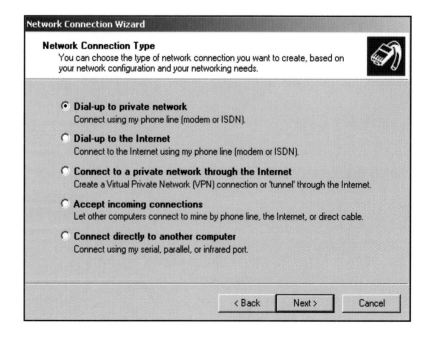

Account policies can be defined as acceptable user practices. A network administrator may have a policy that requires a secure, strong password. The policy may mandate guidelines such as the following:

◆ Users must change their passwords every 45 days.
◆ Passwords must include some combination of letters, numbers, and a special character, such as '@' or '#'.
◆ Passwords must be eight or more characters in length.
◆ Passwords should not be words that appear in a dictionary (in any language).
◆ Passwords should not include personal information, such as a birthday, social security number, license plate number, and so on.
◆ Passwords should be very different from previously used passwords (do not "recycle" a password by changing a character and leaving the rest the same).

Permissions, also called security settings, determine the resources to which a user has access. For example, a new user in the Accounting Department would be permitted to view, but not edit, last year's financial statements. This user would be able to print to the accounting laser printer, but not to the engineering color plotter. Permissions can be set on a per-user basis. However, it is less time-consuming for an administrator to assign permissions to groups of users simultaneously.

Groups

Groups are used to conveniently assign network access permission to many users at a time. Most of the time, a group's boundaries is a department. For example, users in the Computer Aided Drafting (CAD) department could be formed into a CAD Users group (see Figure 13.6).

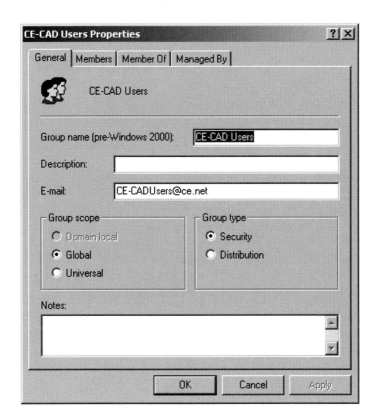

Figure 13.6
Groups make it easy to assign permissions to many users at a time. What are a few advantages of using groups to set permissions?

After a group is established, it can be used as if it were a user account. User or group accounts can be assigned permission settings to resources on the network. Some individuals, such as a manager, may cross several of these imaginary boundaries. A special group can be created, or managers can be added to multiple groups. A user assigned to multiple groups receives whatever permissions each group has.

Scripts can make network resources available to a user based on group memberships. Also, group names can be used to address an e-mail to many individuals at once. In the next You Try It activity, you learn how to view these permission settings.

YOU TRY IT

ACTIVITY 13A Viewing Permissions Settings

Most users on the network do not have permission to determine access to resources on the network. However, if the user has access to a resource, he or she can view the security settings that have been assigned. The following instructions apply to the Windows OS.

❶ Open **Windows Explorer.**

❷ Navigate to a network resource, such as a drive or folder located on a network drive.

❸ Right-click on a folder, then click **Properties.**

❹ Click the **Security** tab as shown in Figure 13.7. At the top of the dialog box, the names of the users and/or group accounts that have access to the folder are displayed.

Figure 13.7
The Security tab shows access rights for user and group accounts.

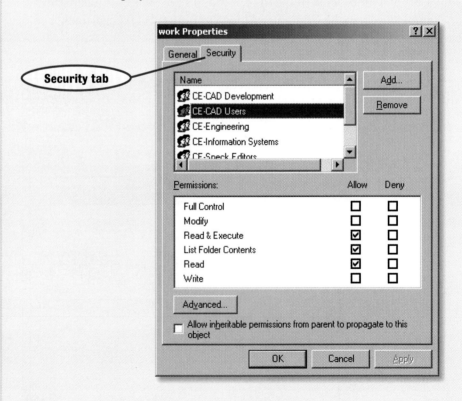

❺ In the Names list, click on one of the names to select it. How can you tell if the name is a single user or a group of users?

6 Look at the Permissions area. Each account can be allowed (or denied) various permissions which give the user the ability to:

- ◆ Have full control (allows the user to do anything)
- ◆ Modify folder structures
- ◆ List folder contents
- ◆ Read files
- ◆ Write files

7 Click on another name in the list and check the permissions for that user or group. Are the permissions the same or different?

8 Do NOT change any of the permissions. Click **OK** to close the dialog box.

9 You can also check the permissions of *files* in the same way as you can for *folders*. Right-click on a file, and click **Properties.**

10 Click the **Security** tab. Click on one of the names. Notice that List Folder Contents does not appear in the Permissions list for a file. Also, when a file is created on a user's computer, the settings may need to be changed so that others may edit the file. The creator of the file can usually set and change these permissions without the assistance of the administrator.

11 Do NOT change any of the permissions. Click **OK** to close the dialog box. Note: If you do not have administrative rights, you can usually view the permissions, but cannot modify them.

Managing the various hardware and all the users on a network is a busy job. In some large organizations, dedicated IT staff are provided whose only job is to manage users' accounts.

Section 13.1 Assessment

Concept Check

1. **Define** Simple Network Management Protocol (SNMP), Management Information Base (MIB), username, account policies, and permissions.

2. **List** at least three devices that could be SNMP agents.

3. **Create** five passwords according to the policies described in this section.

Critical Thinking

4. **Compare and Contrast** Account policies and permissions hold similarities and differences at the same time. What are they?

5. **Formulate** You are trying to determine where a lot of outbound traffic on your network is originating. Explain how your router being SNMP-compliant can help you resolve the issue.

Applying Skills

Identify and Grant Access You need to create user groups for a new organization. Create a table that lists the various departments, the type of data each group might be responsible for, and the type of access each group should have to that data. Simulate granting access, if you have access to a dedicated lab network.

Careers & Technology

NETWORKING CERTIFICATIONS

Many employers expect that you have a specialized certification in one or more networking technologies.

A certification does more than provide proof of generalized computer training. It assures an employer that you have specific skills in a key technology used by that organization.

Professional certifications can enhance your career prospects by making you more employable.

Vendor-Neutral Certifications

A popular vendor-neutral certification program is offered by the Computer Technology Industry Association (CompTIA), an organization serving the IT industry. CompTIA has developed a variety of educational programs designed for IT professionals:

◆ **A+ certification** covers PC hardware maintenance and troubleshooting and operating systems.

◆ **Network+ certification** covers the basics of network architecture and administration.

◆ **i-Net+ certification** focuses on networking technologies essential to Internet and e-commerce networking professionals.

Vendor-Specific Certifications

Several major manufacturers of networking hardware and software offer certifications on their products, sometimes with labels such as "core," "proficient," and "expert." Many employers want their network managers to hold a certification from at least one of the following vendors:

◆ **Microsoft**—Offers networking professionals certification as a Microsoft Certified Professional (MCP), Microsoft Certified Systems Administrator (MCSA), and Microsoft Certified Systems Engineer (MCSE). Each level provides training in a variety of Microsoft operating systems, networking, and management products.

◆ **Novell**—Was one of the first companies to offer certification in the use of its products. The Certified Novell Administrator (CNA), Certified Novell Engineer (CNE), and Master CNE programs are popular among network managers at all levels of industry.

◆ **Cisco**—Is a leading maker of network components, and offers dozens of certifications on topics from routers to internetworking.

Depending on your career goals, you may be interested in a certification in a different area, such as programming, database administration, or electronics. Check with vendors in the area of technology that interests you or with a college or technical school.

Tech Focus

1. Compare and contrast at least three types of networking certifications that are available.

2. Find out more about CompTIA and other organizations, associations, or unions that could be helpful in a networking career.

Section 13.2   Network Monitoring and Maintenance

Guide to Reading

Main Ideas

Log files and auditing tools are used to monitor networks. Proper maintenance of systems includes caring for the physical well-being, as well as upgrading hardware and software. Data should be backed up regularly.

Key Terms

log file
auditing
replication
uninterruptible
   power supply
   (UPS)

Reading Strategy

Identify a monthly schedule of regular maintenance activities that should occur for a system on a network. Create a chart similar to the one below (also available online).

How Often	Maintenance Task

Like a car, networks must be continually monitored and maintained to prevent problems. Cars are taken to the mechanic periodically for tune-ups and oil changes. Regular trips to the mechanic often prevent larger problems from occurring down the road. Network systems must also be monitored and maintained to prevent larger problems.

BASICS OF NETWORK MONITORING

As explained in the first section of this chapter, network hardware and users must be carefully managed. Tools like SNMP and directory services allow an administrator to handle these tasks from anywhere, even remotely. Monitoring tools, such as Performance Monitor and Network Monitor, explained in Chapter 11, are also helpful to keep tabs on server and network performance. In addition to these, other tools are used to manage and monitor the health of the network. Like a carpenter's tools, each type of tool is used for specific purposes.

Logs

When a system develops problems, log files often serve as the first source of diagnostic information. A **log file** is a simple text file that records information about the device, system, or application.

Some log files are created only when problems arise, such as when an application crashes. A utility in the Windows environment, an application called Dr. Watson, logs errors when applications fail. In the Mac OS X environment, the Console application logs errors. The information in the log is quite technical, but provides precise information about what was happening at the time of the crash.

ACTIVITY 13B Viewing Dr. Watson Log Files

In the Windows OS, Dr. Watson records important system information when applications crash. Support personnel often request the log file generated by Dr. Watson to diagnose the cause of the crash.

Figure 13.8
Dr. Watson is an application that records important system information when an application crashes.

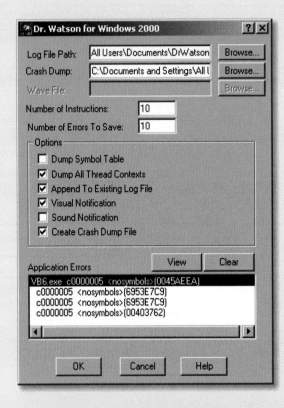

❶ Click **Start** and then click **Run.**

❷ Type drwtsn32 and then click **OK.** The Dr. Watson interface is very simple, as shown in Figure 13.8.

❸ To view the log file, click an error in the Application Errors box, and then click **View.** If you don't find errors, your system and applications are functioning at an optimum level.

❹ A separate window appears showing the contents of the log file (see Figure 13.9).

❺ Click **OK** to close the application.

Figure 13.9
A log file includes important information that can help you resolve problems.

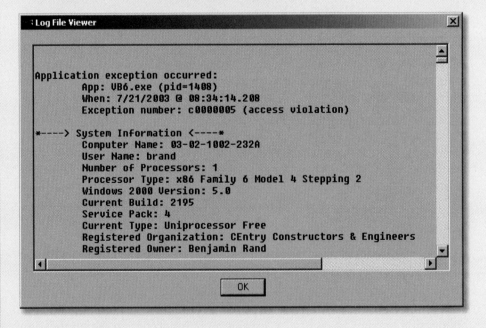

Log files, such as those generated by the Dr. Watson utility, are an important resource for troubleshooting problems.

A boot log file is created when a system boots. These log files record every application and device driver that gets loaded. They can be used to pinpoint a device driver that fails to load and causes the system to stop booting. A log file created by a firewall application can help identify the IP address of a hacker trying to access the system.

System Audits

Auditing is the process of examining and verifying information. Network audits can return information about the hardware and software on the network. System audits are performed for several reasons, including:

- To determine if software licenses are being used illegally
- To record what software is in use throughout the network
- To inventory hardware on a network
- To prepare readiness reports prior to upgrading hardware or software

An audit report is shown in Figure 13.10. This type of report can help administrators identify computers that can migrate to a new operating system. There are many third-party applications that can help system administrators quickly perform entire system audits. The system administrator can perform this without ever leaving his office.

Activity 13.1 Locate Software Auditing Tools Go to networking.glencoe.com for more information about locating software auditing applications.

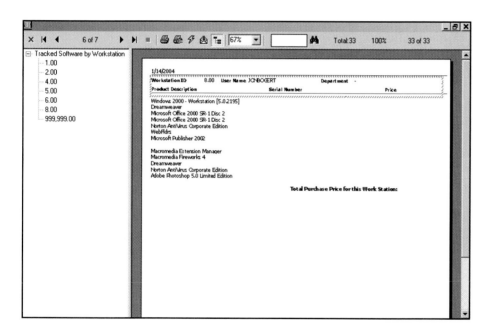

Figure 13.10
Auditing tools, such as Blue Ocean's Track-It!, can survey the entire network and return important information. What are some reasons for performing a system audit?

System Optimization and Improvement

As more users access the network services, it becomes more important to make smart use of those services. This requires a very detailed knowledge of how the system works. The administrator needs to know which settings can be changed to optimize the performance.

For example, some applications allow an administrator to control the amount of system memory the application uses. More memory might improve that application's performance. However, the change may reduce the amount of memory available to other applications. You should never adjust a critical system setting without knowing what it does and why you are doing it.

Traffic Issues

Figure 13.11
Monitoring network activity can help determine usage patterns and identify problems. Why is it important to monitor network traffic on an ongoing basis?

On any network, traffic should be monitored to help IT personnel spot increasing usage trends or identify potential security problems (as shown in Figure 13.11).

Periodic monitoring of network traffic helps administrators establish a baseline of what to expect. Anything outside this baseline can signal a problem that needs resolution. In the event of a virus attack, administrators must take immediate measures.

To effectively monitor large networks, a network operating center (NOC) can be used. For instance, the Indiana University Abilene Network Operations Center has created a 2.5 gigabits per second cross-country backbone. This is an Internet2 backbone. From Indianapolis, Indiana, the NOC can monitor network performance, oversee problems, configuration, network security, quality assurance, and much more. The NOC works twenty-four hours a day, seven days a week to monitor the backbone for over 220 Internet2 universities, corporations, and affiliate members in 50 states, the District of Columbia, and Puerto Rico.

Fault Tolerance and Redundancy

One of a network administrator's highest concerns is ensuring that systems are fault tolerant. This means that critical systems are able to perform their jobs as close to 100 percent of the time as possible. Server applications must recover from problems and maintain services without crashing. For example, if users enter invalid data into a database field, the entire system should not crash. Instead, the software's design reliably handles the error and moves on.

Redundancy can refer to both hardware and data. RAID is one strategy designed to protect data. Another strategy involves **replication,** or copying critical databases to backup servers. For example, important services, such as the logon and directory services provided by a domain controller, can be replicated to backup servers. If the primary domain controller fails, a backup server immediately fills in.

SCHEDULED MAINTENANCE AND UPGRADES

Any complex system requires periodic maintenance to perform at its best. A network administrator has to see to it that maintenance and upgrades follow a schedule.

Maintenance

Regular computer maintenance on all NOSs includes important software and hardware tasks. In the following list, a number of common maintenance tasks are identified.

- Keep virus definitions up-to-date. Many vendors issue these updates weekly. Computers should have a virus utility running at all times. A weekly scan should also be performed.
- Defragment the hard drive. On some OSs, such as the Mac, defragmentation happens automatically in the background. Other OSs should schedule at least a weekly defragmentation.
- Check the case for dust and other debris once per month. You'd be surprised at how much dust can accumulate in the case. This dust can cause cooling fans to clog. This in turn leads to dangerous heat conditions.
- Ensure computers are plugged into a surge protector.
- Servers and other essential systems should be connected to an **uninterruptible power supply (UPS)** device. A UPS is a large rechargeable battery that provides power to connected devices for a period of time if main electrical power goes out.

Implementation of System Upgrades

Another key aspect of computer maintenance is performing necessary upgrades. This may include software upgrades, operating system upgrades, and hardware upgrades. Most software companies make their upgrades, patches, and service releases available for download on the Web.

Software companies normally charge a fee for upgrades. Patches and service releases, on the other hand, normally address bugs or problems with the application. Most often, these are freely available to registered customers. Administrators should keep up-to-date with these.

Hardware upgrades can enhance the system's performance. For example, a system that does not have enough RAM must use the hard drive for extra space. Because the hard drive is many hundreds of times slower at accessing data than RAM is, the system performance slows down. Upgrading the amount of RAM can help the system run much more efficiently. Be sure to check that any upgrade you consider is compatible with your existing hardware and software.

System Backups and Restoring Data

The rule is simple: If you cannot get along without it, back it up. Whether you back up entire disks, selected directories, or files depends on how fast you need to be operational if your system loses important data.

Critical data should be backed up according to daily, weekly, or monthly schedules. How often depends on how critical the data are and how frequently the data are updated. It is best to schedule backups during periods of low system use. An efficient backup plan uses a combination of methods (see Table 13.1 on page 382).

Activity 13.2 Detect Dangerous Network Activity
Akamai's NOCC was one of the first places to notice the dangerous spike in activity caused by the appearance of the Slammer worm in early 2003. You can read more about this interesting story at **networking.glencoe.com**.

READ ME!

Tech Tip Windows computers should have a set of Emergency Repair Disks (ERD) [for Windows 2000] or a set of Automated System Recovery disks (ASR) [for Windows XP] on hand. These disks can help you reboot and recover a Windows computer in the event that something happened and the computer no longer boots normally.

READ ME!

Tech Tip The Windows Update service is used to keep the Windows operating systems up-to-date. This service is used for Windows 98, Me, NT, 2000, and XP.

Table 13.1
Network administrators use a variety of backup methods to back up critical data. What is the primary rule of thumb for determining what data to back up?

| Common Backup Methods | |
Method	Description
Full backup	Backs up all files and marks all files as backed up.
Incremental backup	Backs up any files that have changed since the last backup. Files are marked as backed up. Restoring an entire system requires the full system backup plus each incremental backup since the last full backup.
Differential backup	Backs up any files that have changed since the last full backup. Does not mark files as backed up. Restoring an entire system requires the full system backup and only the last differential backup.

Backup and restore utilities, such as Veritas' Backup Exec, automate the process of scheduling backups and restoring files. Backup applications create a log file that indicates the success or failure of a backup operation. This log file should be consulted often.

Tapes are often used on a rotating, multiple-week cycle. This allows fewer tapes to be used, but still provides adequate backup coverage for a specific amount of time. The longer the cycle, the more tapes that are required. For example, on the first day of the cycle, the administrator performs a full backup and follows with an incremental backup on succeeding days. When the entire cycle has finished, the process begins again. Occasionally (weekly or monthly), a full backup should be stored off-site in the case of some sort of disaster, such as a fire, tornado, or hurricane.

Enrichment **LAB**

Lab 13.1 Creating a Backup Strategy Practice additional hands-on networking skills on page 452.

Section 13.2 Assessment

Concept Check

1. **Define** log file, auditing, replication, and uninterruptible power supply (UPS).

2. **Identify** what type of log file could be consulted to identify problems during the startup of a computer.

3. **List** four things that should be done to properly maintain a computer.

Critical Thinking

4. **Cause and Effect** Explain how files become fragmented on a hard drive and the effect it has on the system.

5. **Analyze** An organization makes a full backup of an important server each week and an incremental backup daily. What if the server crashes on Wednesday? Which tapes must be restored to restore all data on the server?

Applying Skills

Create a Computer Maintenance Schedule Create a calendar that shows each of the various maintenance tasks described in this section. Be sure to schedule important tasks, such as virus scanning, on a regular basis. This calendar should cover a period of three or more months.

Real World Technology

SECURITY AND THE HOME NETWORK

Many people have more than one home computer, and are creating home networks. This is especially common in families with school-age children and a parent who works from home.

Home networks are inexpensive, fun, and convenient. But, they expose home computers to the same security problems faced by businesses.

Benefits and Convenience
Home networks are installed for the same basic reasons as business networks. They allow users to share files, programs, peripherals, and an Internet connection.

Today's home networks are easy to install and can be running in a matter of minutes. Many new homes feature built-in network wiring and a network outlet in each room, allowing a family to quickly connect PCs to a central hub.

The Price of Convenience
Home network users need to become amateur network administrators, armed with special knowledge and tools, to prevent problems like these:

◆ **Viruses**—If a virus infects one computer on the network, it can spread to the others and

beyond. In a home network, each computer should have current antivirus software installed, with all its features activated. Users should keep their virus definitions updated, too.

◆ **Hackers**—Dial-up Internet connections are not terribly vulnerable to hacking because they disconnect periodically. Broadband-connected PCs, however, are connected to the Internet as long as the computer is on. This makes them much easier targets for hackers. The best way to avoid being hacked is to password-protect the computers and install a firewall. Many home networking hubs and routers have built-in firewalls, and are inexpensive protection against attacks.

◆ **Freeloaders**—A wireless network's radio waves can travel outside the home and be picked up by other wireless devices. A neighbor with a wireless device might be able to access files on your disks or even access the Internet through your network! To avoid this, home networks should use a base station equipped with a firewall, which employs the Wired Equivalent Privacy (WEP) protocol to encrypt data transmitted through the network.

Tech Focus

1. Research the various methods used for creating home networks, including wired and wireless. Which method would you choose to create a network in your home? Explain your choice.

2. What problems relate specifically to wireless home computer networks? Focus on a single type of problem, and write a paragraph detailing the steps you would take to avoid this problem on your own home network.

Section 13.3   Basic Scripting

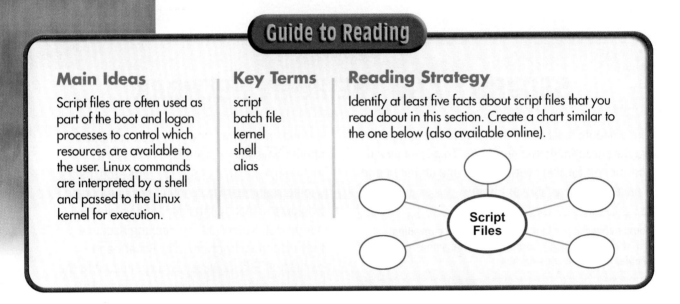

Main Ideas

Script files are often used as part of the boot and logon processes to control which resources are available to the user. Linux commands are interpreted by a shell and passed to the Linux kernel for execution.

Key Terms

script
batch file
kernel
shell
alias

Reading Strategy

Identify at least five facts about script files that you read about in this section. Create a chart similar to the one below (also available online).

Script Files

Scripts are one of the best tools to help administrators do their jobs effectively. A **script** is a set of commands that can be executed without any user interaction. Some scripts are basically a set of prerecorded OS commands. Other scripts are written in a scripting language that enables them to make decisions and execute different portions of the script.

Figure 13.12
Scripting applications provide an easy-to-use, graphical approach to building a script file. Describe some of the benefits of using logon scripts.

SCRIPTS TO MANAGE

Logon scripts often work in conjunction with the domain controller to determine the group to which a user belongs. Resources are made available in the same manner to everyone within the same group.

Third-party scripting applications, such as ScriptLogic Corporation's ScriptLogic, reduce the headache of creating scripts (see Figure 13.12). In the parts to follow, you learn about some common Windows and Linux commands that might be used in a logon script.

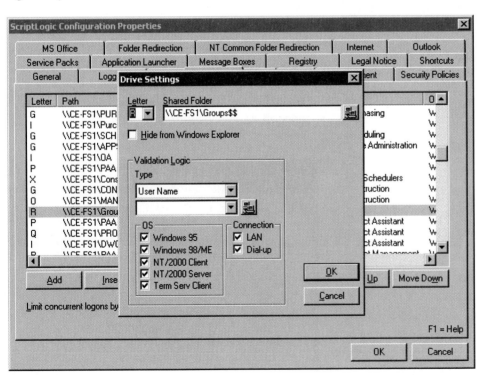

networking.glencoe.com

WINDOWS SCRIPTS

Using Microsoft Active Directory, system administrators can assign individual users, or groups, a customized logon script (see Figure 13.13). This allows a user to have network resources configured and available in whatever arrangement he or she needs.

Specifies the logon script to run whenever this user logs on

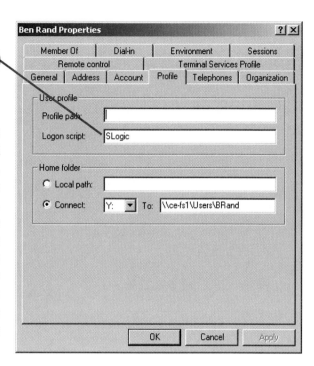

Scripts are simple text files, often stored with a ".bat" extension. This extension identifies the files as a "batch" file. **Batch files** are simple programs that can execute the statements within the file. In the next You Try It activity, you can try your hand at some simple commands that might be used in a logon script.

Figure 13.13
Customized logon scripts can be assigned to individual users. How does a customized logon script benefit a user?

ACTIVITY 13C Working with Windows Batch Commands

YOU TRY IT

You can test commands using the command prompt in the Windows environment on a line-by-line basis. You can learn more about any of the commands by typing the command name, followed by a /?, as shown in the following example:

`echo /?`

After you have verified that a certain command works to your satisfaction, you can add it to a text file with a ".bat" extension to execute them later.

1 Click the **Start** button, and then click **Run.**

2 Type cmd and then click **OK.**

3 At the command prompt, enter echo %username%. The echo command prints a value to the computer screen. In this case, it prints the value stored in the %username% variable.

4 At the command prompt, enter if %username%==funderhill echo "Hello Frodo". Note the two equal symbols in a row. This statement compares your username to "funderhill." If they are equal, then the message "Hello Frodo" is displayed at the command prompt. Unless your username is "funderhill," nothing appears at the command prompt.

Figure 13.14
The username of this
account is holly_allender.

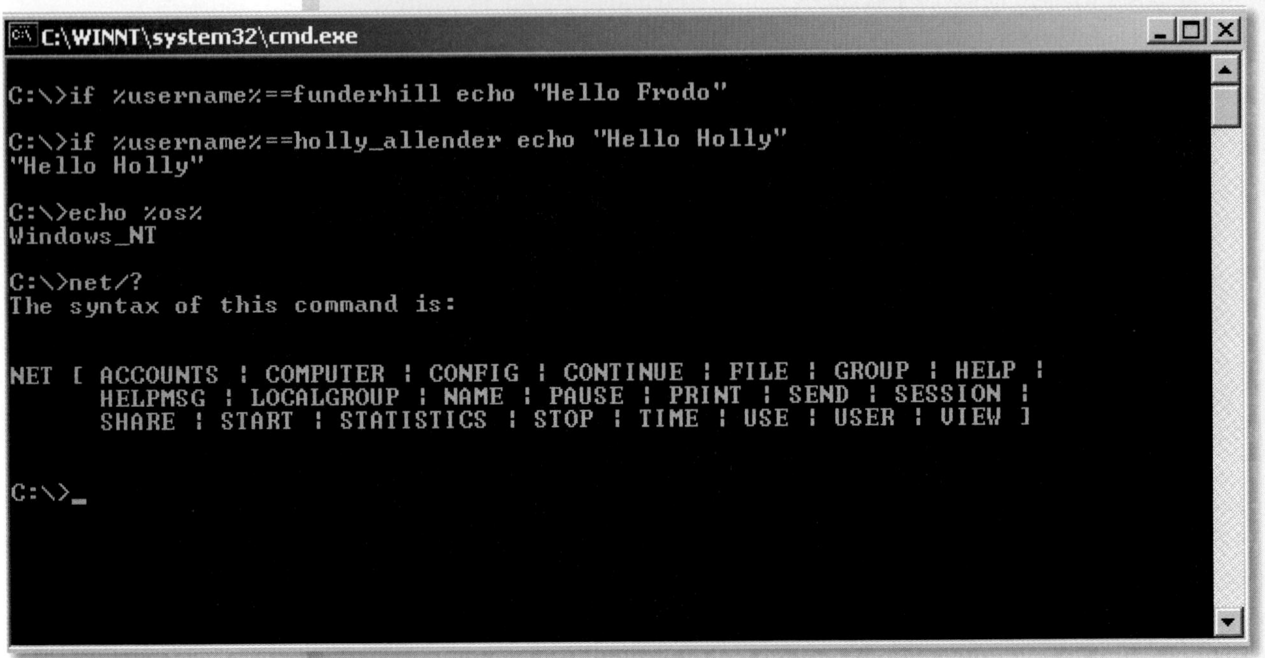

5 Retype the same command, but replace "funderhill" with your own user-name, and "Frodo" with your own first name. This time, you should see "Hello" followed by your own first name, as shown in Figure 13.14.

```
C:\WINNT\system32\cmd.exe                                    _ □ ×

C:\>if %username%==funderhill echo "Hello Frodo"

C:\>if %username%==holly_allender echo "Hello Holly"
"Hello Holly"

C:\>echo %os%
Windows_NT

C:\>net/?
The syntax of this command is:


NET [ ACCOUNTS | COMPUTER | CONFIG | CONTINUE | FILE | GROUP | HELP |
      HELPMSG | LOCALGROUP | NAME | PAUSE | PRINT | SEND | SESSION |
      SHARE | START | STATISTICS | STOP | TIME | USE | USER | VIEW ]


C:\>_
```

6 At the command prompt, enter echo %os%. The name of your operating system should appear at the command prompt. An if statement could determine the correct syntax of commands based on your OS.

7 Type net /? at the command prompt. This family of commands allows you to map and view available network resources. For example, "net name" reveals your computer and username.

8 To map network resources, you can use "net use" followed by the drive letter, followed by the network resource. For example, the command

net use x: \\fs1\datafiles

maps drive X to a shared resource called "datafiles" located on the server named "fs1".

The commands introduced in this section could be stored in a text file with a .bat extension. This file could then be used during the logon process to map network resources to a user's computer.

Obviously, there is a lot to learn about the commands used to create a good logon script. However, most logon scripts are not very complicated. With a little effort, you can learn to be a much more effective administrator by creating your own logon scripts.

To learn more about Windows scripting, go to Help and search for topics scripting. You can investigate other Window scripts to help you manage individual workstations and networks.

LINUX SCRIPTS

Scripts are very important in the Linux operating system. Scripts control how the system works when the computer boots up (starts). After a user logs on, more scripts set important environment variables and system settings, according to the user's preferences.

You need to know a few things about Linux before discussing common script commands. At the heart of the Linux OS is the Linux kernel. The **kernel** is responsible for allocating resources and communicating directly with the hardware. Because the kernel operates at a low level, its "language" is not very accessible to people. For this reason, a shell is used as the interface from a human being to the kernel. The **shell** provides commands that a user can execute. The shell then interprets the user-friendly command into a kernel-friendly command. The kernel then translates the command to something the processor understands (see Figure 13.15).

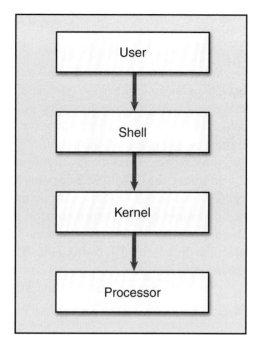

Figure 13.15
Linux can use different shells to provide access to the OS kernel. What purpose does the shell serve?

READ ME!

Jargon A unique feature of Linux is its ability to use different shells to access the kernel. The most commonly used shell in Linux is called BASH, which stands for Bourne-Again SHell.

The "ls" command is the equivalent of the "dir" command in DOS. It displays a list of files in the current directory. An example of its usage is shown next.

```
ls -a
```

The preceding syntax displays a list of all files (hence the –a) in the current directory. Similar to the switches used in the DOS "dir" command, the "ls" command has its own parameters to control the output.

To delete files in DOS, the command "del" is used. In Linux, the command "rm" is used. The example below shows this command and adds a "-i" to prompt the user to confirm the deletion of a file.

```
rm -i
```

To use a drive in Linux, such as a CD-ROM drive, it needs to be mounted. The command to mount a drive is called "mount" and uses the following syntax.

```
mount /mnt/cdrom
```

To eject a CD-ROM, it must be unmounted first. This command is called "umount" and has a similar syntax to the "mount" command.

```
umount /mnt/cdrom
```

READ ME!

Jargon A newbie is someone who is just starting to learn about something new, such as Linux. You will likely encounter the term in many technology-related circles, such as newsgroups or forums.

Commands in Linux often seem long and cryptic, especially to a Linux newbie, or beginner. Fortunately, these commands can be aliased to something easier to remember. An **alias** is basically a shortcut method using a command. Here's an example that would be a great addition to a logon script:

```
alias cdrom="mount /mnt/cdrom"

alias ucdrom="umount /mnt/cdrom"
```

What does all that mean? Let's look at it from the inside out. Inside the quotes on the first line is the command "mount." Mount is used to mount, or make accessible, a drive. In Linux, all mounted drives are listed in the /mnt folder. Before you can access any drive, including a floppy or CD-ROM drive, it must be mounted. The first line creates (aliases) a new command, called "cdrom," that executes the "mount /mnt/cdrom" command.

In Linux, the CD-ROM is locked once it is mounted. This means that you cannot eject the CD-ROM until you unmount it. The second line in the preceding example aliases the command "ucdrom" to unmount the drive. After it is aliased, you simply type "ucdrom" to unmount the CD-ROM so you can eject the disk. After a new disk is inserted, you can type "cdrom" to remount the drive.

Obviously, there is a lot more to learn about scripting in Linux than we have room to cover here. Scripting is an extremely powerful means of controlling and configuring computers and networks using the Linux operating system.

Section 13.3 Assessment

Concept Check

1. **Define** script, batch file, kernel, shell, and alias.

2. **Identify** the command with the correct syntax for mapping a drive in Windows.

   ```
   net use b:\
   \\files\projects

   net use b:
   \\files\projects
   ```

3. **Explain** the benefit of creating and using command aliases.

Critical Thinking

4. **Compare** How does the role of the shell compare to the role of the kernel in an operating system?

5. **Decision Making** How does the "if" statement enhance the capabilities of a script file? Provide two or three examples of how you could use an if statement in a network environment.

6. **Analyze** What advantage is there to Linux's ability to use multiple shells?

Applying Skills

Plan a Windows Script File Using the provided online help, research the **net use** command and write down the code for a simple Windows script file. The script should show the proper syntax for deleting a share on drive g:, then mapping drive g: to a fictional directory called "projects" stored on the server named "Santa."

Section 13.4 Ensuring Network Security

Security planning is an important element in designing a network. It is far easier to implement a secure network from a plan than it is to recover from data loss. This section presents an overview of network security.

PLANNING FOR NETWORK SECURITY

In a networking environment, sensitive data needs to remain private. It is equally important to protect network operations from deliberate or unintentional damage. Maintaining network security requires a balance between facilitating easy access to data by authorized users and restricting access to data by unauthorized users. The network administrator creates this balance.

Four major threats to the security of data on a network are:

◆ Unauthorized access
◆ Electronic tampering
◆ Theft
◆ Intentional or unintentional damage

Despite the seriousness of these threats, data security is not always implemented or supported properly. The administrator's task is to ensure that the network remains reliable and secure, free from those threats.

SECURITY MODELS

Assigning permissions and rights to network resources are at the heart of securing the network. Two security models have evolved for keeping data and hardware resources safe:

◆ Password-protected shares
◆ Access permissions

These models are also called share-level security (for password-protected shares) and user-level security (for access permissions).

Password-Protected Shares

In most peer-to-peer networks, **password-protected shares** are the only type of security available. A password is assigned to each shared resource. Anyone with the correct password gains access to the resource. The types of permissions available may vary, depending on the operating system.

In many OSs, three types of permissions are commonly used (as shown in Table 13.2).

Table 13.2 ⬤──────▶
Most OSs offer three types of permissions. Is the password-protected share system a very secure system? Why or why not?

Common Types of Permissions	
Permission	**Description**
Read Only	Permits users to view, copy, or print documents, but they cannot change the original documents.
Full	Permits users to view, modify, add, and delete files or folders.
Depends On Password	Provides either read or full access depending on the user's password.

The password-protected share system is a simple security method that allows anyone who knows the password to obtain access to that particular resource. It is the less secure of the two models because little can be done to prevent users from sharing passwords.

Access Permissions

Access rights assigned to objects (such as files, folders, and printers) on a per-user basis is known as **access permission.** When a user logs onto the network, a unique identifier is issued according to the username and password combination.

This identifier is checked anytime the user tries to access a resource. The identifier acts just like a security badge. Each resource can look at the "badge" to determine whether to allow the user access.

Access-permission security provides a higher level of control over access rights. Because user-level security is more extensive and can determine various levels of security, it is usually the preferred model in larger organizations.

Resource Security

The administrator determines which users should be allowed to access specific resources. If you have ever been to a concert or professional sports game, you know that the general public is usually admitted through one set of doors. VIPs are given access to the backstage area through another door.

In the same way, an administrator can grant certain types of access to one set of users, whereas other users are granted more (or less) access to the same resource. Table 13.3 on the next page contains common access permissions assigned to shared directories or files.

SHOW ME!

Share-Based Security
View Show Me 13.1 at **networking.glencoe.com** for a presentation on share-based and server-based network security.

Windows Permissions

Permission	Functionality
Full Control	Full control to read, write, modify, and delete files, subfolders, and the folder itself. Can also change permissions for the folder and its files.
Modify	Reads, writes, and modifies files. Cannot delete files or subfolders.
Read and Execute	Reads and copies files in the shared directory. Runs (executes) the files in the directory.
List Folder Contents	Views contents of a folder but cannot open documents or execute files.
Read	Reads files in the directory but cannot execute files. Cannot delete or modify files.
Write	Creates new files in the directory. Cannot delete files.

● Table 13.3
This table outlines the major permissions available on Windows networks. What is the difference between Write and Modify?

SECURITY ENHANCEMENTS

The network administrator can increase the level of security on a network by several means. As discussed in Chapter 10, firewalls and proxies provide one measure of protection. Firewalls monitor traffic flowing into and out of the network, block traffic from certain sites, and can provide information about attempts to gain unauthorized access.

A proxy server manages Internet traffic to and from a local area network (LAN). The proxy server provides access control to the network. Unauthorized attempts to access data are denied by the proxy server. Proxy servers also protect the network using a feature called **Network Address Translation (NAT).** NAT shields the internal IP addresses from the outside world. All outbound network traffic is filtered by the proxy server. The originator's IP address is stripped off and replaced with the proxy's IP address. To anyone on the outside, all the traffic appears to originate from a single IP address.

Another way of monitoring network security is by auditing, or reviewing, security logs generated by a server. Auditing should be a routine element of network security. Audit records list the users that have accessed—or attempted to access—specific resources. Auditing helps administrators identify unauthorized activity. Auditing can track functions such as:

◆ Logon attempts
◆ Connection and disconnection from designated resources
◆ Opening, closing, changing, creating, and deleting files
◆ Creation, modification, or deletion of directories

Encrypting data is another way to secure it. Encryption scrambles the data so that even if someone is able to access it, he or she cannot read it. Using a data-encryption utility, the data are scrambled and cannot be read without the proper code to decrypt the file. E-mail can be encrypted.

Enrichment LAB

Lab 13.2 Preventing the
Spread of Virus Hoaxes
Practice additional hands-on
networking skills on
page 453.

COMPUTER VIRUSES

Computer viruses are written by people with intent to do harm. Viruses are bits of computer programming, or code, that hide in computer programs or on the boot sector of storage devices, such as hard disk drives and floppy disk drives. A virus reproduces itself as often as possible and disrupts the operation of the infected computer or the program. There are two categories of viruses.

◆ **Boot-sector viruses**—When the computer is booted, the virus executes. This is a common method of transmitting viruses from one floppy disk to another. Each time a diseased disk is inserted and accessed, the virus replicates itself onto the new drive.

◆ **File infector viruses**—The virus attaches itself to a file or program and activates any time the file is used. This type of virus spreads most often over the Internet.

The following list describes a few of the more common file infectors:

◆ **Companion virus**—Uses the name of a real program (its companion) but uses a hidden file extension to allow it to be executed in place of the companion file. A common strategy is to make it appear that a file is a picture. When the file is opened, a malicious executable is launched instead.

◆ **Macro virus**—These common viruses are macros written for a specific application, such as Microsoft Outlook. When the user opens a file that contains the virus, the virus attaches itself to the application and then infects any other files accessed by that application.

◆ **Polymorphic virus**—Changes its appearance every time it is replicated. It is more difficult to detect because no two are exactly the same.

◆ **Stealth virus**—Attempts to hide itself from detection. When an antivirus program attempts to find it, the stealth virus intercepts the probe and returns false information indicating it does not exist.

It is critical for network administrators to ensure that all computers on the network are running antivirus software using the latest virus definitions.

Section 13.4 Assessment

Concept Check

1. **Define** password-protected share, access permission, Network Address Translation (NAT), boot-sector virus, and file infector virus.

2. **Identify** the main goals of network security.

3. **List** the four common types of file infector viruses.

Critical Thinking

4. **Cause and Effect** A user complains that he can list the contents of a folder but cannot open any of the files. What is the problem and how can it be corrected?

5. **Generalize** List several security-related functions that can be tracked through network auditing.

Applying Skills

Plan Network Security You have been given the responsibility of planning the network security. Using the information in this chapter and any additional material you can find, write a detailed plan for securing the network.

SECTION 13.1 The Basics of Managing Networks

Key Terms

Simple Network Management Protocol (SNMP), 370
Management Information Base (MIB), 370
username, 372
account policies, 373
permissions, 373

Main Ideas

- SNMP is a protocol used on networks for hardware devices to communicate information about themselves.
- SNMP-compliant devices, called agents, can store information about themselves.
- SNMP management applications can ask agents for information.
- User accounts are established on local computers and on the network.
- Account policies describe acceptable practices.
- Permissions determine what access rights for a given resource are provided to a specific user or group.
- Users can be added to groups to make resource management easier.

SECTION 13.2 Network Monitoring and Maintenance

Key Terms

log file, 377
auditing, 379
replication, 380
uninterruptible power supply (UPS), 381

Main Ideas

- Log files are created by applications and can be used to diagnose problems.
- Auditing can be used to inventory hardware and software on the network.
- Regular system maintenance can help prevent problems.
- Critical data should be backed up on a regular schedule.

SECTION 13.3 Basic Scripting

Key Terms

script, 384
batch file, 385
kernel, 387
shell, 387
alias, 388

Main Ideas

- Scripts are used to automate a series of commands.
- Scripts are often used in network environments to make resources available to users.
- Windows commands can be tested using a command window.
- Linux uses a shell to pass commands to the OS kernel.

SECTION 13.4 Ensuring Network Security

Key Terms

password-protected share, 390
access permission, 390
Network Address Translation (NAT), 391
boot-sector virus, 392
file infector virus, 392

Main Ideas

- Network security must be carefully planned and executed and constantly maintained.
- Password-protected shares, or share-level security, allow access to a resource to anyone with the correct password.
- Access permissions, or user-level security, limit access to a resource to only those users who have been given access to the resource.
- Different types of hardware and software utilities, in conjunction with security policies can be used to help secure the network.
- Computer viruses are malicious programs that infect computer disks and files.

Reviewing Key Terms

1. What does SNMP stand for and what is it used for?
2. What is MIB in a network management concept?
3. Why should servers and essential systems have to use UPS?
4. What responsibility does a kernel have?
5. What are permissions also called?

Understanding Main Ideas

6. **Explain** how a file infector virus infects a computer.
7. **List** two functions of a shell interface.
8. **Explain** why account policies are necessary.
9. **Describe** two types of computer audits.
10. **List** the items that could be mandated by account policies as acceptable user practices.
11. **Describe** how the kernel and shell of an operating system are related.
12. **Relate** *permissions* to *groups* and give examples of each.
13. **Compare** a log file with auditing for the purpose of network monitoring. How are the two related?
14. **Explain** how a proxy server protects its network using a NAT feature.
15. **Describe** why user access is really about managing people.
16. **Find** the relationship between a script file and batch file.
17. **Explain** the difference between password-protected share and access permission for network security.

Critical Thinking

18. **Draw Conclusions** SNMP involves two major components: the SNMP agent and the SNMP management application. How do the two components interact with each other? What role does MIB play in the management process?
19. **Synthesize Information** Redundancy is an effective way to provide fault tolerance so that the network remains running even when some devices are broken down. Summarize two strategies that use redundancy to raise reliability.
20. **Discovering Options** An alias is a shortcut method using a command under Linux environment. It trades off convenience with confusion. Look at the alias example given in your textbook. What are the advantages and disadvantages of creating such an alias?
21. **Examine Scripts** Scripts interact with operating systems and tell them what to do. The language of scripts may vary between operating systems. Look at the script command in the Windows OS and Linux OS for "dir" and discuss the characteristics.
22. **Compare and Contrast** A computer virus is a small code that resides in computer programs or the boot sectors of storage devices; when activated, the code reproduces itself and eventually takes over all the computing resources to disrupt the normal operation. Boot-sector virus and file infector are the two categories of viruses. List their similarities and differences.

e-Review ················

networking.glencoe.com

Study with PowerPoint

To review the main points in this chapter, select **e-Review > PowerPoint Outlines > Chapter 13.**

Online Self Check

Test your knowledge of the material in this chapter by selecting **e-Review > Self Checks > Chapter 13.**

Making Connections

Math – Determine Minimum, Maximum, and Average Values Suppose a network user ignores a company policy to avoid using a word found in a standard dictionary as his password. Suppose also that a hacker uses a dictionary-based utility to break into this user's network account. Assuming a standard English dictionary contains approximately 5,000 words, what is the minimum, the maximum, and the average number of access attempts this utility will make before it discovers the user's password?

STANDARDS AT WORK

Students employ technology in the development of strategies for solving problems in the real world. (NETS-S 6)

Network Monitoring

One common responsibility of network administrators is to monitor the performance of servers and network connections.

Several versions of the Windows operating system include performance monitoring tools, such as Task Manager, that allow users to track CPU, memory, and network utilization. In Windows XP this utility may be accessed on servers and workstations as follows:

a. Press **Ctrl+Alt+Del** to activate the Windows Security dialog, and select **Task Manager.**

b. Click the **Performance** tab to view a graphical representation of your system's CPU utilization and memory usage.

c. Click the **Networking** tab to monitor the utilization of your Local Area Network (LAN) connection.

Perform several common system functions to see how these operations affect your system and/or network performance. For example, copy a large file from one folder to another or from a floppy or CD-ROM disk to your hard drive. On a sheet of paper, note the effects these actions have on overall system performance.

TEAMWORK SKILLS

Creating Linux Aliases

Some network administrators run scripts and perform other functions within a Windows command (DOS) window as well as a Linux command prompt. In order to facilitate this constant switching, some IT personnel will utilize the Linux alias capabilities to create new commands that match their DOS counterparts. For instance, a Linux alias called **dir** can be mapped to the **ls** command to perform a directory listing as it does in a DOS environment.

a. With your teacher's permission, form small groups. This task is best accomplished if groups include at least one member who is familiar with DOS commands and at least one member who has knowledge of UNIX-style commands.

b. Create a list of Linux aliases that could be created to make a Linux system respond to DOS-like commands.

c. Include in your list commands to copy, move, rename, and delete files, and some directory (folder) commands as well.

CHALLENGE YOURSELF

Computing Password Security

Put yourself in a network administrator's position of maintaining maximum password security. To implement the policy, each network user is assigned a password. Suppose that a company executive has asked you to justify a request that the minimum length of these random passwords should be increased from four characters to eight. Using mathematical principles, provide a brief explanation to support your request. If possible, use actual numbers to demonstrate how much additional security this change will provide from random hacker attacks.

(Hint: Each character of the password has 62 possibilities—26 upper case letters + 26 lower case letters + 10 digits. The number of possible passwords that are two characters long is 62 * 62 or 3844. Use this concept to demonstrate the difference in possible passwords that are four characters long versus eight characters long.)

YOU TRY IT

Networking Lab

1. Creating a Windows XP ASR Disk

Several versions of the Windows operating system give users the ability to create a special floppy disk that may be used to recover from a major system failure. In Windows XP, this is called an Automated System Recovery (ASR) disk. You can create the ASR disk with the Windows backup utility as described below. With your teacher's permission, complete following steps:

Ⓐ Open the backup utility from the Windows main menu system by clicking **Start,** select **Programs,** select **Accessories,** choose **System Tools,** and click on **Backup.**

Ⓑ If the backup utility starts in "wizard mode," click the "Advanced Mode."

Ⓒ Click the button labeled **Automated System Recovery Wizard** to initiate the step-by-step wizard that will guide you through the rest of the process.

Ⓓ Insert a floppy disk into your computer's A: drive, or use the CD-RW drive, and follow the instructions that appear on your screen as you proceed through the wizard.

After you have created your Windows ASR disk, it can be used to boot your computer if the primary OS has been damaged and you are unable to reboot. Test the disk if a test computer is available in your networking lab.

2. Setting Permissions for Windows Shares

There are times when the owner of a shared folder may not want the folder to be visible to everyone on the network. Also, there may be times when the owner wants to grant additional permissions to a few specific network users. In Windows XP, the permissions of a shared folder may be set as follows:

Ⓐ Follow the instructions of the Challenge Yourself activity in Chapter 12 to create a shared folder.

Ⓑ Click **Permissions** to open the Permissions dialog as shown here.

Ⓒ To grant access rights to specific users, click **Remove** to remove the "Everyone" group from your Share Permissions list. Then click **Add** to select individual users whom you want to add to your permission list.

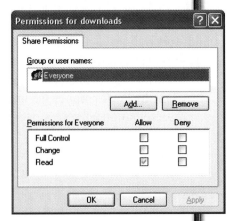

Ⓓ To specify the access rights that the specified users will have (read, change, full control), click the appropriate checkboxes under the "Allow" column of the permissions list.

Ⓔ Click the **OK** button to accept the current permissions, close the Permissions dialog box, and return to the Properties dialog.

You should note that each selected user will have the same set of access permissions granted to them. Display your Permission dialog box for your teacher to show your changes.

Networking Projects

1. Protect a Computer with a Firewall

There are various technologies available that can help protect computer systems from viruses. One common and effective technology is the firewall. The basic purpose of a firewall is to monitor incoming Internet traffic and to prevent any unauthorized access to the receiving server or workstation. Windows XP includes a personal firewall that has proven to be effective against many potentially harmful viruses. This firewall may be activated using the following steps:

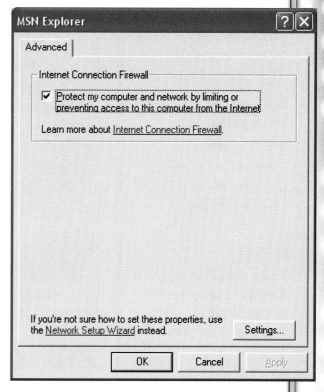

Ⓐ Open the **Control Panel.**

Ⓑ Double-click **Network Connections.**

Ⓒ Right click the active connection manager (such as Local Area Network) and select **Properties** from the pop-up menu. Select **Advanced** to open the dialog box.

Ⓓ Click the checkbox under the heading Internet Connection Firewall to activate the Windows XP personal firewall.

Ⓔ Click the **OK** button to dismiss the dialog.

The Windows XP firewall can help protect computers from many types of Internet malware. However, an administrator would never trust this by itself. This firewall setting should be used in conjunction with an anti-virus product for additional virus detection and prevention capabilities.

2. Create an E-Mail Attachment Policy

Businesses are especially vulnerable to viruses because e-mail attachments can contain viruses. You are the network administrator of a business. It is your responsibility to inform the employees how to deal with e-mail attachments and what the IT department will do.

Compose a memo to your company's employees entitled "E-mail Attachments" and include the following heads in your memo:

◆ Subject
◆ E-mail Attachments and Viruses
◆ How to Avoid Spreading Viruses
◆ How Can You Get Unsolicited E-mail

Troubleshooting Networks

YOU WILL LEARN TO...

WHY IT MATTERS......................................

If you are feeling sick, you might go to the doctor, who then asks you questions about your health. You describe the symptoms: sore throat, headache, and stuffy nose. After drawing upon years of study and experience, the doctor diagnoses the probable cause and prescribes a treatment. Network administrators use a similar, methodical approach to "cure" network problems.

Quick Write Activity

Think about the last time you went to a doctor's office (even if it was just a checkup visit). Write down any questions the doctor asked you. Describe how the role of the doctor is similar to the role of a network troubleshooter.

WHAT YOU WILL DO..

READ TO SUCCEED

How Can You Improve?

What do you do after a test? If you did well, then your study strategies were successful. But if you did poorly, do you think about how to improve for the next test? Think about the process you use to learn material, and discuss study techniques with classmates. But remember that what works for one person might not work for you. Pay attention to your study methods and find out how you learn best.

Guide to Reading

Main Ideas

Troubleshooting requires a planned, methodical approach. Follow the plan and only troubleshoot one thing at a time.

Key Terms

README
system lockup
Event Viewer

Reading Strategy

List each of the five troubleshooting steps and two actions you might take at each step. Create a chart similar to the one below (also available online).

Step	Action 1	Action 2
1. Define the problem	Ask questions to find out more about the problem	Try to reproduce the problem

This section is designed to give you the tools you need to become a skilled network problem solver. If you approach a problem with a plan of action, the cause and its resolution are easier to find. Practicing a structured approach to identifying the problem is the basic element of troubleshooting.

TROUBLESHOOTING STEPS

Troubleshooting is perhaps the most difficult task that network professionals face. Computers never seem to fail at a convenient time. Failures occur in the middle of a project or when there are deadlines, and pressures to fix the problem immediately are intense.

After a problem has been diagnosed, you need to locate resources and follow procedures to correct the problem. But before that diagnosis occurs, it is essential to isolate the true cause of the problem from unrelated factors. As a troubleshooter, you need to learn to quickly and confidently eliminate as many alternative causes as possible. This allows you to focus on the things that might be the cause of the problem. To do this, you must take a systematic approach, as shown in Table 14.1.

Activity 14.1 Troubleshooting Models The five-step model presented here is one example of a troubleshooting methodology. Another commonly referenced model is the Cisco Internetwork Troubleshooting model. For an overview of this model visit networking.glencoe.com.

Table 14.1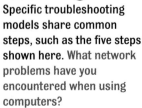
Specific troubleshooting models share common steps, such as the five steps shown here. What network problems have you encountered when using computers?

Troubleshooting Steps

Step	Description
1	Define the problem
2	Isolate the cause
3	Plan the repair
4	Confirm the results
5	Document the outcome

networking.glencoe.com

Step 1: Defining the Problem

The first phase is the most critical, yet most often ignored. Without a complete understanding of the entire problem, you can spend a great deal of time working on the symptoms, without getting to the cause. The only tools required for this phase are a pad of paper, a pen (or pencil), and good listening skills.

Listening to the user is your best source of information. The user's experiences with the problem can give you a head start on narrowing down the possible causes. To help identify the problem, it often helps to ask a series of questions. You might want to create a form with questions to help organize your notes. Table 14.2 lists some general questions to ask the user.

READ ME!

Tech Tip Many networking problems are resolved using the OSI troubleshooting model. This strategy works from "the bottom up," looking for causes first on Layer 1 (the Physical Layer) of the OSI model, then moving to Layer 2 (the Data Link Layer), and so on. As you move up through the layers, the causes and solutions tend to get more difficult.

Common Troubleshooting Questions

Types of Questions	Example of Questions to Ask
Initial questions	◆ What is the problem? ◆ When did you first notice the problem or error? ◆ How long has it been a problem?
Computer's physical aspects	◆ Has the computer recently been moved? ◆ Have there been any recent software or hardware changes? ◆ Has anything happened to the workstation? Was it dropped or was something dropped on it? ◆ Describe any changes in the computer (such as noises, screen changes, disk activity lights).
Details of the problem	◆ When exactly does the problem or error occur? During the startup process? After lunch? Only on Monday mornings? After sending an e-mail message? ◆ What does the problem or error look like?
Reproducing the problem	◆ Can you reproduce the problem or error? ◆ If so, how do you reproduce the problem?

Table 14.2

Using a prepared list of questions can save you time when troubleshooting many common problems. What other relevant questions could you add to this list?

ACTIVITY 14A Creating a Troubleshooting Form

YOU TRY IT

Help desk personnel often use a troubleshooting form to ask a series of questions. The response to each question (usually "Yes" or "No") helps the technician understand the problem. Use information in this chapter or other resources to perform the following:

1 Create a troubleshooting form using a word processing application.

- Write down as many questions as you can think of that could help you identify the cause of a typical computer problem.
- Review your list of questions. If possible, use yes/no questions.

2 After you create your form, work with another student.

- Each student should think of a common computer problem.
- Use your troubleshooting form to identify your partner's problem.

③ Review your troubleshooting session. Were you able to identify the problem? Did you think of other questions as you went?

④ Add, refine, or remove questions as needed.

Creating a troubleshooting form is a good way to help you think through potential problems. Remember that users typically do not have a very technical background, and may have a hard time explaining problems.

Table 14.3 ●

Narrowing the cause of the problem can be very difficult. How do you learn to solve many different types of problems quickly?

Even users with little or no technical background can be helpful as you collect data. Ask users what the network is or is not doing that makes them think it is not functioning correctly. As you continue to ask questions, you can begin to narrow your focus. Table 14.3 provides many example questions and some likely conclusions you can draw from each.

Narrowing Your Focus

Question	Possible Conclusion
Are all users affected or only one?	If only one user has a problem, the user's workstation is probably the cause.
Are the symptoms constant or intermittent?	Intermittent symptoms are a sign of failing hardware.
Did the problem exist before an OS upgrade?	Any change in OS software can cause new problems.
Does the problem appear with all applications or with only one?	If only one application causes problems, focus on the application.
Is this problem similar to a previous problem?	If a similar problem occurred in the past, there might be a documented solution.
Is there new equipment on the network?	Check to verify that new network equipment has been correctly configured.
Was a new application installed before the problem occurred?	Installation and training issues can cause application problems.
Which manufacturers' products are involved?	Some vendors offer telephone, online, or onsite support.
Is there a history of incompatibility among certain vendors and components, such as cards, hubs, disk drives, software, or network operating software?	There might be a documented solution on the vendor's Web site.

Step 2: Isolating the Cause

The next step is to isolate the problem's cause. Eliminate the most obvious causes first. For example, if your computer cannot communicate with the network, check that the network cable is plugged in. Work gradually toward the more complex causes. Your purpose is to narrow your search to one or two general categories. These categories could include the physical aspect of the device, operating system, drivers, or application software.

See the Problem Observe the failure yourself. If possible, have someone demonstrate the failure to you. If it is an operator-induced problem, it is important to observe how it is created, as well as the results.

Re-create the Problem The most difficult problems to isolate are those that are hard to re-create. The only method to resolve these is to re-create the set of circumstances that causes the failure. Sometimes, eliminating causes that are not the problem is the best you can do. This process takes time and patience. Users should be trained to keep detailed records of what is being done before and when the failure occurs. The error message can be a signal to the user to refrain from doing anything with the computer when the problem recurs, except to call you. That way, the "evidence" is not disturbed (see Figure 14.1).

Revisit Baseline and Tests The information you collect provides the foundation for isolating the problem. However, you should also refer to documented baseline information to compare with current network behavior. Rerun tests under the same set of conditions when you created the baseline and compare the two results. Any changes between the two can indicate the source of the problem.

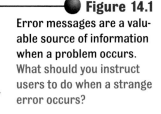
Figure 14.1
Error messages are a valuable source of information when a problem occurs. What should you instruct users to do when a strange error occurs?

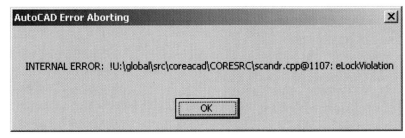

Step 3: Planning the Repair

After you have narrowed your search down to a few categories, the final process of elimination begins. Create a planned approach to isolating the problem based on your knowledge at this point. Start by trying out the most obvious or easiest solution, and continue toward the more difficult and complex. It is important to record each step of the process. Document every action and its results.

After you have created your plan, it is important to follow it through as designed. Jumping ahead and randomly trying things out of order can often lead to problems. If the first plan is not successful (always a possibility), create a new plan based on what you discovered with the previous plan. Be sure to refer to, reexamine, and reassess any assumptions you might have made in the previous plan. After you have located the problem, either repair the defect or replace the defective component.

Step 4: Confirming the Results

No repair is complete without testing to make certain that the problem no longer exists. Ask the user to test the solution and confirm whether it works. You should also make sure that the fix does not generate new problems. Be sure to check that what you have done does not have a negative impact on any other aspect of the network or the user's computer.

Step 5: Documenting the Outcome

Finally, document the problem and the repair. Recording what you have learned provides you with invaluable information. There is no substitute for experience in troubleshooting. Each new problem presents you with an opportunity to expand that experience. Keeping a copy of the repair procedure in

Enrichment **LAB**

Lab 14.1 Human Factors in a Network Practice additional hands-on networking skills on page 454.

your technical library can be useful when the problem (or one like it) occurs again. Documenting the troubleshooting process is one way to build, retain, and share experience.

TYPES OF PROBLEMS

In a network, different types of hardware, software, and even OSs are expected to work together in harmony. Although industry standards go a long way to ensure interoperability, problems occur for many reasons.

Anticipating Problems

No system as complex as a network can run completely trouble-free. In networking, you learn to expect problems. In fact, the best networking personnel are the ones who anticipate potential problems and work to solve them before they reach a critical stage.

Regularly monitoring the network and learning to read important log files are two critical aspects of anticipating problems. Studying to learn more about networking and the various hardware and software in use on your network is important. Experience is also an important teacher.

Configuration Problems

Configuration problems can prevent a computer from starting normally, prevent devices from functioning, or take the entire network down. These problems can occur when devices are not installed correctly (such as a NIC with a jumper set incorrectly) or when configuration settings are incorrect (same computer name or IP address assigned to multiple computers).

When configuring a device, always print, read, and follow the configuration instructions provided. Check the configuration settings for other devices before you begin. For example, if you have to manually assign an IP address for a new employee, you need to know which IP addresses are available on your network.

Figure 14.2 ●
README files tell you the latest information about software or hardware. Where should you look for other information before installation?

Software Problems

Software problems can result from many different causes. There may be a bug in the software. The software may not be compatible with hardware installed in the computer. Or, it may have a conflict caused by the presence of another application.

Prior to installing any software, verify that the hardware meets the recommended configuration. If a **README** file is available (see Figure 14.2), read it before proceeding. The README file included contains last-minute information that may warn you of potential problems. It may also contain important installation and configuration information. Check the manufacturer's Web site for additional information or updates.

Hardware Malfunctions

Hardware can malfunction for a number of different reasons. The primary culprit is overheating. Overheating can result in a variety of symptoms, including spontaneous rebooting and **system lockups.** Lockups make the system unresponsive to any sort of user interaction, including mouse or keyboard activity. Users can often hear a failing fan because it makes a great deal of noise. It should be replaced immediately to ensure adequate cooling to sensitive components such as the CPU. Dust in a manufacturing or construction environment is a common problem. Computers in these types of environments should frequently be cleaned with a can of compressed air.

Another common problem is overloading the computer's internal power supply. Today's processors require a lot of power, and so do the many devices that are connected to the power supply. Many high-end computer configurations now have a CD or DVD burner, a second CD or DVD reader, anywhere from one to four hard drives, as well as a video card that may require additional power directly from the power supply. An underpowered supply can lead to system instability and applications crashing.

RAM can also develop physical problems and report fatal exception errors. These problems can be diagnosed using either special hardware or a software utility that tests the RAM. If errors are detected, the faulty RAM should be replaced right away.

READ ME!

Tech Tip Cables can be misconnected or can be faulty. It is a good idea to keep a supply of spare cables so you can quickly replace or test suspect cables.

Network Malfunctions

Network malfunctions can be difficult to track down. Network technicians use a systematic approach and always start with the most obvious solutions first. For example, if a user complains that she cannot log on to the network, they might check to see if other users are having the same problem. This can help determine if the problem is with the computer or with the network.

If a server experiences problems and needs to be restarted, they monitor the reboot process carefully. They watch for any problems during the reboot. Also, they check the boot log file for any indication of problems. Many times, a failed device on the server prevents the system from performing correctly. Log files are a very important source of event information. Windows **Event Viewer** is an administrative utility you can use to view important log files generated by the Windows OS.

ACTIVITY 14B Viewing Log Files with Event Viewer

YOU TRY IT

The Event Viewer is part of Windows 2000, XP, and Server editions. With this utility, you can view system errors, application errors, and security audit records. Similar Linux utilities also exist.

1 Open the **Control Panel.**

2 Click the link to **Switch to Classic View** (Windows XP only), if necessary.

3 Double-click **Administrative Tools.**

4 Double-click **Event Viewer.**

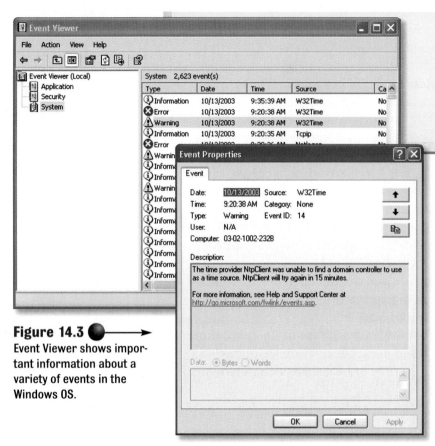

Figure 14.3
Event Viewer shows important information about a variety of events in the Windows OS.

❺ Click **System.** A list of system events appears in the right pane.

❻ Double-click an event to view information about the event (see Figure 14.3).

Log files can be created by many applications and hardware devices and are found in all network operating systems, including NetWare and Linux. Many times, events are logged that eventually lead to more critical failures. Some log files, such as Novell's NSure Audit, even report the seriousness of an event. Check these logs and act on the information to prevent or resolve serious problems.

Section 14.1 Assessment

Concept Check

1. **Define** README, system lockup, and Event Viewer.

2. **List** the five steps of troubleshooting presented in this section. Describe what you should do during each step.

3. **Describe** what an Event Viewer reports.

4. **Explain** the purpose of a README file. Give two examples of when a README file would be useful.

Critical Thinking

5. **Anticipate Problems** You are about to apply an update to a critical system server. What is the single most essential thing you should do before proceeding with the update?

6. **Draw Conclusions** You suspect that your network security has been breached. Where could you look for information that might help you confirm your suspicion?

Applying Skills

Diagnose a Problem
A user complains that applications are opening more slowly than usual, and opening and saving files stored on the computer are also taking longer. Create a list of possible causes and solutions using the five troubleshooting steps and resources such as the Internet, Windows Troubleshooter, reference manuals, and so on.

Ethics & Technology

COMPUTERS AND THE ENVIRONMENT

Think of how much paper you use every day when printing information from your computer. Multiply that figure by hundreds of millions of users to imagine the amount of waste paper being added to our environment.

Recycling is one solution for fighting pollution caused by discarded computers and electrical equipment.

Going Paperless

When computers first became popular, they were supposed to produce a "paperless society." Documents would be written, sent, and read by electronic means. Unfortunately, computers have not reduced paper use at all. In fact, computer printing is so easy and inexpensive that many people are creating more documents than ever.

The trillions of hard copies printed every year lead to deforestation, pollution from paper manufacturing, lots of trash, and wasted electricity. So think before you print.

Poisonous PCs

Millions of out-of-date PCs are thrown out every year. These computers contain many agents that can be harmful to the environment. A cathode-ray tube (CRT) monitor, for example, contains several pounds of lead, which is a known poison.

Only a small fraction of these systems are properly recycled in the United States because the process is expensive and yields a relatively small amount of reusable components or materials.

Recycling Programs

Companies such as Dell and Hewlett-Packard have started their own recycling programs. Some agencies donate their older computers to organizations that are happy to take them, such as schools and community centers. In addition, manufacturers are beginning to design computers with features and material that are less likely to cause waste or environmental damage. States such as California are putting pressure on computer manufacturers to be responsible for safe recycling and disposal of electronics.

Tech Focus

1. How do computers affect the environment? Create a chart that lists computer-related environmental issues, their importance, and possible solutions.

2. Analyze how the widespread use of technology has made recycling an important social issue.

Section 14.2 Finding and Repairing Problems

Guide to Reading

Main Ideas

Software tools can help identify problems. Faulty hardware may need to be replaced. Software problems can sometimes be resolved with a patch or upgrade.

Key Terms

Windows
    Troubleshooter
add-in card
jumper
frequently asked
    questions (FAQ)

Reading Strategy

Create a diagram similar to the one below (also available online) listing at least three of the common problems discussed in this section. For each problem, list a possible cause and a way to resolve the problem.

Problem	Possible Cause	Resolution
Computer won't boot after adding a new video card.	Card improperly seated in slot.	Press card firmly into slot, then reboot.

Isolating the precise cause of the problem is probably the most difficult task in troubleshooting. Users often provide vague answers ("I was doing something and all of a sudden the computer stopped working!") or lack the technical background to describe the problem adequately. Undocumented changes to a workstation, server, or network component can be difficult to identify. For example, a new software patch can be transparent and at the same time cause new problems. In all cases, it is important to have a troubleshooting plan in place, and follow that plan.

FINDING THE PROBLEM

In addition to going through the five troubleshooting steps, some OSs have troubleshooting guides to help resolve most common problems. By studying these guides and how they work, you can learn many valuable lessons for creating your own problem-solving plan.

The **Windows Troubleshooters** for Windows XP are a part of the Help and Support Center. This troubleshooter provides an excellent example of the type of methodology required to identify and resolve technical problems. The troubleshooters are broken down into categories. Each category then asks a series of questions that help identify the cause of the problem and offer suggestions for resolving the problem. If a given solution does not work, the troubleshooter moves on to something else. For other operating systems, consult the help documentation, or look on the Internet for help resolving problems you encounter.

YOU TRY IT

ACTIVITY 14C Using the Windows Troubleshooters

Suppose a user called in with a printing problem. Upon investigation, you learn that the user is using an old MS-DOS-based application. You need to resolve the problem. Using Windows XP Help and Support Center, you can learn more clues about the problem.

❶ Click **Start,** and then click **Help and Support.**

❷ Click the **Fixing a problem** link.

networking.glencoe.com

❸ Click the **Printing problems** link.

❹ Click the **Printing Troubleshooter** link (see Figure 14.4).

❺ Choose "**I cannot print from an MS-DOS-based program...**" and click **Next.**

❻ Read the instructions, select "**No, I still cannot print,**" and click **Next.**

❼ Click the link "**To use the Net.exe command,**" which provides instructions for redirecting print jobs to a network printer.

❽ Read the instructions, select "**Yes, I can print now,**" and then click **Next.**

These troubleshooters, whether Windows-based or from other OSs, cannot resolve every problem you encounter. However, they do a good job of identifying common problems. They also provide an excellent model for developing your own troubleshooting methodology.

● **Figure 14.4**
Windows Troubleshooters provide a great example of troubleshooting methodology.

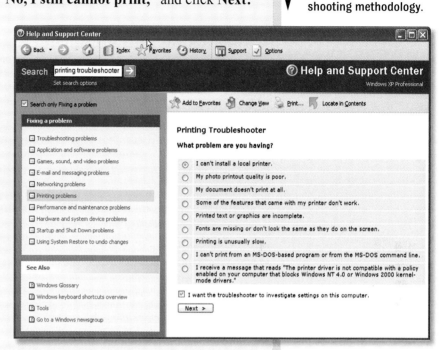

First Response Assistance

First response plans are implemented in many elements of society, including emergency services, such as the paramedic and police services. These plans identify emergency situations, the personnel, and steps that need to be taken immediately to get a situation under control (see Figure 14.5).

In a networking environment, a first response plan does many of the same things. It outlines what steps users should take immediately following a problem. It also outlines how the IT support team begins to resolve the problem. For example, a user cannot connect to the network. The user calls the IT support team. Following a planned procedure, the support person asks a series of questions to identify the cause of the problem. Satisfied that the problem was not a user problem, the error is logged and documented as a potential network problem. More users call, complaining that "the network is down."

At this point, the problem status is bumped up to a more critical level because the problem appears to be affecting more people. Additional support personnel are called in to assist. Each

● **Figure 14.5**
First response plans are valuable to teams who must respond quickly in an emergency, including IT teams. What are some important elements that should be included in a network first response plan?

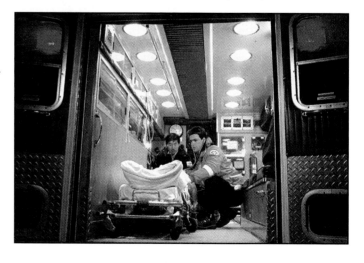

team member follows a preplanned set of instructions to identify the source of the problem. In a critical situation, systems may have to be shut down to prevent the problem from escalating further. For example, there might be a security breach caused by a hacker or virus. However, the problem may simply be traced to a faulty switch that causes users on that segment to lose their connection to the network. After the switch is reset or replaced, the users can go back to work.

Diagnosing and Repairing Hardware Components

Hardware components can have different types of problems. In many cases, a perceived "failure" in the device can be traced to something simple. Thus, most troubleshooting plans always start by checking the most simple, obvious causes of problems. It is surprising how many problems are resolved by plugging in a cable that was disconnected.

Monitors Monitor problems are often fairly serious and must be repaired by certified technicians. However, you can check that the power cable is plugged in, that the cable connected to the video card is securely attached, and that the power is turned on. Before sending the monitor out for repair or replacement, try connecting the monitor to another computer. Sometimes, the problem lies with the video card or the computer, rather than the monitor.

Add-In Cards A common problem with **add-in cards,** such as a video or sound card, is improper seating in the motherboard slots. For example, a video card that is not correctly seated prevents the computer from booting. Add-in cards can suffer from dust or heat buildup. Some top-of-the-line graphics cards actually have more transistors in their Graphic Processing Units (GPUs) than the computer's CPU, which means they generate a lot of heat. Overheating caused by a cooling fan failure can physically damage critical components (see Figure 14.6). Once damaged, these components usually must be replaced.

Figure 14.6 Overheating due to fan failure is one of the most common causes of hardware malfunction. What should be done if a computer fan begins to fail?

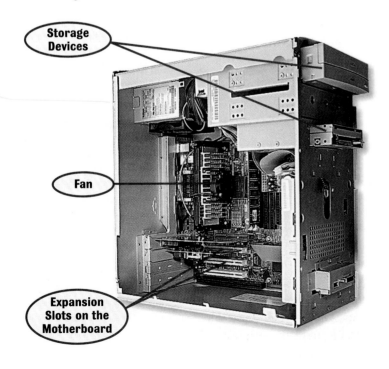

Storage Devices

Fan

Expansion Slots on the Motherboard

Occasionally, the slot that an add-in card or memory chip is plugged into must be an exact slot. Modems seem to be the pickiest about which slot they are plugged into. If your computer does not recognize a new modem, turn off the computer and move the modem to another slot. Turn the computer back on and see if it recognizes the modem.

Storage Devices Hard drives and other storage devices, such as CD or DVD drives, may be set up incorrectly. ATA devices (most home or workstation hard drive and CD/DVD drives are this type) support a maximum of two devices per cable. SCSI devices (most server hard drives are this type) can support many devices attached to one controller. However, each device must be assigned a unique ID number. In addition, a SCSI "chain" of devices must have a terminator at the end of the chain.

External Devices External devices, such as USB devices, sometimes fail to be detected by the OS. In many cases, simply unplugging the device and plugging it back into another USB port causes the OS to recognize the device.

Always eliminate the most obvious causes first. Document every step you take and what the results were. This can help if you have to retrace your steps. More importantly, if you ever have the same problem again, you will not have to spend as much time finding the solution.

REPAIRING THE PROBLEM

In many cases, after the real problem is identified, repairing the problem is relatively straightforward. Finding the true source of the problem is easier said than done. After the problem is identified, you can begin to work on repairing it. Hardware that is malfunctioning can be replaced, software can be patched, or corrupt files can be restored using backup files.

Data Loss

If there were a place where the Ten Rules of Computer Networking were set in stone, rule number one would surely be: You Will Back Up Your Data. Recovering from data loss is never a fun prospect. It is even less fun when data has not been backed up.

Here are some common scenarios that lead to data loss:

◆ A user deletes a file accidentally.
◆ Another user overwrites a file unknowingly.
◆ A hard drive is damaged or crashes.
◆ A laptop is stolen.

In all of these cases, the best solution is to have a backup. With a backup, files can be restored, and entire systems can be rebuilt. Although rebuilding a system can be complicated, the process is much less daunting when a backup is available (see Figure 14.7).

A company needs to prepare for a flood, fire, or other natural disaster. Its hard drives containing valuable data could be physically damaged during a disaster. In such cases, data recovery specialists may be able to recover data from the drive. Most of these companies can, for a small fee, assess the damage to the drive and let you know the probability of recovery. The data recovery itself can be quite costly, but may be your only option when data must be restored.

● **Figure 14.7**
A good backup strategy is absolutely essential to any network. Identify several reasons why a backup strategy needs to be implemented.

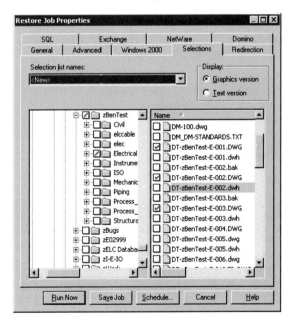

Hardware and Media

Physically damaged computer components are often expensive and difficult to repair. In many cases, such as damaged RAM, the failed component needs to be replaced.

Hardware that is not functioning correctly is not always due to physical damage. Driver issues can prevent the OS from working with the device. Also, configuration settings, such as an improperly set jumper on an add-in card, may prevent the device from working correctly. A **jumper** is a small device used to connect adjacent wire pins on a circuit board. Essentially, jumpers act as on/off switches and are used to alter the configuration of the circuit board or device.

Damage to media, such as CD-ROM or floppy disks, often results in data loss. In some cases where the data are extremely valuable, data recovery specialists might be employed. However, this is an expensive proposition, and data may not be recoverable depending on the extent and type of damage to the media. No matter what, valuable data should be backed up.

Software

Repairing a software problem is often a means of checking to make certain you have the most up-to-date version of the software. For most Windows-based programs, you can click the Help menu, then About. A screen similar to Figure 14.8 appears with the version number of the application.

Next, you can check the software developer's Web site for any patches or updates to the application. It is important to check for a **frequently asked questions (FAQ)** document or a README file that may indicate whether your problem has been addressed. A FAQ document lists frequently asked questions and responses to those questions. You can also try contacting the company's technical support team to report the problem.

Problems with software are often caused by version conflicts with other applications. Sometimes, an application installation installs older files that are incompatible with the files required by a previously installed application. In these situations, you may have to uninstall programs, and reinstall them in a different order to ensure that the most recent version of the shared files is installed last.

Occasionally, software applications do not work with hardware installed in the computer. Checking for driver or software updates is usually the best step.

Figure 14.8
Updating software to the most current version is usually the best option for repairing software problems. What resources are available for resolving problems with a specific software application?

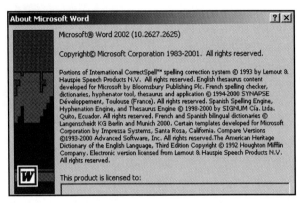

Section 14.2 Assessment

Concept Check

1. **Define** Windows Troubleshooter, add-in card, jumper, and frequently asked questions (FAQ).

2. **Explain** what a first response plan is and why it is useful in a network environment.

3. **Explain** why replacing failing cooling fans is important. How can you tell if a fan is failing?

Critical Thinking

4. **Diagnose a Hardware Problem** You just added a new ATA hard drive on the same cable as the original hard drive. Now the computer is having problems booting. What could be the cause and how would you fix it?

5. **Draw Conclusions** A user calls and says that she cannot print to a network printer. Create a list of several potential problems she might be having.

Applying Skills

Create an Emergency Response Plan With your teacher's permission, work in small groups to make a list of five common computer- or network-related problems. Rank each problem in terms of severity. Next, create a plan for dealing with each problem. Identify the steps you or another person should take to resolve each problem.

EMERGING TECHNOLOGY

THE NEED FOR NEW TECHNOLOGY

You are probably familiar with the saying, "Which came first, the chicken or the egg?" Similarly, one might ask, "Which comes first, the demand for new technology or the technology itself?"

Creating a Demand

When researchers develop a new product, is it because consumers want it? Or, do we only want the newest technology when we see the latest gadgets from manufacturers?

Technology research has reduced the size of computers from room-size to palm-size.

Consider the development of cell phones. Originally, cell phones freed users from land lines, allowing people to make calls from anywhere. But cell phone manufacturers had to come up with new features to compete in the market. Soon, consumers wanted to have cell phones with these features. Today's cell phones offer text messaging, Internet connectivity, built-in voice recorders, and digital cameras.

What to Expect

In the coming years, we might expect these developments:

◆ **The Internet** will evolve as greater, possibly unlimited, bandwidth becomes available. It will provide rapid access to huge amounts of information, making the Internet an even more valuable means of communication and research.
◆ **Medicine** will be practiced online. In the future, surgeons will be able to use virtual reality systems and cameras to control surgical robots and perform surgeries remotely.
◆ **Nanotechnology** will lead to the development of molecule-size supercomputers. Eventually, doctors may be able to treat patients by injecting tiny robots, which will single out and destroy diseased cells. It may also result in paper-thin monitors that roll up and fit in your pocket, and wearable computers built into clothing.

The Technology Life Cycle

There is always a need for new technological developments. Research is motivated by problems with old technologies, competition in the marketplace, and consumer demands. This has created a technology "life cycle" that may never end.

Tech Focus

1. Research the development and evolution of a specific network-related product. How and why has the product changed over time? What effects have these changes had on users?

2. What do you think new technologies will be like in five, ten, or twenty years? Will the technologies lead to positive or negative changes?

Troubleshooting network problems is often accomplished with the help of hardware and software. To troubleshoot effectively, you need to know how these tools can be used to solve network problems.

HARDWARE TOOLS

Hardware tools were once very expensive and difficult devices to use. They are now less expensive and easier to operate. They are helpful to identify performance trends and problems. The following sections describe the most common of these tools.

Figure 14.9
A volt-ohmmeter can be used to verify a cable's ability to carry data. What sorts of problems can be identified with a volt-ohmmeter?

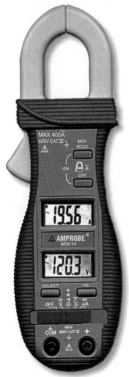

Digital Volt-Ohmmeters

The **digital volt-ohmmeter** (or volt-ohm meter) is the primary, all-purpose electronic measuring tool (see Figure 14.9). It is considered standard equipment for any computer or electronic technician and can reveal far more than just the amount of voltage passing through resistance. Volt-ohmmeters can determine if:

◆ the cable is continuous (has no breaks).
◆ the cable can carry network traffic.
◆ two parts of the same cable are exposed and touching (thereby causing shorts).
◆ an exposed part of the cable is touching another conductor, such as a metal surface.

One of the network administrator's most important functions is to ensure that computer equipment receives a steady supply of power. Electronic equipment is extremely sensitive to the amount of electricity it receives. Too little, and computers may reboot or shut down. Too much, such as when a sudden spike of electricity comes through the line, and equipment can be permanently damaged. To protect against spikes, computers and other network equipment should be plugged into a surge protector. If you experience frequent dips in power, you should connect your equipment to an uninterruptible power supply (UPS). A UPS is essentially a large, rechargeable battery that can allow equipment to continue operating for a short period of time if the electricity goes out.

READ ME!

Tech Tip With any new location or new construction, it is important to check the outlet voltages before connecting any electronic equipment to verify that they are within an acceptable range.

Time-Domain Reflectometers (TDRs)

A **time-domain reflectometer (TDR),** as shown in Figure 14.10, sends sonarlike pulses along cables to locate breaks, shorts, or imperfections. Network performance suffers when the cable is not intact. If the TDR locates a problem, the problem is analyzed and the results are displayed. A TDR can locate a break within a few feet of the actual separation in the cable. TDRs are used frequently during the installation of a new network.

Using a TDR requires special training, and not every maintenance department has this equipment. However, administrators need to know what the capabilities of TDRs are in case the network is experiencing media failure and it is necessary to locate a break.

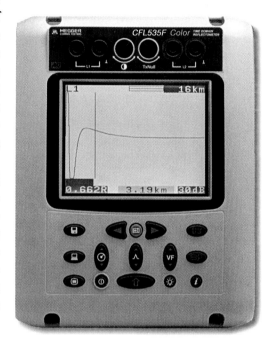

Figure 14.10
A TDR device can help locate breaks or other damage in cables. What problems can occur if a network cable is damaged?

Oscilloscopes

An **oscilloscope** is an electronic instrument that measures the amount of signal voltage per unit of time and displays the result on a monitor. When used with a TDR, an oscilloscope can display:

◆ Shorts
◆ Sharp bends or crimps in the cable
◆ Opens (breaks in the cable)
◆ Attenuation (loss of signal power)

Crossover Cables

A cable used to connect two computers directly with a single cable is a **crossover cable.** Normal patch cables must be connected to an intervening hub. Because the send and receive wires of a crossover cable are reversed on one end, the send wire from one computer is connected to the receive port on the other computer. Crossover cables are useful in troubleshooting network connection problems. Two computers can be directly connected, bypassing the network and making it possible to isolate and test the communication capabilities of one computer, rather than the whole network.

ACTIVITY 14D Creating a Crossover Cable

A crossover cable can be used to network two computers together without an intervening hub. Creating a crossover cable is almost identical to creating a patch cable. The only difference is that two of the wire pairs are crossed. With your instructor's permission, gather the listed supplies and follow the steps below:

- Length of UTP cable, preferably Cat 5 or Cat 5e
- RJ-45 connectors
- Wire stripper
- Wire cutter
- Crimper tool

1 Cut a length of cable appropriate for the distance you need to cover from the computer to the connection device (that is, a hub or switch). Always add a few feet for mistakes or unanticipated rerouting of the cable.

2 Strip approximately 1″ of the cable's outer jacket. Go slowly to avoid cutting into the housing surrounding the wire inside the jacket.

3 Flatten the wires in the following order from left to right: White/Orange (1), Orange (2), White/Green (3), Blue (4), White/Blue (5), Green (6), White/Brown (7), and Brown (8).

Note: You can use a different arrangement, but you must follow the same order on the other end of the cable.

4 Cut off ½″ of the wires, leaving ½″ exposed from the end of the outer jacket.

5 Push the wires into the RJ-45 connector. Ensure that the wires are pushed all the way to the end of the connector.

Note: Always double-check yourself at this point. If you have made a mistake and proceed to crimp the RJ-45 connector, you must cut it off and start over.

6 Plug the RJ-45 connector into the crimper and squeeze the handle. When properly crimped, you should not be able to easily pull the connector off the end of the cable.

7 On the second RJ-45 connector, insert the wires in the following order from left to right: White/Green (1), Green (6), White/Orange (3), Blue (4), White/Blue (5), Orange (6), White/Brown (7), and Brown (8). This is critical or your cable will not work! See Figure 14.11.

Figure 14.11
Crossover cables cross two pair of wires to allow two computers to network together.

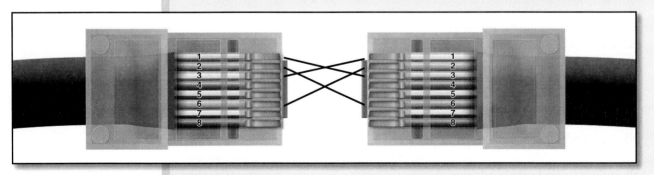

8. When finished, plug one end of your cable into the first computer, and the other end into the second computer.

   - **Note:** Be sure to label your crossover cable because you will not be able to connect a computer to a hub or switch with it.
   - Do not panic if you do not get it right the first time. Just cut the connector off one end and try again.

A crossover cable is a good thing to have in your toolbox when troubleshooting networking problems. Using the crossover cable, you can use a laptop or other computer to connect to a problematic computer to isolate the problem.

Hardware Loopback

One type of serial port connector that enables you to test the communication capabilities of a computer's serial port without having to connect to another computer or peripheral device is a **hardware loopback device.** Instead, using the loopback, data are transmitted to a line, and then returned as received data. If the transmitted data does not return, the hardware loopback detects a hardware malfunction.

GO Online

Activity 14.2 Investigate Wiring Closets Visit **networking.glencoe.com** to learn about wiring closets and the important role they play as a central part of the network.

Tone Generator and Tone Locator

A **tone generator** is a standard tool for wiring technicians in all fields. A tone generator applies an alternating or continuous tone signal to a cable or a conductor. The tone generator is attached to one end of the cable in question. A matching **tone locator** is used to detect the correct cable at the other end of the run. This pair of equipment is sometimes referred to as "fox and hound."

NETWORK UTILITIES

You can use many command-line utilities to help locate problems on the network. Many of these commands are used as part of the TCP/IP suite. Several of these commands, such as the ping command, can be used on most common OSs. Here, we review several of the more important network utilities.

Ping

Ping is used to detect the presence of another computer. If the other computer is available, it sends a message back confirming that it is, indeed, available. The syntax of the ping command is:

```
ping computername
```

where "computername" could be a computer name on your LAN, a domain name such as Google.com, or an IP address. The command returns results that indicate whether communication was successful (see Figure 14.12).

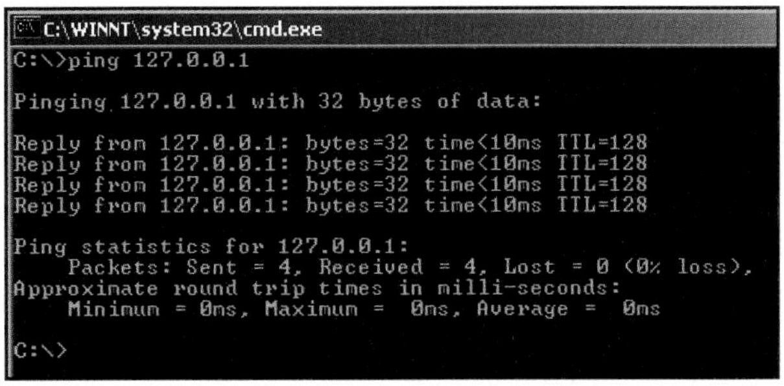
C:\WINNT\system32\cmd.exe
C:\>ping 127.0.0.1
Pinging 127.0.0.1 with 32 bytes of data:
Reply from 127.0.0.1: bytes=32 time<10ms TTL=128
Reply from 127.0.0.1: bytes=32 time<10ms TTL=128
Reply from 127.0.0.1: bytes=32 time<10ms TTL=128
Reply from 127.0.0.1: bytes=32 time<10ms TTL=128
Ping statistics for 127.0.0.1:
Packets: Sent = 4, Received = 4, Lost = 0 (0% loss),
Approximate round trip times in milli-seconds:
Minimum = 0ms, Maximum = 0ms, Average = 0ms
C:\>

Figure 14.12 Ping is used to detect the presence of other computers over the TCP/IP protocol. What are two methods you can use to specify which computer to ping?

Command switches allow you to modify how ping operates. For example,

```
ping computername -t
```

transmits continuously to the other computer, rather than stopping after four packets. This can be useful if you are trying to locate which port on a hub or switch a network device is plugged into, and the cables are not labeled properly. A coworker can unplug one cable at a time until the device stops responding.

TRACERT

Lab 14.2 Using TRACERT to Resolve Response Time Problems Practice additional hands-on networking skills on page 455.

Another useful command is called TRACERT. This command originated in Unix, where it is called Traceroute. This utility sends a packet to a remote computer, and traces the exact route the packet travels along.

The syntax of TRACERT is basically the same as for the ping command:

```
tracert computername
```

where "computername" could be a computer name on your LAN, a domain name such as Google.com, or an IP address. By default, TRACERT attempts to resolve IP addresses to host names. This makes the command run a little slower.

The information provided by TRACERT can help you identify where a communications problem lies. For example, you may not be able to send files to a remote user. Using the TRACERT command, you can see exactly how far a packet gets before it is lost. This can help you determine if a router at your location or the destination is down, or possibly an ISP's router is down somewhere.

TECH TRIVIA

Telnet Alert Telnet is a powerful means of accessing and administering remote computers. However, hackers often use it to access the network. The Telnet server should remain off unless there is a legitimate need to use it.

Telnet

Telnet is a utility used to log on to a remote computer or other network device. Once logged into a Telnet session, the user can browse the remote computer's directories, launch programs, and configure the computer. Telnet requires a Telnet client running on the local machine, a Telnet server running on the remote machine, and a user account established on the remote machine.

Telnet server is a service that permits users to log on and establish Telnet sessions. A session is similar to a telephone call. While the session is open, both computers can communicate with each other. A session is established using the Telnet client on the local computer (see Figure 14.13).

Figure 14.13 ●──→
Telnet is used to remotely access a computer. What risk is there to leaving Telnet server running on a computer that does not need to use it all the time?

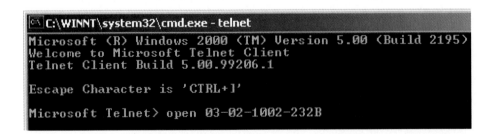

NSLOOKUP

The NSLOOKUP command is used to troubleshoot problems with the DNS server. When you use the NSLOOKUP command, the default DNS server name and IP address are displayed. At the NSLOOKUP prompt, you can issue NSLOOKUP-specific commands, such as LS, which shows a list of computers recorded in the DNS database. In the Windows OS, you can use this command by opening a command prompt window.

ACTIVITY 14E Using the NSLOOKUP Command

YOU TRY IT

The NSLOOKUP command is used to troubleshoot problems with the DNS server. In the Windows OS, do the following:

1 Open a command prompt window, type nslookup, and press **Enter.** The default DNS server name and IP address should appear. The command prompt changes to a special NSLOOKUP prompt.

2 Type help and press **Enter** to view a list of NSLOOKUP-specific commands.

3 Type ls mynetworkdomain.com and press **Enter.** Replace "mynetwork-domain.com" with the name of your school's domain. A list of computer names and IP addresses stored within the DNS server's database appears.

4 Type exit and press **Enter** to exit the NSLOOKUP command.

The NSLOOKUP command offers many ways to query the DNS database, but these are beyond the scope of this book.

NBTSTAT

The NBTSTAT command is used to view statistics of the NetBIOS protocol over TCP/IP connections. As you learned earlier in this book, NetBIOS is a protocol used by Windows networks to resolve Windows computer names to TCP/IP addresses. As such, the NBTSTAT command is only useful on Windows networks.

ACTIVITY 14F Using the NBTSTAT Command

YOU TRY IT

NBTSTAT provides useful information on Windows-based networks. For example, you can resolve a Windows computer name to a TCP/IP address (or vice versa).

1 Open a command prompt window, type nbtstat at the command prompt and press **Enter.** A list of switches you can use with the NBTSTAT command appears.

2 Type nbtstat –n at the command prompt and press **Enter.** Your local computer name, domain name, IP address, and MAC address are displayed.

3 Write down another student's computer name for use in the next step. Type nbtstat –a computername at the command prompt and press **Enter.** Use the other student's computer name in place of "computername." The IP and MAC addresses of the other computer are returned.

Note that the –**a** switch is case sensitive. The –**A** (big A) switch requires the IP address (instead of the Windows name) of the other computer, and returns the Windows name and MAC address.

Using any of these tools can provide information that can help you in the troubleshooting process. When you are troubleshooting a particular problem, carefully document what you do, and how you finally resolve the problem. This can save you from "reinventing the wheel" each time a problem occurs.

SOFTWARE TOOLS

Software tools are needed to monitor trends and identify network performance problems. Software tools are often used to troubleshoot problems, such as those involving the actual data being sent across the network.

Network Monitors

Network monitors track all or a selected part of network traffic. They examine data packets and gather information about packet types, errors, and packet traffic to and from each computer. Network monitors are used to establish a baseline which helps to troubleshoot traffic problems and monitor network usage to determine when it is time to upgrade.

Protocol Analyzers

As data travel around the network, a protocol analyzer (also called "network analyzer") copies packets and saves them for decoding and analysis. Network administrators who work with large networks rely heavily on protocol analyzers. These are the tools used most often to monitor network interactivity.

Sniffers

A **sniffer** is a type of network analyzer that can monitor network traffic. This type of application measures network traffic. Sniffers can gather important LAN traffic statistics, including the amount of traffic and the protocols in use. This information can then be presented in a graphic profile of the LAN.

READ ME!

Tech Tip Although sniffers are great tools for system administrators, they can also be misused. A hacker who gains access to the network could run a sniffer program to intercept data being transmitted across the network.

Section 14.3 Assessment

Concept Check

1. **Define** digital volt-ohmmeter, time-domain reflectometer (TDR), oscilloscope, crossover cable, hardware loop-back device, tone generator, tone locator, and sniffer.

2. **Explain** how the ping command is used to locate a port on a specific computer.

3. **Explain** what type of network the NBTSTAT command is used on and why it is limited to that type of network.

Critical Thinking

4. **Compare and Contrast** How are a crossover cable and a normal patch cable similar? How do they differ?

5. **Resolve Problems** Identify the tool used to monitor network traffic and gather LAN statistics. How could this tool be misused by a hacker?

6. **Hypothesize** Explain how a tone generator/tone locator work and provide an example of why this tool would be used in a network.

Applying Skills

Apply Network Troubleshooting Tools A user calls and complains that she cannot access a file stored on a remote server (located at another site). Write an explanation of how you might find the cause of this problem. Include any tools that might be helpful in your search for the cause.

SECTION 14.1 Troubleshooting Basics

Key Terms

README, 404
system lockup, 405
Event Viewer, 405

Main Ideas

- Effective troubleshooting requires a methodical approach.
- Step one is to gather information and identify the problem.
- Step two is to isolate the cause.
- Step three is to carefully plan and make the repair.
- Step four is to confirm that the repair resolved the problem.
- Step five is to document the problem so that you can easily solve the problem if it recurs.
- Problems are often categorized into types, such as hardware, configuration, software, or network.

SECTION 14.2 Finding and Repairing Problems

Key Terms

Windows Troubleshooter, 408
add-in card, 410
jumper, 411
frequently asked questions (FAQ), 412

Main Ideas

- The Windows Troubleshooter can be a useful way to resolve problems and to begin creating your own troubleshooting strategy.
- Spend time to create a first response plan to deal with critical situations.
- When diagnosing hardware and software problems, always look for the most obvious problem first.

SECTION 14.3 Troubleshooting Tools

Key Terms

digital volt-ohmmeter, 414
time-domain reflectometer (TDR), 415
oscilloscope, 415
crossover cable, 415
hardware loopback device, 417
tone generator, 417
tone locator, 417
sniffer, 420

Main Ideas

- Digital volt-ohmmeters are used to identify problems in network cabling and to confirm source voltage in network equipment.
- TDRs and oscilloscopes can be used to identify physical problems, such as bends or breaks, in network cabling.
- Network monitors are software tools that monitor network traffic.
- Protocol analyzers provide a variety of information about packets being sent around the network.
- Utilities such as ping and TRACERT are used to establish whether a connection between computers is present.
- Telnet is a program that allows one computer to connect to and use another computer remotely.
- NSLOOKUP is used to resolve DNS server problems.
- NBTSTAT is used on Windows networks to view NetBIOS over TCP/IP statistics and information.

Reviewing Key Terms

1. What is a FAQ and what is its role in troubleshooting?
2. What is a jumper used for in a hardware configuration?
3. What is a crossover cable?
4. What is a hardware loopback device?
5. Why are sniffers called "network analyzers"?

Understanding Main Ideas

6. **Explain** when a README file should be read.
7. **Describe** the purposes of a TDR, a digital volt-ohmmeter, and an oscilloscope. How are they used to troubleshoot network problems?
8. **Explain** the most common problem with add-in cards.
9. **List** the steps involved in troubleshooting.
10. **Explain** the reason for categorizing problems.
11. **Describe** what should be included in a first-response plan to deal with a critical situation.
12. **Explain** the similarities and differences of a hardware loopback device and an IP loopback address.
13. **Describe** what can be easily done to check external USB devices that fail.
14. **List** five devices or tools for troubleshooting. At least one device or tool covers each of the areas of hardware, configuration, software, and network problem.

Critical Thinking

15. **Diagnose a Cause** When a device malfunctions, many events are triggered, and it is hard to tell which caused which, that is, which is the root event that caused the problem. What kind of intelligence do you think an event viewer must possess?
16. **Anticipate Problems** Upgrading often introduces problems due to minimum requirements or compatibility. When you add a new hard drive to a computer system, what kinds of problems might you encounter? How would Windows Troubleshooter help?
17. **Categorize Tools** It is important to understand the specific purpose for which a tool is used. Misusing a tool might have consequences similar to a doctor providing a wrong prescription. What categories are provided for troubleshooting tools?
18. **Distinguish Tools** Wiring technicians use a pair of tools called a tone generator and tone locator. They are sometimes referred to as "the fox and the hound." Which is the fox and which is the hound? Why?
19. **Know the Side Effect** As a network administrator, you will need to understand the effects of using various tools. Sniffer, for example, is a double-edged weapon that can be a powerful tool for both the good of the IT staff and the demise of the hacker. Describe the positive and the negative functionality of sniffer.

e-Review ··················
networking.glencoe.com

Study with PowerPoint
To review the main points in this chapter, select **e-Review > PowerPoint Outlines > Chapter 14**.

Online Self Check
Test your knowledge of the material in this chapter by selecting **e-Review > Self Checks > Chapter 14**.

Making Connections

Science – Unlimited Internet Bandwidth
Some computer scientists envision the day in which advanced technologies will provide users around the world with virtually unlimited Internet bandwidth. Assuming that such technologies were available today, explain how they could be used to enhance the effectiveness of system backups. Identify the benefits of being able to store backup data at a remote location.

STANDARDS AT WORK

Students use a variety of media and formats to communicate information and ideas effectively to multiple audiences. (NETS-S 4)

Connecting with FTP
Several software utilities test and establish connections between networked computer systems, such as NSLookup and Telnet. Like Telnet, File Transfer Protocol (FTP) provides remote file management capabilities. With your teacher's permission, perform the following steps:

◆ Click on **Start** and **Run.**
◆ Type ftp into the Open field of the Run dialog and click **OK.** The FTP command window will open.
◆ Use the ftp> command prompt to establish a connection with another computer. Type the command open followed by the network device's name or IP address. For example:

```
open ftp.loc.gov
open 167.19.116.3
```

◆ If the device accepts FTP connections, it will respond with a type of "connected" message. Otherwise, it will give an error message.
◆ Type the command bye at the ftp> prompt and press **Enter** to terminate your FTP session and close the FTP command window.

It is not necessary for you to log on to the device when you use FTP as a connection testing utility.

TEAMWORK SKILLS

Utilize Support Technician Skills
Before hiring a new support technician, many businesses evaluate the candidate's support skills by conducting a "phone test." During a mock support call, the candidate listens to the customer and helps him or her.

Following your teacher's instructions, divide into teams of at least three to four people. One team member will be a customer who needs help with a networking problem. A second team member will be a candidate. The remaining one or two members will evaluate the candidate. Create a performance evaluation sheet that contains a 1-to-5 scale for each skill. Use the troubleshooting guidelines presented in this chapter.

CHALLENGE YOURSELF

IEEE Standards—LAN/MAN (802)
Hardware compatibility is always a network issue. Even devices from the same manufacturer are not guaranteed to be compatible. Devices that meet the same IEEE Standard should be compatible and communicate with each other. Visit the IEEE Web site and navigate to the IEEE Standards Online Web site. Locate the Subscription Portfolio and go to the LAN/MAN pages. There are three types of standard statuses, approved standards, archived standards, and unapproved drafts. Using the Web site, answer the following questions:

◆ What is the number that provides an overview and architecture of the IEEE Standard for LAN/MAN?
◆ What is the number series for bridging standards?
◆ What is the number series for Ethernet standards?
◆ What is the number series for Token Ring standards?
◆ What is the number series for Wireless LANs?
◆ Which number series are for LAN/MAN security?

YOU TRY IT

Networking Lab

1. Troubleshooting with Internet Explorer

As you learned earlier, it is not uncommon for users to experience difficulties accessing information on the Internet, even when their local network connections are working just fine. One resource that network administrators and IT staff have to help resolve such problems is the troubleshooting guide within Internet Explorer. This guide is accessible to users and IT personnel alike, as follows:

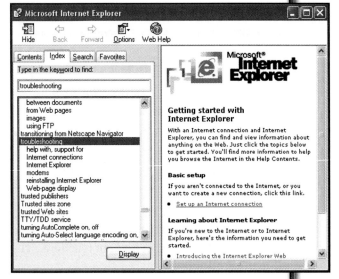

Ⓐ Open **Internet Explorer.**

Ⓑ Click the **Help** menu and then select **Contents and Index.**

Ⓒ Select the **Index** tab of the Help window.

Ⓓ Scroll down the list of index topics to troubleshooting.

Ⓔ Double-click on any subtopic under the troubleshooting keyword to view the available information regarding this subject.

Ⓕ Choose one subtopic. Write a paragraph that identifies two problems and possible solutions according to the information found under the topic.

2. Reviewing System Performance Logs

Not every problem that users report to IT personnel involves a hardware or software failure. Sometimes users complain that their system is functioning, but it is running much slower than usual. Sometimes a performance problem will affect every user on the network, and sometimes it is limited to a single user. One way in which network administrators may investigate a performance problem is by viewing the user's performance logs. In Windows XP, this is done as follows:

Ⓐ Right-click **My Computer** on your Windows desktop and select **Computer Management.**

Ⓑ Click on **Manage** from the pop-up menu.

Ⓒ Locate and expand the **System Tools** entry in the left frame of the window.

Ⓓ Locate the entry **Performance Logs and Alerts** and expand it.

Ⓔ Click on each of the Counter Logs, Trace Logs, or Alerts entries to view a list of logs for that category.

Ⓕ Open a log file by double-clicking it in the right frame of the window.

In a short paragraph, briefly explain your analysis and the purpose of each log.

Networking Projects

1. Create a Decision Tree

There are many methods and philosophies available to help network support technicians service the needs of their customers. One technique that is employed by many companies is called a "decision tree." The purpose of a decision tree is to help technicians ask customers a specific sequence of questions that will guide them to a speedy identification and resolution of the customer's problem. For example:

◆ A customer calls a support line and complains that the computer monitor is blank.
◆ The technician starts by asking a general question, and then asks more and more specific questions based on the customer's answers.
◆ Each question in the decision tree should only have a few possible answers, such as yes or no, one or many, one or two or three, etc.
◆ The support technician might use the following decision tree:

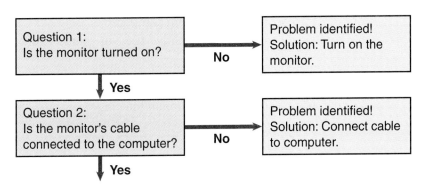

Now refer to the common troubleshooting questions found in Table 14.2 on page 401. Create a set of effective decision trees that are based on these questions.

2. Investigate Computer Viruses

Few tasks are more important to IT professionals than ensuring that their organization's network remains free of harmful computer viruses. There are a number of Web sites that maintain databases on viruses and current patches. As a network administrator or support technician, you will need to be familiar with the latest virus threats and how to fix a computer or network if it becomes infected.

McAfee Security Web site provides information on the latest virus alerts. Visit McAfee's Web site and find the virus database. Using the Web site, answer the following questions:

◆ List three of the latest virus threats.
◆ Describe the different levels of categorizing a virus.
◆ View one of the viruses. Describe who is affected and how it can be fixed.
◆ List five virus hoaxes.

Building 21st Century Skills

Project 1

Decision Making: Design a Network

Plan a home network. Assume you have two desktop computers located in different rooms, plus a laptop that you want to use in different locations throughout the house. Document your decision-making process and answer the following questions.

1. What network media will you use? Why?
2. List the network components you will need.
3. Create a budget detailing how much each component will cost.

Project 2

Critical Thinking: Create Troubleshooting Checklists

Create a set of checklists for troubleshooting the following scenarios. In your checklist, detail the steps that should be taken to diagnose the problem.

1. A user has a virus on his computer.
2. A computer needs to be upgraded to the latest OS.
3. A user reports that the CD drive does not read CDs anymore.
4. A new video card needs to be installed in an old computer.
5. You suspect a hacker has gained access to sensitive files on your network.

Once the preliminary checklists are done, exchange checklists with someone in your class for review. Make any necessary corrections, then submit the final set of checklists to your teacher, or present the information to the class.

Project 3

Analyzing: Monitor Hard Disk Performance

Using Windows 2000 or Windows XP, follow the steps below to monitor your hard drive's performance to see if it is performing optimally.

1. Open **Control Panel,** click **Performance and Maintenance.**
2. Double-click **Administrative Tools.**
3. Double-click **Performance.**
4. Under **Performance Object,** click the down arrow and select **PhysicalDisk.**
5. To find out how much time your hard drive spends reading, writing, and idle, choose **%Disk Read Time, %Disk Write Time,** and **%Idle Time.**
6. Select the drive(s) you want to monitor, then click **Add.**
7. With your teacher's permission, move some large files between folders, copy files to a disk, or copy files to a server to see how well your hard drive is performing.

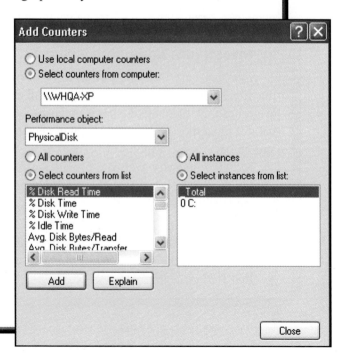

Building Your Portfolio

Network Security

No one wants a disaster that could result in lost or compromised data, or a facility that is destroyed. The damage from even the worst disasters can be minimized to a large extent if a comprehensive plan is in place before the disaster strikes.

If you were placed in charge of your school's network security, what would you do? Prepare a written plan that identifies what measures you would take to prevent and recover from many common network disasters. Use the Network Security Checklist to help you think of important security aspects.

1. Prepare a plan for the following emergencies:
   a. The entire facility is completely destroyed by a tornado.
   b. Portions of the facility are damaged by a fire.
   c. The facility suffers flood damage.
   d. A hacker gains access to student records.
   e. A student inadvertently deletes several important files and now the computer will not boot.
   f. Student accounts have access to the network drive where teachers' files are stored.
   g. A virus infects the network.

2. For each emergency, identify ways in which the network can be protected to prevent the disaster from happening. Discuss each of the following.
   a. Physical protection of the equipment
   b. Data backup
   c. Network security

Network Security Checklist

PHYSICAL PROTECTION OF EQUIPMENT
- ☑ Separate, locked room
- ☑ Low temperature
- ☑ Special fire suppression system (not water!)

DATA BACKUP
- ☑ Critical drives mirrored for redundancy
- ☑ Data backed up regularly
- ☑ Tapes stored off site
- ☑ Disk images to restore machines quickly

SECURITY OF NETWORK
- ☑ Strong password policy
- ☑ User level security
- ☑ Firewall and proxy server monitor Internet traffic

Virus Report

It is vital for networking personnel to keep up to date on the latest viruses and security threats. Use the Internet to research information about recent virus or hacker activity.

1. If you selected a virus to research:
   a. Describe how the virus operates.
   b. Explain how you can clean viruses from systems or prevent systems for getting viruses.

2. If you selected a recent hacker exploit:
   a. Research the security hole that allowed the hacker in.
   b. Explain what could have been done in order to prevent the attack.

Report your findings as a newsletter or newspaper article.

Enrichment Labs Chapter 1

Lab 1.1 Troubleshooting Users' Problems

Purpose
Often, the solutions to users' problems can only be learned by trial and error. It takes practice to know which things to try first, and it is important to keep records of what you have learned in case a similar problem arises.

Scenario
You are the network support technician for a travel agency. A user comes to you and complains that his monitor is not working. You go to his station and observe that the monitor is blank, although the computer is running.

Activity

1 List at least five things to check that might solve this problem immediately.

2 Assume that none of the things you tried solved the problem. You decide to plug another monitor into that computer and see if it works.

3 The second monitor works! What is your analysis of the original problem?

4 If the second monitor did not work, how would you analyze the original problem?

5 Compare your problem-solving checklist with classmates. With your teacher's help, create a class list of successful problem-solving techniques.

Enrichment Labs Chapter 1

Lab 1.2 Comparing and Contrasting Input Devices

Purpose

Learning how to compare different hardware is important in networking because you may have to help make hardware decisions for your company. Understanding hardware is also important when you help users troubleshoot their hardware problems.

Activity

1 Although many people use trackballs, this lab will focus on the two most common types of mice:

◆ **Optical mice** use visible light or infrared to detect changes in position.
◆ **Mechanical mice** use a rolling ball mechanism to detect changes in position.

2 Use some of the following resources to conduct research on the two types of mice:

◆ Dictionaries (online or print)
◆ Catalogs from computer resellers
◆ Internet search (with your teacher's permission)
◆ Hands-on testing and examination of the two types of mice
◆ Textbooks
◆ Computer encyclopedias

3 Research the following:

◆ How each mouse works
◆ How much it costs
◆ How it connects to the computer
◆ How the wear and tear of daily use affects it

4 As you gather information, look for advantages and disadvantages of mouse type. Create tables similar to the ones below to record your notes.

Mechanical Mouse	
Advantages	Disadvantages

Optical Mouse	
Advantages	Disadvantages

5 Based on the information in the tables, which type of mouse would be the best purchase for your classroom or school? Explain your answer.

Enrichment Labs Chapter 2

Lab 2.1   Using System Tools to View System Information in Windows 2000

Purpose

Network administrators and technicians often need to determine system hardware and software resources on a computer. Using Windows 2000, you will explore the Computer Management Console to review your computer system's configuration.

Activity

1 Click **Start,** point to **Programs,** point to **Administrative Tools,** and click **Computer Management.** The Computer Management Console will appear.

2 The System Tools node should already be expanded. If not, click **System Tools.**

3 Double-click **System Information.** (As an alternative, you can click **Start,** click **Run,** and then type MSInfo32.)

4 Create a table similar to the one below. Look in each container (folder) to locate the information in the table. For each item requested, record the name of the container in which you found the item and value of the item.

Item	Container	Value
OS Name		
OS Version		
Network Adapter Name		
Processor		
Total Physical Memory		
Available Physical Memory		
Available Virtual Memory		
CD-ROM Driver		
Disk Driver		
Network Connections		
Problems Devices		
Printing		

5 Now that you have gathered this information, answer the following questions:

Ⓐ What can you do with this information?

Ⓑ What could you do if you wanted to track the information for a group of computers?

Enrichment Labs Chapter 2

Lab 2.2 Saving a Windows 2000 System Information File

Purpose

Technicians must understand their computers' hardware. To increase your understanding, you can create a System Information File. This file provides specific information about your computer's processor. In this lab, you will save a System Information File for your computer, and then view the field.

Activity

1 Click **Start,** point to **Programs,** point to **Administrative Tools,** and then click **Computer Management.** The Computer Management console will appear.

2 Right-click **System Information.**

3 Click **Save As System Information File.**

4 Save the file in a folder of your choice. Type the file name System Info.nfo. It may take a few moments to save the file.

5 Open the System Information File that you just saved.

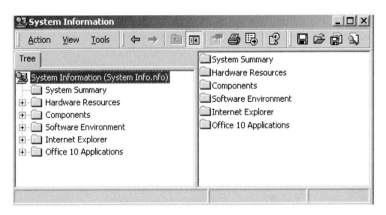

6 Right-click **System Information,** and then click **Find.** In the Windows 2000 System Information File you just created, locate the value of the following:

- ◆ PROCESSOR_ARCHITECTURE
- ◆ PROCESSOR_LEVEL
- ◆ PROCESSOR_IDENTIFIER
- ◆ PROCESSOR_REVISION

7 After you have located the above values, answer the questions below.

Ⓐ What do these values tell you about your computer system?

Ⓑ Do you know what each value means? If you do not, how could you find more information about it?

8 OPTIONAL: If a printer is available in your classroom, print the file contents.

9 Close the Computer Management or System Information console.

Enrichment Labs chapter 3

Lab 3.1 Displaying Local Area Connection Properties in Windows XP

Purpose
Network administrators need to know how to discover the properties of network interface cards (NICs) and information about Internet protocols and online status. In this lab, you will become familiar with the information provided by the Local Area Connection Properties dialog box in Windows XP.

Activity

1 Open the **Control Panel.** Double-click **Network and Internet Connections** and click on **Network Connections.** Right-click on **Local Area Connection** and choose **Properties.**

2 Under **Connect using:** is the name and model of your NIC. Write down this information.

3 Click **Configure.**

4 In the new dialog box titled Network Connection Properties, click the tab labeled **Driver.** Record the following information, then describe what these three values mean to you.

   ◆ Driver Provider
   ◆ Driver Date
   ◆ Driver Version

5 Notice the **Update Driver** button, which helps you update drivers automatically. You can also get updated drivers from Microsoft's Web site, from the NIC manufacturer's site, and from your computer manufacturer's site.

6 Now click the tab labeled **Resources.** Record the following information, then describe what these values mean to you:

   ◆ I/O Range
   ◆ Memory Range
   ◆ IRQ

   IRQ5 is the recommended setting for the NIC card. However, if IRQ5 was being used by another device when the NIC was installed, another IRQ may be used.

7 Click the **General** tab. Look under **Device status.** Does it say that your NIC is working properly? If not, your teacher may wish to help you troubleshoot the problem. Click **Cancel** to close the Network Connections Properties dialog box.

8 Return to the **Local Area Connection Properties** dialog box. Select **Internet Protocol (TCP/IP),** and then click **Properties.** Record which option button is selected: Obtain an IP address automatically, Obtain DNS server address automatically.

9 Click **Cancel** to close the dialog box.

Enrichment Labs Chapter 3

Lab 3.2 Exploring the AppleTalk and TCP/IP Protocols on the Macintosh

Purpose

AppleTalk and TCP/IP are common examples of protocols that connect computers in a local area network and over the Internet. This lab shows how to find information about each protocol on a Macintosh running System 10.x. If your Macintosh is running System 9, you will find AppleTalk and TCP/IP information in the Control Panel under the Apple icon.

Activity

1 Open **System Preferences** and double-click the **Network** icon.

2 Double-click **AppleTalk** to see information for your school's network. Look at the checkbox next to Make AppleTalk Active. Is AppleTalk active on your computer?

Make AppleTalk Active	☐ Yes	☐ No

3 On a separate piece of paper, record the following information, then describe what this information means to you.

- ◆ Computer Name
- ◆ AppleTalk Zone

4 Click the drop-down menu next to **AppleTalk Zone.** What other zones are listed? Be careful not to change the zone by selecting another zone in the drop-down list.

5 Click the drop-down menu next to **Configure.** What is the other option there?

6 Click the button labeled **TCP/IP.** Record the following information:

- ◆ IP Address
- ◆ Subnet Mask
- ◆ DNS Servers

7 What you can do with this information? How can you apply this to a group of computers?

8 You can find more detailed information in the Network Utility application. Double-click your hard drive icon, click **Applications,** click **Utilities,** and double-click **Network Utility.** Click the **AppleTalk** button. Click some of the buttons on the left and then click **Get AppleTalk Information.**

9 Click some of the other buttons such as **Info** to see what information is there.

10 After you have explored various network settings for the Macintosh, answer the following questions:

A Where could you store this information?

B Could you store an entire computer lab's network information in one document? Why would you want to do this?

Enrichment Labs Chapter 4

Lab 4.1 Understanding Network Connectivity

Purpose

Network administrators are constantly reshaping networks to fit the needs of their users. It is important to understand how network components are connected and how the devices that connect them work. In this lab, you will examine the role of the switch, which is very similar to a bridge.

Activity

Refer to the diagram to help answer the questions.

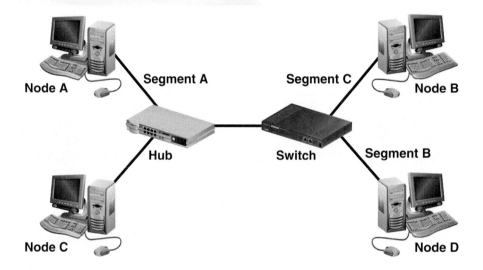

1 Although there are four computers, there are only three segments. Why?

2 Node A on Segment A sends data to Node B on Segment C. The switch gets the first packet of data from Node A, and reads the MAC address. What is the MAC address saved to?

3 At this point, does the switch know where Node B is? If not, where will it send Node A's data?

4 Node C sends information to the switch for Node A. When the switch notes the MAC address for Node C, where is it added? It notes that Node A and Node C are on the same what?

5 Create a table like the one below. Show all the nodes and segments in the diagram.

Routing Table

Node	Segment

Enrichment Labs Chapter 4

Lab 4.2 Troubleshooting New Network Components

Purpose

Network administrators know that upgrades to a network often cause problems. The causes usually relate to incompatible components or damage to some part of the system. Knowing what components to examine first when troubleshooting the problems will help you get the network back up as soon as possible.

Scenario

You are working for a small company that develops software used by the credit-card industry.

◆ You have 20 computers connected in a star-bus topology using active hubs.
◆ Your cabling is UTP Cat5e twisted pair.
◆ You need to add four new employees.
◆ You find a good price for four rebuilt computers.

Your vendor installs the computers over the weekend, along with an additional hub, but when you come in Monday morning you find that the new computers cannot connect to the network.

Activity

1 List two things that could cause each of the following components not to function properly.

◆ Hub
◆ Cable(s)
◆ NICs

2 What could you do to resolve each of the possible causes you listed above?

Hub	UTP Cable	NIC
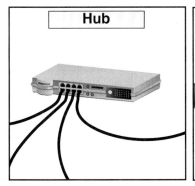	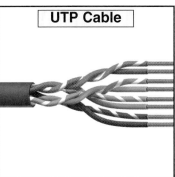	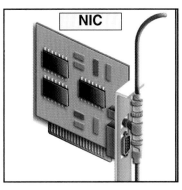

Enrichment Labs Chapter 5

Lab 5.1 Troubleshooting a PC and a Macintosh Network

Purpose

Network troubleshooting skills come with practice. As you solve problems, you will find you have gained skills that can be applied in many different situations. These two scenarios cover very different types of networks, but the solutions are based on a similar core problem.

Scenario A

In the first scenario, you have been called in as a consultant to work on a network for a growing hospital supply company that has Windows 2000 servers and Windows workstations. The network is running the NetBEUI protocol in a single Windows 2000 domain and single physical segment.

Scenario B

In the second scenario, you are a network administrator for an advertising agency. One user calls you in and says that he is trying to use his browser to connect to a Web site, but his Macintosh computer will not connect to any sites at all. No other users on the network are experiencing the same difficulty.

Activity

Read the scenarios above and answer the questions below.

1 For Scenario A, the network administrator has added a router to the network to connect to a new building next door, but he cannot get the traffic to pass through the router. What are the most likely problems? Explain your answers.

2 For Scenario B, what do you think the problem is? Explain your answer.

3 These two scenarios emphasize the importance of one widely used protocol. What is the protocol, and why is it so important?

Enrichment Labs Chapter 5

Lab 5.2 Designing a Token Ring Network

Purpose

The best way to understand a network topology is to work with it and to explain it to someone else. In this lab, you will design a Token Ring network for a specific purpose and describe its functions.

Scenario

You are helping a new non-profit group set up its network. The group is called Kids Compute! and their purpose is to train teenagers who do not have access to computers at home but hope to get computer jobs some day.

A local company has donated 40 computers, cabling, and four MAUs. (They are used to a Token Ring topology and assume you will use the same.) Kids Compute! would like to have four distinct working areas: Word Processing, Page Makeup, Graphics, and Programming.

You have decided to set up the computers in a Token Ring topology using MAUs. Since some of the kids who will be taking classes have expressed an interest in networking, you decide to involve them in setting it up.

Activity

1 First, design the network. Use a computer drawing program, such as Microsoft Visio, or a presentation application, such as PowerPoint. You could also use pencil and paper. You do not have to illustrate every workstation. You can use arrows to indicate many, like this:

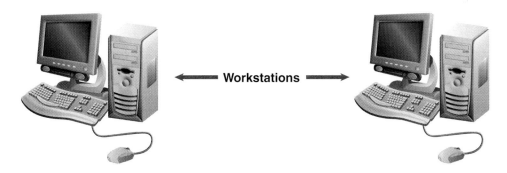

Workstations

2 Write a description of how the network will function. Cover the following topics:

- ◆ Describe the IBM Token Ring topology.
- ◆ Explain how token passing works and how it avoids collisions.
- ◆ Describe the function of the MAUs.
- ◆ Determine how MAUs must be connected.
- ◆ Identify the type of cabling you are using.

3 Present the drawing(s) to the class and refer to your description to explain the network.

Enrichment Labs chapter 6

Lab 6.1 Working with UNIX Commands

Purpose

Anyone who was on the Internet in its early days is familiar with UNIX commands. They were used for communicating between university computers. UNIX is still very much in use, and it is likely you will encounter it. In this lab, you will get a feel for some basic commands.

Activity

1 Find Terminal in the Utilities folder in your Applications folder.

2 Double-click to open **Terminal.** A window will appear containing information like this:

```
Last login: Wed Dec 10 22:27:59 on ttypl
Welcome to Darwin!
[Oldcats-Computer:~] oldcat
```

3 Instead of "oldcat," your username will appear. The vertical gray bar indicates it is waiting for you to type a command. One very important command is **man.** This refers to "manual." It is the help part of the Terminal. Type man ls in the command space.

4 Your screen now shows information about this command, which lists the directories in your User Folder. There are many subcommands, or switches, that can be used with **ls** to get certain types of information. Press **Command-N** to get a new, clear window. Type ls –G. The **–G** parameter sorts your directory types by color.

5 Press **Command-N** to get a new window. Using **man,** find out what some of these commands do. Get a new window after researching each one by pressing **Command-N.**

- ◆ cd   ◆ cp   ◆ mv
- ◆ pwd   ◆ rm   ◆ mkdir

6 Close all windows and open a new one. Type ls to see your directories. To create a new directory, type mkdir Networking. Type ls again to see it in the list. To remove the directory, type rmdir Networking. Type ls again, and you will see that the directory is gone.

7 Follow the instructions above to make and remove a directory of any name you choose.

NOTE: If you have worked with DOS commands, you will notice that many of the UNIX commands are similar.

Enrichment Labs Chapter 6

Lab 6.2 Choosing a Password System

Purpose

Passwords are the first level of security between users and a network. Yet users are notorious for writing passwords down and storing them where they might be found, or for not changing their passwords regularly. In this lab, you will develop a foolproof password system.

Scenario

Users of the network that you administer are required, using the honor system, to change their passwords every month. However, after numerous security violations you are asked to develop a policy that will ensure all users make the change.

Activity

1 Listed below are some possibilities you have considered. Choose the one you think is best.

A Develop a system in which users e-mail you each month with their new passwords, so that you can monitor the results.

B Modify security settings so that passwords expire once a month. Allow five-days before they expire, during which the user must change the password.

C Develop a simple random-alphanumeric generator that automatically creates a new password on the last Friday of each month and e-mails the new password to the user.

2 After you have chosen the best option, answer the following questions:

A Why do you think the option you chose is the best?

B Why are the other options not good choices?

C How you could alter the other two choices to make them better options?

Enrichment Labs Chapter 7

Lab 7.1 Converting Binary Numbers to Decimal Numbers

Purpose

Computer technicians often need to convert binary numbers to decimal numbers. This lab will help you practice an easy way to do these conversions.

Activity

The binary system uses only two digits, 1 and 0. In data transmissions, **1** is also referred to as **true** or **on,** while **0** is **false** or **off.** You will use the terms **true** and **false** in this easy method for converting binary numbers to decimal numbers.

1 Create a table like the one below. Write the binary digits of the number shown in the top row. Use the binary number 1001 0011.

1	0	0	1	0	0	1	1

2 In the second row, write **1** in the **far right** box. Then go from right to left, doubling each number. So 1 doubled is 2, 2 doubled is 4, and so on.

1	0	0	1	0	0	1	1
128	64	32	16	8	4	2	1

3 To fill in the third row, refer back to the top row. Where there is a 1 in the top row, write **true** in the third row, and where there is a 0, write **false.**

1	0	0	1	0	0	1	1
128	64	32	16	8	4	2	1
True	False	False	True	False	False	True	True

4 Any number in the second row that has **true** under it will be used for your final calculation. The numbers with **false** under them will be ignored. Add the "true" numbers together: 128 +16 + 2 +1 = 147. This gives you a decimal number. 147 is equivalent to the binary number 1001 0011.

5 Follow the steps above to convert each binary number to a decimal number.

a. 1011 0000	e. 1111 1110	i. 1001 0000	m. 1101 1110
b. 0010 0000	f. 1100 0110	j. 0000 1110	n. 0010 1111
c. 0000 1000	g. 1010 0100	k. 0001 0100	o. 0111 1100
d. 1000 0111	h. 1001 1111	l. 0000 0110	p. 0101 0000

Enrichment Labs Chapter 7

Lab 7.2 Updating Network Communications

Purpose

Companies can quickly outgrow their networks as their businesses expand. Network administrators need to be ready with solutions. In this lab, you will help one company speed up its communications, both internally and between branches.

Scenario

A clothing designer in New York City has two branch offices: one in Seattle, Washington and one in Ft. Lauderdale, Florida. Each office has a separate internal network. The networks were set up five years ago and each has a coaxial linear-bus topology supporting Ethernet 10 Mbps traffic. The offices stay in touch using phones and express mail.

Lately, the company has developed projects that involve team members from more than one office. Each office has resources that the others do not. The current projects require the resources of both offices.

The management wants a network that is faster internally and provides WAN communication between sites. They want the WAN connection to support about 256 Kbps of data and several analog phone lines (to cut down on high long distance charges).

Activity

Read the scenario above and answer the following questions.

1 Identify at least two network items in each branch office that need upgrading.

2 The separate branch offices need to maintain voice and data communications with each other.

> **A** What type of telecommunication link might you recommend to connect the three sites to each other?

> **B** What type of device could be used to collect the multiple signals from voice and data and put them on the same WAN link?

3 What type of connectivity device should be used to connect each LAN to the multiple paths in the new WAN?

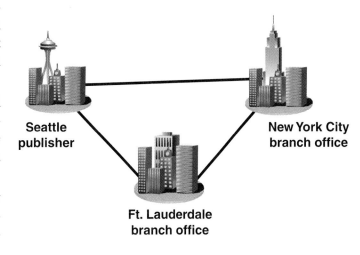

Seattle publisher

Ft. Lauderdale branch office

New York City branch office

Enrichment Labs Chapter 8

Lab 8.1 Choosing a Remote Access Solution

Purpose

When you are setting up network services for a customer, it is important to listen carefully to the customer's goals and needs so that you make not only a workable recommendation, but also one that suits the customer's preferences. In this lab, you will choose a remote access solution.

Scenario

A client who makes sporting equipment has called you in to design a remote access solution for the company's network. The company has offices all over the country. Employees, especially those in marketing, want to be able to use e-mail applications and office files remotely.

The administrator wants to implement a solution that can be managed from the central office. The network is connected to the Internet from the central office, and all users with remote access privileges have a connection to the Internet available to them.

Activity

1 Reread the scenario carefully and then consider these possible solutions:

- ◆ Dial-up connection to the central office
- ◆ Dial-up connections to the individual offices
- ◆ Virtual Private Network

2 Create a table like the one below. Write the advantages and disadvantages of each solution.

Solution	Advantage	Disadvantage
Dial-up connection to central office		
Dial-up connections to individual offices		
Virtual Private Network		

3 Once you decide on the best solution, make your case. Write a report to the customer. Cite all the advantages of your solution.

Enrichment Labs Chapter 8

Lab 8.2 Understanding the Digital Divide

Purpose

The Internet allows us to get to know people from around the world through chat rooms, newsgroups, and online gaming. In this lab, you will examine who is and who is not connected to the Internet and why. You will also learn what you can do to help promote global communications.

Activity

1 Connect to Google, AltaVista, Dogpile, or another search engine to answer the questions below. Search using the queries **global internet access statistics** and **"digital divide" statistics.**

A How many people in the world have Internet access?

B What percentage of the people who have Internet access are in each of the global areas below? Write the information on a sheet of paper.

- Africa
- Asia
- Europe
- Middle East
- North America
- Latin America/Caribbean
- Oceania (Australia, South Pacific Islands, and Antarctica)

C Use a spreadsheet or drawing program to create a bar graph or pie chart to show the information you found in questions A and B in visual form.

2 Even though countries have Internet access, there may not be a high percentage of people actually online. This is true in both developing countries and more developed areas of the world. This is often because of two factors: availability of telecommunications companies and the costs for access.

A Go online and research how people in another country are charged for Internet access and what problems they may have actually getting online. You might word your search request in one of these ways: *country* **Internet access costs,** *country* **Internet access costs statistics,** where *country* is the actual country you are researching. For example, **France Internet access costs.**

B Write a paragraph describing your findings. Compare your findings with those of your classmates.

3 What can you or your school do to increase global communication online? Many non-profit organizations are trying to bridge the global digital divide. Some refurbish used computers to give to those who cannot afford to buy them, while others promote student exchanges.

A Go online and find a program you think is interesting. Search using queries such as **world computer exchange** or **global computer organizations non-profit.**

B Compare your findings with classmates. With your teacher's permission, your class might help one of these programs.

Enrichment Labs Chapter 9

Lab 9.1 Locating IP Addresses with NSLookup

Purpose

Network administrators are often called upon to perform address resolution. Address resolution is the process that uses DNS and its databases to match domain names to IP addresses, which are divided into classes. In this lab, you will use an Internet utility called NSLookup to find IP addresses and their classes.

Activity

1 In Windows XP, open the command prompt and type nslookup and the domain name adobe.com. Press **Enter.**

NOTE: In Mac OS 10.3, go to **Applications, Utilities,** and double-click **Network Utility.** Click **Lookup** in the top menu. Then type in the domain name and click the Lookup button.

The window will show information about your network, and then you will see the following:

> Name: adobe.com
>
> Address: 192.150.14.120

2 You now have the IP address of the Adobe® site. Open your browser and type 192.150.14.120 into the address bar. Press **Enter.** You will be sent to the Adobe home page.

Class	Address Range
A	1–126
B	128–191
C	192–223

NOTE: 127 is reserved for the loopback address.

3 Refer to the address above. What address class is the Adobe IP number?

4 Create a table like the one below. Pick five more domain names of your choice, including small sites.

Domain Name	IP Address	Class

Enrichment Labs Chapter 9

Lab 9.2 Command Prompt FTP

Purpose

FTP was one of the earliest uses of the Internet. In this lab, you will use basic FTP commands that are available on most computers.

Scenario

You are a network administrator. You have a user who can download from an FTP site but cannot upload. Show the user how to use FTP from the command prompt.

Activity

1 In Windows XP, open the command prompt, type ftp, and press **Enter.** You will get a prompt like this: ftp>

This will begin an FTP session.

2 To connect to an FTP site, type open nameofsite.domain.com and press **Enter.** To FTP to the Microsoft site, for example, you will type: open ftp.microsoft.com.

3 Most FTP sites require a login ID and password, or they will accept anonymous connections. This means you actually type anonymous at the name prompt and type your e-mail address for the password.

4 Once in the site, you can type dir or ls to see the files on the remote computer.

5 Now, follow the directions above and connect to the Microsoft FTP site by typing ftp.microsoft.com. Your session should look like the image below:

6 To open a directory, type cd dirname. For example: ftp> cd bussys

7 To download a file, type get filename.txt, where **filename.txt** is the name of the file you are downloading.

8 To upload a file, type put filename.txt. (You do not have uploading privileges on Microsoft.)

```
Command Prompt - ftp                                          _ □ ×
ftp> open ftp.microsoft.com
Connected to ftp.microsoft.com.
220 Microsoft FTP Service
User (ftp.microsoft.com:(none)): anonymous
331 Anonymous access allowed, send identity (e-mail name) as password.
Password:
230-This is FTP.Microsoft.Com
230 Anonymous user logged in.
ftp> ls
200 PORT command successful.
150 Opening ASCII mode data connection for file list.
bussys
deskapps
developr
KBHelp
MISC
MISC1
peropsys
Products
PSS
ResKit
Services
Softlib
226 Transfer complete.
ftp: 101 bytes received in 0.00Seconds 101000.00Kbytes/sec.
ftp>
```

9 If you forget any of the FTP commands, you can type a question mark at the ftp> prompt and it will list the commands. Then you can type the question mark and the command to find out what it does. For example: ftp>? dir.

Enrichment Labs Chapter 10

Lab 10.1 Creating an Intranet Home Page

Purpose

Technicians often need to use a text editor to create HTML tables. In this lab, you will create tables to make a home page for a company's intranet.

Activity

1 The Web page you create will be based on two tables.

2 Open **Microsoft Notepad** or another text editor and type in the following code exactly as shown.

3 Save the file as Intranet1.html. Then open it in your browser. Your Web page should look like the picture to the right. If it does not, then check the HTML code against the one on this page. If you leave off even a closing bracket, it can cause problems.

Enrichment Labs chapter 10

Lab 10.2 Adding Attributes to an Intranet Home Page

Purpose

In the previous lab, you set up a very basic structure for a home page. Now you will use tag attributes to add color and other elements.

Activity

1 Open the text editor you used to make your intranet1.html page in Enrichment Lab 10.1, and open the file.

2 Make the changes to the code as highlighted below.

```
Intranet2 - Notepad
File   Edit   Format   Help

<html>
<head>
<title>Intranet2</title>
</head>
<body bgcolor="#000000">
<table width="85%" border="0">
<tr bgcolor="#FFFFFF">
<td width="32%"></td>
<td width="68%"><font size="7" face="Times New Roman, Times,
serif" color="#000000"><i>Company Intranet</i></font></td>
</tr></table>
<table width="85%" border="0">
<tr>
<td bgcolor="#CC0000" colspan="3"><hr align="center" width="85%"
size="10"></td>
</tr>
<tr bgcolor="#333333" valign="top">
<td width="31%" align="center" valign="top"></td>
<td width="1%" bgcolor="#FFFFFF"></td>
<td width="68%" height="513" align="left" valign=top><br>
<div align="left"></b></font> <br><font size="4" face="Verdana,
Arial, Helvetica, sans-serif" color="#FFFFFF">
Bulletin Board<br><br>
Calendar<br><br>
Phone List<br><br>
Employee Manual<br><br>
Financial<br><br>
Software<br><br>
Network FAQ<br>
</font></div></td>
</tr></table>
</body>
</html>
```

3 Save the file as Intranet2.html. Then open it in your browser. Your Web page should look like the picture to the right. If it does not, check your code against this page.

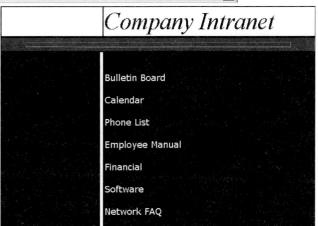

Enrichment Labs Chapter 11

Lab 11.1 Writing Standard Operating Procedures

Purpose

Standard Operating Procedures (SOPs) are an important part of a network administrator's job. An SOP is a document that explains how to do something, such as add a new user to the network. In this lab, you will create an SOP.

Scenario

As you set up or upgrade a network, it is important to record procedures so that they will be systematic and consistent. This is done by creating an SOP. Below is a sample procedure for labeling network cables.

Standard Operating Procedure Networking Division	
Title: Convention for Labeling Network Cables	
Date: October 10, 2002	REV: A
Revision History	
REV A: Initial release of procedure	
Approvals	
Network Administrator	
Operations Manager	
Distribution	
Network Division	
Purpose	To describe conventions and conditions for labeling network cables
Entry and Exit Points Defined	All cables are to be affixed with labels at each entry and exit point. Entry/Exit points occur whenever a cable passes through structural impediments, such as walls and ceilings.
Labeling Conventions	The convention for labeling cables will be source/destination, in which a source is a common connection such as a hub; and a destination is a client workstation, printer, server, and so on.

Activity

1 Think of a task that is commonly done on your school network that should have an SOP. Below are some common tasks you might consider.

- Setting up user accounts
- Setting up peripherals
- Setting up a server
- Changing passwords
- Configuring specific software
- Troubleshooting a printer

2 Write an SOP for the task you chose, following the sample format shown above. If you are not sure how the task is done, ask a network administrator or do research to find out. Create your SOP using a table in your word processing program.

Enrichment Labs Chapter 11

Lab 11.2 Upgrading a Network

Purpose

Upgrading a network involves listening to the client's needs and taking stock of existing equipment. Sometimes your best recommendations do not allow for reusing much of the equipment running the client's present network. In this lab, you will have to replace many items while keeping the client's requirements in mind.

Scenario

You have been assigned to upgrade a network for a small manufacturer. Their network has been in place since 1991.

- ◆ Only minor upgrades or same-model equipment replacements have occurred.
- ◆ The network is configured as peer-to-peer, and there is no file server.
- ◆ The media is coaxial thicknet cable (Standard Ethernet).
- ◆ The network computers are 386-33 PCs.
- ◆ The operating system is Windows for Workgroups 3.11.
- ◆ The company uses shareware word processing applications and spreadsheets as its office software.

The company wants to upgrade to a client/server network. It is adding office space to the building and would like to rewire the network with flexible, inexpensive media. The company is about to begin adding new, powerful design software in its manufacturing process.

Activity

Read the scenario above and answer the questions below.

1 Write your recommendations for each of the following components:

- Ⓐ Server
- Ⓑ Cabling
- Ⓒ Computers
- Ⓓ Software

2 Write a short paragraph for each question:

- Ⓐ What procedure will you follow to do the upgrade with as little downtime as possible?
- Ⓑ After you confirm the installation, what will you need to do?
- Ⓒ Before leaving this job, what kind of information can you leave for the network support team or the network administrator?

Enrichment Labs Chapter 12

Lab 12.1 Executing the Test Life Cycle

Purpose

When you try to identify and solve a problem with your network or with a particular user's computer, there are distinct steps you should take. These steps, or stages, are referred to as the test life cycle. In this lab, you will implement the test life cycle to solve a designer's problem with fonts.

Scenario

One of your designers is using QuarkXPress™ 4.1 on a computer running Macintosh OS 9.2. She complains that fonts appear jagged on her screen. You suspect that downloading and installing Adobe® Type Manager (ATM) Light® might solve the problem, since you know it is required by Quark running in System 9. However, you see that there are red Xs over some fonts in her Suitcase fonts folder.

Activity

Read the scenario above and answer the questions below.

1 Could the red Xs over some fonts be part of the problem? Explain why or why not.

2 Since you know you should test only one thing at a time, you decide to try adding ATM Light. Create a table like the one below. Write a description of each step in your testing. In Stage 5, assume this solution does NOT work.

Test Life Cycle		
Stage	**Step**	**Description**
Stage 1	Test is Planned.	
Stage 2	Test strategy is defined.	
Stage 3	Test plan and test cases are designed.	
Stage 4	Actual execution of the test takes place.	
Stage 5	Results of the test are evaluated and analyzed.	

3 Reread the scenario above. What else did you notice on the user's computer that might contribute to her problem?

Enrichment Labs Chapter 12

Lab 12.2 Re-implementing the Test Life Cycle

Purpose

Sometimes a solution does not work, and you must begin the test life cycle again. In this lab, you will try another solution to the designer's font problem that you worked on in Enrichment Lab 12.1.

Scenario

One of your designers is using QuarkXPress™ 4.1 on a computer running Macintosh OS 9.2. She complains that fonts appear jagged on her screen. You suspect that downloading and installing Adobe® Type Manager (ATM) Light® might solve the problem, since you know it is required by Quark running in System 9. However, you see that there are red Xs over some fonts in her Suitcase fonts folder.

Activity

1 Review the designer's scenario from Enrichment Lab 12.1 as shown above.

2 First, you looked in the documentation for Suitcase and discovered that the red X over a printer icon means that the printer font is missing. Postscript fonts have both a screen and a printer font, and it seems that ATM Light requires both to be installed.

3 Set up a new test cycle that involves installing the printer fonts.

4 Create a table like the one below.

Step 1	
Step 2	
Step 3	
Step 4	
Step 5	

5 Write the steps you will take to solve the problem. This time your result will be a successful one.

6 Since the test had a positive result this time, what should you do next?

Enrichment Labs Chapter 13

Lab 13.1 Creating a Backup Strategy

Purpose

Users accidentally delete files, servers crash, and storms disrupt connections to the network. Network administrators and support technicians need to plan for such events. The backup files may also help when you are upgrading the network or moving the network to a new building. In this lab, you will create a backup strategy.

Scenario

You have recently joined a company whose backup strategy has been to do a full backup every day. However, the backups are now taking so long that they cannot be done overnight, and they are slowing the system for users. You need to develop a new strategy. Your manager's only requirement is that data from a full backup be accessible for two weeks.

Consider how you might utilize these various backup methods: full, incremental, differential. Remember that you cannot do a full daily backup without interfering with employees' work.

Activity

Read the scenario above and answer the questions below.

1 Study the following backup strategy.

2 Explain how it meets the company's needs.

Sa	Su	M	Tu	W	Th	F	Sa	Su	M	Tu	W	Th	F	Sa	Su
A		B	B	B	B	B	C	B	B	B	B	B	B	A	

KEY
A = Full backup
B = Incremental backup
C = Differential

3 Create your own backup strategy for the company. Use a table and key similar to the ones above.

4 Explain your backup strategy in a brief paragraph. Describe the following:

- How your strategy works
- How it is an improvement over the previous strategy
- How it saves time compared to the previous strategy

Enrichment Labs Chapter 13

Lab 13.2 Preventing the Spread of Virus Hoaxes

Purpose

It is bad enough that networks are constantly flooded with new viruses, but they are also flooded with fake viruses, or virus hoaxes. These can take up an administrator's time, especially in a large organization. You will find out how best to handle these annoyances.

Scenario

Have you ever received an e-mail that began with something like this?

Recently a new virus was discovered that was classified by Microsoft and by McAfee Security to be the most damaging of all time! This virus was discovered late yesterday by McAfee and still there is no development of a vaccine!

That is how the "A Virtual Card for You" e-mail hoax begins. The e-mail goes on to tell you how the virus will destroy your hard drive, and instructs you to let as many people know as possible. That means, of course, that many other people end up getting what is essentially a spam e-mail.

A network administrator should be aware of the common hoaxes, which are listed on sites such as the McAfee Security Virus Hoaxes Web site.

Activity

Read the scenario above and answer the questions below.

1 Go to the McAfee Web site and find a list of virus hoaxes. Answer the following questions:

    A How are these virus hoaxes spread?

    B Have you ever received one of those listed? Which one?

2 Write a standard operating procedure (SOP) that warns your users about opening e-mail attachments, about virus hoaxes (reminding them not to send on such e-mails to co-workers and friends), and about the procedure to follow if they discover a real virus.

Enrichment Labs Chapter 14

Lab 14.1 Using TRACERT to Resolve Response Time Problems

Purpose

TRACERT is used to trace a path from the source workstation to a destination IP address. TRACERT is good for troubleshooting network response times. In this lab, you will become familiar with TRACERT results.

Activity

1 You can use either Windows or Macintosh utilities to trace packets.

♦ In Windows, open the **command prompt** window.

♦ In Macintosh OS 10.x, open **Applications, Utilities,** and double-click the **Network Utility.** Click the **Traceroute** tab.

2 You will run a trace from your computer to milwaukee300.org.

♦ If you are using Windows, at the command prompt type TRACERT milwaukeezoo.org and press **Enter.**

♦ If you are using the Macintosh Network Utility, type milwaukeezoo.org in the box. Click the **Trace** button.

You should then see a screen of information similar to the figure below, although it will vary depending on your location. The TRACERT in this example was sent in 13 hops from Boston, MA to Milwaukee, WI.

3 If you look closely at the Macintosh Traceroute, you can see the different parts of the country the packet passed through (New York, Chicago, and so on) and the telecommunications companies that carried it. In the figure shown, point to each city abbreviation you find.

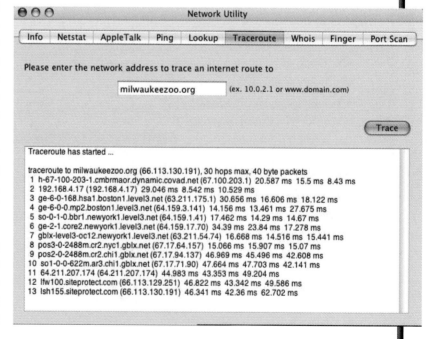

4 The TRACERT shows how many hops are required for the packet to reach the host. It also shows how long each hop takes in milliseconds.

5 Try running TRACERT to other domains you know, both near and far.

Enrichment Labs chapter 14

Lab 14.2 Human Factors in a Network

Purpose

Sometimes your two network resources, people and equipment, clash. Human actions can alter a computer's operating environment. In this lab, you will examine some of these human factors and suggest some preventative measures for each.

Activity

1 Create a table like the one below.

2 In the table, list some common human activities in a computer lab environment and describe how they affect equipment.

3 Fill in your table with other activities and effects of your own.

Human Activity	Effect
Spilling liquids on keyboards and other components	Components can become unusable.
Blocking natural air flow in and around computers	Proper temperatures are not maintained and failures begin.
Using space heaters in under-heated offices	Computers can become overheated. Circuit breakers can be tripped, knocking out power. Possibility of fire.

4 The best preventative measure for these problems is to make computer users aware of the consequences of such behavior.

- ◆ Write a short paragraph about some procedures that will encourage users to be more cautious around equipment. For example, you cannot stop them from drinking coffee at their computers or using heaters if the offices are unbearably cold, but you can suggest keeping the coffee at a distance from the equipment and mandating that heaters be kept on low.
- ◆ Add any other warnings you feel are necessary because of problems you have encountered.

5 Create a poster for one of the problems or solutions identified above. Display all the posters in the computer lab or classrooms at your school.

Certification Programs

WHAT IS CERTIFICATION?

If you have a certification, it means that you passed an exam that demonstrates your knowledge in a specific area of networking. Many certifications are recognized by a wide variety of employers in the field.

Why Should I Get Certified?

Having a certification can go a long way to either help you get that first networking job or to improve your chances of getting a promotion. Generally, the more certifications that you have, the better.

Paths to Certification You can take many different paths to obtain network certification. As shown in the flowchart below, you can start simply with CompTIA's A+ certification and progress through higher levels of certification such as Microsoft MCSA, Cisco CCNA, or Red Hat Certified Engineer.

 There are many companies, including CompTIA, that provide different types of professional certification.

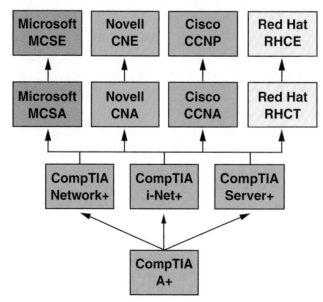

Higher-Level Certifications

| Microsoft MCSE | Novell CNE | Cisco CCNP | Red Hat RHCE |

| Microsoft MCSA | Novell CNA | Cisco CCNA | Red Hat RHCT |

| CompTIA Network+ | CompTIA i-Net+ | CompTIA Server+ |

CompTIA A+

Beginning Certifications

CompTIA

CompTIA provides training and certification for areas such as networking, e-commerce, computer hardware, and computer and network security. This training is *vendor-neutral,* which means that it is not tied to any specific brand or company. The two most popular certifications to obtain for a networking career are CompTIA's A+ and Network+.

A+

The A+ exams focus on computer hardware and operating systems. Passing the two A+ exams demonstrates the knowledge and experience of an entry-level technician with about 500 hours of hands-on experience on the job or in a lab. The A+ exams test areas such as installing, configuring, and upgrading hardware and operating systems. The exams also test troubleshooting, diagnosing problems, and basic networking.

Related job titles:

◆ Computer operator
◆ Field support technician
◆ Hardware installation coordinator
◆ Help desk technician
◆ Network support technician
◆ Operating system specialist
◆ PC technician
◆ Service center technician
◆ Software application technician
◆ Systems analyst
◆ Technical writer

Network+

CompTIA has also created an industry-recognized exam that focuses on networks, called Network+. This exam covers network media and topologies, protocols and standards, network implementation, and network support. For more information about CompTIA Network+, see *Appendix B CompTIA Network+ Certification.*

Related job titles:

◆ Field support technician
◆ Hardware installation coordinator
◆ Internet network specialist
◆ Internet security specialist
◆ Network administrator
◆ Network support technician

For more information about these and other CompTIA exams, visit **comptia.org**.

MICROSOFT

Microsoft offers a number of industry-recognized certifications and training. Two that are particularly related to networking are the **Microsoft Certified Systems Administrator (MCSA)** and the **Microsoft Certified Systems Engineer (MCSE).**

MCSA

Microsoft Certified Systems Administrator (MCSA) is an industry-recognized certification that demonstrates a person's experience and knowledge in implementing, managing, and troubleshooting networks in an existing Microsoft Windows network environment. To obtain experience and knowledge for the MCSA exam, you should first pass the CompTIA Network+ certification and then work in the industry. You can continue studying and gain 6–12 months of hands-on experience with network implementation, administration, and desktop and network operating systems.

Related job titles:

- Network administrator
- Network engineer
- System administrator
- IT engineer
- IT administrator
- Network technician
- Technology support technician

MCSE

Microsoft Certified Systems Engineer (MCSE) is the next level in Microsoft certification. MCSE is for you if you have already passed the MCSA exam and you are looking to plan, design, and implement Microsoft Windows server solutions and architectures in medium- to large-sized companies. You should have at least one year of experience implementing and administering network operating systems and desktop operating systems before taking this exam.

Related job titles:

- Systems engineer
- Network analyst
- Network engineer
- Technical consultant
- Systems analyst

For more information about these and other Microsoft certifications, visit **microsoft.com.**

Before obtaining MCSE certification, you should become MCSA certified.

NOVELL

Novell offers a wide range of certification and training on their various products ranging from network administration to sales. As you are starting your networking career, you may want to take a closer look at two certifications in particular: **Certified Network Administrator (CNA)** and **Certified Network Engineer (CNE).** Visit **novell.com** for more information about Novell training and certification.

CNA

A CNA professional can provide on-site administration for software users of Novell networking products such as NetWare 6, NetWare 5, NetWare 4.11, and Group-Wise. As a CNA, you will be able to perform a variety of tasks such as setting up workstations, managing users and resources in a network environment, automating access to the network, and monitoring network performance.

Related job titles:

◆ Network support technician
◆ Help desk technician
◆ Network administrator

CNE

A step up from CNAs, CNE professionals can create an Internet infrastructure to build a network and perform network planning, installation, and configuration. They can also perform system upgrades and manage network databases.

Related job titles:

◆ Network support technician
◆ Network administrator
◆ Network engineer
◆ Network analyst
◆ Systems analyst
◆ Technical consultant

CISCO

Cisco offers three levels of general certification and training—from Associate to Professional to Expert. These levels are available in various paths (or tracks) and designations. In addition, a variety of Cisco Qualified Specialist focused certifications demonstrate knowledge in specific technologies, solutions, or job roles.

CCNA

A **Cisco Certified Network Associate (CCNA)** is one of the foundation levels of Cisco certification. A CCNA certification demonstrates that a person can install, configure, and operate LAN, WAN, and dial-up access services for small networks. It also certifies that the professional has at least three years of experience.

Related job titles:

◆ Network support specialist
◆ Network technician
◆ Network administrator
◆ Hardware installation coordinator

CCNE

A **Cisco Certified Network Engineer (CCNE)** is the next step in certification after CCNA. It demonstrates that a network professional has advanced knowledge in network installation, configuration, and troubleshooting skills for LANs and WANs in enterprise organizations. A CCNE professional also has knowledge and experience in network security, converged networks, quality of service (QoS), virtual private networks (VPNs), and broadband technologies.

Related job titles:

◆ Network administrator
◆ Network engineer
◆ Network analyst
◆ Systems analyst
◆ System administrator
◆ IT engineer
◆ IT administrator
◆ Technical consultant

Visit **cisco.com** for more information about Cisco certification programs.

RED HAT

Red Hat is one of the most popular open source and Linux providers. The company has created a performance-based training and certification program for Linux. This program has two levels of certification that provide hands-on experience to demonstrate various skills.

RHCT

The first level of certification and training is **Red Hat Certified Technician (RHCT).** The training and certification cover specific skills to production technicians. They are a subset of the next level of certification, **Red Hat Certified Engineer (RHCE).** The RHCT is a test of diagnostic and troubleshooting skills for Red Hat Linux OS.

Related job titles:

◆ Network support technician
◆ Network administrator

RHCE

The **Red Hat Certified Engineer (RHCE)** is the next step after obtaining the RHCT certification. This certification emphasizes experience setting up and managing Red Hat servers that run network services and security.

Related job titles:

◆ Network administrator
◆ Network support technician
◆ Network engineer
◆ Technical consultant

Visit **redhat.com** for more information about Red Hat training and certifications.

CompTIA Network+ Certification

COMPTIA NETWORK+ EXAM

Network+ is a testing program sponsored by the **Computing Technology Industry Association (CompTIA).** This exam certifies the knowledge and ability of individuals with at least nine months of experience in network administration or support.

You can visit the CompTIA Web site to learn more about various certifications.

Development of Network+ certification began in 1995, when a group of technology companies came together to create the IT Skills Project. This committee was formed to help CompTIA identify, classify, and publish skills standards for networking professionals from three types of organizations: information technology companies, channel partners, and business/government firms. Acting on the committee's recommendations, CompTIA defined these job skills through an industry-wide survey. Results and analyses of this survey were used as a foundation for the Network+ certification program.

The Network+ certification demonstrates the knowledge needed to configure and install the TCP/IP client. This exam covers a wide range of vendor and product-neutral networking technologies.

NETWORK+ EXAM OBJECTIVES

The Network+ exam objectives are organized into groups or domains. Each group covers topics such as media and topologies, protocols and standards, network implementation, and network support. A sample of exam objectives is shown below. However, these objectives are reviewed and updated on a regular basis.

To learn more about the exam objectives, visit the CompTIA Network+ Web site.

> ▹ CompTIA Network+ Exam Objectives
>
> ▹ CompTIA Network+ Certification Exam Objective
>
> <<< Back to Intro   Domain 2.0 >>>
>
> **DOMAIN 1.0: Media and Topologies**
>
> 1.1 Recognize the following logical or physical network topologies given a schematic diagram or description:
>
> - Star/Hierarchical
> - bus
> - mesh
> - ring
> - wireless
>
> 1.2 Specify the main features of 802.2 (LLC), 802.3 (Ethernet), 802.5 (token ring), 802.11b (wireless) and FDDI networking technologies, including:
>
> - Speed
> - Access
> - Method
> - Topology
> - Media
>
> 1.3 Specify the characteristics (e.g., speed, length, topology, cable type, etc.) of the following:
>
> - 802.3 (Ethernet) standards
> - 10BASE-T
> - 100BASE-TX
> - 10BASE2
> - 10BASE5
> - 100BASE-FX

REGISTERING FOR THE NETWORK+ EXAM

Anyone who wants to do so can take the Network+ test. There are no specific requirements or prerequisites, except payment of the fee. However, the exam tests the knowledge and ability of individuals with at least nine months of experience in network administration or support. A typical candidate would have CompTIA A+ certification or the equivalent knowledge, but A+ certification is not required. At the time this book was printed, the Network+ exam consisted of 72 questions that must be answered within 90 minutes.

CAREER OPPORTUNITIES

A Network+ certification allows you to stand out as a job candidate. Employers can depend on the certification and the skills that it represents. With a certification in Network+, these entry-level jobs are great places to start your career:

◆ **Field support technician**—Is responsible for installing and upgrading PC and network device hardware, as shown below. The technician usually works in a team with higher-level technicians.

You can visit the CompTIA Web site to learn more about certifications and various job descriptions.

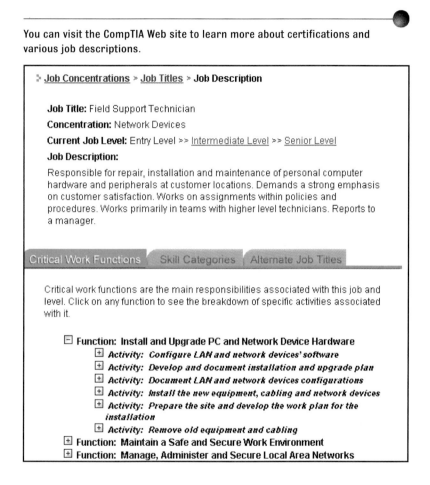

◆ **Hardware installation coordinator**—Works on client machines to connect to the network and assists in problem solving.

◆ **Internet network specialist**—Assists in many aspects of network architecture design and management for enterprise TCP/IP networks. These specialists also identify infrastructure components.

◆ **Internet security specialist**—Secures Windows and Linux-based networks from unauthorized access. The specialist has a fundamental understanding of hackers' methods.

◆ **Network administrator**—Installs, maintains, and configures the network. With other administrators, he or she plans for network growth and implements further hardware and software needs.

◆ **Network support technician**—Documents and troubleshoots users' problems, manages and maintains the network, and works closely with the network administrators.

Network Standards Organizations and Specifications

Standards have been responsible for the success and growth of both the computer and networking products industries. When a vendor subscribes to a set of standards, it means that the vendor is agreeing to make equipment that follows the specifications of the standard.

THE ROLE OF STANDARDS IN NETWORKING

Most networks are a combination of hardware and software from a variety of vendors. This ability to combine the products manufactured by different vendors is made possible by industry standards.

Standards are guidelines that vendors adhere to voluntarily in order to make their products compatible with products from other vendors. In general, those standards address size, shape, material, function, speed, and distance.

More specifically, the standards define physical and operational characteristics of the following:

- Personal computing equipment
- Networking and communication equipment
- Operating systems
- Software

Standards make it possible to buy a network interface card manufactured by one vendor for a computer manufactured by another vendor. The card should be able to do the following:

- Fit into the computer.
- Work with the network cabling.
- Translate signals from the computer and send them out onto the network.
- Receive data from the network and deliver it to the computer.

THE ORIGIN OF STANDARDS

Standards have grown primarily from two sources: popular acceptance (customer driven) and organizational recommendations.

The best example of a customer-driven standard is the term "PC-compatible," which means that a product will work with an IBM Personal Computer or clone. However, as the networking business grew through the mid- and late-1980s, it became apparent that customer-driven popularity was not adequate for creating and imposing standards.

The Influence of the Business Community

In the early years of networking, several large companies, including IBM, Honeywell, and Digital Equipment Corporation (DEC), used their own proprietary standards for how computers could be connected. Those standards describe how to move data from one computer to another, but the standards applied only if all the computers were made by the same company. Getting equipment from one vendor to communicate with equipment from another vendor was difficult.

As networking technology matured, businesses began to trust crucial data to networking. But in the mid-1980s, the same communication problems existed between network vendors that had existed earlier among mainframe vendors. The increasing need for businesses to interact and share data was inescapable.

Computer manufacturers saw this as a business opportunity. They realized that networking technology that enabled communication by conforming to standards would be far more profitable in the long run than equipment that would work only in a single-vendor environment. As a result, standards gradually became a part of the computer and network environment.

The Influence of the Technical Community

Today, certain domestic and international organizations create and define nearly all networking technical standards.

Some of these organizations have existed for many years, and some, such as the SQL Access Group, have evolved more recently as new applications have appeared. These, in turn, created new networking environments that required new guidelines.

Although there are dozens of organizations advocating standards of every description, only a few have gained the recognition required to enlist the support of major computing vendors. The rules of these organizations should be followed or a network will not be accepted. Therefore, network engineers need to be familiar with the names of the organizations and the networking areas they influence.

STANDARDS ORGANIZATIONS

There is no single source for all networking standards. Usually, a standards organization coordinates the specifications for various pieces of equipment or sets the parameters for features or functions. However, sometimes a need for a new standard will set events in motion and eventually result in a standard through agreement or through economic influences.

Most local and international network standards are from a limited number of organizations. Each of these organizations defines standards for a different area of network activity. These organizations are as follows:

- ◆ American National Standards Institute (ANSI)
- ◆ Comité Consultatif Internationale De Télégraphie et Téléphonie (CCITT)
- ◆ Electronics Industries Association (EIA)
- ◆ Institute of Electrical and Electronics Engineers (IEEE)
- ◆ International Organization for Standardization (ISO)
- ◆ Object Management Group (OMG)
- ◆ Open Software Foundation (OSF)
- ◆ SQL Access Group (SAG)

It is important to be aware of these organizations because their acronyms have become common in general networking vocabulary.

AMERICAN NATIONAL STANDARDS INSTITUTE (ANSI)

ANSI is an organization of U.S. industry and business groups dedicated to the development of trade and communication standards. ANSI defines and publishes standards for codes, alphabets, signaling schemes, and communications protocols. ANSI also represents the United States in the International Organization for Standardization (ISO) and the International Telecommunication Union (ITU).

ANSI in Microcomputers

In the microcomputer field, ANSI is commonly encountered in the areas of programming languages and the SCSI interface. Programming languages, such as C, conform to ANSI recommendations to eliminate problems in transporting a program from one type of computer system or environment to another.

ANSI Specifications	
Specifications	**Description**
ANSI 802.1-1985/IEEE 802.5	Token Ring access, protocols, cabling, and interface
ANSI/IEEE 802.3	Coaxial-cable carrier-sense multiple-access with collision detection (CSMA/CD) for Ethernet networks
ANSI X3.135	Structured query language (SQL) database query methods for front-end clients and back-end database services
ANSI X3.92	A privacy and security encryption algorithm
ANSI X12	Electronic data interchange (EDI) defining the exchange of purchase orders, bills of lading, invoices, and other business forms
ANSI X3T9.5	Fiber Distributed Data Interface (FDDI) specification for voice and data transmission over fiber-optic cable at 100 Mbps
SONET	Synchronous Optical Network, a fiber-optic specification defining a global infrastructure for the transmission of synchronous and isochronous (time-sensitive data such as real-time video) information

COMITÉ CONSULTATIF INTERNATIONALE DE TÉLÉGRAPHIE ET TÉLÉPHONIE (CCITT)

The CCITT, which is also known as the International Telegraph and Telephone Consultative Committee, is based in Geneva, Switzerland. It was established as part of the United Nations International Telecommunication Union (ITU), and ITU remains its parent organization. The CCITT studies and recommends communications standards that are recognized throughout the world, and it publishes its recommendations every four years. Each update is distinguished by the color of its cover. CCITT protocols apply to modems, networks, and facsimile transmission (faxes).

The CCITT Study Groups

The CCITT has been divided into study groups for the 1997–2000 study period. Each study group is preparing recommendations for standards in a different subject area. These subject areas include the following:

CCITT Study Groups	
Study Group	**Description**
SG 2	Network and service operation
SG 3	Tariff and accounting principles, including related telecommunications economic and policy issues
SG 4	TMN and network maintenance
SG 5	Protection against electromagnetic effects from the environment
SG 6	Outside plant
SG 7	Data networks and open system communications
SG 8	Characteristics of telematic systems
SG 9	Television and sound transmission
SG 10	Languages and general software aspects for various telecommunication systems
SG 11	Signaling requirements and protocols
SG 12	End-to-end transmission performance of networks and terminals
SG 13	General network aspects
SG 15	Transport networks, systems, and equipment
SG 16	Multimedia services and systems

The V Series

The recommendations for standardizing modem design and operations (transmission over telephone networks) are called the V series. These include the following:

V Series Standards	
Standard	**Description**
V.22	1200 bps full-duplex modem standard
V.22bis	2400 bps full-duplex modem standard
V.28	Defines circuits in RS-232 interface
V.32	Asynchronous and synchronous 4800/9600 bps standard
V.32bis	Asynchronous and synchronous standard up to 14,400 bps
V.35	Defines high data-rates over combined circuits
V.42	Defines error-checking standards
V.90	Defines a standard for 56Kbps modem communication

The X Series

The X series covers **Open Systems Interconnection (OSI)** standards including the following:

X Series Standards

Standard	Description
X.200 (ISO 7498)	OSI reference model
X.25 (ISO 7776)	Packet-switching network interface
X.400 (ISO 10021)	Message handling (e-mail)
X.500 (ISO 9594)	Directory services
X.700 (ISO 9595)	Common Management Information Protocol (CMIP)

ELECTRONICS INDUSTRIES ASSOCIATION (EIA)

The EIA is an organization founded in 1924 by U.S. manufacturers of electronic parts and equipment. It develops industry standards for the interface between data processing and communications equipment. It has published many standards associated with telecommunications and computer communications. The EIA works closely with other associations such as ANSI and ITU (CCITT).

EIA Serial Interface Standards

The EIA standards for the serial interface between modems and computers include the following:

EIA Standards

Standard	Description
RS-232	A standard for serial connections using DB-9 or DB-25 connectors and a maximum cable length of 50 feet. It defines the serial connections between transmitting equipment devices, such as Data Terminal Equipment (DTE), and receiving equipment devices, such as Data Communications Equipment (DCE).
RS-449	A serial interface with DB-37 connections that defines the RS-422 and RS-423 as subsets.
RS-422	A balanced multipoint interface.
RS-423	An unbalanced digital interface.

CCITT Equivalents

EIA standards often have CCITT equivalents. RS-232, for example, is also the CCITT V.24 standard.

INSTITUTE OF ELECTRICAL AND ELECTRONICS ENGINEERS (IEEE)

The **Institute of Electrical and Electronics Engineers (IEEE)** is a U.S.-based society that publishes a variety of standards, including those for data communications.

The 802 Committees

A subgroup of the IEEE, the 802 Committees began developing network specifications in 1980 to ensure low-cost interfaces. These specifications are passed on to the ANSI for approval and standardization within the United States. They are also forwarded to the ISO.

Shortly after the 802 project began, the IEEE realized that a single network standard would be inadequate because it would not include the diverse hardware and new architectures. To adequately cover the wide range of subjects, the society established committees that were to be responsible for defining standards in different networking areas.

802 Committees

Committee	Description
802.1	Internetworking
802.2	Logical Link Control (LLC)
802.3	CSMA/CD Network (Ethernet)
802.4	Token Bus Network
802.5	Token Ring Network
802.6	Metropolitan Area Network (MAN)
802.7	Broadband Technical Advisory Group
802.8	Fiber Optic Technical Advisory Group
802.9	Integrated Voice/Data Networks
802.10	Network Security
802.11	Wireless Network
802.12	Demand Priority Access Network (100VG-AnyLAN)
802.13	Cable TV Access Method and Physical Layer Specification

INTERNATIONAL ORGANIZATION FOR STANDARDIZATION (ISO)

The **International Organization for Standardization (ISO)** is a Paris-based organization of member countries. Each country is represented by its leading standard-setting organization. For example, ANSI represents the United States, and the **British Standards Institution (BSI)** represents the United Kingdom. Other organizations represented at the ISO include the following:

- Governmental bodies such as the U.S. State Department
- Businesses
- Educational institutes
- Research organizations
- CCITT

The ISO works to establish international standards for all services and manufactured products.

ISO Computer Communication Goals

In the area of computing, the ISO's goal is to establish global standards for communications and information exchange. The standards promote open networking environments that let computer systems with products from different venders communicate with one another. These systems will be able to use protocols that have been accepted internationally by the ISO membership.

The ISO Model

The ISO's major achievement in the area of networking and communications has been to define a set of standards known as the **Open Systems Interconnection (OSI)** reference model. This model defines standards for the interaction of computers connected by communications networks.

OBJECT MANAGEMENT GROUP (OMG)

The OMG consists of almost 300 organizations involved in developing a set of languages, interfaces, and protocol standards that vendors can use to create applications that will work with products from different vendors.

The OMG certifies products designed to meet the standards and specifications agreed upon by the OMG members.

In working toward its goals, the OMG developed the **Object Management Architecture (OMA),** a model for object-oriented applications and environments.

The OMG architecture has been adopted by the **Open Software Foundation (OSF),** which is developing portable software environments called the **Distributed Computing Environment (DCE)** and the **Distributed Management Environment (DME).**

OPEN SOFTWARE FOUNDATION (OSF)

The OSF, part of the Open Group, created computing environments by acquiring and combining technologies from other vendors and distributing the results to those who wanted them.

These vendor-neutral environments, referred to as the Open System Software Environment, can be used to create a collection of open systems technologies in which users can incorporate software and hardware from several sources.

The following components comprise the OSF software environment:

OSF Software Components

Component	Description
Distributed Computing Environment (DCE)	This platform simplifies the development of products in a mixed environment.
Distributed Management Environment (DME)	The DME makes tools available for managing systems in distributed and multi-vendor environments.
The Open Software Foundation/1 (OSF/1)	This is a UNIX operating system, based on the Mach kernel, which supports symmetric multiprocessing, enhanced security features, and dynamic configuration.
OSF/Motif	This is a graphical user interface that created a common environment with links to IBM's Common User Access (CUA).
OSF Architecture-Neutral Distribution Format (ADNF)	Developers can use this environment to create a single version of an application that can be used on different hardware architectures.

SQL ACCESS GROUP (SAG)

A part of the ANSI standards, SAG is a group of 39 companies that was founded in 1989 by Hewlett-Packard, Digital, Oracle Corporation, and Sun Microsystems. Its goal is to work with the ISO to create standards covering the interoperability of front- and back-end systems.

SAG's purpose is to promote interoperability among **structured query language (SQL)** standards so that several SQL-based relational databases and tools can work together with database products from different vendors. This interoperability makes it possible for different database applications running on different platforms to share and exchange data.

SAG has developed three technical specifications.

1. **Structured query language**—This is a specification that follows international specifications in implementing the SQL language.
2. **SQL Remote Database Access**—This specification defines communication between a remote database server and an SQL-based client.
3. **SQL Access Call-Level Interface (CLI)**—This group of APIs provides interfacing with SQL-based products.

GLOSSARY

5-4-3 rule A rule that states that a thinnet network can combine as many as five cable segments connected by four repeaters. However, only three segments can have stations attached, which leaves two segments untapped. (p. 138)

A

access permission Access rights assigned to objects (such as files, folders, and printers) on a per-user basis. (p. 391)

account policy Acceptable user practices. (p. 374)

Active Server Page (ASP) A Web page capable of generating customized Hypertext Markup Language (HTML) pages on the fly. (p. 286)

add-in card A component that can be added to a computer to expand its capabilities, such as a video or audio card. (p. 410)

address resolution The process of DNS and its databases matching domain names to IP addresses. (p. 260)

Address Resolution Protocol (ARP) A protocol used to determine the hardware address (MAC address) that corresponds to an IP address. (p. 265)

address space A range of assignable IP addresses technically runs from 0.0.0.0 to 255.255.255.255. (p. 263)

administrative tools The network operating system tools available for network administrators to manage servers, users, and resources from virtually anywhere on the network. (p.179)

Advanced Program to Program Communications (APPC) The SNA mainframe communication model was modified in a specification known as APPC to include mini-computers and personal computers. (p. 84)

Advanced Technology Attachment (ATA) Many hard drives, CD and DVD burners, and other storage devices use the Advanced Technology Attachment (ATA) interface to connect to the motherboard. (p. 351)

alias A shortcut method for using or writing a command. (p. 389)

American National Standards Institute (ANSI) An organization of business and industry groups concerned with fostering the development and adoption of standards in the United States. Among its many concerns, ANSI focuses on various networking technologies. It also represents the United States in the ISO. (p. 240)

American Standard Code for Information Interchange (ASCII) One of the oldest, and most commonly used codes. In this system, each letter, character, or nonprinting character is given a specific numerical code. (p. 210)

analog A signal that travels as a continuously variable wavelike pattern. (p.74)

AppleTalk A protocol stack developed for Macintosh computers that corresponds to five of the seven layers in the OSI reference model. (p. 155)

AppleTalk Data Stream Protocol (ADSP) A protocol used in an AppleTalk network that establishes full, two-way communications sessions. (p. 156)

AppleTalk Transaction Protocol (ATP) A protocol in an AppleTalk network that transports packets. (p. 156)

Application Layer The top (seventh) layer of the OSI reference model that represents the services directly supporting user applications, such as software for file transfers, database access, and e-mail. (p. 79)

ARPANET The Advanced Research Projects Agency Network created in the 1960s made it possible for military and university computers to communicate long distances and to share files through an interconnected network. (p. 13)

array An ordered collection of devices, such as hard drives. (p. 323)

asynchronous communication A form of data transmission that involves a delay of seconds, minutes, or even days. Communication does not happen instantly. (p. 8)

Asynchronous Transfer Mode (ATM) A connection-oriented networking technology. Like frame relay, ATM is designed to take advantage of digital media. (p. 234)

AT command set A special set of Hayes-compatible commands used for controlling modems. (p. 199)

Attached Resource Computer Network (ARCnet) A PC-based LAN architecture that corresponds to the IEEE 802.4 specification. An ARCnet is built using either a bus or a star topology. (p. 143)

attenuation The process of data losing signal strength as the data are transmitted along a cable. (p. 112)

attribute An HTML command that modifies a certain formatting or layout instruction. (p. 298)

auditing The process of examining and verifying information. (p. 381)

Authenticode A technology used to assure end users that the code they are downloading has been created by the group or individual listed on the certificate, and has not been changed since it was created. (p. 292)

B

back end On a file server, behind-the-scenes processes. (p. 40)

backbone A high speed communications path that interconnects many regional networks. (p. 252)

bandwidth Amount of data that can be transmitted in a given amount of time. (p. 46)

barrel connector A component that connects two pieces of cable together to make a longer piece of cable. (p. 58)

base 10 The number of digits that forms the base of the system. Digits from left to right in a decimal number represents a power of ten. (p. 206)

base 16 Hexadecimal base value often noted with a subscript 16. (p. 209)

base 2 The binary system uses only two digits, 1 and 0, which is why it is called base 2. (p. 207)

baseband transmission Transmissions of digital signals over a single channel, typical of most current LANs. One signal at a time travels over the network cable. (p. 75)

baseline A measurement used for determining statistics. For example, a baseline would help determine a server's performance and traffic flow over a period of time. (p. 328)

Basic Rate Interface (BRI) A form of ISDN that is typical in home use. There are two B (bearer) channels that carry data at the rate of 64 Kbps. (p. 216)

batch file A file similar to a script—each line contains instructions that can be read and executed by the operating system. (p. 387)

binary A system of numbers based on two digits, 1 and 0. In computers, the number 0 represents an off electrical state and the number 1 is on. (p. 207)

binding order The sequence in which the operating system runs the protocol. (p. 88)

binding process The process of tying the protocols together to provide data with a route from the application level to the NIC. (p. 88)

bit A binary digit and is the smallest amount of data used by a computer. (p. 207)

bits per second (bps) The measure of transmission speed used in relation to networks and communication lines. (p. 75)

BNC connector A hardware component used to make the connections between the cable and the computers. (p. 112)

boot-on-LAN The process that enables the PC to boot from a server rather than the local hard drive. (p. 122)

boot-sector virus A virus that executes when the computer is booted. (p. 393)

bridge A device used to connect two network segments together. (p. 105)

broadband ISDN (B-ISDN) The next generation of ISDN that is capable of delivering high quantities of data. (p. 236)

broadband transmission Transmissions that rely on an analog signal, a range of frequencies, and a communications medium. Broadband signals can be divided into multiple channels separated by small bands of unused frequencies to avoid interference. (p. 74)

broadcast domain A domain common in Ethernet networks in which the data are broadcast to all other nodes within the network without the need to pass through a router. (p. 108)

brouter A network hybrid device that combines the capabilities of bridges and routers. (p. 108)

budget A summary stating how much money and time will be used toward a specific purpose. (p. 315)

buffer A reserved portion of memory where data is temporarily held until an opportunity to complete its transfer to or from a storage device or Web site is complete. (p. 86)

burst The event that takes place when the network clears of traffic, and data flow freely and quickly using as much bandwidth as needed. (p. 243)

bus A data pathway that connects components in a computer using parallel cabling or wire. (p. 72)

bus network A linear network based on a main trunk line. It is the simplest and easiest topology to implement. (p. 57)

byte A unit of information consisting of 8 bits. In computer processing or storage, a byte is equivalent to a single character, such as a letter, numeral, or punctuation mark. (p. 202)

C

cable modem A modem that uses a cable television connection to get transmission rates that are faster than a dial-up connection. (p. 201)

cache A storage area in memory. (p. 260)

carrier sense The ability of nodes on the network to sense a carrier signal on the line. A carrier signal indicates the network is busy. (p. 138)

carrier sense multiple access with collision avoidance (CSMA/CA) These nodes "listen" to the transmission medium for a chance to transmit. (p. 145)

carrier sense multiple accesses with collision detection (CSMA/CD) The technique used to manage the problem of two nodes on a bus network that transmit data at the same time and the data run into each other. *See also* carrier sense. (p. 57)

carrier services Data transfer services provided by telecommunications companies, such as AT&T, Sprint, or Verizon. (p. 224)

cascading style sheets (CSS) Documents developed to make it easier to apply formatting rules to one or more HTML documents. A single format change can appear throughout a Web site. (p. 300)

cell A fixed-length packet, the basic transmission unit on high-speed networks, such as ATM. (p. 235)

cell relay Used with ATM transmissions, a high-speed transmission method based on fixed-size units that are known as cells. (p. 235)

central processing unit (CPU) The brain, or processor component, of the computer that performs basic functions. (p. 27)

Channel Service Unit (CSU) A device that processes the signals being sent over the digital line and isolates the line from network equipment problems. (p. 215)

circuit-switched network A network that creates a direct physical connection between the sender and receiver. (p. 228)

client A network computer that requests, or orders, information from a server. (p. 36)

Client Services for NetWare (CSNW) A Window NT protocol allows Microsoft clients to connect to file and print resources on NetWare services. (p. 346)

client/server network A network built around one or more dedicated servers and is administered from a central location. It supports many clients and multiple computer platforms. (p. 45)

clustering The grouping of multiple servers in a way that allows them to appear to be a single unit to client computers. Clustering is a means of increasing network capacity and improving data security. (p. 10)

coaxial cable A type of cable that consists of a core of copper wire surrounded by insulation, a braided metal shielding, and an outer cover. (p. 111)

collision When two nodes on a bus network transmit data at the same time and the data collide. (p. 57)

collision detection In the event that two nodes actually transmit simultaneously, the nodes rely on this to resolve the situation. (p. 138)

collision domain A part of the network that includes a segment and its associ-ated nodes created to help reduce the number of collisions over a network. Receives all of the traffic and collisions generated by any node. (p. 108)

Comité Consultatif International Téléphonique et Télégraphique (CCITT) A standards organization now part of the International Telecommunications Union that was instrumental in defining numerous communications-related standards—among them the CCITT V series specifications for modems. (p. 199)

command prompt The location in DOS where system commands are entered. (p. 167)

Common Gateway Interface (CGI) An interface that allows Web servers to interact dynamically with users. Most commonly used to process online forms. (p. 301)

complex instruction set computers (CISC) A type of microprocessor that supports most instructions and is difficult to design and build, leading to somewhat higher costs. (p. 27)

Compressed Serial Line Internet Protocol (CSLIP) A version of SLIP that compresses the TCP header of each packet of data transmitted. Compressed SLIP (CSLIP) reduces the size of the packet, which is important when transmitting small packets of data at low speeds. (p. 214)

computer Any device capable of processing information to produce a desired result. No matter how large or small they are, computers typically perform their work in three well-defined steps (1) accepting input, (2) processing the input according to predefined rules (programs), and (3) producing output. (p. 24)

configuration A design or architecture for how the types of servers and clients are used in the network. (p. 43)

connection A link between two communicating computers. (p. 145)

connectionless protocol A transmission protocol that does *not* establish a complete channel of communications over a set path. The transmission is addressed and broadcasted. It can take multiple routes to the destination. (p. 149)

connection-oriented protocol A transmission protocol that establishes a two-way channel of reliable communications over a set path. (p. 149)

constellation of satellites A group of satellites working together to provide global communications coverage. (p. 202)

contention The competition among stations on a network for the opportunity to use a communication line or network resource. (p. 137)

crossover cable A cable used to connect two computers directly with a single cable. (p. 415)

crosstalk Signal overflow from an adjacent wire that distorts the data signal. (p. 111)

cryptography The encoding of information so that it is unreadable by anyone other than the person(s) holding the key to the code. (p. 291)

cyclical redundancy check (CRC) Error checking used in networks. A sending node performs a mathematical calculation on the packet and the result is attached to the packet's trailer. The receiving node performs the same calculation on the packet it received. If the calculations differ, the CRC signals the source computer to retransmit the packet. (p. 71)

D

data Distinct pieces of information, such as files or entries in a database. (p. 38)

Data Circuit-Terminating Equipment (DCE) Packets are sent here from the DTE or PAD. A DCE might be a modem or packet switch. A DCE is located at each end of the connection. (p. 232)

data encryption standard (DES) A high security level encryption standard, 56 bit keys, used before file transmission. This is no longer the highest level. (p. 293)

data frame An organized, logical structure in which data can be placed. (p. 82)

Data Link Layer The second layer in the OSI reference model. This layer packages raw bits from the physical layer into data frames. (p. 79)

data packet Data that consist of three parts—a header, the data itself, and a trailer. (p. 70)

Data Service Unit (DSU) A device that converts the data from its network-oriented, computer-based format to the form needed for synchronous transmission. The DSU also controls the flow of data to the CSU. (p. 215)

Data Terminal Equipment (DTE) X.25 device terminology. There are no computers, hosts, or nodes. Instead, sending and receiving computers are referred to simply as this. (p. 232)

datagram A packet of data with addressing information, sent through a packet-switching network. (p. 156)

Datagram Delivery Protocol (DDP) A protocol used in an AppleTalk network that delivers packets of data, but provides no means of guaranteeing delivery. Prepares datagrams for routing and delivers them. *See also* datagram. (p. 155)

decapsulation At the receiving end of a transmission, after the packet passes through the layers in reverse order from bottom to top, the process of stripping away all addressing and formatting information passing the data up to the next layer. (p. 80)

decimal A number system based on the use of ten digits (0, 1, 2, 3, 4, 5, 6, 7, 8, and 9). (p. 206)

dedicated server A server that provides a specific type of resource to its clients, such as just printing. (p. 37)

deferral time The amount of time the nodes wait to transmit data. (p. 138)

defragment To optimize the storage space on a hard drive by adjoining scattered files in like clusters. (p. 347)

demodulation The process of converting the analog signal back to a digital signal on the receiving computer. (p. 109)

demultiplexer A device, also known as demux, used to break the high data rate stream back into its original lower rate stream on the receiving end. (p. 203)

Denial of Service (DoS) A type of computer attack that makes it impossible for a receiving computer to function correctly. The attack can cause the recipient to freeze, crash, or reboot, or cause a system to become paralyzed. (p. 334)

deterministic Predictable network transmissions. In certain networks, such as token passing networks, you can calculate how long it will take before a node transmits again. (p. 142)

device driver Software that helps a computer work with a particular device. (p. 140)

dial-up networking (DUN) A client service using regular telephone lines to connect to a network. (p. 224)

digital Signals that encode information numerically, using 0s and 1s and that convey information in separate on/off pulses. (p. 75)

digital data service (DDS) Communication lines that are dedicated, point-to-point connections. Lines transmit digital data, rather than voice calls. (p. 215)

Digital DECnet DECnet by use of its protocol stack defines communication networks over Ethernet LANs, FDDI MANs, and WANs that use private or public data transmission facilities. It can use TCP/IP and OSI protocols as well. (p. 90)

digital divide The gap between people who use technology and those who do not. (p. 237)

digital signature An electronic certi-ficate that verifies the creator of a program or other electronic document. Relies on a private key that is held by the originator, and the public key held by the recipient of the file. (p. 292)

Digital Subscriber Line (xDSL) A family of digital communications technologies. These services provide high-speed network access over the standard copper wires run into homes and offices by the telephone company. (p. 217)

digital volt-ohmmeter An all-purpose electronic measuring tool used in troubleshooting computer problems. (p. 414)

Direct Sequence Spread Spectrum (DSSS) A type of radio signal that breaks data into a pattern of particles, called chips. These chips, which are encrypted, can then be loaded onto the radio signal over a broad range of frequencies. (p. 147)

directory service A network service, installed on server computers, that handles the information databases (directories) required to identify the users and resources on the network. (p. 41)

disk image A complete copy of a configured OS, with all applications and options already set up. (p. 342)

Disk Operating System (DOS) A command driven operating system capable of performing many important tasks, such as file and directory management, disk formatting, and simple text editing. (p. 167)

distributed computing Using the processing power of thousands of idle computers to process large data sets. For example, the primary source of computing power for research into the human genome. (p. 15)

DNS name servers A server that holds and looks through its DNS database to match domain names to IP addresses, then resolves the IP address. (p. 258)

document type definition (DTD) The rules which define the legal tags for an XML document. For an XML file to be valid, it must follow the rules set by the DTD. (p. 300)

domain A grouping of computers and devices that are administered as one unit. (p. 179)

domain controller A Windows server that stores the logon and security information for a network. Another name for a logon server. (p. 344)

Domain Name Server (DNS) Web browsers use this to locate the IP address of the domain name that the user entered in the address bar of the browser (p. 150)

Domain Name System A system based on a tree-like hierarchy and used to uniquely identify Internet sites. This hierarchy includes a top-level domain, a second-level domain, and, often, one or more subdomains. (p. 256)

downstream Delivery of information from a server to a client. (p. 200)

downtime The amount of time a computer or server is out of service due to some problem. (p. 9)

drive assignment Mapping a network folder or drive to a logical drive on a user's computer. (p. 361)

DSL modem A type of fast digital communications technology. The DSL modem is a card installed inside a computer. DSL requires two specialized modems—one connected to the computer accessing the Internet or other network, and another installed at the phone company. (p. 202)

dual-ring topology A topology used in FDDI networks that consist of two counter-rotating rings. (p. 239)

dumb terminal Computers consisting of keyboards for input and screens for output. They are wired directly to the host computer and have little or no processing power of their own. (p. 13)

Dynamic Host Configuration Protocol (DHCP) A protocol used to automatically assign IP addresses within a network. (p. 266)

Dynamic HTML (DHTML) A special type of program code, called script, embed within a regular HTML page. (p. 299)

E

Electronics Industries Association (EIA) A standards organization in the United States that focuses on the development of hardware-related industry standards(p. 468)

encapsulation Packets passed sequentially from one layer to another that gather more information at each layer, such as formatting or addressing information. (p. 80)

encrypt To encode (scramble) information in such a way that it is unreadable to all but those individuals possessing the key to the code. (p. 226)

encryption Scrambling of information so that it is unreadable by anyone other than those possessing the keys, or codes, required to return the information to readable form. (p. 226)

Enhanced Industry Standard Architecture (EISA) A technology created in 1988 by a consortium of companies. This 32-bit bus was backward compatible with the ISA bus, but enhanced its capabilities and speed. (p. 120)

Ethernet A LAN architecture that uses a bus topology and relies on CSMA/CD to regulate traffic on the main communication line. It uses a bus topology and is based on the IEEE 802.3 standard. (p. 137)

EtherTalk A protocol in an AppleTalk network that allows communication over Ethernet networks, an Apple implementation. (p. 156)

Event Viewer An administrative utility you can use to view important log files generated by the Windows OS. (p. 405)

expansion slot Thin, rectangular slots on the motherboard that accepts add-in cards to increase the computer's capabilities. (p. 350)

Extended Binary Coded Decimal Interchange Code (EBCDIC) Code that was developed for use on IBM computers. EBCDIC values were assigned for easy use with punch cards. (p. 210)

Extended File System Version 2 (EXT2) The most common file storage system on Linux systems. (p. 176)

Extensible Markup Language (XML) A markup language used to describe the content structure and not just the appearance of the document that is transmitted. (p. 300)

Extensible Style Sheet (XSL) A document sheet set up for formatting the display of XML data (in a browser, for example). (p. 300)

extranet A Web-like network that makes it possible for employees of a corporation and trusted outside parties to access the network. (p. 290)

F

fault tolerance The ability of computers and network operating systems to withstand severe problems that can bring a network to a standstill, damage hardware, or cause loss of data. (p. 52)

FDDITalk A protocol in an AppleTalk network that allows communication on high-speed, token-passing ring networks over fiber optic cables. (p. 156)

Fiber Distributed Data Interface (FDDI) A standard developed by ANSI for high-speed, fiber optic local area networks. The interface provides specifications for transmission rates of 100 Mbps on networks based on the Token Ring standard. (p. 238)

fiber optic cable A type of cable made up of extremely thin tubes of glass or plastic that allow pulses of light to travel through it to transmit data. (p. 115)

file allocation table (FAT) A file storage system used by the Windows 9x line of operating systems (and optionally by operating systems based on Windows NT). FAT32 is an extension to FAT, which uses 32 bits to store a file's address location. (p. 176)

file infector A virus that attaches itself to a file or program and activates any time the file is used. (p. 393)

file sharing Sharing files between computers; the act of making files on one computer accessible to others on a network. (p. 6)

file system directory A system tool used to display the organizational structure of the files stored on the hard drives, network drives, and other removable storage devices, such as Zip disks or CD-R disks. (p. 175)

File Transfer Protocol (FTP) A protocol that moves files between computers over a network. (p. 150)

firewall A barrier, such as a router, bridge, or gateway, that sits between the network and the outside world. It is designed to keep unacceptable packets from reaching the internal network. (p. 294)

FireWire A bus architecture developed by Apple. It can transfer large amounts of data at very high speeds (400 or 800 Mbps, depending on the version). FireWire is most commonly used in conjunction with digital video (DV) devices, such as DV cameras or external hard drives that require a high rate of transmission. (p. 120)

firmware The term for software routines that are permanently stored on the NIC. This storage is known as read-only memory (ROM) because it cannot be overwritten. (p. 117)

Flash memory A Flash memory device is like a hard drive, but has no moving parts and is penlight to house key size. Stored data remains in memory even when the device has no power. (p. 25)

fractional T1 Part rather than all of the T1 bandwidth. A business often leases this type of bandwidth. (p. 217)

frame A format that Ethernet networks use for transmitting data packets. The frame contains the preamble, source and destination addresses, data, type of protocol used to send the frame, and the CRC. (p. 139)

frame relay A newer form of packet switching that relies on digital technologies, such as fiber optic and ISDN. (p. 233)

Frequency Division Multiplexing (FDM) A multiplexing process that assigns each signal to a different frequency. (p. 203)

Frequency Hopping Spread Spectrum (FHSS) A type of radio sig-nal that requires the transmitter and receiver to hop in unison from one frequency to another. (p. 147)

frequently asked questions (FAQs) document lists frequently asked questions and responses to those questions. (p. 412)

front end On an application server, that information this is processed before the delivery to the desktop client. (p. 40)

G

gateway A dedicated network computer whose job is to convert data packets from one network protocol to another. Enables dissimilar networks to commu-nicate. (p. 108)

Gateway Services for NetWare (GSNW) A protocol that provides a gateway for Microsoft clients and services to access resources on NetWare services. (p. 346)

geostationary earth orbit (GEO) The orbit in which satellites fly at 22,000 miles above the earth in fixed positions. Only about eight satellites are required to cover the entire planet. (p. 202)

gigabyte (GB) Commonly, a thousand megabytes. A gigabyte is 1 billion bytes. A gigabyte can also be either 1000 megabytes or 1024 megabytes, where a megabyte is considered to be 1,048,576 bytes (2 raised to the 20th power). (p. 37)

graphical user interface (GUI) A computer interface that replaces typed commands. Makes computing easy by allowing users to click a mouse and graphical icons to manage files within the OS. (p. 167)

group An account of users. An administrator can easily add or remove users in the group. A group is used to automatically assign permissions to many users at once. (p. 179)

groupware A name that represents a special class of software referred to as "workgroup" software. (p. 183)

H

hard disk One or more inflexible platters coated with material that allows the magnetic recording of computer data. (p. 37)

hardware loopback One type of serial port connector that enables you to test the communication capabilities of a computer's serial port without having to connect to another computer or peripheral device. (p. 417)

hardware technician Entry level individual who set ups, configures, and maintains computer and networking hardware. (p. 23)

Hayes-Compatible Standards The set of transmission signals, commands, used originally by Hayes modems for exchanging status information, such as readiness to send or receive. (p. 199)

header The address part of a packet includes both the sending and the receiving computers. It also includes other information, such as the length of the packet and the time it was sent, to ensure the packet is transmitted appropriately. (p. 71)

hexadecimal A number system based on 16 characters, including the numerals 0 to 9 and the letters A to F. (p. 209)

Hierarchical File System (HFS) A Mac OS file storage system. Files are normally stored as two "forks" or parts. (p. 176)

hop One portion of a transmission's journey between two points. (p. 126)

hub A hardware device that connects the nodes in the arms of a star network. A hub can be active—boosts the signal, or it can be passive—simply relay the signal. (p. 58)

hyperlink Text or image that "links" the user to another document when clicked. (p. 14)

Hypertext Markup Language (HTML) The language used to define the structure and layout of a Web page. HTML acts as a set of instructions that tells browser's software how and where to place the page's content. (p. 269)

Hypertext Transfer Protocol (HTTP) A code that appears at the beginning of every URL clicked or typed with the purpose of visiting a Web site or to request a specific document within the site. (p. 286)

I

icon A picture, or graphic in an OS that represents files, folders, drives, or applications. (p. 168)

IEEE 802.x A series of specifications developed by the IEEE that define numerous networking standards. The x following 802 is a placeholder for individual specifications, including 802.3 (Ethernet), 802.4 (Token Bus), and 802.5 (Token Ring). (p. 136)

Industry Standard Architecture (ISA) An older technology that was used in the IBM PC, XT, and AT computers and their clones. ISA was expanded from an 8-bit bus to a 16-bit bus (16 bits of information could be transmitted simultaneously). (p. 120)

infrared A type of light beam used in wireless networks to transmit the data between devices. (p. 125)

initial sequence number (ISN) In a three-way handshake, it is a number used to verify that data in the packet went through the network successfully. (p. 151)

input Provides some sort of instruction to the computer so that it knows what to do. A device such as a keyboard is an example of an input device. (p. 24)

installation technician Individual responsible for building networks from scratch or expanding current networks. (p. 23)

instant messaging (IM) A type of e-mail process service that enables two (or more) people to establish a private communications channel, similar to calling someone on the phone. (p. 274)

Institute of Electrical and Electronics Engineers (IEEE) A global society of technical professionals. The IEEE (pronounced "eye triple e") focuses on electrical, electronics, computer engineering, and science-related matters. It is especially well known for its development of the IEEE 802.x specifications dealing with networking standards. (p. 136)

Integrated Services Digital Network (ISDN) A technology that delivers different types of information—voice, data, video—in digital form over standard telephone cabling. (p. 145)

Integrated Services LAN (ISLAN) Isochronous LANs aimed at enabling multimedia capabilities on a network. (p. 145)

Integrated Voice/Data (IVD) networks A network capable of transmitting voice or data over the same line cable. (p. 137)

intelligent hub Active hubs with additional capabilities that enable them to monitor the network or perform diagnostic tasks. (p. 143)

interface The connection that provides communication between layers. It also shields neighboring layers from the details of how services are implemented. (p. 80)

International Organization for Standardization (ISO) An international organization made up of standards-setting groups that work to establish global standards for communications and information exchange. The OSI reference model is the organization's best known accomplishment. (p. 79)

Internet Control Message Protocol (ICMP) An Internet protocol used to help hosts control network traffic and respond to various error conditions. (p. 334)

Internet Corporation for Assigned Names and Numbers (ICANN) A nonprofit organization that registers domain names, preserves the operational stability of the Internet, and oversees the Internet's root server system. (p. 261)

Internet Information Services (IIS) Microsoft's Web server that runs on Windows NT and provides services, such as file transfer (FTP), e-mail (SMTP), and Active Server Pages (ASPs). (p. 346)

Internet layer A layer that corresponds to the Network Layer of the OSI model. Routers work at this layer to move packets from one network to another. (p. 150)

Internet Protocol (IP) A protocol responsible for routing packets, sometimes through many different networks. (p. 149)

Internet Protocol version 6 (IPv6) The latest generation of the IP protocol; also called Next Generation IP, or Ipng. (p. 265)

Internet Service Provider (ISP) An online service provider. (p. 253)

Internetwork Packet Exchange/Sequenced Packet Exchange (IPX/SPX) A protocol stack that was designed by Novell for its NetWare networks. (p. 158)

internetworking The transfer and routing of information between and among varied workstations and networks. (p. 84)

interprocess communication (IPC) Another name for Network Basic Input/Output System (NetBIOs) interface. (p. 156)

intranet A Web-like network that can only be accessed by internal users such as employees of a company. (p. 290)

ISDN modem A modem-type device that adapts the signals—which are transmitted in several separate channels—to the communications standards understood by the computer. *See also* Integrated Services Digital Network (ISDN). (p. 201)

isochronos *Iso*—meaning equal and *chronos*—meaning time. *See also* Integrated Services LAN (ISLAN). (p. 145)

iterative query A request that is sent repeatedly (iteratively) through name servers in the domain hierarchy until the complete address—or a "no such site exists" response—is produced. (p. 260)

J

JavaScript A script that utilizes the Java programming language to create dynamic effects that can be added to an HTML page. (p. 301)

jumper A small device used to connect adjacent wire pins on a circuit board. Acts as on/off switch and is used to alter the configuration of the circuit board or device. (p. 411)

K

kernel The part of a program that is responsible for allocating resources and communicating directly with the hardware. (p. 388)

L

latency The time it takes for a transmission to go from one point to another. (p. 202)

legacy application Software that may use older technology, which may be considered outdated compared with today's applications. (p. 318)

license server A server that issues application licenses to clients. After closing the application, the license and application is made available to anyone else on the network. (p.352)

Link Access Balanced Protocol (LAPB) A protocol in X.25 networks that defines how packets are framed and ensures an error-free connection. (p. 233)

Linux A derivative operating system of UNIX. It has gained popularity as an alternative to Microsoft Windows. (p. 170)

local area network (LAN) A network that is relatively limited in size and that usually connects computers in a small geographical area, such as in the same office building. (p. 45)

local user The user at the computer. (p. 51)

LocalTalk A protocol in an AppleTalk network that uses cabling and configuration specially designed for AppleTalk networks. (p. 156)

log file A simple text file that records information about the device, system, or application. (p. 379)

log on To gain access to a network by identifying oneself with a username and a password. (p. 4)

logbook A written record of all changes that affect the network. (p. 361)

Logical Link Control (LLC) A sublayer of the Data Link Layer that is responsible for establishing and terminating links to other computers and sequencing and acknowledging frames and controlling frame traffic. (p. 136)

loopback address A special reserved IP address used to test whether a computer's network capabilities are functioning. (p. 263)

low-earth orbit (LEO) The orbit in which satellites fly between 310 and 1,240 miles above Earth. LEOs have high rates of transmission, but need at least 48 satellites in position before data can be transmitted around the world. (p. 202)

M

Macintosh A model of computer made by Apple. Features a GUI-type OS in which users click graphical icons to manage files. *See also* GUI. (p. 168)

mainframe A large and powerful centralized computer. (p. 43)

Management Information Base (MIB) A database in which information about an SNMP device, called an agent, is stored. (p. 372)

media Physical pieces of equipment used to transport data from one com-puter to another computer or peripheral device on the network. Examples are cables or wireless devices. (p. 38)

Media Access Control (MAC) The lower of two sublayers that make up the Data Link Layer. The MAC manages access to the physical network, delimits frames, and handles error control. (p. 92)

medium-earth orbit (MEO) The orbit in which satellites fly between 6,250 and 12,500 miles above Earth. A group of 20 MEO satellites form a constellation capable of transmitting at speeds greater than GEOs. (p. 202)

menu system A method used primarily in GUI systems to organize commands and information within an application. (p. 174)

mesh network A network topology in which each computer is connected to every other computer by separate cabling. This topology provides redundant paths throughout the network. If one cable fails, another takes over the traffic. (p. 60)

message switching A technology used to route an entire message from one system to another. That message is routed through intermediate (go-between) station and does not involve a direct physical connection between the sender and receiver. (p. 228)

MicroChannel Architecture (MCA) Bus architecture introduced in 1988 with IBM's PS/2 computer. The MCA functions as either a 16-bit or 32-bit bus, but is incompatible with the ISA bus. (p. 120)

Microsoft Active Directory The central database system for administering the network. (p. 180)

microwave Part of the electromagnetic spectrum and a form of radiation that can be used for short- and long-distance communications systems. (p. 126)

mirroring A process of duplicating data on the primary drive to the other drive(s) in the array. (p. 324)

modem A computer-to-computer communication device that converts digital signals from the computer to analog signals for the telephone lines. It derives its name from the two operations it has traditionally handled: modulation and demodulation. (p. 109)

modulation The process on changing the digital signal to an analog signal on the sending computer. (p. 109)

multiple access An instance when more than one node might want to transmit on a network at the same time. (p. 138)

multiplex Multiple transmissions sent through a channel simultaneously and are interwoven into a single signal. (p. 75)

multiplexer A device, also known as a mux, used to divide a transmission into two or more channels. (p. 203)

Multipurpose Internet Mail Extensions (MIME) A widely used Internet protocol designed to allow e-mail messages to include not only text, but sound, graphics, audio, and video. (p. 293)

Multistation Access Unit (MAU) The connection or hub that forms a logical ring. A Token Ring has a logical ring topology. (p. 144)

multitask A computer that works on more than one job at a time. The processor can turn its attention from one job to another if one is held up waiting for input or output. (p. 12)

multiuser dungeon (MUD) A type of game available on the Internet that is an outgrowth of the popular dungeons and dragons type of interactive, multiplayer role playing games (RPGs). (p. 274)

N

Name-Binding Protocol (NBP) In an AppleTalk network, a protocol that makes connections between devices and their network names. (p. 156)

narrowband radio A high-frequency transmission similar to broadcasting from a radio station. The user tunes both the transmitter and the receiver to a certain frequency. (p. 126)

NetBIOS Extended User Interface (NetBEUI) A protocol developed by IBM in the mid-1980s and was designed for LANs of up to 200 computers. (p. 157)

NetWare A software networking product that runs on top of existing hardware, such as that used in the Ethernet and Token Ring networks. *See also* Novell Netware. (p. 158)

NetWare Link (NWLink) The Microsoft implementation of the IPX/SPX protocol. (p. 91)

network A system of two or more computer systems connected together so they can share and exchange data. (p. 6)

Network Access Point (NAP) The major location at which regional networks connect to a national backbone to join the larger Internet. (p. 253)

network address A number that identifies the network and the subnetwork, if any, to which a node belongs. (p. 107)

Network Address Translation (NAT) A network method of shielding the internal IP addresses from the outside world by filtering outbound network traffic. (p. 392)

network administrator Trained individual responsible for installing computers and their operating systems and managing networks on a daily basis. (p. 18)

network architect Highly trained individual who oversees the construction, maintenance, and expansion of a company's network. (p. 19)

Network Basic Input/Output System (NetBIOS) An interface that evolved into a standard method for applications to access protocols in the Transport Layer. (p. 156)

network engineer Highly trained individual responsible for connecting computers to the network and connecting networks to networks. (p. 19)

network interface card (NIC) A hardware component that enables both client computers and servers to communicate with one another. Also known as network adapter card. (p. 50)

network interface layer The layer in the TCP/IP suite that corresponds to the Physical and Data Link Layers of the OSI reference model. This layer provides the interface between the network architecture (such as token ring or Ethernet) and the Internet layer. (p. 150)

Network Layer The third layer of the OSI reference model. This layer is responsible for addressing messages and translating logical addresses and names into physical addresses. This layer also determines the route from the source to the destination computer and manages traffic problems such as switching, routing, and controlling the congestion of data packets on the network. (p. 79)

network monitors Software tools, similar to performance monitors, that track all or a selected part of network traffic. (p. 331)

Network News Transfer Protocol (NNTP) A standard that is used to distribute collections of articles called newsfeeds. (p. 273)

network operating system (NOS) An operating system designed to support networking. A network operating system that must answer the demands of many users, and must do so as quickly and effectively. (p. 52)

network support technician Individual with specialized technical knowledge to troubleshoot the many problems that arise in network usage. (p.19)

newsfeed A collection of news articles delivered through the NNTP protocol by news servers on the Internet. (p. 473)

newsgroup A group of individuals on the Internet with a common interest in a particular subject or set of related subjects. Newsgroups receive and post articles and discussions. (p. 273)

newsreader A software application used to access newsgroup online. (p. 273)

node Each piece of hardware such as, a server, client, and shared peripheral connected to a network. (p. 45)

noise Stray electronic signals that interfere with data transmissions along a cable and slows the transmission speed. (p. 111)

nondedicated server A server that provides many different services to its client computers, such as file retrieval, printing, and e-mailing. (p. 37)

Novell Directory Services (NDS) The central administration application for NetWare-based networks. (p. 180)

Novell NetWare One of the leading network architectures and protocol stacks. *See also* Netware. (p. 90)

NT file system (NTFS) A file storage system used by the Microsoft Windows NT-based operating systems (Windows 2000 and Windows XP). It allows an administrator to set access permissions for directories and/or individual files. (p. 176)

O

online gaming Games available on the Internet that pit players from around the world against one another in real-time. (p. 274)

open source Programming code that is available to anyone. Linux was made of this, which meant that anyone was free to add and improve on the code. (p. 170)

Open Systems Interconnection (OSI) reference model An international standard that is a guide for networking. Defines how data are sent from a computer, through the network, and into a receiving computer. Also called the OSI model. (p. 79)

operating system (OS) The software that closely interacts with the computer hardware and allows the user to interact with the computer. (p. 25)

optical carrier (OC) A signal definition in the SONET standard used by fiber optic media and translated roughly to speed and carrying capacity. (p. 240)

oscilloscope An electronic instrument that measures the amount of signal voltage per unit of time and displays the result on a monitor. (p. 415)

output Data that are displayed for example on a screen or printer, or heard as music from speakers. (p. 25)

outsourcing To hire an outside com-pany to handle various information technology (IT) services, such as technical support. (p. 20)

P
---

packet assembler/disassembler (PAD) A device in X.25 transmissions that prepares packets for transmission and disassembles the packets that come in. (p. 232)

Packet Internet Groper (ping) A simple utility that tests if a network connection is complete, from the server to the workstation, by sending a message to a remote computer. (p. 353)

packet switching A transmission method in which all transmissions are broken into small units and sent over the network. Packets are reassembled at the destination computer. (p. 229)

Packet Switching Exchange (PSE) Go-betweens in the packet switching process. The PSE inspects the packet's destination address, consults a routing table, and forwards the packet at the highest possible speed. (p. 229)

parallel transmission The orderly procession of trans-mitted data in computers in which groups of bits are transferred simultaneously side by side over two or more wires. (p. 72)

parity The detecting of errors in information which increases fault tolerance at the RAID 3 level. (p. 324)

parity bit The signal used for error checking in an asyn-chronous transmission. (p. 204)

partition A part of the usable space on a hard drive that acts as a virtual disk. (p. 344)

password The private string of characters entered by a user to verify his or her identity to the network. Ideally a password is a combination of text, numbers and punctua-tion or other characters that cannot be guessed at or eas-ily cracked by intruders. (p. 10)

password-protected share A security method for keep-ing data and hardware resources safe in which a pass-word is assigned to each shared resource. In most peer-to-peer networks it is the only type of security avail-able. (p. 391)

patch cable A short length of cable with connectors at each end. (p. 320)

PC Card standards Standards developed for personal computer cards and intended for laptop users that target a broad range of devices, including modems. (p. 199)

peer-to-peer network A network that does not require an administrator and whose computers function as both clients and servers. (p. 44)

peripheral A device that is connected to a computer and is controlled by its microprocessor. (p. 38)

Peripheral Component Interconnect (PCI) The most common bus architecture found in today's PC and Mac computers. PCI is generally implemented as a 32-bit archi-tecture. (p. 120)

Peripheral Component Interconnect-Extended (PCI-X) A key component of Gigabit Ethernet. Extends the PCI inter-face to increase data transmission speeds and is more fault tolerant and faster. (p. 120)

permissions Also called security settings. Permissions determine the resources to which a user has access. (p.375)

physical address In networking, a unique numeric address (value) assigned to a network interface card. (p. 152)

Physical Layer The bottommost (first) layer of the OSI reference model. This layer addresses the transmission of the unstructured raw bit stream over a physical medium (the networking cable). The Physical Layer relates the elec-trical/optical, mechanical, and functional interfaces to the cable and also carries the signals that transmit data gen-erated by all of the higher OSI layers. (p. 79)

pilot deployment A period of testing new software or program changes before installation on a network. Also known as a test installation. (p. 324)

Plain Old Telephone Service (POTS) One of the largest and most used networks. Also known as the phone system. (p. 213)

Point-to-Point Protocol (PPP) Point-to-Point Protocol (PPP) provides stable network connections and error-checking features. PPP works at the Data Link Layer. (p. 214)

Point-to-Point Protocol over Ethernet (PPPoE) A proto-col that creates point-to-point communications over Ethernet connections. A typical scenario might be several users on an Ethernet network using a DSL line to connect to the Internet. (p. 214)

Point-to-Point Tunneling Protocol (PPTP) A protocol that creates a Virtual Private Network (VPN) between two computers. With a VPN, a remote user can securely access the network using a public Internet connection. (p. 214)

port A slot or device that enables input devices and out-put devices connect to the computer or network. (p. 24)

portal A Web page that acts as an entryway, or a gateway, to the Web. (p. 291)

Post Office Protocol (POP) A server assigned to receiv-ing and scanning incoming messages and organizing them by the addressee. (p. 182)

Presentation Layer The sixth layer of the OSI reference model. This layer determines the format used to exchange data between networked computers. Manages network security issues by providing services such as data encryp-tion, provides rules for data transfer, and performs data compression to reduce the number of bits that need to be transmitted. (p. 79)

Primary Rate Interface (PRI) A form of ISDN that is gen-erally used to connect a company's telephone network. The line is divided into many channels. (p. 216)

Printer Access Protocol (PAP) A protocol in an AppleTalk network that provides bidirectional communica-tions between PostScript printers and the client computer. (p. 156)

Private Branch Exchange (PBX) The PRI form of ISDN used to connect a company's telephone network to the local or long-distance phone company. (p. 216)

programmable read-only memory (PROM) A chip that contains the hardwired code to start the computer and connect the user to the network. With remote-boot PROMs, diskless workstations can join the network when they start. (p. 122)

protocol Rules that define how network devices communicate with each other and perform specific tasks. (p. 78)

protocol analyzer A tool used to perform real-time network traffic analysis using packet capture, decoding, and transmission data. (p. 331)

protocol stack Multiple layers of protocols that work together. (p. 88)

proxy server A server that forms a barrier between the internal network and the outside world. Presents only one IP address for all the computers on the network. Also known as proxies. (p. 295)

Public Switched Telephone Network (PSTN) A communication service known as the public telephone system. (p. 213)

R

random-access memory (RAM) provides a storage area for data going into and out of the CPU. (p. 27)

README A file included with the software that contains last-minute information that may warn you of potential problems you may encounter. (p. 404)

read-only memory (ROM) A set of prerecorded instructions that tells the computer how to start, look for hardware devices, and check the operating system. (p. 28)

real-time communication Live communication in which people talk with each other at the same time. *See also* synchronous communication. (p. 8)

reduced instruction set computers (RISC) A type of microprocessor that relies on a relatively small set of simplified instructions, allowing them to operate very fast. (p. 27)

redundant network Networks that duplicate data and/or resources to minimize down time and losses in the event of a disaster. (p. 9)

Redundant Array of Inexpensive Disks (RAID) An array of hard drives that mirror or duplicate other drives. Should the primary hard drive fail, the second drive can be substituted for the failed drive with little or no down time. (p. 41)

regional network A collection of small networks. For example, there are regional networks that serve the Northeast, Midwest, West, East, Southeast, Northwest, and Central California. (.p. 253)

reliable network A dependable network user's trust to work. (p. 8)

remote access A direct connection to a network using regular dial-up lines. After the connection is made, the user can work on the network as if in the office. (p. 224)

remote user A user who dials in to the server over modems and telephone lines from a remote location. (p.51)

repeater A device that can be used to connect two cables and that boosts the signal before sending it along. (p. 58)

replication The copying of critical data to backup servers. A backup server can fill in immediately if the primary server fails. (p. 382)

resource Software or hardware, such as a hard drive, printer, or scanner that can be shared over a network. (p. 6)

Return On Investment (ROI) A calculation of how the cost of new equipment or software will result in increased savings or earnings. (p. 357)

Reverse Address Resolution Protocol (RARP) A protocol used to look up the IP address when the hardware, or MAC address, is known. (p. 265)

ring network A network topology that forms a circle, at least as far as the nodes are concerned. (p. 59)

RJ-11 Connector used in twisted-pair cabling to connect telephones and computers to telephones. (p. 113)

RJ-45 Connector used in twisted-pair cabling. RJ-45 connectors house eight cable connections. (p. 113)

root server A DNS server that is responsible for tracking top-level domain names (.com, .org, .net, and so on). (p. 259)

router A network device used to connect networks of different types and that forwards packets from one network to another, even those separated by great distances. A router determines the best route to use to deliver the data. (p. 107)

routing table A database composed of the source and destination of packets and built by a bridge that helps to keep track of the NIC's physical address of the node on the segments the bridge connects. (p. 106)

S

scalable network A network that the hardware or software can grow (scale) up or down to meet an organization's needs. (p. 9)

script A fairly short program that limits interaction within the confines of the Web page and browser. (p. 301)

script A set of commands that can be executed without any user interaction. (p. 386)

search engine A sight that uses automated software to index the Web. (p. 271)

Secure HTTP (HTTPS) An extension to HTTP that adds encryption and security features to HTTP. (p. 288)

Secure Sockets Layer (SSL) An authentication and encryption method developed by Netscape Communications used to protect communications between client and server. (p. 294)

Secure/Multipurpose Internet Mail Extensions (S/MIME) A security-oriented protocol that adds encryption and support for digital signatures to the widely used MIME e-mail protocol. (p. 291)

security The capability of the network operating system to secure data from unauthorized access. (p. 49)

segment A section of the network that includes the cable and nodes that are connected to a device, such as a repeater, hub, or bridge. (p. 105)

Sequenced Packet Exchange (SPX) Part of Novell's IPX/SPX protocol suite for sequenced data. (p. 91)

Serial ATA (S-ATA) A device that can transfer data much more quickly than either ATA or Ultra ATA devices, and uses a thinner cable. (p. 351)

Serial Line Internet Protocol (SLIP) Serial line used to connect to the Internet when modem speeds were limited to 2400 bps. Computers used SLIP to connect to an Internet Service Provider's (ISP) computer, which provided access to the Internet. (p. 214)

serial transmission The procession of transmitted data in which bits are sent over network cables and travel bit by bit one at a time. (p. 73)

server Computers that work behind-the-scenes to provide (serve) shared resources to network users, or clients. (p. 36)

service agreements A contract with an outside business for maintenance and repairs of certain types of equipment, such as printers and copiers. (p. 360)

session A highly structured dialog between two workstations. (p. 81)

Session Layer The fifth layer of the OSI reference model. This layer establishes, uses, and ends a connection between computers and is called a session. It performs name recognition and provides synchronization between user tasks. This layer also implements dialog control between communicating processes, regulating which side transmits, when, for how long, and so on. (p. 79)

shared peripheral Shared hardware devices available on the network, such as printers, copiers, storage drives, and so on. (p. 38)

shareware Software programs you can try before you buy. (p. 347)

shell An interface from a human being to the kernel that provides commands that a user can execute on a processor. (p. 388)

shielded twisted-pair (STP) A type of twisted-pair cabling that uses a woven copper-braid jacket to protect the transmitted data from outside interference. (p. 113)

shielding A layer of covering that grounds a cable and protects it from electric noise and crosstalk. (p. 111)

signal bounce A signal that continues uninterrupted to the end of the bus, and then keeps bouncing back and forth along the cable, preventing other com-puters from sending data. (p. 57)

Simple Mail Transfer Protocol (SMTP) A server assigned to resolving outgoing messages' domain names into IP addresses. (p. 182)

Simple Network Management Protocol (SNMP) A protocol that allows a device on the network to store information about itself, then return that information when asked. SNMP-compliant devices are able to store information about themselves. (p. 372)

sniffer A type of network analyzer that can monitor network traffic. (p. 420)

software Digital instructions that a computer needs to operate. There are instructions that tell systems what to do and those that tell applications what to do. (p. 39)

spread-spectrum radio A transmission technology that broadcasts signals over a range of frequencies, thus providing security for the transmission. (p. 126)

star network A network that stretches out in different directions from a hub in a central location. (p. 58)

star-bus network A combination of the bus and star topologies. In a star-bus network, several star networks are linked together with linear bus trunks. (p. 60)

star-ring network A network similar to the star-bus. Both the star-ring and the star-bus connect at the center to a hub that contains the actual ring or bus. Also called a star-wired ring network. (p. 61)

start bit The signal that frames the bits making up one character. The start bit indicates the start of the character in an asynchronous transmission. (p. 203)

Statistical Time Division Multiplexing (STDM) A multiplexing process that assigns time slots to signals dynamically. This allows the bandwidth to be utilized more fully. (p. 203)

stop bit The signal that marks the end of the character in an asynchronous transmission. (p. 203)

striping A RAID 0 level technique that spreads data across each drive in an array. Increases the array's read and write speeds. (p. 323)

subnet mask A mask used in conjunction with IP addresses to determine the portion of the IP address that identifies the network and the portion that identifies the host. Identifies the first 24 bits as the network address, with the remaining 8 bits identifying the host. (p. 263)

subnetwork A part of a larger network. For example, in a city, it would be the name of the street you live on. (p. 107)

switch A multiport bridge that allows several segments of a network to communicate with one another. (p. 106)

Switched Multimegabit Data Services (SMDS) A broadband public networking service offered by communications carriers. A means for businesses to connect LANs in separate locations. (p. 243)

synchronous communication 1) When people talk to each other at the same time. (p. 8); 2) Communication whose bits are sent and received in a timed method. Digital systems and networks rely on this method that results in faster transmissions, but it is also more complex and more expensive. (p. 204)

Synchronous Digital Hierarchy (SDH) A European standard for the transmission of different types of digital information using optical media—data, voice, and video. (p. 240)

Synchronous Optical NETwork (SONET) An American National Standards Institute (ANSI) standard for the transmission of different types of digital information using optical media—data, voice, and video. (p. 240)

Synchronous Transport Signal (STS) The electrical equivalents of OC levels and are used by nonfiber media. *See also* optical carrier. (p. 240)

system lockup A computer malfunction that makes the system unresponsive to any sort of user interaction, including mouse movement or keyboard activity. (p. 405)

Systems Network Architecture (SNA) IBM's network architecture for mainframe networks. (p. 84)

T

T1 line A high-speed communications line that can handle digital communication and Internet access at a rate of 1.544 Mbps. (p. 216)

tags An HTML command that tells how to display an element, such as text or an image, within a Web browser. (p. 298)

Telnet A TCP/IP protocol that runs on the Application Layer and allows a computer to log on to a remote computer and pretend it is attached directly to the host. (p. 273)

terminal A device with a keyboard and a monitor that connects directly to a mainframe through a communications link or cable. The terminal requests information from the mainframe computer. (p. 13)

terminator A device at the end of a cable that absorbs the signals and keeps them from bouncing back along the line or trunk. (p. 57)

test life cycle Distinct stages of testing a new component goes through before it is deployed on a network. (p. 362)

thin client A network computer that has no local storage and relies on servers for applications, data storage, and administration. (p. 36)

three-way handshake A sequence of steps used by TCP, a connection-based protocol. A link between two computers is established and a reliable connection is created. (p. 151)

throughput The capacity to handle network traffic. A measure for network data transfer performance. (p. 10)

Time Division Multiplexing (TDM) A multiplexing process that assigns each signal a fixed time frame that rotates in a fixed order between each signal. (p. 203)

Time to Live (TTL) A protocol that works at the Internet layer and is called this because a packet must reach its destination in a predetermined period of time or it dies. (p. 150)

time-domain reflectometer (TDR) An electronic device that send sonarlike pulses along cables to locate breaks, shorts, or imperfections. (p. 415)

timesharing In the early days of computers, the concept of running multiple jobs at the same time. The idea of switching the computer's processing from one task to another and incorporating a main, or host computer. (p. 12)

token The small collection of bits computers pass in token passing. (p. 59)

token passing A means of processing a packet, or token, transmission through a network from node to node. (p. 59)

Token Ring An IBM-designed architecture created to connect PC's with IBM's larger midrange and mainframe computers. (p. 144)

TokenTalk A protocol in an AppleTalk network that allows communication over token-passing networks, an Apple implementation. (p. 156)

tone generator A standard tool for wiring that applies an alternating or continuous tone or signal to a cable or a conductor. (p. 417)

tone locator A standard tool for wiring used to detect the correct cable at end of the wire opposite the tone generator. (p. 417)

topology The design or layout of a network. Refers to the way the computers are connected. (p. 56)

Total Cost of Ownership (TCO) The calculation of the initial purchase price of the hardware and software involved in the upgrade and the costs associated with installation, management, training, and insurance. (p. 357)

trailer The end port of a packet that contains the error-checking information to enable the receiving computer to verify that the data arrived intact. (p. 71)

transceiver A device that both transmits and receives signals. In the network interface card (NIC), the transceiver is responsible for receiving and transmitting data. (p. 117)

Transmission Control Protocol (TCP) A protocol that creates a connection between the sending and receiving computers, and then makes sure that all the data arrive safely. (p. 149)

Transmission Control Protocol/Internet Protocol (TCP/IP) reference model An Internet-related network architectural model. (p. 84)

Transport Driver Interface (TDI) A programming interface that allows NetBEUI protocol to communicate with higher level layers (the Session, Presentation, and Application Layers). (p. 157)

Transport Layer The fourth layer of the OSI reference model. It ensures that messages are delivered error free, in sequence, and without losses or duplications. (p. 79)

tree structure A structure in OSs representing the files stored on disk. The drive often represents a "root," or base, that has folders or directories for its branches. (p. 175)

trunk A single main cable in a bus network to which nodes, the client computers and servers, connect. (p. 57)

twisted-pair cable A type of cable that consists of two insulated strands of copper wire twisted around each other. (p. 113)

U

Unicode Code that was developed to combat limitations of systems like the ASCII system. (p. 210)

Uniform Resource Locator (URL) An address used to specify the exact location and name of a resource on the Web. (p. 286)

uninterruptible power supply (UPS) A large rechargeable battery that provides power to connected devices for a period of time if main electrical power goes out. (p. 383)

Uniplex Information and Computing System (UNIX) A uniquely powerful and flexible OS that uses very little assembly language code. (p. 166)

Universal Serial Bus (USB) A bus architecture designed to automatically add and configure new devices on a system without shutting down. The original specification, USB 1.0 was limited to speeds of 1.5 Mbps. Hi-Speed USB (USB 2.0) can transmit data at up to 480 Mbps. (p. 120)

unshielded twisted-pair (UTP) A type of twisted-pair cabling that does not have an extra shielding layer to help eliminate noise interference, however it is highly affordable. (p. 113)

upstream Delivery of information from a client to a server. (p. 200)

uptime The amount of time a computer or server has been running without needing a restart. (p. 9)

Usenet An electronic bulletin board where users can post messages 24 hours a day, 365 days a year. (p. 273)

User Datagram Protocol (UDP) A connectionless transport protocol that is responsible for end-to-end transmission of data. It sends the data, but provides little in the way of error correction. (p. 151)

username A logon name that identifies a specific user on the network. (p. 374)

V

V series Standards that cover today's modems, with speeds up to 56 Kbps. (p. 199)

virtual disk A part of a hard drive that a computer recognizes as an individual disk, even though all the storage space is contained on one physical drive. (p. 344)

Virtual Private Network (VPN) An alternative to using a dial-up network connection. Is a network connection between two computers. With a VPN, a remote user can securely access the internal network from a remote location. (p. 226)

W

Wavelength Division Multiplexing (WDM) A multiplexing process that assigns each signal to a particular wavelength. This type of multiplexing is used in conjunction with fiber optics. (p. 203)

Web browser A software application that functions either in addition to or as part of an operating system to enable use of the Internet, the World Wide Web, and Web technologies implemented on other software, such as word processors and online Help systems. (p. 81)

Wi Fi In wireless network technology, the three standards 802.11a, 802.11b, and 802.11g are commonly referred to as this. (p. 145)

wide area network (WAN) A computer network that uses long-range telecommunication links to connect networked computers across long distances. WANs, in simple terms, are made up of multiple LANs. (p. 45)

Windows A family of OSs created by Microsoft. *See also* GUI. (p. 169)

Windows Internet Naming Service (WINS) A service used to match com-puter names to IP addresses in a Windows network. (p. 266)

Windows Troubleshooter A set of help files that is part of the Help and Support Center. (p. 408)

wired encryption privacy (WEP) A security feature when activated, encrypts the data prior to transmission by the NIC. At the receiving end, the data are decrypted. Most wireless NICs and access points have this security feature built in. (p. 128)

wireless access point (WAP) A transceiver connected to a wired network but used in a wireless network to send and receive signals between the two types of networks. Wireless access points can be thought of as wireless hubs. (p. 122)

wireless local area network (WLAN) A local area network the uses either infrared (IR) light or radio frequencies (RF) to connect the clients and/or peripherals. (p. 46) A network based on 802.11 specifications set standards for wireless LAN communications. These specifications are roughly comparable to Ethernet networks. (p. 136)

X

X.25 A connection-oriented, packet-switching protocol designed for use on analog telephone lines. Computers on an X.25 network can receive and transmit data at the same time. (p. 232)

Z

Zone Information Protocol (ZIP) In an AppleTalk network, a protocol that locates nodes on the network. (p. 156)

INDEX

HTTP, 285–286
HTTPS, 286
Hubs
  active, 105
  as network connectivity
    devices, 104
  hybrid, 105
  in ARCnet, 143
  in star network, 59
  passive, 105
  switched, 105
Hybrid hub, 105
Hybrid networks, 54
Hyperlink, 14
Hypertext Markup Language (HTML),
  269, 296–297
Hypertext Transfer Protocol (HTTP),
  285–286

I

IBM Token Ring architecture, 144
ICANN, 261
ICMP, 332
Icons, 174
IEEE 802.11 standard, 145
IEEE 802.11a standard, 145–146
IEEE 802.11b standard, 145–146
IEEE 802.11g standard, 145–146
IEEE 802.16 standard, 124
IEEE 802.3 standard, 137–139
IEEE 802.9 standard, 144–145
IEEE 802.x standards, 136–137
IIS, 344
IM, 274
Industry Standard Architecture
  (ISA), 120
Information, sharing of in a
  network, 6
Infrared wireless networks, 125–126
Infrastructure, designing within, 319
Input, 24
Input devices, 24
Instant messaging (IM), 274
Integrated Services Digital Network
  (ISDN), 145, 199–200, 214
Integrated Services LAN (ISLAN), 145
Integrated voice/data (IVD)
  networks, 145
Interfaces between communication
  layers, 80
Internet, 14, 250–281
  backbone of, 252–253
  benefits and drawbacks, 287
  for business transactions, 268
  piracy on, 178
Internet Control Message Protocol
  (ICMP), 332

Internet Corporation for Assigned
  Names and Numbers (ICANN), 261
Internet domains, 256–258
Internet Information Services
  (IIS), 344
Internet layer, 150
Internet protocol (IP), 149
Internet Protocol version 6
  (IPv6), 265
Internet Service Provider (ISP),
  253–254
Internet2 research, 16
Internetworking, 84
Internetwork Packet
  Exchange/Sequenced Packet
  Exchange (IPX/SPX), 158
  Novell NetWare using, 344
Interrupt time, 327
Intranets, 288–289
IP addresses, 150, 152–153, 162,
  262–265
  ranges, 264
  resolving, 258, 259–261
IPv6, 265
IPX/SPX,158
  Novell NetWare using, 344
ISA, 120
ISDN, 145, 199–200, 214
ISDN modems, 199–200
ISLAN, 145
Isochronous networks, 144–145
ISP, 253–254
IVD networks, 145

J

JavaScript, 300
Job hunting, 23, 320
Job skills, 20–22
Jumper, 411

K

Kernel, 387
Keyboard shortcuts, 174

L

LANs, 45–46
Latency of satellites, 200
LDAP, 41
Leadership skills, 22, 148
Leased lines, 213
Legacy application, 316
Leisure and recreation and
  networking, 14–15
LEO, 200
License server, 350

Licensing, 350–351
Lightweight directory access
  protocol (LDAP), 41
Line-of-sight networks, 125
Line-of-sight transmission, 146
Linux, 170–171, 210
  kernel, 387
  scripts, 387-388
  shell, 387
Linux scripts, 387–388
LLC sublayer, 92, 136–137
Local area networks (LANs), 45–46
Local user, 51
Log files, 377–379, 405–406
Logbook, 359
Logical Link Control (LLC) sublayer,
  92, 136–137
Loopback address, 263
Low-earth orbit (LEO), 200

M

MAC address, 152–153
MAC sublayer, 92, 136–137, 152
Macintosh operating system,
  168–169
  as a network operating system, 52
  automatic defragmentation of, 381
  built in IPv6 functionality of, 265
  hierarchical filing system of, 176
  installing a network interface card
    using, 119
  log files in, 377
  peer-to-peer capabilities of, 51
  using ping to test network connec-
    tivity, 351–352
Macro virus, 392
Mail servers, 40
Mainframe computers, 12, 43–44
Malware, 172
MAN, 47
Management Information Base
  (MIB), 370
MAU, 144
MCA, 120
Media Access Control (MAC)
  sublayer, 92, 136–137, 152
Media, network, 38
Medium-earth orbit (MEO), 200
Memory, 27–28
Menu systems, 174
MEO, 200
Mesh network, 60
Message switching, 228–229
Metropolitan area network (MAN), 47
MIB, 370
Micro Channel Architecture
  (MCA), 120

PHOTO CREDITS:

Cover and title page; Courtesy of International Business Machines corporation. Unauthorized use not permitted. Cover **(c)** Royalty-free/Ryan McVay/Photodisc/Getty Images cover **(tr)**; Royalty-free/Photodisc/Getty Images cover **(br)**.

Frontmatter; Bob Anderson/Masterfile **iv**; David Chasey/Photodisc/PictureQuest **xiii(t)**; Dex Images/CORBIS **ix**; George B.Diebold/CORBIS **xiii(br)**; Sharon L.Jonz/Photis/PictureQuest **xi**; Lester Lefkowitz/CORBIS **vii(tr)**; Rob Lewine/CORBIS **x**; James Leynse/CORBIS **vii(bl)**; Masterfile **xii**; Jose Luis Pelaez,Inc./ CORBIS **viii**; Royalty-free/Photodisc/Getty Images **xiii(bl), xvi, xxii, H1, H8**; Royalty-free/Corbis Images/ PictureQuest **v, vi(tl)**; SW Productions/Brand X Pictures/PictureQuest **xxiii**; SW Productions/Photodisc/ Getty Images **H6**; Arthur Tilley/Photodisc/Getty Images **H7**; Bill Varie/CORBIS **xv**; Tom Wagner/
CORBIS SABA **vi(br)**.

Text; AMPROBE® 414; Bob Anderson/Masterfile **74(r)**; Cables4Computer.com **122(b), 349(l), 349(r)**; David Chasey/Photodisc/PictureQuest **133**; Ron Chapple/ Thinkstock/PictureQuest **148**; Cooperphoto/CORBIS **100–101**; Donna Cox and Robert Patterson/NCSA/ University Illinois Urbana Champagne **252**; Dex Images/CORBIS **231**; George B.Diebold/CORBIS **74(l)**; Najlah Feanny/CORBIS SABA **368**; Jon Feingersh/Masterfile **17**; Robert W.Ginn/PhotoEdit **134**; Walter Hodges/CORBIS **380**; Courtesy of International Business Machines Corporation.Unauthorized use not permitted. **268, 428, 428 (inset)**; Inc.Gamma Ray Studio/Getty Images **192–193**; Courtesy of Intel Corp. **348(t)**; Photo courtesy of Iomega Corporation **348(b)**; ITStock Int'l/eStock Photo/PictureQuest **146**; Sharon L. Jonz/Photis/PictureQuest **20**; David Kadlubowski/CORBIS **346**; Ed Kashi/CORBIS **308-309**; Krever Studios/Glencoe/McGraw-Hill **410**; Lester Lefkowitz/CORBIS **102**; James Leynse/CORBIS **133**; Romilly Lockyer/Brand X Pictures/ PictureQuest **398**; Masterfile **32**; Stephanie Maze/CORBIS **222**; Ryan McVay/Photodisc/PictureQuest **353**; Courtesy of Megger **415**; Christopher Morris/Black Star Publishing/PictureQuest **68**; Courtesy of Netgear **122(t), 197**; Michael Newman/PhotoEdit **255**; Steve Niedorf Photography/Getty Images **310**; Steve Niedorf/Getty Images **8**; Jose Luis Pelaez,Inc./CORBIS **203**; Anthony Redpath/CORBIS **354**; Mark Richards/PhotoEdit **55**; Jon Riley/Index Stock Imagery **77**; Royalty-free/Blue Moon Stock/SuperStock **287**; Royalty-free/Corbis Images/PictureQuest **19**; Royalty-free/Corbis Images/PictureQuest **190**; Royalty-free/Digital Stock/CORBIS **312**; Royalty-free/Digital Vision/Getty Images **413**; Royalty-free/Digital Vision/PictureQuest **2-3**; Royalty-free/DigitalVision/PictureQuest **407**; Royalty-free/Image Source/PictureQuest **11**; Royalty-free/Stockbyte/PictureQuest **164**; Royalty-free/Thinkstock LLC **320**; Phillip and Karen Smith/SuperStock **194**; Mary Steinbacher/PhotoEdit **280**; Tom StewartCORBIS **409**; iStock Image/SuperStock **383**; Strauss/Curtis/CORBIS **4**; SW Productions/ Brand X Pictures/ PictureQuest **21**; Bill Varie/CORBIS **338**; Tom Wagner/CORBIS SABA **34**; David Young-Wolff/PhotoEdit **23**; Hans Wolff/Getty Images **250**.